SHORTLIST

Barcelona
2007

WHAT'S NEW | WHAT'S ON | WHAT'S NEXT

www.timeout.com/barcelona

Contents

Published by Time Out Guides Ltd
Universal House
251 Tottenham Court Road
London W1T 7AB
Tel: + 44 (0)20 7813 3000
Fax: + 44 (0)20 7813 6001
Email: guides@timeout.com
www.timeout.com

Editorial/Managing Director Peter Fiennes
Series Editor Ruth Jarvis
Deputy Series Editor Lesley McCave
Business Manager Gareth Garner
Guides Co-ordinator Holly Pick
Accountant Kemi Olufuwa

Time Out Guides is a wholly owned subsidiary of Time Out Group Ltd.

© Time Out Group Ltd
Chairman Tony Elliott
Managing Director Mike Hardwick
Financial Director Richard Waterlow
Time Out Magazine Ltd MD David Pepper
Group General Manager/Director Nichola Coulthard
Time Out Communications Ltd MD David Pepper
Production Director Mark Lamond
Group Marketing Director John Luck
Group Art Director John Oakey
Group IT Director Simon Chappell

Time Out and the Time Out logo are trademarks of Time Out Group Ltd.

This edition first published in Great Britain in 2006 by Ebury Publishing

Ebury Publishing is a division of The Random House Group Ltd
Company information can be found on www.randomhouse.co.uk
10 9 8 7 6 5 4 3 2 1

Distributed in USA by Publishers Group West (www.pgw.com)
Distributed in Canada by Publishers Group Canada (www.pgcbooks.ca)
For further distribution details, see www.timeout.com

ISBN Tto 31 December 2006: 1-904978-75-4. From 1 January 2007: 9781904978756

A CIP catalogue record for this book is available from the British Library

Colour reprographics by Wyndeham Icon, 3 & 4 Maverton Road, London E3 2JE

Printed and bound in Germany by Appl

Papers used by Ebury Publishing are natural, recyclable products made from wood
grown in sustainable forests

Barcelona Shortlist

The **Time Out Barcelona Shortlist 2007** is one of a new series of annual guides that draws on Time Out's background as a magazine publisher to keep you current with everything that's going on in town. As well as Barcelona's classic sights and the best of its eating, drinking and entertainment, the guide picks out the most exciting venues to have opened in the last year, and gives a full calendar of events for September 2006 to December 2007. It also includes features on the important news, trends and openings, all compiled by locally based editors and writers. Whether you're visiting for the first time in your life or just the first time since 2006, you'll find the *Time Out Barcelona Shortlist 2007* contains everything you need to know, in a portable and easy-to-use format.

The guide divides central Barcelona into seven areas, each of which contains listings for Sights & museums, Eating & drinking, Shopping, Nightlife and Arts & leisure, along with maps pinpointing all their locations. At the front of the book are chapters rounding up each of these scenes city-wide, and giving a Shortlist of our overall picks in a variety of categories. We also include itineraries for days out, and essentials including transport information and hotels.

Our listings use phone numbers as dialled from within Spain. From abroad, use your country's exit code followed by 34 (the country code for Spain) and the number given. We have noted price categories by using one to four euro signs (€-€€€€),

representing budget, moderate, expensive and luxury. Major credit cards are accepted unless otherwise stated. We also indicate when a venue is NEW , and give **Event highlights**.

All our listings are double-checked but businesses do sometimes close or change their hours or prices, so it's a good idea to call a venue before visiting. While every effort has been made to ensure accuracy, the publishers cannot accept responsibility for any errors this guide may contain.

Venues are marked on the maps using symbols numbered according to their order within the chapter and colour-coded according to the type of venue they represent:

❶ Sights & museums
❶ Eating & drinking
❶ Shopping
❶ Nightlife
❶ Arts & leisure

SHORTLIST
Online

The *Time Out Barcelona Shortlist 2007* is as up to date as it is possible for a printed guidebook to be. And to keep it completely current, it has a regularly updated online companion, at **www.timeout.com/barcelona**. Here you'll find news of the latest openings and exhibitions, as well as picks from visitors and residents – ideal for planning a trip. Time Out is the city specialist, so you'll also find travel information for more than 100 cities worldwide on our site, at www.timeout.com/travel.

Time Out Barcelona Shortlist 2007

EDITORIAL
Editor Ruth Jarvis
Copy Editor Simon Coppock
Researchers John O'Donovan, Patrick Welch
Proofreader Nicholas Royle

STUDIO
Art Director Scott Moore
Art Editor Pinelope Kourmouzoglou
Senior Designer Josephine Spencer
Graphic Designer Henry Elphick
Digital Imaging Dan Conway
Ad Make-up Jenni Prichard
Picture Editor Jael Marschner
Deputy Picture Editor Tracey Kerrigan
Picture Researcher Helen McFarland

ADVERTISING
Sales Director/Sponsorship
 Mark Phillips
International Sales Manager
 Ross Canadé
International Sales Executive
 Simon Davies
Advertising Sales Creative Media Group
Advertising Assistant Kate Staddon

MARKETING
Marketing Manager Yvonne Poon
Marketing & Publicity Manager, US
 Rosella Albanese
Marketing Designer Anthony Huggins

PRODUCTION
Production Manager Brendan McKeown
Production Co-ordinator Caroline Bradford

CONTRIBUTORS
This guide was researched and written by Sally Davies, with further contributions from Nadia Feddo, Michael Kessler and Tara Stevens. Thanks also to the writers of *Time Out Barcelona*.

PHOTOGRAPHY
All photography by Olivia Rutherford, except: page 18 Renaud Visage; page 81 Museu Picasso, Barcelona 2006/Pepe Herrero.
The following images were provided by the featured establishments/artists: pages 2, 29, 32, 63, 89, 163, 168.
Cover photograph: Font Magica. Credit: Pictures Colour Library.

MAPS
JS Graphics (john@jsgraphics.co.uk).

Thanks to Chris Davies, Nick Draper and Taryn Walker.

About Time Out

Founded in 1968, Time Out has expanded from humble London beginnings into the leading resource for those wanting to know what's happening in the world's greatest cities. As well as our influential what's-on weeklies in London, New York and Chicago, we publish more than a dozen other listings magazines in cities as varied as Beijing, Beirut and Mumbai. The magazines established Time Out's trademark style: sharp writing, informed reviewing and bang up-to-date inside knowledge of every scene.

Time Out made the natural leap into travel guides in the 1980s with the City Guide series, which now extends to over 50 destinations around the world. Written and researched by expert local writers and generously illustrated with original photography, the full-size guides cover a larger area than our Shortlist guides and include many more venue reviews, along with additional background features and a full set of maps.

Throughout this rapid growth, the company has remained proudly independent, still owned by Tony Elliott nearly four decades after he started Time Out London as a single fold-out sheet of A5 paper. This independence extends to the editorial content of all our publications, this Shortlist included. No establishment has been featured because it has advertised, and no payment has influenced any of our reviews. And, for our critics, there's definitely no such thing as a free lunch: all restaurants and bars are visited and reviewed anonymously, and Time Out always picks up the bill. For more about the company, see www.timeout.com.

Don't Miss
2007

Sights & Museums

To most visitors, it comes as first a surprise and then something of a relief, that, unlike most phenomenally popular cities, Barcelona does not boast a list of 'must-see' sights to be queued in front of, paid for, ticked off and photographed. The real joy of this sunny and easygoing Mediterranean city lies in its very fabric, thanks to the Catalan love of design, colour and the slightly bizarre.

While no major tourist venues have opened in recent years, there has been a blitz of extraordinary architecture, including Jean Nouvel's Torre Agbar (see box p150), Herzog & de Meuron's Edificio Fòrum (see box p155) and Enric Miralles' Mercat Santa Caterina (p70), which will soon be followed by a glittering new museum building by Frank Gehry in La Sagrera.

Barcelona, then, is the perfect city in which to walk. Most visitors will head first to the Old City, a maze of meandering streets, alleys and squares, where Gothic churches nestle next to lofty palaces, and ancient fountains trickle in quiet *plaças*. Beyond lie the architectural glories of Gaudí and the Modernistas, the long stretch of beach, the hills of Montjuïc and Tibidabo, and parts of the city with a wholly different feel, untouched by the hand of tourism.

Barrio by barrio

Cutting straight through the Old City are La Rambla and

Casa Batlló

SHORTLIST

Must-see art galleries
- Fundació Antoni Tàpies (p122)
- Fundació Joan Miró (p109)
- MACBA (p84)
- Museu Picasso (p72)

Best museum revamps
- CosmoCaixa (p151)
- MNAC (p112)
- Museu Picasso (p72)

Inspirational religious buildings
- Cathedral (p53)
- Monestir de Pedralbes (p152)
- Sagrada Família (p124)
- Santa Maria del Mar (p75)

Best exhibition spaces
- CaixaForum (p108)
- CCCB (p84)
- La Pedrera (p124)

Best for kids
- L'Aquàrium (p104)
- CosmoCaixa (p151)
- Museu de la Xocolata (p72)
- Zoo de Barcelona (p75)

Greatest museum buildings
- Fundació Joan Miró (p109)
- MACBA (p84)
- Museu Marítim (p103)

Prettiest parks
- Jardí Botànic (p110)
- Parc de la Ciutadella (p74)
- Park Güell (p139)

Quirkiest collections
- Museu de Carrosses Fúnebres (p123)
- Museu del Calçat (p53)
- Museu del Perfum (p123)
- Museu Frederic Marès (p55)

Monuments to Modernisme
- Casa Batlló (p122)
- Hospital de la Santa Creu i Sant Pau (p123)
- Palau de la Música Catalana (p74)

Via Laietana. **La Rambla**, once a seasonal riverbed that formed the western limit of the 13th-century city, is now a tree-lined boulevard dividing the medieval buildings and cathedral of the Barri Gòtic from the Raval, home to the MACBA and the CCCB. The nocturnal hugger-mugger of drunks, cutpurses and prostitutes, although not completely without attraction, is redolent of the city's unkempt years as a hard-edged port. Via Laietana, driven through in the 19th century to bring light and air to the slums, is the boundary between the Barri Gòtic, and Sant Pere and the achingly trendy Born, where you'll find the stunning Palau de la Música Catalana, the Museu Picasso and the Parc de la Ciutadella. Between these two thoroughfares is the Plaça Sant Jaume, the heart of the city ever since it was the centre of the Roman fort from which Barcelona grew. Now it is home to two bastions of

coffee from the airport where you left your wallet: £1

(still getting six nonstop hours of sleep: priceless)

Don't worry. MasterCard Global Service™ is available wherever you travel, in any language you speak. So just call the local toll-free number and we'll rush you a new card most anywhere in the world. For a complete list of toll-free numbers, go to www.mastercard.com.

AUSTRIA	0800-21-8235	POLAND	0-0800-111-1211
FRANCE	0-800-90-1387	SPAIN	900-97-1231
GERMANY	0800-819-1040	SWITZERLAND	0800-89-7092
GREECE	00-800-11-887-0303	UK	0800-96-4767
ITALY	800-870-866	USA	1-800-307-7309

From all other countries call collect:
1-636-722-7111

there are some things money can't buy. for peace of mind there's MasterCard®

MACBA p9

government, the Ajuntament (City Hall) and the Generalitat (the regional government).

With the demolition of the medieval walls in 1854, the open fields beyond the choleric city were a blank canvas for urban planners, architects and sculptors. The Eixample (literally, the 'expansion'), with its gridiron layout, is a showcase for the greatest works of Modernisme, including the Sagrada Família, La Pedrera and the Hospital de la Santa Creu i Sant Pau. When the only traffic was the clip-clopping of the horse and cart, these whimsical flights of architectural fancy must have been still more impressive; nowadays the Eixample can be noisy and polluted, as almost every road carries four lanes of traffic. Beyond lies the Park Güell, with Gaudí's emblematic dragon, and *barrios* such as Gràcia, Sants and Sarrià, once independent towns but long since swallowed up and incorporated into the expanding city.

Getting around

The Old City is wonderfully compact and can be crossed on foot in about 20 minutes. The city council runs walking tours on various themes (Modernisme, Picasso, Gourmet and Gothic) at weekends and on other occasional days. For more information, see www.barcelonaturisme.com.

Run by the city council, these popular walking tours have just increased to add a 'gourmet tour', including 13 stops in the city's emblematic cafés, food shops and markets. Tours start in the underground tourist office in Plaça Catalunya. The Gothic tour concentrates on the history and buildings of the Old City, while the Picasso visits the artist's haunts and ends with a visit to the Picasso Museum (entry is included in the price). The Modernisme tour is a circut of the 'Golden Square' in the Eixample, taking in Gaudí's Casa Batlló and La Pedrera. Tours take around 90mins to 2hrs, excluding the museum trip.

Park Güell p11

A fun and eco-friendly way to get around it (and to head to the beach) is to hire a bright yellow Trixi rickshaw. Running noon to 8pm, April to September, and costing €1.50 per person/kilometre, they can be hailed on the street, or booked on 93 310 13 79 or www.trixi.com. The public transport system, including a recently inaugurated tram network, serves every part of the city and is cheap and efficient.

There are two tourist buses seen all over town: the orange Barcelona Tours and the white Bus Turístic. The former is less frequent but less popular, meaning you won't have to queue, while the latter gives a book of discounts for various attractions. Both visit many of the same sights and cost much the same.

Tickets

As well as those given with the Bus Turístic passes, a range of discount passes exists. The Articket (www.articketbcn.com, €20) gives free entry to seven museums and art galleries over three months: Fundació Miró,

MACBA, the MNAC, Espai Gaudí-La Pedrera, the Fundació Tàpies, the CCCB and (a new addition in 2006) the Museu Picasso. The ticket is available from participating venues and tourist offices.

The Barcelona Card (€17) gives one to five days of unlimited transport on the metro and buses, as well as discounts on the airport bus and cable cars, reduced entry to a wide variety of museums and attractions, and discounts at several restaurants, bars and shops. The card is sold at the airport, tourist offices and various participating venues.

A word of warning

Violent crime is almost unknown in Barcelona, but bag-snatching and pickpocketing are rife – the former especially occurs in the Old City and on the beach, the latter on public transport and along La Rambla. Leave whatever you can in your hotel, and be wary of anyone trying to clean something off your shoulder or sell you a posy or a newspaper. Those wanting to swap a coin for one from your country are also wont to empty your wallet.

Andaira

WHAT'S NEW
Eating & Drinking

The first Spanish food revolution came in the early 1980s with a group of enlightened Basque chefs who had the audacity to steal some of the stars and the limelight from their French counterparts. The second is happening now, this time with Catalonia as its powerhouse. Once again the catalyst for change has been a chef, this time Ferran Adrià and his legendary restaurant El Bulli on the Catalan coast.

While his kitchens have spawned many notable alumni, such as Carles Abellan at Comerç 24, the trickle down effect of Adrià's global success – in April 2006 El Bulli was voted 'Best Restaurant in the World' – has also had a huge impact on the gastronomy of the region. Not only is cookery the new rock 'n' roll among young Spaniards, but suddenly gourmet pilgrims from the States, Japan or Australia are showing up with the express intention of splashing some cash in restaurants.

This has led to an increase in quality overall, but also to a rash of new and excellent dining options, among them Andaira, Cinc Sentits, Lasarte, Moo and, in the Hotel Palace, Caelis.

Welcome new additions of a less rarefied nature include the wonderfully cosy Tapioles 53, the excellent tapas at Mam i Teca or just a really good pizza at Ravalo.

Culture clash

The recent accolades afforded to Spanish restaurants have gone a long way towards resolving their image problem. To be fair, the bad press that Spanish restaurants have had until recently was down, in large part, to ignorance or a certain cultural inflexibility on the part of other nations. The oft-heard complaint of the northern tourist regarding the lack of vegetables fails to take into account that these are served first, in order that the meat may be better appreciated. Ironically, this then gives rise to another complaint when a mere plate of vegetables is presented as a starter. 'My water wasn't chilled!' is another, but Spaniards often find water more palatable at room temperature and may assume you prefer it thus.

When the food arrives, if one person hasn't ordered a starter, it's considered only polite to bring their main course to the table together with the other diners' starters. As in France, there is no stigma attached to leaving the cutlery to be used for a second course. The list goes on.

International rescue

Meanwhile, and despite record levels of immigration from around the world, authentic global cuisine is still hard to find in Barcelona. Local resistance to spices and the difficulty of sourcing key ingredients mean that it's difficult to find good Indian, Chinese or Italian food. Middle Eastern and Japanese restaurants have been rather more successful, along with a growing number of Latin American places. Most of the ethnic variety – including good Korean (San Kil), Nepalese (Himali) or Iraqi (Mesopotamia) – is to be found in Gràcia.

SHORTLIST

Best sunny terraces
- Agua (p98)
- Andaira (p98)
- Bestial (p98)
- Cafè de l'Acadèmia (p55)

Best for new-wave cooking
- Alkimia (p125)
- Comerç 24 (p76)
- Moo (p128)

Best for tapas
- Bar Mut (p126)
- Mam i Teca (p87)
- Quimet i Quimet (p116)
- Sureny (p145)

Best rooms for views
- La Miranda del Museu (p99)
- Oleum (p114)
- La Venta (p150)

Best for cocktails
- Dry Martini (p127)
- Gimlet (p77)
- Muebles Ciudad (p57)

Best for old-school charm
- Can Culleretes (p56)
- Envalira (p142)
- Mesón Jesús (p56)
- La Tomaquera (p117)

Best for seafood
- Botafumeiro (p139)
- Can Solé (p99)
- La Paradeta (p78)

Best for vegging out
- La Báscula (p75)
- Organic (p93)
- Sésamo (p88)

Best wine bars
- La Barcelonina de Vins i Esperits (p125)
- Va de Vi (p79)
- La Vinya del Senyor (p80)

Ones to watch
- Andaira (p98)
- Cinc Sentits (p127)
- Oleum (p114)

romantic, welcoming, familiar...

cozy atmosphere with dark wood,
silver, ivory...

fusion tasting menus, mediterranean
flavours, asian touches...

wine packages, national & international
wine cellar, cheese a la carte...

surprise lunch menus, night time with
3 different tasting menus...

● ● ● con gracia

Tapas tips

Along with bullfighting and
flamenco, one of the many and
oft-cited differences between
Barcelona and other Spanish
cities is the dearth of decent
tapas bars. Tapas in Catalonia
are a pale imitation, where they
exist at all, and generally to be
found in the bars belonging to
immigrants from Andalucia, say,
or Galicia. The custom of giving
a free tapa, or just saucer of crisps
and nuts, is almost unheard of in
Catalonia, and hopping from bar
to bar is not as popular as it is in
other regions, so consequently a
caña/canya (draught beer) comes
in a larger measure.

What has caught on big time
in Barcelona are *pintxo* bars – their
Basque origin means that the word
is always given in Euskera – such
as Euskal Extea. A *pintxo* (be
careful not to confuse it with
the Spanish term *pincho*, which
simply refers to a very small tapa)
consists of some ingenious culinary
combination on a small slice of
bread. Platters of them are usually
brought out at particular times,
often around 1pm and again at
8pm. *Pintxos* come impaled on
toothpicks, which you keep on
your plate so that the barman
can tally them up at the end. The
Brits hold the worst reputation for
abusing this eminently civilised
system by 'forgetting' to hand
over all their toothpicks.

Without a decent grasp of the
language, tapas bars can be quite
intimidating unless you know
exactly what you want. Don't be
afraid to seek guidance, but some
of the more standard offerings will
include *tortilla* (potato omelette),

Tapioles 53 p13

patatas bravas (fried potatoes in a spicy red sauce and garlic mayonnaise), *ensaladilla* (Russian salad), *pinchos morunos* (small pork skewers), *champiñones al ajillo* (mushrooms fried in garlic), *gambas al ajillo* (prawns and garlic), *mejillones a la marinera* (mussels in a tomato and onion sauce), *chocos* (squid fried in batter), *almejas al vapor* (steamed clams with garlic and parsley), *pulpo* (octopus) and *pimientos del padrón* (little green peppers, one or two of which will kick like an angry mule).

What happens when

Lunch starts around 2pm and goes on until roughly 3.30pm or 4pm; dinner is served from about 9pm until 11.30pm or midnight. Some restaurants open earlier in the evening, but arriving before 9.30 or 10pm generally means you'll be dining alone or in the company of foreign tourists. Reserving a table is generally a good idea: not only on Friday and Saturday nights, but also on Sunday evenings and Monday lunchtimes, when few restaurants are open. Many also close for lengthy holidays, including about a week over Easter, two or three weeks in August or early September, and often the first week in January. We have listed closures of more than a week wherever we can, but restaurants are fickle, particularly on the issue of summer holidays, so call to check.

Money matters

Eating out in Barcelona is not as cheap as it used to be, but low mark-ups on wines keep the cost relatively reasonable for northern Europeans and Americans. All but the upmarket restaurants are required by law to serve an economical fixed-price *menú del día* (*menú* is not to be confused with the menu, which is *la carta*) at lunchtime; this usually consists of a starter, main course, dessert, bread and something to drink. The idea is to provide cheaper meals for the workers, but while it can be a real bargain, it is not by any means a taster menu or a showcase for the chef's greatest hits; rather, they're a healthier version of what in other countries might amount to a snatched lunchtime sandwich.

Laws governing the issue of prices are routinely flouted, but, legally, menus must declare if the seven per cent IVA (VAT) is included in prices or not (it rarely is), and also if there is a cover charge (generally expressed as a charge for bread). Catalans, and the Spanish in general, tend to tip very little, but tourists should let their conscience decide.

Cinc Sentits p13

Hibernian Books p21

Shopping

Great shopping is nothing new in Barcelona. Ever since the Middle Ages it has been a city of craftsmen and traders, and though modern shoppers may be seeking Camper shoes rather than fishermen's clogs, it remains one of the top commercial destinations on the Mediterranean.

Like any other western city, mall culture is growing and the main shopping arteries are increasingly dominated by chains, but this invasion does not seem to have affected Barcelona's love affair with small speciality stores. Shops in the Old City are just as likely to sell homemade sausage or espadrilles as they are Nike trainers or Levi's.

Barcelona's famous obsession with originality and design is echoed in the incredible number of new openings devoted to boutique fashion, jewellery, furniture and interior decor. Nobody seems to open shops that aren't cool and, as the shoe repairers and ironmongers give way to futon shops and hairdressing salons, one wonders how the city's shoppers can support such a quantity of luxury goods. Not to mention where they might buy something as dully utilitarian as a stopcock or printer cartridge.

Market trends

Market shopping is on the rise among young people, and recent surveys show that over half of citizens aged 25 to 34 regularly shop at municipal markets. This is at least partly due to a huge

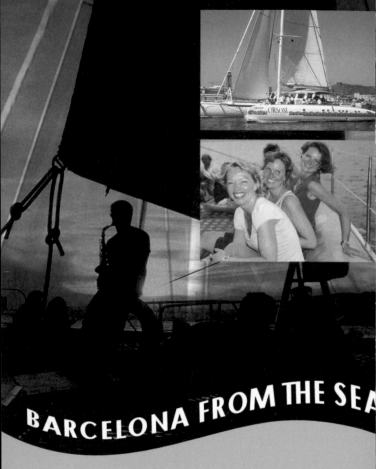

BARCELONA FROM THE SEA

**Relax in the luxury and comfort
of the Catamaran Orsom.**

Daily sails and evening Jazz / Chill out cruises

Tel. (00 34) 93 441 05 37
www.barcelona-orsom.com

municipal advertising campaign and a €50-million programme to reinvent Barcelona's markets. Of the most central, Santa Caterina and Poblenou are newly completed, Barceloneta is due to reopen in March 2007 and the much-loved Mercat Sant Antoni will be closed from 2007 to 2010 while it is transformed into 'the most modern market in Europe'. This being Barcelona, the makeovers are architecturally striking – none more so than Enric Miralles' undulating Mercat de Santa Caterina – and they have also become focal points for urban redevelopment.

Despite all the noise about eating fresh greens, the irony is that the new generation of markets generally hold far fewer stalls than before, with the extra space turned over to incorporate supermarkets, restaurants and even internet cafés.

Speciality stores

Barcelona's rich and thriving scene of tiny speciality shops has attracted an ever-growing number of foreign small traders, be they traders in Moroccan slippers or Chinese calligraphy pens. Barcelona's best source for Spanish farmhouse cheeses, Formatgeria La Seu, is owned by a Scottish woman, while the friendly candymakers boiling and rolling up sweets at Papabubble are Australian. Fertile areas for browsing include the Barri Gòtic, Born, Raval and Gràcia.

Fashion first

It's not all Mango and Zara. Barcelona's reputation as a haven for niche-label designers is growing thanks to the constant stream of new designers from the city's prestigious fashion schools. Young designers to look out for when you're browsing through the

SHORTLIST

Best fashion boutiques
- Adolfo Domínguez (p80)
- Custo Barcelona (p62)
- Giménez y Zuazo (p88)
- Loft Avignon (p64)
- On Land (p82)
- U-Casas (p82)

Best for innovative interior design
- BD Ediciones de Diseño (p130)
- Ici et Là (p82)
- Vinçon (p132)

City classics
- Almacenes del Pilar (p61)
- Herboristeria del Rei (p62)
- Vila Viniteca (p82)

Best for bookish pursuits
- Altaïr (p130)
- Casa del Llibre (p130)
- FNAC (p131)
- Hibernian Books (p146)

Obscure specialists
- Caelum (p61)
- Cereria Subirá (p62)
- El Ingenio (p64)

Best for affordable high-street fashion
- Camper (p130)
- Mango (p132)
- Zara (p65)

Best tasty treats
- Botifarrería de Santa María (p77)
- Casa Gispert (p80)
- Formatgeria La Seu (p62)

Best sweet eats
- Bubó (p80)
- Escribà (p69)
- Papabubble (p64)

Best one-stop shops
- El Corte Inglés (p131)
- Diagonal Mar (p157)
- Maremàgnum (p104)

Camper p19

Custo Barcelona

flash-in-the-pan boutiques around C/Avinyó in the Barri Gòtic, the MACBA area in the Raval or C/Verdi in Gràcia include Raquel Cardona, Juma Alemany, Alberto Tous and Helena Minenko. At the top of the heap, Custodio Dalmau's label, Custo Barcelona, is the city's major success story but other big guns include Josep Font, Lydia Delgado and Antonio Miró, all to be found uptown.

Design for life

Nowhere beats Barcelona for sharp, original design. For anyone who aspires to an apartment resembling a designer bar, Vinçon and BD Ediciones de Diseño have the slickest furniture and household goods and are both located in stunning Modernista buildings. For something quirky, try the eccentric collections at Ici et Là. The Mercado del Borne (www.mercadodelborne.com) grabs the zeitgeist with constantly changing collections of independent design and art from all over the world.

Neighbourhood watch

Shops in Barcelona match their context so neatly that they can almost seem to be part of a giant themed architectural park. The Eixample's expansive boulevards and Modernista architecture complement its wealth of upmarket designer furniture, fashion and homeware stores – here, even the more prosaic pharmacies and grocers' are minor architectural miracles. Passeig de Gràcia is becoming known as one of the world's great shopping avenues, studded with Spanish stars such as the redoubtable Adolfo Domínguez along with countless international luminaries. Running parallel, Rambla de Catalunya boasts lingerie shops, chains and upmarket stores.

The Barri Gòtic's narrow streets and restored medieval spaces are home to a jumble of small craft shops, antique dealers and specialist outlets selling anything from religious candles to carnival masks and anchovy-flavoured bonbons. Crossing over Via Laietana to the Born, the terrain becomes noticeably more design-oriented with an ever-changing selection of boutique fashion, accessories, furniture and shoes. A victim of its own success, the Born buzz has recently been attracting some of the bigger chains.

The new frontier lies across the fashion vacuum of La Rambla, in the Raval, particularly in the newly manicured area between the MACBA and C/Carme where independent designers showcase experimental art and clothes. The rest of the area is noticeably edgier and still holds fast to its bohemian aesthetic with plenty of music shops, second-hand outlets and ethnic wares reflecting the global broil of immigrants who live there.

For a friendly touch, the village-like environments of Sarrià (in the Zona Alta, p151) and Gràcia give an intimacy to antique or clothes shopping while at the other end of the scale, the wide open spaces of Plaça de Catalunya or the shoreline lend themselves to large-scale commerce at malls such as Diagonal Mar and Maremàgnum, not forgetting Spain's department store behemoth, El Corte Inglés.

Opening hours

Increasing numbers of shops are adopting a European timetable and staying open through the siesta period, although most small independent stores still stick to the traditional opening times of 10am-2pm and 5-8pm Monday to Saturday. Don't be surprised to see many shutters down on Saturday afternoons, especially in the summertime. Many shops close for at least two weeks in August. Except for the run up to Christmas, Sunday opening is still limited to shops in tourist zones such as La Rambla and the Maremàgnum. Many newspaper kiosks, bakeries and flower stalls are open Sunday mornings and many convenience stores stay open all day.

Shop tactics

Bargain-hunters should note that sales (*rebaixes* or *rebajas*) begin after the retail orgy of Christmas and Epiphany, running from 7 January to mid February, and again during July and August. Barcelona's tourist offices stock free Shopping Guide booklets with an accompanying map and advice on everything from how to get your VAT refund at the airport to using the Barcelona Shopping Line bus.

Paying away

When the euro came in, anything that had previously cost 100 pesetas was cunningly rounded up to one euro – an overnight price hike of 66 per cent. In other words, cheap shopping in Barcelona is a thing of the past, although at least local wines and home-grown designs like Zara, Mango and Camper are still significantly less pricey here than abroad.

Bargaining should only be attempted at the Els Encants flea-market or when haggling over Sagrada Familia snowglobes on La Rambla; in shops, prices are fixed. As long as you're spending over €10 or so, all but the most cobwebby of places now accept major credit cards. Almost nowhere has chip-and-pin machines installed yet, but you will be required to show some form of picture ID.

City Hall p26

Nightlife

It's increasingly hard to tell where dinner ends and clubbing begins in Barcelona. A trend for multitasking restaurant-bar-club combinations has swept the city and there is a job for every DJ who wants to work. Not so for musicians, however. A city council clampdown on late-night noise has closed over 80 bars, clubs and cultural associations in the last year and even iconic venues like La Boîte and Jazzroom have not escaped the pogrom. Of the bars that have remained open, many, like Barcelona Pipa Club, have ceased to stage live acts out of fear of huge fines.

In terms of music groups, Barcelona has scenes rather than any big emblematic bands. Jazz, indie, *rock català* and electronica are all well represented and local names to look out for at festivals such as BAM, Primavera Sound and Sónar include indie rockers Beef, electro-popper Iris and 12Twelve, an unclassifiable quartet bringing together free jazz, psychedelia and cosmic krautrock. Where Barcelona has had most international success is with *mestizaje* a blend of influences including rock, flamenco, rai, hip hop, and various South American, Asian and African styles. The *mestizaje* top draws at the moment are Ojos de Brujo and the Raval's 08001.

Clubbing

In a city where everybody wants to be a DJ, local standouts are Will Deluxe for electrotech (Club Fellini, p69), Annemiek's dirty house (CDLC, Private Lifestyle events), and DJ Fra, who had a big hit in production duo Ferenc with 'Yes Sir, I Can Hardcore'.

One of the most successful new clubs on the scene has been Fellini, indulging Barcelona's insatiable appetite for all things house and techno. Its older and far more glamorous sister is La Terrrazza – Barcelona's best and best-loved open-air summer club – which reopened after a year closed because of neighbours' complaints in time for its tenth anniversary in May 2006. Also recreating that Ibiza feeling is Private Lifestyle's new all-day (noon-3am) Sunday beachfront party in Shôko (p100). Back indoors, grown-up clubbers heaved a sigh of relief when old-school night, Mond Club, was brought back in April 2006 after a ten-month hiatus. It now lives at Fellini (last Thursday of the month).

Concerts

The main venue for international names (as well as hotly tipped unknowns and local musicians) is the multi-faceted industrial space Razzmatazz, which has recently hosted everything from Arctic Monkeys and Rufus Wainwright to where-are-they-now bands like Sisters of Mercy. Moving into fallback position, the mall-like Bikini still nets some top-notch international names and plenty of local stars. For weirder and less well-known acts, the old dancehalls Sala Apolo, Luz de Gas and La Paloma host several concerts a week. Global superstars perform in Montjuïc's sports stadiums, one of which has recently become the Barcelona Teatre Musical.

When to go

Going out in Barcelona happens so late it's early. People rarely meet for a drink before 11pm and it's not until the bars turf everyone out at 3am that clubs (mumsily known as *discotecas*) get going. As elsewhere, the biggest nights are Thursday to Saturday, but Sunday teatime chill-out sessions are catching on.

SHORTLIST

Best for dancing queens
- Arena (p132)
- La Concha (p94)
- Metro (p135)
- Salvation (p135)

Best for glamour pusses
- CDLC (p100)
- Club Catwalk (p105)
- Elephant (p154)
- Mirablau (p151)

Best for big-name bands
- Razzmatazz (p157)
- Bikini (p149)
- Sala Apolo (p118)

Best for chilling out
- Barcelona Rouge (p115)
- La Caseta del Migdia (p115)
- Spiritual Café (p94)

Best for jazzin' universally
- Harlem Jazz Club (p65)
- Jamboree (p66)
- Jazz Sí Club (p90)

Quirkiest bars
- Bar Pastis (p94)
- La Fira (p134)
- Marsella (p93)

Best for dancehall glamour
- Luz de Gas (p135)
- La Paloma (p91)
- Sala Apolo (p118)

Best pre-club warm-up
- Café Royale (p65)
- Dot (p65)
- Downstairs@Club13 (p65)
- Maumau (p117)

Best for alfresco partying
- Beach *xiringuitos*
- Danzatoria (p151)
- La Terrrazza (p114)

Best Monday-nighters
- City Hall (p133)
- Jamboree (p66)
- Moog (p94)

Palau de la Música Catalana

Arts & Leisure

The last few years have been kind to Barcelona's culture vultures. The vibrancy of Catalan theatre, less dependent on plot or dialogue than on a festive blend of music, choreography, multimedia sleight-of-hand and slick production values, added to the local love for light-hearted mega-productions, has sparked a spectacular growth in attendances in recent years. With television actors serving as theatre box-office draws these days, more and more venues are dedicated to unabashed money-making, with musical comedy at the forefront, but the trickle-down effect is to make people comfortable with the idea of a night out at the theatre.

Classical music has been given a boost of a different kind, with a veritable rash of new concert halls, the latest of which will be a new, 700-seater Sala de Cambra due to open in autumn 2007 in L'Auditori. A couple of years ago

the Palau de la Música Catalana unveiled its new, acoustically excellent, subterranean 500-seater auditorium, while, previous to that, the phoenix-like Liceu opera house spread its wings, Rafael Moneo's stark L'Auditori provided the city with a bleeding-edge concert hall and the Auditori Winterthur became a small, charming outpost in the otherwise soulless business and university district. These venue changes have been supplemented by a subtle switch in repertoire. The canon still reigns, of course. But as a younger generation of cultural programmers takes charge, newer work has found an audience. You no longer have to be dead to get your music heard.

Key players

The last few years have seen the deaths of two leading Catalan composers – Joaquim Homs and

Xavier Montsalvatge – leaving Joan Guinjoan as Catalonia's most important living composer. Another local, manic genius Carles Santos, composes, directs and performs in surreal operatic-theatrical performances that combine sex, psychology and sopranos. Now in his sixties, he still manages to average a new show a year.

Key Catalan theatre players making waves internationally include La Fura dels Baus, Els Comediants and Tricicle, while Dagoll Dagom creates huge money-spinning musicals. And don't forget ever-controversial Calixto Bieito: renowned for his wildly polemical interpretations of *Hamlet* and *Don Giovanni*, he's directed classics at the Edinburgh Festival and worked at the English National Opera.

Dance moves

Barcelona has many thriving contemporary dance companies, but there are few major dance venues and most companies spend their time touring. Performers such as Pina Bausch and the Compañía Nacional de Danza (directed by the revered Nacho Duato) have played to sell-out crowds in the Teatre Nacional (p137) and the Liceu, while the Teatre Nacional has a resident company led by Marta Carrasco and the Teatre Lliure (Plaça Margarida Xirgú, Montjuïc, 93 289 27 70, www.teatrelliure.com) hosts new work. However, it's difficult for companies to find big audiences. Innovative companies such as Sol Picó and Mar Gómez usually run a new show every year, as do influential companies such as Metros, Mudances and Gelabert-Azzopardi.

Festivals

The Festival del Grec (p37), which takes place from June to August, is the mother of all Barcelona

SHORTLIST

Best for an intimate gig
- Auditori Winterthur (p148)
- Mercat de les Flors (p118)
- Metrònom (p82)

Cutting-edge concert halls
- L'Auditori (p137)
- Gran Teatre del Liceu (p69)

Best for catching a movie
- Renoir-Floridablanca (p137)
- Verdi (p146)
- Yelmo Icària Cineplex (p105)

A taste of southern Spain
- Plaza de Toros Monumental (p137)
- El Tablao de Carmen (p118)
- Los Tarantos (p66)

Ultimate Catalan experience
- Nou Camp stadium (p148)
- Palau de la Música (p74)

Best for family fun
- L'Aquàrium (p104)
- IMAX Port Vell (p105)

festivals, calling in impressive musicians, dance troupes and actors from all over the world; its open-air venues are magical on a summer night. The Marató de l'Espectacle (p37) is in June, with a fun but exhausting two nights of non-stop micro performances. Dies de Dansa (p37) offers three days of national and international dance in June and July, in sites such as the Port, the CCCB or the MACBA. Several music festivals are staged, the foremost of which are the Festival de Música Antiga (p34) and the Nous Sons (p34) festival of contemporary music, both in spring. In summer, the focus moves. Various museums hold small outdoor concerts, and there are weekly events in several city parks, particularly as part of July's Clàssics als Parcs season (p37).

Calendar

Sónar p37

Dates highlighted in **bold** are public holidays.

September 2006

3-24 **Festival L'Hora del Jazz**
Various venues
www.amjm.org
Festival of local jazz acts, with free daytime concerts.

11 **Diada Nacional de Catalunya**
All over Barcelona
Flags and marches affirm cultural identity on Catalan National Day.

15-17 **Festival Asia**
Various venues
www.casaasia.es/festival
Shows, music, workshops and stalls from 17 Asian countries.

16-17 **Hipnotik**
CCCB (p84)
www.cccb.org, www.hipnotikfestival.com
Celebrating everything hip hop.

22-24 **Barcelona Arts de Carrer**
Various venues
www.artsdecarrer.org
Street performance festival.

22-24 **Mostra de Vins i Caves de Catalunya**
Moll d'Espanya, Port Vell
Tasting fair, at which you can sample the local wines and Cavas.

22-24 **Barcelona Acció Musical (BAM)**
Various venues
www.bam.es
Around 40 concerts, mostly from local acts, and many free.

CASA BATLLÓ

ANTONI GAUDÍ. BARCELONA

Gaudí

VISITES CULTURALS | DAILY VISITS

 CASA BATLLÓ
ANTONI GAUDÍ. BARCELONA

PASSEIG DE GRÀCIA, 43. Tel. 93 216 03 06

22-25 Festes de la Mercè
All over Barcelona
www.bcn.es
Barcelona's biggest, brightest festival with fire-running, human castles, giants, concerts, an airshow, fireworks on the beach and more.

24 La Mercè

27-1 Oct Festa Major de la Barceloneta
All over Barceloneta
www.cascantic.net
Festival fever fills the fishing quarter.

October 2006

Ongoing Festa Major de la Barceloneta

5-29 LEM Festival
Various venues, Gràcia
www.gracia-territori.com
Multimedia art and experimental electronica music.

12 Dia de la Hispanitat

18-21 Festival de Tardor Ribermúsica
Various venues, Born
www.ribermusica.org
Over 100 free music performances are held in squares, churches, bars and even shops.

26-29 Art Futura
Mercat de les Flors (p118)
www.artfutura.org
Digital and cyber art festival.

31-1 Nov La Castanyada
All over Barcelona
All Saints' Day and the evening before are celebrated with piles of *castanyes* (roast chestnuts).

31-5 Nov In-Edit Beefeater Festival
Cines París, Portal de l'Angel 11-13
www.in-edit.beefeater.es
Musical documentary cinema festival.

November 2006

Ongoing In-Edit Beefeater Festival

1 Tots Sants (All Saints' Day)

1-30 Festival of Pocket Opera
Various venues
www.festivaloperabutxaca.org
Small-scale contemporary opera. This year's featured countries are Belgium and England.

10-18 L'Alternativa
CCCB (p84)
www.alternativa.cccb.org
Indie cinema fest.

10-19 Festival Internacional de Teatre Visual i Titelles
Mercat de les Flors (p118)
www.diba.es/festivaltitellesbcn
International festival of puppetry and theatre.

21-17 Dec BAC!
CCCB (p84) & other venues
www.cccb.org, www.lasanta.org, www.bacfestival.com
Contemporary art festival.

Nov-Dec Els Grans del Gospel
Various venues
www.the-project.net
International gospel festival.

Nov-May AvuiMúsica
Various venues
www.accompositors.com
Contemporary music cycle.

Nov-24 Dec Fair of Sant Eloi
C/Argenteria, Born
Artisan Christmas street fair. Live music from 6-8pm.

Late Nov Wintercase Barcelona
Sala Razzmatazz 1, C/Almogàvers 122, Poblenou
www.wintercase.com
Big-name indie bands.

Late Nov/early Dec Festival Internacional de Jazz de Barcelona
Various venues
www.the-project.net
Jazz from bebop to big band.

December 2006

Ongoing Els Grans del Gospel, AvuiMúsica, Festival Internacional de Jazz de Barcelona, BAC!, Fair of Sant Eloi

BREAD & butter

Europe's coolest city welcomes the return of Europe's coolest urban fashion fair.

As if Barcelona needed any more cool status. Early in 2006 some 45,000 buyers from over 80 countries, 780 labels and a staggering 1,800 journalists descended on the city for its second edition of BREAD & butter, Europe's most cutting-edge urban fashion trade fair. It started life in Germany in 2001 as an alternative buyers' market for selected streetwear brands, launched a Barcelona arm soon afterwards, and in under two years has become the fashion calendar hot date for buyers eager to pounce on the new, the extravagantly throwaway, the hip and the independent.

You won't find the big suppliers here – Mango and Zara take a walk at these events – and buyers instead have the opportunity to browse lesser-known designers, such as Pig, Staf or Kult, in a contemporary cultural setting, with music, art and even food forming part of many exhibitors' stands. DJs, performing chefs, artificial football fields, on-the-spot personalising of video games, jeans and skateboards are all in the mix. A standout in 2006 was the De Puta Madre label, created by a guy who came up with the designs while serving time in a Spanish jail for drug offences. It's that kind of show.

Thanks to the adoring media, it only looks like getting bigger. A second Barcelona fair in July went down a treat and the January 2007 event will be accompanied by a catwalk show. But perhaps most impressive is the city buzz that surrounds the three-day event, infiltrating bars and clubs as the fashionistas rock up en masse, often with DJs in tow. Many parties are private, so you'll have to schmooze for invites – this may also be your best chance of getting into the shows, which are ostensibly for business insiders and the media. Business insiders, the media and their friends, that is.
■ www.breadandbutter.com

DON'T MISS: 2007

2-23 **Fira de Santa Llúcia**
Pla de la Seu & Avda de la
Catedral, Barri Gòtic
www.bcn.es/nadal
Christmas market with trees, decora-
tions and nativity-scene figures.

6 **Día de la Constitución**

8 **La Immaculada**

14-17 **Resfest**
Mercat de les Flors (p118)
www.resfest.com
Festival of innovative film, music, art,
design, fashion and technology.

16-17 **Drap Art**
CCCB (p84)
www.drapart.org
International creative recycling festival, comprising concerts, performances,
workshops and a Christmas market of
recycled goods.

Dec-Feb **Festival Mil·lenni de
Barcelona**
Palau de la Música Catalana (p74)
www.festivalmillenni.com
Music, dance and poetry performances.

21 **BAF (Belles Arts Festival)**
Sala Apolo (p118)
Avant-garde, non-commercial art and
performance with music and DJs until
dawn.

25 **Nadal (Christmas Day)**

26 **Sant Esteve (Boxing Day)**

28 **Día dels Inocents**
Local version of April Fool's Day, with
paper figures attached to the backs of
unsuspecting victims.

31 **Cap d'Any (New Year's Eve)**
Swill Cava and eat a grape for every
chime of the clock at midnight. Wear
red underwear for good luck.

January 2007

Ongoing AvuiMúsica, Festival
Mil·lenni de Barcelona

1 **Any Nou (New Year's Day)**

5 **Cavalcada dels Reis**
All over Barcelona
www.bcn.es/nadal

The three kings (Melchior, Gaspar and
Balthasar) head a grand parade around
town from 5-9pm.

6 **Reis Mags (Three Kings)**

12-21 **Sa Pobla a Gràcia**
Gràcia, around Plaça Diamant
www.bcn.es
Traditional festivities from the island
of Mallorca.

Jan-Apr **Tradicionàrius**
Various locations, mainly in Gràcia
www.tradicionarius.com
Cycle of concert performances of traditional and popular Catalan music.

February 2007

Ongoing AvuiMúsica, Festival
Mil·lenni de Barcelona,
Tradicionàrius

1-21 **Barcelona Visual Sound**
Various venues
www.bcnvisualsound.org
Showcase for untried film talent covering shorts, documentaries, animation
and web design.

9-18 **Santa Eulàlia**
All over Barcelona
www.bcn.es
Blowout winter festival in honour of
Santa Eulàlia, co-patron saint of the
city and a particular favourite of children. Expect many kids' activities.

Feb-Mar **Xcèntric Film Festival**
CCCB (p84)
www.cccb.org/xcentric
Avant-garde festival of rare short films
and videos.

17-21 **Carnestoltes (Carnival)**
All over Barcelona
www.bcn.es
King Carnestoltes leads the fancy dress
parades and street parties before being
burned on Ash Wednesday.

24 **Minifestival de Música
Independent de Barcelona**
C/Teide 20, Nou Barris
www.minifestival.net
An eclectic range of indie sounds from
around the world.

March 2007

Ongoing AvuiMúsica,
Tradicionàrius, Xcèntric
Film Festival

4 Marató Barcelona
Starts & finishes at Plaça
de Espanya
www.maratobarcelona.com
City marathon with revamped route.

Early Mar Festes de Sant Medir de Gràcia
Gràcia
www.santmedir.org
Decorated horse-drawn carts shower
the crowds with blessed boiled sweets.

Mar-Apr Nous Sons – Músiques Contemporànies
L'Auditori (p137) & CCCB (p84)
www.auditori.org
International contemporary music at
the New Sounds festival.

16-20 El Feile
Various venues
www.elfeile.com
Irish festival of music, dance and
stand-up comedy for Saint Patrick's.

April 2007

Ongoing AvuiMúsica,
Tradicionàrius, Nous Sons –
Músiques Contemporànies

2-9 Setmana Santa (Holy Week)
Palm fronds are blessed at the cathedral on Palm Sunday, and children
receive elaborate chocolate creations.

6 Divendres Sant (Good Friday)

9 Dilluns de Pasqua (Easter Monday)

Apr-May BAFF Barcelona Asian Film Festival
Various venues
www.baff-bcn.org
Digital cinema, non-commercial films
and anime from Asia.

Apr-June Festival Guitarra
Various venues
www.the-project.net/festival_guitarra
Guitar festival spanning everything
from flamenco to jazz.

23 Sant Jordi
La Rambla & all over Barcelona
Feast day of Sant Jordi (St George), the
patron saint of Catalonia. Couples
exchange gifts of red roses and books.

Late Apr Feria de Abril de Catalunya
Fòrum area
www.fecac.com
Satellite of Seville's famous fair with
decorated marquees, manzanilla sherry and flamenco.

May 2007

Ongoing AvuiMúsica, BAFF
Barcelona Asian Film Festival,
Festival Guitarra

1 Dia del Treball (May Day)
Various venues
Mass demonstrations are led by trade
unionists.

11 Sant Ponç
C/Hospital, Raval
www.bcn.es
Street market of herbs, honey and
candied fruit to celebrate the day of
Saint Ponç, patron saint of herbalists.

18 Dia Internacional dels Museus
All over Barcelona
www.bcn.es
Free entrance to the city's museums.

May Caminada Internacional de Barcelona
www.euro-senders.com/internacional
The International Walk covers several
routes of various lengths.

May Festival de Música Antiga
L'Auditori (p137)
www.auditori.org
Cycle of ancient music.

May-June Festival Internacional de Percussió
L'Auditori (p137)
www.auditori.org
International percussion festival.

May Loop Festival
Hotel Pulitzer (p174)
www.loop-barcelona.com.
Experimental video art festival.

Festa Major del Raval p37

May **Festival Internacional
de Poesia**
All over Barcelona
www.bcn.es/barcelonapoesia
City-wide poetry festival, with read-
ings in English.

May **Festa Major de Nou Barris**
Nou Barris
www.bcn.es
Neighbourhood festival famous for
outstanding flamenco.

Sun, late May **La Cursa del
Corte Inglés**
All over Barcelona
www.elcorteingles.com
Over 50,000 participants attempt the
seven-mile course.

Late May **Festival de Flamenco
de Ciutat Vella**
CCCB (p84) & other venues
www.tallerdemusics.com
The Old City Flamenco Festival, with
concerts, films and kids' activities.

28 Segona Pascua (Whitsun)

June 2007

Ongoing Festival Guitarra, Festival
Internacional de Percussió

1-30 **Festival de Música Creativa
i Jazz de Ciutat Vella**
All over Old City
www.bcn.es/agenda
The Old City Festival of Creative
Music and Jazz hosts performances at
small intimate venues.

Early June **Festa dels Cors
de la Barceloneta**
Barceloneta
www.bcn.es
Local choirs sing lustily and march in
carnival parades on Saturday morning
and Monday afternoon.

Early June
Mostra Sonora i Visual
Convent Sant Agusti, C/Comerç,
Sant Pere
www.conventagusti.com
Experimental electronica concerts, DJs,
VJs, installations and video art.

June **Primavera Sound**
Fòrum area
www.primaverasound.com
Excellent big-name music festival with a record fair and Soundtrack Film Festival on the side.

June **Marató de l'Espectacle**
Mercat de les Flors (p118)
www.marato.com
Anarchic performance marathon, over two nights, with pieces lasting from three seconds to ten minutes.

June **Festa de la Música**
All over Barcelona
www.bcn.es/icub
Free international music festival with amateur musicians from 100 countries playing in the streets.

June-July **Dies de Dansa**
Various venues
www.marato.com
Dance performances in public spaces dotted around the city.

June-Aug **Festival del Grec**
Various venues
www.bcn.es/grec
Two-month spree of dance, music and theatre all over the city.

15-18 **L'Ou com Balla**
Cathedral cloisters & other venues
www.bcn.es/icub
Corpus Christi processions and the unusual L'Ou Com Balla – for which hollowed out eggs dance on decorated fountains.

Mid June **Sónar**
Various venues
www.sonar.es
The Festival of Advanced Music and Multimedia Art, which encompasses electronic music, urban art and media technologies.

23-**24 Sant Joan**
All over Barcelona
Summer solstice means Cava, all-night bonfires and fireworks.

July 2007

Ongoing Festival del Grec, Dies de Dansa

14-17 **Festa Major del Raval**
Raval
www.bcn.es/icub
Party events include giants, exhibitions, a fleamarket, several children's workshops and free concerts on the Rambla del Raval.

July **Clàssics als Parcs**
Various venues
www.bcn.es/parcsijardin
Free alfresco classical music from young performers in Barcelona's parks.

Mid July **Downtown Reggae Festival**
Jardins de les Tres Ximeneies, Poble Sec
www.nyahbingicrew.com
A free Jamaican music festival puts on dancehall reggae from 5pm-2am.

Mid July **Summercase**
Parc del Fòrum
www.summercase.com
Weekend-long big-name indie festival.

30 **Gran Trobada d'Havaneres**
Passeig Joan de Borbó, Barceloneta
www.bcn.es/icub
Sea shanties with fireworks and *cremat* (flaming spiced rum).

Late July-early Sept **Mas i Mas Festival**
Various venues
www.masimas.com
The best of Latin music in Barcelona.

August 2007

Ongoing Festival del Grec, Mas i Mas Festival

Every Wed **Summer Nights at CaixaForum**
CaixaForum (p108)
www.fundacio.lacaixa.es
All exhibitions are open until midnight with music, films and other activities.

Every Wed & Fri **Jazz in Ciutadella Park**
Parc de la Ciutadella, Born
www.bcn.es/parcsijardins
Free 10pm shows from jazz trios and quartets in front of the fountain.

Clàssics als Parcs p37

Every Tue-Thur **Gandules**
CCCB (p84)
www.cccb.org
A series of outdoor films screened to the deckchair-strewn patio of the CCCB.

12-16 Festa de Sant Roc
Barri Gòtic
www.bcn.es
The Barri Gòtic's party with parades, fireworks, traditional street games and fire-running.

**15 L'Assumpció
(Assumption Day)**

17-24 Festa Major de Gràcia
Gràcia
www.festamajordegracia.org
A best-dressed street competition, along with giants and human castles.

Last week in Aug
Festa Major de Sants
Sants
www.festamajordesants.org
Traditional neighbourhood festival with street parties, concerts and fire-running.

September 2007

Ongoing Mas i Mas Festival

1-31 Festival L'Hora del Jazz
Various venues
www.amjm.org
Festival of local jazz acts, with free daytime concerts.

11 Diada Nacional de Catalunya
All over Barcelona
Flags and marches affirm cultural identity on Catalan National Day.

**20-24 Barcelona Acció
Musical (BAM)**
Various venues
www.bam.es
Around 40 concerts, mostly featuring local acts, and many free.

**22-24 Barcelona Arts
de Carrer**
Raval & La Rambla
www.artsdecarrer.org
Street performances of juggling, magic tricks and acrobatics.

22-24 **Mostra de Vins i Caves de Catalunya**

Moll d'Espanya, Port Vell

Tasting fair, at which you can sample the local wines and Cavas.

22-30 **Festes de la Mercè**

All over Barcelona

www.bcn.es

Barcelona's biggest, brightest festival. You should expect lunatic fire-running, giants, human castles, concerts, an airshow, fireworks on the beach and much more.

24 La Mercè

Last week Sept **Festa Major de la Barceloneta**

All over Barceloneta

www.cascantic.net

Festival fever fills the fishing quarter.

October 2007

Oct **Festival Asia**

Various venues

www.casaasia.es/festival

Up to 150 events from the 17 partici-pating Asian countries.

12 **Dia de la Hispanitat**

Oct **Festival de Tardor Ribermúsica**

Various venues, Born

www.ribermusica.org

Over 100 free music performances are put on in squares, churches, bars and even shops.

Oct **Art Futura**

Mercat de les Flors (p118)

www.artfutura.org

Digital and cyber art festival.

Oct-Nov **LEM Festival**

Various venues, Gràcia

www.gracia-territori.com

Multimedia art exhibits and some 60 electronica concerts.

Late Oct **In-Edit Beefeater Festival**

Cines París, Portal de l'Angel

11-13

www.in-edit.beefeater.es

Musical cinema, ranging from jazz to flamenco.

All in the same boat

Barcelona launches a new round-the-world yacht race.

If you know your bilges from your burgees, then Barcelona is the place to be on 11 November 2007, when the city hosts the Barcelona World Race. It's the first ever two-crew, non-stop, round-the-world race for monohulls, and the missing link in the off-shore racing circuit, bridging the gap between fully crewed races like the Volvo Ocean Race and single-handers such as the Vendée Globe.

Covering 25,000 miles in three months, the event starts and finishes in Barcelona and has attracted some of the world's best professional sailors from both solo and fully crewed disciplines. They will be racing in high-performance Open 60 monohulls, managed by the International Monohull Open Class Association (IMOCA).

The timing of this new global race also acts as a prelude to the Vendée Globe, to be held over the winter of 2008/9, providing an opportunity for skippers to test themselves and their boats fully before their solo circumnavigation.

As well as being host port, Barcelona is a partner in the venture and has established a new organisation known as the Fundació per la Navegació Oceànica de Barcelona (FNO) to promote the city via the sport of sailing. The Barcelona World Race is their first project and is to be run every four years.

■ www.barcelonaworldrace.com

31-1 Nov **La Castanyada**
All over Barcelona
All Saints' Day and the evening before are celebrated with piles of *castanyes* (roast chestnuts).

November 2007

Ongoing LEM Festival

1 Tots Sants (All Saints' Day)

Nov-Dec **Els Grans del Gospel**
Various venues
www.the-project.net
International gospel festival.

Nov **Festival Titelles**
Various venues
www.diba.es/festivaltitellesbcn
Biannual international puppet festival.

Nov-July **AvuiMúsica**
Various venues
www.accompositors.com
A series of 15 small-scale concerts.

Nov **Festival of Pocket Opera**
Various venues
www.festivaloperabutxaca.org
Small-scale contemporary opera.

Nov **L'Alternativa**
CCCB (p84)
www.alternativa.cccb.org
Indie cinema fest.

Nov-Dec **BAC!**
CCCB (p84) & other venues
www.lasanta.org
www.bacfestival.com
Contemporary art festival.

Late Nov/early Dec
Festival International de Jazz de Barcelona
Various venues
www.the-project.net
Jazz from bebop to big band.

Late Nov **Wintercase Barcelona**
Sala Razzmatazz 1, C/Almogàvers 122, Poblenou
www.wintercase.com
Big-name indie bands.

Nov-24 Dec **Fair of Sant Eloi**
C/Argenteria, Born
Artisan Christmas street fair. Live music from 6-8pm.

December 2007

Ongoing Els Grans del Gospel, AvuiMúsica, Festival International de Jazz de Barcelona, BAC!, Fair of Sant Eloi

2-23 **Fira de Santa Llúcia**
Pla de la Seu & Avda de la Catedral, Barri Gòtic
www.bcn.es/nadal
Christmas market with trees, pretty decorations and nativity-scene figures.

6 Día de la Constitució

8 La Immaculada

Dec **Resfest**
Mercat de les Flors (p118)
www.resfest.com
A global travelling festival of innovative film, music, art, design, fashion and technology.

Mid Dec **Drap Art**
CCCB (p84)
www.drapart.org
An international creative recycling festival draws in the punters with concerts, workshops and a market of recyled goods.

Dec-Feb **Festival Mil·lenni de Barcelona**
Palau de la Música Catalana (p74)
www.festivalmillenni.com
Big names from Woody Allen to Sara Baras perform their music, dance and poetry.

Dec **Bellas Artes Festival (BAF)**
Sala Apolo (p118)
www.sala-apolo.com
Avant-garde, non-commercial art and performance with music and DJs until dawn.

25 Nadal (Christmas Day)

26 Sant Esteve (Boxing Day)

28 **Día dels Inocents**
Local version of April Fool's Day, with paper figures attached to the backs of unsuspecting victims.

31 Cap d'Any (New Year's Eve)

Swill Cava and gulp down a grape for every chime of the clock at midnight.

Itineraries

Sagrada Família

To appreciate the sheer scale of this phantasmagorical form emerging from a metropolitan massif, it is best to approach from a distance: the far side of the lake in the Plaça Gaudí is a good spot for a full-length photograph. Take a moment to consider that the current structure will one day be dwarfed by later additions, including a central spire destined to rise 170 metres (560 feet) into the skyline, making the Sagrada Família once again the city's highest building.

An estimated 6,000 people a day pass through the temple, so don't expect the place to yourself. That said, it's worth arriving as the doors open at 9am to beat the worst crowds. Queues tend to be less hectic at the C/Marina entrance as groups are limited to the C/Sardenya entrance on the opposite side. Bear in mind that things are quieter on weekends when there is no construction work. To appreciate the building fully and take in a trip up the spires, you need to allow a full morning.

The first façade to be completed and the most iconic, the **Nativity façade** on C/Marina is a dazzling riot of stone, crammed with religious figures and the flora and fauna of Catalonia, Palestine and the Nile. As the name suggests, this façade is Gaudí's depiction of the story of Christ's genealogy, birth and childhood. From left to right the three portals represent Faith, Charity and Hope, and the story unfolding above them starts at the slaughter of the innocents and ends with Christ preaching in the temple as a young boy. As pieces of sculpture, few of the figures stand up to close aesthetic scrutiny, being (as art critic Robert Hughes puts it) 'devotional cliché'. But taken as a whole, the effect is quite magical.

At the apex, a green cypress symbolises eternity and the doves alighting on it represent blessed souls. Topping the tree, the letter T stands for *theos* (God), the X represents Christ, and the dove represents the Holy Spirit, thus completing the Holy Trinity. At the foot of the tree a pelican ripping open its chest to feed its young is a symbol of the Eucharistic sacrifice. When Gaudí was asked why there was so much detail high up, he replied, 'The angels will see it.'

The façade is partly made of stone from Montserrat mountain, the spiritual heart of Catalonia, and echoes of the rocky fingers of the mountain range are repeated across the façade and in the belltowers.

The visibly newer sculptures of musical angels over the Charity portal are the recent contribution of Japanese sculptor Etsuro Sotoo, whose official conversion to Catholicism while working on the Sagrada Família has been claimed as one of the 'miracles' needed to make Gaudí eligible for sainthood.

Enter the temple through the Nativity façade's **Faith portico** and cross the transept into what will one day be the nave, but is currently a building site filled with scaffolding, machinery and piles of brick and plasterboard. You have to look up for a sense of the project's scale and beauty. Rather than flying buttresses, the vaults are supported by tree-like helicoidal columns splitting into branches and starbursts of foliage ornamented with green and gold ceramic. Jordi Bonet, head architect of the project, has predicted that the apse will be entirely covered by 2007 and that the floor area will be free of scaffolding by 2009, providing congregation space for 15,000 people. The exit brings you out at the Passion façade on the opposite side of the building.

Started in 1952, the **Passion façade** is a brutal counterpart to the baroque fluidity of the Nativity façade. Framed by six tibia-like columns, the façade chronicles the events leading up to Christ's death, following an S-shaped path from the last supper to the crucifixion. It is the work of Josep M Subirachs, a well-known Catalan sculptor who, like Gaudí, has set up a workshop and living space inside the church. His blocky, stylised figures have been widely criticised, not least because one of them depicts a naked Christ on the cross, although Subirachs defended his departure from the original style, saying that his work had nothing to do with Gaudí. Hughes called it 'the most blatant mass of half-digested modernist clichés to be plunked on a notable building within living memory'. Subirachs prevailed, however, and has been commissioned for further work on the Glory façade.

The figure at Christ's feet with an oversized hand and an S on his right arm is thought to be the sculptor's self-portrait. Subirachs also included a portrait of Gaudí over the central doorway, portraying him as a cloaked observer taking notes.

On the left-hand side by the kiss of Judas, the cryptogram or 'magic square' contains 16 numbers offering 310 combinations that all add up to 33, the age of Christ at his death. Just to the left of this is an inscription of Christ's words to Judas (from John 13:27), perhaps also intended as a wink to the famous lengthiness of the project: *El que estàs fent, fes-ho de pressa.* (What thou doest, do it quickly.)

If you feel the need to purchase some cryptogram earrings, the largest of the two souvenir shops on the site is directly to the right of the Passion façade.

No visit is complete without the views from the corn-cob-shaped **belltowers**. Reaching a height of 100 metres (330 feet), they each represent an apostle and the stone 'blinds' are to diffuse the sound of the tubular bells designed by Gaudí and yet to be installed. The cramped spiral stairwells are located on the Nativity façade by the right-hand Faith entrance and are quite literally a tourist trap: only wide enough for single file, once you go up you cannot back down, although a bridge halfway up connects to the descending staircase. For €2 and a long wait you can take one of the two lifts, but you must descend on foot if you take the lift on the Nativity façade. Though the Nativity lift goes a little higher than that inside the Passion façade, in both cases you have to finish the ascent on foot for the views from the very top.

Back on the ground, visit the **subterranean museum**, which offers insight into the history of the construction, scale models and the chance to watch the current sculptors at work. There's also a short film and an exhibition on Gaudí and nature. Finish off with a turn through the wavy-roofed school building on the corner of C/Sardenya and C/Mallorca, which at present serves as an extension of the museum. Gaudí himself is buried to the left of the altar in the neo-Gothic crypt, which has its own entrance through the Sagrada Família's parish church on C/Provença.

Best viewed from the street, the third and final façade will be the main entrance and is to be devoted to the **Resurrection**. This is where building work is currently concentrated. The façade will eventually feature seven bronze doors (representing the seven sacraments), sculpted by Subirachs, and a huge statue of Sant Jordi. The projected *plaça* east of the Glory façade is currently a block of apartments constructed in the early 1970s with the understanding that, eventually, demolition would ensue. C/Mallorca will go underground, although no dates have been set.

At this point, it's time for lunch. Eating opportunities in the area are limited. Ronald McDonald lures in plenty of tired and hungry tourists, as do the truly nasty feeding barns surrounding the temple; for something far more pleasant, head two blocks uptown for excellent home cooking at La Yaya Amelia (C/Sardenya 364, 93 456 45 73), while just down from the Nativity façade there's hearty Galician food at Casa Debasa (C/Marina 241, 93 265 5809). There are pints and pub lunches at the Michael Collins (Plaça Sagrada Família 4, 93 459 46 26) or, for a swanky gourmet treat, Alkimia (p125). For high-quality picnicking, buy ham, cheese and olives from Joaquín Mir (C/València 441, 93 245 10 32) and eat them on the grass at Plaça Gaudí or Plaça Sagrada Família.

If you have any energy after lunch, there is a mercifully tourist-free Modernista jewel a short walk away up the Avda Gaudí. The **Hospital de la Santa Creu i Sant Pau** was designed by Gaudí's contemporary, Lluís Domènech i Montaner, a strong believer in the therapeutic properties of colour and nature. The hospital was built in 1900 as a 'garden city' with plenty of trees, flowers and sylvan glades. The hospital wards were spread over 18 luxurious pavilions, each lavishly adorned with mosaics, sculpture, Mudéjar motifs and polychromatic ceramic tiling. Medical facilities have recently been moved to a newer building nearby, but the public is still free to roam the grounds.

ITINERARIES

Barcelona Head

Street Art

Since time immemorial high design and grand architectural gestures have formed a part of Barcelona's urban planning, most famously when the vast neighbourhood of the Eixample ('Extension') was created to relieve the overcrowding of what is now the Old City. Gaudí and the other Modernista architects were given free rein to create and embellish buildings so fantastical as to provide the perfect counterpoint to the grid-like layout of the streets. A more recent example might be the Born's Mercat Santa Caterina; old, leaking and thoroughly shabby, it was completely overhauled and given a kaleidoscopic undulating roof, which has succeeded in lightening the mood of an entire district, attracting a slew of new shops and businesses in the process.

But what to do when the bricks and mortar have already been in place for centuries? This was the dilemma facing the city planners when it was decided that Barceloneta and the shoreline should be spruced up for the 1992 Olympics. The answer lay in street art, most of which can be enjoyed in a half-day stroll, perhaps with a break for lunch at one of the neighbourhood's many fish restaurants.

The most instantly recognisable piece commissioned at this time, and as emblematic of modern-day Barcelona as the dragon in Park Güell was in its day, is Roy Lichtenstein's pop art **Barcelona Head**, at the junction of Passeig Colom and Via Laietana. This brazen, comic and colourful sculpture features Lichtenstein's trademark use of Benday dots, only

Wounded Star p48

here as ceramic plates in homage to Gaudí's broken-tile technique.

After the irresistible gaiety of this piece, Ulrich Ruckreim's sombre **Four Wedges** in the nearby Pla de Palau is harder to love and slightly puzzling. It consists of two groups of two almost identical stout granite wedges that, despite a local inclination to link them to the four bars of the Catalan flag, are intended to represent nothing but their own purity and strength.

Heading towards the port from here, the next sculpture, Lothar Baumgarten's **Wind Rose**, is best seen from above – and the Museu d'Història de Catalunya (p102) provides the perfect vantage point. Take the lift to the top floor where a practically unknown café boasts the biggest terrace and some of the best views in all of Barcelona. Place an order for coffee and then scrutinise the pavement far below and you'll see giant bronze letters forming words in all directions.

These are the names of the Catalan winds – *tramuntana, llevant, xaloc, migjorn, ponent, garbí, mestral* and *gregal* – positioned according to the direction from which they blow.

Descending to street level, head up Passeig Joan de Borbó, stepping over *gregal* and *llevant* as you go, and halfway up you'll come across Italian artist Mario Merz's line of pink neon numbers under glass, set into the pavement. This piece, **Growing in Appearance**, is more noticeable by night, and 15 years of beach-going traffic have left some of the numbers worse for wear, but keen-eyed mathematicians and fans of *The Da Vinci Code* will make out the Fibonacci sequence.

Continue along this stretch to the Plaça del Mar at the end for one of the most unsettling of this group of sculptures, Juan Muñoz's **A Room Where It Always Rains**. A slatted bronze cage reminiscent of the Umbracle ('shade house') in the Parc de la Ciutadella, it nods to Pirandello's *Six Characters in*

Search of an Author, the expressionless figures within sharing a space but disconnected, conferring an unshakeable air of melancholy on the whole. The original idea was that 'rain' should indeed fall continuously through the bars, but problems with the recycling of the water and leaf fall from above had not been resolved by the time of the sculptor's untimely death in 2001.

Next up, and a little further along the beach, is Rebecca Horn's celebrated **Wounded Star**. This towering stack of rusted cubes is a homage to the fishermen's shacks and *xiringuitos* – makeshift seafood bars – that once filled this stretch of the shore but were torn down in the 1980s to make way for Barcelona's new beach. It's still the essential seaside meeting place – 'We're by the cubes!' is shouted into a hundred mobiles an hour – but is another to have fallen into disrepair, the nautical instruments contained within no longer lit up at night.

This area bristles with old-school seafood restaurants for an outdoor lunch, or you can grab a wrap at nearby La Piadina (p99) on the way to the next sculpture on C/Almirall Cervera, Jannis Kounellis' **Roman Scales**. These also recall the *barrio*'s maritime trading history; six scales hanging from a vertical 18-metre (60-foot) iron beam, each supporting sacks of coffee. The piece initially met with resistance from local residents, but its strength and harmony with its surroundings have become much better appreciated in recent years.

With the exception of *Barcelona Head*, all the sculptures named above are part of a group of pieces commissioned by curator Gloria Moure and collectively known as *Configuracions Urbanes*. The remaining two are a ten-minute walk away, in the Born

neighbourhood. The first is Jaume Plensa's **Born**, on the *passeig* of the same name. Comprising a large iron trunk sitting atop one of the stone benches that line the promenade, and several cast-iron cannon balls bearing apparently random lettering below and around them, it's an unobtrusive but thought-provoking work, attracting double takes from passers-by – those who notice it at all.

The same can be said of James Turrell's **Deuce Coop**, a short walk from here along the C/Comerç. Housed in the entrance to the former Convent Sant Agustí at No.23, it takes the form of a light sculpture and is the most magical of all the pieces, with an almost spiritual quality, particularly late at night, when it's viewed through the slats of the solid iron doors. Different architectural elements are illuminated with coloured lights, the door itself ringed in a neon glow.

All these sculptures make up a tiny part of the 50 or so pieces commissioned in the 1980s as part of the city's grand revamping, and just so happen to be conveniently close to one another. With a few more hours to spare, however, it's also worth visiting **Fallen Sky**, Beverly Pepper's azure land sculptures in the Parc de l'Estació del Nord (p124); Frank Gehry's glittering bronze **Fish** in front of the Hotel Arts (p170), and **Eduardo Chillida's sculptures** in the Plaça del Rei and the Parc de la Creueta del Coll (p153). Most fun of all, though, and certainly worth the metro ride out to Montbau, is Claes Oldenburg's **Matches**. This huge pop art matchbook is one of the city's best-loved and most-photographed pieces, the striking of the flame evoking the lighting of the Olympic torch over on Montjuïc, when the fun began in earnest.

Barcelona by Area

Calle Avinyó

Barri Gòtic

Neither as glacially cool as the Born or as bohemian as the Raval, the Barri Gòtic is nonetheless an essential port of call, with the best preserved medieval quarter in Europe, its ancient splendour surviving the last five centuries virtually intact, huddled around the Gothic **cathedral**.

One of the grander clusters of buildings from the Middle Ages has as its heart the **Plaça del Rei**, where you'll find the former royal palace (**Palau Reial**). The complex houses the **Museu d'Història de la Ciutat** and includes some of Barcelona's most historically important buildings: the **chapel of Santa Àgata** and the 16th-century watchtower (**Mirador del Rei Martí**). Parts of the palace are said to date back to the tenth century,

and there have been many remarkable additions to it since, notably the 14th-century Saló del Tinell, a medieval banqueting hall. It is here that Ferdinand and Isabella are said to have received Columbus on his return from America.

For the last 2,000 years, however, the heart of the city has been Plaça Sant Jaume, where the main Roman axes used to run. At the crossroads of these streets, dominating the forum, was the **Temple of Augustus**, four columns of which can still be seen in C/Pietat. The square now contains the stolid neo-classical façade of the municipal government (**Ajuntament**) and the Renaissance seat of the Catalan regional government (**Palau de la Generalitat**), which stand opposite each other.

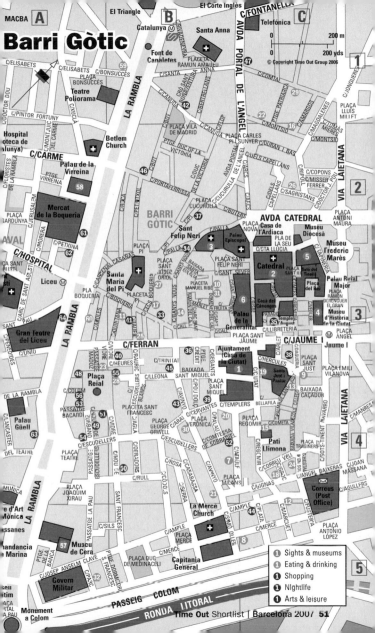

Plaça Sant Just p55

Sights & museums

Ajuntament (City Hall)

Plaça Sant Jaume (93 402 70 00/ special visits 93 402 73 64/www. bcn.es). Metro Liceu or Jaume I. **Open** *Office* 8.30am-2.30pm Mon-Fri. *Visits* 10am-1.30pm Sun. **Admission** free. **Map** p51 C3 ❶

The centrepiece and oldest part of the Casa de la Ciutat is the stately 15th-century Saló de Cent, which is flanked by the semicircular Saló de la Reina Regent, and the Saló de Cròniques, spectacularly painted with murals by Josep Maria Sert. On Sundays there are guided tours every 20 minutes.

Cathedral

Pla de la Seu (93 315 15 54). Metro Jaume I. **Open** *Combined ticket* 1.30-4.30pm daily. *Church* 8am-12.45pm, 5-7.30pm Mon-Fri; 8am-12.45pm, 5-6pm Sat; 8-9am, 5-6pm Sun. *Cloister* 9am-12.30pm, 5-7pm daily. *Museum* 10am-1pm, 5.15-7pm daily. **Admission** *Combined ticket* €4. *Church & cloister* free. *Museum* €1. *Lift to roof* €2. *Choir* €1.50. No credit cards. **Map** p51 C3 ❷

The building is predominantly Gothic, save for the Romanesque chapel of Santa Llúcia to the right of the main façade. The cathedral museum, in the 17th-century chapter house, has paintings and sculptures, including works by the Gothic masters Jaume Huguet, Bernat Martorell and Bartolomé Bermejo. Santa Eulàlia, patron saint of Barcelona, lies in the dramatically lit crypt in an alabaster tomb carved with scenes from her martyrdom. To one side, there's a lift to the roof; take it for a magnificent view of the Old City.

Museu del Calçat (Shoe Museum)

Plaça Sant Felip Neri 5 (93 301 45 33). Metro Jaume I. **Open** 11am-2pm Tue-Sun. **Admission** €2.50; free under-7s. No credit cards. **Map** p51 B2 ❸

One of only three in the world, this tiny footwear museum details the cobbler's craft from Roman times to the present day. Embroidered slippers from the Arabic world, 17th-century

Cathedral

musketeers' boots and delicately hand-painted 18th-century party shoes are all highlights.

Museu d'Història de la Ciutat

Plaça del Rei 1 (93 319 02 22/www. museuhistoria.bcn.es). Metro Jaume I. **Open** *June-Sept* 10am-8pm Tue-Sat; 10am-3pm Sun. *Oct-May* 10am-2pm, 4-8pm Tue-Sat; 10am-3pm Sun. *Guided tours* by appointment. **Admission** *Permanent exhibitions* €4; €2.50 reductions; free under-16s. *Temporary exhibitions* varies. *Both* free 4-8pm 1st Sat of mth. No credit cards. **Map** p51 C3 ❹

The Casa Padellàs is a merchant's palace dating from 1498, underneath which lie extensive Roman remains, including streets, villas and storage vats for oil and wine. The whole underground labyrinth, as far as the cathedral, can be visited as part of the City History Museum. The admission fee also gives you access to the Santa Àgata chapel and the Saló del Tinell,

Caj Chai

at least when there's no temporary exhibition. This majestic room (1370) began life as the seat of the Catalan parliament and was converted in the 18th century into a heavy baroque church, which was dismantled in 1934. Tickets for the museum are also valid for the monastery at Pedralbes (p152).

Museu Frederic Marès

Plaça Sant Iu 5-6 (93 310 58 00/ www.museumares.bcn.es). Metro Jaume I. **Open** 10am-7pm Tue-Sat; 10am-3pm Sun. **Admission** €3; €1.50 reductions; free under-16s. Free 3-7pm Wed, 1st Sun of mth. **Guided tours** noon Sun. No credit cards. **Map** p51 C3 ❺

Founded and once home to obsessive hoarder, kleptomaniac and sculptor Frederic Marès, this is one of the city's most charming museums. The ground floor contains an array of Romanesque crucifixes, virgins and saints, while the first floor takes sculpture up to the 20th century. The basement contains remains from ecclesiastical buildings dating back to Roman times: on the second floor is the 'Gentlemen's Room', stuffed to the gunwhales with walking sticks, key fobs, smoking equipment, matchboxes and opera glasses, while the charming 'Ladies' Room' contains fans, sewing scissors, nutcrackers and perfume flasks.

Event highlights 'Sant Pere de Rodes, the abandonment and restoration of the medieval monastery' (15 Nov 2006-15 Apr 2007).

Palau de la Generalitat

Plaça Sant Jaume (93 402 46 17/ www.gencat.net). Metro Jaume I. **Guided tours** every 30mins 10.30am-1.30pm 2nd & 4th Sun of mth; also 9.30am-1pm, 4-7pm Mon, Fri by appointment. **Admission** free. **Map** p51 C3 ❻

Like the Ajuntament, the Generalitat has a Gothic side entrance on C/Bisbe, with a beautiful relief of St George (Sant Jordi), patron saint of Catalonia, made by Pere Johan in 1418. Inside, the finest features are the first-floor Pati de Tarongers ('Orange Tree Patio') and the magnificent 15th-century chapel.

Eating & drinking

Bar Bodega Teo

NEW *C/Ataulf 18 (93 315 11 59).* **Metro Drassanes or Jaume I. Open** 9.30am-3pm, 5pm-2am Mon-Thur; 9.30am-3pm, 5pm-3am Fri, Sat. **Bar. Map** p51 B4 ❼

An old *bodega* by day, with wine stored in huge oak barrels. At night young foreigners and *barcelonins* sip Moscow Mules amid the eclectic décor – fairy lights, eclectic futuristic insect lamps, a backlit panel of an expressive Mandarin duck and a blaze of stargazer lilies on the bar.

Bar Celta

C/Mercè 16 (93 315 00 06). Metro Drassanes. **Open** *June-Sept* noon-midnight Mon-Sat. *Oct-May* noon-midnight daily. **€. Tapas. Map** p51 C5 ❽

An authentic, no-frills, Galician tapas bar, Bar Celta specialises in food from the region, with good seafood – try the *navajas* (razor clams) or the *pulpo* (octopus) – and crisp Albariño wine served in traditional white ceramic bowls.

Cafè de l'Acadèmia

C/Lledó 1 (93 319 82 53). Metro Jaume I. **Open** 9am-noon, 1.30-4pm, 8.45-11.30pm Mon-Fri. Closed 3 wks Aug. **€€€. Catalan. Map** p51 C3 ❾

The tables outside on the shady little Plaça Sant Just are some of the most sought-after in the city. The regular menu of creative Catalan classics offers superb value and has had no need to change direction over the years, so you can expect to find a home-made pasta (try shrimp and garlic), risotto with duck foie, guineafowl with a tiny tarte tatin and lots of duck.

Caj Chai

NEW *C/Sant Domènech del Call 12 (mobile 610 334 712). Metro Jaume I.* **Open** 4-10pm Mon-Fri; noon-10pm Sat, Sun. No credit cards. **Tearoom. Map** p51 B3 ❿

One for serious drinkers of the brown stuff, Caj Chai is based on a Prague tearoom, where serenity reigns and First Flush Darjeeling is approached with the reverence afforded a vintage wine.

Can Culleretes

C/Quintana 5 (93 317 30 22). Metro Liceu. **Open** 1.30-4pm, 9-11pm Tue-Sat; 1.30-4pm Sun. Closed July. **€€**. **Catalan**. Map p51 B3 ⑪

The rambling dining rooms at the 'house of teaspoons' have been packing them in since 1786, and show no signs of slowing. The secret to the place's longevity is straightforward: honest, hearty cooking and decent wine at the lowest possible prices. Expect sticky boar stew, pork with prunes and dates, goose with apples, partridge escabeche and superbly fresh seafood.

Goa

NEW *C/Ample 46 (93 310 15 22). Metro Jaume I.* **Open** 1-5pm, 7pm-midnight daily. **€€**. **Indian**. Map p51 C4 ⑫

If you're from Brick Lane, Bradford or Bangalore it might not be for you, but Goa is pretty good by local Indian restaurant standards. The pilau rice is underwhelming but naan comes fresh and hot, the rogan josh and chicken jalfrezi will warm the cockles of your heart and veggie accompaniments such as aloo palak are especially tasty.

Ginger

C/Palma de Sant Just 1 (93 310 53 09). Metro Jaume I. **Open** 7pm-2.30am Tue-Thur; 7pm-3am Fri, Sat. Closed 2wks Aug. **€€**. **Tapas/cocktails**. Map p51 C4 ⑬

An elegant, comfortable cocktail bar, Ginger also serves top-notch tapas – try the salmon tartare with horseradish or the wild mushroom filo pastry – and has an impressive selection of mainly Catalan wines by the glass.

La Granja

C/Banys Nous 4 (93 302 69 75). Metro Liceu. **Open** *Sept-July* 9.30am-2pm, 4-9pm Mon-Fri; 9.30am-2pm, 5-9pm Sat; 5-10pm Sun. *Aug* 9.30am-2.30pm, 6.30-9pm Mon-Sat; 6.30-10pm Sun. Closed 2wks Aug. **€**. No credit cards. **Tearoom**. Map p51 B3 ⑭

There are a number of these old *granjes* (milk bars, often specialising in hot chocolate) around town, but this is one of the loveliest, with handsome antique fittings and its very own section of Roman wall at the back. You can stand your spoon in the chocolate, and it won't be to all tastes.

Matsuri

Plaça Regomir 1 (93 268 15 35). Metro Jaume I. **Open** 1.30-3.30pm, 8.30-11.30pm Mon-Fri; 8.30pm-midnight Sat. **€€**. **Asian**. Map p51 C4 ⑮

The trickling fountain, dark shades of terracotta and amber, wooden carvings and wall-hung candles are saved from Asian cliché by the thoroughly occidental lounge soundtrack. Reasonably priced tom yam soup, sushi, pad thai and other Southeast Asian favourites top the list, while less predictable choices include a zingy mango and prawn salad dressed with lime and chilli, and a rich, earthy red curry with chicken and aubergine.

Mercè Vins

C/Amargós 1 (93 302 60 56). Metro Urquinaona. **Open** 8am-5pm Mon-Thur; 8am-5pm, 9.30pm-midnight Fri. **€**. **Catalan**. Map p51 C2 ⑯

With green beams, buttercup walls and fresh flowers, few places are as cosy as Mercè Vins. The standard of cooking on the lunch deals can vary a bit, but occasionally a pumpkin soup or inventive salad might appear, before sausages with garlicky sautéed potatoes. Dessert regulars are flat, sweet *coca* bread with a glass of muscatel, chocolate flan or figgy pudding.

Mesón Jesús

C/Cecs de la Boqueria 4 (93 317 46 98). Metro Jaume I or Liceu. **Open** 1-4pm, 8-11pm Mon-Fri. Closed Aug-early Sept. **€€**. **Spanish**. Map p51 B3 ⑰

The feel is authentic Castilian, with gingham tablecloths, oak barrels, cartwheels and pitchforks hung around the walls, while the waitresses are incessantly cheerful. The dishes are reliably good and inexpensive to boot – try the sautéed green beans with ham to start, then superb grilled prawns or a tasty fish stew.

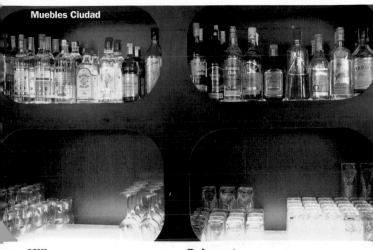

Muebles Ciudad

Milk

NEW *C/Gignas 21 (93 268 09 22).*
Metro Jaume I. **Open** 6.30pm-11.30am
Mon-Thur; 6.30pm-11.30 Fri, Sat; noon-
3am Sun. **€€**. **Fusion/cocktails**.
Map p51 C4 ⓲

Milk's candlelit, low-key baroque look,
charming service and loungey music
make it an ideal location for that first
date. Cocktails are a speciality, as is
good solid home-made bistro grub,
ranging from Caesar salad to fish and
chips. Brunch has been introduced for
idle Sundays.

Muebles Ciudad

NEW *C/Ciutat 5 (93 317 59 89). Metro
Jaume I.* **Open** 10am-2am Mon-Thur,
Sun; 10am-3am Fri, Sat. No credit
cards. **€€**. **Café**. Map p51 C3 ⓳

Be somebody. And if you can't be
somebody, have a Caesar salad. These
are the options that present themselves
in this new café-cum-modelling agency,
a very singular combination, offering a
super-stylish bar downstairs and, on
the mezzanine, a mini-studio where
aspirant TV extras are invited to try
their luck. Leaving the flummery aside,
Muebles Ciudad is a great spot for
breakfast or cocktails.

Peimong

C/Templers 6-10 (93 318 28 73).
Metro Jaume I. **Open** 1-4.30pm, 8-
11.30pm Tue-Sun. **€€**. **Peruvian**.
Map p51 B4 ⓴

With its tapestries of Macchu Pichu
and plastic flowers, Peimong wins no
prizes for design, but makes up for its
rather unforgiving and overlit interior
with some tasty little South American
dishes. Start with stuffed corn tamales,
and then move on to *ceviche*, *pato en aji*
(duck with a spicy sauce and rice) or
the satisfying *lomo sallado* – pork fried
with onions, tomatoes and coriander.

Pitarra

C/Avinyó 56 (93 93 301 16 47/
www.pitarra.com). Metro Liceu.
Open 1-4pm, 8.30-11pm daily.
€€€. **Catalan**. Map p51 B4 ㉑

Once home to Catalan playwright,
Frederic 'Pitarra' Soler, and his watch-
making uncle, this smart, bright traditional restaurant is still a shrine to the
art of horology. Classic dishes include
partridge casserole, pheasant in a
creamy cava sauce and langoustines
with wild mushrooms, but the desserts
are not quite so accomplished.

BARCELONA BY AREA

Milk p57

Els Quatre Gats

C/Montsió 3 bis (93 302 41 40). Metro Catalunya. **Open** *9am-2am daily.* €€€. **Bar/Catalan. Map** p51 C1

This Modernista classic, which was frequented by Picasso and various other luminaries of the period, nowadays caters mainly to tourists. The inevitable consequences include higher prices, so-so food and, worst of all, the house musicians. The place is still dazzling in its design, however, so avoid the worst excesses of touristification and come at lunchtime for a reasonably priced and respectably varied *menú*. And that way you spare yourself 'Bésame Mucho'.

Les Quinze Nits

Plaça Reial 6 (93 317 30 75). Metro Liceu. **Open** *1-3.45pm, 8.30-11.30pm daily.* €€. **Catalan. Map** p51 A3 ㉓

Combining fast-food speed and prices with tablecloths, potted palms and soft lighting has made this chain a legend in its own lunchtime, drawing endless queues. The turnover is brisk, as squadrons of harried waiters serve up good salads and local favourites such as meatballs with squid in black ink, grilled bream with asparagus, *botifarra* and beans, and *crema catalana*. For the best experience choose wisely: the quality of the steaks is variable and the paella can taste mass-produced.
Other locations: La Fonda, C/Escudellers 10 (93 301 75 15).

El Salón

C/Hostal d'en Sol 6-8 (93 315 21 59). Metro Jaume I. **Open** *8.30pm-midnight Mon-Sat. Closed 2wks Aug.* €€€. **Mediterranean. Map** p51 C4 ㉔

Our one and only complaint about this convivial little restaurant, with its air of stylish bohemia, is the chest-height tables. (And that's Nordic chest-height, not Mediterranean.) The food is superb, however, and as varied as it is accomplished, with seafood bisque sharing billing with lamb tagine, burritos, duck magret with ginger, and blackcurrant crumble. A bar and a couple of sofas ensure a full house long after the kitchen closes.

Caption: **Els Quatre Gats**

Schilling

C/Ferran 23 (93 317 67 87). Metro Liceu. **Open** *Sept-July 10am-3am Mon-Sat; noon-2.30am Sun. Aug 5pm-3am daily.* €€. **Café. Map** p51 B3 ㉕

Spacious and utterly elegant, Schilling is no longer as fashionable as it once was, although the supercilious waiters seem not to have realised. Nonetheless, it's an unbeatable place for meeting up, and the window seats remain unchallenged as the city's number one spot for budding travel writers to scribble in their journals.

Shunka

C/Sagristans 5 (93 412 49 91). Metro Jaume I. **Open** *1.30-3.30pm, 8.30-11.30pm Tue-Fri; 2-4pm, 8.30-11.30pm Sat, Sun.* €€€. **Japanese. Map** p51 C2 ㉖

Shunka is one of the better Japanese restaurants in town, and a favourite haunt of Catalan superchef Ferran Adrià. Reserve a table for the sumo-sized set lunch of rich miso soup, a leafy salad topped with salmon and punchy vinegar and teriyaki dressing,

Almacenes del Pilar

followed by vegetable and shrimp tempura and six pieces of maki and extremely good nigiri zushi. The best seats in the house are those up at the counter, where you're right in front of the performing chefs.

Taller de Tapas

Plaça Sant Josep Oriol 9 (93 301 80 20). Metro Liceu. **Open** noon-midnight Mon-Thur, Sun; noon-1am Fri, Sat. €€. **Tapas**. Map p51 B3 ㉗

Useful for tongue-tied tourists and for those who aren't prepared to eat standing three-deep at a bar, this sleek 'tapas workshop' has multilingual menus and plenty of seating, both inside and out. The service can be slow and is occasionally frosty, but the tapas are generally of reliable quality: try the succulent Palamós prawns, for example, or tuck into baby broad beans with ham.

Taxidermista

Plaça Reial 8 (93 412 45 36). Metro Liceu. **Open** 1.30-4pm, 8.30pm-12.30am Tue-Sun. Closed 3wks Jan. €€€. **Mediterranean**. Map p51 B4 ㉘

When this place was a taxidermist's shop, Dalí famously ordered 200,000 ants, a tiger, a lion and a rhinoceros. Nowadays those who leave here stuffed are generally tourists, though this hasn't affected standards, which remain reasonably high. À la carte offerings include foie gras with quince jelly and a sherry reduction; langoustine ravioli with seafood sauce; steak tartare; and some slightly misjudged fusion elements, such as wok-fried spaghetti with vegetables. The lunch *menú* is excellent, with two- or three-course deals.

Tokyo

C/Comtal 20 (93 317 61 80). Metro Catalunya. **Open** 1.30-4pm, 8-11pm Mon-Sat. €€. **Japanese**. Map p51 C1 ㉙

Resist the suggestion that is no *menú*, for this is the way to eat here. A zingy little salad is followed by a mountain of prawn and vegetable tempura and a platter of maki rolls, nigiri and a bowl of miso soup. It's a simple, cosy space, with a reassuring Japanese presence. À la carte, the speciality is edomae (hand-rolled nigiri zushi), but the meat and veg sukiyaki cooked at your table is also good.

La Verònica

C/Avinyó 30 (93 412 11 22). Metro Liceu. **Open** *Sept-July* 7.30pm-1am Mon-Thur; 7.30pm-1.30am Fri; 1.30pm-1am Sat, Sun. *Aug* 7.30pm-1am Mon-Thur; 7.30pm-1.30am Fri; 1.30-7.30pm Sat, Sun. Closed 2wks Feb. **€€. Pizzeria**. **Map** p51 C1 30

With plate glass windows and a high-exposure terrace, this bright orange, gay-friendly pizzeria makes the perfect posing gallery. The pizzas are as thin and well dressed as the clientele, with trendy toppings such as apple and gorgonzola along with the cast-iron classics. Puddings are the competent pan-EU standards of tiramisu, cheese-cake and brownies.

Vinissim

C/Sant Domènec del Call 12 (93 301 45 75). Metro Jaume I or Liceu. **Open** 7pm-1am Tue-Sat. **€€. Tapas/wine bar**. **Map** p51 B3 31

An expertly staffed wine and tapas bar, painted in warm colours and bathed in sunlight, with tables out on a quiet square. The tapas are sublime, from *cochinillo pibil* (spicy, Mexican-style shredded pork) to red peppers filled with cod brandade. Puddings are also excellent, such as delicious fig ice-cream or spiced white chocolate tart with dried fruit.

Xeroga

NEW *C/Parc 1 (93 412 62 75). Metro Drassanes.* **Open** 1-5pm, 8pm-midnight daily. **€€. Chilean**. **Map** p51 A5 32

A Chilean restaurant with a good-natured South American vibe, Xeroga has walls that are hung with bright oil paintings, a gold-stitched sombero and a cracked and burnished guitar. On offer are various empanadas (*pino* is the classic option – meat, olives, egg and raisin), ceviche, *mariscal* (shellfish and hake in a fish broth) and a mighty *bife a lo pobre* – a trucker's breakfast of thin steak, two fried eggs and a stack of chips.

Cereria Subirá p62

Shopping

Almacenes del Pilar

C/Boqueria 43 (93 317 79 84/www.almacenesdelpilar.com). Metro Liceu. **Open** 9.30am-2pm, 4-8pm Mon-Sat. Closed 2wks Aug. **Map** p51 B3 33

At Almacenes del Pilar there's an array of fabrics and accessories for traditional Spanish costumes, on display in a shambolic interior dating back to 1886. Making your way through bolts of material, you'll find richly hued brocades, lace *mantillas* and the high combs over which they are worn, along with fringed, hand-embroidered pure silk *mantones de manila* (shawls) and colourful wooden fans.

Caelum

C/Palla 8 (93 302 69 93). Metro Liceu. **Open** 5-8.30pm Mon; 10.30am-8.30pm Tue-Thur; 10.30am-midnight Fri, Sat; 11.30am-9pm Sun. Closed 2wks Aug. **Map** p51 B2 34

Spain's nuns and monks have a naughty sideline in traditional sweets, including candied saints' bones, sugared egg yolks and drinkable goodies such as eucalyptus and orange liqueur, all of which are beautifully packaged. There's also a taster café downstairs, which is on the site of some medieval Jewish thermal baths.

Cereria Subirá

Baixada de Llibreteria 7 (93 315 26 06). Metro Jaume I. **Open** *Jan-July, Sept-Nov* 9am-1.30pm, 4-7.30pm Mon-Fri; 9am-1.30pm Sat. *Aug* 9am-1.30pm, 4-7.30pm Mon-Fri. *Dec* 9am-1.30pm, 4-7.30pm Mon-Sat. **Map** p51 C3 ③⑤

The interior, dating back to 1761, is stunning, with grand swirling mint-green and gilt-adorned balustrades and torch-wielding maidens, but the range of candles is also impressive. The varieties include simple votive candles, scented and novelty wax creations and tapered classics.

Custo Barcelona

NEW *C/Ferran 36 (93 342 66 98). Metro Jaume.* **Open** 10am-10pm Mon-Sat. **Map** p51 B3 ③⑥

A local predilection for amalgamating loud patterns and prints with an assortment of fabrics culminates in Custo's kaleidoscopic candy-coloured creations. Recent motifs have included 19th-century prints, psychedelic art,

Drap

botanical illustrations and wallpaper. The collections now comprise a full range of casualwear, but the T-shirts remain number one on everybody's wishlists, despite the high prices.

Drap

C/Pi 14 (93 318 14 87). Metro Liceu. **Open** 9.30am-1.30pm, 4.30-8.30pm Mon-Fri; 10am-1.30pm, 5-8.30pm Sat. **Map** p51 B2 ③⑦

A selection of painstakingly crafted dolls' mansions, perfect in every detail down to the doorbells and tiny padded hangers for the hand-carved wardrobes.

Formatgeria La Seu

C/Dagueria 16 (93 412 65 48/www. formatgerialaseu.com). Metro Jaume I. **Open** 10am-2pm, 5-8pm Tue-Fri; 10am-3pm, 5-8pm Sat. Closed Aug. No credit cards. **Map** p51 C3 ③⑧

Formatgeria La Seu stocks a delectable range of Spanish farmhouse olive oils and cheeses, among them a fierce *tou dels til·lers* and a blackcurranty *picón* from Cantabria. On Saturdays, from noon to 3pm, there is a sit-down cheese and oil tasting for €5.85, but you can wash down three cheeses and a glass of wine anytime for €2.40.

Gotham

C/Cervantes 7 (93 412 46 47/www. gotham-bcn.com). Metro Jaume I. **Open** *Sept-July* 11am-2pm, 5-8pm Mon-Fri; 11am-2pm Sat. *Aug* 11am-2pm, 5-8pm Mon-Fri. Closed 2wks end Aug. **Map** p51 B4 ③⑨

Fab 1950s ashtrays in avocado green, some bubble TV sets, teak sideboards, coat stands that look like molecular models… Take a trip down nostalgia lane with Gotham's classic retro furniture from the 1930s, '50s, '60s and '70s in warm cartoon colours.

Herboristeria del Rei

C/Vidre 1 (93 318 05 12). Metro Liceu. **Open** 5-8pm Mon; 10am-2pm, 5-8pm Tue-Sat. Closed 1-2wks Aug. **Map** p51 B3 ④⓪

In 1860 Queen Isabel II named this venerable herbalist official purveyor to the Royal Court, and called in Soler i Rovirosa, a famous theatre-set designer

Subcontinental drift

Bollywood comes to town.

Extravagant Bollywood stories of thwarted love and long-lost brothers interspersed with epic musical numbers and lashings of kohl have found an unlikely home at one of Barcelona's iconic old cinemas. The much-loved Cine Maldà (C/Pi 5, Barri Gòtic, mobile 605 271 379) reopened in August 2006 after extensive remodelling and has become the first cinema in Spain to offer a permanent programme of Indian cinema. The latest releases from Mumbai are screened alongside some classics of the genre, thus continuing the tradition of rereleases for which the Maldà has always been famous.

Offering an alternative to the glitzy Bolly blockbusters, the BAFF (Barcelona Asian Film Festival, p34) is the largest festival of its kind in Europe. India was the featured country in 2006 and Bollywood featured alongside indie projects by little-known directors and respected veterans such as Satyajit Ray. The Bollywood Party has become an established highlight of the BAFF Lounge section of the festival.

Meanwhile, the South Asian Cultural Association, Masala (www.club-masala.com) organises increasingly popular monthly Bollywood Lounge parties at the uptown club, Sweet Café (C/Casanova 75, www.sweetcafebcn.blogspot.com) with music, dancing and Indian snacks. Masala also runs a Sunday movie club along with classes in dancing, cookery and Urdu.

On the other end of the deal, the growing clout of the rupee has attracted the attentions of Barcelona's city council, which is trying to woo the South Asian tourist market by promoting Barcelona as a backdrop for Bollywood. In November 2005 Mayor Joan Clos made an official trip to India to try and close a deal for the shooting of a Bollywood blockbuster in the city, even offering partial financing. Maybe the *sardana* in a sari is not too far away.

Barcelona Pipa Club

of the time, to decorate it. Since then it has remained a local fixture. The shop stocks a couple of hundred medicinal herbs and spices in gorgeous glass jars. You'll also find fine teas, essential oils, natural toiletries, soaps and a selection of health food.

El Ingenio

C/Rauric 6 (93 317 71 38/www. el-ingenio.com). Metro Liceu. **Open** 10am-1.30pm, 4.15-8pm Mon-Fri; 10am-2pm, 5-8.30pm Sat. **Map** p51 B3 ㉛

El Ingenio is a kaleidoscope of magic tricks, puppets, party decorations and wigs. A speciality is carnival outfits and masks, ranging from warty noses to pumpkin-like *capgrosses* (oversized papier-mâché heads).

Le Boudoir

C/Canuda 21 (93 302 52 81/www. leboudoir.net). Metro Catalunya. **Open** *Sept-July* 10am-8.30pm Mon-Fri; 10am-9pm Sat. *Aug* 11am-8.30pm Mon-Sat. **Map** p51 B1 ㊷

Sensuality abounds in Barcelona's classy answer to Agent Provocateur. Sexy lingerie comes with designer labels (and prices), swimwear is not for shrinking violets and fluffy kitten-heeled mules have not been made with practicality in mind.

Loft Avignon

C/Avinyó 22 (93 301 24 20). Metro Jaume I or Liceu. **Open** 10.30am-8.30pm Mon-Sat. **Map** p51 B4 ㊸

A smörgåsbord of top international designers is on the menu at this purveyor of high-end informal fashion for men and women. Think Diesel Style Lab, Indian Rose, Vivienne Westwood and Ungaro, with a gentle sprinkling of Bikkembergs.

Other locations: C/Boters 8 (93 301 37 95); C/Boters 15 (93 412 59 10).

Papabubble

C/Ample 28 (93 268 86 25/www. papabubble.com). Metro Barceloneta or Drassanes. **Open** 10am-2pm, 4-8.30pm Tue-Fri; 10am-8.30pm Sat; 11am-7.30pm Sun. Closed Aug. **Map** p51 C5 ㊹

Tommy and Chris flip, stretch and roll traditionally made hot candy fresh from the kitchen into lollipops, humbugs, sculptures and even edible jewellery in all flavours, from strawberry and lavender to passion fruit and Mojito.

Tribu

C/Avinyó 12 (93 318 65 10). Metro Jaume I or Liceu. **Open** *June-Sept* 11am-2.30pm, 4.30-8.30pm Mon-Fri; 11am-8.30pm Sat. *Oct-May* 11am-2.30pm, 4.30-8.30pm Mon-Sat. **Map** p51 B3 **45**

One of the countless clued-up fashion platforms in town, providing international and homegrown casual labels such as Jocomomola, Nolita, Diesel and Freesoul. Don't miss the designer trainers at the back.

Women's Secret

C/Portaferrissa 7-9 (93 318 92 42/ www.womensecret.com). Metro Liceu. **Open** 10am-9pm Mon-Sat. **Map** p51 B2 **46**

Mix-and-match bras and knickers run the gamut from sexy to sensible. The real winners, however, are the colourful, cheap and cheerful nightwear and bikinis. Quality and durability are not guaranteed, but who cares when you can buy a whole new batch next season?

Zara

Avda Portal de l'Àngel 32-34 (93 317 44 52/www.zara.com). Metro Catalunya. **Open** 10am-9pm Mon-Sat. **Map** p51 A3 **47**

Zara's recipe for success has won over the world, but items are cheaper on its home turf. Well-executed, affordable copies of catwalk styles appear on the rails in a fashion heartbeat. The women's section is the front runner, but the men's and kids' sections cover good ground too. The introduction of the 'Zara Home' department has also been a success.

Nightlife

Barcelona Pipa Club

Plaça Reial 3, pral (93 302 47 32/ www.bpipaclub.com). Metro Liceu. **Open** 10.30pm-2am daily. **Admission** free. No credit cards. **Map** p51 A3 **48**

One of Barcelona's best-loved bars, where Catalan celebrities mingle with the bourgeoisie and American year-abroad students. Licensing problems have put the bar under threat of closure

and the opening hours have been drastically abridged, but it's still worth a shot after-hours. To try, ring the buzzer next to the sign of the pipe.

Café Royale

C/Nou de Zurbano 3 (93 412 14 33). Metro Liceu. **Open** 8.30pm-2.30am Mon-Thur, Sun; 8.30pm-3am Fri, Sat. **Admission** free (1 drink minimum). **Map** p51 A4 **49**

Early in the evening it's a chilled place to slump around on sofas, but even later, when Fred Guzzo's funk, soul and jazz-driven beats and the doorman's snotty attitude are cranked up a notch, the youngish mixed tourist/local crowd seems happier rubbing up against each other in the narrow bar than on the dancefloor.

Dot

C/Nou de Sant Francesc 7 (93 302 70 26/www.dotlightclub.com). Metro Drassanes. **Open** 11pm-2am Tue-Thur, Sun; 9pm-3am Fri, Sat. **Admission** free. No credit cards. **Map** p51 B4 **50**

Dot may be small but it scores large for a combination of great playlist (hip hop, breaks, funk, house... plus a sprinkling of punk and indie) in the hands of resident DJ Kosmos, non-stuffy staff and a cool, yet welcoming, crowd.

Downstairs@Club13

Plaça Reial 13 (93 412 43 27). Metro Liceu. **Open** *Apr-Oct* 2pm-2.30am Mon-Thur, Sun; 2pm-3am Fri, Sat. *Nov-Mar* 6pm-2.30am Mon-Thur, Sun; 6pm-3am Fri, Sat. **Admission** free. **Map** p51 A4 **51**

Sounds glam and, by golly, it is glam. This little nightspot adds a touch of class to grungy Plaça Reial, what with its glittering chandeliers and posh-nosh restaurant. Red flock wallpaper, exposed bricks in the cellar and black leather sofas downstairs make an ideal backdrop for smooth grooves from deep house to nu breaks via hip hop.

Harlem Jazz Club

C/Comtessa de Sobradiel 8 (93 310 07 55). Metro Jaume I. **Open** 8pm-4am Tue-Thur, Sun; 8pm-5am Fri, Sat. *Gigs* 10.30pm, midnight Tue-Thur, Sun;

BARCELONA BY AREA

Downstairs@Club13 p65

11.30pm, 1am Fri, Sat. Closed 2wks Aug. **Admission** free Mon-Thur; €5 (incl 1 drink) Fri-Sun. No credit cards. **Map** p51 B4 ⑤②
An international and studenty crowd braves the oxygen-free atmosphere and crushed space to enjoy what could well be the most eclectic music programming in Barcelona. Despite the name, Harlem Jazz Club hops between genres to encompass everything from klezmer to Moroccan music via flamenco fusion. Unless it succeeds in its bid for public funding, however, it may have to close in 2006/7.

Jamboree/Los Tarantos

Plaça Reial 17 (93 301 75 64/www. masimas.com). Metro Liceu. **Open** 12.30pm-5.30am daily. *Gigs* 10pm Mon; 11pm Tue-Sun. **Admission** (incl 1 drink) €8. *Gigs* €8-€10. **Map** p51 A4 ⑤③
Every night Jamboree hosts jazz, Latin or blues gigs by mainly Spanish groups; when they're over the beards wander off and the beatbox comes out. On Mondays, particularly, the outrageously popular What the Fuck (WTF)

jazz jam session is crammed with a young and local crowd waiting for the funk/hip hop night that follows.

New York

C/Escudellers 5 (93 318 87 30). Metro Drassanes or Liceu. **Open** midnight-5am Thur-Sat. **Admission** (incl 1 drink) €8 with flyer, €10 without. No credit cards. **Map** p51 A4 ⑤④
This ancient former brothel turned rock club now hosts some of the best nights in *musica negra* (black music) – a term that's used for anything from funk to northern soul. Every Friday, Black Magic Sounds covers the ground between ska, rocksteady, reggae, funk, soul and proper 1970s disco for a crowd of diehard followers and late-night wanderers.

Sidecar Factory Club

Plaça Reial 7 (93 302 15 86/www. sidecarfactoryclub.com). Metro Liceu. **Open** 8pm-4.30am Tue-Thur, Sun; 8pm-5am Fri, Sat. *Gigs* (Oct-July) 10.30pm Tue-Sat. **Admission** (incl 1 drink) €6. *Gigs* €5-€10. No credit cards. **Map** p51 B3 ⑤⑤
A basement rock club hosting fledgling Barcelona indie acts as well as intimate concerts by guests ranging from Superchunk-fronted Portastatic to Detroit trash rockers Demolition Doll Rods. Between times, the club holds DJ sessions – with house, techno and electro on Wednesdays, electropop and glam on Thursdays, and the latest pop and rock at weekends.

Arts & leisure

Los Tarantos

Plaça Reial 17 (93 318 30 67/www. masimas.com). Metro Liceu. **Open** *Flamenco show* 8.30pm, 9.30pm, 10.30pm daily. **Admission** €5. **Map** p51 A4 ⑤⑥
This flamenco *tablao* has presented many top stars over the years. It now caters mainly to the tourist trade, but avoids the fripperies of some coach-party venues. Now under new ownership, prices have gone down, but the performers are less experienced.

La Rambla

La Rambla

It used to be said that every true Barcelona citizen was obliged to walk down the mile-long Rambla at least once a day. Today, many locals have become weary of the place, tired of its tawdry souvenir shops, human statues, fortune tellers, card sharps, puppeteers, dancers and tourists (imagine a more theatrical Oxford Street and you're nearly there), but the boulevard remains one of Barcelona's essential attractions.

The Rambla is divided into five parts. First comes the **Font de Canaletes** drinking fountain; if you drink from it, goes the legend, you'll return to Barcelona. Here, too, is where Barça fans converge in order to celebrate their increasingly frequent triumphs. Next comes perhaps the best-loved section of the boulevard, known as **Rambla de les Flors** for its line of magnificent flower stalls, open

into the night. To the right is the **Palau de la Virreina** exhibition and cultural information centre, and the superb Boqueria market. A little further is the **Pla de l'Os** (or **Pla de la Boqueria**), centrepoint of the Rambla, with a pavement **mosaic** created in 1976 by Joan Miró. On the left, where more streets run off into the Barri Gòtic, is the extraordinary **Bruno Quadros** building (1883), with umbrellas on the wall and a Chinese dragon protruding over the street.

The lower half of the Rambla is initially more restrained, flowing between the sober façade of the **Liceu** opera house and the more *fin-de-siècle* (architecturally and atmospherically) **Cafè de l'Opera**. On the right is C/Nou de la Rambla (where you'll find Gaudí's neo-Gothic **Palau Güell**; the promenade then widens into the **Rambla de Santa Mònica**, long a popular haunt of prostitutes.

Chasing the Shadow

On the trail of Barna's Da Vinci Code.

A sprawling thriller with amazing international success, *Shadow of the Wind* may be criticised for its clunky narrative contrivances, hackneyed characters and endless expository dialogue, but it draws in readers with atmospheric descriptions of postwar Barcelona and a ripping good central story. In it, Daniel Sempere is searching for Julián Carax, author of the *Shadow of the Wind*, as a mysterious figure finds and burns all the remaining copies of the novel. And Daniel's copy is the next in his sights.

If you want to walk the book, begin under an archway off La Rambla in C/Arc del Teatre, home to the Cemetery of Forgotten Books, where Daniel first sees the novel. The other side of La Rambla, C/Santa Ana is where he lived 'a stone's throw from the church square', while C/Canuda, running almost parallel, is where Daniel meets Gustavo Barceló in the Ateneo library – with its delightful café. South lies Plaça Reial, home to the unobtainable Clara Barceló; the milk bar she patronises with Daniel is probably Granja Dulcinea at C/Petrixol 2. Julián's would-be lover Nuria Monfort sits to read in Plaça Felip Neri to the east.

Finish with a trip uptown to the creaking mansion where Julián's true love Pénelope met her tragic end. 'Frare Blanc' is now Asador de Aranda, at Avda Tibidabo 31, a Modernista confection that serves a famous roast lamb.

Sights & museums

Museu de Cera

Ptge de la Banca 7 (93 317 26 49/ www.museoceracbn.com). Metro Drassanes. **Open** *July-Sept* 10am-10pm daily. *Oct-May* 10am-1.30pm, 4-7.30pm Mon-Fri; 11am-2pm, 4.30-8.30pm Sat, Sun. **Admission** €6.65; €3.75 children; free under-5s. No credit cards. **Map** p51 A5 ⑤⑦

This is a wax museum that belongs to the so-bad-it's-good school of entertainment. Expect the savvy Playstation generation to be notably underwhelmed by clumsy renderings of Gaudí and Lady Di jumbled in with Frankenstein, neanderthals and ET (mysteriously perched atop the Millennium Falcon).

Palau de la Virreina

La Rambla 99 (93 301 77 75/ www.bcn.es/cultura). Metro Liceu. **Open** 11am-2pm, 4-8pm Tue-Sat; 11am-3pm Sun. **Admission** €3; €1.50 reductions; free under-16s. No credit cards. **Map** p51 A2 ⑤⑧

The Virreina houses the city cultural department, and has lots of information on events and shows, but also boasts strong programming in its two distinct exhibition spaces. Upstairs is dedicated to one-off exhibitions, with the downstairs gallery focused on historical and contemporary photography.

Eating & drinking

Boadas

C/Tallers 1 (93 318 95 92). Metro Catalunya. **Open** *Jan-June, Sept-Dec* noon-2am Mon-Thur; noon-3am Fri, Sat. *July, Aug* noon-3pm, 6pm-2am Mon-Thur; noon-3pm, 6pm-3am Fri, Sat. No credit cards. **Cocktail bar**. **Map** p51 B1 ⑤⑨

Finally the pressure of being 'so classic it's practically a stop on the tourist bus' proved too much for this tiny and well-loved cocktail bar, and it was declared that to enter you must be appropriately dressed. If you do make the cut, this 1930s institution is elegant and relaxing, with sublimely cool barmen from another era.

Café de l'Opera

La Rambla 74 (93 317 75 85).
Metro Liceu. **Open** 8.30am-2.15am
Mon-Thur; 8.30am-2.45am Fri-Sun.
No credit cards. **Café**. **Map** p51 A3 ⑥⓿
Cast-iron pillars, etched mirrors and
bucolic murals create an air of fading
grandeur now incongruous among the
fast-food joints and souvenir shops. A
reasonable selection of tapas is served
by attentive bow-tied waiters. Given
the atmosphere (and the quality of the
competition), there's no better place for
a coffee on La Rambla.

Shopping

La Boqueria

La Rambla 89 (93 318 25 84).
Metro Liceu. **Open** 8am-8.30pm
Mon-Sat. **Map** p51 A2 ⑥①
Barcelona's most central food market
outstrips all the rest. Visitors and residents alike never tire of wandering the
hectic, colourful aisles and ogling the
gory spectacle of tripe and sheep
heads, the flailing pincers of live crabs
and crayfish, bins of nuts, tubs of aromatic olives and sacks of herbs and
spices. Packed under an impressive
vaulted glass and iron structure, the
succession of stalls are a cacophony of
buying and selling – each one brim-
ming with local produce. Don't miss
Llorenç Petràs's woodland stall of
mushrooms and insect goodies, at the
back. If it all makes you hungry, there
are some great places to eat incompa-
rably fresh food, if you can hack the
noise and are prepared to pull up a
stool at a frenzied bar.

However, be sure to steer clear of the
conspicuous stalls near the front, as
their neatly stacked picture-perfect
piles of fruit, mounds of sweets, candied fruit and nuts and ready-to-eat
fruit salads are designed to ensnare
tourists and have the prices to match.
The Barcelona authorities seem to
have cottoned on to the market's potential as tourist attraction and are capi-
talising on it with a range of Boqueria
merchandise, available from a stall
near the entrance.

Escribà

La Rambla 83 (93 301 60 27/
www.escriba.es). Metro Urgell.
Open 8.30am-9pm daily.
Map p51 A3 ⑥②
Antoni Escribà, known as the 'Mozart
of Chocolate', died in 2004, but happily
his legacy lives on. His team produces
jaw-dropping creations for the Easter
displays, from a hulking chocolate
Grand Canyon to a life-size model of
Michelangelo's *David*. Smaller miracles
include cherry liqueur encased in red
chocolate lips.

Nightlife

Club Fellini

La Rambla 27 (93 272 49 80/www.
clubfellini.com). Metro Liceu. **Open**
midnight-6am daily. **Admission**
(incl 1 drink) €9 Mon; €15 Tue-Sun.
With flyer €12. **Map** p51 A4 ⑥③
The prime Rambla location attracts
clubbers of all stripes but Fellini, the
sister club of La Terrrazza (p114),
accommodates most tastes with its
three separate spaces devoted to funk,
house and, above all, techno. The
baroque decor features lashings of red,
fuschia and gold – not that you can see
past the crush of bodies.

Arts & leisure

Gran Teatre del Liceu

La Rambla 51-59, Barri Gòtic
(93 485 99 13/tickets 902 53 33 35/
www.liceubarcelona.com). Metro Liceu.
Map p51 A3 ⑥④
The Liceu has gone from strength to
strength of late, steadily increasing
the number of performances but still
often selling out. The flames that swept
away an outdated, rickety structure a
decade ago cleared the decks for a
fine new opera house. By comparison
with the restrained façade, the 2,340-
seat auditorium is an impressively
elegant, classical affair of red plush,
gold leaf and ornate carvings, but the
mod cons include seat-back subtitles in
various languages that complement
the Catalan surtitles above the stage.

C/Montcada

Born & Sant Pere

The most uptown area of downtown, the Born mixes chapels and shoe shops with enviable élan and now boasts some of the highest property prices in the city. Neighbouring Sant Pere is a little scuzzier and less self-important, but has gained some ground and a little glamour with the new, dazzling Santa Caterina market. The area is demarcated to the east by the **Parc de la Ciutadella**, and to the west by Via Laietana. Sant Pere and the Born are divided by C/Princesa, the former centred around the monastery of **Sant Pere de les Puelles**, which still stands, if greatly altered, in Plaça de Sant Pere.

Sant Pere is undergoing dramatic renovation, with the gradual opening of a continuation of the Avda Francesc Cambó, which will swing around to meet with C/Allada-Vermell, a wide street that was formed when a block was demolished in 1994. The district's market, **Mercat de Santa Caterina**, has been rebuilt to a design by the late Enric Miralles (who also famously designed the Scottish Parliament). South of here, **C/Montcada**, one of the unmissable streets of old Barcelona, leads into the Born. It is lined with a succession of medieval merchants' mansions, the greatest of which house a variety of museums.

Sights & museums

Museu Barbier-Mueller d'Art Precolombí

C/Montcada 14, Born (93 310 45 16/ www.barbier-mueller.ch). Metro Jaume I. **Open** 11am-7pm Tue-Fri; 10am-7pm Sat; 10am-3pm Sun. **Admission** €3; €1.50 reductions; free under-16s. Free 1st Sun of mth. **Map** p71 B4 ❶

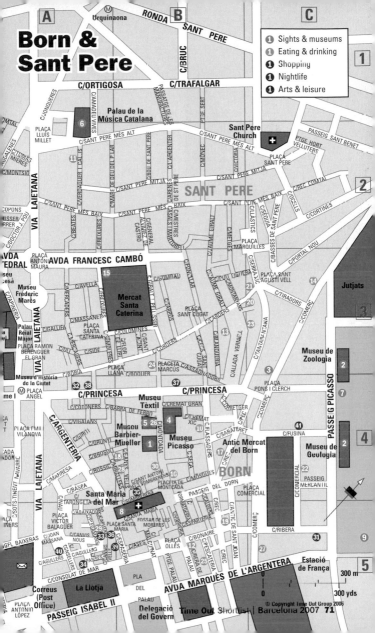

Born & Sant Pere

Museu de la Xocolata

museums in the Parc de la Ciutadella. Both suffer from old-school presentation: dusty glass cases that are filled with moth-eaten stuffed animals and serried rows of rocks. However the zoology museum is redeemed by its location in the Castell dels Tres Dragons, which was built under the aegis of Domènech i Montaner as the café-restaurant for the 1888 Exhibition. The geology part is for aficionados only, with a dry display of minerals, painstakingly classified, alongside explanations of geological phenomena found in Catalonia. More interesting is the selection from the museum's collection of 300,000 fossils, many found locally. A combined ticket also grants entrance to the Jardí Botànic on Montjuïc.

Museu de la Xocolata

C/Comerç 36, Sant Pere (93 268 78 78/www.museudelaxocolata.com). Metro Arc de Triomf or Jaume I. **Open** 10am-7pm Mon, Wed-Sat; 10am-3pm Sun. **Admission** €3.80; €3.20 reductions; free under-7s. **Map** p71 C3 ❸

Made by Barcelona's master *pastissers* for the annual Easter competition, this small collection of chocolate sculptures ranges from models of the Sagrada Família and Montserrat to scenes from *Finding Nemo* or *Ben-Hur*. A brief history of chocolate is pepped up with audio-visual displays and the odd touch-screen computer, but the busiest area is the glass-fronted cookery workshop with classes for all ages and levels. That, and the irresistible chocolate shop.

Located in the 15th-century Palau Nadal, this world-class collection of pre-Columbian art includes frequently changing selections of masks, textiles, jewellery and sculpture, with pieces dating from as far back as the second millennium BC and running up to the early 16th century (showing just how loosely the term 'pre-Columbian' can be used). The Barcelona holdings focus solely on the Americas, representing most of the styles that can be found among the ancient cultures of Meso-America, Central America, Andean America and the Amazon region.

Museu de Ciències Naturals de la Ciutadella

Passeig Picasso, Parc de la Ciutadella, Born (93 319 69 12/www.bcn.es/ museuciencies). Metro Arc de Triomf. **Open** 10am-2pm Tue, Wed, Fri-Sun; 10am-6pm Thur. **Admission** *All exhibitions & Jardí Botànic* €4; €2 reductions. *Museums only* €3; €1.50 reductions. *Temporary exhibitions* €3.50; €1.50 reductions. Free under-12s, 1st Sun of mth. No credit cards. **Map** p71 C3 ❷

The Natural History Museum now comprises the zoology and geology

Museu Picasso

C/Montcada 15-23, Born (93 319 63 10/www.museupicasso.bcn.es). Metro Jaume I. **Open** (last ticket 30mins before closing) 10am-8pm Tue-Sat; 10am-3pm Sun. **Admission** *Permanent collection only* €6; €3 reductions. *With temporary exhibition* €8.50; €5 reductions; free under-16s. Free (museum only) 1st Sun of mth. **Map** p71 B4 ❹

The Picasso Museum takes up a row of medieval mansions, with the main entrance now at the Palau Meca, and

Palau de la Música Catalana p74

the exit at the Palau Aguilar. By no means an overview of the artist's work, it is a record of the vital formative years that the young Picasso spent nearby at La Llotja art school (where his father taught), and later hanging out with Catalonia's fin-de-siècle avant-garde.

The presentation of Picasso's development from 1890 to 1904, from deft pre-adolescent portraits to sketchy landscapes of his Blue Period, is seamless and unbeatable; the collection then leaps to a gallery of mature Cubist paintings from 1917. The pièce de résistance, however, is the complete series of 57 canvases based on Velázquez's famous *Las Meninas*, donated by Picasso himself, and now stretching through three rooms. The display later ends with a wonderful collection of ceramics that were donated by Picasso's widow. Temporary exhibitions are held under the magnificent coffered ceiling of the Palau Finestres. See box p81.

Event highlights Paintings from the Picasso Museum in Antibes (5 July-15 Oct 2006); 'Picasso and the circus': paintings inspired by the artist's love of the big top (15 Nov 2006-18 Feb 2007).

Museu Tèxtil

C/Montcada 12, Born (93 319 76 03/ www.museutextil.bcn.es). Metro Jaume I. **Open** 10am-6pm Tue-Sat; 10am-3pm Sun. **Admission** *Combined admission with Museu de les Arts Decoratives & Museu de Ceràmica* €3.50; €2 reductions; free under-16s. Free 1st Sun of mth. **Map** p71 B4 ❺

The Textile and Clothing Museum occupies two adjacent buildings, the Palau Nadal and Palau dels Marquesos de Lhó; the latter retains some of its original 13th century wooden ceilings. Items on display here include medieval Hispano-Arab textiles, some liturgical vestments and the city's embroidery and lace collection. The real highlight, though, is the historic fashion – from the baroque to the 20th century – that collector Manuel Rocamora donated in the 1960s, and which is one of the finest collections of its type anywhere. Recent important donations include one from Spanish designer Cristóbal Balenciaga, who is famous for the 1958 babydoll dress and pill-box hat. The museum shop is a great place to pick up presents, and there's a nice café outside in the courtyard.

Parc de la Ciutadella

Palau de la Música Catalana

C/Sant Francesc de Paula 2, Sant Pere (93 295 72 00/www.palaumusica.org). Metro Urquinaona. **Open** *Box office* 10am-9pm Mon-Sat. *Guided tours* 9.30am-3pm daily. **Admission** €8; €7 reductions. No credit cards (under €20). **Map** p71 A2 ❻

The façade of Domènech i Montaner's Modernista concert hall, with its bare brick, busts and mosaic friezes representing Catalan musical traditions and composers, is impressive enough, but it is surpassed by the building's staggering interior. Decoration erupts everywhere: the ceiling centrepiece is of multicoloured stained glass; 18 half-mosaic, half-relief figures representing the musical muses appear out of the back of the stage; and on one side, massive Wagnerian carved horses ride out to accompany a bust of Beethoven. The old Palau has been bursting under the pressure of the musical activity going on inside it, and an extension and renovation project by Oscar Tusquets in

the 1980s is being followed by further alterations by the same architect. The rather ugly church next door has been knocked down to make way for the extension of the façade, a subterranean concert hall and a new entrance.

There are guided tours every 30 minutes or so, in either English, Catalan or Spanish. If you do have the chance, though, it's preferable to see the hall by catching a concert.

Parc de la Ciutadella

Passeig Picasso, Born (no phone). Metro Arc de Triomf. **Open** 10am-sunset daily. **Map** p71 C4 ❼

Surprisingly extensive, the park contains a host of attractions: the zoo, the natural history and geology museums, a boating lake and an array of imaginative statuary. The giant mammoth, which can be found at the far side of the boating lake, is a huge hit with kids, as is the group of leaping gazelles. Beside the lake is the *Cascade*, an ornamental fountain on which the young Gaudí worked as assistant to Josep Fontseré, who was the architect of the park. Not to be missed are Fontseré's Umbracle (literally, 'shade house'), which was built in the 1880s with a cast-iron structure reminiscent of his Mercat del Born on C/Comerç and then later restored to provide a pocket of tropical forest within the city, and the elegant Hivernacle ('winter garden').

Santa Maria del Mar

Plaça de Santa Maria, Born (93 310 23 90). Metro Jaume I. **Open** 9am-1.30pm, 4.30-8pm Mon-Sat; 10am-1.30pm, 4.30-8pm Sun. **Admission** free. **Map** p71 B5 **8**

This graceful basilica was built remarkably quickly for a medieval building, and was entirely constructed between 1329 and 1384, with an unusual unity of style for structures from that period. Inside, two rows of perfectly proportioned columns soar up to fan vaults, creating an atmosphere of space. There's also superb stained glass, especially the great 15th-century rose window above the main door. The original window, built only slightly earlier, fell down during an earthquake, an accident that killed 25 people and injured dozens more.

It's perhaps thanks to the group of anti-clerical anarchists who set this magnificent church ablaze in 1936 that its superb features can be appreciated: without the wooden baroque images that clutter so many Spanish churches, the simplicity of its lines can emerge. Try and catch a concert here if you can; particularly stirring are Handel's *Messiah* at Christmas and Mozart's *Requiem* at Easter.

Zoo de Barcelona

Parc de la Ciutadella, Born (93 225 67 80/www.zoobarcelona.com). Metro Barceloneta or Ciutadella-Vila Olímpica. **Open** *Nov-Feb* 10am-5pm daily. *Mar, Oct* 10am-6pm daily. *Apr, Sept* 10am-7pm daily. *May-Aug* 9.30am-7.30pm daily. **Admission** €14; €8.50 3-12s. **Map** p71 C5 **9**

Now that Snowflake the albino gorilla has gone to the swinging tyre in the sky, the zoo is a notably emptier place despite the new multimedia gorilla

museum. Kids still love old favourites like the dolphins, sea lions, elephants, monkeys and hippos, although there's barely enough room to swing a bobcat in some of the enclosures. Child-friendly features include a farmyard petting zoo, pony rides, mini-train and plenty of restaurants, picnic areas and playgrounds. You can rent electric cars from the C/Wellington entrance.

Eating & drinking

La Báscula

C/Flassaders 30, Born (93 319 9866). Metro Jaume I. **Open** 11-11.30pm Tue-Sat. No credit cards. **€**. **Vegetarian**. **Map** p71 B4 **10**

A vegetarian cooperative-run café may not sound like riotous fun, but this former chocolate factory is a real gem, with excellent food and a deceptively large dining room situated out back. An impressively encyclopaedic list of drinks runs from chai to glühwein, taking in cocktails, milkshakes, smoothies and iced tea, and the pasta and cakes are as good as you'll find anywhere.

El Bitxo

NEW *C/Verdaguer i Callís 9, Sant Pere (93 268 17 08). Metro Urquinaona.* **Open** 7pm-1am Mon-Thur, Sun; 7pm-2am Fri, Sat. No credit cards. **€**. **Tapas**. **Map** p71 A2 **11**

A small, lively tapas bar, specialising in excellent cheese and charcuterie from the small Catalan village of Oix. Kick off the evening with a 'Power Vermut' (which is made of red vermouth, Picon, gin and Angostura Bitters), and end it with a bottle of the gutsy house red.

Cal Pep

Plaça de les Olles 8, Born (93 310 79 61). Metro Barceloneta. **Open** 8-11.45pm Mon; 1.30-4pm, 8-11.45pm Tue-Sat. Closed Aug. **€€€**. **Seafood tapas**. **Map** p71 B5 **12**

Cal Pep is always packed: get here early for the coveted seats at the front. There is a cosy dining room at the back, but it's a shame to miss the show behind the bar. Neophytes are steered

Cuines Santa Caterina

towards the *trifásico* – a mélange of fried whitebait, squid rings and shrimp. Other favourites are the exquisite little *tallarines* (wedge clams), and *botifarra* sausage with beans.

Casa Paco
C/Allada Vermell 10, Sant Pere (93 507 37 19). Metro Arc de Triomf or Jaume I. **Open** *Apr-Sept* 9am-2am Mon-Thur, Sun; 9am-3am Fri, Sat. *Oct-Mar* 6pm-2am Tue-Thur, Sun; 6pm-3am Fri, Sat. No credit cards.
Bar. Map p71 B3 ⓭
Sounds like an old man's bar, looks like an old man's bar, but this scruffy yet amiable hole-in-the-wall has been *the* underground hit of recent years, thanks largely to occasional visits from Barcelona's DJ-in-chief, Christian Vogel. Other contributing and crucial factors include a sprawling terrace and the biggest V&Ts in the known world.

Comerç 24
C/Comerç 24, Sant Pere (93 319 21 02). Metro Arc de Triomf. **Open** 1.30-3.30pm, 8.30pm-midnight Mon-Sat. €€€€. **New wave tapas**. Map p71 C3 ⓮

One of the acknowledged masters of the new wave of Catalan cuisine, Carles Abellan was, inevitably, a disciple of Ferran Adrià in the kitchens of El Bulli. Nowadays, however, he ploughs his own, highly successful furrow in this urbane and sexy restaurant. The selection of tiny playful dishes changes seasonally, but might include a 'Kinder egg' (lined with truffle); tuna sashimi and seaweed on a wafer-thin pizza crust; a densely flavoured fish *suquet*; or a fun take on the *bikini* (a cheese and ham toastie).

Cuines Santa Caterina
NEW *Mercat Santa Caterina, Avda Francesc Cambó, Sant Pere (93 268 99 18). Metro Jaume I.* **Open** 1-4pm, 8-11pm Mon-Wed, Sun; 1-4pm, 8pm-midnight Thur-Sat. €€€. **Global**. Map p71 A3 ⓯
To eat at Cuines Santa Caterina is to enter the brave new world of market dining. The menu holds a little of everything you fancy, from langoustine tempura to a baked spud with cheese and *sobrassada* (a soft, spicy sausage from Mallorca). Chocolate tart and a red fruit millefeuille to finish are

good, prices are low (albeit rising), but the quality of the mains and service tends to waver at busy times.

Euskal Etxea

Placeta Montcada 1-3, Born (93 310 21 85). Metro Jaume I. **Open** *Bar* 6.30-11.30pm Mon; 11.30am-4pm, 6.30-11.30pm Tue-Sat. *Restaurant* 8.30-11.30pm Mon; 1.30-4pm, 8.30-11.30pm Tue-Sat. Closed 2wks Aug, 1wk Dec-Jan. **€**. **Tapas**. **Map** p71 B4 ⑯

A Basque cultural centre and *pintxo* bar, where you can help yourself to chicken tempura with saffron mayonnaise, dainty *jamón serrano* croissants, melted provolone with mango and crispy ham, or a mini-brochette of pork. Make sure you hang on to the toothpicks spearing each one: they'll be counted and charged for at the end.

Gimlet

C/Rec 24, Born (93 310 10 27). Metro Jaume I. **Open** 10pm-3am daily. No credit cards. **Cocktails**. **Map** p71 B4 ⑰

On a quiet night, this subdued little wood-panelled cocktail bar has something of an Edward Hopper feel. The long mahogany counter has been burnished by the same well-clad elbows and patrolled by the same laconic barman for many years, and Gimlet is considered something of a classic, but the measures can be a little too ladylike for modern tastes.

Itztli

NEW *C/Mirallers 7, Born (93 319 68 75/www.itztli.com.es). Metro Jaume I.* **Open** noon-11pm Tue-Sun. **€**. **Mexican**. **Map** p71 B4 ⑱

Fortify yourself in the interminable queue for the Picasso Museum with a takeaway chicken burrito from this handily proximate Mexican snack bar. Keenly priced around the €3.50 mark, burritos also come with beef, chilli con carne or veg, as do tacos. Also on offer are quesadillas, wraps, nachos and salads, and there's a good range of Mexican beers, tinned goods and fiery chilli sauces for sale.

Eat the rich

Where to get your foodie fix in the gentrified Born.

As discerning people are attracted to a neighbourhood, discerning provisions are called for – no surprise, then, that Born is now home to myriad specialist food stores, providing rosemary honey, strawberry tartlets and freshly roasted Blue Mountain to its boho-chic denizens.

Some of these shops have been around for decades. Founded in the 1850s, **Casa Gispert** (p80) is a family concern famous for top-quality nuts, dried fruit and coffee, while at **Cafés El Magnífico** (C/Argenteria 64, 93 319 60 81) the Sans family has been importing, roasting and blending coffee since 1919.

Tot Formatge (Passeig del Born 13, 93 319 53 75) has cheeses from all over Catalonia and the rest of Spain, as well as many other parts of Europe. Over the other side of Santa Maria del Mar church, the theatrically arranged windows and counters of **La Botifarrería de Santa María** (C/Santa María 4, 93 319 91 23) glisten pinkly with artisan pates, herb-coated country salami, spicy chorizo, top-quality *pata negra* hams from Jabugo and, of course, the *botifarra* sausage.

Nearby, the Wonkaesque designs for own-made chocolate bars at **Xocoa** (C/Vidrieria 4, 93 319 63 71) make them perfect for the kids back home, but for immediate gratification try the brownies, florentines or truffle-filled shortbread. Similar treats are available at **Bubó** (p80), along with excellent coffee.

Kama

NEW *C/Rec 69, Born (93 268 10 29/www.kamabar.com). Metro Barceloneta.* **Open** 7.30pm-3am Mon, Sun; 12.30pm-3am Tue-Sat. **€€. Indian. Map** p71 B5 ⑲

The default spice setting for Kama's mostly Indian food is mild, paying deference to the Catalan palate, but if owner Ketan hears a British accent, he'll ask if you'd like the heat turned up a little. Once you've factored in rice and naan, the prices can seem a little steep for a Ruby, but you're paying for the Barcelona Treatment: moody lighting, a hot-pink neon bar area, a covetable Kama Sutra frieze and ethno-chillout on the sound system.

Mosquito

C/Carders 46, Sant Pere (93 268 75 69). Metro Arc de Triomf or Jaume I. **Open** 1pm-1am Tue-Thur, Sun; 1pm-3am Fri, Sat. **€€. Asian tapas. Map** p71 C3 ⑳

Don't be put off. The 'exotic tapas' provided at Mosquito are not another lame attempt to sex up fried calamares by way of tower presentation and yucca chips, but tiny versions of good to excellent dishes from the subcontinent and elsewhere in Asia. Food ranges from chicken tikka to Thai omelettes and masala dosas, with Japanese food at lunchtime and late-night on Friday and Saturday.

Mundial Bar

Plaça Sant Agustí Vell 1, Sant Pere (93 319 90 56). Metro Arc de Triomf or Jaume I. **Open** 11am-4pm, 8.30-11.30pm Tue-Fri; noon-4pm, 8.30pm-midnight Sat; noon-3.30pm Sun. Closed Aug. **€€€. Seafood. Map** p71 C3 ㉑

Since 1925 this venerable family establishment has been dishing up no-frills platters of seafood, cheeses and the odd slice of cured meat, amid rather basic decor. People come for the steaming piles of fresh razor clams, shrimp, oysters, fiddler crabs and the like, but there's also plenty of tinned produce, so check on the bar displays to see exactly which is which.

La Paradeta

C/Comercial 7, Born (93 268 19 39). Metro Arc de Triomf or Jaume I. **Open** 8-11.30pm Tue-Fri; 1-4pm, 8pm-midnight Sat; 1-4pm Sun. **€€.** No credit cards. **Seafood. Map** p71 C4 ㉒

Superb seafood, served refectory style. Choose from glistening mounds of clams, mussels, squid, spider crabs and whatever else the boats have brought in, let them know how you'd like it cooked (grilled, steamed or a la marinera), pick a sauce (Marie Rose, spicy local *romesco*, *all i oli* or onion with tuna), buy a drink and wait for your number to be called. A great – and cheap – experience for anyone not too grand to clear their own plate.

Pizza Paco

NEW *C/Allada-Vermell 11, Sant Pere (93 268 25 14). Metro Arc de Triomf.* **Open** 9am-2am Mon-Fri; 1pm-3am Sat, Sun. **€. Pizzeria. Map** p71 C3 ㉓

Spawned from the improbably successful hole-in-the-wall bar opposite, Casa Paco, this one aims to provide ballast. In fact it functions better as a bar than a pizza restaurant (though the pizzas are really pretty good) and you'll struggle to get your order heard over the general hubbub (and the Strokes). One to incorporate into a night on the tiles, rather than an evening's outing in itself.

Re-Pla

C/Montcada 2, Sant Pere (93 268 30 03). Metro Jaume I. **Open** 9pm-midnight Mon-Thur, Sun; 9pm-1am Fri, Sat. **€€€. Global. Map** p71 B3 ㉔

A creditable assortment of hip Asian-Mediterranean fusion, with a wildly varied menu that might include anything from a sushi platter to ostrich with green asparagus, honey and grilled mango slices. Veggie options are clearly marked and desserts are rich and creative. For once, the lighting is wonderfully romantic and the sleek artwork easy on the eye.

La Strada

NEW *C/Pescateria 6, Born (93 268 27 11). Metro Barceloneta.* **Open** 1.30-4pm, 9-11.30pm Mon-Fri; 9-11.30pm Sat. **€€. Italian. Map** p71 B5 ㉕

Thai Café

A peaceful little spot decorated in pale autumnal shades, hidden down an easily missed side street off the Avda Marquès de l'Argentera. Its lunch menu comprises simple Italian food made with high-quality ingredients: bruschetta pomodori; farfalle alla pesto; salmon trout with garlic, chives and toasted almonds, and lemon zabaglione. The set dinner is more of a tasting menu – as well as home-made gnocchi, pasta and risotto are less predictable offerings such as carpaccio of venison with redcurrants.

Tèxtil Cafè

C/Montcada 12, Born (93 268 25 98). Metro Jaume I. **Open** 10am-midnight Tue-Sun. **€€**. **Café**. Map p71 B4 ㉖

Perfectly placed for visitors to the various C/Montcada museums, and with a graceful 14th-century courtyard, Tèxtil Cafè is an elegant place in which to enjoy a coffee in the shade or under gas heaters in winter. There are decent breakfast and lunch menus to boot. For music lovers, a DJ plays on Wednesday and Sunday evenings followed, on Sunday, by live jazz (this attracts a €5 supplement, however).

Thai Café

C/Comerç 27, Born (93 268 39 59). Metro Jaume I. **Open** 12.30-4pm, 8pm-midnight Mon-Thur; 8pm-1am Fri, Sat. **€€€**. **Thai**. Map p71 C5 ㉗

Aromatic tom kha gai soup, fishcakes, pad thai and tangy chicken with chilli and holy basil in a pop art package: hot pink and lime-green candy stripes along the wall, pre-club electronica and ergonomically moulded white chairs where amused-looking media types gesture with chopsticks and cigarettes. In an effort to boost a flagging lunch scene, the restaurant has recently introduced a quick-fix massage service – for an extra €4 you can get a 15-minute back rub before you eat.

Va de Vi

C/Banys Vells 16, Born (93 319 29 00). Metro Jaume I. **Open** 7pm-1am Mon-Wed, Sun; 7pm-2am Thur; 7pm-3am Fri, Sat. **Wine bar**. Map p71 B4 ㉘

Owned by a former sommelier, artist and sculptor, this Gothic-style wine bar lists over 1,000 wines, many by the *cata* (tasting measure). The usual Spanish selections are accompanied by wines from the New World and elsewhere.

La Vinya del Senyor

Plaça Santa Maria 5, Born (93 310 33 79). Metro Barceloneta or Jaume I. **Open** *June-Aug* noon-1am Mon-Thur; noon-2am Fri, Sat; noon-midnight Sun. *Sept-May* noon-1am Tue-Thur; noon-2am Fri, Sat; noon-midnight Sun. **Wine bar**. Map p71 A5 ㉙

Another classic wine bar, this one with an unmatchable position right in front of the basilica of Santa Maria del Mar. With high-quality tapas and so many excellent wines on its list (the selection changes every two weeks), however, it's a crime to do as most tourists do and take up those terrace tables just to take in the view.

El Xampanyet

C/Montcada 22, Born (93 319 70 03). Metro Jaume I. **Open** noon-3.30pm, 7-11.30pm Tue-Sat; noon-3.30pm Sun. Closed Aug. **Bar**. Map p71 B4 ㉚

The eponymous poor man's champagne is actually a fruity and drinkable sparkling white, served here in old-fashioned saucer glasses and best accompanied by the house *tapa*, a little plateful of delicious fresh anchovies from Cantábria. Run by the same family since the 1930s, El Xampanyet is lined with coloured tiles, barrels and antique curios, and with a handful of marble tables.

Shopping

Adolfo Domínguez

C/Ribera 16, Born (93 319 21 59/ www.adolfodominguez.com). Metro Barceloneta. **Open** 11am-9pm Mon-Sat. Map p71 C5 ㉛

Men's tailoring remains Domínguez's forte, with his elegantly cut suits and shirts. The women's line reciprocates with tame but immaculately refined outfits that are also squarely aimed at the 30- to 45-year-old market. The more casual U de Adolfo Domínguez line courts the younger traditionalist, but doesn't quite attain the panache of its grown-up precursor. This under-visited two-storey flagship store is supplemented by several other locations around the city.

Arlequí Mascares

C/Princesa 7, Born (93 268 27 52/ www.arlequimask.com). Metro Jaume I. **Open** 10.30am-8.30pm Mon-Sat; 10.30am-4.30pm Sun. Map p71 A4 ㉜

The walls at Arlequí Mascares drip with masks crafted from papier mâché and leather. Whether gilt-laden or done in feathered commedia dell'arte style, simple Greek tragicomedy versions or traditional Japanese or Catalan varieties, they make striking fancy dress or decorative staples. Other trinkets and toys include finger puppets, mirrors and ornamental boxes.

Bubó

NEW *C/Caputxes 10, Born (93 268 72 24/www.bubo.ws). Metro Jaume I.* **Open** 3-10pm Mon; 10am-10pm Tue, Wed; 10am-11pm Thur; 10am-1am Fri, Sat; 10am-10pm Sun. Map p71 A5 ㉝

Be a hit at any dinner party with a box of Bubó's exquisitely sculpted petits fours or make afternoon tea fashionable again with a tray of its colourful fruit sablés, raspberry and almond brandy snaps, or dreamily rich sachertorte.

Casa Antich SCP

C/Consolat del Mar 27-31, Born (93 310 43 91/www.casaantich.com). Metro Jaume I. **Open** 9am-8.30pm Mon-Fri; 9.30am-8.30pm Sat. Map p71 A5 ㉞

At Casa Antich you will find stacks of hold-alls, briefcases, suitcases and metal steamer trunks that are big enough to sleep in. Also stocked here are travel accessories, backpacks for kids and adults, briefcases, duffles, totes and handbags of all varieties from brands such as Eastpak, Dockers, Samsonite and Superga. And if this isn't enough, bags can also be made to your personal specifications.

Casa Gispert

C/Sombrerers 23, Born (93 319 75 35/ www.casagispert.com). Metro Jaume I. **Open** *Jan-July, Sept* 9.30am-2pm, 4-7.30pm Tue-Fri; 10am-2pm, 5-8pm Sat. *Aug* 10am-2pm, 5-8pm Tue-Sat. *Oct-Dec* 9.30am-2pm, 4-7.30pm Mon-Fri; 10am-2pm, 5-8pm Sat. Map p71 B4 ㉟

It's almost impossible to resist the fine fragrance of roasting coffee beans,

Year of Picasso

Barcelona was home to Picasso from the age of 14 to 21, and is evoked in more of his works than any other place – he himself called it the city 'where everything began'. The city council's 'Picasso 2006 BCN' highlights the vital link between Spain's most famous artist and the Catalan capital. The year (which actually runs until mid 2007) marks the 125th anniversary of Picasso's birth and also the centenary of his return to Barcelona from Paris, an event that marked a sea change in his artistic trajectory and resulted, a year later, in one of the most significant works of the 20th century, *Les Demoiselles d'Avignon*, depicting the prostitutes on Barcelona's Carrer d'Avinyó.

The Picasso Museum (p72) is holding several related exhibitions, including 'The Picasso of the Antibes' (4 July-15 Oct) with over 100 pieces from Picasso's time on the French Riviera, and 'Picasso and the Circus' (15 Nov-18 Feb 2007) which examines Picasso's use of circus motifs, especially the emblematic harlequin figure. In this last exhibition the museum will display its newest acquisition, the rarely seen *Barraca de Feria* (1900). To complement the special events, the museum is offering guided visits to both the permanent and temporary collections.

From 1916 Picasso created sets and costumes for three ballets: *Parade*, *Icarus* and *The Three-Cornered Hat*. These will be performed on 22-23 October by the Ballet de la Ópera de Bordeaux at the Gran Teatre del Liceu (p69), where there will be a display of reviews and photos of the original *Parade* production, considered highly controversial in its time. In February 2007, L'Auditori (p137) presents versions of *The Three-Cornered Hat* and *The Short Life*, and the city council has commissioned a special Picasso-inspired piece by the composer Josep María Mestres.

In early 2007 the Museu d'Història de la Ciutat de Barcelona (p53) hosts 'The Barcelonas of Picasso', an exhibition comparing the street culture and the high art that informed Picasso's work, covering everything from opera to absinthe freshly toasted hazelnuts, pistachios and almonds, and wooden shelves full of spices and teas. The gourmet food baskets make perfect gifts and there are also special DIY packs for local specialities, such as *calçot* sauce, summer *orxata*, Hallowe'en *panellets*, and *crema catalana*.

Ici et Là

Plaça Santa Maria del Mar 2, Born (93 268 11 67/www.icietla.com). Metro Jaume I. **Open** 4.30-8.30pm Mon; 10.30am-8.30pm Tue-Sat. **Map** p71 A5 **36**

An eccentric collection of one-off and/or limited-series handmade furniture and accessories by over 40 artists, all sourced by a French and Spanish female collective. Pieces range from a tribal chair of ostrich leather and antelope horns by Haillard to spiky South African lightbulbs or a table lamp made of chicken wire and beach pebbles.

On Land

C/Princesa 25, Born (93 310 02 11/ www.on-land.com). Metro Jaume I. **Open** *Sept-July* 5-8.30pm Mon; 11am-2pm, 5-8.30pm Tue-Fri; 11am-8.30pm Sat. *Aug* 11am-2pm, 5-8.30pm Tue-Sat. **Map** p71 B4 **37**

Apart from local wonderboy Josep Abril's hip, smart, slouchy menswear, there's recycled urban fashion for men and women by the likes of Cecilia Sörensen, Montse Ibañez and Petit Bateau. T-shirts with mottos are by local outfit Divinas Palabras.

El Rei de la Màgia

C/Princesa 11, Born (93 319 39 20/ www.elreidelamagia.com). Metro Jaume I. **Open** *Sept-July* 10am-2pm, 5-8pm Mon-Fri; 11am-2pm Sat. *Aug* 11am-2pm, 5-8pm Mon-Fri. **Credit** AmEx, MC, V. **Map** p71 A4 **38**

This enclave of illusionism has been enticing wannabe Houdinis into its tiny interior since 1881. In-house professionals produce the tricks of the trade from endless shelves and drawers. Practical jokers are well served, with whoopee cushions, fake turds and more imaginative buffoon material.

U-Casas

C/Espaseria 4, Born (93 310 00 46/ www.casasclub.com). Metro Jaume I. **Open** 10.30am-9pm Mon-Thur; 10.30am-9.30pm Fri, Sat. **Map** p71 A5 **39**

The pared-down, post-industrial decor so beloved of this neighbourhood provides the perfect backdrop for bright and quirky shoes. Strange heels and toes are out in force this season, and after all those snub-nosed winkle-pickers and rubber wedgies from the likes of Helmut Lang, Fly, Fornarina and Irregular Choice, you can rest your weary pins on the giant, shoe-shaped chaise longue.

Vila Viniteca

C/Agullers 7, Born (93 268 32 27/ www.vilaviniteca.es). Metro Jaume I. **Open** *Sept-June* 8.30am-2.30pm, 4.30-8.30pm Mon-Sat. *July-Aug* 8.30am-2.30pm, 4.30-8.30pm Mon-Fri; 8.30am-2.30pm Sat. **Map** p71 A5 **40**

This family-run business has built up a stock of over 6,000 wines and spirits since 1932. With everything from a 1953 Damoiseau rum, which costs as much as €500, through to €6 bottles of table wine, the selection is mostly Spanish and Catalan, but it also takes in some international favourites. The new food shop, situated just next door at No.9, stocks fine cheeses, cured meats and oils.

Arts & leisure

Metrònom

C/Fusina 9, Born (93 268 42 98/ www.metronombcn.org). Metro Arc de Triomf or Jaume I. **Concerts** 10pm. **Admission** free. **Map** p71 C4 **41**

Known predominantly for its exhibitions and installations, Metrònom also hosts concerts of experimental music. The main focus is a week-long series of concerts, featuring key international figures from the experimental music scene. Concerts also take place at other times throughout the year; some are in collaboration with the Barcelona foundation Phonos, which specialises in experimental electro-acoustic music.

Corto Club p90

Raval

Upper Raval

There are streets here that the Barcelona City Council doesn't want you to see. From La Rambla, signposts for the **MACBA** carefully guide visitors along the gentrified 'tourist corridors' of C/Tallers and C/Bonsuccès to a bourgeois bohemian's playground of cafés, galleries and boutiques. Elsewhere, the city's sponge has yet to cleanse this defiantly tough working-class area that doubles as Barcelona's inner city red-light district. The Upper Raval has never had such a louche reputation as the Lower Raval; indeed, in recent years, a plethora of late-night bars and restaurants has made it one of Barcelona's hippest places.

The epicentre of the Upper Raval is the Plaça dels Àngels, where the 16th-century **Convent dels Àngels** houses both the **FAD** design institute and a gigantic almshouse, the **Casa de la Caritat**, that's since been converted into a cultural complex housing the MACBA and the **CCCB**. When the clean, high-culture MACBA opened in 1995, it seemed to embody everything the Raval was not, and was initially mocked as an isolated and isolating social experiment. But over the years, the square and surrounding streets have filled with restaurants, boutiques and galleries; the university students who flock here have changed the character of the place.

Below here is the first part of the Raval to take on an urban character. Behind the Boqueria is the **Antic Hospital de la Santa**

Creu, which took in the city's sick from the 15th century until 1926; it now houses Catalonia's main library, and **La Capella**, an attractive exhibition space.

Sights & museums

Antic Hospital de la Santa Creu & La Capella
C/Carme 47-C/Hospital 56 (no phone/ La Capella 93 442 71 71). Metro Liceu. **Open** 9am-8pm Mon-Fri; 9am-2pm Sat. *La Capella* noon-2pm, 4-8pm Tue-Sat; 11am-2pm Sun. **Admission** free. **Map** p85 B3 ➊

There was a hospital on this site as early as 1024, but in the 15th century it expanded to centralise all the city's hospitals and sanatoriums. By the 1920s it was hopelessly overstretched and its medical facilities moved uptown to the Hospital Sant Pau. One of the last patients was Gaudí, who died here in 1926; it was also here that Picasso painted one of his first important pictures, *Dead Woman* (1903).

The buildings combine a 15th-century Gothic core with baroque and classical additions. They're now given over to cultural institutions, among them Catalonia's main library. Highlights include a neo-classical lecture theatre complete with revolving marble dissection table, and the entrance hall of the Casa de Convalescència, tiled with lovely baroque ceramic murals telling the story of Sant Pau (St Paul); one features an artery-squirting decapitation scene. La Capella, the hospital chapel, was rescued from a sad fate as a warehouse and sensitively converted to an exhibition space for contemporary art. The beautifully shady colonnaded courtyard is a popular spot for reading or eating lunch.

CCCB (Centre de Cultura Contemporània de Barcelona)
C/Montalegre 5 (93 306 41 00/ www.cccb.org). Metro Catalunya. **Open** *Mid June-mid Sept* 11am-8pm Tue-Sat; 11am-3pm Sun. *Mid Sept-mid*

June 11am-2pm, 4-8pm Tue, Thur, Fri; 11am-8pm Wed, Sat; 11am-7pm Sun. **Admission** *1 exhibition* €4.40; €3.30 reductions & Wed. *2 exhibitions* €6; €5.50 reductions & Wed. Free under-16s. **Map** p85 B2 ➋

Spain's largest cultural centre was opened in 1994 at the huge Casa de la Caritat, built in 1802 on the site of a medieval monastery to serve as the city's main workhouse. The massive façade and part of the courtyard remain from the original building; the rest was rebuilt in dramatic contrast, all tilting glass and steel. As a centre for contemporary culture, it picks up whatever falls through the cracks elsewhere: urban culture, early 20th-century art and festivals. The CCCB's exhibitions tend to favour production values over content, but there are occasional gems.

Event highlights 'Bamako '05': photographs from sub-Saharan Africa (3 Oct 2006-28 Jan 2007); 'World Press Photo, the best of the world's photojournalists' (28 Nov-31 Dec 2006).

MACBA (Museu d'Art Contemporani de Barcelona)
Plaça dels Àngels 1 (93 412 08 10/ www.macba.es). Metro Catalunya. **Open** *June-Sept* 11am-8pm Mon, Wed-Fri; 10am-8pm Sat; 10am-3pm Sun. *Oct-May* 11am-7.30pm Mon, Wed-Fri; 10am-8pm Sat; 10am-3pm Sun. *Guided tours* (Catalan/Spanish) 6pm Wed, Sat; noon Sun. **Admission** *Museum* €5.50; €4 reductions. *Temporary exhibitions* €4; €3 reductions. *Combined ticket* €7; €5.50 reductions. **Map** p85 B2 ➌

MACBA was mocked as a triumph of style over substance when it opened in 1995, and it was noted that visitors spent more time photographing Richard Meier's Persil-bright building than they did looking at the paltry exhibits. A decade on, the place has fattened up its holdings considerably, but the wow factor of the triple-level transitional atrium and zigzag ramps still overshadows most of the shows, which are frequently heavily political

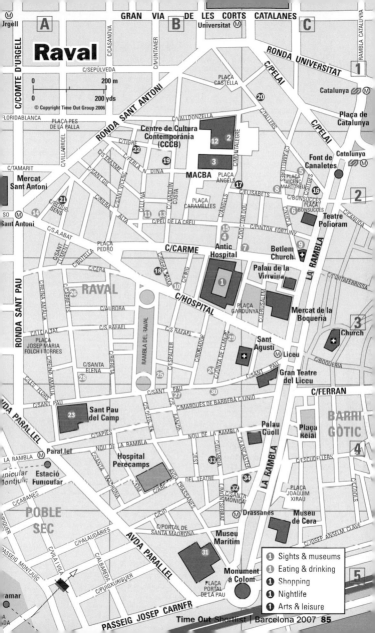

Raval

in concept and occasionally radical to the point of inaccessibility. If you can't or won't see the socio-political implications of, say, a roomful of beach balls, the MACBA may leave you cold. All too often one is left with the feeling that the only really great work of art here is the building itself.

The holdings cover the last 50 years; although there's no permanent collection as such, some of these works are usually on display. The earlier pieces are strong on Spanish expressionists such as Saura and Tàpies (of whom director Manuel Borja-Villel is an ardent fan), alongside Dubuffet, and Basque sculptors Jorge Oteiza and Eduardo Chillida. Works from the last 40 years are more global, with the likes of Beuys, Basquiat and Penk; the contemporary Spanish collection includes Catalan painting (Ferran García Sevilla, Miquel Barceló) and sculpture (Sergi Aguilar, Susana Solano).

Event highlights Galeria Cadaqués, the hugely important gallery that showcased work by Picasso, Dali and Man Ray (22 Sept 2006-8 Jan 2007); Gego, Venezuelan sculptor (20 Oct 2006-1 Feb 2007); Janet Cardiff and Georges Bures Miller, Canadian installation artists (Feb-Apr 2007); Joan Jonas, multimedia artist (Oct 2007-Jan 2008).

Eating & drinking

Ánima

C/Àngels 6 (93 342 49 12). Metro Liceu. **Open** 1-4pm, 9pm-midnight Mon-Sat. **€€€. Mediterranean.** Map p85 B2 ④

A sharp-edged space with a thoughtfully positioned mirror allowing diners to watch the chefs at work. A jumble of sautéed wild mushrooms, and rocket salad with crispy pear are tasty, and sea bass with crab bisque a smooth follow-up. Puddings sound better than they taste, though: apple crumble is actually a patty of apple, banana and crushed almonds, and the pumpkin cake with peppermint ice-cream is just weird. Hit or miss, then, but mostly hit.

Bar Kasparo

Plaça Vicenç Martorell 4 (93 302 20 72). Metro Catalunya. **Open** *May-Aug* 9am-midnight daily. *Sept-Apr* 9am-10pm daily. Closed 1mth Dec-Jan. No credit cards. **€€. Café.** Map p85 C2 ⑤

A summer proposition (there's not any seating available indoors), with tables under shady arcades overlooking a playground for the kids. Run by two Australians, Kasparo has good, cheap food – plenty of soups, salads and pasta, curries Thai and Indian, stews and chilli, with tapas and *bocadillos* available all day.

Buenas Migas

Plaça Bonsuccés 6 (93 318 37 08). Metro Liceu. **Open** *June-Sept* 10am-midnight Mon-Thur, Sun, 10am-1am Fri, Sat. *Oct-May* 10am-11pm Mon-Thur, Sun, 10am-midnight Fri, Sat. **€€. Vegetarian.** Map p85 C2 ⑥

Tables outside sprawl across the square in the shade of acacia trees, while inside has a rustic *Good Life* look, with plenty of pine and Kilner jars, that tells you everything you need to know about the food. Wholesome specialities include focaccia with various toppings, leek and potato or spinach tart, the usual vegetarian-approved cakes – carrot, pear and chocolate brownies – and herbal teas.

Dos Trece

C/Carme 40 (93 301 73 06). Metro Liceu. **Open** 1.30-4pm, 9pm-midnight Tue-Sun. **€€€. Global.** Map p85 C2 ⑦

Is it a bar? Is it a restaurant? Is it a nightclub? Where's my salad? Apart from a little fusion confusion (Thai curry with nachos; cajun chicken with mash; curried sausage with baked apple, and all manner of things with yucca chips), the food's not half bad for the price, but the service could look a little livelier.

Elisabets

C/Elisabets 2-4 (93 317 58 26). Metro Catalunya. **Open** 2-4pm, 7.30-11pm Mon-Fri; 7.30-11pm Sat. Closed 3wks

Aug. €€. No credit cards. **Catalan**.
Map p85 C2 ⑧

Elisabets maintains a sociable local feel, despite the recent gentrification of its street. Dinner is actually a selection of tapas, and otherwise only the set lunch or myriad *bocadillos* are served. The lunch deal is terrific value, however, with osso buco, vegetable and chickpea stew, baked cod with garlic and parsley, and roast pork knuckle all making an appearance on the menu with gratifying regularity.

Granja M Viader

C/Xuclà 4-6 (93 318 34 86). *Metro Liceu*. **Open** 5-8.45pm Mon; 9am-1.45pm, 5-8.45pm Tue-Sat. Closed 2wks Aug. **€€. Tearoom**. **Map** p85 C2 ⑨

The chocolate milk drink Cacaolat was invented in this old *granja* in 1931, and is still on offer, along with strawberry and banana milkshakes, *orxata* (tiger nut milk) and hot chocolate. It's an evocative, charming place with century-old fittings and enamel adverts, but the waiters refuse to be hurried. Popular with Catalan families on the way back from picking up the kids, and couples meeting after work.

Juicy Jones

NEW C/Hospital 76 (93 302 43 30). *Metro Liceu*. **Open** 12.30-11.30pm daily. **€€**. No credit cards. **Vegetarian**. **Map** p85 B3 ⑩

A new branch of this riotously colourful, backpacker-oriented vegan restaurant, with an endless and inventive list of juices, salads and filled baguettes. Staffed, it would seem, by slightly clueless language exchange students, its heart is in the right place, but this is not somewhere you can expect a speedy lunch. Bring a book.

Mam i Teca

C/Lluna 4 (93 441 33 35). *Metro Sant Antoni*. **Open** 1pm-midnight Mon, Wed-Fri, Sun; 8.30pm-midnight Sat. Closed 2wks Aug. **€€. Tapas**. **Map** p85 B2 ⑪

The name comes from an old Catalan expression meaning 'food and drink', and sums up the prevailing spirit of this little yellow and green tapas bar. All the usual tapas, from anchovies to cured meats, are rigorously sourced, and complemented by superb daily specials such as organic *botifarra*, pork confit and asparagus with shrimp.

Dos Trece

El Pati

NEW *C/Montalegre 7 (93 318 65 04).*
Metro Catalunya. **Open** 1-5pm Mon-
Fri. Closed Aug. **€**. **Mediterranean**.
Map p85 B2 ⑫

The charm of this café comes from
its situation in the Pati Manning, an
arcaded 18th-century patio that is decorated with colourful tiling and sgraf-
fiti. The lunch deal is also an agreeable
one, with a mere €10 getting you
spinach ravioli with courgette sauce followed by layers of pork and aubergine
slices in a balsamic vinegar reduction,
or roast chicken with fat wedge chips,
plus a drink and a dessert. Outside
lunch hours, croissants, sandwiches
and similar snacks are served.

Ravalo

NEW *Plaça Emili Vendrell 1/*
C/Peu de la Creu (93 442 01 00).
Metro Sant Antoni. **Open** 8pm-
12.30am Tue-Sun. **€€**. **Pizzeria**.
Map p85 B2 ⑬

Perfect for fans of the thin and crispy
variety, Ravalo's table-dwarfing pizzas
take some beating, thanks to flour, and
a chef, imported from Naples. Most
pizzas, like the Sienna, are furnished
with the cornerstone toppings you'd
expect – in this case mozzarella di
bufala, speck, cherry tomatoes and
rocket – but less familiar offerings
include the Pizza Soufflé, which is filled
with ham, mushrooms and a eggy
mousse (better than it sounds, really).
Ravalo's terrace overlooking a quiet
square is open year-round.

Sésamo

C/Sant Antoni Abat 52 (93 441 64 11).
Metro Sant Antoni. **Open** 1-3.30pm
Mon; 1-3.30pm, 8.30-11.30pm Wed-Sun.
€€. **Vegetarian**. Map p85 A2 ⑭

Another veggie restaurant not to take
itself too seriously (yoga ads, but no
whale song), Sésamo offers a creative
bunch of dishes in a cosy, buzzing back
room. Salad with risotto and a drink is
a bargain at €6.50, or try cucumber
rolls stuffed with smoked tofu and
mashed pine nuts, crunchy polenta
with baked pumpkin, gorgonzola and
radicchio, or the delicious spicy curry

served in popadom baskets with dahl
and wild rice. There is also a selection
of Japanese tapas.

Silenus

C/Àngels 8 (93 302 26 80). Metro
Liceu. **Open** 1.30-4pm, 8.45pm-11.30am
Mon-Thur; 1.30-4pm, 8.45pm-12.30am
Fri, Sat. **€€€**. **Mediterranean**.
Map p85 B2 ⑮

Run by arty types for arty types,
Silenus works hard on its air of scuffed
elegance, with carefully chipped and
stained walls on which the ghost of a
clock is projected and the faded leaves
of a book float up on high. The food,
too, is artistically presented, and never
more so than with the lunchtime tasting menu. This allows a tiny portion of
everything on the menu, from French
onion soup to a flavoursome haricot
bean stew and entrecôte with mash.

Shopping

Discos Castelló

C/Tallers 3, 7, 9 & 79 (93 302 59 46/
www.discoscastello.es). Metro Catalunya.
Open 10am-8.30pm Mon-Sat. **Map**
p85 C2 ⑯

Discos Castelló is a homegrown cluster
of small shops, each with a different
speciality: No.3 is devoted to classical;
the largest, No.7, covers pretty much
everything; No.9 does hip hop, rock
and alternative pop plus T-shirts and
accessories; and No.79 is best for jazz
and 1970s pop. The branch at No.79 is
good for ethnic music and electronica.

Giménez y Zuazo

C/Elisabets 20 (93 412 33 81/www.
gimenezzuazo.com). Metro Catalunya.
Open 10.30am-3pm, 5-8.30pm Mon-Sat.
Map p85 B2 ⑰

This designer duo produces women's
clothes that bring vivid colours and
patterns in T-shirts and tops together
with more elaborate cuts and styles in
their urbanwear. Perennially quirky
designs centre on intricate prints, seemingly casual scribbled drawings and an
almost obsessive attention to detail,
including buttons, lapels and cuffs.

The Wednesday club

Rawal Launch brings midweek madness to La Paloma.

Rawal Launch

It's barely dark on a school-night and the queue trails down three blocks. At its head, the hand-wringing ambassadors of various groups (generally the most attractive female of the party) insist to impervious bouncers that they are, *must* be on the guest list. Others in line edge forward by spotting 'friends' 50 yards ahead. Itinerant beer sellers do a roaring trade.

At the end of all this, through the red velvet curtains and into the hallowed belle époque hall of La Paloma, you might expect a star-studded glamourfest, something as exclusive as, say, the *Vanity Fair* post-Oscars bash. But no – what lies ahead is one of the most unpretentious club nights in the city, combining the colours, sounds, smells and feel-good vibe of a world music festival with the buzz of a private party where everybody knows everybody.

Hippies, lounge lizards, Ibiza throwbacks and even goths throw their differences and ages aside as they wander the stalls selling jewellery, samosas and mint tea, stop for an ayurvedic massage and gaze openmouthed at the bikini-clad maidens doing the rounds entwined in seven-foot pythons. From the ceiling acrobats twirl down bands of crimson fabric, while on stage an improbably bendy doe-eyed Indian goddess gives a warm-up yoga class to the blissed-out group stretched across cushions in front of the stage.

Once the tone of the evening has been established, things start to warm up with 'Bollywood vs Bhangra', where, like rival flocks of birds of paradise, the two groups go head to head in a headspinning kaleidoscope of colour to an ecstatic reception from the crowd, before the club night proper begins, with DJs and live acts from around the world.

If this sounds like your bag, head to **La Paloma** (p92) on the second Wednesday of the month. Not long after lunch

Ravalo p88

Le Swing

C/Riera Baixa 13 (no phone). Metro Liceu. **Open** 11am-2.30pm, 5-9pm Mon-Sat. No credit cards. **Map** p85 B3 ⑱
Today's second-hand is known as 'vintage', and thrift is not on the agenda. Fervent worshippers of Pierre Cardin, YSL, Dior, Kenzo and other fashion deities scour all corners of the sartorial stratosphere and deliver their booty back to this little powder puff of a boutique. The odd Zara number and other mere mortal brands creep in as well.

Nightlife

Benidorm

C/Joaquín Costa 39 (no phone). Metro Universitat. **Open** *Apr-mid Oct* 8pm-2.30am Mon-Thur, Sun; 8pm-3am Fri, Sat. *Mid Oct-Mar* 7pm-2.30am Mon-Thur, Sun; 7pm-3am Fri, Sat. Closed Aug. **Admission** free. No credit cards. **Map** p85 B2 ⑲
This lively, smoky little place is a kitsch paradise of brothel-red walls, crystal lanterns and 1980s disco paraphernalia, boasting the world's smallest toilet, dancefloor and chill-out room. The sounds being absorbed by the mass of humanity packed in here on weekends (watch your wallet) range from hip hop to 1970s stuff, although mostly they are variations on the same electronica theme.

Corto Club

C/Tallers 68 (93 302 27 95). **Open** 9pm-3am Mon-Sat. **Admission** varies. **Credit** V. **Map** p85 C1 ⑳
The people who brought us late-night drinking at the Pipa Club give us another place to whet our palate, this time with music. Live jazz, blues, funk, and bossa nova fill the spaces amid the thought balloons and original drawings of Hugo Pratt's comic-book sailor Corto Maltese. Starry-eyed Argentines wax nostalgic with locals and tourists for the occasional *milonga*, where professionals encourage amateurs to choose a partner and dance to the tango band.

Jazz Sí Club

C/Requesens 2 (93 329 00 21/www. tallerdemusics.com). Metro Sant Antoni. **Open** 5pm-2.30am Mon-Thur, Sun; 5pm-3am Fri, Sat. **Admission** free. No credit cards. **Map** p85 A2 ㉑
This tiny music school auditorium and bar is a space where students, teachers

and music lovers can meet, perform and listen. Every night is dedicated to a different musical genre: there's trad jazz on Monday; pop, rock and blues jams on Tuesday; jazz sessions on Wednesday; Cuban music on Thursday; flamenco on Friday; and rock on Saturday and Sunday.

La Paloma

C/Tigre 27 (93 301 68 97/www.la paloma-bcn.com). Metro Universitat. **Open** 6-9.30pm, 11.30pm-5am Thur; 6-9.30pm, 11.30pm-2am; 2.30am-5am Fri, Sat; 5.45-9.45pm Sun. **Admission** (incl 1 drink) €5-€10. No credit cards. **Map** p85 B2 ㉙

La Paloma recently celebrated its 100th birthday, despite the neighbourhood's efforts to silence it. A walk through the surrealist red velvet-lined foyer reveals a lavishly restored belle époque theatre and dancehall complete with shimmering chandeliers and plush balconies. It's a strange spectacle for those who arrive early – Grandma and Grandpa in full evening wear still foxtrotting after the ballroom sessions finish and the house and broken beats begin. On Thursday nights the Bongo Lounge DJs mix funk and Latin

rhythms with psychedelic lights and live jazz, while Vegas-style go-go dancers compete for attention, while international DJs spin all sorts from electro to acid from 2am Friday to Sunday. The first Wednesday of the month sees the excellent Rawal Launch (see box p89).

Lower Raval

The lower half of the Raval, from C/Hospital downwards, is generally referred to as the **Barrio Chino** ('Barri Xino' in Catalan). The nickname was coined in the 1920s by a journalist comparing it to San Francisco's Chinatown, and referred to its underworld feel rather than to any Chinese population. The authorities have long been working on cleaning up the area. Whole blocks with associations to prostitution or drugs have been demolished, a sports centre, a new police station and office blocks were constructed, and some streets were pedestrianised. But the most dramatic plan was to

Outside MACBA p84

create a 'Raval obert al cel' ('Raval open to the sky'), the most tangible result of which is the sweeping, palm-lined Rambla del Raval, completed in 2000. Current efforts to fill the rather empty new *rambla* include licences for new clubs and bars, Botero's deliciously bulging *Gat* ('Cat') sculpture and an ethnic weekend market.

C/Nou de la Rambla, the area's main street, is home to Gaudí's first major project: **Palau Güell** at Nos.3-5, built for his patron, Eusebi Güell. A fortress-like edifice shoehorned into a narrow six-storey sliver, it was an extension of Güell's parents' house (now a hotel) on La Rambla; it's closed for renovation until spring 2007. Nearby, in C/Sant Pau, is a Modernista landmark, Domènech i Montaner's **Hotel España**, and at the end of the street sits the Romanesque tenth-century church of **Sant Pau del Camp**. Iberian remains dating to 200 BC have been found next to the edifice, marking it as one of the oldest parts of the city. At the lower end of the area were the **Drassanes** (shipyards), now home to the **Museu Marítim**. Along the Paral·lel side of this Gothic building lies the only remaining large section of Barcelona's 14th-century city wall.

Sights & museums

Sant Pau del Camp

C/Sant Pau 101 (93 441 00 01). Metro Paral·lel. **Open** *Visits* noon-1pm; 7.30-8.30pm Mon-Fri. *Mass* 8pm Sat; noon Sun. **Admission** €1. **Map** p85 A4 ㉓
The name, St Paul in the Field, reflects a time when this was still countryside. This little Romanesque church goes back 1,000 years; indeed, the date carved on its most prestigious headstone – that of Count Guifré II Borell, son of Wilfred the Hairy and inheritor of all Barcelona and Girona – is AD 912.

The church's impressive façade includes sculptures of fantastical flora and fauna along with human grotesques. The tiny cloister features extraordinary Visigoth capitals and some triple-lobed arches. Restored after stints serving as a school in 1842, as an army barracks from 1855 to 1890 and as a bomb site during the Civil War, Sant Pau is now a national monument.

Eating & drinking

Biblioteca

C/Junta de Comerç 28 (93 412 62 21). Metro Liceu. **Open** 1-4pm, 9pm-midnight Tue-Sat. Closed 2wks Aug, 1wk Feb. €€€. **Mediterranean**. **Map** p85 B3 ㉔
A very calming, almost meditative space with a minimalist cream decor, Biblioteca is all about food. Food and books about food, that is. From Bocuse to Bourdain, they are all for sale, and their various influences collide in some occasionally sublime cooking. Beetroot gazpacho with live clams and quail's egg is a dense riot of flavour, and the endive salad with poached egg and *romesco* wafers is superb. Mains aren't quite as head-spinning, but are accomplished nevertheless.

Cafè de les Delícies

Rambla del Raval 47 (93 441 57 14). Metro Liceu. **Open** 6pm-2am Mon-Thur, Sun; 6pm-3am Fri, Sat. Closed 3wks Aug. €. No credit cards. **Café**. **Map** p85 B3 ㉕
David Soul! Boney M! Olivia Newton-John! The functioning 1970s jukebox is reason enough to visit this cosy little bar, even without the excellent G&Ts, the chess, the variety of teas, the terrace and the shelves of books for browsing. A coveted alcove with a sofa, low armchairs and magazines is opened at busy times, or there is a quiet dining room at the back.

Las Fernández

C/Carretes 11 (93 443 2043). Metro Paral·lel. **Open** 9pm-1.30am Tue-Fri; 9pm-3am Sat, Sun. €€. **Spanish**. **Map** p85 A3 ㉖

BARCELONA BY AREA

Palau Güell

An inviting entrance, coloured pillar-box red, is a beacon of cheer on one of Barcelona's more insalubrious streets. Inside, the three Fernández sisters have created a bright and unpretentious bar-restaurant that specialises in wine and food from their native León. Alongside regional specialities *cecina* (dried venison), gammon and sausages are lighter, Mediterranean dishes and generous salads; smoked salmon with mustard and dill, pasta filled with wild mushrooms, and sardines with a citrus escabeche.

Marsella

C/Sant Pau 65 (93 442 72 63). Metro Liceu. **Open** 10pm-2.30am Mon-Thur; 10pm-3am Fri, Sat. No credit cards. **Bar**. Map p85 B4 ㉗

A well-loved bar that's been in the same family for five generations. Jean Genet, among other notorious artists and petty thieves, used to come here, attracted, no doubt, by the locally made absinthe, served to this day. Dusty, untapped 100-year-old bottles sit in tall glass cabinets alongside old mirrors and faded William Morris curtains, and chandeliers loom over the cheerful, largely foreign crowd.

Mesón David

C/Carretas 63 (93 441 59 34). Metro Paral·lel. **Open** 1-4.30pm, 8-11.45pm Mon, Tue, Thur-Sun. Closed Aug. €. **Spanish**. Map p85 A3 ㉘

Rough and ready, noisy, chaotic and a lot of fun, Mesón David is also one of the cheapest restaurants in Barcelona. Be prepared to share a table. Mainly Galician dishes include *caldo gallego* (cabbage broth) or fish soup to start, followed by *lechazo* (a vast hunk of roast pork) or grilled calamares. Of the desserts, the almond *tarta de Santiago* battles for supremacy with fresh baby pineapple doused in Cointreau.

Organic

C/Junta de Comerç 1 (93 301 0902). Metro Liceu. **Open** 12.30am-midnight daily. €€. **Vegetarian**. Map p85 B3 ㉙

The last word in refectory chic, Organic is better designed and lighter in spirit (its motto: 'Don't panic, it's organic!') than the majority of the city's vegetarian restaurants. Options include an all-you-can-eat salad bar, a combined salad bar and main course, or the full whammy – salad, soup, main course and dessert. Beware the extras (such as drinks), which hitch up the prices.

Pollo Rico

*C/Sant Pau 31 (93 441 31 84/www.
polloricosl.com). Metro Liceu.* **Open**
10am-1am Mon, Tue, Thur-Sun. €.
Roast chicken. **Map** p85 B4 ③⓪
A Raval institution, the 'Tasty Chicken'
has the best rotisserie fowl in the city
twirling away in its windows. Picnickers
can take away a golden-skinned quarter for just €3 while local characters
and tourists all troop upstairs for
heartier portions, litre jugs of wicked
sangria, or the €3 plate of *botifarra* and
beans. The only downsides are the
supermarket lighting and the droopy,
greasy chips.

Spiritual Café

*Museu Marítim, Avda Drassanes
(mobile 677 634 031/reservations
93 317 52 56). Metro Drassanes.*
Open *May-mid Oct* 9pm-3am Wed-
Sun. €€€. **Café**. **Map** p85 B5 ③①
Deliciously different, this late-night
alfresco lounge bar fills the patio of the
Maritime Museum in summer with
chilled sounds and zephyrs of incense.
Low, round tables scrawled with
Arabic script and lit with candles float
on a sea of rugs and cushions, while a
team of student waiters offers massages, acrobatics, juggling, Tibetan
chants, and poetry.

Nightlife

Bar Pastis

*C/Santa Mònica 4 (93 318 79 80).
Metro Drassanes.* **Open** 7.30pm-
2.30am Tue-Thur, Sun; 7.30pm-
3.30am Fri, Sat. **Bar**. **Map** p85 B4 ③②
This quintessentially Gallic bar once
served pastis to visiting sailors and the
denizens of the Barrio Chino underworld. It still has a louche Marseilles
feel, floor-to-ceiling indecipherable oil
paintings (by the original owner when
drunk, apparently), Edith Piaf on the
stereo, and latter-day troubadours on
Tuesdays, Wednesdays and Sundays.

La Concha

*C/Guàrdia 14 (93 302 41 18).
Metro Drassanes.* **Open** 5pm-2.30am
Mon-Thur, Sun; 5pm-3am Fri, Sat.
Admission free. No credit cards.
Map p85 B4 ③③
Manager Rashid has made such an
impressive turnaround of this classic
bar that these days it's talked about
from Ronda to Rio, with as many in-
the-know tourists as locals and drag
queens taking up space along the bar.
Spanish screen siren Sara Montiel
remains immortalised in a hundred
faded photographs, while the exotic
Arabic music mixes with flamenco.

Moog

*C/Arc del Teatre 3 (93 301 72 82/
www.masimas.com). Metro Drassanes.*
Open midnight-5am daily.
Admission €8. **Map** p85 C4 ③④
Moog has been programming electronic music for years with admirable
consistency. Residents Omar, Robert X
and Juan B share deck space with guest
DJs on Wednesdays, while Sunday's
Affair guarantees eclecticism. A bar in
the entryway, a few tables, a small
downstairs dancefloor for house and
techno and a chill-out room (of sorts)
upstairs combine to form a compact
and scaled-down club.

Sant Pau del Camp p92

Barceloneta & the Ports

Barceloneta

Now that it's crowded with sunbathers, it's hard to believe that Barceloneta's beach was once a filthy Hell's Bathroom of sewage, heavy industry and warehouses. Once the 1992 Olympics opened Barcelona's eyes to the vast commercial potential of its shoreline, the beaches were swiftly cleared and filled with tons of golden sand, imported palm trees, drainage systems, flood lighting and landscaped promenades.

The area has also been the beneficiary of a quite staggering amount of sculpture, particularly around the Port Vell (see p46). Lothar Baumgarten's **Rosa dels Vents** has the names of Catalan winds embedded in the pavement, and, at the other end of Passeig Joan de Borbó, is Juan Muñoz's disturbing sculpture of five caged figures known as **Una habitació on sempre plou** (*A Room Where It Always Rains*). Heading left at the end of Passeig Joan de Borbó, you'll reach Barceloneta beach and Rebecca Horn's tower of rusty cubes, **Estel Ferit** (*Wounded Star*), which pays homage to the much-missed *xiringuitos*. The Passeig Marítim esplanade runs north from here, to Frank Gehry's shimmering copper **Fish**, the U-shaped biomedical research park and the twin skyscrapers of the exoskeletal Hotel Arts and the Torre Mapfre, which form an imposing gateway to the Port Olímpic.

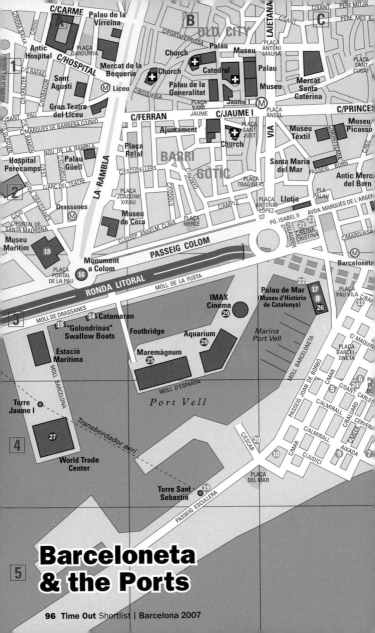

Barceloneta & the Ports

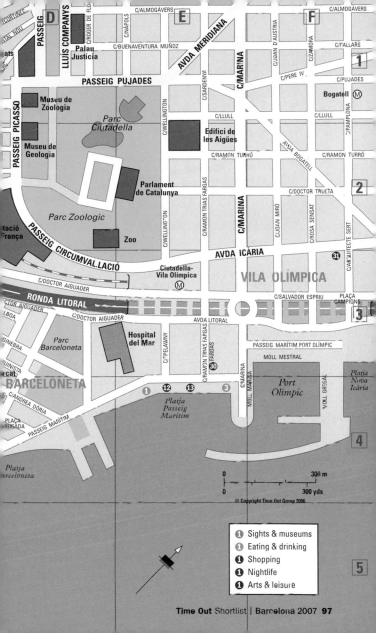

D **E** **F**

C/ALMOGÀVERS

PASSEIG LLUÍS COMPANYS
C/ROGER DE FLOR
C/NÀPOLS
C/ALMOGÀVERS

Palau Justícia
C/BUENAVENTURA MUÑOZ

AVDA MERIDIANA

C/MARINA
C/JUAN D'AUSTRIA
C/ZAMORA
C/PALLARS

1

PASSEIG PUJADES
C/SARDENYA
C/PERE IV
C/PUJADES

Museu de Zoologia

Parc Ciutadella

C/WELLINGTON
C/LLULL
C/LLULL
C/PAMPLONA

Bogatell Ⓜ

PASSEIG PICASSO

Edifici de les Aigües

Museu de Geologia
C/RAMON TURRÓ
C/RAMON TURRÓ

AVDA BOGATELL

Parlament de Catalunya
C/WELLINGTON
C/RAMON TRIAS FARGAS
C/MARINA
C/DOCTOR TRUETA

2

ació França

Parc Zoologic
C/JUAN MIRÓ
C/ROSA SENSAT
C/ARQUITECTE SERT

PASSEIG CIRCUMVAL.LACIÓ

Zoo

AVDA ICÀRIA

㉛

ación bía

C/DOCTOR AIGUADER
Ciutadella-Vila Olímpica Ⓜ

VILA OLÍMPICA

RONDA LITORAL

TOR AIGUADER
LBOA
L/DOCTOR AIGUADER
AVDA LITORAL
C/SALVADOR ESPRIU
PLAÇA CAMPIONS

3

GINEBRA

Parc Barceloneta

Hospital del Mar
C/P'ELAMNY
C/RAMON TRIAS FARGAS
FARGAS
PASSEIG MARÍTIM PORT OLÍMPIC

UINISTA cat

㉚
C/MARINA
MOLL MESTRAL

BARCELONETA
C/ANDREA DÒRIA

MOLL MARINA

MOLL GREGAL

Port Olímpic

Platja Nova Icària

PLAÇA RUGADA
PASSEIG MARÍTIM
① ⑫ ⑬ ③
Platja Passeig Marítim

4

Platja arceloneta

0   300 m
0   300 yds
© Copyright Time Out Group 2006

5

① Sights & museums
① Eating & drinking
① Shopping
① Nightlife
① Arts & leisure

Can Solé

Eating & drinking

Agua

Passeig Marítim 30 (93 225 12 72).
Metro Barceloneta. **Open** 1.30-4pm,
8.30pm-midnight Mon-Thur; 1.30-4pm,
8.30pm-1am Fri; 1.30-5pm, 8.30pm-1am
Sat; 1.30-5pm, 8.30pm-midnight Sun.
€€€. **Mediterranean**. Map p97 E4 **1**
Let down by some front-of-house chaos
that means a long wait even with a
booking, Agua is otherwise one of the
freshest, most relaxed places to eat in
the city, with a large terrace smack on
the beach and an animated sunny
interior. The menu rarely changes, but
regulars never tire of the competently
executed monkfish tail with *sofregit*,
the risotto with partridge, and fresh
pasta with juicy prawns. Scrummy
puddings include marron glacé mousse
and sour apple sorbet.

Andaira

NEW *C/Vilajoiosa 52-54 (93 221 16 16/*
www.andaira.com). Metro Barceloneta.
Open 1.15-3.30pm, 9-11.30pm daily.
€€€€. **Mediterranean**. Map
p96 C4 **2**
Dishes include succulent lamb baked
for 24 hours and served with mint and
spinach jus; eggs poached – like the
lamb, at the gastronomically modish
temperature of 65° – and served up
with sea urchins and chickpea broth,

and monkfish paired with bergamot
mayonnaise. The restaurant itself has
a relaxed minimalist look, with pale
grey pinstripes and flickering tealights,
but the best tables are on the terrace
overlooking the beach.

Bestial

C/Ramón Trias Fargas 2-4 (93 224
04 07). Metro Barceloneta. **Open**
1.30-4pm, 8.30pm-midnight Mon-Wed;
1.30-5pm, 8.30pm-1am Thur-Sat.
€€€. **Italian**. Map p97 E4 **3**
Its tiered wooden decking and ancient
olive trees make Bestial a peerless spot
for alfresco seaside dining. At weekends, coloured lights play over the
tables as a DJ takes to the decks. The
food is modern Italian: dainty mini-
pizzas, rocket salads with parma ham
and a lightly poached egg, tuna with
black olive risotto and all the puddings
you'd expect to find – panna cotta,
tiramisu and limoncello sorbet.

Can Maño

C/Baluard 12 (93 319 30 82). Metro
Barceloneta. **Open** noon-4pm, 8-11pm
Mon-Fri; noon-5pm Sat. Closed Aug.
€. No credit cards. **Seafood**.
Map p96 C3 **4**
With a roaring telly, fruit machines
and tables so cramped the waiters have
to frisbee the food at you, this neigh-
bourhood caff is a local institution,

catering principally to hungry local workers. The huge portions of market-fresh cuttlefish, red mullet or bream usually come with chips, although you can request aubergine or fried tomatoes (if you can keep the waiter's attention that long). Arrive early.

Can Solé

C/Sant Carles 4 (93 221 50 12). Metro Barceloneta. **Open** 1.30-4pm, 8-11pm Tue-Sat; 1.30-4pm Sun. Closed 2wks Aug. **€€€. Seafood. Map** p96 C4 ⑤
Located in a charming old fisherman's cottage, this lavishly tiled restaurant has been serving traditional harbour-side food for over a century. Regulars, usually of port-quaffing age themselves, tuck into plates of shrimp, wild mackerel, stewed lobster and superb paellas cooked almost under their noses in the bustling open kitchen. The decor is elegant yet not overboard, with plenty of photos of former fans like Santiago Rusiñol and Joan Miró.

La Cova Fumada

C/Baluard 56 (93 221 40 61). Metro Barceloneta. **Open** 8.30am-3.30pm Mon-Wed; 8.30am-3.30pm, 6-8.30pm Thur, Fri; 8.30am-1.30pm Sat. Closed Aug. **€.** No credit cards. **Tapas. Map** p96 C4 ⑥
This cramped little *bodega* is the birth-place of the potato *bomba*, served with a fiery chilli sauce. Especially tasty are the chickpeas with morcilla sausage, roast artichokes and the marinated sardines. Its huge following of lunching workers means it's hard to get a table after 1pm.

Daguiri

NEW *C/Grau i Torras 59, corner of C/Almirall Aixada (93 221 51 09). Metro Barceloneta.* **Open** *June-Oct* 11am-2am daily. *Nov-May* 11am-2.30am Mon, Thur-Sun. **€€. Café. Map** p96 C4 ⑦
Daguiri works hard to avoid being a one-trick pony. Along with a seaside summer terrace, there's a raft of mea-sures aimed squarely at foreign resi-dents. Wi-Fi connections, a language exchange, Murphy's, Guinness and a stack of international newspapers fea-ture among them. Throughout the day, there's cheesy garlic bread, delectable filled ciabatta, tapas, dolmades and dips, and home-made chocolate or carrot cake.

La Miranda del Museu

Museu d'Història de Catalunya, Plaça Pau Vila 3 (93 225 50 07). Metro Barceloneta. **Open** 10am-7pm Tue, Wed; 10am-7pm, 9-11pm Thur-Sat; 10am-4pm Sun. **€€. Café. Map** p96 C3 ⑧
Don't go spreading this about, but there's a secret café with terrific views, cheap and reasonable food and a vast terrace, sitting right at the edge of the marina, perched high above the humdrum tourist traps. Stroll into the Catalan History Museum and take the lift to the top floor. You don't need a ticket.

La Piadina

NEW *C/Meer 48 (mobile 660 806 172). Metro Barceloneta.* **Open** *Jan-Mar* 1-11pm Thur-Sun. *Apr-Oct* 1-11pm daily. **€.** No credit cards. **Italian. Map** p96 C4 ⑨
A *piadina* is a warmed Italian wrap, made using something akin to a large pitta. Fillings here come in 30 different permutations on the basic tomato, mozzarella, ham, rocket and mushroom theme. To find the place, turn inland at Rebecca Horn's tower of rusting cubes on the beach.

El Suquet de l'Almirall

Passeig Joan de Borbó 65 (93 221 62 33). Metro Barceloneta. **Open** 1-4pm, 9-11pm Tue-Sat; 1-4pm Sun. Closed 2wks Aug. **€€€. Seafood. Map** p96 C4 ⑩
El Suquet remains a friendly family concern despite the smart decor and mid-scale business lunchers. Fishy favourites range from *xató* salad to *arròs negre* and a variety of set menus, including the 'blind' selection of tapas, a gargantuan taster menu and, most popular, the *pica-pica*, which includes roast red peppers with anchovies, a bowl of steamed cockles and clams, and a heap of *fideuà* with lobster.

BARCELONA BY AREA

El Vaso de Oro

C/Balboa 6 (93 319 30 98). Metro
Barceloneta. **Open** 9am-midnight
daily. Closed Sept. No credit cards.
€€. **Tapas**. **Map** p96 C3 ⑪

The enormous popularity of this long,
narrow, cruise ship style-bar tells you
everything you need to know about the
tapas, but also means that he who hesitates is lost when it comes to ordering.
Elbow out a space and demand, loudly, *chorizitos*, *patatas bravas*, cubed
steak (*solomillo*) or spicy tuna (*atún*).

Nightlife

CDLC

Passeig Marítim 32 (93 224 04
70/www.cdlcbarcelona.com). Metro
Ciutadella-Vila Olímpica. **Open** noon-
2.30am Mon-Wed; noon-3am Thur-Sun.
Admission free. **Map** p97 E4 ⑫

Carpe Diem Lounge Club is the darling
of the Barça football team (it's owned
by the wife of ex-Barça man Patrick
Kluivert) and other celebs staying at
the Hotel Arts. It works hard to be the
most exclusive club on the circuit,
sometimes even going so far as to
refuse entry to its own invited VIPs.
But, hey, if Rod Stewart got in, you
should be able to. There's a space to
suit any kind of lounge lizard – from
the swanky bed-size sofas to the
fast-moving dancefloor and beachfront
terrace. Resident DJ Anne-Miek and
guests play soulful, vocal house.

Shôko

Passeig Marítim 36 (93 225 92 03/
www.shoko.biz). Metro Ciutadella-Vila
Olímpica. **Open** midnight-3am Wed-
Sun. **Admission** free. **Map** p97 E4 ⑬

Another Jekyll and Hyde restaurant-
club, where the staff look miserable in
their role as waiters, but once it's party
time their joie de vivre knows no
bounds. The restaurant has had hor-
rendous reports, but thanks largely to
its attempt at a harmonious oriental
atmosphere (the decor has been feng
shui-ed) the club is an oasis of good
vibes in the notoriously snooty or
seedy Port Olimpic.

Port Vell

Over the last 15 years Port Vell (the
'Old Port') has changed beyond
recognition from an industrial
dockyard to a palm-fringed
paradigm of urban integration,
attracting over 16 million visitors a
year. The clean-up has extended the
whole seven kilometres (four miles)
of city seashore, which is now a
virtually continuous strip of modern
construction: new docks, beaches,
marinas, hotels, the Diagonal Mar
area, conference centres and cruise
and ferry harbours are soon to be
joined by Ricard Bofill's Nova
Bocana development, with its new
maritime esplanade and sail-shaped
luxury hotel.

To the south sits the **Moll
d'Espanya**, an artificial island
linked to land by the undulating
Rambla de Mar footbridge housing
the **Maremàgnum** mall, an **IMAX**
cinema and the **aquarium**. Beyond
this is the **World Trade Center**,
a hulking, ship-shaped construction
built on a jetty and housing offices
and a five-star hotel. At the
approach to the jetty, Andreu
Alfaro's enormous **Onas** (*Waves*)
cheers up the gridlocked
roundabout of Plaça de la
Carbonera, where a grim basin
of coal commemorates where the
steamboats once refuelled. To the
right, beyond the busy ferry and
cruise ports, is the grandly named
Porta d'Europa, the longest
drawbridge in Europe, which
curtains off the vast container port.

Sights & museums

Catamaran Orsom

Portal de la Pau, Port de Barcelona (93
441 05 37/www.barcelona-orsom.com).
Metro Drassanes. **Sailings** (approx 1hr
20mins) Mar-Oct noon-8pm 3-4 sailings
daily. All sailings subject to weather
conditions. **Tickets** €12; €6-€9

Taking the piss

Goodbye to alfresco drinking and urinating.

Mayor Joan Clos, the old smoothie, likes to talk about social cohesion. He loves to claim that Barcelona is run by its citizens and he rarely misses an opportunity to mention tolerance. Imagine the recent surprise then of one *Time Out* reader who, enjoying a quiet beer on the beach with his girlfriend, was approached by a couple of policemen and fined €70. His crime was not causing a disturbance, or even drinking alcohol in a public place, it was drinking alcohol *from a can* in a public place.

This is one of a raft of often impenetrable new bylaws introduced in 2006 and designed to counteract '*incivisme*' in the city, and attracting ridicule and opprobrium in equal measure. The category hitting the headlines has been prostitution, with the offering or accepting of sexual services being outlawed where it is likely to impede public use of a street or space (this is, of course, open to a thousand interpretations), but there are several others likely to affect the unwitting tourist.

Consumption of alcohol in a public space (apart from pavement bars or café tables) is forbidden where 'this may cause a nuisance' and where it comes 'in a bottle or a can'. Fines can reach an impressive €1,500. Bodily functions are also in the Mayor's sights, with spitting, defecating and urinating in the street (vomiting was removed at the eleventh hour) attracting penalties of up to €300. And don't even think about spraypainting a wall, handing out leaflets or flyposting (€120 €3,000) or skateboarding over street furniture (€750 to €3,000).

Most egregious penalty, though, must surely be that imposed on anyone using shampoo in a beach shower. The fine for this is €1,500. The justification for this is even more irrational, stating 'For reasons of hygiene, the use of soaps or other personal hygiene products is forbidden', narrowly pipped to the post for most absurd wording by the bylaw forbidding citizens to 'be tempted by... tricksters'.

Remember that people, and just say no.

Maremàgnum p104

reductions; free under-4s. *Jazz cruises* €14; €7-€10 reductions. No credit cards. **Map** p96 A3 ⓴

Departing from the jetty by the Monument a Colom, this 23-metre (75ft) catamaran chugs round the Nova Bocana harbour development, before unfurling its sails and peacefully gliding across the bay. There are 8pm jazz cruises from June to September or the catamaran can be chartered for private trips along the Costa Brava.

Las Golondrinas

Moll de Drassanes (93 442 31 06/ www.lasgolondrinas.com). Metro Drassanes. **Tickets** €9.20; €4-€6.50 reductions; free under-4s. **Map** p96 A3 ⓯

For over 115 years the 'swallow boats' have chugged all around the harbour, giving passengers a bosun's-eye view of Barcelona's now rapidly changing seascape. The fleet is made up of three double-decker pleasure boats and two glass-bottomed catamarans, moored next to the Orsom catamaran. Boats leave around every 35 minutes for the shorter trip, and approximately every hour for the longer trip.

Monument a Colom

Plaça Portal de la Pau (93 302 52 24). Metro Drassanes. **Open** 9am-8.30pm

daily. **Admission** €2.20; €1.40 reductions; free under-4s. No credit cards. **Map** p96 A3 ⓰

The end of La Rambla is marked by the Columbus monument, designed for the 1888 Great Exhibition, and inspired by Nelson's Column, complete with four majestic lions. A tiny lift takes you up inside the column to a circular viewing bay for a panoramic view of city and port. Claustrophobes and vertigo sufferers should stay away; the slight sway is particularly unnerving.

Museu d'Història de Catalunya

Plaça Pau Vila 3 (93 225 47 00/ www.mhcat.net). Metro Barceloneta. **Open** 10am-7pm Tue, Thur-Sat; 10am-8pm Wed; 10am-2.30pm Sun. **Admission** €3; €2.10 reductions; free under-7s. Free to all 1st Sun of mth. No credit cards. **Map** p96 C3 ⓱

Located in a lavishly converted 19th-century port warehouse, the Museum of Catalan History's compass runs from the Paleolithic era right up to Jordi Pujol's proclamation as President of the Generalitat in 1980. With very little in the way of original artefacts, it is more a virtual chronology of the region's past revealed through two floors of text, photos, film, animated models and reproductions of everything from a medieval shoemaker's shop to a 1960s bar. Hands-on activities such as trying to lift a knight's armour or irrigating lettuces with a Moorish water wheel add a little pzazz to the rather dry displays. Every section has a decent introduction in English, but the reception desk will also lend copies of the more detailed museum guide. Upstairs is a café with terrace and an unbeatable view.

Museu Marítim

Avda de les Drassanes (93 342 99 29/www.diba.es/mmaritim). Metro Drassanes. **Open** 10am-7pm daily. **Admission** €5.40; €2.70 reductions; free under-7s. *Temporary exhibitions varies. Combined ticket with Las Golondrinas* (35 mins) €6.60; €4-€5.10 reductions; free under-4s. (1hr30mins) €10.10; €5.70-€7.70 reductions; free under-4s. **Map** p96 A2 ⑱

One of the finest examples of civil Gothic architecture in Spain, the medieval shipyards, or *drassanes*, are a wonderful setting for this spacious nautical museum. The mainstay of the collection is a full-scale replica of the Royal Galley, in which Don Juan of Austria led the Holy League to a resounding victory against the Turkish navy in the Battle of Lepanto in 1571. Stand on the platform over the poop deck with your audio-guide and like magic a group of ghostly galley slaves will appear in front of you. The museum also shows you how shipbuilding and cartography techniques have developed over the years through an absorbing range of maps and models, and there is a curious collection of figureheads. A ticket to the museum also allows you access to the three-masted *Santa Eulàlia* schooner docked in the Moll de la Fusta.

Transbordador Aeri

Torre de Sant Sebastià, Barceloneta (93 441 48 20). Metro Barceloneta. Also Torre de Jaume I, Port Vell, to Ctra Miramar, Montjuïc. Metro Drassanes. **Open** *Mid June-mid Sept* 10.45am-7.15pm daily. *Mid Sept-mid*

June 10.30am-5.45pm daily. **Tickets** €7.50 single; €9 return; free under-3s. No credit cards. **Map** p96 B4 ⑲

Take the lift up the Sant Sebastià tower at the very far end of Passeig Joan de Borbó or the Jaume I tower in front of the World Trade Center to jump on one of the battered old cable cars, which run over the port to Montjuïc. To ensure a clear view, try to avoid mid morning and mid afternoon, when you'll be jostling for window space.

Eating & drinking

Bar Colombo

C/Escar 4 (93 225 02 00). Metro Barceloneta. **Open** noon-3am daily. Closed 2wks Jan-Feb. No credit cards. **Bar**. **Map** p96 B4 ⑳

Deckshod yachties and moneyed locals stroll by all day, oblivious to this unassuming little bar and its sunny terrace overlooking the port. In fact, nobody seems to notice it, odd given its fantastic location and generous portions of *patatas bravas*. The only drawback is the nerve-jangling techno that occasionally fetches up on the stereo.

Can Paixano

C/Reina Cristina 7 (93 310 08 39). Metro Barceloneta. **Open** 9am-10.30pm Mon-Sat. Closed 3wks Aug-Sept. No credit cards. **Bar**. **Map** p96 C2 ㉑

It's impossible to talk, get your order heard or move your elbows, yet the 'Champagne Bar', as it's invariably known, has a global following. Its smoky confines are always mobbed with Catalans and adventurous tourists making the most of dirt-cheap house Cava and sausage *bocadillos* (you can't buy a bottle without a couple). A must.

Luz de Gas – Port Vell

Opposite the Palau de Mar, Moll del Dipòsit (93 484 23 26). Metro Barceloneta or Jaume I. **Open** *Apr-Oct* noon-3am daily. Closed Nov-Mar. **Bar**. **Map** p96 C3 ㉒

It's cheesy, but this boat/bar also has its romantic moments. By day, bask in the sun with a beer on the upper deck, or rest in the shade below. With nightfall, candles are brought out, wine is uncorked and, if you can blot out the Lionel Richie, it's everything a holiday bar should be.

Set Portes

Passeig d'Isabel II 14 (93 319 30 33). Metro Barceloneta. **Open** 1pm-1am daily. €€€. **Seafood**. Map p96 C2 ㉓

The eponymous seven doors open on to as many dining salons, all kitted out in elegant 19th-century decor. Regional dishes are served in enormous portions and include a stewy fish *zarzuela* with half a lobster, and a different paella daily (shellfish, for example, or with rabbit and snails). Reservations are only available for certain tables (two to three days in advance is recommended); without one, get there early or expect a long wait outside.

Somorrostro

NEW *C/Sant Carles 11, Barceloneta (93 225 00 10). Metro Barceloneta.* **Open** 7-11.30pm Mon, Thur-Sun. €€€. **Global**. Map p96 C4 ㉔

Named after the shanty town of Andalucian immigrants that once stood nearby on the beach, Somorrostro is a refreshingly non-fishy, non-traditional restaurant for these parts. Its bare-bricked walls and red and black decor attract a young, buzzy crowd, attended to by permanently confused waiters. The food ranges from cucumber, tomato and yoghourt soup with home-made bread, to an unexpectedly successful tandoori duck magret.

Shopping

Maremàgnum

Moll d'Espanya (93 225 81 00/ www.maremagnum.es). Metro Drassanes. **Open** 10am-10pm daily. Map p96 B3 ㉕

After years of declining popularity, the Maremàgnum shopping centre has been spruced up, ditched most of the bars and discos and taken a step upmarket with shops such as Xocoa (for mouthwatering chocolate), Calvin Klein and Parisian accessories from boudoirish Lollipops. The high-street staples are all present and correct – Mango, H&M, Women's Secret and so on – and the ground floor still focuses on the family market with sweets, clothes for kids and a Barça shop. There's also a Starbucks and a handful of tapas bars and restaurants.

Nightlife

Le Kasbah

Plaça Pau Vilà (Palau del Mar) (93 238 07 22/www.ottozutz.com). Metro Barceloneta. **Open** 10.30pm-3am daily. **Admission** free. Map p96 C3 ㉖

A white awning heralds the entrance to this louche bar beind the Palau de Mar. Inside, a North African harem look seduces a young and up-for-it mix of tourists and students on to its plush cushions for a cocktail or two before going out. As the night progresses so does the music, from chill-out early on to full-on boogie after midnight.

Sugar Club

NEW *World Trade Center, Moll de Barcelona (93 508 83 25/www.sugar club-barcelona.com). Metro Drassanes.* **Open** 8pm-4am Wed-Sat. **Admission** free. Map p96 A4 ㉗

Grupo Salsitas continues its quest to rule all that's cool. Beautiful people and a twinkling view across the marina provide the decoration in this otherwise minimal couple of spaces, one small and intimate with a splash of smooth and soulful vocal house, the other a large dancefloor with sofas. DJs blend tribal, electro and tech house beats with the odd remixed 1980s classic thrown in to keep the well-dressed 25- to 35-year-old Sugar babes sweet.

Arts & leisure

L'Aquàrium

Moll d'Espanya (93 221 74 74/www. aquariumbcn.com). Metro Barceloneta or Drassanes. **Open** Oct-May 9.30am-9pm Mon-Fri; 9.30am-9.30pm Sat, Sun. June, Sept 9.30am-9.30pm daily. July, Aug 9.30am-11pm daily. **Admission** €14.50; €9.50 reductions; free under-4s. Map p96 B3 ㉘

The main draw here is the Oceanari, a giant shark-infested tank traversed via a glass tunnel. Many of the larger tanks are surrounded by benches for lingering observation; smaller animals, such as starfish and the newly expanded collection of sea horses, are at kids'-eye level.

IMAX Port Vell

Moll d'Espanya (93 225 11 11/www. imaxportvell.com). Metro Barceloneta or Drassanes. Tickets €7-€10. Map p96 B3 **29**

A squat white hulk in the middle of the marina, the IMAX has yet to persuade many that it's anything more than a gimmick. Its predictable programming, immediately recognisable from similar enterprises the world over, covers fish, birds, ghosts and adventure sports, possibly in 3D.

Vila Olímpica

In the two years preceding the 1992 Olympics, the 'Olympic Village' was transformed from an industrial wasteland into a model neighbourhood, with accommodation for 15,000 athletes, parks, a metro stop, a multiplex cinema, four beaches and a leisure marina. The result is a spacious and comfortable district but the lack of cafés and shops leaves it devoid of Mediterranean charm and bustle, unless you count the weekend skaters and cyclists.

Most social activity takes place in the seafront Port Olímpic, home to docked sailboats, restaurants, beaches, a large casino, and a waterfront strip of cheesy nightclubs and theme pubs. Wide empty boulevards lend themselves well to large-scale sculpture and landmark pieces include a jagged **pergola** on Avda Icària by Enric Miralles and Carme Pinós, in memory of the ripped-up industrial railway tracks, and Antoni Llena's abstract **David i Goliat** in the Parc de les Cascades.

Nightlife

Around the right-angled quayside of the Port Olímpic, you'll find dance bars interspersed with seafood restaurants, fast-food outlets, ice-cream parlours, coffee shops and mock-Irish pubs; with video screens, glittery lights and go-go girls and boys in abundance, it makes little difference which one you choose.

Club Catwalk

C/Ramon Trias Fargas s/n (93 221 61 61/www.clubcatwalk.net). Metro Ciutadella-Vila Olímpica. Open *midnight-5.30am Thur-Sun.* Admission *Thur, Sun free. Fri, Sat €9.* Credit DC, MC, V. Map p97 E3 **30**

The fashionable sashay over from neighbouring CDLC and Shôko to strut their stuff in this A-list hedonist paradise. Get past the impassive doormen to enter two separate dancefloors, one house and the other hip hop and R&B. White canopied sofas where anything goes set the tone for its South Beach inspired glam. Once a month the fine Subliminal Sessions play host to Erick Morillo and other DJs from the New York house label.

Arts & leisure

Yelmo Icària Cineplex

C/Salvador Espriú 61, Vila Olímpica (information 93 221 75 85/tickets 902 22 09 22/www.yelmocineplex.es). Metro Ciutadella Vila Olímpica. Tickets *Mon €4.90. Tue-Sun €6.10; €4.90 before 3pm & reductions.* No credit cards. Map p97 F3 **31**

In a sterile shopping mall beside the Olympic port, this massive 15-screen multiplex is low on atmosphere but high on choice. Films are mostly mainstream and American, with the odd Spanish or European movie thrown in for a bit of variation. Weekends are seat-specific, so queues tend to be slow-moving; it's worth booking your place on the internet before you go.

Font Màgica de Montjuïc p109

Montjuïc & Poble Sec

Though it wasn't always the case, Montjuïc is Barcelona's Xanadu, a pleasure ground of gardens, museums and galleries, perfect for a leafy stroll with majestic views over the city. Calatrava's Olympic needle and the other buildings of the 1992 Games are scattered over the landward side, while facing the sea is the lighthouse and enormous cemetery. A reminder of the city's violent past lurks on top of it all, scarcely visible from below: the squat and heavily fortified Castell de Montjuïc, a place full of dark memories for the city's older citizens (see box p111).

The long axis from **Plaça d'Espanya** is still the most popular means of access to the park, with the climb now eased by a sequence of open-air escalators. In the centre of Plaça d'Espanya itself is a monument that was designed by Josep Maria Jujol (who created the wrought-iron balconies on La Pedrera). The Las Arenas bullring, in a neo-Mudéjar style, is currently being remade into a shopping and leisure centre by architect Richard Rogers.

The many parks and gardens include the **Jardins Mossèn Costa i Llobera**, which abound in tropical plants, but particularly cacti; they lie just below Miramar,

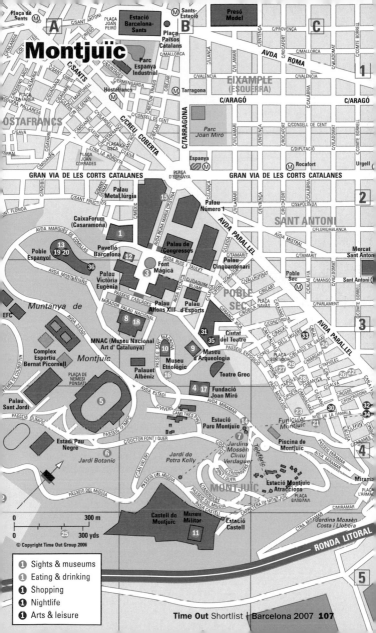

Montjuïc

CaixaForum

on the steep flank nearest the port. Not far above are the **Jardins del Mirador**, from where you can enjoy a spectacular view over the harbour. One of the newest parks is the nearby **Jardins de Joan Brossa**, which features humorous, hands-on contraptions where children can manipulate water-courses and do creative adventure sports. Walk down towards the funicular station and you will reach the **Jardins Cinto Verdaguer**, with its lovely quiet pond, beautiful water lilies and grassy slopes.

Sights & museums

CaixaForum

Casaramona, Avda Marquès de Comillas 6-8 (93 476 86 00/ www.fundacio.lacaixa.es). Metro Espanya. **Open** 10am-8pm Tue-Sun. **Admission** free. **Map** p107 B1 ❶ Back in 1911 Puig i Cadafalch designed the creative brickwork of this former mattress factory. It spent most of the last century in a sorry state, acting briefly as a police barracks and then falling into dereliction. Fundació La Caixa, the charitable arm of Catalonia's largest savings bank, bought it and gave it a huge rebuild. The brick factory was supported while the ground below was excavated to house an entrance plaza by Arata Isozaki (who designed the Palau Sant Jordi on the other side of the hill), a Sol LeWitt mural, a 350-seat auditorium, bookshop and library. In addition to the smaller permanent contemporary art collection, upstairs there are three impressive spaces for temporary exhibitions – often among the most interesting in the city.
Event highlights 'The Arab World' (Oct 2006-Feb 2007); French rococo painter Jean-Honoré Fragonard (Nov 2006-Feb 2007).

Cementiri del Sud-oest

C/Mare de Déu de Port 54-58 (93 484 17 00). Bus 38. **Open** 8am-6pm daily. **Admission** free. **Map** p107 A4 ❷

This enormous necropolis, perched at the side of the motorway out of town, serves as a daily reminder to commuters of their own mortality. It has housed the city's dead since 1883, originally placing them in four sections: one for Catholics, one for Protestants, one for non-Christians and a fourth for abortions. It now stretches over the entire south-west corner of the mountain, with family tombs stacked five or six storeys high. Many, especially those belonging to the gypsy community, are a riot of colour and flowers.

Font Màgica de Montjuïc

Plaça d'Espanya (93 316 10 00/ www.bcn.es/fonts). Metro Espanya. **Fountain** May-Sept 8pm-midnight Thur-Sun; music every 30mins 9.30pm-midnight. Oct-Apr 7-9pm Fri, Sat; music every 30mins 7-9pm. **Map** p107 B3 ❸

Still using its original art deco waterworks, the 'magic fountain' works its wonders with the help of 3,600 pieces of tubing and over 4,500 light bulbs. Summer evenings after nightfall see the multiple founts swell and dance to various hits ranging from Sting to the *1812 Overture*, showing off its kaleidoscope of pastel colours, while searchlights play in a giant fan pattern over the palace dome.

Fundació Joan Miró

Parc de Montjuïc (93 329 19 08/ www.bcn.fjmiro.es). Metro Paral·lel then Funicular de Montjuïc/bus 61. **Open** July-Sept 10am-8pm Tue, Wed, Fri, Sat; 10am-9.30pm Thur; 10am-2.30pm Sun. Oct-June 10am-7pm Tue, Wed, Fri, Sat; 10am-9.30pm Thur; 10am-2.30pm Sun. *Guided tours* 11.30pm Sat, Sun. **Admission** *All exhibitions* €7.20; €5 reductions. *Temporary exhibitions* €4; €3 reductions. Free under-14s. **Map** p107 B4 ❹

Josep Lluís Sert, who spent the years of the dictatorship as Dean of Architecture at Harvard University, designed one of the world's great museum buildings on his return. Approachable, light and airy, these white walls and arches house a

Joan Miró

Fundació Joan Miró

collection of more than 225 paintings, 150 sculptures and all of Miró's graphic work, plus some 5,000 drawings. The permanent collection, highlighting Miró's trademark use of primary colours and simplified organic forms symbolising stars, the moon, birds and women, occupies the second half of the space. On the way to the sculpture gallery is Alexander Calder's lovely reconstructed *Mercury Fountain*, which was originally seen at the Spanish Republic's Pavilion at the 1937 Paris Fair. In other works, Miró is shown as a Cubist (*Street in Pedralbes*, 1917), Naïve (*Portrait of a Young Girl*, 1919) or Surrealist (*Man and Woman in Front of a Pile of Excrement*, 1935). Downstairs are works donated to the museum by 20th-century artists. In the upper galleries large, black-outlined paintings from the final period precede a room of works with political themes. **Event highlights** Carles Santos, the multi-disciplined Valencian artist (23 June 2006-5 Nov 2006); 'Miró, the final years' (Nov 2006-Feb 2007).

Galeria Olímpica

Estadi Olímpic, Parc de Montjuïc (93 426 06 60/www.fundaciobarcelona olimpica.es). Metro Espanya/bus all routes to Plaça d'Espanya. **Open** *Apr-Sept* 10am-2pm, 4-7pm Mon-Fri. *Oct-Mar* (by appointment) 10am-1pm, 4-6pm Mon-Fri. **Admission** €2.70; €2.40-€1.50 reductions. **Map** p107 A4 ⑤

Of fairly limited interest, this is a hotch-potch of imagery and paraphernalia that commemorates the 1992 Olympics, including fancy costumes from the opening ceremony and the ubiquitous mascot Cobi.

Jardí Botànic

C/Doctor Font i Quer (93 426 49 35). Metro Espanya. **Open** *Apr-June, Sept* 10am-5pm Mon-Fri; 10am-8pm Sat, Sun. *July, Aug* 10am-8pm daily. *Oct-Mar* 10am-5pm daily. **Admission** €4; €2 reductions; free under-16s. Free last Sun of mth. No credit cards. **Map** p107 A4 ⑥

The botanic garden was opened in 1999, with the idea of collecting plants from seven global regions that share a western Mediterranean climate. The result is highly impressive. Everything about the futuristic design, from the angular concrete pathways to the raw sheet-steel banking (and including even such small details as the design of the bins), is the complete antithesis of the more naturalistic, Jekyll-inspired gardens of England. It is meticulously kept, with the added advantage of wonderful views across the city.

Jardins Mossèn Costa i Llobera

Ctra de Miramar 1. Metro Drassanes or Paral·lel. **Open** 10am-sunset daily. **Admission** free. **Map** p107 B4 ⑦

The port side of Montjuïc is protected from the cold northerly wind, which creates a microclimate that is some two degrees warmer than the rest of the city. This has made it perfect for 800 species of the world's cactus. It is said to be the most complete collection of its type in Europe.

BARCELONA BY AREA

Las Arenas bullring p106

Who captures the castle?

Barcelona refuses to relinquish Montjuïc castle.

The saga of the handover of the 17th-century Montjuïc castle from the Spanish government to the city of Barcelona is a permanent resident in local headlines. A potent symbol of repression – it was used to bombard the Catalans into submission in 1842 and as a prison, torture centre and execution site for dissidents during the dictatorship – its ownership is a loaded issue.

Prime minister José Luis Zapatero promised the restitution of the castle to the city in June 2004 and negotiations were going smoothly until the last minute in February 2006, when José Bono, Spanish Minister of Defence, imposed three conditions: the presence of a military detachment, the maintenance of some military antennae and, most gallingly, to keep the Spanish flag flying rather than the Catalan flag because 'Montjuïc is Spanish territory.'

Barcelona flatly rejected this proposal but stalemate was averted when Bono announced his resignation in April 2006. Barely able to conceal its glee, the Barcelona town council is confident (at the time of writing) that a deal is imminent. One plan floated for the castle's future is to counter its unsavoury history by turning it into an institution devoted to peace studies.

Most visitors come for the spectacular views over Barcelona, and the parkland surrounding the castle has been extensively relandscaped to make the area more accessible. Inside, the military museum (**Museu Militar**, p113) is little visited by tourists, despite having rid its giftshop of unsavoury fascist paraphernalia and stashed away its Franco statue (the last in the city). The museum collection itself contains the usual assortment of military paintings and dozens of rooms of uniforms, armour, weapons and grim instruments of war. If you don't mind an uphill walk after, the port-crossing cable car is a spectacular way to reach the castle.

MNAC (Museu Nacional d'Art de Catalunya)

Palau Nacional, Parc de Montjuïc (93 622 03 76/www.mnac.es). Metro Espanya. **Open** 10am-7pm Tue-Sat; 10am-2.30pm Sun. **Admission** *Permanent exhibitions* €8.50; €5.95 reductions. *Temporary exhibitions* €3. *Combined entrance with Poble Espanyol* €12. Free under-7s. Free 1st Thur of mth. **Map** p107 B3 ❽

After a renovation that overran even the most pessimistic estimates of time and expense, the MNAC now houses a dizzying overview of Catalan art from the 12th to 20th centuries. The highlight is still the extraordinary collection of Romanesque murals – especially the tremendous *Crist de Taüll*, from the 12th-century church of Sant Climent de Taüll. The art is set into freestanding wood supports or reconstructed church interiors. Even 'graffiti' scratchings (probably by monks) of crosses, animals and labyrinths have been preserved.

The Gothic collection at MNAC is also excellent, and starts with some late 13th-century frescoes that were discovered in 1961 and 1997 when two palaces in the city were being renovated. There are some stunning carvings and paintings from Catalonian churches, including works of the indisputable Catalan masters of the Golden Age, Bernat Martorell and Jaume Huguet. The highlight of the Thyssen collection is Fra Angelico's *Madonna of Humility* (c1430s), while the Cambó bequest contains some stunning old masters – some fine works by Titian, Rubens and El Greco among them.

Event highlights Humberto Rivas, Argentine photographer (Sept 2006-Dec 2006).

Museu d'Arqueologia de Catalunya

Passeig de Santa Madrona 39-41 (93 423 21 49/93 423 56 01/www. mac.es). Metro Poble Sec. **Open** 9.30am-7pm Tue-Sat; 10am-2.30pm Sun. **Admission** €2.40; €1.80 reductions; free under-16s. No credit cards. **Map** p107 B3 ❾

La Canadença p114

The time frame for this archaeological collection starts with the Palaeolithic period, and there are relics of Greek, Punic, Roman and Visigoth colonisers, up to the early Middle Ages. A massive Roman sarcophagus is carved with scenes of the rape of Persephone, and an immense statue of Aesculapius, the god of medicine, towers over one room. The display ends with the marvellous, jewel-studded headpiece of a Visigoth king. One of the best-loved pieces, perhaps inevitably, is an alarmingly erect Priapus, found during building work in Sants in 1848 and kept under wraps 'for moral reasons' until 1986.

Museu Etnològic

Passeig de Santa Madrona s/n (93 424 68 07/www.museuetnologic.bcn.es). Metro Poble Sec. **Open** 10am-7pm Tue, Thur; 10am-2pm Wed, Fri-Sun. **Admission** €3; €1.50 reductions; free under-16s, over-65s. No credit cards. **Map** p107 B3 ❿

The ethnology museum has recently been renovated and expanded in order to display more pieces from its vast collections of artefacts. The basement storage room has been spruced up and opened to the public, and makes for an enjoyable wander through glass-fronted cabinets, stuffed with all manner of objects from across the world. Of the displays upstairs, most outstanding are the Moroccan, Japanese and Philippine holdings, though there are also some interesting pre-Columbian finds.

Museu Militar

Castell de Montjuïc, Ctra de Montjuïc 66 (93 329 86 13). Metro Paral.lel, then funicular & cable car. **Open** *Apr-Oct* 9.30am-8pm Tue-Sun. *Nov-Mar* 9.30am-5pm Tue-Fri; 9.30am-8pm Sat, Sun. **Admission** €2.50; €1-€1.25 reductions; free under-7s. No credit cards. **Map** p107 B5 ⓫
See box p111.

Pavelló Mies van der Rohe

Avda Marquès de Comillas (93 423 40 16/www.miesbcn.com). Metro Espanya. **Open** 10am-8pm daily. **Admission** €3.50; €2 reductions; free under-18s. No credit cards. **Map** p107 B2 ⓬
Mies van der Rohe built the Pavelló Alemany (German Pavilion) for the 1929 Exhibition not as a gallery, but as a simple reception space, sparsely furnished by his trademark 'Barcelona Chair'. The pavilion was a founding monument of modern rationalist architecture, with its flowing floor plan and a revolutionary use of materials. Though the original was demolished after the Exhibition, a fine replica was built on the same site in 1986, the simplicity of its design setting off the warm tones of the marble and expressive Georg Kolbe sculpture in the pond.

Poble Espanyol

Avda Marquès de Comillas (93 325 78 66/www.poble-espanyol.com). Metro Espanya. **Open** 9am-8pm Mon; 9am-2am Tue-Thur; 9am-4am Fri, Sat; 9am-midnight Sun. **Admission** €7.50; €5.50 reductions; €15 family ticket; free under-7s. **Map** p107 A2 ⓭

Another legacy of the 1929 Exhibition, this time an enclosed area showing examples of traditional architecture from every region in Spain. A Castilian square leads to an Andalucían church, then on to village houses from Aragon, and so on. There are numerous bars and restaurants, and 60-plus shops and workshops. The Poble is unmistakably aimed at tourists, but it has been working to raise its cultural profile, as with the Fundació Fran Daurel collection of contemporary art and the recent opening of a quality gallery of Iberian arts and crafts.

Telefèric de Montjuïc

Estació Funicular, Avda Miramar (93 443 08 59/www.tmd.net). Metro Paral.lel, then funicular. **Map** p107 B4 ⓮
The Telefèric, with its four-person cable cars, is closed for renovations until the beginning of 2007, after which it will extend down to the port. In the meantime there is a replacement bus service (11am-7.15pm daily, every 15mins), running from the funicular to the castle.

Tren Montjuïc

Plaça d'Espanya (information 93 415 60 20). Metro Espanya. **Open** *Apr-mid June, 1st 2wks Sept* 10am-8.30pm Sat, Sun. *Mid June-Aug* 10am-8pm daily. Closed mid Sept-Mar. **Tickets** *All-day* €3.20; €2-€2.55 reductions. No credit cards. **Map** p107 B2 ⓯
This isn't a train but an open trolley pulled by a truck that goes up Montjuïc to Miramar every half hour through the day, passing all the hilltop sights along the way.

Eating & drinking

La Font del Gat

Passeig Santa Madrona 28 (93 289 04 04). Funicular Parc Montjuïc/bus 55. **Open** 1-6pm Tue-Sun. €€. **Catalan**. **Map** p107 B3 ⓰
A much-needed watering hole perched high on Montjuïc between the Miró and ethnological museums. A small and informal-looking restaurant, it has a

surprisingly sophisticated menu: ravioli with truffles and wild mushrooms, for example, or foie gras with Modena caramel. Tables outside attract a surcharge, but enjoy a fantastic view of the city.

Fundació Joan Miró
Parc de Montjuïc (93 329 07 68). Metro Paral·lel, then Funicular de Montjuïc. **Open** 10am-7pm Tue-Sat; 10am-2.30pm Sun. €€. **Café**. **Map** p107 B4 ⑰

Inside the Miró museum is this pleasant restaurant and café; the former overlooks the sculpture garden, while the latter has tables outside in a grassy courtyard dotted with Miró's pieces. The sandwiches made with 'Arab bread' are expensive but huge; there are also pasta dishes and daily specials.

Oleum
NEW *MNAC, Palau Nacional, Montjuïc (93 289 06 79). Metro Espanya.* **Open** 1-4pm Tue-Sun. €€€€. **Modern Mediterranean**. Map p107 B3 ⑱

That the MNAC's new restaurant is to be considered a serious contender is indicated by the two Antoni Tàpies canvases flanking the stunning view across the city. Dishes run the gamut from scallops on squid ink noodles with lime foam to suckling pig with an onion tarte tatin, or St Peter's fish poached in a fennel broth. Despite one or two teething troubles (distracted service and a couple of deliquescent foams), your average museum caff this is not.

Nightlife

Discothèque
Poble Espanyol, Avda Marquès de Comillas (93 511 57 64). Metro Espanya. **Open** midnight-6am Fri, Sat. **Admission** (incl 1 drink) €12 with flyer, €18 without. **Map** p107 A2 ⑲

New promoters have taken on the arduous task of keeping Discothèque at the forefront of the A-list clubs. A snaking queue of the young and the beautiful use kiosks and attitude to blag their way in. Nights with names like 'Ken loves you' or 'Fuck me, I'm famous' mix up

house and techno in the main room, while hip hop and R&B fill the smaller room. Projections, drag queens, podium dancers and a VIP bar create the Ibiza-when-it-was-still-hot vibe.

La Terrrazza
Poble Espanyol, Avda Marquès de Comillas (93 272 49 80/www.nightsungroup.com). Metro Espanya. **Open** *Mid Oct-mid May* midnight-6am Thur-Sat. **Admission** (incl 1 drink) €15 with flyer, €18 without. **Map** p107 A2 ⑳

The city's best-loved club returned in fine style in 2006 after a year exiled to the coast after noise complaints – it can be hard to soundproof an alfresco dancefloor. Beautiful (or at least young, or at least gay) people queue up out front all summer to dance under the stars. You don't have to dress up but you may skip the queue or the ticket price if you do. Guests like house DJs Dimitri from Paris and Miguel Migs share the decks with resident DJs.

Poble Sec & Paral·lel

Poble Sec is a friendly, working-class residential area of quiet streets and leafy squares. On the stretch of the Avda Paral·lel opposite the city walls three tall chimneys stand amid modern office blocks. They are all that remain of the Anglo-Canadian-owned power station known locally as La Canadença ('The Canadian'). This was the centre of the city's largest general strike, in 1919. Beside the chimneys an open space has been created and dubbed the **Parc de les Tres Xemeneies** ('Park of the Three Chimneys'). It is now particularly popular with skateboarders and Pakistani expat cricketers.

Towards the Paral·lel are some distinguished Modernista buildings, which local legend has maintained were built for *artistas* from the nude cabarets by their rich sugar daddies. At C/Tapioles 12 is a beautiful, narrow wooden Modernista door with particularly lovely writhing ironwork, while at C/Elkano 4 is **La Casa de les Rajoles**, which is known for its peculiar mosaic façade. Incongruous in such a central area is the small neighbourhood of single family dwellings with quaint gardens, off the upper reaches of C/Margarit.

Sights & museums

Refugi Antiaeri del Poble Sec

C/Nou de la Rambla 175 (93 319 02 22). Metro Paral·lel. **Open** *Guided tour* 11am 1st Sat of mth (by appointment only). Call to book 10am-2pm Mon-Fri; 4-6pm Tue, Thur. *Meeting place* Biblioteca Francesc Boix, C/Blai 34. **Admission** €3.20; free under-7s. **Map** p107 C4 ㉑

About 1,500 Barcelona civilians were killed during the vicious air bombings of the Civil War, a fact that the government long silenced. As Poble Sec particularly suffered the effects of bombing, a large air-raid shelter was built partially into the mountain at the top of C/Nou de la Rambla; one of some 1,200 in the entire city. Now converted into a museum, it is worth a visit. The guided tour takes 90 minutes.

Eating & drinking

Barcelona Rouge

C/Poeta Cabanyes 21 (93 442 49 85). Metro Paral·lel. **Open** 11pm-4am Tue-Sat. **Admission** free. No credit cards. **Bar**. **Map** p107 C3 ㉒

A hidey-hole of a place, small enough to get packed even though it's little known, hard to get into and hard on the wallet. Once inside there's ambient music, good cocktails and battered sofas draped with foreign and local thirtysomethings – those with a bit of money and a bit of class who want to avoid the more obvious nightspots. Ring the buzzer to get in.

Bar Primavera

C/Nou de les Rambla 192 (93 329 30 62). Metro Paral·lel. **Open** *Apr-Oct* 8am-10pm Tue-Sun. *Nov-Mar* 8am-7pm Tue-Sun. Closed 3wks Dec-Jan. No credit cards. **Bar**. **Map** p107 C4 ㉓

While this emphatically isn't a destination bar, it does have its own charm, and makes for a perfect pit stop on the climb up Montjuïc, with a quiet, vine-covered terrace from which to look back over the city while munching on rather basic *bocadillos*.

La Bella Napoli

C/Margarit 14 (93 442 50 56). Metro Paral·lel. **Open** 8.30pm-midnight Tue; 1.30-4pm, 8.30pm-midnight Wed-Sun. **€€**. **Pizzeria**. **Map** p107 C3 ㉔

The welcoming Neapolitan waiters can talk you through the long, long list of antipasti and pasta dishes, but you can't go wrong with the crispy baked pizzas. Portions of all dishes are generous and everything is very fresh, bar the dull pudding menu of bought-in ice-cream desserts; for the own-made cheesecake and tiramisu you have to ask. The beer is Moretti and the wine all Italian. A recent expansion means booking is no longer necessary.

La Caseta del Migdia

Mirador de Migdia, Passeig del Migdia s/n, Montjuïc (mobile 617 956 572). Bus 55 or bus Parc de Montjuïc/ funicular de Montjuïc, then 10min walk. Follow signs to Mirador de Montjuïc. **Open** *June-Sept* 8.30pm-2.30am Thur, Fri; 10am-2.30am Sat; 10.30am-1am Sun. *Oct-May* 10am-6pm Sat, Sun. No credit cards. **Bar**. **Map** p107 A5 ㉕

Follow the Camí del Mar footpath around Montjuïc castle to find one of the few vantage points in Barcelona from which to watch the sun set. Completely alfresco, high up in a clearing among the pines, this is a magical space, scattered with deckchairs, some hammocks and candlelit tables. DJs spinning funk, rare groove and lounge music alternate in a surreal fashion with a faltering string quartet.

BARCELONA BY AREA

La Soleá

Quimet i Quimet

C/Poeta Cabanyes 25 (93 442 31 42).
Metro Paral·lel. **Open** noon-4pm, 7-
10.30pm Mon-Fri; noon-4pm Sat. Closed
Aug. €€. **Tapas**. Map p107 C3 26
Packed to the rafters with dusty bottles of wine, this minuscule bar makes
up for in tapas what it lacks in space.
The speciality is preserved clams,
cockles, mussels and so on, which are
not to all tastes, but the *montaditos*,
sculpted tapas served on bread, are
spectacular. Try salmon sashimi with
cream cheese, honey and soy, or cod,
passata and black olive pâté.

La Soleá

NEW *Plaça del Sortidor 14 (93 441*
01 24). Metro Poble Sec. **Open** noon-
midnight Tue-Sat; noon-4pm Sun.
€€. No credit cards. **Global**. Map
p107 C3 27
From the name to the sprawling terrace
and the cheerful waiters to the orange
and yellow decor, everything about La

Soleá radiates sunshine. There's barely
a continent that hasn't been visited on
the menu, which holds houmous,
tabouleh and goat's cheese salad
alongside juicy burgers served with
roquefort or mushrooms, smoky tandoori chicken, Mexican tacos, vegetable
samosas and slabs of Argentine beef.

Tapioles 53

NEW *C/Tapioles 53 (93 329 22 38/*
www.tapioles53.com). Metro Paral·lel
or Poble Sec. **Open** 9-11.30pm daily.
€€€. **Global**. Map p107 C3 28
Eating at Tapioles 53 would be just
like eating at a friend's house; if, that
is, you had any friends who could cook
this well and had as canny an eye for
seductive lighting. It's the brainchild of
Australian chef Sarah Stothart, who
wanted to create a cosy atmosphere
with accomplished but unpretentious
food – such dishes as fabulous home-
made bread with wild mushroom soup;
boeuf bourgignon; fresh pasta with

baby broad beans and artichokes; rose-water rice pudding with pomegranate, or ginger and mascarpone cheesecake.

La Tomaquera

C/Margarit 58 (no phone). Metro Poble Sec. **Open** *1.30-3.45pm, 8.30-10.45pm Tue-Sat. Closed Aug.* €€. *No credit cards.* **Spanish.** **Map** p107 C3 ㉙
Like a curmudgeonly but beloved old uncle, the more obstreperous La Tomaquera is, the more popular it becomes. It's bright, it's loud, its waiters are brusque, there is no booking or telephone, there is only house wine, there are no soft drinks, there is only grilled meat with weapons-grade *all i oli* (unless you count the snails) and no, you can't pay with Visa. If you don't like it, you can go elsewhere. Of course, nobody does.

Nightlife

Maumau

C/Fontrodona 33 (93 441 80 15/ www.maumaunderground.com). Metro Paral·lel. **Open** *11pm-2.30am Thur; 11pm-3am Fri, Sat; 7pm-midnight Sun.* **Admission** *Membership* €5. *No credit cards.* **Map** p107 C4 ㉚
Behind the anonymous grey door (ring the bell), first-timers to this likeable little chill-out club pay €5 to become members, though in practice it rarely charges out-of-towners. Inside, a large warehouse space is humanised with colourful projections, IKEA sofas and scatter cushions, and a friendly, laid-back crowd. DJ Wakanda schools us in the finer points of deep house, jazz, funk or whatever takes his fancy.

Pocket Club

Mercat de les Flors, C/Lleida 59 (93 426 18 75/21 02/www.pocketbcn.com). Metro Espanya or Poble Sec. **Open** *9.30pm-2am every other Thur.* **Admission** €9. *Gigs varies.* *No credit cards.* **Map** p107 B3 ㉛
Mercat de les Flors is normally the host for performances programmed for one festival or another, but it has appeared on the urban hipster's radar recently as one of the venues for Pocket

Straight up

The rebuilding of Puig i Cadafalch's columns.

As a highly controversial new Catalan statute stokes the fires of regional pride, the city council is planning some very appropriate public statuary: the 60-foot-high (200-foot) *Quatre Barres* ('Four Columns') by Josep Puig i Cadafalch. Built in 1919, they represent the four stripes of the Catalan flag, and were demolished in 1928 by evil Spanish dictator General Primo de Rivera for being too overtly symbolic of Catalan independence.

Puig i Cadafalch had impeccable Catalan credentials: as well as designing iconic Modernista buildings – Casa Amatller on Passeig de Gràcia, Fàbrica Casaramona (now the CaixaForum, p108) and, on Avda Diagonal, Casa de les Punxes ('House of Spikes', Nos.416-20) and Palau Baró de Quadras (No.373) – he was president of the Mancomunitat (the semi-autonomous government of Catalonia) from 1917 to 1923.

The 1929 World Exhibition was the catalyst for Puig's urbanisation of Montjuïc, with the four ionic columns intended as its central showpiece. They stood in front of where the 'magic fountain' now plays to the crowds, and a favourite contender for their new site is just behind the fountain in the Plaça de les Cascades.

The columns should be reinstated in 2007, part of the 'Year of Puig i Cadafalch' that is to mark the 50th anniversary of his death – though he actually died on 23 December 1956.

Club. This bi-monthly night features the most independent of musical performers, from beardy folk twiddler Iron and Wine to laptop-wielding, mash-up audio guerrilla Jason Forrest.

Sala Apolo

C/Nou de la Rambla 113 (93 441 40 01/ www.sala-apolo.com). Metro Paral·lel. **Open** midnight-5am Wed, Thur; midnight-7am Fri, Sat; 10.30pm-3am Sun. **Admission** varies. No credit cards. **Map** p107 C4 ❷

This 1940s dancehall is a curious and rather musty backdrop for some eclectic alternative music programming. Local bands and international groups from Lee Scratch Perry to Gotan Project play from Thursday to Saturday (be warned, the sound system is not what it might be) before the club sessions kick off the night proper. Wednesday's Canibal Sound System night stretches the term Latin music to include hip hop and funk. Thursday is funk night in the Powder Room. Friday and Saturday's Nitsa Club is an elder statesman of city's techno scene.

Tinta Roja

C/Creu dels Molers 17 (93 443 32 43/ www.tintaroja.net). Metro Poble Sec. **Open** *Bar* 8pm-1.30am Wed, Thur; 8pm-3am Fri, Sat. *Shows* 10pm-midnight Wed-Sat. Closed 2wks Aug. **Admission** *Bar* free. *Shows* (incl 1 drink) €8-€10. No credit cards. **Map** p107 C3 ❸

Push through the depths of the bar to find yourself transported to a Buenos Aires bordello/theatre/circus/cabaret by plush red velvet sofas, smoochy niches and an ancient ticket booth. It's an atmospheric place for a late-ish drink, and a distinctly different entertainment experience from Friday to Sunday when you can take in live performances of tango, jazz and flamenco in a small theatre at the back.

Arts & leisure

Cine Ambigú

Sala Apolo, C/Nou de la Rambla 113 (93 441 40 01/www.retinas.org). Metro

Paral·lel. **Shows** 8.30pm, 10.30pm Tue. Closed June-Sept. **Tickets** €4-€6.50 (incl 1 drink). No credit cards. **Map** p107 C4 ❸

This charming 1930s music hall, which is reminiscent of a louche, candlelit cabaret, hosts weekly screenings of accessible but alternative art-house cinema from all round Europe, usually on Tuesdays. Seating is somewhat monastic, but you can dull the discomfort with alcohol, and smoking of all types is permitted.

Mercat de les Flors

Plaça Margarida Xirgú, C/Lleida 59, Montjuïc (93 426 18 75/www.mercat flors.com). Metro Poble Sec. **Box office** 1hr before show. Advance tickets also available from Palau de la Virreina. **Tickets** varies. No credit cards. **Map** p107 B3 ❸

A huge converted flower market housing three performance spaces, the Mercat is one of the most innovative venues in town. Performances here experiment with unusual formats and mix new technologies, pop culture and the performing arts. Film nights and DJ sessions also feature; events include June's Marató de l'Espectacle and the Festival Asia in autumn.

El Tablao de Carmen

Poble Espanyol, Avda Marquès de Comillas, Montjuïc (93 325 68 95/ www.tablaodecarmen.com). Metro Espanyas. **Open** 8pm-2am Tue-Sun. *Shows* 9.30pm, 11.30pm Tue-Thur, Sun; 9.30pm, midnight Fri, Sat. Closed Jan. **Admission** *Show & 1 drink* €30. *Show & dinner* €57. **Map** p107 A3 ❸

This rather sanitised version of the traditional flamenco tablao sits in faux-Andalucían surroundings in the Poble Espanyol. You'll find both established stars and new young talent, displaying the various styles of flamenco singing, dancing and music. The emphasis is on panache rather than passion, so you might prefer your flamenco with a bit more spit and a little less polish. You must reserve in advance, which will allow you to enter the Poble Espanyol free after 7pm.

Rambla de Catalunya

Eixample

Plaça Catalunya, the hub of the city, links the old medieval quarter to the vast, grid-patterned Eixample ('enlargement'). Largely built in the late 19th century, it's a gold mine of elegant palaces and swanky shops, and the spiritual centre of bourgeois Barcelona. This huge area is bisected by the **Passeig de Gràcia**, one of Europe's most sophisticated shopping streets. It's the highlight of the **Quadrat D'Or** (Golden District), a square mile between C/Muntaner and C/Roger de Flor that contains 150 protected buildings, many of them Modernista gems.

The period of the *barrio*'s construction, around the end of the 19th century, coincided with Barcelona's golden age of architecture: the city's bourgeoisie employed Gaudí, Puig i Cadafalch, Domènech i Montaner and the like

to build them ever more daring townhouses in an orgy of avant-garde one-upmanship. The result is extraordinary.

Unfortunately it is also dull to negotiate on foot. The lack of open spaces and abundance of traffic lights can, at times, give you the feeling that you're caught inside an enormous industrial waffle iron.

The overland railway that once ran down C/Balmes has traditionally been the dividing line through the middle of the Eixample. The fashionable **Dreta** ('Right') contains the most distinguished Modernista architecture, the most important museums and the shopping avenues. The **Esquerra** ('Left'), meanwhile, was built slightly later; it contains some great markets and some of the less well-known Modernista sights.

Eixample

Hospital de la Santa Creu i Sant Pau

Sights & museums

Casa Batlló

Passeig de Gràcia 43 (93 216 03 06/ www.casabatllo.es). Metro Passeig de Gràcia. **Open** 9am-8pm daily. **Admission** *Apartment only* €10; €8 reductions; free under-6s. *Complete visit* €16; €12.80 reductions; free under-6s. **Map** p120 C3 ❶

For many people the Casa Batlló is the most telling example of Gaudí's pre-eminence over his Modernista contemporaries; the comparison is easy, since it sits in the same block as masterworks by his two closest rivals, Puig i Cadafalch and Domènech i Montaner. Opinions differ on what the building's remarkable façade represents, most particularly its polychrome shimmering walls, the sinister skeletal balconies and the humpbacked, scaley roof. Some maintain it shows the spirit of carnival, others insist it is a cove on the Costa Brava. The most popular theory, however, which takes into account the architect's patriotic feelings, is that it depicts Sant Jordi and the dragon. The idea is that the cross on top of the building is the knight's lance, the roof is the back of the beast, and the balconies below are the skulls and bones of its hapless victims.

Exploring the interior (at a cost) offers the best opportunity of understanding how Gaudí, who is sometimes considered the lord of the bombastic and overblown, was really the master of tiny details. Witness the ingenious ventilation in the doors and the amazing natural light reflecting off the azure walls of the inner courtyard, or the way in which the brass window handles are curved to fit precisely the shape of a hand. An apartment within Casa Batlló is now open to the public, as, more recently, have been the attic and the roof terrace: the whitewashed arched rooms of the top floor, which were originally used for washing and hanging clothes, are among the master's most atmospheric spaces.

Fundació Antoni Tàpies

C/Aragó 255 (93 487 03 15/www. fundaciotapies.org). Metro Passeig de Gràcia. **Open** 10am-8pm Tue-Sun. **Admission** €4.20; €2.10 reductions; free under-16s. **Map** p120 C3 ❷

Antoni Tàpies is Barcelona's most celebrated living artist. In 1984 he set up the Tàpies Foundation in the former publishing house of Muntaner i Simon, dedicating it to the study and appreciation of contemporary art. He promptly crowned the building with a glorious tangle of aluminium piping and ragged metal netting (*Núvol i Cadira*, meaning 'cloud and chair'). This was a typically contentious act by an artist whose work, a selection of which remains on permanent display on the top floor of the gallery, has been causing controversy ever since he burst on to the art scene in the 1960s. 'Give the organic its rights', he proclaimed, and thus devoted his time to making the seemingly insignificant significant, using materials such as mud, string, rags and cardboard to build his rarely pretty but always striking works.

Fundació Francisco Godia

*C/València 284 pral (93 272 31 80/
www.fundacionfgodia.org). Metro
Passeig de Gràcia.* **Open** 10am-
8pm Mon, Wed-Sun. Closed Aug.
Admission €4.50; €2.10 reductions;
free under-5s. *Combined ticket with
Museu Egipci €8.50; €6.50 reductions.*
No credit cards. **Map** p121 D3 ❸

Godia's first love was motor-racing: he
was a Formula 1 driver for Maserati in
the 1950s. His second, though, was art,
which is how this private museum has
come to house an interesting selection
of medieval religious art, historic
Spanish ceramics and modern painting. Highlights include Alejo de
Vahia's medieval *Pietà* and a baroque
masterpiece by Lucio Giordano, along
with some outstanding Romanesque
sculptures, and 19th-century oil paintings by Joaquin Sorolla and Ramon
Casas. The modern collection has
works by Miró, Julio González, Tàpies
and Manolo Hugué.

Hospital de la Santa Creu i Sant Pau

*C/Sant Antoni María Claret 167 (93
291 90 00/www.santpau.es/www.ruta
delmodernisme.com). Metro Hospital
de Sant Pau.* **Map** p121 F2 ❹

Doctors in their white coats mingle
with recovering patients and camera-
wielding tourists in the green and
pleasant grounds of Domènech i
Montaner's 'garden city' of a hospital,
a collection of pavilions abundantly
adorned with the medieval flourishes
that characterise the architect's style.
The hospital, which is composed of 18
pavilions and connected by an underground tunnel system, is a short walk
from the madding crowds at the
Sagrada Família. Domènech i Montaner
built the hospital very much with its
patients in mind, convinced that pleasant surroundings and aesthetic
harmony were good for the health.
Unfortunately, the old buildings don't
entirely suit the exigencies of modern
medicine: by the end of 2006 all patient
care will be phased out and moved to
a blocky white monstrosity of a building on the north side of the hospital
grounds. The public has free access to
the grounds; guided tours (€5) are
offered every morning.

Museu de Carrosses Fúnebres

*C/Sancho de Avila 2 (93 484 17 10).
Metro Marina.* **Open** 10am-1pm,
4-6pm Mon-Fri; 10am-1pm Sat, Sun
(wknds call to check). **Admission**
free. **Map** p121 F5 ❺

Ask at the reception desk of the
Ajuntament's funeral service and, eventually, a security guard will take you
down to a perfectly silent and splen-
didly shuddersome basement housing
the world's biggest collection of funeral
carriages and hearses, dating from the
18th century through to the 1950s.
There are ornate baroque carriages and
more functional Landaus and Berlins,
and a rather wonderful silver Buick.
The white carriages were designed
for children and virgins, and there's a
windowless black-velour mourning
carriage for the forlorn mistress.

Museu del Perfum

*Passeig de Gràcia 39 (93 216 01 21/
www.museodelperfume.com). Metro
Passeig de Gràcia.* **Open** 10.30am-
1.30pm, 4.30-8pm Mon-Fri; 11am-2pm
Sat. **Admission** €5; €3 reductions.
Map p120 C4 ❻

Nearly 5,000 scent bottles, cosmetic
flasks and related objects. One part
shows all manner of unguent vases and
essence jars in chronological order,
from a tube of black eye make-up from
pre-dynastic Egypt to Edwardian
atomisers and a double flask pouch
prized by Marie Antoinette. The second
section exhibits perfumery brands such
as Guerlain and Dior; some in rare
bottles – among them a garish Dali creation for Schiaparelli and a set of rather
disturbing golliwog flasks for Vigny.

Museu Egipci de Barcelona

*C/València 284 (93 488 01 88/www.
fundclos.com). Metro Passeig de Gràcia.*
Open 10am-8pm Mon-Sat; 10am-2pm
Sun. **Admission** *Museum* €5.50; €4.50

BARCELONA BY AREA

reductions; free under-5s. *Combined ticket with Fundació Godia* €8.50; €6.50 reductions. **Map** p121 D3 **7**

Two floors of this museum showcase a well-chosen collection that spans some 3,000 years of Nile-drenched culture. Exhibits run from religious statuary, such as the massive baboon heads used to decorate temples, to everyday copper mirrors or alabaster headrests. Outstanding pieces include painstakingly matched fragments from the Sixth Dynasty Tomb of Iny, a bronze statuette of the goddess Osiris breastfeeding her son Horus, and mummified cats, baby crocodiles and falcons.

Parc de l'Estació del Nord

C/Nàpols (no phone). Metro Arc de Triomf. **Open** 10am-sunset daily. **Admission** free. **Map** p121 F5 **8**

This slightly shabby space is perked up by three pieces of land art in glazed blue ceramic by New York sculptor Beverley Pepper. Along with a pair of incongruous white stone entrance walls, *Espiral Arbrat* (*Tree Spiral*) is a spiral bench set under the shade of lime-flower trees and *Cel Caigut* (*Fallen Sky*) is a 7m-high (23ft) ridge rising from the grass, while the tilework recalls Gaudí's *trencadís* smashed-tile technique.

Parc Joan Miró (Parc de l'Escorxador)

C/Tarragona (no phone). Metro Tarragona or Espanya. **Open** 10am-sunset daily. **Map** p120 A3 **9**

The demolition of the old slaughterhouse provided some much-needed urban parkland, although there's precious little greenery here. The rows of stubby *palmera* trees and grim cement lakes are dominated by a library and Miró's towering phallic sculpture *Dona i Ocell* (*Woman and Bird*).

La Pedrera (Casa Milà)

Passeig de Gràcia 92-C/Provença 261-5 (93 484 59 00/www.caixacatalunya.es). Metro Diagonal. **Open** 10am-8pm daily. **Admission** €8; €4.50 reductions; free under-12s. **Guided tours** (in English) 4pm Mon-Fri. **Map** p121 D3 **10**

The last secular building designed by Antoni Gaudí, the Casa Milà (usually referred to as La Pedrera, 'the stone quarry') is a stupendous and daring feat of architecture, the culmination of the architect's experimental attempts to recreate natural forms with bricks and mortar. Its marine feel is complemented by Jujol's tangled balconies, doors of twisted kelp ribbon, sea-foamy ceilings and interior patios as blue as a mermaid's cave. Ridiculed when it was completed in 1912, it has become one of Barcelona's best loved buildings, and is adored by architects for its extraordinary structure: it is supported entirely by pillars, without a single master wall, allowing the vast asymmetrical windows of the façade to invite in great swathes of natural light.

There are three exhibition spaces. The first-floor art gallery hosts free exhibitions of eminent artists, you can visit a reconstructed Modernista flat on the fourth floor, and the attic holds a museum dedicated to an insightful overview of Gaudí's career. Best of all is the chance to stroll on the roof of the building amid its *trencadís*-covered ventilation shafts: their heads are shaped like the helmets of medieval knights, which led the poet Pere Gimferrer to dub the spot 'the garden of warriors'.

Sagrada Família

C/Mallorca 401 (93 207 30 31/www.sagradafamilia.org). Metro Sagrada Família. **Open** *Mar-Sept* 9am-8pm daily. *Oct-Feb* 9am-6pm daily. **Admission** €8; €5 reductions; €3 7-10 years; free under-6s. Lift to spires €2. No credit cards. **Map** p121 F3 **11**

The Temple Expiatori de la Sagrada Família manages to be both Europe's most fascinating building site and Barcelona's most emblematic creation. The 1930s anarchists managed to set fire to Gaudí's intricate plans and models for the building; ongoing work is a matter of conjecture and controversy, with the finishing date of 2020 looking increasingly optimistic. The church's first mass is scheduled for Sant Josep's day (19 March) 2007, 125 years after its foundation stone was laid. (There's a detailed guide to the church on p42.)

Gaudí, who is buried beneath the nave, dedicated over 40 years to the project, the last 14 exclusively, and the crypt, the apse and the nativity façade, which were completed in his lifetime, are the most beautiful elements of the church. The latter, facing C/Marina, looks at first glance as though some careless giant has poured candlewax over a Gothic cathedral, but closer inspection shows every protuberance to be an intricate sculpture of flora, fauna or human figure, combining to form an astonishingly moving stone tapestry depicting scenes from Christ's life. The other completed façade, the Passion, which faces C/Sardenya, is more austere, with vast diagonal columns in the shape of bones and haunting sculptures by Josep Maria Subirachs. Japanese sculptor Etsuro Sotoo has chosen to adhere more faithfully to Gaudí's intentions, and has fashioned six more modest musicians at the rear of the temple, as well as the exuberantly coloured bowls of fruit to the left of the nativity façade. The highlight of any trip, however, is a vertiginous hike up one of the towers (you can take a lift), affording unprecedented views through archers' windows.

Eating & drinking

Alkimia

C/Indústria 79 (93 207 61 15).
Metro Joanic or Sagrada Família.
Open 1.30-3.30pm, 9-11pm Mon-Fri; 9-11pm Sat. Closed 3wks Aug €€€€.
Catalan. Map p121 F2 ⑫

A great way to explore what this Michelin-starred restaurant has to offer is to sample the gourmet menu, which offers four savoury courses, including complex dishes that play with Spanish classics – for instance, liquid *pa amb tomàquet* with *fuet* sausage, wild rice with crayfish, strips of tuna on a bed of foamed mustard – and a couple of desserts. An excellent wine cellar adds to the experience.

La Pedrera

Astoria

C/Paris 193 (93 414 47 99). Metro Hospital Clínic. **Open** 9pm-midnight Tue-Sat. Closed Aug. €€€. **Modern European. Map** p120 C2 ⑬

Party like it's 1985 in this stunning converted theatre, kitted out in red and blue neon and plush black upholstery, and with tables overlooking the dance floor. Portions are small, but what there is is delectable: mango and tiger prawn salad, lobster claws on green beans, steak tartar, or médaillons of prime, pan-fried sirloin. All are a worthy precursor to the hot chocolate soufflé or sweet-and-sour truffles.

La Barcelonina de Vins i Esperits

C/València 304 (93 215 70 83).
Metro Passeig de Gràcia. **Open** Sept-June 6pm-2am Mon-Fri; 7.30pm-2am Sat; 8pm-1am Sun. July, Aug 6pm-2am Mon-Fri; 7.30pm-2am Sat.
Wine bar. Map p121 D3 ⑭

With hundreds of bottles sitting behind chicken wire and bright lighting that's

Dolso

a dentist's delight, La Barcelonina is one of a rare breed: unpretentious wine bars. Oenophiles and local workers alike rub shoulders at the bar, poring over a long wine list that includes some excellent Cavas, and preparing for the night ahead with a handful of tapas or maybe a salad.

Bar Mut

NEW C/Pau Claris 192 (93 217 43 38). *Metro Diagonal*. **Open** 8am-midnight Mon-Sat; 8am-5pm Sun. **Bar**. **Map** p121 D2 ⑮

There's more than a soupçon of the 16ème arrondissement in this smart, traditional bar; well-heeled Catalans, BCBG to the core, chatter loudly and dine on excellent, well-sourced tapas – foie, wild sea bass and *espardenyes* (sea cucumbers). The wine selection is similarly upmarket and displayed so seductively behind glass that you may find yourself drinking and spending rather more than you bargained for.

Bauma

C/Roger de Llúria 124 (93 459 05 66). *Metro Diagonal*. **Open** 8am-midnight Mon-Fri, Sun. Closed 3wks Aug. €€. **Café**. **Map** p121 D2 ⑯

Bauma is an old-style café-bar that's perfect for lazy Sunday mornings, with its battered leather seats, ceiling fans and an incongruous soundtrack of acid jazz. Along with well-priced, substantial dishes such as baked cod, and wild boar stew, there's an impressive list of tapas and sandwiches.

La Bodegueta

Rambla de Catalunya 100 (93 215 48 94). *Metro Diagonal*. **Open** 8am-2am Mon-Sat; 6.30pm-1am Sun. Closed 2wks Aug. €€. No credit cards. **Tapas**. **Map** p120 C3 ⑰

Resisting the rise of the surrounding area, this former wine bodega is un-reconstructed, dusty and welcoming, supplying students, businessmen and everyone in between with reasonably priced wine, vermouth on tap and prime-quality tapas amid the delicate patterns of century-old tiling. In summer, tables are outside on the almost pedestrianised Rambla de Catalunya.

Café Berlin

C/Muntaner 240-242 (93 200 65 42). *Metro Diagonal*. **Open** 10am-2am Mon-Wed; 10am-3am Thur, Fri; 11am-3am Sat. €€. **Café**. **Map** p120 B2 ⑱

Downstairs, low sofas fill up with amorous couples while upstairs all is sleek and light, with brushed steel, dark leather and a Klimtesque mural. A rack of newspapers and plenty of sunlight make it popular for coffee or snacks all day; as well as tapas there are pasta dishes, *bocadillos* and cheesecake, but beware the 20% surcharge for pavement tables.

Casa Calvet

C/Casp 48 (93 412 40 12). *Metro Urquinaona*. **Open** 1-3.30pm, 8.30-11pm Mon-Sat. €€€€. **Catalan**. **Map** p121 D4 ⑲

One of Gaudí's more understated buildings from the outside, Casa Calvet has an interior full of glorious detail in the carpentry, stained glass and tiles. The food is up to par, with surprising combinations almost always hitting the mark: squab with puréed pumpkin, risotto of duck confit and truffle with yoghurt ice-cream, and smoked foie gras with mango sauce. The puddings are supremely good, particularly the pine nut tart with foamed *crema catalana*.

Cervesería Catalana

C/Mallorca 236 (93 216 0368). Metro Passeig de Gràcia. **Open** 8am-1.30am Mon-Fri; 9am-1.30am Sat, Sun. **€€**. **Tapas**. **Map** p120 C3 ⑳

The Catalan beer house lives up to its name with a winning selection of brews from around the world, but the real reason to come is the tapas. A vast array is yours for the pointing; only hot *montaditos*, such as bacon, cheese and dates, have to be ordered from the kitchen. Arrive early for a seat at the bar, even earlier for a pavement table.

Cinc Sentits

C/Aribau 58 (93 323 94 90/www.cinc sentits.com). Metro Passeig de Gràcia or Universitat. **Open** 1.30-3.30pm Mon; 1.30-3.30pm, 8.30-11pm Tue-Sat. **€€€€**. **Modern Spanish**. **Map** p120 B3 ㉑

Most reasonably priced of the city's top-end restaurants, the 'Five Senses' should be on everyone's dining agenda. Globally sourced ingredients, from Danish beef to Australian river salt, have been placed together in uplifting combinations, cooked with meticulous precision and served in elegant but unstuffy surroundings. Lamb cutlets with a porcini crust are inspired, but crisp suckling pig with apple and a Priorat reduction is superb. To finish, try the artesanal Catalan cheese pairings or the officially unfinishable trio of chocolate ganaches. Suggested wine pairings are impeccable throughout.

Cremeria Toscana

NEW *C/Muntaner 161 (93 539 38 25). Metro Hospital Clínic.* **Open** 1pm-midnight Tue-Thur; 1pm-1am Fri, Sat; noon-10pm Sun. No credit cards. **Ice-cream**. **Map** p120 B2 ㉒

In this charming little ice-cream parlour, with its lovely, antique-strewn mezzanine, around 20 authentically Italian

Casa Calvet

flavours are made daily, ranging from zingy mandarin to impossibly creamy coconut. 'I dopocena' ('after dinner') are miniature gourmet sundaes, mixing parmesan and pear flavours; mascarpone and tiramisu; chocolate and pistachio; or liquorice and mint.

Dolso

NEW *C/València 227 (93 487 59 64). Metro Passeig de Gràcia.* **Open** 9am-10.30pm Mon; 9am-11.30pm Tue-Thur; 9am-1am Fri; noon-1am Sat; 6-11.30pm Sun. **€€**. **Desserts**. **Map** p120 C3 ㉓

Heaven on earth for the sweet of tooth, Dolso is a 'pudding café', where even the retro-baroque wallpaper is chocolate-coloured. Desserts run from light (a gin and tonic rendered in clear jelly, lemon sorbet, candied peel and juniper berries) to wickedly indulgent (chocolate fondant with sherry reduction and passion fruit sorbet). A short range of sandwiches and topped ciabatta keeps the spoilsports happy.

Dry Martini

C/Aribau 162-166 (93 217 50 72). FGC Provença. **Open** 1pm-2.30am

BARCELONA BY AREA

Camper p130

Mon-Thur; 1pm-3am Fri; 6.30pm-3am Sat; 6pm-2.30am Sun. **Credit** AmEx, DC, MC, V. **Map** p120 B2 ㉔
A shrine to the eponymous cocktail, honoured in Martini-related artwork and served in a hundred forms. All the trappings of a traditional cocktail bar are here – bow-tied staff, leather banquettes, drinking antiques and wooden cabinets displaying a century's worth of bottles – but the stuffiness is absent: music owes more to trip hop than middle-aged crowd-pleasers, and the barmen welcome all comers.

Gaig

Hotel Cram, C/Aragó 214 (93 429 10 17). Metro Passeig de Gràcia. **Open** 1.30-3.30pm, 9-11pm Mon-Sat. €€€€.
Modern Catalan. Map p120 B3 ㉕
Housed in the 1980s-style steely grey decor of the Hotel Cram, Carles Gaig's cooking never fails to thrill, from the crayfish tempura amuse-gueule, served with a dip of creamed leek salted with a piece of pancetta, through to a shot-glass holding layers of tangy lemon syrup, *crema catalana* mousse, caramel ice-cream and topped with burnt sugar

(to be eaten by plunging the spoon all the way down). All this pleasure comes at a price, however.

Lasarte

C/Mallorca 259 (93 445 32 42/www. restaurantlasarte.com). Metro Passeig de Gràcia. **Open** 1.30-3.30pm, 8.30-11.30pm Mon-Fri. Closed Aug. €€€€.
Modern Basque. Map p120 C3 ㉖
See box p136.

Moo

C/Rosselló 265 (93 445 40 00). Metro Diagonal. **Open** 1.30-4pm, 8.30-11pm Mon-Sat. €€€€. **Modern European**. Map p120 C3 ㉗
Superbly inventive cooking is overseen by renowned Catalan chef Joan Roca and designed as 'half portions', the better to experience the full range, from sea bass with lemongrass to exquisite suckling pig with a sharp Granny Smith purée. Wines from a list of 500 are suggested to go with every course, and many dishes are even built around them: you can finish, for example, with 'Sauternes', the wine's bouquet perfectly rendered in mango ice-cream, saffron custard and grapefruit jelly.

Noti

*C/Roger de Llúria 35 (93 342
66 73). Metro Passeig de Gràcia or
Urquinaona.* **Open** 1.30-4pm, 8.30pm-
midnight Mon-Fri; 8.30pm-midnight
Sat. **€€€€. Mediterranean. Map**
p121 D4 ②

Centrally positioned tables surrounded
by reflective glass and gold panelling
make celebrity-spotting unavoidable,
but myriad other reasons for coming
here include a rich and aromatic
fish soup with velvety rouille; lobster
carpaccio with crispy seaweed; smoky
hunks of seared tuna; and a succulent
lamb brochette with spiced couscous
and spring vegetables. Jazz gives way
to house as the night progresses and the
restaurant becomes a bar for the city's
most gorgeous.

Ot

*C/Corsega 537 (93 435 80 48). Metro
Sagrada Família.* **Open** 1.30-3.30pm,
8.30-11pm Tue-Sat. Closed 3wks Aug.
€€€€. Modern Mediterranean.
Map p121 F2 ②

It's the extras that make the Ot experience memorable: an olive-oil tasting
to start; a shot of cauliflower soup
speckled with herring eggs as an
amuse-bouche, or the sweet and sour
layers of coconut and hibiscus flower
foam with the coffee. There is no à la
carte menu, just a couple of set-price
deals, but these are very safe hands in
which to leave yourself; when they say
chocolate soufflé needs basil ice-cream,
by Jove, they're right.

La Paninoteca Cremoni

NEW *C/Rosselló 112 (93 451 03 79).
Metro Hospital Clínic.* **Open** 9.30am-
5pm, 7.30pm-midnight Mon-Fri; 1-5pm,
8.30pm-midnight Sat. **€€. Panini.**
Map p120 B2 ③

Named after the 19th-century inventor
of the celebrated Italian sandwich, this
is a sunny spot, with a white-painted
rustic look that is enlivened by a huge
photograph of Sienna. Neither the
owners nor the ingredients can make
much claim to Italian provenance, but
panini such as the *siciliano* – consist-
ing of olive bread, mozzarella, tomato,

aubergine and basil – make a wonderful change nonetheless from endless
bocadillos de jamón.

Saüc

NEW *Passatge Lluis Pellicer 12 (93
321 01 89). Metro Hospital-Clínic.*
Open 1.30-3.30pm, 8.30-10.30pm
Tue-Sat. **€€€€. Modern Catalan.**
Map p120 B2 ③

Book early for one of the coveted tables
at Saüc ('elderberry'), particularly for
lunch. The classy €20 set lunch holds
accomplished Catalan comfort food in
the shape of spicy Mallorcan sausage
with potatoes and poached egg to more
sophisticated fare such as cod with
apple aïoli, cherry tomatoes and
spinach. Excellent bread, a shot glass
of pepper and potato soup with
pancetta as an *aperitivo* and home-
made petits fours are also unexpected
touches in a *menú del día.*

Semproniana

*C/Rosselló 148 (93 453 18 20).
Metro Hospital Clínic.* **Open**
1.30-4pm, 9-11.30pm Mon-Thur; 1.30-
4pm, 9pm-midnight Fri, Sat. **€€€.**
Mediterranean. Map p120 B2 ③

The Old Curiosity Shop meets Tate
Modern in this former printing house,
which is wall-papered with defunct
leaflets and pages from old books. The
combination of antique furniture with
arty mobiles made out of tortured
kitchen utensils is as offbeat as the
food, which might include such dishes
as an all-white 'monochrome of cod
and chickpeas'; turbot with passion
fruit and *escopinyes* (cockles); or a green
salad served with a mad scientist's test-
tube rack of 14 aerosol dressings.

Tragaluz

*Ptge de la Concepció 5 (93 487
01 96). Metro Diagonal.* **Open**
1.30-4pm, 8.30pm-midnight Mon-Wed,
Sun; 1.30-4pm, 8.30pm-12.30am Thur-
Sat. **€€€€. Mediterranean. Map**
p120 C3 ③

Tragaluz is the stylish flagship for an
extraordinarily successful group of
restaurants (which includes Agua,
Bestial and Omm). Prices have risen a

BARCELONA BY AREA

bit recently and the wine mark-up is hard to swallow, but there's no faulting tuna tataki with a cardamom wafer and a dollop of ratatouille-like *pisto*; monkfish tail in a sweet tomato *sofrito* with black olive oil; or juicy braised oxtail with cabbage. Finish with the cherry consommé or a thin tart of white and dark chocolate.

Ty-Bihan

Ptge Lluís Pellicer 13 (93 410 90 02). Metro Hospital Clínic. **Open** 1.30-3.30pm Mon; 1.30-3.30pm, 8.30-11.30pm Tue-Fri; 8.30-11.30pm Sat. **€€.**
Breton. Map p120 B2 ❸❹
Functioning both as crêperie and Breton cultural centre, Ty-Bihan has chosen a smart, spacious look over wheat sheaves and pitchforks. A long list of sweet and savoury galettes (crêpes made with buckwheat flour) are followed up with scrumptious little blinis smothered in strawberry jam and cream and crêpes suzettes served in a pool of flaming Grand Marnier. The Petite menu will take care of *les enfants*, while a bowl of cider takes care of the grown-ups.

Windsor

C/Còrsega 286 (93 415 84 83). Metro Diagonal. **Open** 1-4pm, 8.30-11pm Mon-Fri; 8.30-11pm Sat. Closed Aug. **€€€€. Modern Catalan. Map** p120 C2 ❸❺
Let down by a smart but drab dining room and a preponderance of foreign businessmen, Windsor nevertheless serves some of the most creative food around. Start with an amuse-gueule or a tomato reduction with pistachio; warm up with wild mushroom cannelloni in truffle sauce or divine foie gras on thin slices of fruit cake; and peak with a dense, earthy dish of cod on black lentils followed by a foamed *crema catalana*. Then come down to earth with the bill.

Shopping

Altaïr

Gran Via de les Corts Catalanes 616 (93 342 71 71/www.altair.es). Metro
Universitat. **Open** 10am-2pm, 4.30-8.30pm Mon-Fri; 10am-3pm, 4-8.30pm Sat. **Map** p120 C4 ❸❻
The outstanding selection of travel books at Altaïr includes guidebooks, maps, literature, children's books and the shop's own superb glossy magazine. What's more, you can buy world music CDs and DVDs. A relaxed vibe, helpful staff and comfy armchairs for sampling books before you buy make it hard to leave.

BD Ediciones de Diseño

Casa Tomas, C/Mallorca 291 (93 458 69 09/www.bdbarcelona. com). Metro Passeig de Gràcia. **Open** 10am-2pm, 4-8pm Mon-Fri; 10am-2pm, 4.30-8pm Sat. Closed Aug. **Map** p121 D3 ❸❼
A Modernista masterpiece by architect Domènech i Muntaner is an appropriately lavish setting for this prominent design centre. Best known for its reproductions of classic pieces by design deities, this is the place where anyone with a few thousand euros to spare can buy Gaudí's curving Calvet armchair or Dalí's magenta-coloured Gala love seat. Also showcases new designers alongside contemporary big guns such as Javier Mariscal and Oscar Tusquets.

Camper

C/Pelai 13-37 (93 302 41 24/www. camper.com). Metro Catalunya. **Open** 10am-10pm Mon-Sat. **Map** p121 D3 ❸❽
Now internationally coveted, these bright, round-toed durable shoes in quasi-childish styles started out as Mallorcan peasant (*camper*) shoes. Some of the more extraordinary new lines include bright, plastic wellies, boots inspired by boxing gloves, and wobbly rubber high heels for the girls. **Other locations**: Plaça del Àngels 6 (93 342 41 41); Rambla de Catalunya 122 (93 217 23 84); C/València 249 (93 215 63 90).

Casa del Llibre

C/Passeig de Gràcia 62 (93 272 34 80/ www.casadellibro.com). Metro Passeig de Gràcia. **Open** 9.30am-9.30pm Mon-Sat. **Map** p121 D3 ❸❾

Vinçon p132

Part of a well-established Spanish chain, Casa del Llibro is a general bookstore that offers an assortment of titles, including some fiction in English. Glossy coffee-table tomes on a range of Barcelona themes – and thus with good gift potential – sit by the front right-hand entrance.

El Corte Inglés

Plaça Catalunya 14 (93 306 38 00/ www.elcorteingles.es). Metro Catalunya. **Open** 10am-10pm Mon-Sat. **Map** p121 D5 ⓴

With its cult-like grip on the Spanish consumer consciousness, El Corte Inglés has become synonymous with the phrase 'department store' since gobbling the last of the competition in the early 1990s. The monolithic Plaça Catalunya branch has nine floors of fashion, beauty and home decor, a seventh-floor café and a decent supermarket in the basement with services from currency exchange to key-cutting. The branch on Portal de l'Àngel has six floors of music, electronics, mobile phone services, books and sporting goods; there are red-jacketed stewards by the doors who will point you in the right direction.

Other locations: Avda Diagonal 471-473 (93 493 48 00); Avda Diagonal 617 (93 366 71 00); L'Illa, Avda Diagonal 545 (93 363 80 90).

FNAC

El Triangle, Plaça Catalunya 4 (93 344 18 00/www.fnac.es). Metro Catalunya. **Open** 10am-10pm Mon-Sat. *Newsstand* 10am-10pm daily. **Map** p120 C5 ㊸

At FNAC you'll find a sweeping book selection in several languages, and at low prices. On other floors of this French multimedia megastore, there are CDs, DVDs, hi-fis, TVs, computers, mobile phones, film processing and so on. The first-rate international newsstand and café on the ground floor is a pleasant place in which to have a coffee or leaf through magazines on a Sunday afternoon. The downside of the FNAC shopping experience is the mainly young, surly and sketchily informed staff.

Other locations: L'Illa, Avda Diagonal 545-557, Eixample (93 444 59 00).

L'Illa

*Avda Diagonal 545-557, Eixample
(93 444 00 00/www.lilla.com). Metro
Maria Cristina.* **Open** 10am-9.30pm
Mon-Sat. *Supermarket* 9.30am-9.30pm
Mon-Sat. **Map** p120 A1 ⓬

It looks more like an iceberg than an
island (*illa*), but this popular commercial and business centre caters to a
fashionable clientele with over 130
shops, among them outposts of FNAC,
Camper, Diesel, Decathlon and Mango.
There are fast-food restaurants, a food
market on the ground floor and a
Caprabo hypermarket.

Mango

*Passeig de Gràcia 65 (93 215 75 30/
www.mango.es). Metro Passeig de
Gràcia.* **Open** 10am-9pm Mon-Sat.
Credit AmEx, DC, MC, V. **Map**
p120 C3 ⓭

A small step up from Zara in quality
and price, Mango's womenswear is less
chameleon-like but still victim to the
catwalks. Strong points include tai-
lored trouser suits and skirts, knitwear
and stretchy tops. Unsold items end up
at the Mango Outlet, which are packed
with frenzied girls on a mission.
Other locations: Passeig de Gràcia
8-10 (93 412 15 99).

Purificación García

*Passeig de Gràcia 21 (93 487 72 92/
www.purificaciongarcia.es). Metro
Passeig de Gràcia.* **Open** 10am-8.30pm
Mon-Sat. **Map** p120 C4 ⓮

Purificación's sleek, sophisticated
creations occasionally take off on brief
flights of fancy. The conservatively cut
men's garments are jazzed up with a
wide palette of colours and inventive
use of fabrics; the slightly more whimsical women's styles flirt maturely with
informality and bohemian chic. Yet, on
the whole, Purificación's collections
remain anchored in pure and understated designs.

Vinçon

*Passeig de Gràcia 96 (93 215 60 50/
www.vincon.com). Metro Diagonal.*
Open 10am-8.30pm Mon-Sat. **Map**
p121 D2 ⓯

Your first stop for Catalan interior
design. The ground floor has lighting,
kitchen and bathroom goods; everything related to the bedroom is in a
nearby branch. Furniture is on the
Modernista upper floor, where pieces
of interest, such as Emili Padrós's
stools made from motorbike seats, are
accompanied by blurb on the designer.
Other locations: TincÇon, C/Rosselló
246 (93 215 60 50).

Nightlife

Antilla BCN Latin Club

*C/Aragó 141 (93 451 45 64/
www.antillasalsa.com). Metro Urgell.*
Open 11pm-4am Mon-Thur, Sun;
11pm-5.30am Fri, Sat. Gigs around
11.30pm. **Admission** (incl 1 drink
minimum) €10. No credit cards.
Map p120 A3 ⓰

The Antilla prides itself on being a
'Caribbean cultural centre', but its true
calling lies in being the self-proclaimed
best *salsateca* in town, offering dance
classes (including acrobatic salsa and
Afro-Cuban styles) and a solid programme of live music, which covers all
Latin flavours from *son* to merengue
and Latin jazz.

Arena

Classic & Madre *C/Diputació 233.*
Map p120 C4 ⓱
VIP & Dandy *Gran Via de les Corts
Catalanes 593.* **Map** p120 C4 ⓲
Both *93 487 83 42/www.arena
disco.com. Metro Universitat.* **Open**
12.30am-5am Fri, Sat. **Admission** (incl
1 drink) €5 Fri; €10 Sat. No credit cards.
The four Arena discos offer variations
on well-worn gay themes; you can
switch between them freely after getting your hand stamped on entrance.
Of the four, Classic is the most light-
hearted, playing 1980s and '90s classics, with a campy-kitsch atmosphere
and a healthy mix of the sexes. The
cavernous Madre has a darkroom,
pounding house and current chart hits.
It attracts a younger crowd, and is
more of a cattle market. VIP and
Dandy are probably the tackiest and
are the most mixed; again, youthful

Luz de Gas p135

venues with lots of space, but nonetheless heaving at weekends. VIP does its bit for the Spanish retro pop industry, while Dandy bangs away with house.

Buda

C/Pau Claris 92 (93 318 42 52/ www.budarestaurante.com). Metro Catalunya. **Open** 9pm-3am daily. **Admission** free. **Map** p121 D4 ⑲
The glamorous Buda has lots of throne-style furniture and gilded wall paper, topped off with a colossal chandelier. The laid-back nature of the staff (dancing on the bar seems completely acceptable) and upbeat house music make it excellent for drinks and an ogle. Tuesday is 'Model's night' (which model isn't clear), Wednesday is ballroom dancing night, and every second Thursday is Asian night, complete with geishas.

City Hall

Rambla Catalunya 2-4 (93 317 21 77/www.grupo-ottozutz.com). Metro Catalunya. **Open** midnight-6am Tue-Sun. **Admission** (incl 1 drink) €12. **Map** p120 C4 ⑳

A venue that packs in a sweaty stream of clubbers thanks to its cutting-edge musical selection on any given day of the week. Catch Old is Cool night on Mondays or acid and electro house on a Wednesday, while Soul City provides hip hop and R&B on Thursdays and Underground Sessions hosts ambassadors of house such as Derrick L Carter on Fridays and Saturdays, .

Danzarama

Gran Via de les Corts Catalanes 604 (93 301 97 43/reservations 93 342 5070/www.gruposalsitas.com). Metro Universitat. **Open** 7am-3am Mon-Sat. **Admission** free. **Map** p120 C4 ㉑
The ever-expanding Salsitas group takes the restaurant-club concept to the extreme at Danzarama, opening from 7am for breakfast and serving snacks, lunches and dinner throughout the day into the night. From 6pm Café Chillout eases you into the evening with lounge music and infusions. Each evening sees a different event, such as special singles nights or perhaps a comedy performance. Resident DJs, including

Metro

local muso legend David Mas, play grown-up house for clubbers who've grown out of glowsticks.

Distrito Diagonal

Avda Diagonal 442 (mobile 607 113 602/www.distritodiagonal.com). Metro Diagonal. **Open** 11pm-4am Thur; 11pm-6am Fri, Sat. **Admission** free Thur, before 3am Fri-Sun; (incl 1 drink) €15 after 3am Fri-Sun. No credit cards. **Map** p121 D2 52
Housed in the stunning Casa Comalat, Distrito Diagonal attracts a slightly older crowd with an easygoing atmosphere bathed in red light, sounds from nu jazz to deep house, and plenty of chairs to sink into. It is a sought-after venue for small promoters and one-off parties, which means the music veers from Bollywood to hip hop. On a Thursday night, Cabaret Club educates listeners with the latest indietronica.

Domèstic

C/Diputació 215 (93 453 16 61). Metro Universitat. **Open** 7.30pm-2.30am Tue-Thur; 7.30pm-3am Fri, Sat. **Admission** free. **Credit** AmEx, MC, V. **Map** p120 C4 53

Domèstic is another multi-tasking venue, this time combining a rather half-hearted restaurant, a bar/club and an occasional live venue. The colours are bold, the crowd is studenty and the music is laid-back, ranging from electro-pop to tribal house, with a new roster of DJs every month. Domèstic tends to be more of a meeting place than a destination, although you might find the cosy, battered leather chairs are hard to leave.

La Fira

C/Provença 171 (mobile 650 855 384). Metro Hospital Clínic. **Open** 10pm-3am Tue-Thur; 10pm-4.30am Fri, Sat. **Admission** free before 1am; €10 (incl 1 drink) after 1am. No credit cards. **Map** p120 B3 54
It's called a 'bar-museum', but don't worry, you don't get served a history lesson along with your pint of lager. The exhibits are old fairground rides: bumper cars, merry-go-rounds, crazy mirrors… which can all seem a little bit spooky when you're in a dark, warehouse-sized space and surrounded by beered-up students flirting to a soundtrack of tacky pop.

Luz de Gas

C/Muntaner 246 (93 209 77 11/www.
luzdegas.com). FGC Muntaner. **Open**
11.30pm-5am daily. *Gigs* 12.30am Mon-
Sat; midnight Sun. **Admission** (incl
1 drink) €15. **Map** p120 B1 ⑤

This lovingly converted old music hall,
garnished with chandeliers and classical friezes, occasionally hosts classic
MOR acts: maybe Phil Collins or Bill
Wyman's Rhythm Kings. Between
these visits from international 'names',
you'll find nightly residencies: blues on
Mondays, Dixieland jazz on Tuesdays,
cover bands on Wednesdays, Saturdays
and Sundays, soul on Thursdays and
rock on Fridays.

Metro

C/Sepúlveda 185 (93 323 52 27/
www.metrodisco.bcn). Metro
Universitat. **Open** midnight-5am
daily. **Admission** (incl 1 drink) €12.
Map p120 B4 ⑥

Another gay classic, this one for a
slightly older crowd. The smaller
dancefloor plays retro pop classics,
while the packed main area focuses
on house. The darkroom gets rammed:
watch your pockets. There are drag
shows on Monday nights, and on those
dark winter Tuesdays strippers are
there to warm you up; other events
include foam parties and bingo.

Salvation

Ronda Sant Pere 19-21 (93 318 06
86/www.matineegroup.com). Metro
Urquinaona. **Open** midnight-5am
Fri, Sat; 6pm-5am Sun. **Admission**
(incl 1 drink) €12. No credit cards.
Map p121 D5 ⑤

One of the two large dancefloors at
Salvation sees disdainful barebacked
Muscle Marys pumping to house
among swirls of dry ice, while the other
reverberates to cheesy disco. On a
Sunday night, the club becomes La
Madame, with a fun-loving gay/straight
mix. Again, watch your wallet in the
claustrophobic darkroom.

Santa Locura

C/Consell de Cent 294 (93 487 77
22). Metro Passeig de Gràcia. **Open**
midnight-5.30am Thur-Sat.
Admission (incl 1 drink) €10.
No credit cards. **Map** p120 C1 ⑤

Perhaps Barcelona's most extraordinary clubbing experience, Santa Locura
has three floors filled with weird and
wonderful nocturnal pleasures: you
can get married at the bar; watch a
Chippendale-style show; plead guilty
at the confessional box; and hit the
dancefloor to the music of Kylie and
Sophie Ellis-Bextor.

Space Barcelona

C/Tarragona 141-147 (93 426 84
44/www.spacebarcelona.com). Metro
Tarragona. **Open** midnight-6am Fri,
Sat. **Admission** (incl 1 drink) €15;
€12 with flyer. No credit cards.
Map p120 A3 ⑤

Space? There's actually not too much
of it in this version of the Balearic
superclub, but that isn't about to stop
Barcelona's youngest citizens, who
parade the latest H&M designer
imposter threads and head to this meat
market of raging hormones to relive
memories of last summer in Ibiza.
The decor is Bauhaus, and Space's four
ample bars make for a short wait. The
DJ sets orbit around house, with occasional guests like the Basement Boys
bringing in an older crowd.

The Pop Bar

C/Aribau 103 (93 451 29 58). Metro
Hospital Clínic. **Open** 9pm-3.30am
Wed-Sun. **Admission** free. **Credit**
AmEx, DC, MC, V. **Map** p120 B3 ⑥

Balls to house, hip hop and all the rest
of it. Come here and you can have pure,
unadulterated pop and one-hit wonders
that you never thought you'd hear
again – we're talking early Kylie, Rick
Astley and Donna Summer. The retro
decor is appropriate to the sounds –
which means funky brown, orange
and white, augmented by things like
polka dot toilets, and deep orange sofa
booths. This place also gets two
thumbs up for its big screens showing
FashionTV – it makes a welcome
change from those darned projections
that you find absolutely everywhere
else these days.

Berasategui in Barcelona

Spain's finest chef opens a new restaurant in the city.

Lasarte

To many gastronomes, Spain's finest chef is neither much renowned experimentalist Ferran Adrià nor much-loved grandfather of modern Spanish cooking Juan Mari Arzak, but an unassuming young man called Martín Berasategui. Berasategui has not been slow in garnering all possible stars in the Michelin galaxy, and many who learnt their trade in his kitchens have gone on to earn their own rosettes. His cooking is hard to pin down, eschewing fireworks but never less than supremely creative, emphasising the light and healthy without skimping on the luxurious ingredients typically revered by gourmets – the foies, the truffles and gamey meats.

The restaurant carrying Berasategui's name sits in a sleepy suburb (Lasarte) ten miles south of San Sebastián. For most people that meant a taste of his genius required at the very least a flight to Bilbao, where he directs the restaurant at the Guggenheim, and from there a trip to San Sebastián and a long taxi ride. Happily for Barcelona, however, Berasategui has finally established a culinary outpost (also called **Lasarte**, p128) here, in the Hotel Condes de Barcelona (p171), overseeing a menu that incorporates many of his signature dishes.

One of the most spectacular of these is the layered terrine of foie gras, smoked eel and caramelised apple – such is the demand for this that Berasategui has pledged never to remove it from the menu. Other dishes of note include a succulent pigeon breast with creamed wild mushrooms and a foie gras prepared from its own liver or – more typical of his trademark light touch – roast sea bass with hot citrus viniagrette and creamed 'marrowbone' of cauliflower.

Unusually for a Spanish restaurant, however, it is with the final course that Lasarte really excels. Puddings range from superbly refreshing – apple 'ravioli' in a mint and lime jus with coconut ice-cream and rum granita – to impossibly indulgent – a rich bread and butter pudding with coffee ice-cream and plum compôte.

■ www.restaurantlasarte.com

242

C/Entença 37 (www.dosquatredos.com).
Metro Espanya or Rocafort. **Open**
varies. **Admission** varies. No credit
cards. **Map** p120 A4 ❻❶
Once a goth-friendly joint playing dark
European electronica by the likes of
Depeche Mode, 242 has lightened up a
bit since then, with the studded dog
collars now sharing dancefloor space
with the glitter of electroclash. Local
lovers of Brit music old enough to
remember the original release of 'Blue
Monday' come here to shug to anything electronic, from Peaches to the
Postal Service via the Pet Shop Boys.
Check out the website for your free
entry password and the wildly varying
opening hours.

Arts & leisure

L'Auditori

C/Lepant 150 (93 247 93 00/www.
auditori.org). Metro Marina. **Open**
Information 8am-10pm daily. *Box*
office noon-9pm Mon-Sat; 1hr before
performance Sun. *Performances* 8pm
Mon-Thur; 9pm Fri; 7pm Sat; 11am
Sun. **Map** p121 F5 ❻❷
Rafael Moneo's sleek design is anodyne
to the point of anonymity, all pale beech
and sharp lines, and the Auditori is
never likely to arouse the same
affection as the Palau de la Música.
Nevertheless, the 2,400-seat hall has
provided the city with a world-class
music venue and a home to its orchestra, the OBC. The Museu de la Música
is expected to open here at the end of
2006, as is a new 600-seat auditorium,
which will add more variety to an
already impressive programme that
covers not just classical music but jazz,
contemporary and world music.

Méliès Cinemes

C/Villarroel 102 (93 451 00 51/www.
cinesmelies.blogspot.com). Metro Urgell.
Tickets Mon €2.70. Tue-Sun €4. No
credit cards. **Map** p120 B4 ❻❸
More accessible than art-house but
more eclectic than a commercial cinema,
the Méliès is run by and for film lovers.
Programming is an eccentric combina-

tion of classic movies, contemporary
works and whatever else the owner
might feel like screening. There are up
to eight films shown per week, with
regular seasons organised by director,
star or theme.

Plaza de Toros Monumental

Gran Via de les Corts Catalanes 749
(93 245 58 04/93 215 95 70). Metro
Monumental. **Open** *Bullfights* Apr-Sept
5.30-7pm Sun. *Museum* Apr-Sept 11am-
2pm, 4-8pm Mon-Sat; 10.30am-1.30pm
Sun. **Admission** *Bullfights* €18-€95.
Museum €4; €3 reductions. No credit
cards. **Map** p121 F4 ❻❹
In 2004 the council voted the city to be
anti-taurino (anti-bullfighting), though
this was largely a symbolic gesture:
100 bulls are still killed every year
at the city's one remaining bullring.
Corridas take place on Sundays in
summer, largely in front of tourists and
homesick Andalucians.

Renoir-Floridablanca

C/Floridablanca 135 (93 228 93 93/
www.cinesrenoir.com). Metro Sant
Antoni. **Map** p120 B5 ❻❺
This is the closest first-run original-
version cinema you'll find to the centre
of town. Renoir-Floridablanca has four
screens and shows up to eight independent, off-beat foreign and Spanish
films per day, though make note that
programming can tend towards the
worthy, rather than the particularly
exciting. Be prepared to be educated.

Teatre Nacional de Catalunya (TNC)

Plaça de les Arts 1 (93 306 57 00/
www.tnc.es). Metro Glòries. **Box office**
3-9pm Tue-Sun. **Tickets** €15-€25;
€10-€15 reductions. **Map** p121 F4 ❻❻
Funded by the Generalitat and designed
by architect Ricard Bofill, the huge
Parthenon-like TNC has three superb
performance spaces. Its main stage
promotes large-scale Spanish classical
theatre, while more contemporary
European theatre and works by new
writers are normally staged in the more
experimental Sala Tallers.

Plaça Rius i Taulet

Gràcia

A favourite hangout of the city's bohemians, Gràcia holds many workshops and studios, and the numerous small, unpretentious bars are frequented by artists, designers and students. However, it really comes into its own for a few days each August, when its famous *festa major* grips the entire city. The streets are festooned with startlingly original home-made decorations and all of Barcelona turns up in a party mood. Open-air meals are laid on for the residents of Gràcia, and entertainment is laid on for everybody: from street parties for the old-timers singing along to *habaneros* (shanties) to amusements to the resident squatters who get to pogo to punk bands.

Much of Gràcia was built in the heyday of Modernisme, something evident in the splendid main drag, the C/Gran de Gràcia. Many of the buildings are rich in nature-inspired curves and fancy façades, but the finest example is Lluís Domènech i Montaner's **Casa Fuster** at No.2, recently reopened as a luxury hotel. Gaudí's disciple Francesc Berenguer was responsible for much of the civic architecture, most notably the **Mercat de la Llibertat** (Barcelona's oldest covered market, but, dating back to before the annexation, it is decorated with the coat of arms of the independent Gràcia) and the old **Casa de la Vila** (Town Hall) in Plaça Rius i Taulet.

However, the district's most overwhelming Modernista gem is one of Gaudí's earliest and most fascinating works, the **Casa Vicens** of 1883-8, hidden away in C/Carolines. The building is a private residence and thus not open to visitors, but the castellated red brickwork and colourful tiled exterior with Indian and Mudéjar influences should not be missed; notice, too, the spiky wrought-iron leaves on the gates.

Sights & museums

Fundació Foto Colectània

C/Julián Romea 6, D2 (93 217 16 26/www.colectania.es). FGC Gràcia. **Open** 5-8.30pm Mon; 11am-2pm, 5-8.30pm Tue-Sat. Closed Aug. **Map** p140 B4 ❶

Dedicated to the promotion of photo collecting, this private photography foundation promotes the collections of other important galleries and museums. The Fundació also shows major Spanish and Portuguese photographers from the 1950s.

Park Güell

C/Olot (Casa-Museu Gaudí 93 219 S8 11). Metro Lesseps/bus 24, 25. **Open** 10am-sunset daily. *Museum* Apr-Sept 10am-7.45pm daily. Oct-Mar 10am-5.45pm daily. **Admission** *Park* free. *Museum* €4; €3 concessions; free under-9s. No credit cards. **Map** p141 F1 ❷

Park Güell is a fairytale of a place, and the fantastical exuberance of Gaudí's imagination is truly breathtaking. The two gatehouses were based on designs the architect made earlier for the opera *Hansel and Gretel*, one of them featuring a red and white mushroom for a roof. From here, walk up a splendid staircase flanked by multicoloured battlements, past the iconic mosaic dragon, to what would have been the marketplace. Here, a hundred palm-shaped pillars hold up a roof, reminiscent of the hypostyle hall at Luxor. On top of this structure is the esplanade, a circular concourse surrounded by undulating benches decorated with shattered tiles.

The park is itself magical, with twisted stone columns supporting curving colonnades or merging with the natural structure of the hillside. Gaudí lived for a time in one of the two

houses built on the site. The house was actually designed by his student Berenguer, but has since become the Casa-Museu Gaudí; guided tours, some in English, are given. The best way to get to the park is on the 24 bus; if you go via Lesseps metro, be prepared for a steep uphill walk.

Eating & drinking

La Baignoire

C/Verdi 6 (mobile 606 330 460). Metro Fontana or Joanic. **Open** *June-Sept* 8pm-2am Mon-Thur, Sun; 8pm-3am Fri, Sat. *Oct-May* 6pm-2am Mon-Thur, Sun; 6pm-3am Fri, Sat. No credit cards. **Bar**. **Map** p141 D4 ❸

It means 'bathtub', which goes some way towards giving you an idea of the size, but the staff are unfailingly friendly and slide projections and lounge music complement the mellow vibe. Fresh fruit juices are served in summer, while cocktails and decent wine are available year-round.

Bodega Manolo

C/Torrent de les Flors 101 (93 284 43 77). Metro Joanic. **Open** 9.30am-7pm Tue, Wed; 9.30am-1am Thur, Fri; 12.30-4.30pm, 8.30pm-1am Sat; 10.30am-3pm Sun. Closed Aug. No credit cards. **€€**. **Tapas**. **Map** p141 E3 ❹

Another old family *bodega* with faded, peeling charm, barrels on the wall and rows of dusty bottles, Manolo specialises not only in wine, but in classy food: we recommend the foie gras with port and apple. At the other end of the scale, but certainly holding its own, comes the 'Destroyer': egg, bacon, sausage and chips.

Botafumeiro

C/Gran de Gràcia 81 (93 218 42 30). Metro Fontana. **Open** 1pm-1am daily. **€€€€**. **Galician**. **Map** p140 C4 ❺

Love it or hate it (and the size, racket and overwhelmingly *arriviste* diners mean no one leaves undecided), there's no denying Botafumeiro's success, and its literally dozens of tables are rarely empty for very long. The speciality is

BARCELONA BY AREA

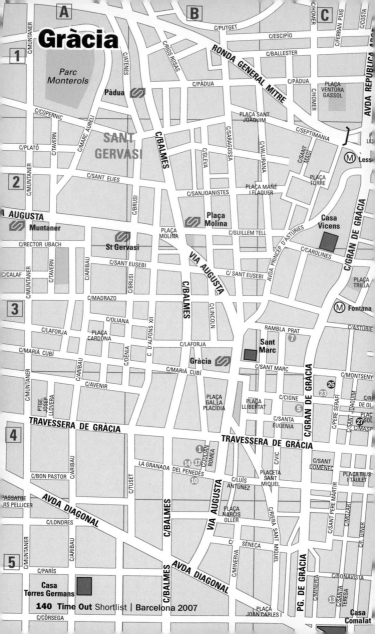

Gràcia

D · E · F

BAIXADA GLÒRIA
DIEU DEL COLL
C/VERDI
C/SOSTRES
C/ULOT
Casa Museu Gaudí
Park Güell ②
CTRA CARMEL
C/RAMIRO DE MAE

AVDA HOSPITAL MILITAR
C/ALBIGESOS
C/MARE DE
C/MAIGNON
C/VALLDOREIX
C/SANT CUGAT
AVDA COLL DEL PORTELL
C/MERCEDES
RAMBLA MERCEDES
C/MARIANAO
C/LLARRARD
1

C/ANTEQUERA
C/MOLIST
RAMBLA CAN TODA
AVDA POMPEU FAL

C/SANTA PERPÈTUA
C/VERDI
AVDA SANT JOSEP DE LA MUNTANYA
Hospital
C/MARE DE DÉU DE LA SALUT

TRAVESSERA DE DALT

RONDA DE GUINARDÓ
2

C/TORRENT DE L'OLLA
C/VERDI
CA LA GRANJA
C/CARDENER
C/SANT SALVADOR
TORRENT DE LES FLORS
C/CAMÈLIES
C/ESCORIAL
CALEGRE DE DALT
C/CAMÈLIES
C/BALCELLS
C/SECRETARI COLOMA

C/MARTÍ
PLAÇA NORD
C/PROVIDÈNCIA
PASSEIG AMUNT
C/MARTÍ

C/POPAZ ⑯
GRÀCIA
④
PLAÇA ROVIRA I TRIAS
㉒
C/LEGALITAT
C/PROVIDÈNCIA
3

PLAÇA DIAMANT
⑯
PLAÇA VIRREINA
C/REIG I BONET
CALEGRE DE DALT

C/L'OR
C/VERDI ㉘
⑳ ⑥
C/L'ENCARNACIÓ
C/ESCORIAL
C/L'ENCARNAC

⑧⑱
C/PERLA
C/SANT LLUIS
C/L'ENCARNAC
C/GUTEMBERG
TORRENT DE LA VIDAL
C/SANT LLUIS
C/PI I MARGALL
C/IAXDIRT

⑲
❸
C/VERDI
C/TORRIJOS
C/FONTANA
TORRENT DE LES FLORS
C/SECRETARI COLOMA
C/ROMANS
⑳
C/BRUNIQUER
PLAÇA JOANIC
4
C/P. LÁINEZ

⑳ REVOLUCIÓ SETEMBRE 1868
C/RAMON Y CAJAL
Ⓜ **Joanic**

TRAVESSERA DE GRÀCIA

C/PUIGMARTÍ
PLAÇA JOHN LENNON

⑫
C/SIRACUSA
PLAÇA RASPALL
C/TORDERA
C/BANYOLES
C/BAILEN
PASSEIG SANT JOAN
ALIÓ
C/ROGER DE FLOR
⑳
C/TORRENT DE L'OLLA
C/FRATERNITAT
C/TORRES
C/MILA I FONTANALS
C/MONISTROL
PASSATGE
5

C/LLIBERTAT
C/SANTA EULÀLIA
C/PERILL
C/CAMPRODON

C/CÒRSEGA
C/CÒRSEGA

Time Out Shortlist | Barcelona 2007 **141**

❶ Sights & museums
❶ Eating & drinking
❶ Shopping
❶ Nightlife
❶ Arts & leisure

0 ___ 200 m
0 ___ 200 yds
© Copyright Time Out Group 2006

Parc Güell p139

excellent Galician seafood, served with military precision by the fleet of nautically clad waiters. Non-fishy dishes include a rich *caldo gallego* (cabbage and pork broth) and *lacón con grelos* (gammon with turnip tops).

Cantina Machito

C/Torrijos 47 (93 217 34 14).
Metro Fontana or Joanic. **Open**
1-4pm, 7pm-12.30am daily. **€€**.
Mexican. Map p141 D3 ⑥
One of life's perpetual mysteries is whether Mexican desserts are any good or not, given that no one has ever had room for one. Here, for example, 'your starter for ten' takes on a whole new meaning with the tasty but unfinishable *orden de tacos*, while mains largely comprise *enmoladas* or *enchiladas* the size of wine bottles, beached next to a sea of thick *mole* sauce. The tequila shots and Margaritas go without saying.

Casa Quimet

Rambla de Prat 9 (93 217 53 27).
Metro Fontana. **Open** 6.30pm-2am
Tue-Sun. Closed Aug. **No credit cards**. Map p140 C3 ⑦
Yellowing jazz posters cover every inch of wallspace, dozens of ancient guitars are suspended from the ceiling and a succession of ticking clocks compete to be heard over the voice of Billie Holiday. This other-worldly 'Guitar Bar' (as the place is invariably known to locals) occasionally springs to life with an impromptu jam session, but most of the time it remains a perfect study in melancholy.

Emu

C/Guilleries 17 (93 218 45 02). Metro Fontana. **Open** 7pm-2am Mon-Thur; 7pm-3am Fri, Sat. **€€€**. No credit cards. **Asian**. Map p141 D3 ⑧
Run by two Australians and known locally as a Thai restaurant, Emu is really, well, Australian, meaning that its pad thai and red curry are complemented by Malaysian beef rendang, Vietnamese spring rolls with spicy peanut sauce and a very convincing but thoroughly occidental Caesar salad. The wine list is largely antipodean too, with some smooth reds and fruity whites also available by the glass. There are only seven tables, so get there early or book ahead.

Envalira

Plaça del Sol 13 (93 218 58 13).
Metro Fontana. **Open** 1.30-4pm, 9pm-midnight Tue-Sat; 1.30-5pm Sun. Closed Aug. **€€**. **Spanish**. Map p140 C4 ⑨

Old-school Spain lives on as penguin-suited waiters solemnly hand out brown PVC menus at plastic teak-effect tables under painfully austere lighting. But it's all worth it for the food: as traditionally brown as the drab decor, it runs the full gamut of hefty Iberian classics. Start with fish soups or lentils and go on to paellas, roast meats and seafood stews, followed by serious, own-made *crema catalana* or *tarta de Santiago*.

Flash Flash

C/Granada del Penedès 25 (93 237 09 90). FGC Gràcia. **Open** 1.30pm-1.30am daily. **€€€**. **Tortillas/cocktails**. Map p140 B4 ⑩

Opened in 1970, this bar was a design sensation in its day, with its white leatherette banquettes and walls that are still imprinted with silhouettes of a life-size frolicking, Twiggy-like model. They call it a *tortilleria*, which means there are 60 or so tortilla variations, alongside a list of kid-friendly dishes and adult-friendly cocktails.

Folquer

C/Torrent de l'Olla 3 (93 217 43 95). Metro Diagonal or Verdaguer. **Open** 1-4pm, 9-11.30pm Mon-Fri; 9-11.30pm Sat. Closed 3wks Aug. **€€€**. **Catalan**. Map p141 D5 ⑪

Filled with an animated, older clientele, it's ultimately a welcoming space, however, with daffodil yellow wood panelling and huge splashy artworks. The inventive food is well executed and reasonably priced, never more so than in the lunch deals: the 'Executive' is a sturdy main, such as entrecôte, with a salad, pudding and wine for €14, while the normal menú is cheaper and still creative, with a gourmet hamburger and wild mushrooms, or *suquet de pop* (octopus stew).

Himali

C/Milà i Fontanals 68 (93 285 15 68). Metro Joanic. **Open** noon-4pm, 8pm-midnight Tue-Sun. **€€**. **Nepalese**. Map p141 D4 ⑫

Cocking a snook at the many mediocre Indian restaurants around, Barcelona's first Nepalese eaterie has become a hit. Faced with an alien and impenetrable menu, the set meals seem tempting, but they aren't always the best option: press the waiters for recommendations or try *mugliaco kukhura* (barbecued butter chicken in creamy tomato sauce) or *khasi masala tarkari* (baked spicy lamb). Meat cooked in the tandoori oven (*txulo*) is also worth a try, and there are plenty of vegetarian choices.

Jean Luc Figueras

C/Santa Teresa 10 (93 415 28 77). Metro Diagonal. **Open** 1.30-3pm, 8.30-11.30pm Mon-Sat. **€€€€**. **Catalan/French**. Map p140 C5 ⑬

A superb Michelin-starred restaurant set in the palatial old atelier of fashion deity Balenciaga. Figueras' innovative Catalan-French cuisine might include a dish of fresh foie on fig bread with a reduction of aniseted and ratafia, fried prawn and ginger pasta in mango and mustard sauce, or sea bass with cod and black pudding. Desserts, such as parfait of peanuts and the caramelised banana with milk chocolate sorbet, are sumptuous blends of temperature and texture.

Laurak

C/Granada del Penedès 14-16 (93 218 71 65). FGC Gràcia. **Open** 1-4pm, 9-11.30pm Mon-Sat. **€€€**. **Basque**. Map p140 B4 ⑭

When Basques aren't eating or forming new gastronomic societies, they're opening restaurants, and sleek, elegant Laurak is one of the finest. Living up to Basque cuisine's reputation, dishes include a heavenly salad of tender pigs' trotters with octopus, caramelised suckling pig with pistachio mousse or a *porrusalda* (cod, potato and leek soup) deconstructed into foams, slices and swirls. The indecisive should try the five-course traditional menu or even the seven-dish taster menu.

Mesopotamia

C/Verdi 65 (93 237 15 63). Metro Fontana. **Open** 8.30pm-midnight Tue-Sat. Closed 2wks Apr. **€€**. No credit cards. **Iraqi**. Map p141 D3 ⑮

The menu at Barcelona's only Iraqi restaurant is based on Arab 'staff of life' foods, such as yoghurt and rice. Best value is the enormous taster menu, which includes great Lebanese wines, a variety of dips for your *riqaq* bread, bulgur wheat with aromatic roast meats and vegetables, sticky baklawa and Arabic teas. Also good are the potato croquettes stuffed with minced meat, almonds and dried fruit.

Noise i Art

C/Topazi 26 (93 217 50 01). Metro Fontana. **Open** 6pm-2.30am Tue-Thur, Sun; 7pm-3am Fri, Sat. Closed 2wks end Aug. No credit cards. **Bar/café**. **Map** p141 D3 ⑯

It's known locally as the 'IKEA bar', which, although some of the plastic fittings do look strangely familiar, doesn't really do justice to the colourful, pop art interior. A chilled and convivial atmosphere is occasionally livened up with a flamenco session, and all the usual Gràcia staples such as houmous and tabbouleh are served along with various salads and pasta dishes.

Octubre

C/Julián Romea 18 (93 218 25 18). FGC Gràcia/metro Diagonal. **Open** 1.30-3.30pm, 9-11pm Mon-Fri; 9-11pm Sat. Closed Aug. **€€**. **Catalan**. **Map** p140 B4 ⑰

Time stands still in this quiet little spot, with quaint old-fashioned decor, swathes of lace and brown table linen. Time often stands still, in fact, between placing an order and receiving any food, but this is all part of Octubre's sleepy charm, along with a roll-call of reasonably priced and mainly Catalan dishes. The beef in mustard sauce is excellent, and wild mushroom risotto, while not outstanding, is decent enough for the price.

Puku Café

C/Guilleries 10 (93 601 32 37). Metro Fontana. **Open** *June-Sept* 7pm-1.30am Mon-Thur; 7pm-3am Fri, Sat. *Oct-May* 6.30pm-1am Mon-Wed; 6.30pm-2am Thur; 7pm-3am Fri, Sat. No credit cards. **Bar/café**. **Map** p141 D3 ⑱

The Puku Café has two very different vibes. During the week it's a colourful meeting place, where the casually hip hang out over a bottle of wine and maybe some cactus and lime ice-cream. At weekends, however, the amber walls and deep orange columns prop up a younger, scruffier crowd, nodding along to some of the city's best DJs spinning a varied playlist based around electropop.

Saint-Germain

C/Torrent de l'Olla 113 (93 218 04 13). Metro Fontana. **Open** 6pm-2.30am Mon-Thur, Sun; 6pm-3am Fri, Sat. No credit cards. **Bar**. **Map** p141 D4 ⑲

Get here early for a leather armchair from which to survey assembled young hip Americans sipping Caipirinhas, picking at ham and cheese crêpes, and making noises of recognition at the soundtrack of Kruder & Dorfmeister. Decent salads, quiches and sandwiches are served until midnight.

Salambó

C/Torrijos 51 (93 218 69 66). Metro Fontana or Joanic. **Open** noon-2.30am Mon-Thur, Sun; noon-3am Fri, Sat. **Café**. **Map** p141 D3 ⑳

The time-honoured meeting place for Verdi cinema-goers, Salambó is a large and ever so slightly staid split-level café that serves coffee, teas and filled ciabatta to the *barrio*'s more conservative element. At night, those who are planning to eat are given preference when it comes to bagging a table.

Samsara

C/Terol 6 (93 285 36 88). Metro Fontana or Joanic. **Open** *June-Sept* 8.30pm-2am Mon-Thur; 8.30pm-3am Fri; 8.30pm-3am Sat. *Oct-May* 1.30-4pm, 8.30pm-2am Mon-Thur; 1.30-4pm, 8.30pm-3am Fri; 8.30pm-3am Sat. **€€€**. **Tapas**. **Map** p141 D4 ㉑

A combination of Moroccan-themed decor and intelligent cooking, Samsara has built up quite a following among Gràcia foodies. Its tapas are diminutive but don't want for flavour or imagination: try monkfish ceviche with mango

Cantina Machito p142

or watermelon gazpacho with basil oil. Photos line the walls, and a DJ plays lounge and the smoothest of house later in the week.

San Kil

C/Legalitat 22 (93 284 41 79). Metro Fontana or Joanic. **Open** noon-4pm, 8pm-midnight Mon-Sat. Closed 2wks Aug. **€€. Korean. Map** p141 E3
If you've never eaten Korean before, it pays to gen up before you head to this bright, spartan restaurant. *Panch'an* is the ideal starter: four little dishes containing vegetable appetisers, one of which will be tangy *kimch'i* (fermented cabbage with chilli). Then try mouthwatering *pulgogi* – beef served sizzling at the table and eaten rolled into lettuce leaves – and maybe *pibimbap* – rice with vegetables (and occasionally meat) topped with a fried egg.

Shojiro

C/Ros de Olano 11 (93 415 65 48). Metro Fontana. **Open** 1.30-3.30pm Mon; 1.30-3.30pm, 9-11.30pm Tue-Sat. Closed 2wks Apr, 2wks Aug. **€€€. Catalan/Japanese. Map** p140 C4
A curious but successful mix of Catalan and Japanese applies to the decor as much as the food, with original 'mosaic' flooring and dark green paintwork setting off a clean feng-shui look. There are only set meals (water, wine, coffee and tax are all included in the price at lunch), starting with an amuse-bouche, then offering sushi with strips of nori, sticky rice and salad, or courgette soup and pancetta as a starter, with salmon teriyaki or spring chicken confit with potato dauphinois as mains. Puddings might include a wonderfully refreshing own-made apple ice-cream.

Sureny

Plaça de la Revolució 17 (93 213 75 56). Metro Fontana or Joanic. **Open** *Oct-July* 8.30pm-midnight Tue-Thur; 8.30pm-1am Fri; 1-3.30pm, 8pm-midnight Sat, Sun. *Aug, Sept* 8.30pm-midnight Tue-Thur; 8.30pm-1am Fri; 8pm-midnight Sat, Sun. Closed last wk Sept, 1st wk Oct, 2wks Dec-Jan. **€€. Tapas. Map** p141 D4
A well-kept gastronomic secret, Sureny boasts superb tapas and waiters who know what they're talking about. As well as the usual run-of-the-mill tortilla 'n' calamares, look out for tuna marinated in ginger and soy, partridge and venison in season, and a sublime duck foie with redcurrant sauce.

La Tarantella

C/Fraternitat 37, Gràcia (93 284 98 57). Metro Fontana. **Open** 8pm-midnight Tue; 1.30-4pm, 8pm-midnight Wed-Sun **€€. Pizzeria. Map** p141 D5

Verdi

Forge your way through the brightly lit and unpromising tunnel of a bar into the cosy, low-ceilinged back room, which is warmed with beams, yellow paintwork and oil paintings. Here you can dine on decent budget Italian grub (salads, pasta and pizzas). Toppings are generous, rather too much so at times. The house pizza, for example, comes slathered in mozzarella, ham, mushrooms and onion, while the Extremeño is a mountain of mozzarella, chorizo and egg.

Shopping

Hibernian Books

C/Pere Serafí 33-35 (93 217 47 96/
www.hibernian-books.com). Metro
Fontana. **Open** 4-8pm Mon; 10.30am-
8.30pm Tue-Sat. No credit cards.
Map p140 C4 26
Hibernian Books opened its doors in 2004 with over 30,000 titles, displaying everything from popular fiction by Danielle Steel to more cultured works. A kiddies' corner, armchairs, packed shelves and tea and coffee furnish this bookworm's lair, which operates a part-exchange system for those keen on offloading some suitcase ballast.

Nightlife

Mond Bar

Plaça del Sol 21 (93 272 09 10/www.
mondclub.com). Metro Fontana. **Open**
8.30pm-3am daily. **Admission** free.
No credit cards. **Map** p140 C4 27
This tiny two-level bar gets sweaty and smoky as the coolest cats in Gràcia pack in for an early drink. Recent problems with the neighbours saw the DJs replaced with a jukebox.

Arts & leisure

Verdi

C/Verdi 32, Gràcia (93 238 79 90/
www.cines-verdi.com). Metro Fontana.
No credit cards. **Map** p141 D3 28
A long-standing champion of foreign cinema, the original five-screen Verdi, plus its four-screen annexe Verdi Park on the next street over, offer a diverse programme of interesting, accessible cinema from around the world, concentrating on Asia and Europe, as well as some Spanish repertoire. At peak times, chaos reigns; arrive early and make sure you don't mistake the line to enter for the ticket queue.
Other locations: Verdi Park,
C/Torrijos 49 (93 238 79 90).

Parc de l'Espanya Industrial p148

Other Districts

Sants & Les Corts

For many arriving by bus or train, Estació de Sants is their first sight of Barcelona. Most take one look at the forbidding **Plaça dels Països Catalans**, which looks like it was designed with skateboard tricks in mind, and get the hell out of the area. In the 19th century this was the industrial motor of the city, housing giant textile factories. Nearby **Plaça de Sants**, with Jorge Castillo's *Ciclista* statue, is the hub of the district, right in the middle of the C/Sants high street. Also worth checking out are the showy Modernista buildings at Nos.12, 130, 145 and 151, all designed by local architect Modest Feu. However, the more humble workers' flats nearby in the narrow streets off C/Premià are more typical of this very working-class area. From there, C/Creu Coberta, an old Roman road once known as the Camí d'Espanya, 'the road to Spain', runs to Plaça d'Espanya.

Row after row of apartment blocks now obscure any trace of the rustic origins of Les Corts (literally, 'cowsheds' or 'pigsties'), as the village itself was swallowed up by Barcelona in the late 19th century. But search and you will find **Plaça de la Concòrdia**, a quiet square dominated by a 40-metre (131-foot) bell tower. This is an anachronistic oasis housing the civic centre Can Deu, formerly a farmhouse and now home to a great bar that hosts jazz acts every other Thursday. The area is much better known, though, for what happens every other weekend, when tens of thousands pour in to watch FC

Auditori Winterthur

A charming, intimate venue in the unlikely setting of L'Illa, a monolithic shopping centre. Though it hosts few concerts, they're generally of high quality; the Schubert cycle and series of song recitals, both annual events, are well worth catching.

Nou Camp – FC Barcelona

Nou Camp, Avda Arístides Maillol, access 9, Les Corts (93 496 36 00/08/ www.fcbarcelona.com). Metro Collblanc or Palau Reial. **Ticket office** 9am-1.30pm, 3.30-6pm Mon-Thur; 9am-2.30pm Fri; from 11am match days. Tickets available from 2wks before each match. **Tickets** €19-€125. **Museum** *Open* 10am-6.30pm Mon-Sat; 10am-2pm Sun. *Admission* €5.30; €3.70 reductions; free under-5s. *Guided tour* €9.50; €6.60 reductions. No credit cards.

There hasn't been a better time to be a Barça fan since the golden Cruyff days of the early 1990s. Barcelona walked the Spanish league in 2005/6 and won the European Champions' League, along the way enhancing their reputation as the team everyone wants to watch. Ronaldinho is hands-down the world's greatest player, Eto'o is lethal in front of goal and incoming Argentine Leo Messi is the most authentic new Maradona since Maradona himself. Around 4,000 tickets usually go on sale on the day of the game: phone to find out when, and join the queue an hour or so beforehand at the intersection of Travessera de les Corts and Avda Arístides Maillol. If you can't get to the stadium on matchday but love the team, it's well worth visiting the club museum. A guided tour of the stadium will take you through the players' tunnel to the dugouts and up to the President's box.

Barcelona, whose **Nou Camp** stadium takes up much of the west of the *barrio*.

Sights & museums

Parc de l'Espanya Industrial

Passeig de Antoni (no phone). Metro Sants-Estació. **Open** 10am-sunset daily.

A puzzling space, designed by Basque Luis Peña Ganchegui, with ten watchtowers looking over a boating lake with a statue of Neptune in the middle, flanked by a stretch of mud that is used mainly for walking dogs. By the entrance kids can climb over Andrés Nagel's *Drac,* a massive and sinister black dragon.

Arts & leisure

Auditori Winterthur

L'Illa, Avda Diagonal 547, Les Corts (93 290 11 02/www.winterthur.es). Metro Maria Cristina. **Open** *Information* 9am-1.30pm, 3-7pm Mon-Fri.

Shopping

Enric Rovira Shop

Avda Josep Tarradellas 113, Les Corts (93 419 25 47/www.enricrovira.com). Metro Entença. **Open** 10am-2.30pm, 5-8pm Tue-Fri; 10am-2.30pm Sat. Closed Aug.

Enric Rovira is definitely the most deluxe of Barcelona's growing tribe of chocolate boutiques, producing velvety smooth, hazelnut-studded versions of Gaudí's hexagonal pavement slabs, pink peppercorn truffles, Cabernet Sauvignon bonbons and twisty blocks of Christmas *turrón* in a number of unusual flavours.

Nightlife

Bikini

C/Déu i Mata 105, Les Corts (93 322 08 00/www.bikinibcn.com). Metro Les Corts or Maria Cristina. **Open** midnight-5am Wed-Sun. **Admission** (incl 1 drink) €15.

Bikini is hard to find in the soulless streets behind the L'Illa shopping centre, but it's worth seeking out for top-flight gigs by serious musicians of any stripe, from Femi Kuti to Thievery Corporation, Marianne Faithfull to Amp Fiddler. After the gigs, stay for club nights with house, funk and hip hop on the turntables.

Tibidabo & Collserola

The ugly, neo-Gothic **Sagrat Cor** temple crowning the peak of the Collserola massif has become one of the city's most recognisable landmarks; it's clearly visible for miles around. At weekends, thousands of people head to the top of the hill, with its sweeping views over the whole of Barcelona to the sea in order to whoop and scream at the **funfair**. Nowadays the only one in Barcelona, it's been running since 1921 and has changed little since: the rides are creaky and old-fashioned, but very quaint.

Getting up to the top on the clanking old **Tramvia Blau** (Blue Tram) and then the **funicular railway** is part of the fun; Plaça Doctor Andreu between the two is a great place for an alfresco drink. For the best view of the city, either take a lift up the needle of Norman Foster's communications tower, the **Torre de Collserola**, or up to the *mirador* at the feet of Christ atop the Sagrat Cor.

The vast **Parc de Collserola** is more a series of forested hills than a park; its shady paths through holm oaks and pines open out to spectacular views. It's most easily reached by FGC train on the Terrassa–Sabadell line from Plaça Catalunya or Passeig de Gracia, getting off at **Baixador de Vallvidrera** station.

Sights & museums

Funicular de Tibidabo

Plaça Doctor Andreu to Plaça Tibidabo (93 211 79 42). FGC Avda Tibidabo, then Tramvia Blau. **Open** As funfair (see below), but starting 30mins earlier. **Tickets** *Single* €2; €1.50 reductions. *Return* €3, €2 reductions. No credit cards.

This art deco vehicle offers occasional glimpses of the city below as it winds through the pine forests up to the summit. The service has been running since 1901, but only according to a complicated timetable. Alternatively, it's nearly an hour's (mostly pleasant) hike up from Plaça Doctor Andreu for those who are feeling energetic.

Tibidabo funfair

Plaça del Tibidabo, Tibidabo (93 211 79 42/www.tibidabo.es). FGC Avda Tibidabo **Open** *Nov-mid Dec, mid Jan-Feb* noon-6pm Sat, Sun. *Mar, Apr* noon-7pm Sat, Sun. *May, June* noon-8pm Sat, Sun. *July* noon-8pm Wed-Fri; noon-11pm Sat, Sun. *Aug* noon-10pm Mon-Thur; noon-11pm Fri-Sun. *1st 2wks Sept* noon-8pm Wed-Fri; noon-9pm Sat, Sun. *2nd 2wks Sept* noon-9pm Sat, Sun. *Oct* noon-7pm Sat, Sun. Closed mid Dec-mid Jan. **Admission** *Rides* €11. *Unlimited rides* €22; €9-€16 reductions; free children under 90cm.

Dating back to 1889, this charming, mountain-top fairground has more than 30 rides, ranging from bumper cars and rollercoasters to the wonderful

Tower records

Jean Nouvel changes the cityscape.

Some are calling it Barcelona's 'gherkin', while many others have a less generous – and unprintable – nickname for Jean Nouvel's Torre Agbar. Completed in 2005, it juts into the city's skyline with verve and audacity that owe nothing to Norman Foster's Swiss Re tower.

Designed and built for the city's water authority, the Torre Agbar comprises two concrete cylindrical structures, the inner to house the lifts and facilities and the other forming the outer wall. The elliptical space between is filled with light- and air-filled offices, separated by glass walls and without pillars, creating a curious floating sensation.

The idea was to create a 'human' and ecologically sound working environment. The materials used are recyclable (the building even incorporates its own water-recycling system) and the 4,400 louvre windows are designed in such a way as to create a natural ventilation system that all but does away with the need for air-conditioning.

What really sets the 142m (466ft) tower apart, however, is the façade; the reds, greens and blues of the profiled aluminium encasing the building shimmer through glass slats, creating new effects with the changing angle of the sun. For all the local sniggers over its undeniably phallic profile, it's a worthy monument to Barcelona's love of colour and sinuous form.

Aeromàgic (a stunning mountain ride) and the 1928 Avió, the world's first popular flight simulator. Few are hair-raising by today's standards, but more attractions are being added, such as a multimedia 'experience' that enables children to become part of a cartoon. Don't miss the antique mechanical puppets and contraptions at the Museu d'Autòmats or hourly puppet shows at the Marionetàrium (from 1pm).

Torre de Collserola

Ctra de Vallvidrera al Tibidabo (93 406 93 54/www.torredecollserola.com). FGC Peu Funicular, then funicular. **Open** *Apr-June, Sept* 11am-2.30pm, 3.30-7pm Wed-Fri; 11am-7pm Sat, Sun. *July, Aug* 11am-2.30pm, 3.30-8pm Mon-Fri; 11am-8pm Sat, Sun. *Oct-Mar* 11am-2.30pm, 3.30-6pm Mon-Fri; 11am-6pm Sat, Sun. **Admission** €5; €4 reductions; free under-4s.

Just five minutes' walk from the Sagrat Cor is its main rival as Barcelona's most visible landmark, Norman Foster's communications tower, built in 1992 to transmit images of the Olympics around the world. Visible from just about everywhere in the city and always flashing at night, the tower is loved and hated in equal measure, but its stunning views of Barcelona and the Mediterranean are undeniable.

Eating & drinking

Merbeyé

Plaça Doctor Andreu, Tibidabo (93 417 92 79). FGC Avda Tibidabo, then Tramvia Blau/bus 60. **Open** noon-2.30am Mon-Thur; noon-3.30am Fri, Sat; noon-2am Sun. **Bar**.

Merbeyé is a cocktail bar straight from central casting: moodily lit, plush with red velvet and hung with prints of jazz maestros. In summer there's also a peaceful, stylish terrace for alfresco fun. The clientele runs from shabby gentility to flashy Barça players and their bling-encrusted wives.

La Venta

Plaça Doctor Andreu (93 212 64 55). FGC Avda Tibidabo, then Tramvia

Blau. **Open** 1.30-3.15pm, 9-11.15pm
Mon-Sat. **€€€**. **Mediterranean**.
Perched high above the city mayhem,
La Venta's Moorish-influenced interior
plays second fiddle to the terrace
for every season: shaded by day and
uncovered by night in summer, sealed
and warmed with a wood-burning
stove in winter. Complex starters
include lentil and spider crab salad;
sea urchins au gratin (a must); and
langoustine ravioli, filled with leek and
foie mousse. Simpler, but high-quality
mains run from rack of lamb to delicate
monkfish in filo pastry with pesto.

Nightlife

Danzatoria

*Avda Tibidabo 61 (93 272 00 40/
www.gruposalsitas.com). FGC Avda
Tibidabo, then 10min walk.* **Open**
9pm-2.30am Tue-Sat; 8pm-2.30am
Sun. **Admission** free.
The uptown location attracts an
upscale crowd to this spectacular converted manor house on a hill overlooking Barcelona. The hipness factor goes
up as you climb the club's glamour-
glutted storeys. Preened *pija* flesh is
shaken on hot-house dancefloors, or
laid across sofas hanging from the ceiling in the chill-out lounges. We've had
reports of snotty staff, but who cares
when you're lounging in one of the
layers of palm-filled gardens, accompanied by some gorgeous creature and
some (very expensive) champagne.

Mirablau

*Plaça Doctor Andreu 1, Tibidabo
(93 418 58 79). FGC Avda Tibidabo,
then Tramvia Blau.* **Open** 11am-
4.30am Mon-Thur; 11am-5.30am
Fri-Sun. **Admission** free. **Credit** V.
It doesn't get any more uptown than
this, either geographically or socially.
Located at the top of Tibidabo, this
small bar is packed with the high rollers
of Barcelona, from local footballers
living on the hill to international businessmen on the company card, as well
as young *pijos* stopping by for a drink
before heading off to nearby Danzatoria

on daddy's ride. Apart from the cheesy
Spanish pop, its only attraction is the
breathtaking view.

Zona Alta

Zona Alta (the 'upper zone',
or 'uptown') is the name given
collectively to a series of smart
neighbourhoods, including **Sant
Gervasi**, **Sarrià**, **Pedralbes**
and **Putxet**, that stretch out
across the lower reaches of the
Collserola hills. The centre of
Sarrià and the streets of old
Pedralbes around the monastery
retain a flavour of the sleepy
country towns these once were.
    Gaudí fans are rewarded by
a trip up to the **Pavellons de la
Finca Güell** at Avda Pedralbes 15;
its extraordinary and rather
frightening wrought-iron gate
features a dragon into whose
gaping mouth the foolhardy can
fit their heads. Once inside the
gardens, via the main gate on Avda
Diagonal, make sure to look out for
a delightful fountain designed by
the master himself. Across near
Putxet is Gaudí's relatively sober
Col·legi de les Teresianes
(C/Ganduxer 85-105), while up
towards Tibidabo, just off Plaça
Bonanova, rises his remarkable
Gothic-influenced **Torre Figueres**
or **Bellesguard**.

Sights & museums

CosmoCaixa

*C/Teodor Roviralta 47-51 (93 212
60 50/www.fundacio.lacaixa.es).
Bus 60/FGC Avda Tibidabo, then
Tramvia Blau.* **Open** 10am-8pm Tue-
Sun. **Admission** €3; €2 reductions;
free under-3s. *Planetarium* €2; €1.50
reductions; free under-3s.
The long and eagerly awaited revamp
of the Fundació La Caixa's science
museum and planetarium, to create the
biggest in Europe, was only partially
successful. First off, its size is a little

CosmoCaixa p151

misleading: apart from a couple of spaces – the Flooded Forest, a reproduction of a bit of Amazonia complete with flora and fauna, and the Geological Wall – the collection has not been proportionally expanded to fit the new building. A glass-enclosed spiral ramp runs down an impressive six floors, but actually represents quite a long walk to reach the main collection five floors down. What's more, for all the fanfare made by the museum about taking exhibits out of glass cases and making scientific theories accessible, many of the displays still look very dated.

On the plus side, the installations for children are quite excellent: the Bubble Planetarium pleases kids aged three to eight, and the wonderful Clik (aimed at ages three to six) and Flash (for ages seven to nine) introduce kids to science through games. Toca Toca! ('Touch! Touch!') educates children about which animals and plants are safe and which should be avoided. One of the real highlights, for kids and adults, remains the

hugely entertaining sound telescope, which is situated outside on the Plaça de la Ciència.

Event highlights 'Einstein, 100 Years of Physics' (until 28 Feb 2007).

Monestir de Pedralbes

Baixada del Monestir 9 (93 203 92 82). FGC Reina Elisenda. **Open** 10am-5pm Tue-Sat; 10am-3pm Sun. **Admission** €4; €2.50 reductions; free under-12s. Free 1st Sun of mth.

In 1326 the widowed Queen Elisenda de Montcada used her inheritance to buy this land and build a convent for the 'Poor Clare' order of nuns, which she soon joined. The result is a jewel of Gothic architecture, with an understated single-nave church with fine stained-glass windows and a beautiful three-storey 14th-century cloister. The place was out of bounds to the general public until 1983 when the nuns, a closed order, opened it up as a museum in the mornings (they escape to a nearby annexe).

The site offers a fascinating insight into life in a medieval convent, taking you through its kitchens, pharmacy and refectory with its huge vaulted ceiling. To one side is the tiny chapel of Sant Miquel, with murals dating to 1343 by Ferrer Bassa, a Catalan painter and student of Giotto. In the former dormitory next to the cloister is a selection of hitherto undisplayed objects belonging to the nuns. Among them are illuminated books, furniture and objects reflecting the artistic and religious life of the community.

Museu de Ceràmica & Museu de les Arts Decoratives

Palau Reial de Pedralbes, Avda Diagonal 686 (93 280 16 21/www. museuceramica.bcn.es/www.museu artsdecoratives.bcn.es). Metro Palau Reial. **Open** 10am-6pm Tue-Sat; 10am-3pm Sun. **Admission** *Combined admission with Museu Tèxtil* €3.50; €2 reductions; free under-16s. Free 1st Sun of mth. No credit cards.

These two collections – accessible, along with the Textile Museum, on the same ticket – are housed in the august Palau Reial; originally designed for the family of Eusebi Güell, Gaudí's patron, it was later used as a royal palace. The Museum of Decorative Arts is informative and fun, and looks at the different styles informing the design of artefacts in Europe since the Middle Ages, from Romanesque to art deco and beyond. A second section is devoted to post-war Catalan design of objects as diverse as urinals and man-sized inflatable pens.

The Ceramics Museum is equally fascinating, showing how Moorish ceramic techniques from the 13th century were developed after the Reconquista with the addition of colours (especially blue and yellow) in centres such as Manises (in Valencia) and Barcelona. Two 18th-century murals are of sociological interest: one, La Xocolatada, shows the bourgeoisie at a garden party, while the other, by the same artist, depicts the working classes at a bullfight in the Plaza Mayor in Madrid. Upstairs is a section showing 20th-century ceramics, which includes a room dedicated to Miró and Picasso. The two museums, along with the Textile Museum and several smaller collections, are to be merged in the future in a Museu de Disseny (Design Museum) as part of the cultural overhaul of the Plaça de les Glòries.

Parc de la Creueta del Coll

C/Mare de Déu del Coll (no phone). Metro Penitents. **Open** 10am-sunset daily. **Admission** free.

This park was created from a quarry in 1987 by Josep Matorell and David Mackay, the team that went on to design the Vila Olímpica. It boasts a sizeable swimming pool, complete with its own 'desert island', and an interesting sculpture by Eduardo Chillida: called *In Praise of Water*, it consists of a 50-ton lump of curly granite that's suspended on cables.

Tramvia Blau (Blue Tram)

Avda Tibidabo (Plaça Kennedy) to Plaça Doctor Andreu (93 318 70 74/www.tramvia.org/tramviablau). FGC Avda Tibidabo. **Open** *Mid June-mid Sept* 10am-8pm daily. *Mid Sept-mid June* 10am-6pm Sat. **Frequency** 20mins. **Tickets** €2.10 single; €3.10 return. No credit cards.

Barcelonins and tourists have been clanking 1,225m (4,000ft) up Avda Tibidabo in the 'blue trams' since 1902. In the winter months, when the tram only operates on weekends, a rather more prosaic bus takes you up (or you can walk it in 15 minutes).

Eating & drinking

Vivanda

C/Major de Sarrià 134 (93 205 47 17). Metro FGC Reina Elisenda. **Open** 9-11.30pm Mon; 1.30-3.30pm, 9-11.30pm Tue-Sat. **€€€. Catalan**.
As if the leafy garden, dappled with sunlight, weren't reason enough to come here, the waiters are charming and the chefs skilled. Starters are a

Elephant

light and healthy bunch, with crisp salads and baby vegetables, but mains are more traditionally Catalan. Oxtail is stuffed with cured duck with shallot jam, or there are more straightforward choices of pork with mustard sauce, hake, sea bass, bonito or, bizarrely, ostrich. Try the own-made pistachio ice-cream to finish.

Nightlife

Elephant

Passeig dels Til·lers 1 (93 334 02 58/ www.elephantbcn.com). Metro Palau Reial. **Open** 11.30pm-4am Wed; 11.30pm-5am Thur-Sat. **Admission** free Wed, Thur, Sun; €12 Fri, Sat.
If you have a Porsche and a model girlfriend, this is where you meet your peers. Housed in a converted mansion, Elephant is as elegant and high-design as its customers. The big attraction is the outdoor bar and terrace dancefloor, though the low-key and low-volume (due to neighbours' complaints) house music doesn't inspire much hands-in-the-air action.

Otto Zutz

C/Lincoln 15 (93 238 07 22/www. grupo-ottozutz.com). FGC Gràcia.

Open midnight-5am Wed; midnight-5.30am Thur-Sat. **Admission** (incl 1 drink) €15.
Nightclubs and supermodels go hand in hand, so it's no wonder that a club would give its name to a modelling agency. Its young superbabes come here to spend their hard-earned cash posing and strutting on the distinct dancefloors. Hip hop and R&B are the choice rhythms in one, there's deep house in the Velvet Room, while electro and tech house prevail on the main floor, where every month the Poker Flat boys lend their technical wizardry.

Pacha

Avda Doctor Marañon 17 (93 334 32 33/www.clubpachabcn.com). Metro Zona Universitaria. **Open** 11.30pm-4.30am Wed; midnight-7am Thur-Sat; 8pm-2am Sun. **Admission** (incl 1 drink) €15.
The international überclub lands in Barcelona and loses none of its charm in doing so. This Pacha is massive and brightly lit, and boasts one of the best sound systems in town – not a penny has been spared in creating the club's six bars, two VIP areas, chill-out room and terrace. The crowd is mainly young, made up of a mix of students

and fresh-faced foreign tourists. Sunday is Sundown 'Teadance' sessions day, with big-in-Ibiza guest DJs playing uplifting house from 8pm till late.

Universal

C/Marià Cubi 182 bis-184 (93 201 35 96/www.grupocostaeste.com). FGC Muntaner. **Open** 11pm-5.30am Mon-Sat. **Admission** free.

One of a very few clubs in the city that cater to an older, well-dressed crowd, Universal doesn't charge admission to get in, but the drink prices are steep as a result. Recent renovations by the designer of the Salsitas chain have brought about aquatic slide projections in the upstairs chill-out area, along with a sharper look downstairs. As it gets later, the music moves from downtempo to soft house, which works the crowd up to a gentle shimmy.

Poblenou

Poblenou has been many things in its time: a farming community, a fishing port, the site of heavy industry factories and a trendy post-industrial suburb. Now it's also a burgeoning technology and business district, snappily tagged '22@'. Many of the factories around here closed down in the 1960s; these days the buildings that have not already been torn down or converted into office blocks are used as schools, civic centres, workshops, open spaces or, increasingly, coveted lofts.

On its northern edge **Plaça de les Glòries** holds the area's most striking landmark in the shape of French architect Jean Nouvel's hugely phallic **Torre Agbar** (see box p150). With this the *plaça* has become the gateway to a new commercial and leisure area on the shoreline (see box right), known as the Fòrum after the event in 2004 for which it was created. Many detractors of the Fòrum, a six-month cultural

What future for the Fòrum?

Marketed as a forum on peace, sustainability and cultural diversity, the 2004 Universal Forum of Cultures (www.barcelona2004.org) turned into Barcelona's biggest ghetto purge and urban speculation bonanza since the 1992 Olympics. The Fòrum's legacy – besides public debt that will not be paid off until 2014 – is an enormous and somewhat sterile shoreline site containing Herzog & de Meuron's triangular blue Edifici Fòrum, a new marina, a 'Peace Park', a plaza almost as large as Tiananmen Square and southern Europe's largest convention centre (www.ccib.es).

The problem is what to do with it. After the speeches were over and the Chinese acrobats had gone home, the site sat virtually unused. To allay increasing public disgust, the Ajuntament has been furiously sexing up the Fòrum by hijacking some of the city's largest cultural events, including Primavera Sound (p37), the Feria de Abril (p34) and the Sant Joan summer solstice party (p37). The conference centre has become something of a corporate Shangri-La, while the Fòrum building has a new high-end restaurant. The beachfront lido incorporates Pangea Island 60m (200ft) off the coast – only accessible by swimming – and activities such as inflatables and kayaks. You'll almost certainly have it all to yourself.

Torre Agbar p155

symposium, felt that its real purpose was to regenerate this post-industrial wasteland. Certainly, a large element of its legacy is enormous conference halls and hotels that it is hoped will draw many wealthy business clients into the city – as well as a scarcely believable increase in real-estate values.

Eating & drinking

Els Pescadors

Plaça Prim 1 (93 225 20 18). Metro Poblenou. **Open** 1-3.45pm, 8.30pm-midnight daily. **€€€. Catalan.**
Sit at large, luxuriously laid terrace tables or in one of two elegant dining rooms at Els Pescadors to enjoy some of the most imaginatively prepared seafood in the city. The house speciality is succulently fresh cod, which is to be found in dishes such as 'green' paella with *kokotras* (tender throat flesh) or cod with garlic mousseline, while starters include the likes of sautéed green asparagus with foie gras or creamy leek soup with rock mussels.

Shopping

Barcelona Glòries

Avda Diagonal 208, Eixample (93 486 04 04/www.lesglories.com). Metro Glòries. **Open** Shops 10am-10pm Mon-Sat.
Since opening in 1995, this mall, office and leisure centre has become the focus of local life. There's a seven-screen cinema (films are mostly dubbed into Spanish) and over 220 shops, including a Carrefour supermarket, an H&M, a Mango and a Disney Store, facing on to a large, café-filled square decorated with jets of coloured water. Family-oriented attractions include a free pram-lending service, play areas and entertainment such as bouncy castles and trampolines.

Diagonal Mar

Avda Diagonal 3 (902 53 03 00/www. diagonalmar.com). Metro El Maresme-Forum. **Open** Shops 10am-10pm Mon-Sat. Food court & entertainment 10am-midnight Mon-Thur; 10am-2am Fri, Sat; 11am-midnight Sun.
This three-level mall has an airy marine theme and a sea-facing roof terrace filled with cafés and restaurants of the fast-food variety. Business is a little slow (except at the giant Alcampo supermarket), so it's a good queue-free option. Other anchor stores here include Zara, Mango and FNAC. There are also a bowling alley, exhibitions, concerts and, every Sunday at 12.30pm, children's entertainment.

Nightlife

Oven

C/Ramon Turró 126 (93 221 06 02). Metro Poblenou. **Open** 1.30pm-4am Mon-Wed; 1.30-4pm, 9pm-3am Thur-Sat. **Admission** free.
The slickest outfit in the newly hip Poblenou, Oven is a bit tiresome to get to but worth the effort, especially if you make a night of it by having some fine cocktails and dinner here first. The industrial interior segues into grown-up clubland come midnight, when the tables are cleared to make way for dancing, and Barcelona's best-known DJ, Professor Angel Dust, hits the decks with his own mix of house and Afro-Latin tunes.

Razzmatazz

C/Almogàvers 122 (93 320 82 00). Metro Bogatell or Marina. **Open** 1-5am Fri, Sat. **Admission** (incl 1 drink) €12.
Five thousand clubbers can't be wrong. The mother of all warehouse superclubs, not to mention the best live venue in Barcelona, Razzmatazz now offers clubbers the chance to take in all of its five spaces for a single admission price. Whether they're goths, punks, mods, technophiles or electrotrash, young Catalans from Badalona and beyond trek here to dance until they drop. This is a place Jarvis Cocker, Miss Kittin and Dave Clark, as well as bands from Air to Blur, call home when they visit the city.

BARCELONA BY AREA

Your places to stay in Barcelona

BARCELONA CITY CENTRE - the hostel that is like a hotel

Just three blocks from Ramblas and Catalunya square and one block away from Passeig de Gracia and Gaudí´s buildings. This hostel is like a little hotel. Rooms with tv, satellite, air-conditioned, heating... and with bathroom ensuite.
BARCELONA CITY CENTRE, 60, Balmes street. Entlo., Barcelona

BARCELONA CITY URQUINAONA - a simple and charming hostel

Perfect for "Ryanair" travellers to Barcelona, as it is just two street away from the bus station to Girona´s airport. A peaceful, clean, simple and charming guesthouse where you will feel totally at home. Its strategic postion will allow you to be five minutes away from the most interesting parts of Barcelona.
BARCELONA CITY URQUINAONA, 13, Bailen street. Pral 1ª. Barcelona

BARCELONA CITY RAMBLAS - our "low cost" hostel

A simple and clean hostel in a superb central location between the Ramblas street and Catalunya square, the central square of Barcelona. We have recently renovated the establishment, giving it a new modern personality but keeping details of its classic style
BARCELONA CITY RAMBLAS (PENSIÓN CANALETAS), 133rd, Ramblas street. 3rd floor, Barcelona

Visit
www.barcelonacityhostels.com
to book your perfect accommodation today
info: +34 65 39 000 39

Essentials

Casa Camper p167

Hotels

The issue of Barcelona's mushrooming hotel construction has been hugely controversial in recent years, as Old City blocks of flats are cleared of any remaining tenants to make way for more four-stars, and towering business hotels spring up around the periphery. Oddly, this massive increase in the number of beds has not seen a fall in prices, and it can still be difficult to find a room in Barcelona outside the winter months, especially in mid-range to budget establishments.

Booking in advance – by at least two weeks, and more in summer – is strongly advised, at least in those places where it's possible: many of the cheaper hotels won't accept reservations. It's always worth calling a few days before your arrival to reconfirm the booking (get it in writing if you can; many

of our readers have reported having problems), and to check the cancellation policy. Often you will lose at least the first night.

To be sure of getting a room with natural light or a view, ask for an outside room (*habitación exterior*), which will usually face the street. Many of Barcelona's buildings are built around a central patio or airshaft, and the inside rooms (*habitación interior*) around them can be quite gloomy, albeit quieter.

Accommodation in Catalonia is divided into two official categories: hotels (H) and *pensiones* (P). To be a hotel (star-rated one to five), a place must have en suite bathrooms in every room. Ratings are based on physical attributes rather than levels of service; often the only difference between a three- and a four-star hotel is the presence of a meeting room. *Pensiones*, usually

ESSENTIALS

cheaper and often family-run, are star-rated one or two, and are not required to have en suite bathrooms (though many do). Some *pensiones* are called *hostales*, but, confusingly, are not youth hostels; those are known as *albergues*.

Prices can vary considerably depending on the time of year; always check for special deals. All bills are subject to seven per cent IVA (value added tax) on top of the basic price; this is not normally included in the advertised rate. Breakfast is not usually included outside special offers.

Barri Gòtic & La Rambla

Duc de la Victòria
C/Duc de la Victòria 15 (93 270 34 10/ fax 93 412 77 47/www.nh-hotels.com). Metro Catalunya. €€€.
The trusty NH chain has high standards of comfort and service, and this good-value downtown branch is no exception. The 156 rooms, with blue and beige colour scheme, may be unexciting, but the location a stone's throw from La Rambla is unbeatable.

H1898
NEW *La Rambla 109 (00 34 93 552 95 52/www.nnhotels.es). Metro Plaça Catalunya.* €€€€.
A dapper new hotel in a splendid 19th-century building, famously the former Philippine Tobacco Company headquarters. Rooms are subject to Henley Regatta-type colour schemes; one floor is all perky green and white stripes, another is red and white, and so on. The more expensive rooms have generously sized wooden-decked terraces, while some of the suites have private plunge pools. All guests can use the spa, gym and indoor and outdoor pools.

Hostal Fontanella
Via Laietana 71, 2° (telephone/fax 93 317 59 43/www.hostalfontanella.com). Metro Urquinaona. €€.

ESSENTIALS

Unremarkable – aside from a splendid Modernista lift – but more than adequate, this 11-room *hostal* has got enough chintz, lace and dried flowers to give even Laura Ashley a serious run for her money. The downside of the Fontanella's central location is that outward-facing rooms are abuzz with the sound of busy traffic. However, it's a clean and comfortable place to stay, and double-glazing has recently been installed.

Hostal Jardí

Plaça Sant Josep Oriol 1 (93 301 59 00/ fax 93 342 57 33). **€€**.
The Hostal Jardí offers somewhat spartan accommodation but is located in an excellent central position within the Barri Gòtic. The decor is rather clinical (make sure you avoid, especially, the dark *interior* rooms), but the rooms are all kept clean, and they all have en suite bathrooms. The best, which are certainly worth the extra expense, have balconies overlooking the pretty *plaça*.

Hostal Lausanne

Avda Portal de l'Àngel 24, 1° 1ª (telephone/fax 93 302 11 39). Metro Catalunya. **€**.
Situated on one of downtown Barcelona's busiest shopping streets, this *hostal* occupies the first floor of a fine old building. Of the 17 basic rooms, four have en suite bathrooms. Furniture is dated, but it's a friendly and safe place, with a fun backpacker vibe. The street is as quiet at night as it is busy during the day.

Hostal Maldà

C/Pi 5, 1° 1ª (93 317 30 02). Metro Liceu. **€**.
Once you've found the entrance (in a shopping arcade), negotiated several flights of stairs, you'll discover that this friendly *hostal* harbours a startling number of rooms (around 30) in the architectural equivalent of Mary Poppins's handbag. Some of the rooms are small and pretty gloomy, and only one room has (very basic) en suite facilities, but at these prices, you weren't expecting any frills, right?

Hostal Noya

La Rambla 133, 1° (93 301 48 31). Metro Catalunya. **€**.
This cheerful cheapo has a smiling *mamá* on hand to greet you, fake ferns in the doorways and handsome old tiles on the floor. The lone bathroom is white, weathered and worn, and can get busy since it's shared between 12 rooms (there is a separate WC), but all bedrooms do have their own sinks.

Hostal Rembrandt

C/Portaferrissa 23, pral 1ª (telephone/fax 93 318 10 11/www. hostalrembrandt.com). Metro Liceu. **€**.
A charming 28-room *hostal*: fairly stylish (for the price) with lots of wood panelling and soft lighting. An added bonus is the pretty interior courtyard, which makes for a pleasant chill-out zone/eating area. Rooms out front can be a little noisy.

Hotel Colón

Avda Catedral 7 (93 301 14 04/fax 93 317 29 15/www.hotelcolon.es). Metro Jaume I. **€€€**.
With its chintzy furnishings, thick carpets and walls bedecked in bright floral prints, the Colón is not the most trendy hotel, but it's eminently dependable. Its great location, on the square in front of the cathedral, is best enjoyed in the rooms that overlook the magnificent Gothic edifice, some of which have balconies.

Hotel Le Meridien Barcelona

La Rambla 111 (93 318 62 00/fax 93 301 77 76/www.barcelona.lemeridien. com). Metro Liceu. **€€€€**.
An elegant and genteel hotel, Le Meridien is famed for having the best (and most expensive) suites in town, and therefore draws an accordingly star-studded clientele. Despite its size (it has 233 rooms), it manages to retain an air of intimacy thanks to its helpful, friendly staff. Renovations have included new wood floors and leather furnishings, along with Egyptian cotton bedlinen, rain showers and plasma-screen TVs.

Pampering and panoramas

Six Senses Spa

As the success of the city's bid to attract a better class of tourist than the stag-party animals and besuited conference-goers of yesteryear becomes all too clear, the swishest of its hotels have adapted to the demands of the weary jet set.

The Six Senses Spa sits high on the 43rd floor of the **Hotel Arts** (p170), offering dazzling views of the big blue from its black marble, his and hers wet-rooms, complete with jacuzzi, fiendishly hot Finnish sauna and eye-watering 'ice shower' for a seriously stimulating scrubdown. Luxury treatments based on organic lotions and potions include hot stones and four-handed massages, while the post-pamper lounges are havens of calm, with ginger tea, fruit and magazines to complement yet more stunning views.

With equally breathtaking views, but further from the centre, the **Gran Hotel La Florida** (p176) is for those who like a little isolation. The L-shaped, indoor-outdoor steel infinity pool is reason enough for a

visit, but there's also a supremely well appointed Turkish bath as well as a stack of high-class beauty treatments. Finish a virtuous detox chilling on a sofa with a Mai Tai in one hand.

The much anticipated Spaciomm at the **Hotel Omm** (p173) is finally open, with Zen-like natural decor in wood, stone, iron and coconut matting. Personalised sessions follow a consultation and include specialist treatments such as a Tibetan facial to cure headaches, and shiatsu or reflexogy for pre menstrual tension.

Finally, the Metropolitan spa in Richard Roger's newly opened **Hesperia Tower** (see box p168) is the biggest in town, covering a whopping 4,000sq m (43,000sq ft). As well as offering personal training and an Olympic-sized swimming pool, it has state-of-the-art aqua spa circuits including Turkish baths, water beds and neck jets, while the beauty spa specialises in stimulating facial and body treatments to shave off the years and pounds.

Hotel Neri

*C/Sant Sever 5 (93 304 06 55/fax
93 304 03 37/www.hotelneri.com).
Metro Jaume I.* €€€.

A handsome boutique hotel, in a former
18th-century palace. The lobby, which
teams flagstone floors and wooden
beams with funky designer fixtures,
red velvet and lashings of gold leaf,
gives a taste of what's to come in the 22
rooms, where neutral tones, natural
materials and rustic finishes (untreated
wood and unpolished marble) stand
in stylishly orchestrated contrast with
satins, velvets and high-tech perks
(hi-fis, plasma-screen TVs).

Hotel Nouvel

*C/Santa Anna 20 (93 301 82 74/fax
93 301 83 70/www.hotelnouvel.com).
Metro Catalunya.* €€€.

Opened in 1917, the Nouvel has bags
of old-world charm. Guestrooms don't
quite live up to the lobby, which features carriage lanterns, ornately
embossed ceilings and curved wooden
fittings. But they are airy, comfortable
and decorated in a neutral classic style,
with spacious bathrooms, a few of
which preserve the original tiled floors.
The rooms on the top floor are the
brightest and most luxurious.

Hotel Oriente

*La Rambla 45 47 (93 302 25 58/
fax 93 412 38 19/www.husa.es).
Metro Liceu.* €€€.

It was inaugurated as Barcelona's first
'grand hotel' in 1842, but the Oriente
has been fairly ordinary for a number
of years, though a renovation has
brightened things up. All rooms now
have pale wood floors, minimalist
design and sleek electrical gadgetry, in
striking contrast to the ritzy old-world
ballroom and dining room. Sadly, no
amount of renovation can do away
with the noise from La Rambla; light
sleepers should ask for a room at the
back of the hotel.

Hotel Rivoli Ramblas

*La Rambla 128 (93 481 76 76/fax
93 317 50 53/www.rivolihotels.com).
Metro Catalunya or Liceu.* €€€.

Hotel Neri

The peaceful Rivoli is a world apart
from the bustle outside. The rooms are
comfortable and classy, and sound-
proofed windows block out most of the
noise in the ones facing La Rambla. The
Blue Moon cocktail bar is a slick place
to start or end an evening, and guests
have use of the rooftop pool and terrace
across the street at Hotel Ambassador.
Discounts are frequently given.

H10 Racó del Pi

*C/Pi 7 (93 342 61 90/fax 93 342 61 91/
www.h10.es). Metro Liceu.* €€€.

Part of the H10 chain, Racó del Pi offers
spacious rooms with parquet floors,
handsome terracotta-tiled bathrooms
and an elegant glass conservatory on
the ground floor. It can be a bargain out
of season, when rates can be substan-
tially cheaper than those given here.
Check their website for details.

Pensión Hostal Mari-Luz

*C/Palau 4 (phone/fax 93 317 34 63/
www.pensionmariluz.com). Metro
Jaume I or Liceu.* €.

You'll have to climb several flights of
a grand stone staircase to reach the

ESSENTIALS

Grand Hotel Central

Mari-Luz, but the effort is well worth it for the smiling service and the cosy atmosphere. Stripped wood doors and old floor tiles add character to the otherwise plain but quiet rooms, some of which face a plant-filled inner courtyard. There are dorms as well as some double and triple rooms (No.4 and No.6 have good en suite bathrooms).

Born & Sant Pere

Banys Orientals
C/Argenteria 37 (93 268 84 60/fax 93 268 84 61/www.hotelbanysorientals. com). Metro Jaume I. €€€.
Banys Orientals remains one of the best deals in town. It exudes cool, from its location at the heart of the Born to the deeply stylish shades-of-grey minimalism of its rooms, and touches such as free mineral water on the landings. The downside is the smallish size of some of the double rooms. Plans to create a luxurious new service by tapping into the eponymous thermal baths that lie underneath the hotel are in the pipeline.

Grand Hotel Central
NEW *Via Laietana 30 (00 34 93 295 79 00/grandhotelcentral.com). Metro Jaume I.* €€€€.
Another of the recent wave of hotels in the city to adhere to the unwritten code that grey is the new black. The shadowy, Hitchcockian corridors of the Grand Hotel Central open on to sleek and well-appointed rooms with flat-screen TVs, DVD players and Molton Brown toiletries, but the real charm of the hotel lies on its roof. Here you can sip a cocktail while you admire simply fabulous views from the vertiginous infinity pool.

Pensión Francia
C/Rera de Palau 4 (93 319 03 76). Metro Barceloneta. €.
The only frills at Pensión Francia are on the bedspreads: many of the 18 simple, spotless rooms are very small, particularly the singles. Some have a shower, sink and toilet; others have one or more of these facilities outside the room. On the plus side, staff are amiable and the location, just off a lively square, is excellent. Rooms are spread over two upper floors; there's no lift.

Pensió 2000
C/Sant Pere Més Alt 6, 1° (93 310 74 66/fax 93 319 42 52/www.pension 2000.com). Metro Urquinaona. €€.
One of Barcelona's best-value *pensiones* opposite the Palau de la Música.

Only two of its six bright and airy rooms are en suite, but the communal facilities are truly sparkling. With tall windows, buttercup-yellow walls and a lounge peppered with books and toys, it's a cheery sunbeam of a place, with a relaxed atmosphere. The large rooms also make it a good bet for holidaying families.

Raval

Casa Camper

C/Elisabets 11 (93 342 62 80/fax 93 342 75 63/www.casacamper.com). Metro Catalunya. €€€.
Another of the Mallorcan footwear giant's diversification ventures, this is a holistic concept-fest of a boutique hotel where Mediterranean simplicity meets contemporary cool. High-tech features (including plasma TVs, DVDs and CD players) and quirky touches (a healthy snack and breakfast included in the room rate; hammocks; and specially designed bicycles available for rent at €15/day) are underscored by functionality and environmental awareness, though the starkness of its rooms won't be to everybody's tastes.

Hostal Gat Raval

C/Joaquin Costa 44, 2ª (93 481 66 70/fax 93 342 66 97/www.gat accommodation.com). Metro Universital. €€.
Gat Raval embodies everything that 21st-century budget accommodation should be: smart, clean and funky, with bright, sunshiney rooms that each boast a work by a local artist. Some rooms have balconies while others have views of the MACBA. Nearly all the bathrooms are communal (though they are very clean).

Hostal Gat Xino

C/Hospital 155 (93 324 88 33/ www.gataccommodation.com). Metro Sant Antoni. €€.
Added extras in the newest member of the Gat family include a bright, breezy breakfast room with apple-green polka dot walls, a wood-decked patio and a sprawling roof terrace, its fate yet undecided. There's more bright green in the bedrooms (all of which are en suite) with comfortable beds, crisp white linen and flat-screen TVs. The best rooms have small terraces.

Hostal La Terrassa

C/Junta de Comerç 11 (93 302 51 74/ fax 93 301 21 88). Metro Liceu. €.
Clean, friendly and, above all, cheap, La Terrassa is a typical backpackers' joint; it's also the top choice, it would appear, for travelling skateboarders. There's no air-conditioning, but all the rooms have fans. It's child-friendly, and there's a scruffy terrace at the back of the building, which is perfect for soaking up the sun while making new friends over a refreshing beer.

Hostal-Residencia Ramos

C/Hospital 36 (93 302 07 23/fax 93 302 04 30/www.hostalramos.com). Metro Liceu. €€.
This family-run hostal offers one of the best deals in the Raval. There's no air-conditioning, but plenty of windows and balconies keep it cool. Rooms (all en suite) are basic, but light and airy. The best rooms have balconies looking on to the plaça, though not for the faint-hearted, as they can get quite noisy.

Hosteria Grau

C/Ramelleres 27 (93 301 81 35/fax 93 317 68 25/www.hostalgrau.com). Metro Catalunya. €€.
This charming, family-run hostal oozes character, with a tiled spiral staircase and fabulous 1970s-style communal areas. The open fireplace is a luxury if you visit in the winter. Rooms are basic, comfortable and fairly quiet. If you're after self-catering accommodation, the family also has apartments that are available for rent.

Hotel Ambassador

C/Pintor Fortuny 13 (93 342 61 80/fax 93 302 79 77/www.rivolihotels.com). Metro Catalunya. €€€€.
The four-star Ambassador slipped into relative obscurity after the 1992 Olympics, which is odd because it's one

ESSENTIALS

High times

Richard Rogers brings a little glamour to the 'burbs.

The **Hesperia Tower** (p176) is unpromisingly located on the side of a motorway, on a unkempt housing estate miles from the centre of town (aka the 'new financial district' if you believe everything you read) and with the airport as its only nearby tourist attraction. It would not seem, perhaps, the most auspicious beginning for a five-star landmark hotel. But thanks to its impeccable design and architectural credentials, courtesy of Richard Rogers, it has already been earmarked by the travel glamorati as the next destination stop-over, with folks booking in from all over the globe to experience the wonders of Barcelona's newest skyscraper.

The rooms are spacious and plush with plummy wine colours, splashes of gold and immense floor-to-ceiling windows providing knuckle-biting views down on to the matchstick world below. But on top of some inspiring interiors, what the Hesperia Tower does really well is facilities, which range from the Metropolitan spa – the most extensive in the city – to a state-of-the-art conference centre and auditorium. Indeed, there's a whole micro-city in there, with a Martini bar in the lobby, a casual-dining restaurant in the form of the wine-centric Bouquet, and a club lounge for those on expense accounts. If you want to razzle-dazzle 'em though, the 'hanging bar' with lift-only access is a true work of engineering genius and the perfect precursor to triple-starred chef Santi Santamaria's flying saucer, rooftop restaurant, which must surely rank as the most eye-popping in town.

Since the Tower is predominantly a business hotel, good weekend deals are there for the taking. And although there might not be much happening in the immediate area, there's plenty to keep the discerning traveller amused for a night or two without actually needing to leave.

■ www.hesperia-tower.com

of the nicest hotels in the area. It's recently been refurbished, and now boasts a heady blend of water features, gold paint and smoked glass, a glittering colossus of a chandelier and a free-standing Modernista bar that dominates the lounge area. Rooms are sleek and comfortable; there's also a pool and a jacuzzi on the rooftop.

Hotel España
C/Sant Pau 9-11 (93 318 17 58/fax 93 317 11 34/www.hotelespanya.com). Metro Liceu. **€€€**.
The lower floors at this Modernista landmark were designed by architect Domènechi Montaner in 1902. The main restaurant is decorated with floral tiling and elaborate woodwork; the larger dining room beyond it features extravagant murals of river nymphs by Ramon Casas. The bedrooms might disappoint after all this grandeur, but they have been considerably improved of late. All are en suite, and the better rooms open on to a bright interior patio.

Hotel Gaudí
C/Nou de la Rambla 12 (93 317 90 32/ fax 93 412 26 36/www.hotelgaudi.es). Metro Liceu. **€€€**.
In a nod to the great architect (the Palau Güell is right opposite), the Hotel Gaudí has a replica of the palace's roof in the lobby, but you can feast your eyes on the real thing if you book into one of the upper rooms with a small terrace. Rooms are cool and comfortable, and all have good-sized bathrooms.

Hotel Mesón Castilla
C/Valldonzella 5 (93 318 21 82/fax 93 412 40 20/www.mesoncastilla.com). Metro Universitat. **€€€**.
This chocolate-box hotel opened in 1952; before then, it was a private house belonging to an aristocratic Catalan family. Public areas are full of antiques and curious artworks, but the rooms are fairly uniform, with cosy soft furnishings to contrast with the tiled floors. The best have tranquil terraces, with a delightful plant-packed one off the breakfast room.

Hotel Peninsular
C/Sant Pau 34-36 (93 302 31 38/fax 93 412 36 99/www.hpeninsular.com). Metro Liceu. **€€**.
This colonial-style hotel is housed in a building that once belonged to Augustinian monks and spans several floors, with a breakfast cafeteria on ground level. The handsome, fern-filled interior patio is a great space for writing postcards, but the rooms have seen better days; if you opt for a cheaper room, with communal bathroom, expect the basics, though they do have air-conditioning and heating.

Hotel Principal
C/Junta de Comerç 8 (93 318 89 74/ fax 93 412 08 19/www.hotelprincipal. es). Metro Liceu. **€€-€€€**.
The Principal distinguishes itself by the wonderfully ornate furniture in its 120 renovated rooms, all of which have good bathrooms, and its sunny, communal roof terrace. Bedrooms are comfortable and boast the odd piece of very chintzy furniture. The best rooms are those facing the street (all with balconies).

Hotel Sant Agustí
Plaça Sant Agustí 3 (93 318 16 58/fax 93 317 29 28/www.hotelsa.com). Metro Liceu. **€€€**.
With its buff, sandstone walls and huge, arched windows looking on to the *plaça*, not to mention the pink marble lobby filled with forest-green furniture, this imposing hotel is the most handsome in the Raval and the oldest in Barcelona. Housed in the former convent of St Augustine, it was converted into a hotel in 1840. Rooms are nice, but there's no soundproofing.

Barceloneta

Grand Marina Hotel
Edificio World Trade Center, Moll de Barcelona (93 603 90 00/fax 93 603 90 90/www.grandmarinahotel.com). Metro Drassanes. **€€€€**.
For business people, this five-star hotel in the World Trade Center at the end of the pier in the Port Vell couldn't be

ESSENTIALS

more convenient, and its location – within easy reach of the Old City, yet isolated from its chaos – is also good for tourists. All the 278 rooms are spacious, with minimalist furnishings, jacuzzis and views over the sea or city. Facilities include a rooftop gym and pool, an elegant piano bar and a restaurant.

Hotel Arts

C/Marina 19-21 (93 221 10 00/fax 93 221 10 70/www.ritzcarlton.com). Metro Ciutadella-Vila Olímpica. €€€€.

The 44-storey, Ritz-Carlton-owned Arts has spruced up all its rooms, and still scores top marks for service. Plush robes, Bang & Olufsen CD players, sea views and a 'Club' floor for VIPs just some of the hedonistic perks awaiting guests. Even seasoned travellers are dazzled by the personal service, art-filled hallways and the city's only beachfront pool, which overlooks Frank Gehry's bronze fish sculpture. The luxury duplex apartments have chef services and round-the-clock butlers.

Hotel Duquesa de Cardona

Passeig Colom 12 (93 268 90 90/ fax 93 268 29 31/www.hduquesade cardona.com). Metro Drassanes or Jaume I. €€€.

This elegantly restored 16th-century palace is furnished in wood, leather and stone – complemented by a soft colour scheme that reflects the original paintwork. Cosy bedrooms make it the ideal hotel for a romantic stay, and if guests can't quite face the walk to the beach, they can take the lift up to the wood-decked roof terrace where they can sunbathe and cool off in the pool while taking in the amazing views.

Montjuïc

Hostal Restaurante Oliveta

C/Poeta Cabanyes 18 (93 329 23 16/ chesycar@yahoo.es). Metro Paral·lel. €.

These six diminutive and basic rooms, tucked away above a family-run bar-restaurant, are all modern and fresh, but renovation is nevertheless on the

cards for 2006. Bonuses include air-con in all rooms and 24-hour service from the bar downstairs. Only two of the rooms have en suite bathrooms, but communal facilities are squeaky clean.

Eixample

Hotel Astoria

C/París 203 (93 209 83 11/fax 93 202 30 08/www.derbyhotels.es). Metro Diagonal. €€€.

Built in 1954 and renovated in the 1990s, the 117 rooms here have undergone a recent slick facelift, though vintage features have been preserved. The classic lobby's domed ceiling is supported by columns and adorned with frescoed dolphins, while the bar is all marble floors, chandeliers and Chesterfield sofas. There's also a delightful room that features an antique pool table and vintage posters. Recent additions to the hotel are a sauna and rooftop swimming pool.

Hotel Atrium Palace

Gran Via de les Corts Catalanes 656 (93 342 80 00/fax 93 342 80 01/www. hotel-atriumpalace.com). Metro Passeig de Gràcia. €€€.

Housed in an attractive old building, this is a modern, light-filled and cutting-edge hotel with an unstuffy atmosphere. Rooms, decorated in a minimalist attire of creams and browns, narrowly sidestep sterility thanks to plenty of wood and token fresh flowers. Budget airline-style pricing strategies mean that rates are lower the earlier you book and, unusually, drop on weekdays.

Hotel Axel

C/Aribau 33 (93 323 93 93/fax 93 323 93 94/www.hotelaxel.com). Metro Universitat. €€€.

Behind the fetching Modernista façade is this funky boutique hotel for discerning gays (but everyone's welcome). The slinky lobby and restaurant set the scene, but bedrooms are lighter on the senses, with ivory walls, bleached flooring and the odd splash of colour. Functional modular furniture plays second fiddle to the mighty king-size

Hotel Astoria

beds, while plasma-screen TVs and hi-fis keep the technophiles happy. But the rooftop is where it's all happening, with a little pool, a jacuzzi, a bar and a relaxing sundeck.

Hotel Balmes

C/Mallorca 216 (93 451 19 14/fax 93 451 00 49/www.derbyhotels.es). Metro Passeig de Gràcia. €€€.
The star feature of this well-groomed three-star is its lush patio garden, which boasts a cute pool, a handful of tables and a discreet bar. Displays of African art, some duplex rooms and plant-filled interior patios are charismatic signature touches of the Claris family (see below, Hotel Claris). However, the chic but slightly out-moded rooms can be quite small and beds err on the short side.

Hotel Claris

C/Pau Claris 150 (93 487 62 62/fax 93 215 79 70/www.derbyhotels.es). Metro Passeig de Gràcia. €€€€.
With its neo-classical exterior, plush antique furniture, eclectic art collection (the Claris holds the largest private collection of Egyptian art in Spain) and sleek steel and glass fixtures, it's little wonder that so many hold the

Claris dear. In the bedrooms, antique artworks and Chesterfield sofas sit alongside elegant modern installations, while Warhol prints liven up the East 47 restaurant. Sidle past the glorious rooftop pool to the bar, where a DJ will soundtrack your cocktail.

Hotel Condes de Barcelona

Passeig de Gràcia 73-75 (93 445 00 00/fax 93 445 32 32/www.condes debarcelona.com). Metro Passeig de Gràcia. €€€€.
The family-owned Condes is made up of two buildings that face each other on C/Mallorca at the intersection of Passeig de Gràcia. The north building occupies a 19th-century palace and has a plush dipping pool on the roof, where the terrace offers evening dining and jazz. In the newer building, rooms on the seventh floor have terraces and a bird's-eye view of La Pedrera. Lodgings range from comfortable standard rooms to themed suites that boast extras such as jacuzzis. For the new restaurant, Lasarte, see box p136.

Hotel Constanza

C/Bruc 33 (93 270 19 10/fax 93 317 40 24/www.hotelconstanza.com). Metro Urquinaona. €€€.
A stylish, boutique hotel that doesn't cost the earth. The lobby looks like the chill-out lounge of an exclusive night-club, with boxy, white sofas, dark wood and Japanese silk screens separating the breakfast room from the main area. Upstairs, wine-coloured corridors lead to sumptuous bedrooms, with dark wood, leather furnishings and huge pillows. Bathrooms are just as chic and go overboard on the toiletries. Rooms at the back are quietest, and some have their own private terraces.

Hotel Ginebra

Rambla Catalunya 1, 3° 1ª (93 317 10 63/fax 93 317 55 65). Metro Catalunya. €€.
The 12 rooms in this dusky old *hostal* are very reasonable, with old-fashioned floral decor and en suite bathrooms, but it's the central location on Plaça

Catalunya that's the real plus. Eight rooms have balconies looking over the city's hub, but sliding shutters inside the windows keep the din to a low buzz.

Hotel Inglaterra

C/Pelai 14 (93 505 11 00/fax 93 505 11 09/www.hotel-inglaterra.com). Metro Universitat. €€€.
The Inglaterra is surprisingly peaceful considering the hubbub filling the street outside. With blond wood hallways, and neat, minimalist bedrooms with meditative Japanese characters sunk into the walls, it's a simple and elegant place. Star features here include a leafy roof terrace and a comfortable living room and cafeteria. Guests may use the swimming pool at the Majestic (see below).

Hotel Jazz

C/Pelai 3 (93 552 96 96/fax 93 552 96 97/www.nnhotels.es). Metro Catalunya. €€€.
Rooms at the Jazz are decked out in neutral greys, beiges and black, softened with parquet floors, and spiced up with dapper pinstripe cushions and splashes of funky colour. Beds are roomy and bathrooms are super-sleek, with cool, polished black tiles. The latest technology comes naturally to this newbie, which boasts flat-screen TVs and wireless internet. A rooftop pool and sundeck top things off.

Hotel Majestic

Passeig de Gràcia 68 (93 488 17 17/fax 93 488 18 80/www.hotelmajestic.es). Metro Passeig de Gràcia. €€€€.
Behind a neo-classical façade lies a panoply of perks, such as a service that allows you to print a selection of the day's newspapers from all over the world. A rooftop pool and gym offer stunning views over the city, and the opulent guestrooms, decorated with classical flair, are impressive. The Drolma restaurant is one of the finest, and most expensive, in the city.

Hotel Omm

C/Rosselló 265 (93 445 40 00/fax 93 445 40 04/www.hotelomm.es). Metro Diagonal. €€€€.

Hotel Arts p170

The Omm is part space-age movie set, part feng shui lounge, offering everything the world's beautiful people could possibly need for a slick metropolitan getaway. The open-plan lobby is perfect for people-watching, while the rooftop plunge pool offers fabulous views of Gaudí's landmark buildings. Bedrooms are super-stylish with cool, natural materials, two bathrooms and every gadget imaginable, from high tech illumination to state-of-the-art hi-fis.

Hotel Palace

Gran Via de les Corts Catalanes 668 (93 318 52 00/fax 93 318 01 48/ www.ritzbcn.com). Metro Passeig de Gràcia. €€€€.
In its heyday, the Ritz, as this was called until recently, was peopled by the likes of Frank Sinatra, Ava Gardner and Salvador Dalí, who famously had a horse brought up to his room. It's looking a little the worse for wear these days, but it remains the grande dame of Barcelona's hotels; a bastion of old-school luxury, it sparkles with gilded edges and teardrop chandeliers. Other

notable features include open fireplaces, as well as mosaic 'Roman baths' and four-poster beds. The brand new junior suites are sleek and modern, for those who find this kind of grandeur oppressive. Chef Romain Fornell, the youngest person ever to be awarded a Michelin star, heads up the kitchen.

Hotel Podium

C/Bailén 4-6 (93 265 02 02/fax 93 265 05 06/www.nh-hotels.com). Metro Arc de Triomf. €€€€.
Attractively located behind an early 20th-century façade but essentially a business hotel, the Podium is worth checking for discounts at weekends and other off-peak times. The rooms are smart and comfortably equipped (with Playstations!); the rooftop funland includes a bar and, unusually, a pool big enough for swimming as opposed to just dipping.

Hotel Pulitzer

C/Bergara 6-8 (93 481 67 67/fax 93 481 64 64/www.hotelpulitzer.es). Metro Catalunya. €€€.
An unprepossessing façade reveals an impressive lobby that's stuffed with comfortable white leather sofas, a reading area that's overflowing with glossy picture books, a swanky bar and a restaurant. The rooftop terrace is a fabulous spot for a sundowner, with squishy loungers, scented candles and tropical plants. The rooms themselves are not terribly spacious, but are sumptuously decorated with cool elephant-grey marble (which is *very* now), fat fluffy pillows and kinky leather trim.

Hostal de Ribagorza

C/Trafalgar 39 (telephone/fax 93 319 19 68/www.hostalribagorza.com). Metro Urquinaona. €.
Pedro and his mother give this lacy one-floor *hostal* a very homely feeling, with flowers and plants, a cosy lounge and conversation on tap. Modernista elements jazz up the 11 simple rooms, four of which have en suite bathrooms. Most of the rooms face on to a big avenue and can consequently be noisy. (Interior rooms are quiet but devoid of

charm.) Room 106 is recommended for its light-filled gallery.

Hostal d'Uxelles

Gran Via de les Corts Catalanes 688, pral (93 265 25 60/fax 93 232 85 67/ www.hotelduxelles.com). Metro Tetuán. €€.
A delightfully pretty *hostal*, and a steal at the price. The angels above reception are a hint of what's to come: pine floors or Modernista tiles, cream walls with gilt-framed mirrors, antique furnishings and bright, Andaluz-tiled bathrooms (all en suite). Pastels rule and plush drapes hang romantically above the bedsteads. The best rooms have plant-filled balconies with tables and chairs. The second wing is housed in a building down the road.

Hostal Girona

C/Girona 24, 1° 1ª (93 265 02 59/fax 93 265 85 32/www.hostalgirona.com). Metro Urquinaona. €€.
This gem of an *hostal* is filled with antiques, chandeliers and oriental rugs. Simple rooms follow suit, with tall windows, pretty paintwork and tiled floors. It's worth splashing out on rooms in the refurbished wing, with en suite bathrooms, although rooms in the older wing are equally charming and some have en suite showers. Brighter, outward-facing rooms have small balconies overlooking C/Girona or bigger balconies on to a huge and quiet patio. Gorgeous and good value.

Hostal Goya Principal

C/Pau Claris 74, 1° (93 302 25 65/fax 93 412 04 35/www.hostalgoya.com). Metro Urquinaona. €€.
Its renovations now completed, this *hostal* represents excellent value. Upstairs guests have use of an airy TV room with free internet access, sofas and sleek palms, as well as a terrace. Bedrooms are done out in chocolates and creams, with comfy beds, chunky duvets and cushions. Bathrooms have a real Habitat feel – no bad thing – and on the whole, the Goya Principal puts other *hostals* of its ilk to shame.

the5rooms

Hostal San Remo

C/Ausiàs Marc 19, 1º 2ª (93 302 19 89/ fax 93 301 07 74/www.hostalsanremo. com). Metro Urquinaona. €€.
Staying in this bright, neat and peaceful apartment feels a bit like staying with an amenable relative. Friendly owner Rosa and her fluffy white dog live on site and take good care of guests. All seven of the rooms are equipped with air-conditioning, blue and white-striped bedspreads and modern wooden furniture; five have en suite bathrooms and most have a little balcony and double-glazing.

Market Hotel

NEW *C/Comte Borrell 68, Eixample (00 34 93 325 12 05/www.markethotel. com.es). Metro Sant Antoni.* €€.
The people that brought us the wildly successful 'Quinze Nits' chain of restaurants apply their low-budget, hi-design approach to this new hotel, singlehandedly filling the €60 to €100 accommodation gap in the process. The monochrome rooms, though not exactly huge, are comfortable and stylish for this kind of money and downstairs is a handsome and keenly priced restaurant typical of the group. The noisy dawn arrival of the stall-holders of the nearby Mercat Sant Antoni is the only drawback.

Prestige Paseo de Gràcia

Passeig de Gràcia 62 (93 272 41 80/ fax 93 272 41 81/www.prestigehotels. com). Metro Passeig de Gràcia. €€€€.
The Prestige Paseo de Gràcia was born when architect Josep Juanpere took a 1930s building and revamped it with funky and oriental-inspired minimalist design and Japanese gardens. Work in perks such as Bang & Olufsen plasma screen TVs, intelligent lighting, free minibars and even umbrellas in every room, add the effortlessly handsome 'Zeroom' lounge-cum-bar-cum-library, where expert concierges are always on hand, and you get Barcelona's ultimate designer boutique hotel.

Residencia Australia

Ronda Universitat 11, 4º 1ª (93 317 41 77/fax 93 317 07 01/ www.residenciaustralia.com). Metro Universitat. €€.
Maria, who is the owner of Residencia Australia, fled from Franco's Spain to Australia in the 1950s, and returned after the Generalisimo's death to carry on the family business and open this small, friendly, home-from-home *pensión*. There are just four cute rooms (one en suite); all are cosy and clean and simply done. There's a minimum two-night stay. The family also has two apartments nearby that can be booked if rooms are full.

the5rooms

NEW *C/Pau Claris 72 (93 342 78 80/fax 93 342 78 80/www.thefiverooms.com). Metro Catalunya or Urquinaona.* €€€.
A welcome new addition to Barcelona's rather dreary hotel scene, the5rooms is a chic and comfortable B&B, where the delightful Jessica Delgado makes every effort to make her guests feel at home. Books and magazines are dotted around the stylish sitting areas and bedrooms, and breakfast is served at any time of day. No questions asked. Jessica is also a very useful source of information on the city.

ESSENTIALS

Gràcia

Casa Fuster

Passeig de Gràcia 132 (93 255 30 00/
fax 93 255 30 02/www.hotelcasafuster.
com). Metro Diagonal. €€€€.

The Casa Fuster was designed by
Modernista Domènechi Montaner for
the aristocratic Fuster family. It has also
served as the home of Catalan poet
Salvador Espriu, as boutiques, a
chic café and a cinema. These days, the
96 opulent rooms have sleek, modern
designs, cutting-edge technology and
original architectural features. Suites
have king-size beds and wrought-iron
balconies, while rooms have flat-screen
TVs and remote-controlled lighting.

Hotel Confort

Travessera de Gràcia 72 (93 238 68
28/fax 93 238 73 29/www.medium
hoteles.com). Metro Diagonal
or Fontana. €€€.

The Confort is light-years ahead of
other two-star establishments, with 36
simple but smart modern bedrooms
with curvy light wood furnishings and
gleaming marble bathrooms. All the
rooms get lots of light, thanks to the
several interior patios. There's a bright
dining room and lounge, with a large
leafy terrace that makes a lovely
setting for a sunny summer breakfast
or a cool drink on a balmy night.

Other districts

Gran Hotel La Florida

Carretera de Vallvidrera al Tibidabo
83-93 (93 259 30 00/fax 93 259 30
01/www.hotellaflorida.com). €€€€.

The Florida reopened in 2003, with
lavish suites, terraces and gardens, an
outdoor nightclub and a luxury spa.
Perched atop Tibidabo, it offers brac-
ing walks in the hills and breathtaking
360-degree views, which culminate in
the jaw-dropping infinity pool. Getting
a cab to take you back from town at
night can be tricky: the free shuttle service only runs until 8pm in summer,
and earlier in winter (though this is
subject to change).

Hesperia Tower Hotel

Gran Via 144, L'Hospitalet de Llobregat
(93 413 5000/fax 93 413 50 10/
www.hesperia-tower.com). €€€€
See box p168.

Hotel Catalonia Barcelona Plaza

Plaça d'Espanya 6-8 (93 426 26 00/
fax 93 426 04 00/www.hoteles-
catalonia.com). Metro Espanya.
€€€€.

This monolithic business hotel has 347
rooms, which are spread over 11 floors,
and a range of services including an
on-site bank and travel agency. The
standard rooms are grey-carpeted feats
of blandness, though they're highly
comfortable and very well equipped.
There are stunning panoramic views
from the vantage point of the rooftop
swimming pool, even in winter, when
it dons a glass cover and is heated.

Hotel Guillermo Tell

C/Guillem Tell 49 (93 415 40 00/
fax 93 217 34 65/www.hotelguillermo
tell.com). Metro Fontana/FGC Plaça
Molina. €€€.

The 'William Tell' is a neat little
uptown three-star hotel with 61 trim,
comfortable and generally spacious
rooms each classically decked out in
ecru and sky-blue stripes. Located on
the periphery of the Zona Alta, it's only
a ten-minute walk to Gràcia or a short
metro ride to the city centre.

Petit Hotel

C/Laforja 67, 1° 2ª (93 202 36 63/
fax 93 202 34 95/www.petit-hotel.net).
FGC Muntaner. €€.

Located in the smart neighbourhood
of Sant Gervasi, this charming and
convivial B&B has four neat, fresh-
feeling bedrooms that are set around
a comfortable and softly lit lounge.
Although only two of the rooms are
en suite, all the others have large,
immaculately clean and modern bathrooms located outside each room. The
hotel's owners, Rosa and Leo, are
always happy to chat to guests and
provide insider information on the
city. Breakfast is served all day.

Getting Around

Arriving & leaving

By air

Aeroport de Barcelona

93 298 38 38/www.aena.es.
Barcelona's airport is at El Prat, just south-west of the city. Each airline works from one of the three main terminals (A, B or C) for all arrivals and departures. There are tourist information desks and currency exchanges in terminals A and B.

Aerobús

The airport bus (information 93 415 60 20) runs from each terminal to Plaça Catalunya, with stops at Plaça d'Espanya, C/Urgell and Plaça Universitat. Buses to the airport go from Plaça Catalunya (in front of El Corte Inglés), stopping at Sants station and Plaça d'Espanya. Buses run every 12-13mins, leaving the airport from 6am-midnight Mon-Fri and 6.30am-midnight on weekends, returning from Plaça Catalunya 5.30am-11.15pm Mon-Fri and 6am-11.15pm at weekends. The trip takes 35-45mins; a single is €3.60, a return (valid one week) €6.15. At night the slower, local 106 runs every 75mins between the airport (from 10.15pm) and Plaça d'Espanya (from 10.55pm). Last airport departure is 4.22am (from Plaça d'Espanya 3.50am).

Airport trains

A long overhead walkway between the terminals leads to the airport train station. Trains stop at Sants, Plaça Catalunya, Arc de Triomf and Clot-Aragó, all of which are also metro stops. Trains leave the airport at 13mins and 43mins past the hour, 6.13am-11.40pm Mon-Fri. Trains to the airport leave Plaça Catalunya at 8mins and 38mins past the hour, 5.38am-10.11pm Mon-Fri

(5mins later from Sants). Weekend times vary slightly, but there are still usually trains every 30mins, mostly leaving Plaça Catalunya at 11mins and 41mins past the hour. The journey takes 17-30mins and costs €2.30 one way (there are no return tickets). Be aware that tickets are only valid for 2hrs after purchase. A little-publicised fact is that the T-10 metro pass can also be used.

Taxis from the airport

The basic taxi fare from the airport to central Barcelona should be €18-€26, including a €3 airport supplement. Fares are about 15% higher after 10pm and at weekends. There is a 90¢ supplement for each large piece of luggage placed in the car boot. All licensed cab drivers use the ranks outside the terminals.

By bus

Most long-distance coaches (both national and international) stop or terminate at **Estació d'Autobusos Barcelona-Nord** (C/Ali Bei 80, 902 26 06 06, www.barcelonanord.com). The **Estació d'Autobusos Barcelona-Sants** at C/Viriat, between Sants rail station and Sants-Estació metro stop, is only a secondary stop for many coaches, though some international Eurolines services (information 93 490 40 00, www.eurolines.es) begin and end journeys at Sants.

By train

Most long-distance services operated by the Spanish state railway company **RENFE** run from **Barcelona-Sants** station, easily reached by metro. A few services from the French border or south to Tarragona stop at the **Estació de França** in the Born, near the Barceloneta metro but it's otherwise sparsely served. Many trains stop at **Passeig de Gràcia**, which can be the handiest for the city centre and also has a metro stop.

RENFE

National 902 24 02 02/international 902 24 34 02/www.renfe.es. **Open** *National* 5am-10pm daily. *International* 7am-midnight daily.
RENFE tickets can be bought at train stations, travel agents or reserved over the phone and delivered to an address or hotel for a small extra fee. They have some English-speaking phone operators.

Public transport

Although it's run by different organisations, Barcelona public transport is now highly integrated, with the same tickets valid for up to four changes of transport on bus, tram, local train and metro lines as long as you do it within 75 minutes. The **metro** is generally the quickest and easiest way of getting around the city. All metro lines operate from 5am to midnight Monday to Thursday, Sunday and public holidays; 5am to 2am Friday, Saturday. **Buses** run throughout the night and to areas not covered by the metro system. Local buses and the metro are run by the city transport authority (**TMB**). Two underground train lines connect with the metro but are run by Catalan government railways, the **FGC**. One runs north from Plaça Catalunya; the other runs west from Plaça d'Espanya to Cornellà. Two tramlines are of limited use to visitors.

FGC information

Vestibule, Plaça Catalunya FGC station (93 205 15 15/www.fgc.net). **Open** 7am-9pm Mon-Fri.

Other locations: FGC Provença (open 9am-7pm Mon-Fri, closed Aug); FGC Plaça d'Espanya (open 9am-2pm, 4-7pm Mon-Fri).

TMB information

Main vestibule, Metro Universitat, Eixample (93 318 70 74/www.tmb.net). **Open** 8am-8pm Mon-Fri.
Other locations: vestibule, Metro Sants Estació & Sagrada Família (both 7am-9pm Mon-Fri; Sants also open 9am-7pm Sat, 9am-2pm Sun); vestibule, Metro Diagonal (8am-8pm Mon-Fri).

Buses

Many city bus routes originate in or pass through the city centre, at Plaça Catalunya, Plaça Universitat and Plaça Urquinaona. However, they often run along different parallel streets, due to the city's one-way system. Not all stops are labelled and street signs are not always easy to locate. Most routes run 6am-10.30pm daily except Sundays. There's usually a bus every 10-15mins, but they're less frequent before 8am, after 9pm and on Saturdays. On Sundays, buses are less frequent still; a few do not run at all.

Board at the front and disembark through the middle or rear doors. Only single tickets can be bought from the driver; if you have a *targeta,* insert it into the machine behind the driver as you board.

Fares and tickets

Travel in the Barcelona urban area has a flat fare of €1.15 per journey, but multi-journey tickets or *targetes* are better value. The basic ten-trip *targeta* is the **T-10** (Catalan *Te-Deu*, Spanish *Te-Diez*) for €6.65, which can be shared by any number of people travelling simultaneously; the ticket is validated in the machines on the metro, train or bus once per person per journey. The T-10 offers access to all five of the city's main transport systems (local

RENFE and FGC trains within the main metropolitan area, the metro, tram and buses). To transfer, insert your card into a machine a second time; unless 75 minutes have elapsed since your last journey, another unit will not be deducted. Single tickets don't allow free transfers.

You can buy T-10s in newsagents and Servi-Caixa cashpoints as well as metro and train stations (from ticket office or machine), but not on buses.

Trams

Lines **T1**, **T2** and **T3** go from Plaça Francesc Macià, Zona Alta to the outskirts of the city. T1 goes to Cornellà via Hospitalet and Esplugues de Llobregat; T2 goes the same way, but contines further to Sant Joan Despí; and T3 runs to Sant Just Desvern. **T4** runs from Ciutadella-Vila Olímpica (also a metro stop), via Glòries and the Fòrum, on to Sant Adrià (also a RENFE train station).

All trams are fully accessible for wheelchair-users and are part of the integrated TMB *targeta* system: simply insert the ticket into the machine as you board. You can buy integrated tickets and single tickets from the machines at tram stops.

Tram information

Trambaix (902 19 32 75/www.tram bcn.com). **Open** 9am-2pm, 4-7pm Mon-Thur; 9am-2pm Fri.

Taxis

It's usually easy to find one of the 10,300 black and yellow taxis. There are ranks at railway and bus stations, in main squares and throughout the city, but taxis can also be hailed on the street when they show a green light on the roof and a sign saying *'lliure/libre'* (free) behind the windscreen. Information on taxi fares, ranks and regulations can be found at www.emt-amb.com.

Fares

Current rates and supplements are shown inside cabs on a sticker in the rear side window (in English). The basic fare for a taxi hailed in the street to pick you up is €1.30 (or €1.40 at nights, weekends and holidays), which is what the meter should register when you set off. The basic rates (eg 74¢/km) apply 7am-9pm Mon-Fri; at other times, including public holidays, the rate is 20%-30% higher. There are supplements for luggage (90¢), for the airport (€3) and the port (€2), and for 'special nights' such as New Year's Eve (€3), as well as a waiting charge. Taxi drivers are not required to carry more than €20 in change; few accept credit cards.

Radio cabs

These companies take bookings 24 hours daily. Phone cabs start the meter when a call is answered but, by the time it picks you up, it should not display more than €2.93 during weekdays and €3.66 at night, at weekends or public holidays.

Autotaxi Mercedes Barcelona *93 303 32 66.*
Barnataxi *93 357 77 55.*
Fono-Taxi *93 300 11 00.*
Ràdio Taxi '033' *93 303 30 33.*
Servi-Taxi *93 330 03 00.*
Taxi Groc *93 322 22 22.*
Taxi Miramar *93 433 10 20.*

Driving

Car & motorbike hire

Car hire is relatively pricey, but it's a competitive market so shop around. Check carefully what's included: ideally, you want unlimited mileage, 16% VAT (IVA) included and full insurance cover (*seguro todo riesgo*) rather than the third-party minimum (*seguro obligatorio*). You'll need a credit card as a guarantee. Most companies require you to have had

ESSENTIALS

a licence for at least a year; many also enforce a minimum age limit.

Pepecar *807 41 42 43, www.pepecar.com.*
Europcar *93 491 48 22, reservations 902 10 50 30, www.europcar.com.*
Motissimo *93 490 84 01, www.motissimo.es.*
Vanguard *93 439 38 80, www.vanguardrent.com.*

Parking

Parking is fiendishly complicated, and municipal police are quick to hand out tickets or tow away cars. In some parts of the old city, access is limited to residents for much of the day. In some old city streets, time-controlled bollards pop up, meaning your car may get stuck. Wherever you are, don't park in front of doors signed '*Gual Permanent*', indicating an entry with 24-hour right of access.

Pay and display areas

In effect from 2006, the Area Verde contains zones exclusively for residents' use (most of the old city), and 'partial zones' (found in Gràcia, Barceloneta and the Eixample) where non-residents pay €2.75 an hour with a two-hour maximum stay.

If you overstay by no more than an hour, you can cancel the fine by paying an extra €6; to do so, press *Anul·lar denúncia* on the machine, insert €6, then press *Ticket*. In areas denoted with an orange hand, the limit is an hour and the rate is €2.50. Some machines accept credit cards (MC, V); none accepts notes or gives change. For information, call 010.

Car parks

Car parks ('*parkings*') are signalled by a white 'P' on a blue sign. **SABA** (Plaça Catalunya, Plaça Urquinaona, Rambla Catalunya, Avda Catedral, airport and elsewhere; 902 28 30 80, www.saba.es) costs around €2.30/hr, while **SMASSA** car parks (Plaça Catalunya 23, C/Hospital 25-29, Avda

Francesc Cambó 10, Passeig de Gràcia 60, and elsewhere; 93 409 20 21, www.bsmsa.es/mobilitat) cost €1.60-€2.30/hr. The €5 fare at the **Metro-Park** park-and-ride facility (Plaça de les Glòries, Eixample, 93 265 10 47, open 4.30am-12.30am Mon-Sat) includes a day's unlimited travel on the metro and buses.

Towed vehicles

If the police have towed your car, they should leave a triangular sticker on the pavement where it was. The sticker should let you know to which pound it's been taken. If not, call 902 36 41 16; staff generally don't speak English. Recovering your vehicle within 4hrs costs €134, with each extra hour costing €1.75, or €17.50 per day. On top of this, you'll have to pay a fine to the police, which varies. You'll need your passport and documentation, or the rental contract, to prove it's your car.

Petrol

Most *gasolineres* (petrol stations) have unleaded (*sense plom/sin plomo*), regular (*super*) and diesel (*gas-oil*). Petrol is considerably cheaper in Spain than it is in most northern European countries.

Cycling

There's a network of bike lanes (*carrils bici*) along major avenues and by the seafront; local authorities are keen to promote cycling. However, weekday traffic can be risky, despite legislation that states that drivers must slow down near cyclists. No more than two bikes may ride side by side. There's information on cycling in Barcelona at www.bcn.es/bicicleta.

Al punt de trobada (bicycle hire)

C/Badajoz 24, Poblenou (93 225 05 85). Metro Llacuna. **Open** 9am-2pm, 4-8pm Mon-Fri; 9am-2pm Sat; 10am-3pm Sun.

Resources A-Z

Accident & emergency

The following lines are available 24 hours a day.

Emergency services *112.*
Police, fire or ambulance.
Ambulance/Ambulància *061*
In a medical emergency, go to the casualty department (*Urgències*) of any of the main public hospitals. All are open 24 hours daily.

Centre d'Urgències Perecamps
Avda Drassanes 13-15, Raval (93 441 06 00). Metro Drassanes or Paral·lel.
Hospital Clínic *C/Villarroel 170, Eixample (93 227 54 00). Metro Hospital Clínic.*
Hospital Dos de Maig *C/Dos de Maig 301, Eixample (93 507 27 00). Metro Hospital de Sant Pau.*
Hospital del Mar *Passeig Marítim 25-29, Barceloneta (93 248 30 00). Metro Ciutadella-Vila Olímpica.*
Hospital de Sant Pau *C/Sant Antoni Maria Claret 167, Eixample (93 291 90 00). Metro Hospital de Sant Pau.*

Pharmacies

Pharmacies (*farmàcies/farmacias*) are signalled by large green and red neon crosses. Most are open 9am 1.30pm and 4.30-8pm weekdays, and 9am-1.30pm on Saturdays. About a dozen operate around the clock, while more have late opening hours; some of the most central are listed below. The full list of chemists that stay open late (usually until 10pm) and overnight on any given night is posted daily outside every pharmacy door and given in the day's newspapers. You can also call the 010 and 098 information lines. At night, duty pharmacies often appear closed, but knock on the shutters and you'll be attended to.

Farmàcia Alvarez *Passeig de Gràcia 26, Eixample (93 302 11 24). Metro Passeig de Gràcia.* **Open** 8am-11pm Mon-Thur; 8am-midnight Fri; 9am-midnight Sat.
Farmàcia Cervera *C/Muntaner 254, Eixample (93 200 09 96). Metro Diagonal/FGC Gràcia.* **Open** 24hrs daily.
Farmàcia Clapés *La Rambla 98, Barri Gòtic (93 301 28 43). Metro Liceu.* **Open** 24hrs daily.
Farmàcia Vilar *Vestibule, Estació de Sants, Sants (93 490 92 07). Metro Sants Estació.* **Open** 7am-10.30pm Mon-Fri; 8am-10.30pm Sat, Sun.

Consulates

A full list of consulates is in the phone book under '*Ambaixades i consolats/Embajadas y consulados*'.

Australian Consulate *Plaça Gal.la Placidia 1-3, 1º, Gràcia. (93 490 90 13/fax 93 411 09 04/www.spain. embassy.gov.au). FCG Gràcia.* **Open** 10am-noon Mon-Fri. Closed Aug.
British Consulate *Avda Diagonal 477, 13º Eixample (93 366 62 00/fax 93 366 62 21/www.ukinspain.com). Metro Hospital Clínic.* **Open** Mid Sept-md June 9.30am-2pm Mon-Fri. Mid June-mid Sept 9am-1.30pm Mon-Fri.
Canadian Consulate *C/E de Pinós 10, Zona Alta (93 204 27 00/fax 93 204 27 01/www.canada-es.org). FGC Reina Elisenda.* **Open** 10am 1pm Mon Fri.
Irish Consulate *Gran Via Carles III 94, Zona Alta (93 491 50 21/fax 93 490 09 86). Metro Maria Cristina.* **Open** 10am-1pm Mon-Fri.
New Zealand Consulate *Travessera de Gràcia 64, 2º, Gràcia (93 209 03 99/ fax 93 202 08 90). Metro Diagonal.* **Open** 9am-2pm, 4-7pm Mon-Fri.
South African Consulate *Travessera de Gràcia 43, Zona Alta (93 366 10 25/93 366 10 26). FGC Gràcia.* **Open** 9am-noon Mon-Fri.
US Consulate *Passeig Reina Elisenda 23, Zona Alta (93 280 22 27/fax 93 205 52 06/www.embusa.es). FGC Reina Elisenda.* **Open** 9am-1pm Mon-Fri.

Credit card loss

Each of these lines has English-speaking staff and is open for 24 hours a day.
American Express 902 11 11 35.
Diners Club 901 10 10 11.
MasterCard 900 97 12 31.
Visa 900 99 11 24.

Customs

Customs declarations are not usually necessary if you arrive in Spain from another EU country and are carrying only legal goods for personal use. The amounts given below are guidelines only: if you approach these maximums in several different categories, you may still have to explain your personal habits.

- 800 cigarettes, 400 small cigars, 200 cigars or 1kg loose tobacco
- 10 litres of spirits (over 22% alcohol), 90 litres of wine (under 22% alcohol) or 110 litres of beer

If you are coming from a non-EU country or the Canary Islands, you can bring:

- 200 cigarettes, 100 small cigars, 50 regular cigars or 250g (8.82oz) of tobacco
- 1 litre of spirits (over 22% alcohol) or 2 litres of wine or beer (under 22% alcohol)
- 50g (1.76oz) of perfume
- 500g coffee; 100g tea

Visitors can also carry up to €6,000 in cash without having to declare it. Non-EU residents are able to reclaim VAT (IVA) on some large purchases when they leave.

Disabled travellers

Run by a British expat wheelchair-user who now lives in Barcelona, **www.accessiblebarcelona.com** is a useful resource.

Institut Municipal de Persones amb Disminució

Avda Diagonal 233, Eixample (93 413 27 75/www.bcn.es/imd). Metro Glòries or Monumental/56, 62 bus. **Open** 8.30am-2.30pm Mon-Fri.
The city's organisation for the disabled has information on access to venues, and can provide a map with wheelchair-friendly itineraries.

Transport

Access for disabled people to local transport still leaves quite a lot to be desired. For wheelchair-users, buses and taxis are usually the best bets. There is a transport information phone line (below), and transport maps, which you can pick up from transport information offices (pp178-9) and some metro stations, indicate wheelchair access points and adapted bus routes. For more, check www.tmb.net.

Centre d'Informació de Transport Adaptat

Information 93 486 07 52/fax 93 486 07 53. **Open** *Sept-July* 9am-9pm Mon-Fri; 9am-3pm Sat. *Aug* 9am-9pm Mon-Fri.
The TMB's disabled transport information department. English speakers are usually available.

Electricity

The standard current in Spain is 220V. Plugs are of the type that have two round pins. You'll need a plug adaptor to use British-bought electrical devices. If you have US (110V) equipment, you will need a current transformer as well as an adaptor.

Estancs/estancos

Government-run tobacco shops, known as an *estanc/estanco* (at times, just '*tabac*') and identified by a brown and yellow sign, are very important institutions. As well as tobacco, they will also supply postage stamps and envelopes, public transport *targetes* and phonecards.

Internet

There are internet centres all over Barcelona. Some libraries have internet points.

Bornet Internet Cafè

C/Barra de Ferro 3, Born (93 268 15 07/fax 93 511 45 10/www.bornet bcn.com). Metro Jaume I. **Open** 10am-10pm Mon-Fri; 3pm-10pm Sat, Sun. No credit cards.

There are ten terminals in this small café and six more for laptops. One hour is €2.60; but you're really paying for atmosphere.

easyEverything

La Rambla 31, Barri Gòtic (93 301 75 07/www.easyeverything.com). Metro Drassanes or Liceu. **Open** 8am-2.30am daily. No credit cards.

There are 330 terminals here and 240 at Ronda Universitat 35 (open 8am-2am daily). Buy credit from the machines; price then increases with demand.

Police

If you're robbed or attacked, report the incident as soon as possible at the nearest police station (*comisaría*), or dial 112. In the centre, the most convenient is the 24hr **Guàrdia Urbana** station (La Rambla 43, 092 or 93 344 13 00), which often has English-speaking officers on duty; they may eventually transfer you to the **Policía Nacional** (C/Nou de la Rambla 76, 091 or 93 290 28 49) to formally report the crime.

To do this, you'll need to make an official statement (*denuncia*). It's highly improbable that you will recover your property, but

you need the *denuncia* to make an insurance claim. You can also make this statement over the phone or online (902 10 21 12, www.policia.es; except for crimes involving physical violence, or if the author has been identified). You'll still have to go to the *comisaría* within 72 hours to sign the *denuncia*, but you'll skip some queues.

Post

Letters and postcards weighing up to 20g cost 29¢ within Spain; 57¢ to the rest of Europe; 78¢ to the rest of the world – though anything in a non-rectangular envelope costs more. Prices will normally rise on 1 Jan. It's usually easiest to buy stamps at *estancs* (p182). Mail sent abroad is slow: 5-6 working days in Europe, 8-10 to the USA. Postboxes in the street are yellow, sometimes with a white or blue horn insignia. Postal information is available at www.correos.es or on 902 197 197.

Correu Central

Plaça Antonio López, Barri Gòtic (93 486 80 50). Metro Barceloneta or Jaume I. **Open** 8.30am-9.30pm Mon-Fri; 8.30am-2pm Sat. **Other locations:** Ronda Universitat 23, Eixample; C/Aragó 282, Eixample (both 8.30am-8.30pm Mon-Fri, 9.30am-1pm Sat).

Poste restante

Poste restante letters should be sent to Lista de Correos, 08080 Barcelona, Spain. Pick-up is from the main post office; you'll need your passport.

Smoking

Laws were passed in 2006 that required all bars and restaurants over 100sq m (1,080sq ft) to have a non-smoking area; smaller establishments can elect to be non-smoking or not, but those that are not can no longer admit under-18s. Usually only upmarket hotels have non-smoking rooms or floors. Smoking bans in cinemas, theatres and on trains are generally respected, though smoking in banks, offices and on station platforms is still quite common.

Telephones

Normal Spanish phone numbers have nine digits; the area code (93 in the province of Barcelona) must be dialled with all calls, both local and long-distance. Spanish mobile numbers always begin with 6. Numbers starting 900 are freephone lines, while other 90 numbers are special-rate services.

International and long-distance calls

To make an international call, dial 00 and then the country code, followed by the area code (omitting the first zero in UK numbers), and then the number. Country codes are as follows: Australia 61; Canada 1; Irish Republic 353; New Zealand 64; South Africa 27; United Kingdom 44; USA 1. To phone Spain from abroad, you should dial the international access code, followed by 34, followed by the number.

Public phones

The most common type of payphone accepts coins (5¢ up), phonecards and credit cards. There is a multilingual digital display (press 'L' to change language) and written instructions in English and other languages. Calls to directory enquiries on 11818 are free from payphones, but you'll usually have to insert a coin to make the call (it will be returned when you hang up).

Telefónica phonecards (*tarjetas telefónica/targetes telefònica*) are sold at newsstands and *estancs*

(p182). Other cards sold at phone centres, shops and newsstands give cheaper rates on all but local calls. This latter type of card contains a toll-free number to call from any phone.

Time

Spain is one hour ahead of London, six hours ahead of New York, eight hours behind Sydney and 12 hours behind Wellington. In all EU countries clocks are moved forward one hour in early spring and back again in late autumn.

Tipping

There are no fixed rules for tipping in Barcelona, but locals generally don't tip much. It's fair to leave 5-10% in restaurants, but if you think the service has been bad, don't feel you have to. People sometimes leave a little change in bars: not expected, but appreciated. In taxis, tipping is not standard, but if the fare works out at a few cents below a euro, many people will round up. It's usual to tip hotel porters.

Tickets

FNAC (p131) has an efficient ticket desk on its ground floor: it sells tickets to theme parks and sights, but it's especially good for contemporary music concerts and events (it's also one of the main outlets for tickets to Sónar, p37). Concert tickets for smaller venues are often sold in record shops and at the venues themselves; check posters for further details. If you want to get tickets to the football, see the listings on p148.

Servi-Caixa – La Caixa
902 33 22 11/www.servicaixa.com.

Use the special Servi-Caixa ATMs (most larger branches of La Caixa have them), dial 902 33 22 11 or check the website to purchase tickets for cinemas, concerts, plays, museums, amusement parks and Barça games. You'll need the card with which you made the payment when you collect the tickets.

Tel-entrada – Caixa Catalunya

902 10 12 12/www.telentrada.com. Through Tel-entrada you can purchase tickets for theatre performances, cinemas (including the IMAX), concerts, museums and sights over the phone, online or over the counter at any branch of the Caixa Catalunya savings bank. Tickets can be collected from Caixa Catalunya ATMs or the tourist office at Plaça Catalunya (below).

Tourist Information

Oficines d'Informació Turística

Plaça Catalunya, Eixample (information 807 11 72 22/from outside Spain +34 93 285 38 34/www.bcn.es/www.barcelona turisme.com). Metro Catalunya. **Open** *Office* 9am-9pm daily. *Call centre* 9am-8pm Mon-Fri.
The main office of the city tourist board is underground on the Corte Inglés side of the square: look for big red signs with 'i' in white. It has information, money exchange, a shop and a hotel booking service, and sells phonecards, tickets for shows, sights and public transport. **Other locations**: C/Ciutat 2, Barri Gòtic; C/Sardenya (opposite the Sagrada Familia), Eixample; Plaça Portal Pau (opposite Monument a Colom), Port Vell; Sants station; La Rambla 115; cnr of Plaça d'Espanya and Avda Maria Cristina; airport.

Palau Robert

Passeig de Gràcia 107, Eixample (93 238 40 00/80 91/www.gencat.net/ probert). Metro Diagonal. **Open** 10am-7pm Mon-Sat; 10am-2.30pm Sun.

The Generalitat's lavishly equipped centre has maps and other essentials for the whole of Catalonia.

Centre d'Informació de la Virreina

Palau de la Virreina, La Rambla 99, Barri Gòtic (93 301 77 75/information 93 316 10 00/www.bcn.es/cultura). Metro Liceu. **Open** 10am-8pm Mon-Sat; 11am-3pm Sun. *Ticket sales* 11am-8pm Tue-Sat; 11am-3pm Sun.
The information office of the city's culture department, with details of shows, exhibitions and special events.

010 phoneline

Open 8am-10pm Mon-Sat.
This city-run information line is aimed mainly at locals, but it manages to do an impeccable job of answering all kinds of queries. There are sometimes English-speaking operators.

Visas

EU nationals and citizens of the US, Canada, Australia and New Zealand do not need visas for stays of up to three months. For EU citizens a passport or national ID card valid for travel abroad is sufficient; non-EU citizens must have full passports.

What's on

The main papers have daily 'what's on' listings, with entertainment supplements on Fridays (most run TV schedules on Saturdays). For monthly listings, see *Metropolitan* and freesheets such as *Mondo Sonoro* and *AB* (found in bars and music shops).

Guía del Ocio

This is a weekly listings magazine. Available at any kiosk, its listings aren't always up to date or accurate. You can also consult their website at www.guiadelociobcn.es.

ESSENTIALS

Spanish Vocabulary

Although many locals prefer to speak Catalan, everyone in the city can speak Spanish. The Spanish familiar form for 'you' (*tú*) is used very freely, but it's safer to use the more formal *usted* with older people and strangers (verbs below are given in the *usted* form).

Useful expressions

hello *hola*; good morning *buenos días*; good afternoon, good evening *buenas tardes*; good evening (after dark), good night *buenas noches* goodbye *adiós*
please *por favor*; very good/OK *muy bien* thank you (very much) (*muchas*) *gracias*; you're welcome *de nada*; do you speak English? *¿habla inglés?*; I'm sorry, I don't speak Spanish *no hablo castellano* I don't understand *no entiendo* what's your name? *¿cómo se llama?* Sir/Mr *señor (sr)*; Madam/Mrs *señora (sra)*; Miss *señorita (srta)* excuse me/sorry *perdón*; excuse me, please *oiga* (to attract someone's attention, politely; literally, 'hear me'); OK/fine *vale*
where is…? *¿dónde está…?* why? *¿porqué?*; when? *¿cuándo?*; who? *¿quién?*; what? *¿qué?*; where? *¿dónde?*; how? *¿cómo?* who is it? *¿quién es?*, is/are there any…? *¿hay…?* very *muy*; and *y*; or *o*; with *con*; without *sin;* enough *bastante* open *abierto*; closed *cerrado*; entrance *entrada*; exit *salida* I would like *quiero*; how many would you like? *¿cuántos quiere?*; how much is it *¿cuánto es?* I like *me gusta*; I don't like *no me gusta*
good *bueno/a*; bad *malo/a*; well/badly *bien/mal*; small *pequeño/a*; big *gran, grande*; expensive *caro/a*; cheap *barato/a*; hot (food, drink) *caliente*; cold *frío/a*; something *algo*; nothing *nada* more/less *más/menos*; more or less *más o menos* toilets *los servicios*

Getting around

a ticket *un billete*; return *de ida y vuelta*; the next stop *la próxima parada* left *izquierda*; right *derecha* here *aquí*; there *allí*; straight on *recto*; to the end of the street *al final de la calle*; as far as *hasta*; towards *hacia*; near *cerca*; far *lejos*

Time

now *ahora*; later *más tarde;* yesterday *ayer*; today *hoy*; tomorrow *mañana*; tomorrow morning *mañana por la mañana* morning *la mañana*; midday *mediodía*; afternoon/evening *la tarde*; night *la noche*; late night (roughly 1-6am) *la madrugada* at what time…? *¿a qué hora…?* at 2 *a las dos*; at 8pm *a las ocho de la tarde*; at 1.30 *a la una y media*; at 5.15 *a las cinco y cuarto*; in an hour *en una hora*

Numbers

0 *cero*; 1 *un, uno, una*; 2 *dos*; 3 *tres*; 4 *cuatro*; 5 *cinco*; 6 *seis*; 7 *siete*; 8 *ocho*; 9 *nueve*; 10 *diez*; 11 *once*; 12 *doce*; 13 *trece*; 14 *catorce*; 15 *quince*; 16 *dieciséis*; 17 *diecisiete*; 18 *dieciocho*; 19 *diecinueve*; 20 *veinte*; 21 *veintiuno*; 22 *veintidós*; 30 *treinta*; 40 *cuarenta*; 50 *cincuenta*; 60 *sesenta*; 70 *setenta*; 80 *ochenta*; 90 *noventa*; 100 *cien*; 200 *doscientos*; 1,000 *mil*

Days & months

Monday *lunes*; Tuesday *martes*; Wednesday *miércoles*; Thursday *jueves*; Friday *viernes*; Saturday *sábado*; Sunday *domingo* January *enero*; February *febrero*; March *marzo*; April *abril*; May *mayo*; June *junio*; July *julio*; August *agosto*; September *septiembre*; October *octubre*; November *noviembre*; December *diciembre*

Catalan Vocabulary

Catalan phonetics are significantly different from those of Spanish, with a wider range of vowel sounds and soft consonants. Catalans use the familiar (*tu*) rather than the polite (*vosté*) second-person forms very freely, but for convenience verbs are given here in the polite form.

Useful expressions

hello *hola*; good morning *bon dia*; good afternoon, good evening *bona tarda*; good night *bona nit*; goodbye *adéu*
please *si us plau*; very good/OK *molt bé* thank you (very much) (*moltes*) *gràcies*; you're welcome *de res*
do you speak English? *parla anglés?*; I'm sorry, I don't speak Catalan *ho sento, no parlo català*
I don't understand *no entenc* what's your name? *com es diu?* Sir/Mr *senyor (sr)*; Madam/Mrs *senyora (sra)*; Miss *senyoreta (srta)*; excuse me/sorry *perdoni/disculpi*; excuse me, please *escolti* (literally, 'listen to me'); OK/fine *val/d'acord* how much is it? *quant és?*
why? *perquè?*; when? *quan?*; who? *qui?*; what? *qué?*; where? *on?*; how? *com?*; where is...? *on és...?*; who is it? *qui és?*; is/are there any...? *hi ha...?/n'hi ha de...?*
very *molt*; and *i* or *o*; with *amb*; without *sense*; enough *prou* open *obert*; closed *tancat* entrance *entrada*; exit *sortida* I would like *vull*; how many would you like? *quants en vol?* I like *m'agrada*; I don't like *no m'agrada* good *bo/bona*; bad *dolent/a*, well/badly *bé/malament*; small *petit/a*; big *gran*; expensive *car/a*; cheap *barat/a*; hot (food, drink) *calent/a*; cold *fred/a* something *alguna cosa*; nothing *res*; more *més*; less *menys*; more or less *més o menys* toilet *el bany/els serveis/el lavabo*

Getting around

a ticket *un bitllet*; return *d'anada i tornada*; left *esquerra*; right *dreta*; here *aquí*; there *allí*; straight on *recte*; at the corner *a la cantonada*; as far as *fins a*; towards *cap a*; near *a prop*; far *lluny*; is it far? *és lluny?*

Time

now *ara*, later *més tard*; yesterday *ahir*; today *avui*; tomorrow *demà*; tomorrow morning *demà pel matí*; morning *el matí*; midday *migdia*; afternoon *la tarda*; evening *el vespre*; night *la nit*; late night (roughly, 1-6am) *la matinada*; at what time...? *a quina hora...?* in an hour *en una hora*; at 2 *a les dues*, at 8pm *a les vuit del vespre*; at 1.30 *a dos quarts de dues/a la una i mitja* (can also be referred to as quarters of the next hour: in this case, two quarters of 2); at 5.15 *a un quart de sis/a les cinc i quart*; at 22.30 *a vint i dos-trenta*

Numbers

0 *zero*; 1 *u, un, una*; 2 *dos, dues*; 3 *tres*; 4 *quatre*; 5 *cinc*; 6 *sis*; 7 *set*; 8 *vuit*; 9 *nou*; 10 *deu*; 11 *onze*; 12 *dotze*; 13 *tretze*; 14 *catorze*; 15 *quinze*; 16 *setze*; 17 *disset*; 18 *divuit*; 19 *dinou*; 20 *vint*; 21 *vint-i-u*; 22 *vint-i-dos, vint-i-dues*; 30 *trenta*; 40 *quaranta*; 50 *cinquanta*; 60 *seixanta*; 70 *setanta*; 80 *vuitanta*; 90 *noranta*; 100 *cent*; 200 *dos-cents, dues-centes*; 1,000 *mil*

Days & months

Monday *dilluns*; Tuesday *dimarts*; Wednesday *dimecres*; Thursday *dijous*; Friday *divendres*; Saturday *dissabte*; Sunday *diumenge* January *gener*; February *febrer*; March *març*; April *abril*; May *maig*; June *juny*; July *juliol*; August *agost*; September *setembre*; October *octobre*; November *novembre*; December *desembre*

Menu Glossary

Basics

Catalan	Spanish	English
una cullera	una cuchara	a spoon
una forquilla	un tenedor	a fork
un ganivet	un cuchillo	a knife
una ampolla de	una botella de	a bottle of
vi negre	vino tinto	red wine
vi rosat	vino rosado	rosé
vi blanc	vino blanco	white wine
una altra	otra	another (one)
més	más	more
pa	pan	bread
oli d'oliva	aceite de oliva	olive oil
sal i pebre	sal y pimienta	salt and pepper
amanida	ensalada	salad
truita	tortilla	omelette
(note: *truita* refers to either an omelette or a trout.)		
la nota	la cuenta	the bill
un cendrer	un cenicero	ashtray
bon profit	aproveche	enjoy your meal
sóc...	soy...	I'm a...
vegetarià/ana	vegetariano/a	vegetarian
diabètic/a	diabético/a	diabetic

Cooking terms

Catalan	Spanish	English
a la brasa	a la brasa	char-grilled
a la graella/planxa	a la plancha	grilled on a hot metal plate
a la romana	a la romana	fried in batter
al forn	al horno	baked
al vapor	al vapor	steamed
fregit	frito	fried
rostit	asado	roast
ben fet	bien hecho	well done
a punt	medio hecho	medium
poc fet	poco hecho	rare

Carn/Carne/Meat

Catalan	Spanish	English
bou	buey	beef
cabrit	cabrito	kid
conill	conejo	rabbit
embotits	embotidos	cold cuts
fetge	hígado	liver
garrí	cochinillo	suckling pig
llebre	liebre	hare
llengua	lengua	tongue
llom	lomo	loin (usually pork)
pernil (serrà)	jamón serrano	dry-cured ham
pernil dolç	jamón york	cooked ham
peus de porc	manos de cerdo	pigs' trotters
porc	cerdo	pork
porc senglar	jabalí	wild boar
vedella	ternera	veal
xai/be	cordero	lamb

Aviram/Aves/Poultry

Catalan	Spanish	English
ànec	pato	duck
gall dindi	pavo	turkey
guatlla	codorniz	quail
oca	oca	goose
ous	huevos	eggs
perdiu	perdiz	partridge
colomí	pichón	pigeon
pintada	gallina de Guinea	guinea fowl
pollastre	pollo	chicken

Peix/Pescado/Fish

Catalan	Spanish	English
anxoves	anchoas	anchovies
bacallà	bacalao	salt cod
besuc	besugo	sea bream
caballa	verat	mackerel
llenguado	lenguado	sole
llobarro	lubina	sea bass
lluç	merluza	hake
moll	salmonete	red mullet

ESSENTIALS

alvocat	aguacate	avocado
bolets	setas	wild mushrooms
carbassós	calabacines	courgette
carxofes	alcachofas	artichokes
ceba	cebolla	onion
cigrons	garbanzos	chickpeas
col	col	cabbage
enciam	lechuga	lettuce
endivies	endivias	chicory
espinacs	espinacas	spinach
mongetes blanques	judías blancas	haricot beans
mongetes verdes	judías verdes	French beans
pastanagues	zanahorias	carrot
patates	patatas	potatoes
pebrots	pimientos	peppers
pèsols	guisantes	peas
porros	puerros	leek
tomàquets	tomates	tomatoes
xampinyons	champiñones	mushrooms

rap	rape	monkfish
rèmol	rodaballo	turbot
salmó	salmón	salmon
sardines	sardinas	sardines
tonyina	atún	tuna
truita	trucha	trout

(note: **truita** can also mean omelette.)

Marisc/Mariscos/Shellfish

Catalan	Spanish	English
calamarsos	calamares	squid
cloïsses	almejas	clams
cranc	cangrejo	crab
escamarlans	cigalas	crayfish
escopinyes	berberechos	cockles
espardenyes	espardeñas	sea cucumbers
gambes	gambas	prawns
llagosta	langosta	spiny lobster
llagostins	langostinos	langoustines
llamàntol	bogavante	lobster
musclos	mejillones	mussels
navalles	navajas	razor clams
percebes	percebes	barnacles
pop	pulpo	octopus
sípia	sepia	squid
tallarines	tallarinas	wedge clams

Verdures/Legumbres/Vegetables

Catalan	Spanish	English
albergínia	berenjena	aubergine
all	ajo	garlic

Postres/Postres/Desserts

Catalan	Spanish	English
flam	flan	crème caramel
formatge	queso	cheese
gelat	helado	ice-cream
música	música	dried fruit and nuts served with muscatel
pastis	pastel	cake
tarta	tarta	tart

Fruita/Fruta/Fruit

Catalan	Spanish	English
figues	higos	figs
gerds	frambuesas	raspberries
maduixes	fresas	strawberries
pera	pera	pear
pinya	piña	pineapple
plàtan	plátano	banana
poma	manzana	apple
préssec	melocotón	peach
prunes	ciruelas	plums
raïm	uvas	grapes
taronja	naranja	orange

ESSENTIALS

Index

ESSENTIALS

ESSENTIALS

Enjoy a real Irish pub in the **PORT OLIMPIC, BARCELONA**

Live music everyday at midnight*. Great bands playing covers, pop-rock, and Irish pub songs.
5 huge screens, **to enjoy all sporting events.***
*For timetable & information visit our website www.kennedybcn.com

KENNEDY IRISH SAILING CLUB
PORT OLIMPIC - BARCELONA
Open every day from 6.00 p.m. to 3.30 am

Where we are:

METRO L4 "Vila Olímpica" - TRAM T4 "Vila Olímpica"
BUS Line 10-157-36-45-57-59 -71-92 - Bus turistic "Vila Olímpica"

Moll Mestral 26-27-28, Port Olimpic - Barcelona - Spain
Tel. Number: +34 932 210 039 - e-mail: hello@kennedybcn.com

GUINNE

Selected and introduced by

HAROLD CLURMAN

FAMOUS
AMERICAN PLAYS
OF THE

1930s

THE LAUREL DRAMA SERIES

Published by Dell Publishing Co., Inc.
1 Dag Hammarskjold Plaza
New York, N.Y. 10017
Copyright © 1959 by Harold Clurman
Laurel ® TM 674623, Dell Publishing Co., Inc.

ISBN: 0-440-32478-5

Previous Dell Edition #2478
New Dell Edition

First printing—January, 1968
Second printing—February, 1970
Third printing—August, 1970
Fourth printing—November, 1971
Fifth printing—August, 1972
Sixth printing—May, 1973
Seventh printing—October, 1974
Eighth printing—October, 1975
Ninth printing—July, 1976
Tenth printing—October, 1977
Eleventh printing—October, 1978
Twelfth printing—April 1980

Contents

Introduction

There is a tendency nowadays to downgrade the thirties. The reason for this is that the prevailing mood of the thirties was what used to be called "left of center." Beginning with the late forties—from the time the phrase about the "iron curtain" became part of the common vocabulary—our "intelligentsia" sounded the retreat. The Roosevelt administration, subjected to sharp criticism not infrequently close to slander, seemed to be in bad odor. "Left of center" might be construed as something worse than liberalism. To be "radical" implied that one might be tainted with some degree of "pink."

A good many of the writers, artists and theatre folk in the thirties were inclined to radicalism. (Had not the Roosevelt administration sponsored the Projects for writers, artists and theatre?) In the early forties the fervor of the thirties was gradually absorbed by the pressures of the war. Since Russia was one of our allies there was less strictly political feeling: everyone was chiefly concerned with victory and the return to peaceful prosperity.

Shortly after the peace conference suspicion of the Soviet Union increased. Radicalism of any sort might be interpreted as "softness" toward the potential enemy. Our artists and writers, including theatre people, had not only shown too much sympathy for social experiment but had also been too emphatic about the real or supposed shortcomings of their own country. At best the enthusiasm of the thirties was now considered a sign of juvenile simple-mindedness, at worst something close to treason.

Around the year 1953 this reaction to the thirties had come close to hysteria. Today there is certainly more calm but the notion that the thirties was a foolish period persists.

Presumably we are now far sounder in our thinking and work than we were then.

There is another aspect to the rather low esteem in which much of the dramatic work of the thirties is now held. The immediate past in the theatre always makes a poor impression. Writing about the twenties, which every student of our theatre history regards as a high point of the American theatre both in volume of activity and in achievement, Joseph Wood Krutch in the early thirties said that the record no longer seemed as bright as it once appeared. Very few of the best plays of that time would endure.

What most of us fail to note in this connection is that very few plays measured in the light of decades or generations have ever "endured." Shakespeare as we know Shakespeare is a nineteenth-century discovery! (He was neglected or disgracefully altered during the seventeenth and eighteenth centuries.) The number of plays which have come down to us from the Greeks of the fifth century B.C. and from the Elizabethan era are a paltry few compared to the number produced. How cavalier was the attitude of our drama critics toward Marlowe's *Tamburlaine* because he was not equal to Shakespeare!

We may explain this paradox through our own theatregoing experience. A play may be both enjoyable and important to us at the moment we see it, but when the circumstances of our lives have changed, it may well have lost its appeal. One of the most popular plays the American theatre has ever produced is the dramatization of *Uncle Tom's Cabin*. No one can deny its importance for its day even if we no longer have much regard for it as literature.

It is downright stupid to sneer at our erstwhile excitement over *Waiting for Lefty* because today a good many people (in Europe at any rate) are waiting for Godot. As theatre-goers we are very rarely able to estimate a play in the present as we shall view it twenty-five years hence. What appeared a very inconsiderable play to England's finest dramatic critic, Bernard Shaw, Oscar Wilde's *The Importance of Being Earnest*, has proved durable beyond anyone's belief when it was first presented.

I recall having seen Robert Sherwood's *The Petrified Forest* (1935) in the company of one of our country's most astute men of letters. He enjoyed it thoroughly. A few days later we spoke on the phone. He remarked that the theatre was a hoax: he had been "taken in" by the play as he watched it, he said, but on further reflection he realized the play's flaws in thought and plot. Most readers who are also playgoers are like that.

We enjoy the "show," but we *think* about the play. There is often a disparity of judgment between the two activities. For though we are intellectually aware that literature and theatre are not identical, we are prone to assume that the text of a play is equivalent to the texture of its production. But a play in the theatre communicates qualities beyond— sometimes, in a bad performance, less than—what we find on the printed page. Thus to evaluate the theatre of any period only with regard to its texts is a falsification.

The plays of the thirties sharpen certain tendencies that were already evident, and comparatively new, in the plays of the twenties. For the twenties, which may be said to represent America's second coming of age in literature (the first might be dated around 1850) and its true coming of age in the theatre, were marked by a rather harsh critical realism. What such men as Frank Norris and Theodore Dreiser had been saying about us in their novels began to be said somewhat more lyrically (though no less vehemently) in the plays of Eugene O'Neill. The theatre is ideologically almost always behind the times because it is a mass medium. It takes a while for people to acknowledge publicly what a few individuals may think and say privately.

It was the artistic pleasure of the twenties to deride, curse, bemoan the havoc, spiritual blindness and absurdity of America's materialistic functionalism with its concomitant acquisitiveness and worship of success.

Another marked feature of the theatrical twenties was the fact that plays which had previously satisfied audiences with the mere tracing of types (or stereotypes) began to strike them as increasingly hollow. Characters began to show their faces on the stage. Psychology was "introduced."

Men and women were no longer heroes or villains but "human," a mixture of contradictory traits. The standardized Puritanism typified by the old anti-vice societies became an object of scorn and ridicule.

The sentiment against war in *What Price Glory?* of the twenties was converted into the poignant and pointed satire of Paul Green's *Johnny Johnson* in the thirties. The sense of loneliness which informs O'Neill's pieces is rendered more acute and more general in Steinbeck's *Of Mice and Men* some ten years later. The plight of the colored people in the Heywards' *Porgy* or in Green's *In Abraham's Bosom* is intensified in John Wexley's *They Shall Not Die* in the thirties. The playful probing of Behrman's *The Second Man* in 1927 is given a social connotation in the same author's *Biography* and other of his later plays in the thirties. The laborer as a symbol of inner disharmony within the apparent health of the American commonwealth which we observe in O'Neill's *The Hairy Ape* (1922) becomes a leading theme on a more concrete basis in the thirties.

The most significant difference between the theatre of the twenties and that of the thirties is the emphasis in the later period on the social, economic and political background of the individual psychological case. The Wall Street crash of 1929, the Great Depression of the early thirties with its attendant scar of widespread unemployment, the hopeful attempt to remedy this bitter condition which ensued are the effective causes for the abrupt and drastic change.

The plays included in this volume are not all necessarily the "best" of the thirties, but all are representative. Space and other factors of publication permitting, I should certainly have included O'Neill's *Mourning Becomes Electra* (1931), an Irish play of Denis Johnston's, *The Moon in the Yellow River* (1932), Maxwell Anderson's *Winterset* (1935), Sidney Kingsley's *Dead End* (1935), Thornton Wilder's *Our Town* (1938), Robert Sherwood's *Abe Lincoln in Illinois* (1938), Lillian Hellman's *The Little Foxes* (1939).

Of the plays included one had to be the work of Clifford

Odets. Historically speaking he is the dramatist of the thirties *par excellence*. His immediate sources of inspiration, his point of view, his language, his import and perhaps some of his weaknesses are typical of the thirties.

I am not at all sure that *Awake and Sing!*, first presented by the Group Theatre on February 19, 1935, is the best of Odets' plays. The 1937 *Golden Boy* has a more striking story line and is more varied and personal in its meaning. But *Awake and Sing!* contains the "seed" themes of the Odets plays and indicates most unaffectedly the milieu and the quality of feeling in which his work is rooted. One might even go so far as to say that there is hardly another play of the thirties—except perhaps John Howard Lawson's *Success Story* (1932)— which so directly communicates the very "smell" of New York in the first years of the depression.

The keynotes of the period are struck in *Awake and Sing!* as never again with such warm intimacy. There is first of all the bafflement and all-pervading worry of lower middle-class poverty. This is conveyed in language based on common speech and local New York (including Jewish) idiom, but it is not precisely naturalistic speech, for Odets' writing is a personal creation, essentially lyric, in which vulgarity, tenderness, energy, humor and a headlong idealism are commingled.

What is Odets' basic impulse; what is his "program"? They are contained in Jacob's exhortation to his grandson, "Go out and fight so life shouldn't be printed on dollar bills," and in another reflection, "Life should have some dignity." It seems to me that not only is most of Odets expressed in these bare words but the greater part of the whole cry of the American "progressive" movement—its radicalism if you will—as the artists of the thirties sensed it, is summed up in these innocent mottoes.

The "biblical" fervor in *Awake and Sing!* impels a "revolutionary" conviction expressed in Jacob's comment, "It needs a new world," which leads his grandson to take heart and proclaim, "Fresh blood, arms. We've got 'em. We're glad we're living." This was the "wave" of the thirties. If that wave did not carry us on to the millennium, it is surely the height of folly to believe that it had no vital force and accomplished nothing of value in the arts as well as in our community life.

S. N. Behrman's *End of Summer,* produced by the Theatre Guild on February 17, 1936, gives us the depression period seen from another angle: that of the "privileged" classes. It is a comedy of manners which besides its merits in the way of urbane dialogue, etc., presents a central character who (apart from having a decided semblance to the play's author) is kin to most of the folk who buy the best seats in our metropolitan theatres. Leonie, says Behrman, "is repelled by the gross and the voluptuary: this is not hypocrisy. . . . In the world in which she moves hypocrisy is merely a social lubricant, but this very often springs from a congenital and temperamental inability to face anything but the pleasantest and most immediately appealing and the most flattering aspect of things, in life and in her own nature."

What *End of Summer* presents is the spectacle of such a person confronted by the unhappy phenomenon of mass unemployment, nascent radicalism, spectres of fascism and the ambiguities of the psychoanalysts. The treatment is characteristic of Behrman—joshing, debonair, slightly more lighthearted than the author actually feels.

The lady of the play for the first time meets "the young radicals our colleges are said to be full of nowadays." One such radical, a somewhat fictitious Irish Catholic young fellow, tells the lady, "The world is middle-aged and tired," at which the lady queries, "Can you refresh us?" The young man rejoins, "Refresh you! Leonie, we can rejuvenate you." That was another hope of the youth which during the thirties had reached the ages of twenty-five to thirty-five. It was not altogether a vain hope for, as I have already indicated and shall continue to indicate, there was a young and invigorating spirit that relieved the thirties of its blues and led to concrete benefits.

One of the faults easily spotted in *End of Summer* is also evident in Robert Sherwood's *Idiot's Delight,* produced by the Theatre Guild in the spring of 1936. Just as the young radicals of Behrman's play seem to be known by hearsay rather than by intimate acquaintance, so in *Idiot's Delight*

Sherwood's grasp of the European political situation is informed as it were by headlines rather than truly experienced. Thus he makes his French pacifist a Radical-Socialist who speaks of the workers' uprising and alludes to Lenin with reverence, whereas any knowledgeable foreign correspondent could have told Sherwood that the Radical-Socialists of France are the party of small business, abhor Lenin's doctrines and are neither radical nor socialist.

This slight error is worth mentioning because it is symptomatic of a not uncommon failing in American playwrights when they generalize or "intellectualize" on social or ethical themes. It is a species of dilettantism which consists of dealing with subjects in which one is certainly interested but not truly familiar.

More cogent than this flaw is the sentiment which inspired Sherwood to write *Idiot's Delight*. It echoes the American fear of and profound estrangement from the facts of European intrigue which led to war. One merit of Sherwood's play is that it gives us an inkling of the moral climate in our country shortly after the Italian-Ethiopian conflagration and at the outset of the Spanish civil conflict—two omens of the future scarcely understood by an average citizen. Sherwood's "solution" to the problem in his play is the idealistic injunction "You can refuse to fight."

This is significant because it shows that the attitude of our dramatists, generally speaking, was fundamentally moral rather than, as some are now inclined to believe, political. This explains why Sherwood, whose *Idiot's Delight* might indicate the opposition to war of the "conscientious objector," took a very different stand when Nazism threatened to engulf Europe and the world. The play also marks the transition from skepticism and pessimism in regard to modern life, suggested by several of Sherwood's earlier plays, to the willingness to be engaged in political struggle and an acceptance of war, exemplified by his *Abe Lincoln in Illinois*.

Sherwood was a shrewd showman: *Idiot's Delight* gives striking evidence of this. He himself is supposed to have said, "The trouble with me is that I start off with a big message and end with nothing but good entertainment." *Idiot's Delight* was good entertainment, particularly in the acting opportunities it afforded Alfred Lunt and Lynn Fontanne, just as Leonie in *End of Summer*, in itself a charming characterization, was given special fragrance by Ina Claire's delightful talent.

John Steinbeck's *Of Mice and Men*, produced by Sam H. Harris on November 23, 1937, is a parable of American loneliness and of our hunger for "brotherhood"—two feelings the depression greatly enhanced. This play, unlike most of the others we have cited, concentrates on the unemployed of the farm lands, the itinerants and ranch workers, while it alludes to the bus and truck drivers whose travels through the country permitted them to observe the state of the nation in its broad horizon.

The American theatre, centered in New York, is on the whole cut off from the rest of the country. The thirties was the time when the theatre, along with the other arts, rediscovered America. *Green Grow the Lilacs* (1931) is one of the several Lynn Riggs Oklahoma plays, Erskine Caldwell's *Tobacco Road* (1933), Osborn's *Morning's at Seven* (1939)—to mention only a few—are among the many which in one way or another perform a similar function. One of the reasons why Steinbeck's parable carries conviction on naturalistic grounds is that the author shares the background and the earthiness of his characters.

Steinbeck knows our longing for a home, not a mere feeding place. He has the same true sympathy for the lonesome devil whose sole companion is a mangy old dog as for the Negro cut off by his fellow workers because of his color. He suggests with something iike an austere sorrow that America's "underprivileged" will never reach the home they crave till they arrive at greater consciousness.

Speaking of "austerity" I should point out that one of the ground tones of American art and theatre (particularly the latter) is sentimentality. This is also true of Steinbeck's play, though he tries to control his sentimentality. Now sentimentality is usually accounted a vice, because it bespeaks a propensity to express a greater degree of feeling than a specific situation warrants. But sentimentality need not be a vital flaw; it isn't in *Of Mice and Men*. It is often the characteristic of a young and vigorous people whose experience of life is, so to speak, still new and uncontaminated by too frequent disillusionment. In this sense our history makes us a sentimental people and it is only natural that our arts, particularly our folk arts, should reveal this quality.

This brings us to the last play of this volume: William Saroyan's *The Time of Your Life*, presented by the Theatre Guild in association with Eddie Dowling on October 25, 1939. This sentimental comedy is by way of being a little classic. It marks the deliquescence of the aggressive mood of the thirties. For though the moralistic and critical rationale of the thirties is still present in *The Time of Your Life*, it is there in a lyrically anarchistic manner, a sort of sweet (here and there mawkish) dream.

Another way, distinctly 1959, of describing this play is to call it pre-beatnik! "I believe dreams more than statistics," one character says. "Everybody is behind the eight ball," says another. Money appears as the root of most evil—anyway it is the filthiest thing that goes and "there's no foundation all the way down the line," as the old man from the Orient mutters throughout the play.

In a way *The Time of Your Life* is a social fable: it turns its head away from and thumbs its nose at our monstrously efficient society which produces arrogance, cruelty, fear, headaches, constipation and the yammering of millions of humble folk, only to conclude that "all people are wonderful." Though this evinces more bewilderment than insight, it is nevertheless honestly American in its fundamental benevolence.

What saves this play, or rather what "makes" it, is its infectious humor, its anti-heroism (an oblique form of rebelliousness), its San Francisco colorfulness, its succulent dialogue, its wry hoboism and nonconformity. Though it is of another time, one still reads it with a sense of relief.

No account of the theatre of the thirties can convey any sense of its true nature and its contribution to our culture without emphasizing certain purely theatrical factors which played as decisive a role as the plays themselves.

The importance of the Group Theatre (1931–1941), whose origins may be traced back to the late twenties, can hardly be overestimated. (The first unofficial "group" meetings were held in 1928.) The Group Theatre was important not alone because it developed Odets from among its acting members, or even because it presented Sidney Kingsley's first play, *Men in White* (1933), Saroyan's first play, *My Heart's in the Highlands* (1939) as well as various plays by Paul Green, John Howard Lawson, Irwin Shaw and Robert Ardrey, but also because it organized its actors as a permanent company and trained them in a common craftsmanship which not only became emblematic for the era but which in many ways influenced the course of our theatre practice in the ensuing years.

Among the actors, directors, producers, designers, teachers trained or brought into prominence by the Group Theatre were: Stella Adler, Luther Adler, Boris Aronson, Harold Clurman, Lee Cobb, Cheryl Crawford, Morris Carnovsky, John Garfield, Elia Kazan, Mordecai Gorelik, Robert Lewis, Lee Strasberg, Franchot Tone.

The Group Theatre in certain respects continued a tradition established by such pioneer organizations as the Provincetown Players, the Theatre Guild, the Neighborhood Playhouse. In another way the Group served as a model for such organizations as the Theatre Union, the Theatre Collective, the Theatre of Action, which were "workers' theatres" with a more specifically political orientation. These were valuable organizations, particularly the Theatre Union, offering vivid productions of social plays. Our theatre needs more such organizations (there are none at present) which commit themselves to definite ideals or policies rather than wallowing in hit-or-miss show-shop opportunism.

Far more important than these special organizations was the Federal Theatre Project (1935–1939). Its rudest critics will not deny the interest of such productions as the "Living Newspaper," *One Third of a Nation,* the Negro *Macbeth,* Marlowe's *Dr. Faustus,* T. S. Eliot's *Murder in the Cathedral,* and the attempted production of Marc Blitzstein's momentous musical play, *The Cradle Will Rock*—ultimately presented under different auspices.

The Federal Theatre Project brought much excellent theatre fare to a national public at nominal prices, a public the greater part of which was barely acquainted with any form of "live" theatre. This was the first government-sponsored theatre in our history and it indicated how beneficial such an effort could be, even when circumstances were far from favorable.

Orson Welles was given his first opportunity as a director under the Federal Theatre Project. Because of his success there he was enabled to establish (with John Houseman) the short-lived but animated Mercury Theatre which produced a remarkably provocative *Julius Caesar* in the spirit of the times (1937).

Looking back from the vantage point of 1959 we may say that although admirable work still continues to be done on our constantly harassed and considerably shrunken stage, there are two virtues which may be claimed for the theatre of the thirties conspicuously lacking today. The theatre of the thirties attempted to make the stage an instrument of public enlightenment through a passionate involvement with the national scene. It made valiant and, to a remarkable degree, effective efforts to bring order and discipline into the helter-skelter of our theatre's artistic and financial organization.

An intelligent and successful Broadway producer of today recently said to me, "The theatre at present is twenty times more 'commercial' than it was in the thirties. For one thing, you could reach the hearts and souls of actors, playwrights, designers, etc., with good sense and considerations of sound craftsmanship. Today these people, whatever their personal dispositions, appear encircled by an iron ring forged by agents who protect their clients from all thought beyond income, percentages and publicity."

The lean days and hungry nights of the thirties were a brave time. Aren't we a little torpid now?

HAROLD CLURMAN

AWAKE AND SING!

by Clifford Odets

For my Father and Mother

From *Six Plays of Clifford Odets.*
Copyright 1935 by Clifford Odets.
Reprinted by permission of Random House, Inc.

*First production, February 19th, 1935,
at the Belasco Theatre, New York,
with the following cast from the
Group Theatre Acting Company:*

MYRON BERGER, *Art Smith*
BESSIE BERGER, *Stella Adler*
JACOB, *Morris Carnovsky*
HENNIE BERGER, *Phoebe Brand*
RALPH BERGER, *Jules Garfield*
SCHLOSSER, *Roman Bohnen*
MOE AXELROD, *Luther Adler*
UNCLE MORTY, *J. E. Bromberg*
SAM FEINSCHREIBER, *Sanford Meisner*

*The entire action takes place in an apartment
in the Bronx, New York City.*

The Characters of the Play

All of the characters in Awake and Sing!
share a fundamental activity:
a struggle for life amidst petty conditions.

BESSIE BERGER, *as she herself states, is not only the
mother in this home but also the father. She is constantly arranging and taking care of her family. She
loves life, likes to laugh, has great resourcefulness and
enjoys living from day to day. A high degree of energy
accounts for her quick exasperation at ineptitude. She
is a shrewd judge of realistic qualities in people in the
sense of being able to gauge quickly their effectiveness.
In her eyes all of the people in the house are equal.
She is naïve and quick in emotional response. She is
afraid of utter poverty. She is proper according to her
own standards, which are fairly close to those of most
middle-class families. She knows that when one lives in
the jungle one must look out for the wild life.*

MYRON, *her husband, is a born follower. He would like
to be a leader. He would like to make a million dollars. He is not sad or ever depressed. Life is an even
sweet event to him, but the "old days" were sweeter
yet. He has a dignified sense of himself. He likes people. He likes everything. But he is heartbroken without being aware of it.*

HENNIE *is a girl who has had few friends, male or female. She is proud of her body. She won't ask favors.
She travels alone. She is fatalistic about being trapped,
but will escape if possible. She is self-reliant in the best*

sense. Till the day she dies she will be faithful to a loved man. She inherits her mother's sense of humor and energy.

RALPH *is a boy with a clean spirit. He wants to know, wants to learn. He is ardent, he is romantic, he is sensitive. He is naïve too. He is trying to find why so much dirt must be cleared away before it is possible to "get to first base."*

JACOB, *too, is trying to find a right path for himself and the others. He is aware of justice, of dignity. He is an observer of the others, compares their activities with his real and ideal sense of life. This produces a reflective nature. In this home he is a constant boarder. He is a sentimental idealist with no power to turn ideal to action.*

With physical facts—such as housework—he putters. But as a barber he demonstrates the flair of an artist. He is an old Jew with living eyes in his tired face.

UNCLE MORTY *is a successful American business man with five good senses. Something sinister comes out of the fact that the lives of others seldom touch him deeply. He holds to his own line of life. When he is generous he wants others to be aware of it. He is pleased by attention—a rich relative to the* BERGER *family. He is a shrewd judge of material values. He will die unmarried. Two and two make four, never five with him. He can blink in the sun for hours, a fat tomcat. Tickle him, he laughs. He lives in a penthouse with a real Japanese butler to serve him. He sleeps with dress models, but not from his own showrooms. He plays cards for hours on end. He smokes expensive cigars. He sees every Mickey Mouse cartoon that appears. He* is a 32-degree Mason. He is really deeply intolerant finally.

MOE AXELROD *lost a leg in the war. He seldom forgets that fact. He has killed two men in extra-martial activity. He is mordant, bitter. Life has taught him a disbelief in everything, but he will fight his way through. He seldom shows his feelings: fights against his own sensitivity. He has been everywhere and seen everything. All he wants is* HENNIE. *He is very proud. He scorns the inability of others to make their way in life, but he likes people for whatever good qualities they possess. His passionate outbursts come from a strong but contained emotional mechanism.*

SAM FEINSCHREIBER *wants to find a home. He is a lonely man, a foreigner in a strange land, hypersensitive about this fact, conditioned by the humiliation of not making his way alone. He has a sense of others laughing at him. At night he gets up and sits alone in the dark. He hears acutely all the small sounds of life. He might have been a poet in another time and place. He approaches his wife as if he were always offering her a delicate flower. Life is a high chill wind weaving itself around his head.*

SCHLOSSER, *the janitor, is an overworked German whose wife ran away with another man and left him with a young daughter who in turn ran away and joined a burlesque show as chorus girl. The man suffers rheumatic pains. He has lost his identity twenty years before.*

SCENE—*Exposed on the stage are the dining room and adjoining front room of the* BERGER *apartment. These two rooms are typically furnished. There is a curtain between them. A small door off the front room leads to* JACOB'S *room. When his door is open one sees a picture of Sacco and Vanzetti on the wall and several shelves of books. Stage left of this door presents the entrance to the foyer hall of the apartment. The two other bedrooms of the apartment are off this hall, but not necessarily shown.*

Stage left of the dining room presents a swinging door which opens on the kitchen.

> *Awake and sing,* ye that dwell in dust:
>   ISAIAH—26:19

Act one

TIME. *The present; the family finishing supper.*
PLACE. *An apartment in the Bronx, New York City.*

RALPH. Where's advancement down the place? Work like crazy! Think they see it? You'd drop dead first.

MYRON. Never mind, son, merit never goes unrewarded. Teddy Roosevelt used to say—

HENNIE. It rewarded you—thirty years a haberdashery clerk!

[*Jacob laughs.*]

RALPH. All I want's a chance to get to first base!

HENNIE. That's all?

RALPH. Stuck down in that joint on Fourth Avenue— a stock clerk in a silk house! Just look at Eddie. I'm as good as he is—pulling in two-fifty a week for forty-eight minutes a day. A headliner, his name in all the papers.

JACOB. That's what you want, Ralphie? Your name in the paper?

RALPH. I wanna make up my own mind about things . . . be something! Didn't I want to take up tap dancing, too?

BESSIE. So take lessons. Who stopped you?

RALPH. On what?

BESSIE. On what? Save money.

RALPH. Sure, five dollars a week for expenses and the rest in the house. I can't save even for shoe laces.

BESSIE. You mean we shouldn't have food in the house, but you'll make a jig on the street corner?

RALPH. I mean something.

BESSIE. You also mean something when you studied on the drum, Mr. Smartie!

RALPH. I don't know. . . . Every other day to sit around with the blues and mud in your mouth.

MYRON. That's how it is—life is like that—a cake-walk.

RALPH. What's it get you?

HENNIE. A four-car funeral.

RALPH. What's it for?

JACOB. What's it for? If this life leads to a revolution it's a good life. Otherwise it's for nothing.

BESSIE. Never mind, Pop! Pass me the salt.

RALPH. It's crazy—all my life I want a pair of black and white shoes and can't get them. It's crazy!

BESSIE. In a minute I'll get up from the table. I can't take a bite in my mouth no more.

MYRON [*restraining her*]. Now, Mamma, just don't excite yourself—

BESSIE. I'm so nervous I can't hold a knife in my hand.

MYRON. Is that a way to talk, Ralphie? Don't Momma work hard enough all day?

[BESSIE *allows herself to be reseated.*]

BESSIE. On my feet twenty-four hours?

MYRON. On her feet—

RALPH [*jumps up*]. What do I do—go to night-clubs with Greta Garbo? Then when I come home can't even have my own room? Sleep on a day-bed in the front room! [*Choked, he exits to front room.*]

BESSIE. He's starting up that stuff again. [*Shouts to him.*] When Hennie here marries you'll have her room—I should only live to see the day.

HENNIE. Me, too. [*They settle down to serious eating.*]

MYRON. This morning the sink was full of ants. Where they come from I just don't know. I thought it was coffee grounds . . . and then they began moving.

BESSIE. You gave the dog eat?

JACOB. I gave the dog eat.

[HENNIE *drops a knife and picks it up again.*]

BESSIE. You got dropsy tonight.

HENNIE. Company's coming.

MYRON. You can buy a ticket for fifty cents and win fortunes. A man came in the store—it's the Irish Sweepstakes.

BESSIE. What?

MYRON. Like a raffle, only different. A man came in—

BESSIE. Who spends fifty-cent pieces for Irish raffles? They threw out a family on Dawson Street today. All the furniture on the sidewalk. A fine old woman with gray hair.

JACOB. Come eat, Ralph.

MYRON. A butcher on Beck Street won eighty thousand dollars.

BESSIE. Eighty thousand dollars! You'll excuse my expression, you're bughouse!

MYRON. I seen it in the paper—on one ticket—765 Beck Street.

BESSIE. Impossible!

MYRON. He did . . . yes he did. He says he'll take his old mother to Europe . . . an Austrian—

HENNIE. Europe . . .

MYRON. Six per cent on eighty thousand—forty-eight hundred a year.

BESSIE. I'll give you money. Buy a ticket in Hennie's name. Say, you can't tell—lightning never struck us yet. If they win on Beck Street we could win on Longwood Avenue.

JACOB [*ironically*]. If it rained pearls—who would work?

BESSIE. Another county heard from.

[RALPH *enters and silently seats himself.*]

MYRON. I forgot, Beauty—Sam Feinschreiber sent you a present. Since I brought him for supper he just can't stop talking about you.

HENNIE. What's that "mockie" bothering about? Who needs him?

MYRON. He's a very lonely boy.

HENNIE. So I'll sit down and bust out crying " 'cause he's lonely."

BESSIE [*opening candy*]. He'd marry you one two three.

HENNIE. Too bad about him.

BESSIE [*naïvely delighted*]. Chocolate peanuts.

HENNIE. Loft's week-end special, two for thirty-nine.

BESSIE. You could think about it. It wouldn't hurt.

HENNIE [*laughing*]. To quote Moe Axelrod, "Don't make me laugh."

BESSIE. Never mind laughing. It's time you already had in your head a serious thought. A girl twenty-six don't grow younger. When I was your age it was already a big family with responsibilities.

HENNIE [*laughing*]. Maybe that's what ails you, Mom.

BESSIE. Don't you feel well?

HENNIE. 'Cause I'm laughing? I feel fine. It's just funny —that poor guy sending me presents 'cause he loves me.

BESSIE. I think it's very, very nice.

HENNIE. Sure . . . swell!

BESSIE. Mrs. Marcus' Rose is engaged to a Brooklyn boy, a dentist. He came in his car today. A little dope should get such a boy.

[*Finished with the meal,* BESSIE, MYRON *and* JACOB *rise. Both* HENNIE *and* RALPH *sit silently at the table, he eating. Suddenly she rises.*]

HENNIE. Tell you what, Mom. I saved for a new dress, but I'll take you and Pop to the Franklin. Don't need a dress. From now on I'm planning to stay in nights. Hold everything!

BESSIE. What's the matter—a bedbug bit you suddenly?

HENNIE. It's a good bill—Belle Baker. Maybe she'll sing "Eli, Eli."

BESSIE. We was going to a movie.

HENNIE. Forget it. Let's go.

MYRON. I see in the papers [*as he picks his teeth*] Sophie Tucker took off twenty-six pounds. Fearful business with Japan.

HENNIE. Write a book, Pop! Come on, we'll go early for good seats.

MYRON. Moe said you had a date with him for tonight.

BESSIE. Axelrod?

HENNIE. I told him no, but he don't believe it. I'll tell him no for the next hundred years, too.

MYRON. Don't break appointments, Beauty, and hurt people's feelings.

[*Bessie exits.*]

HENNIE. His hands got free wheeling. [*She exits.*]

MYRON. I don't know . . . people ain't the same. N-O. The whole world's changing right under our eyes. Presto! No manners. Like the great Italian lover in the movies. What was his name? The Shiek. . . . No one remembers? [*Exits, shaking his head.*]

RALPH [*unmoving at the table*]. Jake . . .

JACOB. Noo?

RALPH. I can't stand it.

JACOB. There's an expression—"strong as iron you must be."

RALPH. It's a cock-eyed world.

JACOB. Boys like you could fix it some day. Look on the world, not on yourself so much. Every country with starving millions, no? In Germany and Poland a Jew couldn't walk in the street. Everybody hates, nobody loves.

RALPH. I don't get all that.

JACOB. For years, I watched you grow up. Wait! You'll graduate from my university.

[*The others enter, dressed.*]

MYRON [*lighting*]. Good cigars now for a nickel.

BESSIE [*to* JACOB]. After take Tootsie on the roof. [*To* RALPH.] What'll you do?

RALPH. Don't know.

BESSIE. You'll see the boys around the block?

RALPH. I'll stay home every night!

MYRON. Momma don't mean for you—

RALPH. I'm flying to Hollywood by plane, that's what I'm doing.

[*Doorbell rings.* MYRON *answers it.*]

BESSIE. I don't like my boy to be seen with those tramps on the corner.

MYRON [*without*]. Schlosser's here, Momma, with the garbage can.

BESSIE. Come in here, Schlosser. [*Sotto voce.*] Wait, I'll give him a piece of my mind. [MYRON *ushers in* SCHLOSSER *who carries a garbage can in each hand.*] What's the matter, the dumbwaiter's broken again?

SCHLOSSER. Mr. Wimmer sends new ropes next week. I got a sore arm.

BESSIE. He should live so long your Mr. Wimmer. For seven years already he's sending new ropes. No dumbwaiter, no hot water, no steam— In a respectable house, they don't allow such conditions.

SCHLOSSER. In a decent house dogs are not running to make dirty the hallway.

BESSIE. Tootsie's making dirty? Our Tootsie's making dirty in the hall?

SCHLOSSER [*to* JACOB]. I tell you yesterday again. You must not leave her—

BESSIE [*indignantly*]. Excuse me! Please don't yell on an old man. He's got more brains in his finger than

you got—I don't know where. Did you ever see—he
should talk to you an old man?

MYRON. Awful.

BESSIE. From now on we don't walk up the stairs no
more. You keep it so clean we'll fly in the windows.

SCHLOSSER. I speak to Mr. Wimmer.

BESSIE. Speak! Speak. Tootsie walks behind me like a
lady any time, any place. So good-bye . . . good-bye,
Mr. Schlosser.

SCHLOSSER. I tell you dot—I verk verry hard here. My
arms is . . . [*Exits in confusion.*]

BESSIE. Tootsie should lay all day in the kitchen maybe.
Give him back if he yells on you. What's funny?

JACOB [*laughing*]. Nothing.

BESSIE. Come. [*Exits.*]

JACOB. Hennie, take care. . . .

HENNIE. Sure.

JACOB. Bye-bye.

[HENNIE *exits.* MYRON *pops head back in door.*]

MYRON. Valentino! That's the one! [*He exits.*]

RALPH. I never in my life even had a birthday party.
Every time I went and cried in the toilet when my
birthday came.

JACOB [*seeing* RALPH *remove his tie*]. You're going to
bed?

RALPH. No, I'm putting on a clean shirt.

JACOB. Why?

RALPH. I got a girl. . . . Don't laugh!

JACOB. Who laughs? Since when?

RALPH. Three weeks. She lives in Yorkville with an
aunt and uncle. A bunch of relatives, but no parents.

JACOB. An orphan girl—tch, tch.

RALPH. But she's got me! Boy, I'm telling you I could
sing! Jake, she's like stars. She's so beautiful you
look at her and cry! She's like French words! We

went to the park the other night. Heard the last band concert.

JACOB. Music . . .

RALPH [*stuffing shirt in trousers*]. It got cold and I gave her my coat to wear. We just walked along like that, see, without a word, see. I never was so happy in all my life. It got late . . . we just sat there. She looked at me—you know what I mean, how a girl looks at you—right in the eyes? "I love you," she says, "Ralph." I took her home. . . . I wanted to cry. That's how I felt!

JACOB. It's a beautiful feeling.

RALPH. You said a mouthful!

JACOB. Her name is—

RALPH. Blanche.

JACOB. A fine name. Bring her sometimes here.

RALPH. She's scared to meet Mom.

JACOB. Why?

RALPH. You know Mom's not letting my sixteen bucks out of the house if she can help it. She'd take one look at Blanche and insult her in a minute—a kid who's got nothing.

JACOB. Boychick!

RALPH. What's the diff?

JACOB. It's no difference—a plain bourgeois prejudice—but when they find out a poor girl—it ain't so kosher.

RALPH. They don't have to know I've got a girl.

JACOB. What's in the end?

RALPH. Out I go! I don't mean maybe!

JACOB. And then what?

RALPH. Life begins.

JACOB. What life?

RALPH. Life with my girl. Boy, I could sing when I think about it! Her and me together—that's a new life!

JACOB. Don't make a mistake! A new death!

RALPH. What's the idea?

JACOB. Me, I'm the idea! Once I had in *my* heart a dream, a vision, but came marriage and then you forget. Children come and you forget because—

RALPH. Don't worry, Jake.

JACOB. Remember, a woman insults a man's soul like no other thing in the whole world!

RALPH. Why get so excited? No one—

JACOB. Boychick, wake up! Be something! Make your life something good. For the love of an old man who sees in your young days his new life, for such love take the world in your two hands and make it like new. Go out and fight so life shouldn't be printed on dollar bills. A woman waits.

RALPH. Say, I'm no fool!

JACOB. From my heart I hope not. In the meantime— [*Bell rings.*]

RALPH. See who it is, will you? [*Stands off.*] Don't want Mom to catch me with a clean shirt.

JACOB [*calls*]. Come in. [*Sotto voce.*] Moe Axelrod. [MOE *enters.*]

MOE. Hello girls, how's your whiskers? [*To* RALPH.] All dolled up. What's it, the weekly visit to the cat house?

RALPH. Please mind your business.

MOE. Okay, sweetheart.

RALPH [*taking a hidden dollar from a book*]. If Mom asks where I went—

JACOB. I know. Enjoy yourself.

RALPH. Bye-bye. [*He exits.*]

JACOB. Bye-bye.

MOE. Who's home?

JACOB. Me.

MOE. Good. I'll stick around a few minutes. Where's Hennie?

JACOB. She went with Bessie and Myron to a show.

MOE. She what?!

JACOB. You had a date?

MOE [*hiding his feelings*]. Here—I brought you some halavah.

JACOB. Halavah? Thanks. I'll eat a piece after.

MOE. So Ralph's got a dame? Hot stuff—a kid can't even play a card game.

JACOB. Moe, you're a no-good, a bum of the first water. To your dying day you won't change.

MOE. Where'd you get that stuff, a no-good?

JACOB. But I like you.

MOE. Didn't I go fight in France for democracy? Didn't I get my goddam leg shot off in that war the day before the armistice? Uncle Sam give me the Order of the Purple Heart, didn't he? What'd you mean, a no-good?

JACOB. Excuse me.

MOE. If you got an orange I'll eat an orange.

JACOB. No orange. An apple.

MOE. No oranges, huh?—what a dump!

JACOB. Bessie hears you once talking like this she'll knock your head off.

MOE. Hennie went with, huh? She wantsa see me squirm, only I don't squirm for dames.

JACOB. You came to see her?

MOE. What for? I got a present for our boy friend, Myron. He'll drop dead when I tell him his gentle horse galloped in fifteen to one. He'll die.

JACOB. It really won? The first time I remember.

MOE. Where'd they go?

JACOB. A vaudeville by the Franklin.

MOE. What's special tonight?

JACOB. Someone tells a few jokes . . . and they forget the street is filled with starving beggars.

MOE. What'll they do—start a war?

JACOB. I don't know.

MOE. You oughta know. What the hell you got all the books for?

JACOB. It needs a new world.

MOE. That's why they had the big war—to make a new world, they said—safe for democracy. Sure every big general laying up in a Paris hotel with a half dozen broads pinned on his mustache. Democracy! I learned a lesson.

JACOB. An imperial war. You know what this means?

MOE. Sure, I know everything!

JACOB. By money men the interests must be protected. Who gave you such a rotten haircut? Please [*fishing in his vest pocket*], give me for a cent a cigarette. I didn't have since yesterday—

MOE [*giving one*]. Don't make me laugh. [*A cent passes back and forth between them,* MOE *finally throwing it over his shoulder.*] Don't look so tired all the time. You're a wow—always sore about something.

JACOB. And you?

MOE. You got one thing—you can·play pinochle. I'll take you over in a game. Then you'll have something to be sore on.

JACOB. Who'll wash dishes?

[*Moe takes deck from buffet drawer.*]

MOE. Do 'em after. Ten cents a deal.

JACOB. Who's got ten cents?

MOE. I got ten cents. I'll lend it to you.

JACOB. Commence.

MOE [*shaking cards*]. The first time I had my hands on a pack in two days. Lemme shake up these cards. I'll make 'em talk.

[JACOB *goes to his room where he puts on a Caruso record.*]

JACOB. You should live so long.

MOE. Ever see oranges grow? I know a certain place—

One summer I laid under a tree and let them fall right in my mouth.

JACOB [*off, the music is playing; the card game begins*]. From "L'Africana" . . . a big explorer comes on a new land—"O Paradiso." From act four this piece. Caruso stands on the ship and looks on a Utopia. You hear? "Oh paradise! Oh paradise on earth! Oh blue sky, oh fragrant air—"

MOE. Ask him does he see any oranges?

[BESSIE, MYRON *and* HENNIE *enter.*]

JACOB. You came back so soon?

BESSIE. Hennie got sick on the way.

MYRON. Hello, Moe . . .

[MOE *puts cards back in pocket.*]

BESSIE. Take off the phonograph, Pop. [*To* HENNIE.] Lay down . . . I'll call the doctor. You should see how she got sick on Prospect Avenue. Two weeks already she don't feel right.

MYRON. Moe . . . ?

BESSIE. Go to bed, Hennie.

HENNIE. I'll sit here.

BESSIE. Such a girl I never saw! Now you'll be stubborn?

MYRON. It's for your own good, Beauty. Influenza—

HENNIE. I'll sit here.

BESSIE. You ever seen a girl should say no to everything. She can't stand on her feet, so—

HENNIE. Don't yell in my ears. I hear. Nothing's wrong. I ate tuna fish for lunch.

MYRON. Canned goods . . .

BESSIE. Last week you also ate tuna fish?

HENNIE. Yeah, I'm funny for tuna fish. Go to the show —have a good time.

BESSIE. I don't understand what I did to God He blessed me with such children. From the whole world—

MOE [*coming to aid of* HENNIE]. For Chris' sake, don't kibitz so much!

BESSIE. You don't like it?

MOE [*aping*]. No, I don't like it.

BESSIE. That's too bad, Axelrod. Maybe it's better by your cigar store friends. Here we're different people.

MOE. Don't gimme that cigar store line, Bessie. I walked up five flights—

BESSIE. To take out Hennie. But my daughter ain't in your class, Axelrod.

MOE. To see Myron.

MYRON. Did he, did he, Moe?

MOE. Did he what?

MYRON. "Sky Rocket"?

BESSIE. You bet on a horse!

MOE. Paid twelve and a half to one.

MYRON. There! You hear that, Momma? Our horse came in. You see, it happens, and twelve and a half to one. Just look at that!

MOE. What the hell, a sure thing. I told you.

BESSIE. If Moe said a sure thing, you couldn't bet a few dollars instead of fifty cents?

JACOB [*laughs*]. "Aie, aie, aie."

MOE [*at his wallet*]. I'm carrying six hundred "plunks" in big denominations.

BESSIE. A banker!

MOE. Uncle Sam sends me ninety a month.

BESSIE. So you save it?

MOE. Run it up. Run-it-up-Axelrod, that's me.

BESSIE. The police should know how.

MOE [*shutting her up*]. All right, all right— Change twenty, sweetheart.

MYRON. Can you make change?

BESSIE. Don't be crazy.

MOE. I'll meet a guy in Goldman's restaurant. I'll meet 'im and come back with change.

MYRON [*figuring on paper*]. You can give it to me to-morrow in the store.

BESSIE [*acquisitive*]. He'll come back, he'll come back!

MOE. Lucky I bet some bucks myself. [*In derision to* HENNIE.] Let's step out tomorrow night, Par-a-dise. [*Thumbs his nose at her, laughs mordantly and exits.*]

MYRON. Oh, that's big percentage. If I picked a winner every day . . .

BESSIE. Poppa, did you take Tootsie on the roof?

JACOB. All right.

MYRON. Just look at that—a cake-walk. We can make—

BESSIE. It's enough talk. I got a splitting headache. Hennie, go in bed. I'll call Dr. Cantor.

HENNIE. I'll sit here . . . and don't call that old Ignatz 'cause I won't see him.

MYRON. If you get sick Momma can't nurse you. You don't want to go to a hospital.

JACOB. She don't look sick, Bessie, it's a fact.

BESSIE. She's got fever. I see in her eyes, so he tells me no. Myron, call Dr. Cantor.

[MYRON *picks up phone, but* HENNIE *grabs it from him.*]

HENNIE. I don't want any doctor. I ain't sick. Leave me alone.

MYRON. Beauty, it's for your own sake.

HENNIE. Day in and day out pestering. Why are you always right and no one else can say a word?

BESSIE. When you have your own children—

HENNIE. I'm not sick! Hear what I say? I'm not sick! Nothing's the matter with me! I don't want a doctor.

[BESSIE *is watching her with slow progressive under-standing.*]

BESSIE. What's the matter?

HENNIE. Nothing, I told you!

BESSIE. You told me, but— [*A long pause of examination follows.*]

HENNIE. See much?

BESSIE. Myron, put down the . . . the . . . [*He slowly puts the phone down.*] Tell me what happened. . . .

HENNIE. Brooklyn Bridge fell down.

BESSIE [*approaching*]. I'm asking a question. . . .

MYRON. What's happened, Momma?

BESSIE. Listen to me!

HENNIE. What the hell are you talking?

BESSIE. Poppa—take Tootsie on the roof.

HENNIE [*holding* JACOB *back*]. If he wants he can stay here.

MYRON. What's wrong, Momma?

BESSIE [*her voice quivering slightly*]. Myron, your fine Beauty's in trouble. Our society lady . . .

MYRON. Trouble? I don't under—is it—?

BESSIE. Look in her face. [*He looks, understands and slowly sits in a chair, utterly crushed.*] Who's the man?

HENNIE. The Prince of Wales.

BESSIE. My gall is busting in me. In two seconds—

HENNIE [*in a violent outburst*]. Shut up! Shut up! I'll jump out the window in a minute! Shut up! [*Finally she gains control of herself, says in a low, hard voice:*] You don't know him.

JACOB. Bessie . . .

BESSIE. He's a Bronx boy?

HENNIE. From out of town.

BESSIE. What do you mean?

HENNIE. From out of town!!

BESSIE. A long time you know him? You were sleeping by a girl from the office Saturday nights? You slept good, my lovely lady. You'll go to him . . . he'll marry you.

HENNIE. That's what you say.

BESSIE. That's what I say! He'll do it, take *my* word he'll do it!

HENNIE. Where? [*To* JACOB.] Give her the letter.

[JACOB *does so.*]

BESSIE. What? [*Reads.*] "Dear sir: In reply to your request of the 14th inst., we can state that no Mr. Ben Grossman has ever been connected with our organization . . ." You don't know where he is?

HENNIE. No.

BESSIE [*walks back and forth*]. Stop crying like a baby, Myron.

MYRON. It's like a play on the stage. . . .

BESSIE. To a mother you couldn't say something before. I'm old-fashioned—like your friends I'm not smart—I don't eat chop suey and run around Coney Island with tramps. [*She walks reflectively to buffet, picks up a box of candy, puts it down, says to* MYRON:] Tomorrow night bring Sam Feinschreiber for supper.

HENNIE. I won't do it.

BESSIE. You'll do it, my fine beauty, you'll do it!

HENNIE. I'm not marrying a poor foreigner like him. Can't even speak an English word. Not me! I'll go to my grave without a husband.

BESSIE. You don't say! We'll find for you somewhere a millionaire with a pleasure boat. He's going to night school, Sam. For a boy only three years in the country he speaks very nice. In three years he put enough in the bank, a good living.

JACOB. This is serious?

BESSIE. What then? I'm talking for my health? He'll come tomorrow night for supper. By Saturday they're engaged.

JACOB. Such a thing you can't do.

BESSIE. Who asked your advice?

JACOB. Such a thing—

BESSIE. Never mind!

JACOB. The lowest from the low!

BESSIE. Don't talk! I'm warning you! A man who don't believe in God—with crazy ideas—

JACOB. So bad I never imagined you could be.

BESSIE. Maybe if you didn't talk so much it wouldn't happen like this. You with your ideas—I'm a mother. I raise a family, they should have respect.

JACOB. Respect? [*Spits.*] Respect! For the neighbors' opinion! You insult me, Bessie!

BESSIE. Go in your room, Papa. Every job he ever had he lost because he's got a big mouth. He opens his mouth and the whole Bronx could fall in. Everybody said it—

MYRON. Momma, they'll hear you down the dumbwaiter.

BESSIE. A good barber not to hold a job a week. Maybe you never heard charity starts at home. You never heard it, Pop?

JACOB. All you know, I heard, and more yet. But Ralph you don't make like you. Before you do it I'll die first. He'll find a girl. He'll go in a fresh world with her. This is a house? Marx said it— abolish such families.

BESSIE. Go in your room, Papa.

JACOB. Ralph you don't make like you!

BESSIE. Go lay in your room with Caruso and the books together.

JACOB. All right!

BESSIE. Go in the room!

JACOB. Some day I'll come out, I'll— [*Unable to continue, he turns, looks at* HENNIE, *goes to his door and there says with an attempt at humor:*] Bessie, some day you'll talk to me so fresh . . . I'll leave the house for good! [*He exits.*]

BESSIE [*crying*]. You ever in your life seen it? He should dare! He should just dare say in the house another word. Your gall could bust from such a man. [*Bell rings,* MYRON *goes.*] Go to sleep now. It won't hurt.

HENNIE. Yeah?

[MOE *enters, a box in his hand.* MYRON *follows and sits down.*]

MOE [*looks around first—putting box on table*]. Cake. [*About to give* MYRON *the money, he turns instead to* BESSIE.] Six fifty, four bits change . . . come on, hand over half a buck. [*She does so. Of* MYRON.] Who bit him?

BESSIE. We're soon losing our Hennie, Moe.

MOE. Why? What's the matter?

BESSIE. She made her engagement.

MOE. Zat so?

BESSIE. Today it happened . . . he asked her.

MOE. Did he? Who? Who's the corpse?

BESSIE. It's a secret.

MOE. In the bag, huh?

HENNIE. Yeah . . .

BESSIE. When a mother gives away an only daughter it's no joke. Wait, when you'll get married you'll know. . . .

MOE [*bitterly*]. Don't make me laugh—when I get married! What I think a women? Take 'em all, cut 'em in little pieces like a herring in Greek salad. A guy in France had the right idea—dropped his wife in a bathtub fulla acid. [*Whistles.*] Sss, down the pipe! Pfft—not even a corset button left!

MYRON. Corsets don't have buttons.

MOE [*to* HENNIE]. What's the great idea? Gone big time, Paradise? Christ, it's suicide! Sure, kids you'll have, gold teeth, get fat, big in the tangerines—

HENNIE. Shut your face!

MOE. Who's it—some dope pullin' down twenty bucks a week? Cut your throat, sweetheart. Save time.

BESSIE. Never mind your two cents, Axelrod.

MOE. I say what I think—that's me!

HENNIE. That's you—a lousy fourflusher who'd steal the glasses off a blind man.

MOE. Get hot!

HENNIE. My God, do I need it—to listen to this mutt shoot his mouth off?

MYRON. Please. . . .

MOE. Now wait a minute, sweetheart, wait a minute. I don't have to take that from you.

BESSIE. Don't yell at her!

HENNIE. For two cents I'd spit in your eye.

MOE [*throwing coin to table*]. Here's two bits.

[HENNIE *looks at him and then starts across the room.*]

BESSIE. Where are you going?

HENNIE [*crying*]. For my beauty nap, Mussolini. Wake me up when it's apple blossom time in Normandy. [*Exits.*]

MOE. Pretty, pretty—a sweet gal, your Hennie. See the look in her eyes?

BESSIE. She don't feel well. . . .

MYRON. Canned goods . . .

BESSIE. So don't start with her.

MOE. Like a battleship she's got it. Not like other dames—shove 'em and they lay. Not her. I got a yen for her and I don't mean a Chinee coin.

BESSIE. Listen, Axelrod, in my house you don't talk this way. Either have respect or get out.

MOE. When I think about it . . . maybe I'd marry her myself.

BESSIE [*suddenly aware of* MOE]. You could— What do you mean, Moe?

MOE. You ain't sunburnt—you heard me.

BESSIE. Why don't you, Moe? An old friend of the

family like you. It would be a blessing on all of us.

MOE. You said she's engaged.

BESSIE. But maybe she don't know her own mind. Say, it's—

MOE. I need a wife like a hole in the head. . . . What's to know about women, I know. Even if I asked her. She won't do it! A guy with one leg—it gives her the heebie-jeebies. I know what she's looking for. An arrow-collar guy, a hero, but with a wad of jack. Only the two don't go together. But I got what it takes . . . plenty, and more where it comes from. . . . [*Breaks off, snorts and rubs his knee.*]

[*A pause. In his room* JACOB *puts on Caruso singing the lament from "The Pearl Fishers."*]

BESSIE. It's right—she wants a millionaire with a mansion on Riverside Drive. So go fight City Hall. Cake?

MOE. Cake.

BESSIE. I'll make tea. But one thing—she's got a fine boy with a business brain. Caruso! [*Exits into the front room and stands in the dark, at the window.*]

MOE. No wet smack . . . a fine girl. . . . She'll burn that guy out in a month. [MOE *retrieves the quarter and spins it on the table.*]

MYRON. I remember that song . . . beautiful. Nora Bayes sang it at the old Proctor's Twenty-third Street—"When It's Apple Blossom Time in Normandy." . . .

MOE. She wantsa see me crawl—my head on a plate she wants! A snowball in hell's got a better chance. [*Out of sheer fury he spins the quarter in his fingers.*]

MYRON [*as his eyes slowly fill with tears*]. Beautiful . . .

MOE. Match you for a quarter. Match you for any goddam thing you got. [*Spins the coin viciously.*] What the hell kind of house is this it ain't got an orange!!

SLOW—CURTAIN

Act two

*One year later, a Sunday afternoon. The front room.
JACOB is giving his son MORDECAI (UNCLE MORTY) a
haircut, newspapers spread around the base of the
chair. MOE is reading a newspaper, leg propped on a
chair. RALPH, in another chair, is spasmodically reading a paper. UNCLE MORTY reads colored jokes. Silence,
then BESSIE enters.*

BESSIE. Dinner's in half an hour, Morty.

MORTY [*still reading jokes*]. I got time.

BESSIE. A duck. Don't get hair on the rug, Pop. [*Goes
to window and pulls down shade.*] What's the matter the shade's up to the ceiling?

JACOB [*pulling it up again*]. Since when do I give a
haircut in the dark? [*He mimics her tone.*]

BESSIE. When you're finished, pull it down. I like my
house to look respectable. Ralphie, bring up two
bottles seltzer from Weiss.

RALPH. I'm reading the paper.

BESSIE. Uncle Morty takes a little seltzer.

RALPH. I'm expecting a phone call.

BESSIE. Noo, if it comes you'll be back. What's the matter? [*Gives him money from apron pocket.*] Take
down the old bottles.

RALPH [*to JACOB*]. Get that call if it comes. Say I'll
be right back.

[JACOB *nods assent.*]

MORTY [*giving change from vest*]. Get grandpa some
cigarettes.

RALPH. Okay. [*Exits.*]

JACOB. What's new in the paper, Moe?

MOE. Still jumping off the high buildings like flies—
the big shots who lost all their cocoanuts. Pfft!

JACOB. Suicides?

MOE. Plenty can't take it—good in the break, but can't
take the whip in the stretch.

MORTY [*without looking up*]. I saw it happen Monday in my building. My hair stood up how they
shoveled him together—like a pancake—a bankrupt
manufacturer.

MOE. No brains.

MORTY. Enough . . . all over the sidewalk.

JACOB. If someone said five-ten years ago I couldn't
make for myself a living, I wouldn't believe—

MORTY. Duck for dinner?

BESSIE. The best Long Island duck.

MORTY. I like goose.

BESSIE. A duck is just like a goose, only better.

MORTY. I like a goose.

BESSIE. The next time you'll be for Sunday dinner I'll
make a goose.

MORTY [*sniffs deeply*]. Smells good. I'm a great boy for
smells.

BESSIE. Ain't you ashamed? Once in a blue moon he
should come to an only sister's house.

MORTY. Bessie, leave me live.

BESSIE. You should be ashamed!

MORTY. Quack quack!

BESSIE. No, better to lay around Mecca Temple playing cards with the Masons.

MORTY [*with good nature*]. Bessie, don't you see Pop's
giving me a haircut?

BESSIE. You don't need no haircut. Look, two hairs he
took off.

MORTY. Pop likes to give me a haircut. If I said no he

don't forget for a year, do you, Pop? An old man's like that.

JACOB. I still do an A-1 job.

MORTY [*winking*]. Pop cuts hair to fit the face, don't you, Pop?

JACOB. For sure, Morty. To each face a different haircut. Custom built, no ready made. A round face needs special—

BESSIE [*cutting him short*]. A graduate from the B.M.T. [*Going.*] Don't forget the shade. [*The phone rings. She beats* JACOB *to it.*] Hello? Who is it, please? . . . Who is it, please? . . . Miss Hirsch? No, he ain't here. . . . No, I couldn't say when. [*Hangs up sharply.*]

JACOB. For Ralph?

BESSIE. A wrong number.

[JACOB *looks at her and goes back to his job.*]

JACOB. Excuse me!

BESSIE [*to* MORTY]. Ralphie took another cut down the place yesterday.

MORTY. Business is bad. I saw his boss Harry Glicksman Thursday. I bought some velvets . . . they're coming in again.

BESSIE. Do something for Ralphie down there.

MORTY. What can I do? I mentioned it to Glicksman. He told me they squeezed out half the people. . . .

[MYRON *enters dressed in apron.*]

BESSIE. What's gonna be the end? Myron's working only three days a week now.

MYRON. It's conditions.

BESSIE. Hennie's married with a baby . . . money just don't come in. I never saw conditions should be so bad.

MORTY. Times'll change.

MOE. The only thing'll change is my underwear.

MORTY. These last few years I got my share of gray hairs. [*Still reading jokes without having looked up once.*] Ha, ha, ha— Popeye the sailor ate spinach and knocked out four bums.

MYRON. I'll tell you the way I see it. The country needs a great man now—a regular Teddy Roosevelt.

MOE. What this country needs is a good five-cent earthquake.

JACOB. So long labor lives it should increase private gain—

BESSIE [*to* JACOB]. Listen, Poppa, go talk on the street corner. The government'll give you free board the rest of your life.

MORTY. I'm surprised. Don't I send a five-dollar check for Pop every week?

BESSIE. You could afford a couple more and not miss it.

MORTY. Tell me jokes. Business is so rotten I could just as soon lay all day in the Turkish bath.

MYRON. Why'd I come in here? [*Puzzled, he exits.*]

MORTY [*to* MOE]. I hear the bootleggers still do business, Moe.

MOE. Wake up! I kissed bootlegging bye-bye two years back.

MORTY. For a fact? What kind of racket is it now?

MOE. If I told you, you'd know something.

[HENNIE *comes from bedroom.*]

HENNIE. Where's Sam?

BESSIE. Sam? In the kitchen.

HENNIE [*calls*]. Sam. Come take the diaper.

MORTY. How's the Mickey Louse? Ha, ha, ha . . .

HENNIE. Sleeping.

MORTY. Ah, that's life to a baby. He sleeps—gets it in the mouth—sleeps some more. To raise a family nowadays you must be a damn fool.

BESSIE. Never mind, never mind, a woman who don't

raise a family—a girl—should jump overboard. What's she good for? [*To* MOE—*to change the subject.*] Your leg bothers you bad?

MOE. It's okay, sweetheart.

BESSIE [*to* MORTY]. It hurts him every time it's cold out. He's got four legs in the closet.

MORTY. Four wooden legs?

MOE. Three.

MORTY. What's the big idea?

MOE. Why not? Uncle Sam gives them out free.

MORTY. Say, maybe if Uncle Sam gave out less legs we could balance the budget.

JACOB. Or not have a war so they wouldn't have to give out legs.

MORTY. Shame on you, Pop. Everybody knows war is necessary.

MOE. Don't make me laugh. Ask me—the first time you pick up a dead one in the trench—then you learn war ain't so damn necessary.

MORTY. Say, you should kick. The rest of your life Uncle Sam pays you ninety a month. Look, not a worry in the world.

MOE. Don't make me laugh. Uncle Sam can take his *seventy* bucks and— [*Finishes with a gesture.*] Nothing good hurts. [*He rubs his stump.*]

HENNIE. Use a crutch, Axelrod. Give the stump a rest.

MOE. Mind your business, Feinschreiber.

BESSIE. It's a sensible idea.

MOE. Who asked you?

BESSIE. Look, he's ashamed.

MOE. So's your Aunt Fanny.

BESSIE [*naïvely*]. Who's got an Aunt Fanny? [*She cleans a rubber plant's leaves with her apron.*]

MORTY. It's a joke!

MOE. I don't want my paper creased before I read it. I want it fresh. Fifty times I said that.

BESSIE. Don't get so excited for a five-cent paper—our star boarder.

MOE. And I don't want no one using my razor either. Get it straight. I'm not buying ten blades a week for the Berger family. [*Furious, he limps out.*]

BESSIE. Maybe I'm using his razor too.

HENNIE. Proud!

BESSIE. You need luck with plants. I didn't clean off the leaves in a month.

MORTY. You keep the house like a pin and I like your cooking. Any time Myron fires you, come to me, Bessie. I'll let the butler go and you'll be my housekeeper. I don't like Japs so much—sneaky.

BESSIE. Say, you can't tell. Maybe any day I'm coming to stay.

[HENNIE *exits.*]

JACOB. Finished.

MORTY. How much, Ed. Pinaud? [*Disengages self from chair.*]

JACOB. Five cents.

MORTY. Still five cents for a haircut to fit the face?

JACOB. Prices don't change by me. [*Takes a dollar.*] I can't change—

MORTY. Keep it. Buy yourself a Packard. Ha, ha, ha.

JACOB [*taking large envelope from pocket*]. Please, you'll keep this for me. Put it away.

MORTY. What is it?

JACOB. My insurance policy. I don't like it should lay around where something could happen.

MORTY. What could happen?

JACOB. Who knows, robbers, fire . . . they took next door. Fifty dollars from O'Reilly.

MORTY. Say, lucky a Berger didn't lose it.

JACOB. Put it downtown in the safe. Bessie don't have to know.

MORTY. It's made out to Bessie?

JACOB. No, to Ralph.

MORTY. To Ralph?

JACOB. He don't know. Some day he'll get three thousand.

MORTY. You got good years ahead.

JACOB. Behind.

[RALPH *enters.*]

RALPH. Cigarettes. Did a call come?

JACOB. A few minutes. She don't let me answer it.

RALPH. Did Mom say I was coming back?

JACOB. No.

[MORTY *is back at new jokes.*]

RALPH. She starting that stuff again? [BESSIE *enters.*] A call come for me?

BESSIE [*waters pot from milk bottle*]. A wrong number.

JACOB. Don't say a lie, Bessie.

RALPH. Blanche said she'd call me at two—was it her?

BESSIE. I said a wrong number.

RALPH. Please, Mom, if it was her tell me.

BESSIE. You call me a liar next. You got no shame—to start a scene in front of Uncle Morty. Once in a blue moon he comes—

RALPH. What's the shame? If my girl calls I wanna know it.

BESSIE. You made enough mish mosh with her until now.

MORTY. I'm surprised, Bessie. For the love of Mike tell him yes or no.

BESSIE. I didn't tell him? No!

MORTY [*to* RALPH]. No!

[RALPH *goes to a window and looks out.*]

BESSIE. Morty, I didn't say before—he runs around steady with a girl.

MORTY. Terrible. Should he run around with a foxie-woxie?

BESSIE. A girl with no parents.

MORTY. An orphan?

BESSIE. I could die from shame. A year already he runs around with her. He brought her once for supper. Believe me, she didn't come again, no!

RALPH. Don't think I didn't ask her.

BESSIE. You hear? You raise them and what's in the end for all your trouble?

JACOB. When you'll lay in a grave, no more trouble. [*Exits.*]

MORTY. Quack quack!

BESSIE. A girl like that he wants to marry. A skinny consumptive-looking . . . six months already she's not working—taking charity from an aunt. You should see her. In a year she's dead on his hands.

RALPH. You'd cut her throat if you could.

BESSIE. That's right! Before she'd ruin a nice boy's life I would first go to prison. Miss Nobody should step in the picture and I'll stand by with my mouth shut.

RALPH. Miss Nobody! Who am I? Al Jolson?

BESSIE. Fix your tie!

RALPH. I'll take care of my own life.

BESSIE. You'll take care? Excuse my expression, you can't even wipe your nose yet! He'll take care!

MORTY [*to* BESSIE]. I'm surprised. Don't worry so much, Bessie. When it's time to settle down he won't marry a poor girl, will you? In the long run common sense is thicker than love. I'm a great boy for live and let live.

BESSIE. Sure, it's easy to say. In the meantime he eats out my heart. You know I'm not strong.

MORTY. I know . . . a pussy cat . . . ha, ha, ha.

BESSIE. You got money and money talks. But without the dollar who sleeps at night?

RALPH. I been working for years, bringing in money here—putting it in your hand like a kid. All right, I can't get my teeth fixed. All right, that a new suit's like trying to buy the Chrysler Building. You never in your life bought me a pair of skates even—things I died for when I was a kid. I don't care about that stuff, see. Only just remember I pay some of the bills around here, just a few . . . and if my girl calls me on the phone I'll talk to her any time I please. [*He exits.* HENNIE *applauds.*]

BESSIE. Don't be so smart, Miss America! [*To* MORTY.] He didn't have skates! But when he got sick, a twelve-year-old boy, who called a big specialist for the last $25 in the house? Skates!

JACOB [*just in. Adjusts window shade*]. It looks like snow today.

MORTY. It's about time—winter.

BESSIE. Poppa here could talk like Samuel Webster, too, but it's just talk. He should try to buy a two-cent pickle in the Burland Market without money.

MORTY. I'm getting an appetite.

BESSIE. Right away we'll eat. I made chopped liver for you.

MORTY. My specialty!

BESSIE. Ralph should only be a success like you, Morty. I should only live to see the day when he rides up to the door in a big car with a chauffeur and a radio. I could die happy, believe me.

MORTY. Success she says. She should see how we spend thousands of dollars making up a winter line and winter don't come—summer in January. Can you beat it?

JACOB. Don't live, just make success.

MORTY. Chopped liver—ha!

JACOB. Ha! [Exits.]

MORTY. When they start arguing, I don't hear. Suddenly I'm deaf. I'm a great boy for the practical side. [*He looks over to* HENNIE *who sits rubbing her hands with lotion.*]

HENNIE. Hands like a raw potato.

MORTY. What's the matter? You don't look so well . . . no pep.

HENNIE. I'm swell.

MORTY. You used to be such a pretty girl.

HENNIE. Maybe I got the blues. You can't tell.

MORTY. You could stand a new dress.

HENNIE. That's not all I could stand.

MORTY. Come down to the place tomorrow and pick out a couple from the "eleven-eighty" line. Only don't sing me the blues.

HENNIE. Thanks. I need some new clothes.

MORTY. I got two thousand pieces of merchandise waiting in the stock room for winter.

HENNIE. I never had anything from life. Sam don't help.

MORTY. He's crazy about the kid.

HENNIE. Crazy is right. Twenty-one a week he brings in—a nigger don't have it so hard. I wore my fingers off on an Underwood for six years. For what? Now I wash baby diapers. Sure, I'm crazy about the kid too. But half the night the kid's up. Try to sleep. You don't know how it is, Uncle Morty.

MORTY. No, I don't know. I was born yesterday. Ha, ha, ha. Some day I'll leave you a little nest egg. You like eggs? Ha?

HENNIE. When? When I'm dead and buried?

MORTY. No, when *I'm* dead and buried. Ha, ha, ha.

HENNIE. You should know what I'm thinking.

MORTY. Ha, ha, ha, I know.

[MYRON *enters.*]

MYRON. I never take a drink. I'm just surprised at myself, I—

MORTY. I got a pain. Maybe I'm hungry.

MYRON. Come inside, Morty. Bessie's got some schnapps.

MORTY. I'll take a drink. Yesterday I missed the Turkish bath.

MYRON. I get so bitter when I take a drink, it just surprises me.

MORTY. Look how fat. Say, you live once. . . . Quack, quack. [*Both exit.* MOE *stands silently in the doorway.*]

SAM [*entering*]. I'll make Leon's bottle now!

HENNIE. No, let him sleep, Sam. Take away the diaper. [*He does. Exits.*]

MOE [*advancing into the room*]. That your husband?

HENNIE. Don't you know?

MOE. Maybe he's a nurse you hired for the kid—it looks it—how he tends it. A guy comes howling to your old lady every time you look cock-eyed. Does he sleep with you?

HENNIE. Don't be so wise!

MOE [*indicating newspaper*]. Here's a dame strangled her hubby with wire. Claimed she didn't like him. Why don't you brain Sam with an axe some night?

HENNIE. Why don't you lay an egg, Axelrod?

MOE. I laid a few in my day, Feinschreiber. Hardboiled ones too.

HENNIE. Yeah?

MOE. Yeah. You wanna know what I see when I look in your eyes?

HENNIE. No.

MOE. Ted Lewis playing the clarinet—some of those high crazy notes! Christ, you coulda had a guy with some guts instead of a cluck stands around boilin' baby nipples.

HENNIE. Meaning you?

MOE. Meaning me, sweetheart.

HENNIE. Think you're pretty good.

MOE. You'd know if I slept with you again.

HENNIE. I'll smack your face in a minute.

MOE. You do and I'll break your arm. [*Holds up paper.*] Take a look. [*Reads.*] "Ten-day luxury cruise to Havana." That's the stuff you coulda had. Put up at ritzy hotels, frenchie soap, champagne. Now you're tied down to "Snake-Eye" here. What for? What's it get you? . . . a two by four flat on 108th Street . . . a pain in the bustle it gets you.

HENNIE. What's it to you?

MOE. I know you from the old days. How you like to spend it! What I mean! Lizard-skin shoes, perfume behind the ears. . . . You're in a mess, Paradise! Paradise—that's a hot one—yah, crazy to eat a knish at your own wedding.

HENNIE. I get it—you're jealous. You can't get me.

MOE. Don't make me laugh.

HENNIE. Kid Jailbird's been trying to make me for years. You'd give your other leg. I'm hooked? Maybe, but you're in the same boat. Only it's worse for you. I don't give a damn no more, but you gotta yen makes you—

MOE. Don't make me laugh.

HENNIE. Compared to you I'm sittin' on top of the world.

MOE. You're losing your looks. A dame don't stay young forever.

HENNIE. You're a liar. I'm only twenty-four.

MOE. When you comin' home to stay?

HENNIE. Wouldn't you like to know?

MOE. I'll get you again.

HENNIE. Think so?

MOE. Sure, whatever goes up comes down. You're easy —you remember—two for a nickel—a pushover! [*Suddenly she slaps him. They both seem stunned.*] What's the idea?

HENNIE. Go on . . . break my arm.

MOE [*as if saying "I love you"*]. Listen, lousy.

HENNIE. Go on, do something!

MOE. Listen—

HENNIE. You're so damn tough!

MOE. You like me. [*He takes her.*]

HENNIE. Take your hand off! [*Pushes him away.*] Come around when it's a flood again and they put you in the ark with the animals. Not even then—if you was the last man!

MOE. Baby, if you had a dog I'd love the dog.

HENNIE. Gorilla! [*Exits.* RALPH *enters.*]

RALPH. Were you here before?

MOE [*sits*]. What?

RALPH. When the call came for me?

MOE. What?

RALPH. The call came.

[JACOB *enters.*]

MOE [*rubbing his leg*]. No.

JACOB. Don't worry, Ralphie, she'll call back.

RALPH. Maybe not. I think somethin's the matter.

JACOB. What?

RALPH. I don't know. I took her home from the movie last night. She asked me what I'd think if she went away.

JACOB. Don't worry, she'll call again.

RALPH. Maybe not, if Mom insulted her. She gets it on both ends, the poor kid. Lived in an orphan asylum most of her life. They shove her around like an empty freight train.

JACOB. After dinner go see her.

RALPH. Twice they kicked me down the stairs.

JACOB. Life should have some dignity.

RALPH. Every time I go near the place I get heart failure. The uncle drives a bus. You oughta see him—like Babe Ruth.

MOE. Use your brains. Stop acting like a kid who still wets the bed. Hire a room somewhere—a club room for two members.

RALPH. Not that kind of proposition, Moe.

MOE. Don't be a bush leaguer all your life.

RALPH. Cut it out!

MOE [*on a sudden upsurge of emotion*]. Ever sleep with one? Look at 'im blush.

RALPH. You don't know her.

MOE. I seen her—the kind no one sees undressed till the undertaker works on her.

RALPH. Why give me the needles all the time? What'd I ever do to you?

MOE. Not a thing. You're a nice kid. But grow up! In life there's two kinds—the men that's sure of themselves and the ones who ain't! It's time you quit being a selling-plater and got in the first class.

JACOB. And you, Axelrod?

MOE [*to* JACOB]. Scratch your whiskers! [*To* RALPH.] Get independent. Get what-it-takes and be yourself. Do what you like.

RALPH. Got a suggestion?

[MORTY *enters, eating.*]

MOE. Sure, pick out a racket. Shake down the cocoanuts. See what that does.

MORTY. We know what it does—puts a pudding on your nose! Sing Sing! Easy money's against the law. Against the law don't win. A racket is illegitimate, no?

MOE. It's all a racket—from horse racing down. Marriage, politics, big business—everybody plays cops and robbers. You, you're a racketeer yourself.

MORTY. Who? Me? Personally I manufacture dresses.

MOE. Horse feathers!

MORTY [*seriously*]. Don't make such remarks to me

without proof. I'm a great one for proof. That's why I made a success in business. Proof—put up or shut up, like a game of cards. I heard this remark before —a rich man's a crook who steals from the poor. Personally, I don't like it. It's a big lie!

MOE. If you don't like it, buy yourself a fife and drum —and go fight your own war.

MORTY. Sweatshop talk. Every Jew and Wop in the shop eats my bread and behind my back says, "a sonofabitch." I started from a poor boy who worked on an ice wagon for two dollars a week. Pop's right here he'll tell you. I made it honest. In the whole industry nobody's got a better name.

JACOB. It's an exception, such success.

MORTY. Ralph can't do the same thing?

JACOB. No, Morty, I don't think. In a house like this he don't realize even the possibilities of life. Economics comes down like a ton of coal on the head.

MOE. Red rover, red rover, let Jacob come over!

JACOB. In my day the propaganda was for God. Now it's for success. A boy don't turn around without having shoved in him he should make success.

MORTY. Pop, you're a comedian, a regular Charlie Chaplin.

JACOB. He dreams all night of fortunes. Why not? Don't it say in the movies he should have a personal steamship, pyjamas for fifty dollars a pair and a toilet like a monument? But in the morning he wakes up and for ten dollars he can't fix the teeth. And millions more worse off in the mills of the South— starvation wages. The blood from the worker's heart. [MORTY *laughs loud and long.*] Laugh, laugh . . . tomorrow not.

MORTY. A real, a real Boob McNutt you're getting to be.

JACOB. Laugh, my son. . . .

MORTY. Here is the North, Pop.

JACOB. North, south, it's one country.

MORTY. The country's all right. A duck quacks in every pot!

JACOB. You never heard how they shoot down men and women which ask a better wage? Kentucky 1932?

MORTY. That's a pile of chopped liver, Pop.

[BESSIE *and others enter.*]

JACOB. Pittsburgh, Passaic, Illinois—slavery—it begins where success begins in a competitive system.

[MORTY *howls with delight.*]

MORTY. Oh, Pop, what are you bothering? Why? Tell me why? Ha ha ha. I bought you a phonograph . . . stick to Caruso.

BESSIE. He's starting up again.

MORTY. Don't bother with Kentucky. It's full of moonshiners.

JACOB. Sure, sure—

MORTY. You don't know practical affairs. Stay home and cut hair to fit the face.

JACOB. It says in the Bible how the Red Sea opened and the Egyptians went in and the sea rolled over them. [*Quotes two lines of Hebrew.*] In this boy's life a Red Sea will happen again. I see it!

MORTY. I'm getting sore, Pop, with all this sweatshop talk.

BESSIE. He don't stop a minute. The whole day, like a phonograph.

MORTY. I'm surprised. Without a rich man you don't have a roof over your head. You don't know it?

MYRON. Now you can't bite the hand that feeds you.

RALPH. Let him alone—he's right!

BESSIE. Another county heard from.

RALPH. It's the truth. It's—

MORTY. Keep quiet, snotnose!

JACOB. For sure, charity, a bone for an old dog. But in Russia an old man don't take charity so his eyes turn black in his head. In Russia they got Marx.

MORTY [*scoffingly*]. Who's Marx?

MOE. An outfielder for the Yanks.

[MORTY *howls with delight.*]

MORTY. Ha ha ha, it's better than the jokes. I'm telling you. This is Uncle Sam's country. Put it in your pipe and smoke it.

BESSIE. Russia, he says! Read the papers.

SAM. Here is opportunity.

MYRON. People can't believe in God in Russia. The papers tell the truth, they do.

JACOB. So you believe in God . . . you got something for it? You! You worked for all the capitalists. You harvested the fruit from your labor? You got God! But the past comforts you? The present smiles on you, yes? It promises you the future something? Did you found a piece of earth where you could live like a human being and die with the sun on your face? Tell me, yes, tell me. I would like to know myself. But on these questions, on this theme—the struggle for existence—you can't make an answer. The answer I see in your face . . . the answer is your mouth can't talk. In this dark corner you sit and you die. But abolish private property!

BESSIE [*settling the issue*]. Noo, go fight City Hall!

MORTY. He's drunk!

JACOB. I'm studying from books a whole lifetime.

MORTY. That's what it is—he's drunk. What the hell does all that mean?

JACOB. If you don't know, why should I tell you.

MORTY [*triumphant at last*]. You see? Hear him? Like all those nuts, don't know what they're saying.

JACOB. I know, I know.

MORTY. Like Boob McNutt you know! Don't go in the park, Pop—the squirrels'll get you. Ha, ha, ha . . .

BESSIE. Save your appetite, Morty. [*To* MYRON.] Don't drop the duck.

MYRON. We're ready to eat, Momma.

MORTY [*to* JACOB]. Shame on you. It's your second childhood.

[*Now they file out.* MYRON *first with the duck, the others behind him.*]

BESSIE. Come eat. We had enough for one day. [*Exits.*]

MORTY. Ha, ha, ha. Quack, quack. [*Exits.*]

[JACOB *sits there trembling and deeply humiliated.* MOE *approaches him and thumbs the old man's nose in the direction of the dining room.*]

MOE. Give 'em five. [*Takes his hand away.*] They got you pasted on the wall like a picture, Jake. [*He limps out to seat himself at the table in the next room.*]

JACOB. Go eat, boychick. [RALPH *comes to him.*] He gives me eat, so I'll climb in a needle. One time I saw an old horse in summer . . . he wore a straw hat . . . the ears stuck out on top. An old horse for hire. Give me back my young days . . . give me fresh blood . . . arms . . . give me—

[*The telephone rings. Quickly* RALPH *goes to it.* JACOB *pulls the curtains and stands there, a sentry on guard.*]

RALPH. Hello? . . . Yeah, I went to the store and came right back, right after you called. [*Looks at* JACOB.]

JACOB. Speak, speak. Don't be afraid they'll hear.

RALPH. I'm sorry if Mom said something. You know how excitable Mom is. . . . Sure! What? . . . Sure, I'm listening. . . . Put on the radio, Jake. [JACOB *does so. Music comes in and up, a tango, grating with an insistent nostalgic pulse. Under the cover of the music* RALPH *speaks more freely.*] Yes . . . yes . . . What's the matter? Why're you crying? What happened? [*To* JACOB.] She's putting her uncle on. Yes? . . . Listen, Mr. Hirsch, what're you trying to do? What's the big idea? Honest to God. I'm in no mood for joking! Lemme talk to her! Gimme Blanche! [*Waits.*] Blanche? What's this? Is this a joke? Is that true? I'm coming right down! I know, but— You wanna do that? . . . I know, but— I'm coming down . . . tonight! Nine o'clock . . . sure . . . sure . . . sure. . . . [*Hangs up.*]

JACOB. What happened?

MORTY [*enters*]. Listen, Pop. I'm surprised you didn't— [*He howls, shakes his head in mock despair, exits.*]

JACOB. Boychick, what?

RALPH. I don't get it straight. [*To* JACOB]. She's leaving. . . .

JACOB. Where?

RALPH. Out West— To Cleveland.

JACOB. Cleveland?

RALPH. . . . In a week or two. Can you picture it? It's a put-up job. But they can't get away with that.

JACOB. We'll find something.

RALPH. Sure, the angels of heaven'll come down on her uncle's cab and whisper in his ear.

JACOB. Come eat. . . . We'll find something.

RALPH. I'm meeting her tonight, but I know—

[BESSIE *throws open the curtain between the two rooms and enters.*]

BESSIE. Maybe we'll serve for you a special blue plate supper in the garden?

JACOB. All right, all right.

[BESSIE *goes over to the window, levels the shade and on her way out, clicks off the radio.*]

MORTY [*within*]. Leave the music, Bessie.

[*She clicks it on again, looks at them, exits.*]

RALPH. I know. . . .

JACOB. Don't cry, boychick. [*Goes over to* RALPH.] Why
should you make like this? Tell me why you should
cry, just tell me. . . . [JACOB *takes* RALPH *in his arms
and both, trying to keep back the tears, trying fear-
fully not to be heard by the others in the dining
room, begin crying.*] You mustn't cry. . . .

[*The tango twists on. Inside the clatter of dishes and
the clash of cutlery sound.* MORTY *begins to howl
with laughter.*]

CURTAIN

SCENE II

That night. The dark dining room.
AT RISE JACOB *is heard in his lighted room, reading
from a sheet, declaiming aloud as if to an audience.*

JACOB. They are there to remind us of the horrors—
under those crosses lie hundreds of thousands of
workers and farmers who murdered each other in
uniform for the greater glory of capitalism. [*Comes
out of his room.*] The new imperialist war will send
millions to their death, will bring prosperity to the
pockets of the capitalist—aie, Morty—and will bring
only greater hunger and misery to the masses of
workers and farmers. The memories of the last
world slaughter are still vivid in our minds. [*Hearing a noise he quickly retreats to his room.* RALPH
comes in from the street. He sits with hat and coat
on.* JACOB *tentatively opens the door and asks:*]
Ralphie?

RALPH. It's getting pretty cold out.

JACOB [*enters room fully, cleaning hair clippers*]. We should have steam till twelve instead of ten. Go complain to the Board of Health.

RALPH. It might snow.

JACOB. It don't hurt . . . extra work for men.

RALPH. When I was a kid I laid awake at nights and heard the sounds of trains . . . far-away lonesome sounds . . . boats going up and down the river. I used to think of all kinds of things I wanted to do. What was it, Jake? Just a bunch of noise in my head?

JACOB [*waiting for news of the girl*]. You wanted to make for yourself a certain kind of world.

RALPH. I guess I didn't. I'm feeling pretty, pretty low.

JACOB. You're a young boy and for you life is all in front like a big mountain. You got feet to climb.

RALPH. I don't know how.

JACOB. So you'll find out. Never a young man had such opportunity like today. He could make history.

RALPH. Ten p.m. and all is well. Where's everybody?

JACOB. They went.

RALPH. Uncle Morty too?

JACOB. Hennie and Sam he drove down.

RALPH. I saw her.

JACOB [*alert and eager*]. Yes, yes, tell me.

RALPH. I waited in Mount Morris Park till she came out. So cold I did a buck'n wing to keep warm. She's scared to death.

JACOB. They made her?

RALPH. Sure. She wants to go. They keep yelling at her—they want her to marry a millionaire, too.

JACOB. You told her you love her?

RALPH. Sure. "Marry me," I said. "Marry me tomorrow." On sixteen bucks a week. On top of that I had to admit Mom'd have Uncle Morty get me fired in a second. . . . Two can starve as cheap as one!

JACOB. So what happened?

RALPH. I made her promise to meet me tomorrow.

JACOB. Now she'll go in the West?

RALPH. I'd fight the whole goddam world with her, but not her. No guts. The hell with her. If she wantsa go—all right—I'll get along.

JACOB. For sure, there's more important things than girls. . . .

RALPH. You said a mouthful . . . and maybe I don't see it. She'll see what I can do. No one stops me when I get going. . . . [*Near to tears, he has to stop. JACOB examines his clippers very closely.*]

JACOB. Electric clippers never do a job like by hand.

RALPH. Why won't Mom let us live here?

JACOB. Why? Why? Because in a society like this today people don't love. Hate!

RALPH. Gee, I'm no bum who hangs around pool parlors. I got the stuff to go ahead. I don't know what to do.

JACOB. Look on me and learn what to do, boychick. Here sits an old man polishing tools. You think maybe I'll use them again! Look on this failure and see for seventy years he talked, with good ideas, but only in the head. It's enough for me now I should see your happiness. This is why I tell you—DO! Do what is in your heart and you carry in yourself a revolution. But you should act. Not like me. A man who had golden opportunities but drank instead a glass tea. No . . . [*A pause of silence.*]

RALPH [*listening*]. Hear it? The Boston air mail plane. Ten minutes late. I get a kick the way it cuts across the Bronx every night.

[*The bell rings:* SAM, *excited, disheveled, enters.*]

JACOB. You came back so soon?

SAM. Where's Mom?

JACOB. Mom? Look on the chandelier.

SAM. Nobody's home?

JACOB. Sit down. Right away they're coming. You went in the street without a tie?

SAM. Maybe it's a crime.

JACOB. Excuse me.

RALPH. You had a fight with Hennie again?

SAM. She'll fight once . . . some day. . . . [*Lapses into silence.*]

JACOB. In my day the daughter came home. Now comes the son-in-law.

SAM. Once too often she'll fight with me, Hennie. I mean it. I mean it like anything. I'm a person with a bad heart. I sit quiet, but inside I got a—

RALPH. What happened?

SAM. I'll talk to Mom. I'll see Mom.

JACOB. Take an apple.

SAM. Please . . . he tells me apples.

RALPH. Why hop around like a billiard ball?

SAM. Even in a joke she should dare say it.

JACOB. My grandchild said something?

SAM. To my father in the old country they did a joke . . . I'll tell you: One day in Odessa he talked to another Jew on the street. They didn't like it, they jumped on him like a wild wolf.

RALPH. Who?

SAM. Cossacks. They cut off his beard. A Jew without a beard! He came home—I remember like yesterday how he came home and went in bed for two days. He put like this the cover on his face. No one should see. The third morning he died.

RALPH. From what?

SAM. From a broken heart . . . Some people are like this. Me too. I could die like this from shame.

JACOB. Hennie told you something?

SAM. Straight out she said it—like a lightning from the sky. The baby ain't mine. She said it.

RALPH. Don't be a dope.

JACOB. For sure, a joke.

RALPH. She's kidding you.

SAM. She should kid a policeman, not Sam Feinschreiber. Please . . . you don't know her like me. I wake up in the nighttime and she sits watching me like I don't know what. I make a nice living from the store. But it's no use—she looks for a star in the sky. I'm afraid like anything. You could go crazy from less even. What I shall do I'll ask Mom.

JACOB. "Go home and sleep," she'll say. "It's a bad dream."

SAM. It don't satisfy me more, such remarks, when Hennie could kill in the bed. [JACOB *laughs.*] Don't laugh. I'm so nervous—look, two times I weighed myself on the subway station. [*Throws small cards to table.*]

JACOB [*examining one*]. One hundred and thirty-eight —also a fortune. [*Turns it and reads.*] "You are inclined to deep thinking, and have a high admiration for intellectual excellence and inclined to be very exclusive in the selection of friends." Correct! I think maybe you got mixed up in the wrong family, Sam.

[MYRON *and* BESSIE *now enter.*]

BESSIE. Look, a guest! What's the matter? Something wrong with the baby? [*Waits.*]

SAM. No.

BESSIE. Noo?

SAM [*in a burst*]. I wash my hands from everything.

BESSIE. Take off your coat and hat. Have a seat. Excitement don't help. Myron, make tea. You'll have a glass tea. We'll talk like civilized people. [MYRON *goes.*] What is it, Ralph, you're all dressed up for a party? [*He looks at her silently and exits. To* SAM.] We saw a very good movie, with Wallace Beery. He acts like life, very good.

MYRON [*within*]. Polly Moran too.

BESSIE. Polly Moran too—a woman with a nose from here to Hunts Point, but a fine player. Poppa, take away the tools and the books.

JACOB. All right. [*Exits to his room.*]

BESSIE. Noo, Sam, why do you look like a funeral?

SAM. I can't stand it. . . .

BESSIE. Wait. [*Yells.*] You took up Tootsie on the roof.

JACOB [*within*]. In a minute.

BESSIE. What can't you stand?

SAM. She said I'm a second fiddle in my own house.

BESSIE. Who?

SAM. Hennie. In the second place, it ain't my baby, she said.

BESSIE. What? What are you talking?

[MYRON *enters with dishes.*]

SAM. From her own mouth. It went like a knife in my heart.

BESSIE. Sam, what're you saying?

SAM. Please, I'm making a story? I fell in the chair like a dead.

BESSIE. Such a story you believe?

SAM. I don't know.

BESSIE. How you don't know?

SAM. She told me even the man.

BESSIE. Impossible!

SAM. I can't believe myself. But she said it. I'm a second fiddle, she said. She made such a yell everybody heard for ten miles.

BESSIE. Such a thing Hennie should say—impossible!

SAM. What should I do? With my bad heart such a remark kills.

MYRON. Hennie don't feel well, Sam. You see, she—

BESSIE. What then?—a sick girl. Believe me, a mother knows. Nerves. Our Hennie's got a bad temper. You'll let her she says anything. She takes after me —nervous. [*To* MYRON.] You ever heard such a remark in all your life? She should make such a statement! Bughouse.

MYRON. The little one's been sick all these months. Hennie needs a rest. No doubt.

BESSIE. Sam don't think she means it—

MYRON. Oh, I know he don't, of course—

BESSIE. I'll say the truth, Sam. We didn't half the time understand her ourselves. A girl with her own mind. When she makes it up, wild horses wouldn't change her.

SAM. She don't love me.

BESSIE. This is sensible, Sam?

SAM. Not for a nickel.

BESSIE. What do you think? She married you for your money? For your looks? You ain't no John Barrymore, Sam. No, she liked you.

SAM. Please, not for a nickel.

[JACOB *stands in the doorway.*]

BESSIE. We stood right here the first time she said it. "Sam Feinschreiber's a nice boy," she said it, "a boy he's got good common sense, with a business head." Right here she said it, in this room. You sent her two boxes of candy together, you remember?

MYRON. Loft's candy.

BESSIE. This is when she said it. What do you think?

MYRON. You were just the only boy she cared for.

BESSIE. So she married you. Such a world . . . plenty of boy friends she had, believe me!

JACOB. A popular girl . . .

MYRON. Y-e-s.

BESSIE. I'll say it plain out—Moe Axelrod offered her plenty—a servant, a house . . . she don't have to pick up a hand.

MYRON. Oh, Moe? Just wild about her . . .

SAM. Moe Axelrod? He wanted to—

BESSIE. But she didn't care. A girl like Hennie you don't buy. I should never live to see another day if I'm telling a lie.

SAM. She was kidding me.

BESSIE. What then? You shouldn't be foolish.

SAM. The baby looks like my family. He's got Feinschreiber eyes.

BESSIE. A blind man could see it.

JACOB. Sure . . . sure. . . .

SAM. The baby looks like me. Yes . . .

BESSIE. You could believe me.

JACOB. Any day . . .

SAM. But she tells me the man. She made up his name too?

BESSIE. Sam, Sam, look in the phone book—a million names.

MYRON. Tom, Dick and Harry.

[JACOB *laughs quietly, soberly.*]

BESSIE. Don't stand around, Poppa. Take Tootsie on the roof. And you don't let her go under the water tank.

JACOB. Schmah Yisroeal. Behold! [*Quietly laughing he goes back into his room, closing the door behind him.*]

SAM. I won't stand he should make insults. A man eats out his—

BESSIE. No, no, he's an old man—a second childhood. Myron, bring in the tea. Open a jar of raspberry jelly.

[MYRON *exits.*]

SAM. Mom, you think—?

BESSIE. I'll talk to Hennie. It's all right.

SAM. Tomorrow, I'll take her by the doctor.

[RALPH *enters.*]

BESSIE. Stay for a little tea.

SAM. No, I'll go home. I'm tired. Already I caught a cold in such weather. [*Blows his nose.*]

MYRON [*entering with stuffs*]. Going home?

SAM. I'll go in bed. I caught a cold.

MYRON. Teddy Roosevelt used to say, "When you have a problem, sleep on it."

BESSIE. My Sam is no problem.

MYRON. I don't mean . . . I mean he said—

BESSIE. Call me tomorrow, Sam.

SAM. I'll phone supper time. Sometime I think there's something funny about me.

[MYRON *sees him out. In the following pause Caruso is heard singing within.*]

BESSIE. A bargain! Second fiddle. By me he don't even play in the orchestra—a man like a mouse. Maybe she'll lay down and die 'cause he makes a living?

RALPH. Can I talk to you about something?

BESSIE. What's the matter—I'm biting you?

RALPH. It's something about Blanche.

BESSIE. Don't tell me.

RALPH. Listen now—

BESSIE. I don't wanna know.

RALPH. She's got no place to go.

BESSIE. I don't want to know.

RALPH. Mom, I love this girl. . . .

BESSIE. So go knock your head against the wall.

RALPH. I want her to come here. Listen, Mom, I want you to let her live here for a while.

BESSIE. You got funny ideas, my son.

RALPH. I'm as good as anyone else. Don't I have some

rights in the world? Listen, Mom, if I don't do something, she's going away. Why don't you do it? Why don't you let her stay here for a few weeks? Things'll pick up. Then we can—

BESSIE. Sure, sure. I'll keep her fresh on ice for a wedding day. That's what you want?

RALPH. No, I mean you should—

BESSIE. Or maybe you'll sleep here in the same bed without marriage.

[JACOB *stands in his doorway, dressed.*]

RALPH. Don't say that, Mom. I only mean . . .

BESSIE. What you mean, I know . . . and what I mean I also know. Make up your mind. For your own good, Ralphie. If she dropped in the ocean I don't lift a finger.

RALPH. That's all, I suppose.

BESSIE. With me it's one thing—a boy should have respect for his own future. Go to sleep, you look tired. In the morning you'll forget.

JACOB. "Awake and sing, ye that dwell in dust, and the earth shall cast out the dead." It's cold out?

MYRON. Oh, yes.

JACOB. I'll take up Tootsie now.

MYRON [*eating bread and jam*]. He come on us like the wild man of Borneo, Sam. I don't think Hennie was fool enough to tell him the truth like that.

BESSIE. Myron!

[*A deep pause.*]

RALPH. What did he say?

BESSIE. Never mind.

RALPH. I heard him. I heard him. You don't needa tell me.

BESSIE. Never mind.

RALPH. You trapped that guy.

BESSIE. Don't say another word.

RALPH. Just have respect? That's the idea?

BESSIE. Don't say another word. I'm boiling over ten times inside.

RALPH. You won't let Blanche here, huh. I'm not sure I want her. You put one over on that little shrimp. The cat's whiskers, Mom?

BESSIE. I'm telling you something!

RALPH. I got the whole idea. I get it so quick my head's swimming. Boy, what a laugh! I suppose you know about this, Jake?

JACOB. Yes.

RALPH. Why didn't you do something?

JACOB. I'm an old man.

RALPH. What's that got to do with the price of bonds? Sits around and lets a thing like that happen! You make me sick too.

MYRON [*after a pause*]. Let me say something, son.

RALPH. Take your hand away! Sit in a corner and wag your tail. Keep on boasting you went to law school for two years.

MYRON. I want to tell you—

RALPH. You never in your life had a thing to tell me.

BESSIE [*bitterly*]. Don't say a word. Let him, let him run and tell Sam. Publish in the papers, give a broadcast on the radio. To him it don't matter nothing his family sits with tears pouring from the eyes. [*To* JACOB.] What are you waiting for? I didn't tell you twice already about the dog? You'll stand around with Caruso and make a bughouse. It ain't enough all day long. Fifty times I told you I'll break every record in the house. [*She brushes past him, breaks the records, comes out.*] The next time I say something you'll maybe believe it. Now maybe you learned a lesson.

[*Pause.*]

JACOB [*quietly*]. Bessie, new lessons . . . not for an old dog.

[MOE *enters.*]

MYRON. You didn't have to do it, Momma.

BESSIE. Talk better to your son, Mr. Berger! Me, I don't lay down and die for him and Poppa no more. I'll work like a nigger? For what? Wait, the day comes when you'll be punished. When it's too late you'll remember how you sucked away a mother's life. Talk to him, tell him how I don't sleep at night. [*Bursts into tears and exits.*]

MOE [*sings*]. "Good-bye to all your sorrows. You never hear them talk about the war, in the land of Yama Yama. . . ."

MYRON. Yes, Momma's a sick woman, Ralphie.

RALPH. Yeah?

MOE. We'll be out of the trenches by Christmas. Putt, putt, putt . . . here, stinker. . . . [*Picks up Tootsie, a small, white poodle that just then enters from the hall.*] If there's reincarnation in the next life I wanna be a dog and lay in a fat lady's lap. Barrage over? How 'bout a little pinochle, Pop?

JACOB. Nnno.

RALPH [*taking dog*]. I'll take her up. [*Conciliatory.*]

JACOB. No, I'll do it. [*Takes dog.*]

RALPH [*ashamed*]. It's cold out.

JACOB. I was cold before in my life. A man sixty-seven. . . . [*Strokes the dog.*] Tootsie is my favorite lady in the house. [*He slowly passes across the room and exits. A settling pause.*]

MYRON. She cried all last night—Tootsie—I heard her in the kitchen like a young girl.

MOE. Tonight I could do something. I got a yen . . . I don't know.

MYRON [*rubbing his head*]. My scalp is impoverished.

RALPH. Mom bust all his records.

MYRON. She didn't have to do it.

MOE. Tough tit! Now I can sleep in the morning. Who the hell wantsa hear a wop air his tonsils all day long!

RALPH [*handling the fragment of a record*]. "O Paradisol"

MOE [*gets cards*]. It's snowing out, girls.

MYRON. There's no more big snows like in the old days. I think the whole world's changing. I see it, right under our very eyes. No one hardly remembers any more when we used to have gaslight and all the dishes had little fishes on them.

MOE. It's the system, girls.

MYRON. I was a little boy when it happened—the Great Blizzard. It snowed three days without a stop that time. Yes, and the horse cars stopped. A silence of death was on the city and little babies got no milk . . . they say a lot of people died that year.

MOE [*singing as he deals himself cards*].
    "Lights are blinking while you're drinking,
    That's the place where the good fellows go.
    Good-bye to all your sorrows,
    You never hear them talk about the war,
    In the land of Yama Yama.
    Funicalee, funicala, funicalo. . . ."

MYRON. What can I say to you, Big Boy?

RALPH. Not a damn word.

MOE [*goes "ta ra ta ra" throughout.*]

MYRON. I know how you feel about all those things, I know.

RALPH. Forget it.

MYRON. And your girl . . .

RALPH. Don't soft soap me all of a sudden.

MYRON. I'm not foreign born. I'm an American, and

yet I never got close to you. It's an American father's duty to be his son's friend.

RALPH. Who said that—Teddy R.?

MOE [*dealing cards*]. You're breaking his heart, "Litvak."

MYRON. It just happened the other day. The moment I began losing my hair I just knew I was destined to be a failure in life . . . and when I grew bald I was. Now isn't that funny, Big Boy?

MOE. It's a pisscutter!

MYRON. I believe in Destiny.

MOE. You get what-it-takes. Then they don't catch you with your pants down. [*Sings out.*] Eight of clubs. . . .

MYRON. I really don't know. I sold jewelry on the road before I married. It's one thing to— Now here's a thing the druggist gave me. [*Reads.*] "The Marvel Cosmetic Girl of Hollywood is going on the air. Give this charming little radio singer a name and win five thousand dollars. If you will send—"

MOE. Your old man still believes in Santy Claus.

MYRON. Someone's got to win. The government isn't gonna allow everything to be a fake.

MOE. It's a fake. There ain't no prizes. It's a fake.

MYRON. It says—

RALPH [*snatching it*]. For Christ's sake, Pop, forget it. Grow up. Jake's right—everybody's crazy. It's like a zoo in this house. I'm going to bed.

MOE. In the land of Yama Yama . . . [*Goes on with ta ra.*]

MYRON. Don't think life's easy with Momma. No, but she means for your good all the time. I tell you she does, she—

RALPH. Maybe, but I'm going to bed.

[*Downstairs doorbell rings violently.*]

MOE [*ring*]. Enemy barrage begins on sector eight seventy-five.

RALPH. That's downstairs.

MYRON. We ain't expecting anyone this hour of the night.

MOE. "Lights are blinking while you're drinking, that's the place where the good fellows go. Good-bye to ta ra tara ra," etc.

RALPH. I better see who it is.

MYRON. I'll tick the button. [*As he starts, the apartment doorbell begins ringing, followed by large knocking.* MYRON *goes out.*]

RALPH. Who's ever ringing means it.

[*A loud excited voice outside.*]

MOE. "In the land of Yama Yama, Funicalee, funicalo, funic—"

[MYRON *enters followed by* SCHLOSSER *the janitor.* BESSIE *cuts in from the other side.*]

BESSIE. Who's ringing like a lunatic?

RALPH. What's the matter?

MYRON. Momma . . .

BESSIE. Noo, what's the matter?

[*Downstairs bell continues.*]

RALPH. What's the matter?

BESSIE. Well, well . . . ?

MYRON. Poppa . . .

BESSIE. What happened?

SCHLOSSER. He shlipped maybe in de snow.

RALPH. Who?

SCHLOSSER [*to* BESSIE]. Your fadder fall off de roof. . . . Ja.

[*A dead pause.* RALPH *then runs out.*]

BESSIE [*dazed*]. Myron . . . Call Morty on the phone . . . call him. [MYRON *starts for phone.*] No. I'll do it myself. I'll . . . do it.

[MYRON *exits.*]

SCHLOSSER [*standing stupidly*]. Since I was in dis country . . . I was pudding out de ash can . . . The snow is vet. . . .

MOE [*to* SCHLOSSER]. Scram.

[SCHLOSSER *exits.*]

[BESSIE *goes blindly to the phone, fumbles and gets it.* MOE *sits quietly, slowly turning cards over, but watching her.*]

BESSIE. He slipped. . . .

MOE [*deeply moved*]. Slipped?

BESSIE. I can't see the numbers. Make it, Moe, make it. . . .

MOE. Make it yourself. [*He looks at her and slowly goes back to his game of cards with shaking hands.*]

BESSIE. Riverside 7— . . . [*Unable to talk she dials slowly. The dial whizzes on.*]

MOE. Don't . . . make me laugh. . . . [*He turns over cards.*]

CURTAIN

Act three

A week later in the dining room. MORTY, BESSIE *and* MYRON *eating. Sitting in the front room is* MOE *marking a "dope sheet," but really listening to the others.*

BESSIE. You're sure he'll come tonight—the insurance man?

MORTY. Why not? I shtupped him a ten-dollar bill. Everything's hot delicatessen.

BESSIE. Why must he come so soon?

MORTY. Because you had a big expense. You'll settle

once and for all. I'm a great boy for making hay while the sun shines.

BESSIE. Stay till he'll come, Morty. . . .

MORTY. No, I got a strike downtown. Business don't stop for personal life. Two times already in the past week those bastards threw stink bombs in the showroom. Wait! We'll give them strikes—in the kishkas we'll give them. . . .

BESSIE. I'm a woman. I don't know about policies. Stay till he comes.

MORTY. Bessie—sweetheart, leave me live.

BESSIE. I'm afraid, Morty.

MORTY. Be practical. They made an investigation. Everybody knows Pop had an accident. Now we'll collect.

MYRON. Ralphie don't know Papa left the insurance in his name.

MORTY. It's not his business. And I'll tell him.

BESSIE. The way he feels. [*Enter* RALPH *into front room.*] He'll do something crazy. He thinks Poppa jumped off the roof.

MORTY. Be practical, Bessie. Ralphie will sign when I tell him. Everything is peaches and cream.

BESSIE. Wait for a few minutes. . . .

MORTY. Look, I'll show you in black on white what the policy says. *For God's sake, leave me live!* [*Angrily exits to kitchen. In parlor,* MOE *speaks to* RALPH, *who is reading a letter.*]

MOE. What's the letter say?

RALPH. Blanche won't see me no more, she says. I couldn't care very much, she says. If I didn't come like I said. . . . She'll phone before she leaves.

MOE. She don't know about Pop?

RALPH. She won't ever forget me she says. Look what she sends me . . . a little locket on a chain . . . if she calls I'm out.

MOE. You mean it?

RALPH. For a week I'm trying to go in his room. I guess he'd like me to have it, but I can't. . . .

MOE. Wait a minute! [*Crosses over.*] They're trying to rook you—a freeze-out.

RALPH. Who?

MOE. That bunch stuffin' their gut with hot pastrami. Morty in particular. Jake left the insurance—three thousand dollars—for you.

RALPH. For me?

MOE. Now you got wings, kid. Pop figured you could use it. That's why . . .

RALPH. That's why what?

MOE. It ain't the only reason he done it.

RALPH. He done it?

MOE. You think a breeze blew him off?

[HENNIE *enters and sits.*]

RALPH. I'm not sure what I think.

MOE. The insurance guy's coming tonight. Morty "shtupped" him.

RALPH. Yeah?

MOE. I'll back you up. You're dead on your feet. Grab a sleep for yourself.

RALPH. No!

MOE. Go on! [*Pushes boy into room.*]

SAM [*whom* MORTY *has sent in for the paper*]. Morty wants the paper.

HENNIE. So?

SAM. You're sitting on it. [*Gets paper.*] We could go home now, Hennie! Leon is alone by Mrs. Strasberg a whole day.

HENNIE. Go on home if you're so anxious. A full tub of diapers is waiting.

SAM. Why should you act this way?

HENNIE. 'Cause there's no bones in ice cream. Don't touch me.

SAM. Please, what's the matter. . . .

MOE. She don't like you. Plain as the face on your nose . . .

SAM. To me, my friend, you talk a foreign language.

MOE. A quarter you're lousy. [SAM *exits.*] Gimme a buck, I'll run it up to ten.

HENNIE. Don't do me no favors.

MOE. Take a chance. [*Stopping her as she crosses to doorway.*]

HENNIE. I'm a pushover.

MOE. I say lotsa things. You don't know me.

HENNIE. I know you—when you knock 'em down you're through.

MOE [*sadly*]. You still don't know me.

HENNIE. I know what goes in your wise-guy head.

MOE. Don't run away. . . . I ain't got hydrophobia. Wait. I want to tell you. . . . I'm leaving.

HENNIE. Leaving?

MOE. Tonight. Already packed.

HENNIE. Where?

MORTY [*as he enters followed by the others*]. My car goes through snow like a dose of salts.

BESSIE. Hennie, go eat. . . .

MORTY. Where's Ralphie?

MOE. In his new room. [*Moves into dining room.*]

MORTY. I didn't have a piece of hot pastrami in my mouth for years.

BESSIE. Take a sandwich, Hennie. You didn't eat all day. . . . [*At window.*] A whole week it rained cats and dogs.

MYRON. Rain, rain, go away. Come again some other days. [*Puts shawl on her.*]

MORTY. Where's my gloves?

SAM [*sits on stool*]. I'm sorry the old man lays in the rain.

MORTY. Personally, Pop was a fine man. But I'm a great

boy for an honest opinion. He had enough crazy
ideas for a regiment.

MYRON. Poppa never had a doctor in his whole life. . . .
[*Enter* RALPH.]

MORTY. He had Caruso. Who's got more from life?

BESSIE. Who's got more? . . .

MYRON. And Marx he had.

[MYRON *and* BESSIE *sit on sofa.*]

MORTY. Marx! Some say Marx is the new God today.
Maybe I'm wrong. Ha ha ha . . . Personally I
counted my ten million last night. . . . I'm sixteen
cents short. So tomorrow I'll go to Union Square and
yell no equality in the country! Ah, it's a new generation.

RALPH. You said it!

MORTY. What's the matter, Ralphie? What are you
looking funny?

RALPH. I hear I'm left insurance and the man's coming
tonight.

MORTY. Poppa didn't leave no insurance for you.

RALPH. What?

MORTY. In your name he left it—but not for you.

RALPH. It's my name on the paper.

MORTY. Who said so?

RALPH [*to his mother*]. The insurance man's coming tonight?

MORTY. What's the matter?

RALPH. I'm not talking to you. [*To his mother.*] Why?

BESSIE. I don't know why.

RALPH. He don't come in this house tonight.

MORTY. That's what *you* say.

RALPH. I'm not talking to you, Uncle Morty, but I'll
tell you, too, he don't come here tonight when
there's still mud on a grave. [*To his mother.*]
Couldn't you give the house a chance to cool off?

MORTY. Is this a way to talk to your mother?

RALPH. Was that a way to talk to your father?

MORTY. Don't be so smart with me, Mr. Ralph Berger!

RALPH. Don't be so smart with *me*.

MORTY. What'll you do? I say he's coming tonight. Who says no?

MOE [*suddenly, from the background*]. Me.

MORTY. Take a back seat, Axelrod. When you're in the family—

MOE. I got a little document here. [*Produces paper.*] I found it under his pillow that night. A guy who slips off a roof don't leave a note before he does it.

MORTY [*starting for* MOE *after a horrified silence*]. Let me see this note.

BESSIE. Morty, don't touch it!

MOE. Not if you crawled.

MORTY. It's a fake. Poppa wouldn't—

MOE. Get the insurance guy here and we'll see how— [*The bell rings*]. Speak of the devil . . . Answer it, see what happens.

[MORTY *starts for the ticker.*]

BESSIE. Morty, don't!

MORTY [*stopping*]. Be practical, Bessie.

MOE. Sometimes you don't collect on suicides if they know about it.

MORTY. You should let . . . You should let him. . . .

[*A pause in which* ALL *seem dazed. Bell rings insistently.*]

MOE. Well, we're waiting.

MORTY. Give me the note.

MOE. I'll give you the head off your shoulders.

MORTY. Bessie, you'll stand for this? [*Points to* RALPH.] Pull down his pants and give him with a strap.

RALPH [*as bell rings again*]. How about it?

BESSIE. Don't be crazy. It's not my fault. Morty said he should come tonight. It's not nice so soon. I didn't—

MORTY. I said it? Me?

BESSIE. Who then?

MORTY. You didn't sing a song in my ear a whole week to settle quick?

BESSIE. I'm surprised. Morty, you're a big liar.

MYRON. Momma's telling the truth, she is!

MORTY. Lissen. In two shakes of a lamb's tail, we'll start a real fight and then nobody won't like nobody. Where's my fur gloves? I'm going downtown. [*To* SAM.] You coming? I'll drive you down.

HENNIE [*to* SAM, *who looks questioningly at her*]. Don't look at me. Go home if you want.

SAM. If you're coming soon, I'll wait.

HENNIE. Don't do me any favors. Night and day he pesters me.

MORTY. You made a cushion—sleep!

SAM. I'll go home. I know . . . to my worst enemy I don't wish such a life—

HENNIE. Sam, keep quiet.

SAM [*quietly; sadly*]. No more free speech in America? [*Gets his hat and coat.*] I'm a lonely person. Nobody likes me.

MYRON. I like you, Sam.

HENNIE [*going to him gently; sensing the end*]. Please go home, Sam. I'll sleep here. . . . I'm tired and nervous. Tomorrow I'll come home. I love you. . . . I mean it. [*She kisses him with real feeling.*]

SAM. I would die for you. . . . [SAM *looks at her. Tries to say something, but his voice chokes up with a mingled feeling. He turns and leaves the room.*]

MORTY. A bird in the hand is worth two in the bush. Remember I said it. Good night. [*Exits after* SAM.]

[HENNIE *sits depressed.* BESSIE *goes up and looks at the picture calendar again.* MYRON *finally breaks the silence.*]

MYRON. Yesterday a man wanted to sell me a saxophone with pearl buttons. But I—

BESSIE. It's a beautiful picture. In this land, nobody works. . . . Nobody worries. . . . Come to bed, Myron. [*Stops at the door, and says to* RALPH.] Please don't have foolish ideas about the money.

RALPH. Let's call it a day.

BESSIE. It belongs for the whole family. You'll get your teeth fixed—

RALPH. And a pair of black and white shoes?

BESSIE. Hennie needs a vacation. She'll take two weeks in the mountains and I'll mind the baby.

RALPH. I'll take care of my own affairs.

BESSIE. A family needs for a rainy day. Times is getting worse. Prospect Avenue, Dawson, Beck Street—every day furniture's on the sidewalk.

RALPH. Forget it, Mom.

BESSIE. Ralphie, I worked too hard all my years to be treated like dirt. It's no law we should be stuck together like Siamese twins. Summer shoes you didn't have, skates you never had, but I bought a new dress every week. A lover I kept—Mr. Gigolo! Did I ever play a game of cards like Mrs. Marcus? Or was Bessie Berger's children always the cleanest on the block?! Here I'm not only the mother, but also the father. The first two years I worked in a stocking factory for six dollars while Myron Berger went to law school. If I didn't worry about the family who would? On the calendar it's a different place, but here without a dollar you don't look the world in the eye. Talk from now to next year—this is life in America.

RALPH. Then it's wrong. It don't make sense. If life made you this way, then it's wrong!

BESSIE. Maybe you wanted me to give up twenty years

ago. Where would you be now? You'll excuse my expression—a bum in the park!

RALPH. I'm not blaming you, Mom. Sink or swim—I see
it. But it can't stay like this.

BESSIE. My foolish boy . . .

RALPH. No, I see every house lousy with lies and hate.
He said it, Grandpa— Brooklyn hates the Bronx.
Smacked on the nose twice a day. But boys and girls
can get ahead like that, Mom. We don't want life
printed on dollar bills, Mom!

BESSIE. So go out and change the world if you don't
like it.

RALPH. I will! And why? 'Cause life's different in my
head. Gimme the earth in two hands. I'm strong.
There . . . hear him? The air mail off to Boston. Day
or night, he flies away, a job to do. That's us and it's
no time to die.

[*The airplane sound fades off as* MYRON *gives alarm
clock to* BESSIE *which she begins to wind.*]

BESSIE. "Mom, what does she know? She's old-fashioned!" But I'll tell you a big secret: My whole life
I wanted to go away too, but with children a woman
stays home. A fire burned in *my* heart too, but now
it's too late. I'm no spring chicken. The clock goes
and Bessie goes. Only my machinery can't be fixed.
[*She lifts a button: the alarm rings on the clock; she
stops it, says "Good night" and exits.*]

MYRON. I guess I'm no prize bag. . . .

BESSIE [*from within*]. Come to bed, Myron.

MYRON [*tears page off calendar*]. Hmmm . . . [*Exits to
her.*]

RALPH. Look at him, draggin' after her like an old
shoe.

MOE. Punch drunk. [*Phone rings.*] That's for me. [*At*

phone.] Yeah? . . . Just a minute. [*To* RALPH.] Your
girl . . .

RALPH. Jeez, I don't know what to say to her.

MOE. Hang up?

[RALPH *slowly takes phone.*]

RALPH. Hello. . . . Blanche, I wish. . . . I don't know
what to say. . . . Yes . . . Hello? . . . [*Puts phone
down.*] She hung up on me. . . .

MOE. Sorry?

RALPH. No girl means anything to me until . . .

MOE. Till when?

RALPH. Till I can take care of her. Till we don't look
out on an airshaft. Till we can take the world in two
hands and polish off the dirt.

MOE. That's a big order.

RALPH. Once upon a time I thought I'd drown to death
in bolts of silk and velour. But I grew up these last
few weeks. Jake said a lot.

MOE. Your memory's okay?

RALPH. But take a look at this. [*Brings armful of books
from* JACOB'S *room—dumps them on table.*] His
books, I got them too—the pages ain't cut in half of
them.

MOE. Perfect.

RALPH. Does it prove something? Damn tootin'! A ten-
cent nail-file cuts them. Uptown, downtown, I'll
read them on the way. Get a big lamp over the bed.
[*Picks up one.*] My eyes are good. [*Puts book in
pocket.*] Sure, inventory tomorrow. Coletti to Driscoll to Berger—that's how we work. It's a team down
the warehouse. Driscoll's a show-off, a wiseguy, and
Joe talks pigeons day and night. But they're like me,
looking for a chance to get to first base too. Joe
razzed me about my girl. But he don't know why. I'll
tell him. Hell, he might tell me something I don't

know. Get teams together all over. Spit on your hands and get to work. And with enough teams together maybe we'll get steam in the warehouse so our fingers don't freeze off. Maybe we'll fix it so life won't be printed on dollar bills.

MOE. Graduation Day.

RALPH [*starts for door of his room, stops*]. Can I have . . . Grandpa's note?

MOE. Sure you want it?

RALPH. Please— [MOE *gives it.*] It's blank!

MOE [*taking note back and tearing it up*]. That's right.

RALPH. Thanks! [*Exits.*]

MOE. The kid's a fighter! [*To* HENNIE.] Why are you crying?

HENNIE. I never cried in my life. [*She is now.*]

MOE [*starts for door. Stops*]. You told Sam you love him. . . .

HENNIE. If I'm sore on life, why take it out on him?

MOE. You won't forget me to your dyin' day—I was the first guy. Part of your insides. You won't forget. I wrote my name on you—indelible ink!

HENNIE. One thing I won't forget—how you left me crying on the bed like I was two for a cent!

MOE. Listen, do you think—

HENNIE. Sure. Waits till the family goes to the open air movie. He brings me perfume. . . . He grabs my arms—

MOE. You won't forget me!

HENNIE. How you left the next week?

MOE. So I made a mistake. For Chris' sake, don't act like the Queen of Roumania!

HENNIE. Don't make me laugh!

MOE. What the hell do you want, my head on a plate? Was my life so happy? Chris', my old man was a bum. I supported the whole damn family—five kids and Mom. When they grew up they beat it the hell away like rabbits. Mom died. I went to the war; got clapped down like a bedbug; woke up in a room without a leg. What the hell do you think, anyone's got it better than you? I never had a home either. I'm lookin' too!

HENNIE. So what?

MOE. So you're it—you're home for me, a place to live! That's the whole parade, sickness, eating out your heart! Sometimes you meet a girl—she stops it— that's love. . . . So take a chance! Be with me, Paradise. What's to lose?

HENNIE. My pride!

MOE [*grabbing her*]. What do you want? Say the word —I'll tango on a dime. Don't gimme ice when your heart's on fire!

HENNIE. Let me go!

[*He stops her.*]

MOE. WHERE?!

HENNIE. What do you want, Moe, what do you want?

MOE. You!

HENNIE. You'll be sorry you ever started—

MOE. You!

HENNIE. Moe, lemme go— [*Trying to leave.*] I'm getting up early—lemme go.

MOE. No! . . . I got enough fever to blow the whole damn town to hell. [*He suddenly releases her and half stumbles backwards. Forces himself to quiet down.*] You wanna go back to him? Say the word. I'll know what to do. . . .

HENNIE [*helplessly*]. Moe, I don't know what to say.

MOE. Listen to me.

HENNIE. What?

MOE. Come away. A certain place where it's moonlight and roses. We'll lay down, count stars. Hear the big ocean making noise. You lay under the trees. Champagne flows like— [*Phone rings.* MOE *finally answers the telephone.*] Hello? . . . Just a minute. [*Looks at* HENNIE.]

HENNIE. Who is it?

MOE. Sam.

HENNIE [*starts for phone, but changes her mind*]. I'm sleeping. . . .

MOE [*in phone*]. She's sleeping. . . . [*Hangs up. Watches* HENNIE *who slowly sits.*] He wants you to know he got home O.K. . . . What's on your mind?

HENNIE. Nothing.

MOE. Sam?

HENNIE. They say it's a palace on those Havana boats.

MOE. What's on your mind?

HENNIE [*trying to escape*]. Moe, I don't care for Sam— I never loved him—

MOE. But your kid—?

HENNIE. All my life I waited for this minute.

MOE [*holding her*]. Me too. Made believe I was talkin' just bedroom golf, but you and me forever was what I meant! Christ, baby, there's one life to live! Live it!

HENNIE. Leave the baby?

MOE. Yeah!

HENNIE. I can't. . . .

MOE. You can!

HENNIE. No. . . .

MOE. But you're not sure!

HENNIE. I don't know.

MOE. Make a break or spend the rest of your life in a coffin.

HENNIE. Oh, God, I don't know where I stand.

MOE. Don't look up there. Paradise, you're on a big boat headed south. No more pins and needles in your heart, no snake juice squirted in your arm. The whole world's green grass and when you cry it's because you're happy.

HENNIE. Moe, I don't know. . . .

MOE. Nobody knows, but you do it and find out. When you're scared the answer's zero.

HENNIE. You're hurting my arm.

MOE. The doctor said it—cut off your leg to save your life! And they done it—one thing to get another.

[*Enter* RALPH.]

RALPH. I didn't hear a word, but do it, Hennie, do it!

MOE. Mom can mind the kid. She'll go on forever, Mom. We'll send money back, and Easter eggs.

RALPH. I'll be here.

MOE. Get your coat . . . get it.

HENNIE. Moe!

MOE. I know . . . but get your coat and hat and kiss the house good-bye.

HENNIE. The man I love. . . . [MYRON *entering*.] I left my coat in Mom's room. [*Exits*.]

MYRON. Don't wake her up, Beauty. Momma fell asleep as soon as her head hit the pillow. I can't sleep. It was a long day. Hmmm. [*Examines his tongue in a buffet mirror*.] I was reading the other day a person with a thick tongue is feebleminded. I can do anything with my tongue. Make it thick, flat. No fruit in the house lately. Just a lone apple. [*He gets apple and paring knife and starts paring*.] Must be something wrong with me—I say I won't eat but I eat. [HENNIE *enters dressed to go out*.] Where you going, little Red Riding Hood?

HENNIE. Nobody knows, Peter Rabbit.

MYRON. You're looking very pretty tonight. You were a beautiful baby too. 1910, that was the year you was born. The same year Teddy Roosevelt come back from Africa.

HENNIE. Gee, Pop; you're such a funny guy.

MYRON. He was a boisterous man, Teddy. Good night.
[*He exits, paring apple.*]

RALPH. When I look at him, I'm sad. Let me die like a
dog, if I can't get more from life.

HENNIE. Where?

RALPH. Right here in the house! My days won't be for
nothing. Let Mom have the dough. I'm twenty-two
and kickin'! I'll get along. Did Jake die for us to
fight about nickels? No! "Awake and sing," he said.
Right here he stood and said it. The night he died,
I saw it like a thunderbolt! I saw he was dead and I
was born! I swear to God, I'm one week old! I want
the whole city to hear it—fresh blood, arms. We got
'em. We're glad we're living.

MOE. I wouldn't trade you for two pitchers and an outfielder. Hold the fort!

RALPH. So long.

MOE. So long.

[*They go and* RALPH *stands full and strong in the doorway, seeing them off, as the curtain slowly falls.*]

CURTAIN

END OF SUMMER

by S. N. Behrman

For May and Harold Freedman

From *Four Plays by S. N. Behrman.*
Copyright 1936 by Samuel N. Behrman.
Reprinted by permission of Random House, Inc.

*First production, February 17, 1936,
at the Guild Theatre, New York,
with the following cast:*

WILL DEXTER, *Shepperd Strudwick*
MRS. WYLER, *Mildred Natwick*
PAULA FROTHINGHAM, *Doris Dudley*
ROBERT, *Kendall Clark*
LEONIE FROTHINGHAM, *Ina Claire*
SAM FROTHINGHAM, *Minor Watson*
DR. KENNETH RICE, *Osgood Perkins*
DENNIS MCCARTHY, *Van Heflin*
DR. DEXTER, *Herbert Yost*
BORIS, COUNT MIRSKY, *Tom Powers*

SCENE

*The action of the play takes place in the
living room of Bay Cottage, the Frothinghams'
summer place in Northern Maine.*

TIME—*The present.*

Act one

SCENE—*The verandah-living room of the Frothingham estate, Bay Cottage, in Northern Maine. It is a charmingly furnished room with beautiful old distinguished pieces. A chintz couch and chairs give the room an air of informality. Beyond the door back you see a spacious, more formal room. Through the series of glass windows over the curving window seat on the right wall you see the early budding lilac and sumach. Woodbine and Virginia creeper are sprawling over the fence of native stone. Silver birch and maple are beginning to put out their leaves. The tops of red pine and cedar are visible over the rocks which fall away to the sea.*

TIME. *The present. A lovely afternoon in May.*

AT RISE. MRS. WYLER, *a very old lady and* WILL DEXTER, *an attractive, serious boy, are engaged in conversation.* MRS. WYLER *is knitting.*

WILL. When you were a young girl in Cleveland, did you see much of Mr. Rockefeller?

MRS. WYLER. Not much. Of course my husband saw him every day at the office. But he never came to our house. We were young and worldly. He was strict and religious.

WILL. Did you suspect, in those days, how rich you were going to be?

MRS. WYLER. Mercy no! We debated a long time before we moved up to Cleveland from Oil City. My mother thought Oil City was no place to bring up a young girl. She finally persuaded my father to let us move up to Cleveland. But there was a lot of talk about the expense.

WILL. Was Oil City lively?

MRS. WYLER [*demurely*]. It was pretty rough! I remember the celebration when they ran the first pipe-line through to Pittsburgh. That was a celebration!

WILL. The oil just poured, didn't it? Gushed out of the ground in great jets, and the people swarmed from everywhere to scoop it up.

MRS. WYLER. I remember we had a gusher in our back-yard. We put a fence around it to keep the cows from lapping up the oil.

WILL. Were you excited?

MRS. WYLER. Not by the oil.

WILL. I should think you would have been!

MRS. WYLER [*dryly*]. We weren't. Oil was smelly. We wanted to get away from it. We discovered bath-salts.

WILL. You didn't know it was the true fountain of your —dynasty?

MRS. WYLER. We left it to the men—as I look back over my life the principal excitement came from houses— buying and building houses. The shack in Oil City to the mansion on Fifth Avenue. We had houses everywhere—houses in London, houses in Paris, Newport and this—and yet, it seemed to me, we were always checking in and out of hotels.

WILL. It seems strange to think—

MRS. WYLER. What?

WILL. This golden stream—that you stumbled on so accidentally—it's flowing still—quenchless—and you

on it—all you dynastic families—floating along in it
—in luxurious barges!

MRS. WYLER. When I read these books about the early
days of oil—these debunking books, you call them—
they make me smile.

WILL. Do they? Why? I'd like to know that.

MRS. WYLER. They're so far from the truth.

WILL. Are they?

MRS. WYLER. Of course they are!

WILL. Why?

MRS. WYLER. Because they're written from a foreign
point of view—not *our* point of view. We did as well
as anybody could have done according to our lights.

WILL. Yes, but what sort of lights were they?

MRS. WYLER [*tolerantly*]. There you are!

WILL. How lucky you were!

MRS. WYLER [*teasing him*]. Our young men didn't moon
about. They made opportunities for themselves!

WILL. Or did the opportunities make them? All you
had to do was pack your week-end bag and pioneer.

MRS. WYLER. Is the world quite exhausted then?

WILL. Possibly not, but our pioneering might take a
form you would find—unpalatable.

MRS. WYLER. Yes yes. [*Benevolently.*] I suppose you're
one of those young radicals our colleges are said to
be full of nowadays. Tell me, what do you young
radicals stand for?

WILL. I haven't decided exactly what I'm for, but I'm
pretty certain what I'm against.

MRS. WYLER [*pumping him*]. Most young people are
bored by the past. You're full of curiosity. Why is
that?

WILL [*not committing himself*]. I'm interested.

MRS. WYLER. At my age to be permitted to talk of one's
youth is an indulgence. Ask me anything you like.
At my age also one has no reason for restraint. I have

had the bad judgment to survive most of my contemporaries.

WILL. I love talking to you, Mrs. Wyler. I think you're
very wise.

MRS. WYLER [*with a sigh*]. Go on thinking so—I'll try
not to disillusion you! [*A moment's pause.*] Are you
staying on here at Bay Cottage?

WILL. Oh, no, I have to go back to Amherst to get my
degree.

MRS. WYLER. And after that?

WILL [*humorously*]. The dole!

[*The old lady laughs.*]

MRS. WYLER. My daughter tells me she's invited your
father here.

WILL. Yes.

MRS. WYLER. I shall be so glad to meet him. He's an inventor, isn't he?

WILL. He's a physicist. Specializes in—

MRS. WYLER. Don't tell me—in spite of my great wisdom
I can't keep up with science. Whenever anybody
makes a scientific explanation to me I find there are
two things I don't know instead of just one.

WILL [*cheerfully*]. Anyway, Dad's been fired.

MRS. WYLER. I am very sorry to hear that.

WILL. He's been working on a method for improving
high-speed steel.

MRS. WYLER. Did he fail?

WILL. He succeeded. [MRS. WYLER *is surprised.*] They
decided that his discovery, if perfected and marketed, might increase the technological unemployment. They have decided therefore to call a halt on
scientific discovery—especially in those branches
where it might have practical results. That is one
of the differences, Mrs. Wyler, between my day—
and yours—in your day, you put a premium on in-
vention—we declare a moratorium on it.

[*The old lady gives him a shrewd look.*]

MRS. WYLER. Yes, yes. I am perfectly sure that you're in for a hard time, Will.

WILL. [*lightly, shrugging his shoulders*]. As I have been elected by my class as the one most likely to succeed, I am not worrying, Mrs. Wyler. All I have to do is bide my time.

MRS. WYLER [*amused*]. I am perfectly certain you'll come out! Paula tells me you and your friend, Dennis McCarthy, want to start some kind of magazine.

WILL. Yes. A national magazine for undergraduate America. You see, Mrs. Wyler, before the rift in our so-called system, college men were supposed to live exclusively in a world of ukuleles, football slogans, and petting-parties—*College Humor* sort of thing. But it was never entirely true. Now it is less true than ever. This magazine—if we can get it going— would be a forum for intercollegiate thought. It would be the organ of critical youth as opposed—to the other.

MRS. WYLER. What other?

WILL. The R.O.T.C., the Vigilantes and the Fascists— the Youth Movement of guns and sabres—

MRS. WYLER. I see. Well, I wish you luck, Will.

WILL. Thank you.

[PAULA FROTHINGHAM *comes in, a lovely young girl in gay summer slacks.*]

PAULA [*to* WILL]. Aren't you swimming? Hello, Granny.

WILL. Your grandmother and I have been discussing life.

PAULA. With a capital L, I suppose?

WILL. Enormous! I've been getting data on the pioneer age. Your grandmother thinks the reason we're in the condition we're in is because we're lazy.

MRS. WYLER [*mildly*]. Lazy? Did I say that?

WILL. In a way.

MRS. WYLER. If I said it, it must be so. Everybody over seventy is infallible!

PAULA [*nestling to her*]. Darling.

MRS. WYLER. Survival is quite a knack. You children don't realize it.

WILL. Oh, don't we though! It's getting harder every day.

MRS. WYLER. Nonsense! At your age you can't help it.

WILL. In your stately opulence that's what you think, Mrs. Wyler. You just don't know!

MRS. WYLER. Nonsense! Do you think your generation has a monopoly on hard times?

WILL. Now please don't tell me we've had depressions before?

MRS. WYLER [*rising to go*]. Paula, your young man is impertinent. Don't have anything to do with him. [*She goes out.*]

PAULA. What a conquest you've made of Granny! Way and ahead of all my beaus!

WILL. That undistinguished mob! Who couldn't?

PAULA. As long as you admit there is a mob . . .

WILL. Why wouldn't there be? Everybody loves you for your money!

PAULA [*confidently*]. I know it! And of all the fortune-hunters I've had dangling after me you're easily the most . . .

WILL. Blatant!

PAULA. That's it! Blatant! Like my new slacks?

WILL. Love 'em.

PAULA. Love me?

WILL. Loathe you.

PAULA. Good! Kiss? [*They kiss quickly.*]

WILL. Funny thing about your grandmother . . .

PAULA. Now I won't have you criticizing Granny . . .

WILL. I'm crazy about her. You feel she's been through everything and that she understands everything. Not this though. Not the essential difference between her times and ours.

PAULA. Oh dear! Is it the end of the world then?

WILL. The end of this world.

PAULA [*goes to window seat right, with a sigh*]. Such a pretty world. [*She points through windows at the garden and sea beyond.*] Look at it! Too bad it has to go! Meantime before it quite dissolves let's go for a swim. [*She starts for door.*]

WILL [*abstracted*]. All right . . . [*Following her to window seat.*]

PAULA [*she turns back*]. What's on your mind?

WILL. Wanted to speak to you about something. . . .

PAULA. What?

WILL [*embarrassed slightly*]. Er—your mother. . . .

PAULA. What's Mother gone and done now? Out with it. Or is it you? My boy-friends are always in love with Mother. I've had to contend with that all my life. So if it's that you needn't even mention it . . . come on.

WILL. No, but really, Paula. . . .

PAULA. Well then, out with it! What is it!

WILL. This. [*He gives her note.*] Found it on my breakfast tray this morning in a sealed envelope marked "Confidential."

PAULA [*reading note aloud, rather bewildered*]. "To give my little girl a good time with. Leonie Frothingham."

WILL. And this! [*He hands her check.* PAULA *takes it and looks at it.*]

PAULA. A hundred dollars. Does Mother think her little girl can have a good time with *that?* She doesn't know her little girl!

WILL. But what'll I do with it? How'll I get it back to her?

PAULA. Over my dead body you'll get it back to her!

You'll spend it on Mother's little girl. Now come on
  swimming!

WILL. Does your mother put one of these on every
  breakfast tray?

PAULA. Argue it out with her.

WILL. I can't. It would seem ungracious. You must give
  it back to her for me.

PAULA. Catch me! Don't take it too seriously. She slips
  all the kids something every once in a while. She
  knows my friends are all stony. You overestimate the
  importance of money, Will—it's a convenience, that's
  all. You've got a complex on it.

WILL. I have! I've got to have. It's all right to be dainty
  about money when you've lots of it as you have. . . .

PAULA. Rotten with it is the expression, I believe. . . .

WILL. I repudiate that expression. It is genteel and
  moralistic. You can't be rotten with money—you can
  only be *alive* with it.

PAULA. You and the rest of our crowd make me feel it's
  bad taste to be rich. But what can I do? I didn't ask
  for it!

WILL. I know. But look here . . . I've got a brother out
  of college two years who's worked six weeks in that
  time and is broke and here I am in an atmosphere
  with hundred-dollar bills floating around!

PAULA [*with check*]. Send him that!

WILL. Misapplication of funds!

PAULA [*warmly*]. Mother would be only too . . .

WILL. I know she would—but that isn't the point. . . .
  You know, Paula—

PAULA. What?

WILL. Sometimes I think if we weren't in love with each
  other we should be irreconcilable enemies—

PAULA. Nothing but sex, eh?

WILL. That's all.

PAULA. In that case— [*They kiss.*]

WILL. That's forgiving. But seriously, Paula—

PAULA. Seriously what?

WILL. I can't help feeling I'm here on false pretenses. What am I doing with a millionaire family—with you? If your mother knew what I think, and what I've let you in for in college—she wouldn't touch me with a ten-foot pole. And you too—I'm troubled about the superficiality of your new opinions. Isn't your radicalism—acquired coloring?

PAULA. I hope not. But—so is all education.

WILL. I know but—!

PAULA. What are you bleating about? Didn't I join you on that expedition to Kentucky to be treated by that sovereign state as an offensive foreigner? My back aches yet when I remember that terrible bus ride. Didn't I get my name in the papers picketing? Didn't I give up my holiday to go with you to the Chicago Peace Congress? Didn't I?

WILL [*doubtfully*]. Yes, you did.

PAULA. But you're not convinced. Will darling, don't you realize that since knowing you and your friends, since I've, as you say, acquired your point of view about things, my life has had an excitement and a sense of reality it's never had before. I've simply come alive—that's all! Before then I was bored—terribly bored without knowing why. I wanted something more—fundamental—without knowing what. You've made me see. I'm terribly grateful to you, Will darling. I always shall be.

WILL. You are a dear, Paula, and I adore you—but—

PAULA. Still unconvinced?

WILL. This money of yours. What'll it do to us?

PAULA. I'll turn it over to you. Then you can give me an allowance—and save your pride.

WILL. I warn you, Paula—

PAULA. What?

WILL. If you turn it over to me, I'll use it in every way I can to make it impossible for anyone to have so much again.

PAULA. That's all right with me, Will.

WILL. Sometimes you make me feel I'm taking candy from babies.

PAULA. The candy is no good for the baby, anyway. Besides, let's cross that bridge when we come to it.

[ROBERT, *the butler, enters.*]

ROBERT. I beg your pardon, Miss Frothingham.

PAULA. Yes, Robert?

ROBERT. Telephone for you.

PAULA. Thank you, Robert. [*She crosses to table back of sofa for telephone. At phone.*] Yes—this is Paula— Dad!—Darling!—Where are you? . . . but how wonderful . . . I thought you were in New York . . . well, come right over this minute. . . . Will you stay the night? . . . Oh, too bad! . . . I'll wait right here for you. Hurry, darling! Bye! [*She hangs up.*] Imagine, Dad! He's motoring up to Selena Bryant's at Murray Bay—I'm dying to have you meet him. He's the lamb of the world.

WILL. Not staying long, is he?

PAULA. No. He wants to see Mother he says. I wonder . . . oh, dear!

WILL. What?

PAULA. I was so excited I forgot to tell him. . . .

WILL. What?

PAULA. That a new friend of Mother's is coming.

WILL. The Russian?

PAULA. The Russian's here. He dates from last winter. You're behind the times, Will.

WILL. Who's the new friend?

PAULA. I'm not sure about it all yet. Maybe Mother isn't either. But I've had some experience in watching them come and go and my instinct tells me Dr. Rice is elected.

WILL. Who is Dr. Rice?

PAULA. Psychoanalyst from New York. [*Burlesquing slightly.*] The last word, my dear—

[*At this point the object of* PAULA'S *maternal impulse comes in, running a little and breathless, like a young girl.* LEONIE FROTHINGHAM, *as she has a daughter of nearly twenty, must be herself forty, but, at this moment, she might be sixteen. She is slim, girlish, in a young and quivering ecstasy of living and anticipation. For* LEONIE, *her daughter is an agreeable phenomenon whom she does not specially relate to herself biologically—a lovely apparition who hovers intermittently in the wild garden of her life. There is something, for all her gaiety, heartbreaking about* LEONIE, *something childish and childlike—an acceptance of people instantly and uncritically at the best of their own valuation. She is impulsive and warm-hearted and generous to a fault. Her own fragile and exquisite loveliness she offers to the world half shyly, tentatively, bearing it like a cup containing a precious liquid of which not a drop must be spilled. A spirituelle amoureuse, she is repelled by the gross or the voluptuary; this is not hypocrisy—it is, in* LEONIE, *a more serious defect than that. In the world in which she moves hypocrisy is merely a social lubricant but this myopia—alas for* LEONIE!—*springs from a congenital and temperamental inability to face anything but the pleasantest and the most immediately appealing and the most flattering aspects of things—in life and in her own nature. At this moment, though, she is the loveliest fabrication of Nature, happy in the summer sun and loving all the world.*]

LEONIE. My darlings, did you ever know such a day?

WILL [*he is a shy boy with her*]. It's nice!

LEONIE. Nice! It's . . . [*Her gesture conveys her utter inadequacy to express the beauties of the day.*] It's— radiant! It knows it's radiant! The world is pleased with herself today. Is the world a woman? Today she is—a lovely young girl in blue and white.

WILL. In green and white.

LEONIE [*agreeing—warmly*]. In green and white!—it depends where you look, doesn't it? I'm just off to the station to meet Dr. Rice. Will, you'll be fascinated by him.

PAULA [*cutting in—crisply*]. Sam telephoned.

LEONIE. Sam!

PAULA. Your husband. My father. Think back, Leonie.

LEONIE. Darling! Where is he?

PAULA. He's on his way here. He telephoned from Miller's Point.

LEONIE. Is he staying?

PAULA. No.

LEONIE. Why not?

PAULA. He's going on to Selena Bryant's.

LEONIE. What is this deep friendship between Sam and Selena Bryant?

PAULA. Now, Leonie, don't be prudish!

LEONIE [*appealing for protection to* WILL]. She's always teasing me. She's always teasing everybody about everything. Developed quite a vein. I must warn you, Paula—sarcasm isn't feminine. In their hearts men don't like it. Do you like it, Will? Do you really like it?

WILL. I hate it!

LEONIE [*in triumph to* PAULA]. There you see! He hates it!

PAULA [*tersely*]. He doesn't always hate it!

LEONIE [*her most winning smile on* WILL]. Does she

bully you, Will? Don't let her bully you. The sad
thing is, Paula, you're so charming. Why aren't you
content to be charming? Are you as serious as Paula,
Will? I hope not.

WILL. Much more.

LEONIE. I'm sorry to hear that. Still, for a man, it's all
right, I suppose. But why are the girls nowadays so
determined not to be feminine? Why? It's coming
back you know—I'm sure of it—femininity is due for
a revival.

PAULA. So are Herbert Hoover and painting on china.

LEONIE. Well I read that even in Russia ... the women
... [*She turns again to* WILL *whom she feels sympathetic*.] It isn't as if women had done such marvels
with their—masculinity! Have they? Are things better because women vote? Not that I can see. They're
worse. As far as I can see the women simply rein-
force the men in their—mistakes.

WILL [*to* PAULA]. She has you there!

LEONIE [*with this encouragement warming to her
theme*]. When I was a girl the calamities of the
world were on a much smaller scale. It's because the
women, who, after all, are half of the human race,
stayed at home and didn't bother. Now they do
bother—and look at us!

PAULA. Well, that's as Victorian as anything I ever—

LEONIE. I'd love to have been a Victorian. They were
much happier than we are, weren't they? Of course
they were.

PAULA [*defending herself to* WILL]. It's only Mother
that brings out the crusader in me—[*to* LEONIE.]
When you're not around I'm not like that at all.
Am I, Will?

[*But* WILL *is given no chance to answer because* LEONIE
is holding a sprig of lilac to his nostrils.]

LEONIE. Smell. [WILL *smells*.] Isn't it delicious?

WILL. It's lovely.

LEONIE. Here . . . . [*She breaks off a sprig and pins it into his lapel. While she is doing it she broaches a delicate subject quite casually to* PAULA.] Oh, by the way, Paula . . .

PAULA. Yes, Mother?

LEONIE. Did you mention to Sam that—that Boris—

PAULA. I didn't, no. It slipped my mind.

LEONIE. It doesn't matter in the least.

PAULA. Father isn't staying anyway. . . .

LEONIE. Well, why shouldn't he? You must make him. I want him to meet Dr. Rice. He's really a most extraordinary man.

PAULA. Where'd you find *him?*

LEONIE. I met him at a party at Sissy Drake's. He *saved* Sissy.

PAULA. From what?

LEONIE. From that awful eye-condition.

PAULA. Is he an oculist too?

LEONIE [*to* WILL]. She went to every oculist in the world—she went to Baltimore and she went to Vienna. Nobody could do a thing for her—her eyes kept blinking—twitching really in the most unaccountable way. It was an ordeal to talk to her—and of course she must have undergone agonies of embarrassment. But Dr. Rice psychoanalyzed her and completely cured her. How do you suppose? Well, he found that the seat of the trouble lay in her unconscious. It was too simple. She blinked in that awful way because actually she couldn't bear to look at her husband. So she divorced Drake and since she's married to Bill Wilmerding she's as normal as you or me. Now I'll take you into a little secret. I'm having Dr. Rice up to see Boris. Of course Boris mustn't know it's for him.

PAULA. What's the matter with Boris?

LEONIE. I'm not sure. I think he's working too hard.

WILL. What's he working at?

LEONIE. Don't you know? Didn't you tell him, Paula? His father's memoirs. He's the son, you know, of the great Count Mirsky!

WILL. I know.

LEONIE. I must show you the photographs of his father —wonderful old man with a great white beard like a snow-storm—looks like Moses—a Russian Moses— and Boris is sitting on his knees—couldn't be over ten years old and wearing a fur cap and boots— boots!—and they drank tea out of tall glasses with raspberry jelly in—people came from all over the world, you know, to see his father . . . !

WILL. Isn't it strange that Count Mirsky's son should find himself in this strange house on this odd headland of Maine—Maine of all places!—writing his father's life? It's fantastic!

PAULA [*with some malice*]. Is Dr. Rice going to help you acclimate him?

LEONIE. I hope so. You and Paula will have to entertain him—you young intellectuals. Isn't it a pity I have no mind? [*She rises and crosses to table right to arrange lily-of-the-valley sprigs in a vase.*]

PAULA [*to* WILL]. She knows it's her greatest asset. Besides she's a fake.

WILL [*gallantly*]. I'm sure she is.

LEONIE. Thank you, my dears. It's gallant of you. [*She crosses to* PAULA—*embraces her from behind.*] But I'm not deceived. I know what Paula thinks of me— she looks down on me because I won't get interested in sociology. There never were any such things about when I was a girl. The trouble is one generation never has any perspective about another generation.

WILL. That's what your mother was saying to me just a little while ago.

LEONIE. Was she? [*She sits left of* WILL.] I'm sure though Mother and I are much closer—that is, we understand each other better than Paula and I. Don't you think so, Paula?

PAULA [*considering it*]. Yes. I do think so.

LEONIE. I knew you'd agree. Something's happened between my generation and Paula's. New concepts. I don't know what they are exactly but I'm very proud that Paula's got them.

PAULA [*laughing helplessly*]. Oh, Mother! You reduce everything to absurdity!

LEONIE [*innocently*]. Do I? I don't mean to. At any rate it's a heavenly day and I adore you and I don't care about anything so long as you're happy. I want you to be happy.

PAULA [*helplessly*]. Oh dear!

LEONIE. What's the matter?

PAULA. You're saying that!

LEONIE. Is that wrong? Will—did I say something wrong?

PAULA. You want me to be happy. It's like saying you want me to be eight feet tall and to sing like Lily Pons.

LEONIE. Is it like that? Why? Will . . .

WILL [*gravely feeling he must stand up for* PAULA, *but hating to*]. Paula means . . . [*Pause.*]

LEONIE. Yes . . . ?

WILL [*miserable*]. She means—suppose there isn't any happiness to be had? Suppose the supply's run out?

LEONIE. But, Will, really . . . ! On a day like this! Why don't you go swimming? [*Rises.*] Nothing like sea-water for—morbidity! Run out indeed! And to-day of all days! Really! [*Gets gloves.*] I'm disappointed in you, Will. I counted on you especially . . .

WILL [*abjectly*]. I was only fooling!

LEONIE. Of course he was. [*Sits on arm of sofa beside WILL.*] Will, I rely on you. Don't let Paula brood. Can't she drop the sociology in the summer? I think in the fall you're much better—braced—for things like that. Keep her happy, Will.

WILL. I'll do my best now that—thanks to you—I have the means.

LEONIE. Oh . . . [*Remembering.*] Oh, you didn't mind, did you? I hope you didn't mind.

WILL [*embarrassed*]. Very generous of you.

LEONIE. Generous! Please don't say that. After all— we who are in the embarrassing position nowadays of being rich must do something with our money, mustn't we? That's why I'm helping Boris to write this book. *Noblesse oblige.* Don't you think so, Will? Boris tells me that the Russians—the *present* Russians—

WILL. You mean the Bolsheviks?

LEONIE. Yes, I suppose I do. He says they don't like his father at all any more and won't read his works because in his novels he occasionally went on the assumption that rich people had souls and spirits too. You don't think like that too, do you, Will—that because I'm rich I'm just not worth bothering about at all— No, you couldn't! [*The appeal is tremulous. WILL succumbs entirely.*]

WILL [*bluntly*]. Mrs. Frothingham, I love you!

LEONIE [*rises from arm of sofa and sits in sofa beside WILL. To PAULA*]. Isn't he sweet? [*To WILL.*] And I love you, Will. Please call me Leonie. Do you know how Mother happened to name me Leonie? I was born in Paris, you know, and I was to be called Ruhama after my father's sister. But Mother said

no. No child of mine, she said, shall be called Ruhama. She shall have a French name. And where
do you think she got Leonie?

WILL. From the French version of one of those Gideon
Bibles.

LEONIE [*as breathless as if it happened yesterday*]. Not
at all. From a novel the nurse was reading. She asked
the nurse what she was reading and the nurse gave
her the paper book and Mother opened it and found
Leonie!

WILL. What was the book?

LEONIE. Everyone wants to know that . . . But I don't
know. Mother didn't know. She kept the book to
give to me when I grew up. But one day she met M.
Jusserand on a train—he was the French Ambassador
to Washington, you know—and he picked up the
book in Mother's compartment and he read a page
of it and threw it out of the window because it was
trash! You see what I've had to live down.

WILL. Heroic!

LEONIE. I hope you stay all summer, Will. I won't hear
of your going anywhere else.

WILL. Don't worry. I have nowhere else to go!

LEONIE. Tell me—that magazine you and Dennis want
to start—will it be gay?

WILL. Not exactly.

LEONIE. Oh, dear! I know. Columns and columns of
reading matter and no pictures. Tell me—your father
is coming to dine, isn't he? I am so looking forward
to meeting him. I love scientific men. They're usually so nice and understanding. Now, I've really got
to go. [*Rises and starts out.*]

PAULA. Dennis will be on that train.

LEONIE. Oh, good! I like Dennis. He makes me laugh
and I like people around who make me laugh, but I
do wish he'd dress better. Why can't radicals be

chic? I saw a picture of Karl Marx the other day
and he looks like one of those advertisements before you take something. I'll look after Dennis, Will
—save you going to the station— [*To* PAULA.] And
Paula, tell Sam—

PAULA. Yes?

LEONIE [*forgetting the message to* SAM]. You know, I
asked Dr. Rice if he would treat me professionally
and he said I was uninteresting to him because I was
quite normal. Isn't that discouraging? Really, I must
cultivate something. Good-bye, darlings. [*She runs
out.*]

WILL. But what was the message to Sam? [*He sits.*]

PAULA [*helplessly*]. I'll never know. Neither will she.
[WILL *laughs.*] What can you do with her? She makes
me feel like an opinionated old woman. And I worry
about her.

WILL. Do you?

PAULA. Yes. She arouses my maternal impulse.

WILL [*who feels he can be casual about* LEONIE *now
that she is gone*]. She relies rather too much on
charm!

PAULA [*turning on him bitterly*]. Oh, she does, does
she! [*Goes over to sofa and sits right of* WILL.] You
renegade. You ruin all my discipline with Mother.
You're like a blushing schoolboy in front of her . . .

WILL [*protesting sheepishly*]. Now, Paula, don't exag-
gerate!

PAULA. You are! I thought in another minute you were
going to ask her to the frat dance. And where was
all that wonderful indignation about her leaving
you the check? Where was the insult to your pride?
Where was your starving brother in Seattle? Where?
Where?

WILL. I don't know but somehow you can't face your
mother with things like that. It seems cruel to face

her with realities. She seems outside of all that.

PAULA [*conceding that*]. Well, you're going to be no help to me in handling Mother, I can see that!

WILL [*changing subject—a bit sensitive about having yielded so flagrantly to* LEONIE]. This Russian—

PAULA. What about him?

WILL [*gauche*]. Platonic, do you suppose?

PAULA. Don't be naïve!

[*Enter* SAM FROTHINGHAM, PAULA's *father, a very pleasant-faced, attractive man between forty-five and fifty.*]

SAM. Oh, hello.

[WILL *rises.*]

PAULA [*flying to him*]. Darling!—

SAM [*they meet center and embrace*]. Hello, Paula. Delighted to see you.

PAULA. This is Will Dexter.

SAM [*shaking hands with* WILL]. How do you do?

WILL. I'm delighted to meet you.

PAULA [*to* WILL]. Wait for me at the beach, will you, Will?

WILL. No, I'll run down to the station and ride back with the others.

PAULA. Okay.

[SAM *nods to him.* WILL *goes out.*]

SAM [*crosses to front of sofa*]. Nice boy. [*Follows her.*]

PAULA. Like him?

SAM. Do you?

PAULA. I think so.

SAM. Special?

PAULA. Sort of.

SAM. Very special?

PAULA [*sits right end of sofa*]. Well—not sure.

SAM. Wait till you are. You've lots of time.

PAULA. Oh, he's not exactly impulsive.

SAM. Then he's just a fool.

PAULA. How are you, darling?

SAM. Uneasy.

PAULA. With me!

SAM. Especially.

PAULA. Darling, why?

SAM. I'll tell you. That's why I've come.

PAULA. Everything all right?

SAM. Oh, fine.

PAULA [*mystified*]. Then . . . ?

SAM [*switching off*]. How's Leonie?

PAULA. Fine. Delighted you were coming.

SAM. Was she?

PAULA. She really was. She's off to Ellsworth to meet a doctor.

SAM. Doctor?

PAULA. Psychoanalyst she's having up to massage her Russian's complexes.

SAM [*laughing*]. Oh— [*With a sigh.*] What's going to happen to Leonie?

PAULA. Why? She's on the crest!

SAM. She needs that elevation. Otherwise she sinks.

PAULA. Well—you know Mother . . .

SAM. Yes. [*A moment's pause.*] Paula?

PAULA. Yes, Dad.

SAM. The fact is—it's ridiculous I should feel so nervous about telling you—but the fact is . . .

PAULA. What?

SAM. I've fallen in love. I want to get married. There! Well, thank God that's out! [*He wipes his forehead, quite an ordeal.*] Romance at my age. It's absurd, isn't it?

PAULA. Selena Bryant?

SAM. Yes.

PAULA. She has a grown son.

SAM [*smiling at her*]. So have I—a grown daughter.

PAULA. You'll have to divorce Mother.

SAM. Yes.

PAULA. Poor Leonie!

SAM. Well, after all—Leonie—you know how we've lived for years.

PAULA. Has Leonie hurt you?

SAM. Not for a long time. If this with Selena hadn't happened we'd have gone on forever, I suppose. But it has.

PAULA. You know, I have a feeling that, in spite of everything, this is going to be a shock to Leonie.

SAM. Paula?

PAULA. Yes.

SAM. Do you feel I'm deserting you?

[*She turns her head away. She is very moved.*]

PAULA. No—you know how fond I am of you—I want you to be . . .

SAM [*deeply affected*]. Paula . . . !

PAULA. Happy. [*A silence. She is on the verge of tears.*]

SAM. I must make you see my side, Paula.

PAULA [*vehemently*]. I do!

SAM. It isn't only that—you're so young—but somehow —we decided very soon after you were born, Leonie and I, that our marriage could only continue on this sort of basis. For your sake we've kept it up. I thought I was content to be an—appendage—to Leonie's entourage. But I'm not—do you know what Selena—being with Selena and planning with Selena for ourselves has made me see—that I've never had a home. Does that sound mawkish?

PAULA. I thought you loved Bay Cottage.

SAM. Of our various ménages this is my favorite—it's the simplest. And I've had fun here with you— watching you grow up. But very soon after I married Leonie I found this out—that when you marry a very rich woman it's always *her* house you live in. [*A moment's pause.*]

PAULA. I'm awfully happy for you, Sam, really I am. You deserve everything but I can't help it, I . . .

SAM. I know. [*A pause.*] Paula . . .

PAULA. Yes, Dad?

SAM. You and I get on so well together—always have—Selena adores you and really—when you get to know her . . .

PAULA. I like Selena enormously. She's a dear. Couldn't be nicer.

SAM. I'm sure you and she would get on wonderfully together. Of course, Leonie will marry again. She's bound to. Why don't you come to live with us? When you want to . . .

PAULA. Want to!

SAM. All the time then. Leonie has such a busy life.

PAULA. It's awfully sweet of you.

SAM. Sweet of me! Paula!

PAULA. Where are you going to live?

SAM. New York. Selena has her job to do.

PAULA. She's terribly clever, isn't she?

SAM. She's good at her job.

PAULA. It must be wonderful to be independent. I hope I shall be. I hope I can make myself.

SAM. No reason you can't.

PAULA. It seems to take so much—

SAM. What sort of independence?

PAULA. Leonie's independent, but that independence doesn't mean anything somehow. She's always been able to do what she likes.

SAM. So will you be.

PAULA. That doesn't count somehow. It's independence in a vacuum. No, it doesn't count.

SAM. Maybe it isn't independence you want then?

PAULA. Yes, it is. I want to be able to stand on my own feet. I want to be—justified.

SAM [*understandingly*]. Ah! That's something else. [*A little amused.*] That's harder!

PAULA. I mean it, really I do— [*Pause.*] It's curious— how—adrift—this makes me feel. As if something vital, something fundamental had smashed. I wonder how Mother'll take it. I think—unconsciously— she depends on you much more than she realizes. You were a stabilizing force, Sam, in spite of everything and now . . .

SAM [*seriously*]. *You* are the stabilizing force, if you ask me, Paula. . . .

PAULA. I don't know.

SAM. What's worrying you, Paula? Is it this Russian?

PAULA. Oh, I think he's harmless really.

SAM. What then?

PAULA. That one of these days—

SAM. What?

PAULA. That one of these days—now that you're going —somebody will come along—who won't be harmless.—You know, I really love Leonie.

[LEONIE *comes running in just ahead of* DR. KENNETH RICE, DENNIS *and* WILL. LEONIE *is in the gayest spirits.* DR. RICE *is handsome, dark, magnetic, quiet, masterful. He is conscious of authority and gives one the sense of a strange, genius-like intuition.* DENNIS *is a flamboyant Irishman, a little older than* WILL, *gawky, black-haired, slovenly, infinitely brash.* SAM *and* PAULA *rise.* LEONIE *comes down to center with* KENNETH *at her left.* WILL *remains back of sofa.* DENNIS *follows down to right center.*]

LEONIE. Oh, Sam, how perfectly . . . This is Dr. Rice— my husband Sam Frothingham—and my daughter Paula! Sam, Dennis McCarthy.

DENNIS. How do you do?

[*No one pays any attention to him.* DR. RICE *shakes*

hands with SAM *and* PAULA. LEONIE *keeps bubbling, her little laugh tinkling through her chatter.*]

LEONIE. It's courageous of me, don't you think, Dr. Rice, to display such a daughter? Does she look like me? I'll be very pleased if you tell me that she does. Sit down, sit down, everybody.

DENNIS [*holding up his pipe*]. You don't mind if I—?

LEONIE. No, no, not at all— [*She sits center chair,* PAULA *sits on right end sofa,* DENNIS *sinks into chair, right, by table.*] Sam! How well you're looking! Are you staying at Selena's? How is Selena?

SAM. She's very well.

LEONIE. Dr. Rice knows Selena.

KENNETH. Yes, indeed!

LEONIE. I envy Selena, you know, above all women. So brilliant, so attractive and so self-sufficient. That is what I envy in her most of all. I have no resources— I depend so much on other people. [*Turns to* RICE.] Do you think, Dr. Rice, you could make me self-sufficient?

KENNETH. I think I could.

LEONIE. How perfectly marvelous!

KENNETH. But I shouldn't dream of doing it!

LEONIE. But if I beg you to?

KENNETH. Not even if you beg me to.

LEONIE. But why?

KENNETH. It would deprive your friends of their most delightful avocation.

LEONIE. Now that's very grateful. You see, Sam, there are men who still pay me compliments.

SAM. I can't believe it!

LEONIE. You must keep it up, Dr. Rice, please. So good for my morale. [*To* PAULA.] Oh, my dear, we've been having the most wonderful argument— [*To* DENNIS.] Haven't we?

DENNIS. Yes.

LEONIE. All the way in from Ellsworth— [*To* RICE.] Really, Doctor, it's given me new courage. . . .

PAULA. New courage for what?

LEONIE. I've always been afraid to say it for fear of being old-fashioned—but Dr. Rice isn't afraid.

KENNETH [*explaining to* SAM]. It takes great courage, Mr. Frothingham, to disagree with the younger generation.

SAM. It does indeed.

PAULA. Well, what is it about?

LEONIE. Yes—what *was* it about, Dennis?

DENNIS. Statistics and theology. Some metaphysics thrown in.

SAM. Good heavens! [*Sits.*]

DENNIS. Statistics as a symbol.

WILL. Dr. Rice still believes in the individual career.

KENNETH. I hang my head in shame!

DENNIS. He doesn't know that as a high officer of the National Student Federation, I have at my fingers' ends the statistics which rule our future, the statistics which constitute our horizon. Not your future, Paula, because you are living parasitically on the stored pioneerism of your ancestors.

PAULA. Forgive me, Reverend Father!

DENNIS. I represent, Doctor, the Unattached Youth of America—

KENNETH. Well, that's a career in itself!

[*They laugh.*]

DENNIS [*imperturbable*]. When we presently commit the folly of graduating from a benevolent institution at Amherst, Massachusetts, there will be in this Republic two million like us. Two million helots. [*Leaning over* LEONIE.] But Dr. Rice pooh-poohs statistics.

LEONIE [*arranging his tie*]. Does he Dennis?

DENNIS. He says the individual can surmount statistics, violate the graphs. Superman!

WILL. Evidently Dr. Rice got in just under the wire.

KENNETH. I'd never submit to statistics, Mr. Dexter— I'd submit to many things but not to statistics.

LEONIE. Such dull things to submit to—

DENNIS. You must be an atheist, Dr. Rice.

KENNETH. Because I don't believe in statistics?—the new God?

LEONIE. Well, *I'm* a Protestant and I don't believe in them either.

DENNIS. Well, Protestant is a loose synonym for atheist —and I, as an Irishman—and a—

KENNETH. Young man—

DENNIS. Yes?

KENNETH. Have you ever heard Bismarck's solution of the Irish problem?

DENNIS. No. What?

KENNETH. Oh, it's entirely irrelevant.

LEONIE. Please tell us. I adore irrelevancies.

KENNETH. Well, he thought the Irish and the Dutch should exchange countries. The Dutch, he thought, would very soon make a garden out of Ireland, and the Irish would forget to mend the dikes.

[*They laugh.*]

LEONIE. That's not irrelevant—

DENNIS. It is an irrelevance, but pardonable in an adversary losing an argument.

KENNETH [*to* PAULA]. Miss Frothingham, you seem very gracious. Will you get me out of this?

PAULA. No, I'm enjoying it.

LEONIE. Whatever you may say, Dennis, it's an exciting time to be alive.

DENNIS. That is because your abnormal situation renders you free of its major excitement.

LEONIE. And what's that, Dennis?

DENNIS. The race with malnutrition.

KENNETH. But that race, Mr.—?

DENNIS. McCarthy.

KENNETH. Is the eternal condition of mankind. Perhaps mankind won't survive the solution of that problem.

WILL [*with heat*]. It's easy to sit in this living room—and be smug about the survival of the fittest—especially when you're convinced you're one of the fittest. But there are millions who won't concede you that superiority, Dr. Rice. There are millions who are so outrageously demanding that they actually insist on the right to live! They may demand it one day at the cost of your complacency.

LEONIE. Will! We were just chatting.

WILL. I'm sorry! The next thing Dr. Rice'll be telling us is that war is necessary also—to keep us stimulated —blood-letting for the other fellow.

KENNETH. Well, as a matter of fact, there's something to be said for that too. If you haven't settled on a career yet, Mr. Dexter, may I suggest evangelism?

DENNIS. But Dr. Rice—!

KENNETH. And now, Mrs. Frothingham, before these young people heckle me too effectively, may I escape to my room?

LEONIE [*rising*]. Of course. Though I don't think you need be afraid of their heckling, Doctor. You say things which I've always believed but never dared say.

KENNETH [*as they walk out*]. Why not?

LEONIE. I don't know—somehow—I lacked the—the authority. I want to show you your rooms myself. [*Leaving the room, followed by* RICE.] I'll be right back, Sam—[RICE *nods to them and follows her out. As they go out she keeps talking to him.*] I am giving you my father's rooms—he built the wing especially so that when he wanted to work he'd be away from the rest of the house—you have the sea *and* the garden— [*They are off. A moment's pause.*]

PAULA. Well, that's a new type for Leonie!

DENNIS. There's something Rasputinish about him. What's he doing in Maine?

WILL. What, for the matter of that, are you and I doing in Maine? We should be in New York, jockeying for position on the bread-line. Let's go to the beach, Dennis. Pep us up for the struggle.

DENNIS. In that surf? It looks angry. I can't face life today.

PAULA. Swim'll do you good.

DENNIS [*starting for garden*]. It's not a swim I want exactly but a float—a vigorous float. Lead me to the pool, Adonais—

WILL. All right.

[*As he starts to follow* DENNIS, DR. DEXTER, WILL'S *father, comes in ushered by* ROBERT. *He is a dusty little man with a bleached yellow Panama hat. He keeps wiping his perspiring face with an old handkerchief. He doesn't hear very well.*]

DENNIS. Ah, the enemy—!

[PAULA *and* SAM *rise.*]

WILL. Hello, Dad. You remember Paula.

DEXTER. Yes . . . yes, I do.

WILL [*introducing* SAM]. My father—Mr. Frothingham.

SAM. Very glad to see you.

DEXTER [*shaking hands*]. Thank you.

DENNIS [*pointing dramatically at* DEXTER]. Nevertheless I repeat—the enemy!

PAULA. Dennis!

WILL. Oh, he's used to Dennis!

DEXTER [*wipes his forehead*]. Yes, and besides it was very dusty on the road.

PAULA. Won't you sit down?

[DEXTER *does so, in center chair. The others remain standing.*]

WILL. How long did it take you to drive over, Dad?

DEXTER. Let's see—left New Brunswick at two. . . .

WILL [*looks at watch*]. Three and one half hours— pretty good—the old tin Lizzie's got life in her yet.

DEXTER. You young folks having a good time, I suppose? [*He looks around him absent-mindedly.*]

PAULA. Dennis has been bullying us.

DEXTER. He still talking? [*Mildly.*] It's the Irish in him.

DENNIS [*nettled*]. You forgot to say shanty!

DEXTER [*surprised*]. Eh? Why should I say that?

WILL. Dennis is a snob. Wants all his titles.

DENNIS. You misguided children don't realize it—but here—in the guise of this dusty, innocent-seeming man—sits the enemy.

DEXTER [*turning as if stung by a fly—cupping his hand to his ear*]. What? What did he say?

DENNIS. The ultimate enemy, the true begetter of the fatal statistics—Science. You betray us, Paula, by having him in the house; *you* betray us, Will, by acknowledging him as a father.

DEXTER [*wiping his forehead*]. Gosh, it's hot!

SAM [*sensing a fight and urging it on—solemnly*]. Can all this be true, Dr. Dexter?

DEXTER. What be true?

SAM. Dennis's accusation.

DEXTER. I am slightly deaf and McCarthy's presence always fills me with gratitude for that affliction.

DENNIS. It's perfectly obvious. You've heard of technological unemployment. Well, here it sits, embodied in Will's father. Day and night with diabolical ingenuity and cunning he works out devices to unemploy us. All over the world, millions of us are being starved and broken on the altar of Science.

We Catholics understand that. We Catholics repudiate the new Moloch that has us by the throat.

WILL. Do you want us to sit in medieval taverns with
Chesterton and drink beer?

[DEXTER *turns to* DENNIS; *as if emerging suddenly from
an absent-minded daze, he speaks with great authority, casually but with clarity and precision.*]

DEXTER. The fact is, my voluble young friend, I am not
the Moloch who is destroying you but that you and
the hordes of the imprecise and the vaguely trained
—are destroying me! I have, you will probably be
pleased to learn, just lost my job. I have been interrupted in my work. And why? Because I am successful. Because I have found what, with infinite patience and concentration, I have been seeking to
discover. From the elusive and the indeterminate
and the invisible, I have crystallized a principle
which is visible and tangible and—predictable. From
the illimitable icebergs of the unknown I have
chipped off a fragment of knowledge, a truth which
so-called practical men may put to a use which will
make some of your numbers unnecessary in the
workaday world. Well—what of it, I say?—who de-
crees that you shall be supported? Of what importance are your lives and futures and your meandering aspirations compared to the firmness and the
beauty and the cohesion of the principles I seek, the
truth I seek? None—none whatever! Whether you
prattle on an empty stomach or whether you prattle
on a full stomach can make no difference to anybody that I can see. [*To* PAULA *abruptly, rising.*]
And now, young woman, as I have been invited here
to spend the night, I'd like to see my room!

PAULA [*crossing to him*]. Certainly! Come with me. I'll
have Robert show you your room. [*They go to door*

back. She calls.] Robert! [ROBERT *enters.*] Will you take Dr. Dexter to his room?

[DEXTER *follows* ROBERT *out.*]

SAM. Gosh! I thought he was deaf!

WILL. He can hear when he wants to! [*To* DENNIS.] Now will you be good!

DENNIS. I'm sorry—I didn't know he'd lost his job or I wouldn't have . . .

WILL. Oh, that's all right. Well, Dennis, how does it feel to be superfluous?

DENNIS [*sourly*]. The man's childish! [*He goes out, door right through garden.*]

PAULA. Isn't he marvelous? Don't you love Will's father?

SAM. Crazy about him. He's swell.

WILL. He's a pretty good feller. He seems absent-minded but actually he's extremely present-minded. If you'll excuse me, I'm going out to soothe Dennis. [*He follows* DENNIS *out.*]

[*A pause.*]

SAM. That young man appears to have sound antecedents.

PAULA. Oh, yes—Will's all right, but—oh, Sam—!

SAM. What?

PAULA. With you gone—I'm terrified for Leonie. I really am! When I think of the foolish marriages Leonie would have made if not for you!

SAM. It's a useful function, but I'm afraid I'll have to give it up!

PAULA [*with new determination*]. Sam . . .

SAM. Yes, Paula.

PAULA. If Leonie goes Russian—

SAM. Well?

PAULA. Or if she goes Freudian—?

SAM. In any case you and this boy'll probably be getting married.

PAULA. That's far from settled yet.

SAM. Why?

PAULA. Will's scared.

SAM. Is he?

PAULA. Of getting caught in Leonie's silken web.

SAM. That's sensible of him.

[LEONIE *comes back, half running, breathless.*]

LEONIE. Well! Isn't Dr. Rice attractive?

SAM [*rising*]. Very.

PAULA [*rising*]. And so depressed about himself! [*She goes out—door right.*]

LEONIE. Isn't it extraordinary, Dr. Rice having achieved the position he has—at his age? He's amazing. And think of it, Sam—not yet forty.

SAM. Anybody under forty is young to me!

LEONIE. How old are you, Sam?

SAM. Forbidden ground, Leonie.

LEONIE. I should know, shouldn't I, but I don't. I know your birthday—I always remember your birthday. . . .

SAM. You do indeed!

LEONIE. It's June 14. But I don't know how old you are.

SAM. Knowledge in the right place—ignorance in the right place!

LEONIE [*meaning it*]. You're more attractive and charming than ever.

SAM. You're a great comfort.

LEONIE. It's so nice to see you!

SAM. And you too! [*He is not entirely comfortable—not as unself-conscious and natural as she is.*]

LEONIE. Sometimes I think Paula should see more of you. I think it would be very good for her. What do you think of her new friends?

SAM. They seem nice.

LEONIE. They're all poor and they're very radical. They

look on me—my dear, they have the most extraordinary opinion of me. . . .

SAM. What is that?

LEONIE. I'm fascinated by them. They think of me as a hopeless kind of spoiled Bourbon living away in a never-never land—a kind of Marie Antoinette. . . . [*She laughs.*] It's delicious!

SAM. Is Paula radical too?

LEONIE. I think she's trying to be. She's a strange child.

SAM. How do you mean?

LEONIE. Well, when I was a child I was brought up to care only if people were charming or attractive or . . .

SAM. Well-connected . . .

LEONIE. Yes . . . These kids don't care a hoot about that.

SAM. I think the difference between their generation and ours is that we were romantic and they're realistic.

LEONIE. Is that it?

SAM. I think so.

LEONIE. What makes that?

SAM. Changes in the world—the war—the depression . . .

LEONIE. What did people blame things on before—the war?

SAM [*smiling*]. Oh, on the tariff and on the Republicans—and on the Democrats! Leonie—

LEONIE. Yes, Sam.

SAM. I—I really have something to tell you.

LEONIE [*looks up at him curiously*]. What? [*Pause.*]

SAM. I am in love with Selena Bryant. We want to get married.

LEONIE [*pause—after a moment*]. Human nature is funny! Mine is!

SAM. Why?

LEONIE. I know I ought to be delighted to release you. Probably I should have spoken to you about it myself before long—separating. And yet—when you tell me—I feel—a pang. . . .

SAM. That's very sweet of you.

LEONIE. One's so possessive—one doesn't want to give up anything.

SAM. For so many years our marriage has been at its best—a friendship. Need that end?

LEONIE. No, Sam. It needn't. I hope truly that it won't.

SAM. What about Paula?

LEONIE. Did you tell Paula?

SAM. Yes . . .

LEONIE. Did she . . . ?

SAM [*rising*]. Leonie . . .

LEONIE [*pauses*]. Yes, Sam.

SAM. A little while ago you said—you thought Paula ought to see more of me.

LEONIE. Yes . . . I did. . . . [*She is quite agitated suddenly. The thought has crossed her mind that perhaps* PAULA *has told* SAM *that she would prefer to go with him. This hurts her deeply, not only for the loss of* PAULA *but because, from the bottom of her being, she cannot bear not to be loved.*]

SAM. Don't you think then . . . for a time at least . . .

LEONIE [*defeatist in a crisis*]. Paula doesn't like me! [*It is a sudden and completely accepted conviction.*]

SAM. Leonie!

LEONIE. She'd rather go with you!

SAM. Not at all—it's only that . . .

LEONIE. I know what Paula thinks of me. . . .

SAM. Paula adores you. It's only that . . .

LEONIE. It's only that what—

SAM. Well, for instance—if you should get married—

LEONIE. What if I did?

SAM [*coming to stand close to her left*]. It would mean

a considerable readjustment for Paula—wouldn't it?
You can see that.

LEONIE [*rising*]. But it would too with you and Selena.

SAM [*taking step toward her*]. She knows Selena. She
admires Selena.

LEONIE [*rising and walking down to front of sofa*].
What makes you think she wouldn't admire—whom-
ever I married?

SAM [*after a moment, completely serious now*]. There's
another aspect of it which I think for Paula's sake
you should consider most carefully.

LEONIE. What aspect?

SAM [*coming down to her*]. Paula's serious. You know
that yourself. She's interested in things. She's not
content to be a Sunday-supplement heiress—floating along—she wants to do things. Selena's a working woman. Selena can help her.

LEONIE. I know. I'm useless.

SAM. I think you ought to be unselfish about this.

LEONIE. Paula can do what she likes, of course. If she
doesn't love me . . .

SAM. Of course she loves you.

LEONIE. If she prefers to live with you and Selena I
shan't stand in her way.

[*Her martyrish resignation irritates* SAM *profoundly.
He feels that really* LEONIE *should not be allowed
to get away with it.*]

SAM. You're so vain, Leonie.

LEONIE [*refusing to argue*]. I'm sorry.

[*This makes it worse.* SAM *goes deeper.*]

SAM. After all, you're Paula's mother. Can't you look
at her problem—objectively?

LEONIE. Where my emotions are involved I'm afraid I
never know what words like that mean.

[*He blunders in worse, farther than he really means
to go.*]

SAM [*flatly*]. Well, this sort of thing isn't good for Paula.

LEONIE [*very cold, very hurt*]. What sort of thing? [*A moment's pause. He is annoyed with himself at the ineptitude of his approach.*] Be perfectly frank. You can be with me. What sort of thing?

SAM. Well—Leonie— [*With a kind of desperate bluntness.*] You've made a career of flirtation. Obviously Paula isn't going to. You know you and Paula belong to different worlds. [*With some heat.*] And the reason Paula is the way she is is because she lives in an atmosphere of perpetual conflict.

LEONIE. Conflict? Paula?

SAM. With herself. About you.

LEONIE [*rising*]. That's too subtle for me, I'm afraid.

SAM. Paula's unaware of it herself.

LEONIE. Where did you acquire this amazing psychological insight? You never used to have it. Of course! From Selena. Of course!

SAM. I've never discussed this with Selena.

LEONIE. No?

SAM. She's told me she'd be happy to have Paula but . . .

LEONIE. That's extremely generous of her—to offer without discussion. . . .

SAM [*she has him there; he loses his temper*]. It's impossible for you to consider anything without being personal.

LEONIE. I am afraid it is. I don't live on this wonderful, rarefied, intellectual plane inhabited by Selena and yourself—and where you want to take Paula. I'm sorry if I've made Paula serious, I'm sorry she's in a perpetual conflict about me. I'm sorry I've let her in for—this sort of thing! I'm sorry! [*She is on the verge of tears. She runs out.*]

SAM. Leonie . . . ! [*He follows her to door back, call-*

ing.] Leonie! [*But it is too late. She is gone. He turns back into room.*] Damn!

[PAULA *comes in—from beach, door right.*]

PAULA. Where's Leonie?

SAM. She just went upstairs.

PAULA. I've been showing Dr. Rice our rock-bound coast.

SAM. What's he like?

PAULA. Hard to say. He's almost too sympathetic. At the same time—

SAM. What?

PAULA. At the same time—he is inscrutable! I can't tell whether I like him or dislike him. You say Selena knows him. What does she say about him?

SAM. Selena isn't crazy about him.

PAULA. Why not?

SAM. Brilliant charlatan, she says—also a charmer.

PAULA. I gather that, and I resent him. How'd you come out with Leonie?

SAM. I've made a mess of it. I'm a fool!

PAULA. My going with you, you mean?

SAM. Yes.

PAULA. Sam . . .

SAM. Yes?

PAULA. Will you mind very much . . .

SAM. What?

PAULA. If I don't go with Selena and you?

SAM. But I thought you said—and especially if she marries somebody—

PAULA [*slowly*]. That's just what I'm thinking of—

SAM. What's happened?

PAULA. There's no way out of it, Sam—I've got to stay.

SAM. But why?

PAULA [*simply, looking up at him*]. Somebody's got to look after Leonie. . . .

[KENNETH *enters.*].

KENNETH. My first glimpse of Maine. A masculine Riviera.

PAULA. It's mild now. If you want to see it really virile —come in the late fall.

KENNETH. You've only to crook your little finger. I'll be glad to look at more of Maine whenever you have the time. [*Sits, facing her.*]

PAULA. Of course. Tomorrow?

KENNETH. Yes. Tomorrow. [*To* SAM.] You know, from Mrs. Frothingham's description— [*Looking back at* PAULA, *intently.*] I never could have imagined her. Not remotely.

[ROBERT *enters.*]

SAM. What is it, Robert?

ROBERT. Mrs. Frothingham would like to see Dr. Rice in her study.

KENNETH [*rising*]. Oh, thank you. [*He walks to door back.*] Excuse me. [*He goes upstairs.*]

[PAULA *and* SAM *have continued looking front. As* KENNETH *starts upstairs they slowly turn and look at one another. The same thought has crossed both their minds—they both find themselves looking suddenly into a new and dubious vista.*]

CURTAIN

Act two

SCENE I

SCENE. *The same.*
TIME. *Midsummer—late afternoon.*
AT RISE: KENNETH *is at a bridge table working out a*

chess problem. He hears voices and footsteps approaching. Gets up, unhurried, and looks off into garden. Sees BORIS *and* LEONIE *approaching. As they come in he strolls off—they do not see him.* LEONIE'S *arms are full of flowers. She is looking for* KENNETH. COUNT MIRSKY *follows her in.*

COUNT MIRSKY, *a Russian, is very good-looking, mongoloid about the eyes. His English is beautiful, with a slight and attractive accent. He is tense, jittery—a mass of jangled nerves—his fingers tremble as he lights one cigarette after another. He is very pale—his pallor accentuated by a dark scarf he wears around his neck.*

BORIS [*stopping center*]. It appears he is not here either.

LEONIE. He? Who? [*Crossing to table behind sofa to put some flowers in vase.*]

BORIS. When you're in the garden with me you think— perhaps he is in the house. When you are in the house you think perhaps he is in the garden.

LEONIE. Boris, darling, you have the odd habit of referring to mysterious characters without giving me any hint who they are. Is that Russian symbolism? There will be a long silence; then you will say: He would not approve, or they can't hear us. It's a bit mystifying.

BORIS [*crossing to stand near her*]. You know who I mean.

LEONIE [*going to table right to put flowers in vase*]. Really, you flatter me. I'm not a mystic, you know, Boris. I'm a simple extrovert. When you say "he," why can't it refer to someone definite—and if possible to someone I know.

BORIS [*crossing to back of table, facing her across it*]. You know him, all right.

LEONIE. There you go again! *Really,* Boris!

BORIS [*moving closer to her around table*]. You've been

divorced now for several weeks. You're free. We were only waiting for you to be free—

LEONIE [*moving away, sitting in chair, right*]. Now that I am free you want to coerce me. It's a bit unreasonable, don't you think?

[BORIS *walks to end of windowseat and sits. Enter* KENNETH, *door back*.]

KENNETH [*strolling across stage toward* LEONIE]. Hello, Leonie. Count Mirsky—

LEONIE. Kenneth—I haven't seen you all day.

KENNETH. I've been in my room slaving away at a scientific paper.

LEONIE. My house hums with creative activity. I love it. It gives me a sense of vicarious importance. What's your paper on?

KENNETH. Shadow-neurosis.

LEONIE. Shadow-neurosis. How marvelous! What does it mean?

KENNETH [*looking at* BORIS]. It is a sensation of non-existence.

LEONIE. Is it common?

KENNETH. Quite. The victim knows that he exists and yet he feels that he does not!

LEONIE. In a curious way I can imagine a sensation like that—do you know I actually can. Isn't it amusing?

BORIS. The doctor is so eloquent. Once he describes a sensation it becomes very easy to feel it.

LEONIE. That's an entrancing gift. Why are you so antagonistic to Kenneth? He wants to help you but you won't let him. I asked him here to help you.

KENNETH [*to* BORIS]. Your skepticism about this particular disease is interesting, Count Mirsky, because, as it happens, you suffer from it.

BORIS [*bearing down on* KENNETH]. Has it ever occurred to you that you are a wasted novelist?

KENNETH. Though I have not mentioned you in my article I have described you.

LEONIE [*rising and crossing left to table behind sofa*]. You should be flattered, Boris.

BORIS. I am!

LEONIE. Another case history! I've been reading some of Kenneth's scientific textbooks. Most fascinating form of biography. Who was that wonderful fellow who did such odd things—Mr. X.? You'd never think you could get so interested in anonymous people. I'd have given anything to meet Mr. X.—though I must say I'd feel a bit nervous about having him in the house.

KENNETH. How is your book getting along, Count Mirsky?

BORIS. Very well. Oh—so—

KENNETH. Far along in it?

BORIS. Quite.

LEONIE. I'm crazy to see it. He's dedicating it to me but he hasn't let me see a word of it!

KENNETH. For a very good reason.

LEONIE. What do you mean?

KENNETH. Because there is no book. There never has been a book.

LEONIE [*she lets flowers drop*]. Kenneth!

KENNETH. Isn't that true, Count Mirsky?

BORIS. It is not!

KENNETH. Then why don't you let us see a bit of it?

LEONIE. Oh, do! At least the dedication page.

KENNETH. A chapter—

BORIS. Because it isn't finished yet.

LEONIE. Well, it doesn't have to be finished. We know the end, don't we? The end belongs to the world.

KENNETH. Let us see it, Count.

BORIS. I can't.

KENNETH. What are you calling the book?

BORIS. I haven't decided yet.

KENNETH. May I suggest a title to you—?

LEONIE. Oh, do! What shall we call it, Kenneth?

KENNETH. "The Memoirs of a Boy Who Wanted to Murder His Father."

LEONIE. What!

BORIS [*gripping arms of chair*]. I am not a hysterical woman, Doctor—and I'm not your patient!

LEONIE. But Kenneth—Boris worshipped his father.

KENNETH. No, he hated him. He hated him when he was alive and he hates him still. He grew up under the overwhelming shadow of this world-genius whom, in spite of an immense desire to emulate and even surpass—he felt he could never emulate and never surpass—nor even equal— Did you worship your father, Count Mirsky?

BORIS. It's true! I hated him!

LEONIE. Boris!

BORIS. I hated him!

KENNETH. Now you can let us see the book, can't you—now that we know the point of view—just a bit of it?

LEONIE. I'm more crazy than ever to see it now. I can tell you a little secret now, Boris. I was afraid—I was rather afraid—that your book would be a little like one of those statues of an ancestor in a frock-coat. Now it sounds really exciting. You hated him. But how perfectly marvelous! I can't wait to see it now. Do run up to your study and bring it down, Boris—do!

BORIS. No.

LEONIE. That's very unpleasant of you.

BORIS. You might as well know it then. There isn't any book. There never will be. Not by me.

LEONIE. But I don't understand—every day—in your room working—all these months!

BORIS [*facing her*]. One wants privacy! Possibly you can't realize that. You who always have to have a house full of people.

LEONIE [*goes back to flowers at table*]. Boris!

KENNETH [*rising*]. Why don't you write the book anyway, Count Mirsky? There is a vogue these days for vituperative biography.

BORIS. I am not interested in the vogue.

KENNETH. We are quite used nowadays to children who dislike their fathers. The public—

BORIS. To titillate the public would not compensate me for forcing myself to recall the atmosphere of saintly sadism in which my childhood was spent—I can still smell that living room, I can still smell those stinking, sexless pilgrims who used to come from all over the world to get my saintly father's blessing. I used to sit with my mother in a room no bigger than a closet to get away from the odor of that nauseating humanitarianism. There was no privacy in the Villa Mirskovitch. Oh, no—it was a Mecca—do you understand—a Mecca!

KENNETH. Yes, I think I understand.

BORIS. Well, I have been paying the haloed one back. I have been getting privacy at his expense at last.

LEONIE. Why have you never told me before that you felt this way about your father?

BORIS. I never said anything about him. It was you who did the talking. You always raved about the great man with that characteristic American enthusiasm for what you don't know.

LEONIE. Nevertheless, the world recognizes your father as a great man. The books are there to prove it. There they are. You can't write books like that without greatness—no matter what you say. You are a petulant child. Your father was a great man.

BORIS. It makes no difference how great he was—those pilgrims stank!

[LEONIE *turns away*.]

KENNETH. I suggest that to write that book, even if no one ever sees the manuscript but you, might amuse you—a kind of revenge which, when you were a boy, you were in no position to take.

BORIS. Are you trying to cure me, Doctor? Please don't trouble. I don't need your particular species of professionalism. I do not need any help from you. [*He goes to door back, turns to* LEONIE. LEONIE *looks bewilderedly at* KENNETH. BORIS *goes out*.]

LEONIE. How did you know? You're uncanny!

KENNETH. All in the day's work.

LEONIE. Why is it I always get myself involved with men weaker than myself? I certainly am no tower of strength.

KENNETH. Possibly not—but you are generous and impulsive. You have a tendency to accept people at the best of their own valuation.

LEONIE. I want to help them. I do help them. After they get used to my help, after they get to count on my help, I get impatient with them. Why, I ask myself, can't people help themselves?

KENNETH. And very natural.

LEONIE. I seem to attract people like that!

KENNETH. Leonie—you are the last woman on earth Count Mirsky should marry. He would only transfer his hatred of his father to you.

LEONIE. I don't think I understand you, Kenneth— really I don't—and I do so want to understand things.

KENNETH. Well—your charm, your gaiety, your position, your wealth, your beauty—these would oppress him. Again, he cannot be himself.—Or, if he

is himself, it is to reveal his nonentity, his infe-
riority—again the secondary role—Leonie Frothingham's husband—the son of Count Mirsky—the husband of Leonie Frothingham. Again the shadow—
again, eternally and always—non-existence. Poor
fellow. [*Pause.*]

LEONIE. I'm so grateful to you, Kenneth.

KENNETH. Nonsense. You mustn't be grateful to me
because I—exercise my profession.

LEONIE. I want to express my gratitude—in some tangible form. I've been thinking of nothing else lately.
I can't sleep for thinking of it.

KENNETH. Well, if it gives you insomnia, you'd better
tell me about it.

LEONIE. I want to make it possible for you to realize
your ambition.

KENNETH. Ambition? What ambition?

LEONIE. Ah! You've forgotten, haven't you? But you
let it slip out one day—you pump me professionally
—but I do the same to you—non-professionally.

KENNETH. You terrify me!

LEONIE. That night last winter when we went to dinner in that little restaurant where you go with your
doctor friends . . . you told me your dream.

KENNETH. My censor must have been napping.

LEONIE. He was. Or she was. What sex is your censor?

KENNETH. That's none of your business.

LEONIE. I'm sorry.

KENNETH. Which of my dreams was I so reckless as to
reveal to you?

LEONIE. To have a sanatorium of your own one day—
so you can carry out your own ideas of curing patients.

KENNETH. Oh, that! Out of the question.

LEONIE. Why?

KENNETH. To do it on the scale I visualize, would cost

more than I'm ever likely to save out of my practice.

LEONIE. I'll give you the sanatorium. I've never given anyone anything like that before. What fun!

KENNETH. Will I find it all wrapped up in silver foil on Christmas morning?

LEONIE. Yes. You will! You will! We'll have a suite in it for Mr. X.—for all your anonymous friends—we'll entertain the whole alphabet!

KENNETH. You see, Leonie!

LEONIE. What do you mean? I thought you'd be—

KENNETH. Of course, it's terribly generous of you. I'm deeply touched. But . . .

LEONIE. But . . . ?

KENNETH. I'm a stranger to you.

LEONIE. Kenneth!

KENNETH. Outside of my professional relation—such as I have with scores of patients—little more than that.

LEONIE. I thought—

KENNETH. And yet you are willing to back me in a venture that would cost a sizeable fortune—just on that. Leonie! Leonie!

LEONIE. It would be the best investment I've ever made. Paula's always telling me I have no social consciousness. Well, this would be.—It would keep me from feeling so useless. I do feel useless, Kenneth. Please!

KENNETH. I'm sorry. I couldn't hear of it. Of course, it's out of the question.

LEONIE. It isn't. I can afford it. Why shouldn't I? It would be helping so many people—you have no right to refuse. It's selfish of you to refuse.

KENNETH. I distrust impulsive altruism. You will forgive me, Leonie, but it may often do harm.

LEONIE. How do you mean, Kenneth?

KENNETH. I gather you are about to endow a radical magazine for the *boys*—

LEONIE. Will and Dennis! I thought it would be nice to give them something to do!

KENNETH. Yes. You are prepared to back them in a publication which; if it attained any influence, would undermine the system which makes you and your people like you possible.

LEONIE. But it never occurred to me anyone would read it.

KENNETH. There is a deplorably high literacy in this country. Unfortunately it is much easier to learn to read than it is to learn to think.

LEONIE. Well, if you don't think it's a good idea, Kenneth, I won't do it. But this sanatorium is different.

KENNETH. Why?

LEONIE. Because, if you must know it, it would be helping you—and that means everything in the world to me. There, I've said it. It's true! Kenneth —are you terrified?

KENNETH. You adorable child!

LEONIE. It's extraordinary, Kenneth—but you are the first strong man who's ever come into my life— [*Enter* PAULA, DENNIS, WILL, *door back.*] Oh, I'm very glad to see you! Will! Hullo, Dennis. You all know Dr. Rice. Mr. Dexter, Mr. McCarthy. Sit down, everybody. Well, children, how is New York?

[DENNIS *crosses down front of them to chair left by sofa and sits.*]

WILL. Stifling, thank you.

LEONIE. Any luck yet?

WILL. I am available, but New York is dead to its chief opportunity.

LEONIE. Then you can stay here for a bit. You can both stay here.

DENNIS. That was all right when we were in college, Mrs. Frothingham. Can't do it now.

LEONIE. Oh, you're working. I'm so glad!

DENNIS. I beg your pardon. Did you say working?

LEONIE. Well, then! I don't see why you can't stay here and take a holiday.

WILL. From what?

LEONIE. Since none of you are doing anything in town, you might as well stay here and do nothing and be comfortable.

DENNIS. Yes, but it's an ethical question. When we're in New York doing nothing, we belong to the most respectable vested group going! The unemployed. As such we have a status, position, authority. But if we stay here doing nothing—what are we? Low-down parasites.

KENNETH. No jobs about anywhere, eh?

WILL. Extinct commodity.

DENNIS. I did pretty well last week.

LEONIE. Really?

DENNIS. I was rejected by seven newspapers—including the *Bronx Home News* and the *Yonkers Herald*—six magazines and trade papers—a total of twenty-eight rejections in all, representing a net gain over the previous week of seven solid rejections. I submit to you, gentlemen, that's progress—pass the cigars, Will.

LEONIE. Couldn't you stay here and be rejected by mail?

DENNIS. Doesn't give you that same feeling somehow—that good, rich, dark-brown sensation of not being wanted!

LEONIE. You know, Kenneth, in a curious way, Dennis reminds me a bit of Mr. X.

DENNIS. And who's X.?

LEONIE. A sporting acquaintance.

DENNIS. There's one thing I'd like to ask Dr. Rice. . . . Do you mind?

KENNETH. At your service.

DENNIS [*turning chair and facing* KENNETH *upstage*]. In the psychoanalytic hierarchy Freud is the god, isn't he?

KENNETH. Of one sect, yes.

DENNIS. Well, the original sect—

KENNETH. Yes . . .

DENNIS. Now, every psychoanalyst has to have himself analyzed. That's true, isn't it, Doctor?

KENNETH. Generally speaking—yes.

DENNIS. As I understand it, the highest prices go to those nearest the Master himself.

KENNETH. This boy is irreverent . . .

DENNIS. I know whereof I speak. I prepared an article on the subject for *Fortune.*

WILL. Rejection number three hundred.

DENNIS. I am afraid, Will, that you are a success worshipper!

LEONIE. Dennis is an *enfant terrible,* and he exhausts himself keeping it up!

DENNIS. I have examined the racket with a microscopic patience and this I find to be true: at the top of the hierarchy is the Great Pan-Sexualist of Vienna. To be an orthodox and accepted Freudian, you must have been analyzed by another of the same. Now what I am burning to know is this: Who analyzed Sig Freud himself? Whom does he tell his repressions to? Why, the poor guy must be lonely as hell!

LEONIE. What would you do with him, Kenneth? He has no repressions whatever!

KENNETH. He needs some badly.

LEONIE. I wonder what Dennis would confess to his psychoanalyst that he isn't always shouting to the world?

DENNIS. I'd make the psychoanalyst talk. [*To* KENNETH. *Beckoning.*] Tell me, Doctor, what did you dream last night?

KENNETH [*behind his cupped hand*]. Not in public.

DENNIS [*rises and crosses straight right*]. You see—he's repressed! I tell you these psychoanalysts are repressed. They've got nobody to talk to! I'm going swimming. It's pathetic! [*He goes out.*]

LEONIE. I'm going too. He makes me laugh. How about you, Kenneth?

KENNETH. Oh, I'll watch.

LEONIE [*to others*]. Come along with us. There's plenty of time for a swim before dinner.

[KENNETH *starts out with* LEONIE, *stops on the way.*]

KENNETH. I suppose you and your Irish friend edited the comic paper at college?

WILL. No, we edited the serious paper.

KENNETH. Just the same it must have been very funny. [*He goes out after* LEONIE.]

WILL. Don't think that feller likes me much.

PAULA. You're psychic.

WILL. Well, for the matter of that I'm not crazy about him either.

PAULA. Don't bother about him. Concentrate on me!

WILL. How are you, darling?

PAULA. Missed you.

WILL [*pulls her to sofa and sits with her.* PAULA *left end sofa*]. And I you. Pretty lousy in town without you.

PAULA. Oh, poor darling!

WILL. Although my star is rising. I did some book-reviews for *The New York Times* and the *New Masses*.

PAULA. What a gamut!

WILL. I made, in fact, a total of eleven dollars. The student most likely to succeed in the first four months since graduation has made eleven dollars.

PAULA. Wonderful!

WILL. My classmates were certainly clairvoyant. As a matter of fact, I shouldn't have told you. Now I'll be tortured thinking you're after me for my money.

PAULA. You'll never know!

WILL [*putting arm around her shoulders and drawing her to him*]. What've you been doing?

PAULA. Lying in the sun mostly.

WILL. Poor little Ritz girl.

PAULA. Wondering what you do every night.

WILL. Forty-second Street Library mostly. Great fun! Voluptuary atmosphere!

PAULA. Is your life altogether so austere?

WILL. Well, frankly, no. Not altogether.

PAULA. Cad!

WILL. What do you expect?

PAULA. Loyalty.

WILL. I am loyal. But you go around all day job-hunting. You find you're not wanted. It's reassuring after that to find a shoulder to lean on, sort of haven where you *are* wanted. Even the public library closes at ten. You have to go somewhere. If I'm ever Mayor of New York, I'll have the public libraries kept open all night . . . the flop-houses of the intellectuals!

PAULA. Is it anyone special . . . ?

WILL. Just a generalized shoulder.

PAULA. Well, you're going to have a special one from now on—mine! You know, the way you're avoiding the issue is all nonsense.

WILL. You mean my gallant fight against you?

PAULA. I've decided that you are conventional and bourgeois. You're money-ridden.

WILL. Eleven dollars. They say a big income makes you conservative.

PAULA. I don't mean your money. I mean—my money. It's childish to let an artificial barrier like that stand between us. It's also childish to ignore it.

WILL [*rising*]. I don't ignore it. That's what worries me. I count on it. Already I find myself counting on it. I can't help it. Sitting and waiting in an office for some bigwig who won't see me or for some underling who won't see me I think: "Why the hell should I wait all day for this stuffed shirt?" I don't wait. Is it because of you I feel in a special category? Do I count on your money? Is that why I don't wait as long as the other fellow? There's one consolation: the other fellow doesn't get the job either. But the point is disquieting!

PAULA. What a Puritan you are!

WILL [*sitting beside her again*]. Will I become an appendage to you—like your mother's men?

PAULA. You're bound to—money or no money.

WILL [*taking her into his arms*]. I suppose I might as well go on the larger dole—

PAULA. What?

WILL. Once you are paid merely for existing—you are on the dole. I rather hoped, you know—

PAULA. What?

WILL. It's extraordinary the difference in one's thinking when you're in college and when you're out—

PAULA. How do you mean?

WILL. Well, when I was in college, my interest in the—"movement"—was really impersonal. I imagined myself giving my energies to the poor and the downtrodden in my spare time. I didn't really believe I'd be one of the poor and down-trodden myself. In my heart of hearts, I was sure I'd break through the iron law of Dennis's statistics and land a job somewhere. But I can't—and it's given a tremendous jolt to my self-esteem.

PAULA. But you'll come through. I'm sure of it. I wish you could learn to look at my money as a means rather than an end.

WILL. I'd rather use my own.

PAULA. You're proud.

WILL. I am.

PAULA. It's humiliating but I'm afraid I've got to ask you to marry me, Will.

WILL. It's humiliating but considering my feelings I see no way out of accepting you.

PAULA. You submit?

WILL [*kissing her hand*]. I submit.

PAULA. After a hard campaign—victory!

WILL. You *are* a darling.

PAULA [*getting up and crossing to center*]. I can't tell you what a relief it'll be to get away from this house.

WILL. Why?

PAULA. I don't know. It's getting very complicated.

WILL. Leonie?

PAULA. *And* Boris. *And* Dr. Rice. Funny thing how that man . . .

WILL. What?

PAULA. Makes you insecure somehow.

WILL. Supposed to do just the opposite.

PAULA. He answers every question—and yet he's secretive. I've never met a man who—who—

WILL. Who what?

PAULA. Really, I can't stand Dr. Rice.

WILL. I believe he fascinates you.

PAULA. He does. I don't deny that. And I can't tell

you how I resent it. Isn't it silly? [*The old lady*
WYLER *in a wheel chair is propelled in by a nurse.
The old lady is much wasted since the preceding
summer; she is touched with mortality.*] Granny!

MRS. WYLER. Paula! How are you, my dear?

PAULA. I came up to see you before, but you were
asleep.

MRS. WYLER. Nurse told me.

[*Exit* NURSE, *door left.*]

PAULA. You remember Will?

WILL. How do you do, Mrs. Wyler?

MRS. WYLER. Of course. How do you do, young man?

PAULA. Well, this is quite an adventure for you, isn't
it, Granny?

MRS. WYLER. You're the boy who was always so curious
about my youth.

WILL. Yes.

MRS. WYLER. I've forgotten most of it. Now I just live
from day to day. The past is just this morning. [*A
moment's pause.*] And I don't always remember
that very well. Aren't there insects who live only
one day? The morning is their youth and the afternoon their middle age. . . .

PAULA. You don't seem yourself today. Not as cheerful
as usual.

MRS. WYLER. Can't I have my moods, Paula? I am
pleased to be reflective today. People are always
sending me funny books to read. I've been reading
one and it depressed me.

PAULA. Well, I'll tell you something to cheer you up,
Granny— Will and I are going to be married.

MRS. WYLER. Have you told your mother?

PAULA. Not yet. It's a secret.

[*Enter* KENNETH.]

KENNETH. Well, Mrs. Wyler! Wanderlust today?

MRS. WYLER. Yes! Wanderlust!

KENNETH. Paula, if you're not swimming, what about our walk, and our daily argument?

MRS. WYLER. What argument?

KENNETH. Paula is interested in my subject. She hovers between skepticism and fascination.

PAULA. No chance to hover today, Kenneth. Will's improving his tennis. Sorry.

KENNETH. So am I.

MRS. WYLER. I've a surprise for you, Paula.

PAULA. What?

MRS. WYLER. Your father's coming.

PAULA. No!

MRS. WYLER. Yes.

PAULA. But how—! How do you know?

MRS. WYLER. Because I've sent for him, and he wired me he's coming. He's driving from Blue Hill. He should be here now.

PAULA. That's too—! Oh, Granny, that's marvelous! Will, let's drive out to meet him, shall we? Does Mother know?

MRS. WYLER. I only had Sam's wire an hour ago.

PAULA. Granny, you're an angel.

MRS. WYLER. Not quite yet. Don't hurry me, child.

PAULA. Come on, Will. [*Exit* PAULA *and* WILL.]

MRS. WYLER. I can see you are interested in Paula. You are, aren't you, Dr. Rice?

KENNETH. Yes. She's an extraordinary child. Adores her father, doesn't she?

MRS. WYLER. How would you cure that, Doctor?

KENNETH. It's quite healthy.

MRS. WYLER. Really? I was hoping for something juicy in the way of interpretation.

KENNETH. Sorry!

MRS. WYLER. What an interesting profession yours is, Dr. Rice.

KENNETH. Why particularly?

MRS. WYLER. Your province is the soul. Strange region.

KENNETH. People's souls, I find are, on the whole, infinitely more interesting than their bodies. I have been a general practitioner and I know.

MRS. WYLER. These young people—don't they frighten you?

KENNETH. Frighten!

MRS. WYLER. They are so radical—prepared to throw everything overboard—every tradition—

KENNETH. Paula's friends have nothing to lose, any change would be—in the nature of velvet for them.

MRS. WYLER. What do you think of Will?

KENNETH. I'm afraid I've formed no strongly defined opinion on Will.

MRS. WYLER. Oh, I see— That is a comment in itself.

KENNETH. He's nondescript.

MRS. WYLER. Do you mean to point that out to Paula?

KENNETH. I don't think so. That won't be necessary.

MRS. WYLER. Why not?

KENNETH. Blood will tell.

MRS. WYLER. That's very gracious of you, Doctor. [*Pause.*] And what do you think of Leonie?

KENNETH. Very endearing—and very impulsive.

MRS. WYLER. For example—I mean of the latter—

KENNETH. She offered to build me a sanatorium—a fully equipped modern sanatorium.

MRS. WYLER. Did she? Convenient for you.

KENNETH. Except that I refused.

MRS. WYLER. Wasn't that quixotic?

KENNETH. Not necessarily.

[PAULA *and* SAM *enter, door-back.*]

PAULA. Here he is!

MRS. WYLER. Sam!

SAM. Louise!

PAULA. He wouldn't come if I'd ask him. He said so shamelessly. You know Dr. Rice?

SAM. Of course.

KENNETH. Excuse me. [KENNETH *goes out.*]

SAM. Well, Louise!

MRS. WYLER. Hello, Sam.

[SAM *kisses her.*]

SAM. How's she behaving?

PAULA. Incorrigible. Dr. Prentiss tells her to rest in her room. You see how she obeys him. She'll obey you though.

SAM. Well, I'll sneak her away from Dr. Prentiss and take her abroad.

MRS. WYLER. I want to go to Ethiopia. Run along, dear. I want to talk to Sam.

PAULA. Keep him here, Granny. Pretend you're not feeling well.

MRS. WYLER. I'll try. [*Exit* PAULA *door back.*] Well, Sam—

SAM. I got your wire last night. Here I am.

MRS. WYLER. It's nice of you.

SAM. Oh, now, Louise. You know you're the love of my life.

MRS. WYLER. Yes, Sam, I know—but how is Selena?

SAM. Flourishing.

MRS. WYLER. You're all right then?

SAM. Unbelievably.

MRS. WYLER. I knew you would be.

SAM. And you?

MRS. WYLER. I'm dying, Sam.

SAM. Not you—

MRS. WYLER. Don't contradict me. Besides, I'm rather looking forward to it.

SAM. Is Dr. Prentiss—?

MRS. WYLER. Dr. Prentiss soft-soaps me. I let him. It relieves his. mind. But that's why I've sent for you.

SAM. You know, my dear—

MRS. WYLER. Yes, Sam. I know I can count on you. I'm

dying. And I'm dying alone. I have to talk to somebody. You're the only one.

SAM. Is anything worrying you?

MRS. WYLER. Plenty.

SAM. What, dear?

MRS. WYLER. The future. Not my own. That's fixed
or soon will be. But Leonie's—Paula's—

SAM. Aren't they all right?

MRS. WYLER. I am surrounded by aliens. The house is
full of strangers. That Russian upstairs; this doctor.

SAM. Rice? Are you worried about him?

MRS. WYLER. What is he after? What does he want? He
told me Leonie offered to build him a sanatorium—

SAM. Did he accept it?

MRS. WYLER. No. He refused. But something tells me
he will allow himself to be persuaded.

SAM. I don't think Rice is a bad feller really. Seems
pretty sensible. Are you worried about this boy—
Dexter, and Paula?

MRS. WYLER. Not in the same way. I like the boy. But
Paula—I'm worried about what the money'll do
to her. We know what it's done to Leonie. You
know, Sam, in spite of all her romantic dreams Leonie has a kind of integrity. But I often wonder
if she's ever been really happy.

SAM. Oh, now, Louise, this pessimism's unlike you—

MRS. WYLER. This money we've built our lives on—it
used to symbolize security—but there's no security
in it any more.

SAM. Paula'll be all right. I count on Paula.

MRS. WYLER. In the long run. But that may be too late.
One can't let go of everything, Sam. It isn't in nature. That's why I've asked you to come. I want
you to remain as executor under my will.

SAM. Well, I only resigned because—since I'm no
longer married to Leonie—

MRS. WYLER. What has that got to do with it?

SAM. All right.

MRS. WYLER. Promise?

SAM. Certainly.

MRS. WYLER. I feel something dark ahead, a terror—

SAM. Now, now, you've been brooding.

MRS. WYLER. Outside of you—Will is the soundest person I'll leave behind me, the healthiest—but in him too I feel a recklessness that's just kept in—I see a vista of the unknown—to us the unknown was the West, land—physical hardship—but he's hard and bitter underneath his jocularity—he isn't sure, he says, what he is— Once he is sure, what will he do?—I want you to watch him, Sam, for Paula's sake.

SAM. I will.

MRS. WYLER. They're all strange and dark. . . . And this doctor. A soul doctor. We didn't have such things—I am sure that behind all this is a profound and healing truth. But sometimes truths may be perverted, and this particular doctor—how are we to know where his knowledge ends and his pretension begins? Now that I am dying, for the first time in my life I know fear. Death seems easy and simple, Sam—a self-indulgence—but can I afford it? [*She smiles up at him. He squeezes her hand.*]

SAM. Everything will be all right. Trust me.

MRS. WYLER. I do. [*A pause.*] You'll stay the night?

SAM. Of course.

MRS. WYLER. Now I feel better.

SAM. That's right. [*Pause.*]

MRS. WYLER. I'd like to live till autumn.

SAM. Of course you will. Many autumns.

MRS. WYLER. Heaven forbid. But this autumn. The color—the leaves turn. [*Looking out window.* SAM *looks too.*] The expression seems strange. What do they turn to?

SAM [*softly, helping her mood*]. Their mother. The earth.

MRS. WYLER. I'm happy now. I'm at peace.

SAM [*puts arm around her and draws her to him*]. That's better.

MRS. WYLER [*smiling up at him*]. It's very clever of me to have sent for you, Sam. I'm pleased with myself. Now, Sam, let 'em do their worst—

SAM [*smiling back at her and patting her hands*]. Just let 'em . . . !

CURTAIN

SCENE II

SCENE. *The same.*

TIME. *A few hours later—before dinner.* LEONIE *is standing in doorway looking out.* BORIS *center; he is fatalistically quiet at first.*

BORIS. What it comes to is this then! You're through with me. You want me to go!

LEONIE. I'm no good to you! I can no longer help you.

BORIS. Frustrated altruist!

LEONIE. You hate me!

BORIS. That would be encouraging!

LEONIE. We have nothing more for each other.

BORIS. Less than we had in the beginning!

LEONIE. Less than I thought we had.

BORIS [*walking toward her*]. And the man of science?

LEONIE. What?

BORIS [*still bearing down on her*]. This intricate man of science. You fluctuate so, Leonie. [*Facing her.*]

LEONIE. Please, Boris. I've failed. Can't we part—beautifully?

BORIS. What do you want to do? Go out on the bay and say farewell before the villagers in a barge drawn by a flock of swans? Shall we have a little orchestra to play—with the strings sobbing—and the bassoon off key?

LEONIE. You are bitter and cruel. Why? I've tried to help you. Why are you bitter?

BORIS [*moving close to her*]. At least I'm honest. Can you say the same?

LEONIE [*breaking away from him*]. I don't know what you mean by that.

BORIS [*getting in front of her*]. Yes, you do.

LEONIE. You're eating yourself up. You're killing yourself. There's the great lovely world outside and you sit in your room hating—

BORIS. What do you recommend? Cold showers and Swedish massage? What does the man of science prescribe for me?

LEONIE. Why do you hate Kenneth so?

BORIS. I'm jealous, my dear!

LEONIE. Poor Boris. You're beyond a simple emotion like that, aren't you?

BORIS. I envy you, Leonie. All like you.

LEONIE. Do you?

BORIS. I envy all sentimental liars who gratify their desires on high principle. It makes all your diversions an exercise in piety. You're sick of me and want to sleep with the man of science. [LEONIE *turns away. He seizes her arms and turns her to him.*] Does this suffice for you? No. It must be that you can no longer help me. [*Little silent laugh.*] My sainted father was like that! God!

LEONIE. This is the end, Boris.

BORIS. Of course it is. I tell you this though: Beware of him, Leonie. Beware of him.

LEONIE. Your hatred of Kenneth—like all your hatreds

—they're unnatural, frightening. I'm frightened of you. [*Turning from him.*]

BORIS [*crossing before her, closing door so she can't escape*]. Much better to be frightened of him. You know what I think. What does he think? Does he tell you? Do you know?

LEONIE. Yes, I know.

BORIS. You know what he tells you. This clairvoyant who gets rich profoundly analyzing the transparent. [*Enter* KENNETH, *door back.*]

KENNETH. Your mother would like to see you, Leonie.

LEONIE. Is she all right?

[BORIS *goes upstage to small table. Gets cigarette.*]

KENNETH. Oh, very chipper, Mr. Frothingham is with her.

LEONIE. She sent for Sam, didn't she? I wonder why.

BORIS. Perhaps she felt the situation too complicated —even for *you*, Dr. Rice.

KENNETH. I don't think so.

BORIS. You are so Olympian, Dr. Rice. Would it be possible to anger you?

KENNETH. Symptoms, my dear Count, never anger me. I study them.

BORIS. Really, you are in a superb position. I quite envy you. One might cut oneself open in front of you—and it would be a symptom. Wouldn't it?

LEONIE. Boris, please—what's the good?

BORIS [*crossing slowly to* LEONIE]. You are quite right, my dear, no good—no good in the world. Give your mother this message for me. Tell her that under the circumstances I shall simplify the situation by withdrawing.

LEONIE. You make me very unhappy, Boris.

BORIS. How agreeable then that you have Dr. Rice here —to resolve your unhappiness. [*Crosses quickly to table behind sofa and puts out cigarette.*]

LEONIE [*following him*]. Where will you be in case I—in case you—Boris?

BORIS. Don't worry about me. A magazine syndicate has offered me a great deal for *sentimental* reminiscences of my father. Imagine that, sentimental! They have offered me—charming Americanism—a ghost-writer. It will be quaint—one ghost collaborating with another ghost. [*Raising hand like Greek priest.*] My blessings, Leonie. [*Kisses her hand.*] You have been charming. Dr. Rice— [*He bows formally. Exit* BORIS.]

LEONIE. Poor Boris— [*She sinks into a chair, overcome.*]

KENNETH. He's part of the past. You must forget him.

LEONIE. Poor Boris!

KENNETH. You will forget him.

LEONIE. I'll try.

KENNETH. Exorcised!

LEONIE. You know, Kenneth, I feel you are the only one in the world I can count on.

KENNETH. Not me.

LEONIE. Whom else?

KENNETH. Yourself!

LEONIE. Light reed! Fragile! Fragile!

KENNETH. Pliant but unbreakable.

LEONIE. No. Don't think much of myself, Kenneth. Really I don't. My judgment seems to be at fault somehow. Paula thinks so too. She's always lecturing me. [*Sits right end of sofa.*]

KENNETH. Paula can't abide me.

LEONIE. It's not true!

KENNETH. You know, Leonie, I have an instinct in these matters—so, also, has your daughter.

LEONIE. Don't you like Paula?

KENNETH. I love her. Everyone connected with you.

LEONIE. Kenneth! How dear of you! Of course Paula and I are poles apart. Look at her friends!

KENNETH. Raffish!

LEONIE [*a little taken aback by this*]. Oh, do you think so? All of them? Don't you like Will?

KENNETH. Nice enough. Clever in his way. With an eye to the main chance.

LEONIE. Really?

KENNETH. Naturally—penniless boy.

LEONIE. I've always encouraged Paula to be independent. I've never tried to impose my ideals or my standards on her. Have I done wrong to give her her own head this way? She's such a darling, really. She's killing, you know. So superior, so knowing. The other day—the other day, Kenneth . . . I took her to lunch in town and she criticized me—now what do you think about?

KENNETH [*sitting on arm of chair*]. For once my intuition fails me.

LEONIE. About my technique with men. She said it was lousy. Isn't it delicious?

KENNETH. Not more specific than simply lousy?

LEONIE. She said I threw myself at men instead of reversing the process.

KENNETH. But I should think she would have approved of that. She makes such a fetish of being candid!

LEONIE. That's just what I said—exactly. I said I couldn't pretend—that I couldn't descend to—technique. I said that when my feelings were involved I saw no point in not letting the other person see it. I reproached her for deviousness. Strange ideas that child has—strange!

KENNETH. I'm afraid her generation is theory-ridden! [*Pause.*]

LEONIE. Kenneth?

KENNETH. Yes, Leonie?

LEONIE. It's true of course.

KENNETH. What?

LEONIE. Paula's—criticism. I can't conceal my feelings. Least of all—from you. [*Slight pause.*]

KENNETH. Why should you?

LEONIE. Oh, Kenneth, I'm so useless! You know how useless I am!

KENNETH. I know only that you are gracious and lovely —and that you have the gift of innocence.

LEONIE. I hate my life. It's been so scattered—emotionally.

KENNETH. Whose isn't?

LEONIE. You are such a comfort. Really it's too much now to expect me to do without you. Kenneth?

KENNETH. Yes . . . Leonie.

LEONIE. Will you be a darling—and marry me?

KENNETH. Leonie?

LEONIE [*returning his gaze*]. Yes, Kenneth.

KENNETH. Have you thought this over?

LEONIE. It's the first time—the very first time—that I've ever been sure.

KENNETH. You are so impulsive, Leonie.

LEONIE. Kenneth, don't you think we'd have a chance —you and I—don't you think?

[*Enter* PAULA, *door back.*]

PAULA [*realizes she has interrupted a tête-à-tête*]. Oh, sorry—!

LEONIE. Paula dear, have you been with Mother?

PAULA. Yes. Granny wants to see you, as a matter of fact.

LEONIE. Oh, I forgot! Is she all right? Cheerful?

PAULA. Oh, very.

LEONIE. I'll be right there. Stay and talk to Kenneth, Paula. He thinks you don't like him. Prove to him it isn't true. Do you think you could be gracious, Paula? Or is that too old-fashioned? [*Exit* LEONIE *door back.*]

[*In the following scene* PAULA *determines to get rid of*

the tantalizing and irritating mixed feelings she has
about KENNETH, *her sense of distrusting, disliking*
and simultaneously being fascinated by him—she
feels he has something up his sleeve; she is playing a
game to discover what it is and yet she becomes in-
creasingly conscious that game is not unpleasant to
her because of her interest in her victim.]

PAULA. Leonie's all a-flutter. What is it?

KENNETH. She was just telling me—she envies you your
poise.

PAULA. Your intentions are honorable, I hope.

KENNETH. Old hat, Paula.

PAULA. I beg your pardon.

KENNETH. Undergraduate audacity. Scott Fitzgerald.
Old hat.

PAULA. We don't like each other much, do we?

KENNETH. That's regrettable.

PAULA. And yet—I'm very curious about you.

KENNETH. What would you like to know?

PAULA. Your motive.

KENNETH. Ah!

PAULA. And yet even if you told me—

KENNETH. You wouldn't believe it?

PAULA [*facing him*]. No. Now why is that? Even when
you are perfectly frank, your frankness seems to me
—a device. Now why is that?

KENNETH. I'll tell you.

PAULA. Why?

KENNETH. Because you yourself are confused, muddled,
unsure, contradictory. I am simple and co-ordinated.
You resent that. You dislike it. You envy it. You
would like such simplicity for yourself. But, as you
are unlikely to achieve it, you soothe yourself by
distrusting me.

PAULA. You say I'm muddled. Why am I muddled?

KENNETH. You've accepted a set of premises without

examining them or thinking about them. You keep
them like jewels in a box and dangle them. Then
you put them back in the box, confident that they
belong to you. But as they don't you feel an occasional twinge of insecurity—

PAULA. Do you mind dropping the parables—?

KENNETH. Not at all—

PAULA. Why am I muddled? For example—

KENNETH. You're a walking contradiction in terms—

PAULA. For example?

KENNETH. For example—for example—your radicalism.
Your friends. Your point of view. Borrowed. Unex-
amined. Insincere.

PAULA. Go on.

KENNETH. You are rich and you are exquisite. Why are
you rich and exquisite? [*Walking back to face her.*]
Because your forebears were not moralistic but ruthless. Had they been moralistic, had they been concerned, as you pretend to be, with the "predatory
system"—this awful terminology—you'd be working
in a store somewhere wrapping packages or waiting
on querulous housewives with bad skins or teaching
school. Your own origins won't bear a moralistic investigation. You must know that. Your sociology
and economics must teach you that.

PAULA. Suppose I repudiate my origins?

KENNETH. That takes more courage than you have.

PAULA. Don't be so sure.

KENNETH. But why should you? If you had a special
talent or were a crusader there might be some sense
in it. But you have no special talent and you are
not a crusader. Much better to be decorative. Much
better for a world starving for beauty. Instead of
repudiating your origins you should exult in them
and in that same predatory system that made you

possible. [*Crossing to table behind sofa for cigarette.*]

[*Pause.*]

PAULA. What were your origins?

KENNETH [*lighting cigarette*]. Anonymous.

PAULA. What do you mean?

KENNETH. I was discovered on a doorstep.

PAULA. Really?

KENNETH. Like Moses.

PAULA. Where were you brought up?

KENNETH. In a foundling asylum in New England. The place lacked charm. This sounds like an unpromising beginning but actually it was more stimulating than you might imagine. I remember as a kid of twelve going to the library at Springfield and getting down the *Dictionary of National Biography* and hunting out the bastards. Surprising how many distinguished ones there were and are. I allied myself early with the brilliant and variegated company of the illegitimate.

PAULA. You don't know who your parents were?

KENNETH. No.

PAULA. Did you get yourself through college?

KENNETH. *And* medical school.

PAULA. Did you practice medicine?

KENNETH. For a bit. I devoted myself—when the victims would let me—to their noses and throats. It was a starveling occupation. But I gave up tonsillectomy for the soul. The poor have tonsils but only the rich have souls. My instinct was justified—as you see.

PAULA. You've gone pretty far.

KENNETH. Incredible journey!

PAULA. Having come from—from—

KENNETH. The mud—?

PAULA. Well—I should think you'd be more sympathetic to the under-dogs.

KENNETH. No, why should I? The herd bores me. It interests me only as an indication of the distance I've traveled.

PAULA. Will would say that you are a lucky individual who—

KENNETH. Yes, that is what Will would say. It always satisfies the mediocrity to call the exceptional individual lucky.

PAULA. You don't like Will?

KENNETH. I despise him.

PAULA. Why?

KENNETH. I detest these young firebrands whose incandescence will be extinguished by the first job! I detest radicals who lounge about in country-houses.

PAULA. You're unfair to Will.

KENNETH. I have no interest in being fair to him. We were discussing you.

PAULA. You are too persuasive. I don't believe you.

KENNETH. My advice to you is to find out what you want before you commit yourself to young Mr. Dexter.

PAULA. But I have committed myself.

KENNETH. Too bad.

PAULA. For him or for me?

KENNETH. For both of you; but for him particularly.

PAULA. Why?

KENNETH. I see precisely the effect your money will have on him. He will take it and the feeling will grow in him that in having given it you have destroyed what he calls his integrity. He will even come to believe that if not for this quenching of initiative he might have become a flaming leader of the people. At the same time he will be aware that both these comforting alibis are delusions—because he has no integrity to speak of nor any initiative to speak of. Knowing they are lies he will only proclaim them the louder, cling to them the harder. He will hate you as the thief of his character—petty larceny, I must say.

PAULA [*jumping up, taking several steps away from him*]. That's a lie.

KENNETH. Will is an American Puritan. A foreigner—Boris, for example—marries money, feeling that he gives value received. Very often he does. But young Dexter will never feel that—and maybe he'll be right.

PAULA. You hate Will.

KENNETH. You flatter him.

PAULA. How did you get to know so much about people? About what they feel and what they will do?

KENNETH. I began by knowing myself—but not lying to myself. [*A silence. He looks at her. He takes in her loveliness. He speaks her name, in a new voice, softly.*] Paula—

PAULA [*she looks at him fixedly*]. What?

KENNETH. Paula—

PAULA. What?

KENNETH. Do you know me any better now? Do you trust me any better now?

PAULA. I don't know.

[*Enter* WILL.]

KENNETH. Paula, Paula, Paula— [PAULA *starts toward door back.*] Don't go, Paula!

WILL. Oughtn't you to be changing for dinner? [PAULA *stops upstage.*] Hello, Doctor. What's the matter?

KENNETH. May I congratulate him?

WILL. What's he been saying?

KENNETH. Paula told me she is going to marry you.

PAULA. The doctor is a cynic.

KENNETH. We were discussing the European and American points of view toward money marriages—There's a great difference. The European fortune hunter, once he has landed the bag, has no more twinge of conscience than a big-game hunter when he has made his kill. The American—

WILL. Is that what you think I am, Doctor?

KENNETH [*to* PAULA *amiably*]. You see. He resents the mere phrase. But, my dear boy, that is no disgrace. We are all fortune hunters—

PAULA [*pointedly*]. Not all, Kenneth—!

KENNETH. But I see no difference at all between the man who makes a profession of being charming to rich ladies—or any other—specialist. The former is more arduous.

PAULA. Are you defending Will or yourself?

KENNETH. I am generalizing. [*To* WILL.] Congratulations! I admit that to scatter congratulations in this way is glib, but we live in a convention of glibness. Good God, we congratulate people when they marry and when they produce children—we skim lightly over these tremendous hazards— Excuse me. [*Exit* KENNETH.]

WILL. God damn that man!

PAULA. Will!

WILL. I can't stand him—not from the moment I saw him—because he's incapable of disinterestedness himself, he can't imagine it in others. He's the kind of cynical, sneering— He's a marauder. The adventurer with the cure-all. This is just the moment for him. And this is just the place!

PAULA. I've never seen you lose your temper before, Will.

WILL. You know why, don't you?

PAULA. Why?

WILL. Because he's right! While he was talking I felt like hitting him. At the same time a voice inside me said: Can you deny it? When I came in here he was saying your name. He was looking at you—it seems he hasn't quite decided, has he?

PAULA. I'm worried about him and Leonie—

WILL. He's got Leonie hook, line and sinker. That's obvious.

PAULA. She mustn't! Will, she mustn't!

WILL. You can't stop it—you can't do anything for Leonie. Nobody can do anything for anybody. Nobody should try.

PAULA. Will—you mustn't go back to New York. You must stay and help me.

WILL. Sorry. Nothing doing.

PAULA. Will!

WILL. I have a feeling you'll rather enjoy saving Leonie from the doctor.

PAULA. Will! That's not fair, Will!

WILL. It may not be fair but it is obvious. Also, it is obvious that the doctor won't mind being saved.

PAULA. It's lucky for both of us that one of us has some self-control.

WILL. No, I won't stay here. I hate the place, I hate Dr. Rice, I hate myself for being here!

PAULA. Don't let me down, Will—I need you terribly just now—

WILL [*at white heat*]. I haven't quite the technique of fortune hunting yet—in the European manner. Which of the two is he after—you or Leonie? Will he flip a coin?

PAULA. I hate you! I hate you!

WILL. Well, we know where we are at any rate.

PAULA. Yes. We do!

[LEONIE *comes running in. She wears an exquisite summer evening frock. She is breathless with happiness.*]

LEONIE. Paula! Why aren't you dressed? I want you to wear something especially lovely tonight! Do you like this? It's new. I haven't worn it before. [*She twirls for them.*] I've a surprise for you, Will. You'll know what it is in a minute. I was thinking of you and it popped into my mind. You know, Will, I'm very, very fond of you. And I think you are equally fond of me. I can't help liking people who like me. I suppose you think I'm horribly vain. But then, everybody's vain about something. [BUTLER *comes in with cocktails and sandwiches, to table right of fireplace.*] If they're not, they're vain about their lack of vanity. I believe that's a mot! Pretty good for a brainless— Here, Will, have a cocktail— [WILL *takes cocktail.*] Paula—what's your pet vanity? She thinks mine's my looks but it's not. If I had my way I shouldn't look at all the way I look.

[*Enter* DR. DEXTER, *door back. He wears a sea-green baggy dinner-suit; he looks as "hicky" and uncertain as ever.*]

DEXTER. Good evening, Mrs. Frothingham.

LEONIE. Dr. Dexter—how good of you to come. Delighted to see you.

DEXTER. Good evening. Hello, Will.

WILL. Dad!

DEXTER. Mrs. Frothingham invited me. Didn't you know?

LEONIE [*takes* DEXTER'S *arm and goes to* WILL]. You told me you had to leave tomorrow to visit your father in Brunswick so I just called him up in Brunswick—

DEXTER. She sent the car all the way for me. Nice car. Great springs.

LEONIE [*to* WILL]. Now you won't have to leave tomorrow. You can both spend the week-end here.

WILL [*walking away a little right*]. Awfully nice of you, Leonie.

LEONIE [*following him.* DEXTER *sits on sofa*]. You see, Will, I leave the big issues to the professional altruists. I just do what I can toward making those around me happy. And that's *my* vanity!

[*Enter* DENNIS, *door back.*]

DENNIS. Well! Well! Fancy that now, Hedda!

LEONIE. Oh, hello, Dennis, just in time for a cocktail. [LEONIE *leads him over to sofa.* WILL *is isolated down right center.*]

DENNIS [*to* DEXTER]. How are you?

DEXTER [*not friendly*]. I'm all right.

DENNIS. Complicated week-end! You and the Healer! Faraday and Cagliostro. That'll be something.

LEONIE [*takes* DENNIS'S *arm*]. Everybody tells me to like you, Dennis. I'm in such a mood that I'm going to make the effort.

DENNIS. I've been waiting for this. I'm thrilled!

LEONIE [*strolling with him across stage front*]. Something tells me you could be very charming if you wanted to. Tell me, Dennis, have you ever tried being lovable and sweet?

DENNIS. For you, Mrs. Frothingham, I would willingly revive the age of chivalry!

LEONIE. But there's no need of that. I just want you to be nice. Here, have a cocktail. Give you courage.

DENNIS. Just watch me from now on, Mrs. Frothingham.

LEONIE. I will. Passionately. [*Hands him cocktail.*] I'll be doing nothing else.

[BUTLER *crosses back of sofa, offers* DEXTER *and* PAULA *cocktails.* DR. RICE *comes in.*]

DENNIS [*stage sigh*]. A-h-h! The doctor! Just in time to look at my tongue, Doctor.

KENNETH. That won't be necessary, young man. I can tell— It's excessive.

LEONIE [*crossing to* KENNETH]. Kenneth—you remember Will's father—Dr. Dexter.

KENNETH. How do you do?

[*They shake hands. A second* BUTLER *has come in and he and* ROBERT *are passing cocktails and hors d'oeuvres.* LEONIE *keeps circulating among her guests.* KENNETH *and* DEXTER *are in the center—*DENNIS, *obeying a malicious impulse, presides over them. Announces a theme on which he eggs them on to utter variations.*]

DENNIS. A significant moment, ladies and gentlemen— the magician of Science meets the magician of Sex— The floating libido bumps the absolute! What happens?

DEXTER [*cupping his hand to his ear*]. What?

[WILL *crosses to door and looks out moodily.*]

DENNIS. The absolute hasn't got a chance. Isn't that right, Dr. Rice?

KENNETH. I shouldn't venture to contradict a young intellectual. Especially a very young intellectual.

LEONIE [*crosses front of* KENNETH, *to* DENNIS]. There, you see, I'm afraid, after all, I'll have to give you up, Dennis. You can't be lovable. You can't be sweet.

DENNIS. But I didn't promise to be winsome to everybody, only to you.

LEONIE. You really must treat him, Kenneth. He has no censor at all.

DENNIS. My censor is the Catholic tradition. We Catholics anticipated both Marx and Freud by a little matter of nineteen centuries. Spiritually, we have a Communion in the Holy Ghost—Communion. As for Dr. Rice, he offers confession without absolution. He is inadequate.

[LEONIE *returns with tray of canapes.*]

LEONIE. It seems such bad taste to discuss religion at cocktail time. Try a stuffed olive.

DEXTER. By the time you get your beautiful new world, true science will have perished.

LEONIE. Aren't you too pessimistic, Dr. Dexter? Too

much science has made you gloomy. Kenneth, the
depression hasn't stopped your work, has it? Depression or no depression—

[WILL *springs up.*]

WILL [*tensely*]. That's right, Leonie. [*Everyone faces
WILL.*] Depression or no depression—war or peace—
revolution or reaction—Kenneth will reign supreme!

[KENNETH *stares at him.* WILL *confronts him.*]

LEONIE. Will!

WILL. Yes, Leonie. His is the power and the glory!

LEONIE. Dennis, this is your influence—

WILL. I admire you unreservedly, Doctor. Of your kind
you are the best. You are the essence.

KENNETH. You embarrass me.

WILL. Some men are born ahead of their time, some behind, but you are made pat for the instant. Now is
the time for you—when people are unemployed and
distrust their own capacities—when people suffer
and may be tempted—when integrity yields to despair—now is the moment for you!

KENNETH [*strolling closer to him so they are face to
face*]. When, may I ask, is the moment for you—
when if ever?

WILL. After your victory. When you are stuffed and
inert with everything you want, then will be the
time for me. [*He goes out.*]

PAULA [*running after WILL*]. Will . . . Will . . .Will . . .
[*She follows him out.*]

LEONIE [*devastated by this strange behavior*]. What is
it? I don't like it when people stand in the middle
of the floor and make speeches. What's the matter
with him? Dennis, do you know?

DENNIS [*with a look at KENNETH*]. I can guess.

LEONIE. Has he quarreled with Paula? Paula is so in-
ept. She doesn't know how to . . . At the same time,

if he had a grievance, why couldn't he have kept it until after dinner?

[*Enter* ROBERT.]

ROBERT. Dinner is served. [*Exit* ROBERT.]

LEONIE. Well, we'll do what we can. Sam is dining with Mother in her room, Boris has a headache. Dennis, you and Dr. Dexter—

DENNIS. You've picked me, Dr. Dexter. I congratulate you.

DEXTER. Thank God, I can't hear a word you say. [*Exit* DEXTER, *door back*.]

DENNIS [*sadistically*]. Oh, yes, he can. And we'll fight it out on these lines if it takes all dinner. [*He follows* DEXTER *out*.]

LEONIE. What extraordinary behavior! What do you suppose, Kenneth—shall I go after them?

KENNETH. I wouldn't. It's their problem. Give them time.

LEONIE [*reassured*]. You are so wise, Kenneth. How did I ever get on without you? I have that secure feeling that you are going to be my last indiscretion. When I think how neatly I've captured you—I feel quite proud. I guess my technique isn't so lousy after all. [*She takes his arm and swings along beside him as they waltz in to dinner.*]

CURTAIN

Act three

SCENE. *The same.*

TIME. *Late that fall. The trees have turned. The sumach have put out the brilliant red flowers of autumn.*

AT RISE. WILL *and* DENNIS *have just arrived, and are standing at fireplace, back.* LEONIE *comes in to greet them.* SAM *strolls in with her.*

LEONIE. I'm so glad to see you! [*She shakes hands with each of them warmly.*] Will! How are you? [*To* DENNIS.] It's so good of you to come.

SAM [*shaking hands with* WILL]. Very glad to see you.

WILL. Thanks.

[SAM *shakes hands with* DENNIS.]

LEONIE. Sam drove over for a few hours from Blue Hill to talk business to me. He hasn't had much luck so far. It's simply wonderful having you boys here— it's like old times. I didn't tell Paula. [*To* SAM.] I did all this on my own. It's a surprise for Paula.

DENNIS. She'll be overcome when she sees me. Maybe you should prepare her.

WILL. Where is Paula?

LEONIE. Isn't it provoking! She and Kenneth went for a walk. They should have been back long before this. [*Turning back to them.*] Paula hasn't been at all herself, Will. I thought you would cheer her up.

DENNIS. I will be very glad to do what I can, of course. Several very stubborn cases have yielded to my charm.

LEONIE. I'm sure! Do sit down. [*She sits.*]

DENNIS [*taking out his pipe*]. Do you mind?

[WILL *sits.*]

LEONIE. Oh, please—I can't tell you how I appreciate your coming—

DENNIS [*the harassed business man*]. Well, as a matter of fact, Leonie, it wasn't easy to get away from the office—

LEONIE. Are you in an office?

DENNIS. Sometimes as many as fifteen in a day. [LEONIE

laughs.] But when I got your appealing letter—*and* the return tickets—I'm chivalrous at heart, you know, Leonie—

LEONIE. I know you are!

SAM. How's town?

WILL. Very hot.

SAM. I'm just on my way down. Stopped by to go over several things with Leonie—

LEONIE. Poor Sam's been having an awful time with me. He keeps putting things in escrow. Where is escrow?

DENNIS. It's where squirrels put nuts in the wintertime.

LEONIE. I see! Dennis is much more lucid than you, Sam.

DENNIS. I have a knack for making the abstruse translucent. Especially in economics. Now, would you like to know why England went off gold?

LEONIE. No, I wouldn't.

DENNIS. I shall yield to your subconscious demand and tell you.

LEONIE [*to others*]. Help!

DENNIS. I see that there is no audience for my peculiar gift.

LEONIE. You know, Will, I've thought perhaps you were angry with us.

WILL. Why?

LEONIE. You haven't been here for so long. [*To* SAM.] Since Granny died—none of them have been here. Did Paula write you about Granny's funeral?

WILL. No. She didn't.

LEONIE. Of course I hate funerals—I can't bear them— but this was so—natural. Mother wanted to live till the fall and she did. It was a dreaming blue sky and there was that poignant haze over the hills and over the bay, and the smell of burning wood from somewhere. Burning wood never smells at any other time the way it does in Indian summer. And the colors that day! Did you ever, Sam, see such a day?

SAM. It was beautiful.

LEONIE. They say the colors of autumn are the colors of death, but I don't believe that. They were in such strength that day. I cried—but not on account of Mother—that kind of day always makes me cry a little bit anyway. You couldn't cry over consigning anyone you loved to an earth like that—on a day like that. I put some blazing leaves over her, but when I passed there the other day, they were withered and brown—

SAM [*chiding her*]. Now, Leonie—

LEONIE. Sam thinks I shouldn't talk about Mother. But I don't see why. She doesn't depress me. I think of her with joy. She had a wonderful life.

SAM. She was a wonderful woman.

LEONIE [*to* WILL]. Imagine, Will—when Sam was here last time—you were here that week-end—she *knew*. She asked Sam to be executor of her will.

SAM [*very annoyed at her for bringing this up*]. Leonie—

LEONIE. Why didn't you tell me, Sam, then?

SAM. Seemed no point.

LEONIE. She didn't want me to know, did she?

SAM. No. She didn't want to distress you. [*A moment's pause.*]

LEONIE. What can be keeping Paula? [*She glances out of the window.*] Sam, do you want to talk business to me some more?

SAM. I'd like to talk to Will a minute.

LEONIE. Oh—yes. Well, Dennis, wouldn't you like me to show you to your room? [*She rises, goes to door into hallway.* DENNIS *follows.*]

DENNIS. Thanks. I've got to answer a chain letter.

LEONIE. I've given you a room you've never had. The tower room.

DENNIS. Is it ivory? I won't be comfortable if it isn't ivory.

LEONIE. Well just this once you're going to be uncomfortable—and like it! [*She goes out.*]

DENNIS [*tragically*]. And for this I gave up a superb view of the gas-house on 149th Street. [*He goes out.*]

SAM [*rises and goes up toward fireplace*]. Will—

WILL. Yes, Mr. Frothingham.

SAM. Oh—call me Sam.

WILL. All right.

SAM. I'll have to be pushing off in an hour or so. I rather wanted to talk to you.

WILL. Yes—

SAM [*wipes his forehead*]. Gosh, Leonie's a difficult woman to talk business to. [*Sits.*]

WILL. I can imagine that. She's not interested in business.

SAM. *She—is—not!!!*

WILL. What do you want to speak to me about?

SAM. Paula.

WILL. What about Paula?

SAM. As I'm her father—I hope you won't think me—

WILL. Of course not—

SAM. It's not altogether easy—

WILL. Do you want me to help you?

SAM. Yes. I wish you would!

WILL. You're worried about Paula and me, aren't you? So was her grandmother. You think me irresponsible. Less responsible for example—[*as if making a random comparison*] than Dr. Rice?

SAM. Well, as a matter of fact, I've rather gotten to know Dr. Rice, and in many respects, he's a pretty sound feller. [*Rising and going to stand above*

WILL.] Hang it all, Will, I like you, and I don't like to preach to you, you know.

WILL. Go on.

SAM. Well, there are—from my point of view at least— a lot of nonsensical ideas knocking about. I'd like to point out just one thing to you. Your radicalism and all that— Well, the point is this—if you marry Paula —and I hope you do, because I like you—and, what is more important, Paula likes you—you'll have responsibilities. Paula will be rich. Very rich. Money means responsibility. Now, I shouldn't, for example, like you to start radical magazines with it. I shouldn't like you to let money drift through your fingers in all sorts of aimless, millennial directions that won't get anywhere.

WILL. Who told you that was my intention?

SAM. A little bird.

WILL. With a black moustache?

SAM. Does that matter?

WILL. No.

SAM [*putting hand on* WILL.'s *shoulder*]. As a matter of fact, I'm not worried about you at all. Money, I expect, will do to you what getting power does to radical opposition, once it gets office—

WILL. Emasculate me, you mean?

SAM. Well, hardly. Mature you. Once you're rich, I have no doubt you'll be—

WILL. Sound.

SAM. Yes. Sound. But your friends—this McCarthy boy—

WILL. Well, I can easily cut Dennis—all my poor and unsound friends—

SAM [*quietly*]. I'm sorry you're taking this tone with me, Will. I'm the last person in the world to ask you to drop anybody. I'd be ashamed of you if you did. Only—

WILL. Only?

SAM. I must tell you that I am in position—by virtue of the will left by Mrs. Wyler—to keep Paula's money from being used for any purpose that might be construed as—subversive.

WILL. From whose point of view?

SAM [*quietly*]. From mine.

WILL. I see.

SAM. Possibly you may not believe this—but I trust you, Will. Mrs. Wyler trusted you.

WILL. You needn't worry. Paula seems to have other interests apparently.

SAM. What do you mean?

WILL. Sounder interests—

[DENNIS *enters, through door back.*]

DENNIS. The tower room lets in light on four sides, but nothing to look at. Just the sea and the landscape.

SAM. What did you do with Leonie?

DENNIS. She's gone to her mother's room to potter around.

SAM. Maybe I can get her attention while she's pottering. Excuse me. [SAM *goes out.*]

DENNIS. Poor Leonie—she's the last of the lovely ladies. The inheritance taxes'll get 'em soon. You know we were by way of getting our magazine from Leonie when Dr. Rice spiked our guns. So I'm leaving. My time is too valuable. But the Healer won't last forever, and when he goes, I shall return. Take heart, my good man. I know you feel a little tender about this, but remember, my lad, it's the Cause that counts. Remember what Shaw says: "There is no money but the devil's money. It is all tainted and it might as well be used in the service of God." [*A moment—*WILL *is obviously thinking of something else.*] What's the matter?

WILL. Nothing.

DENNIS [*bringing down chair to sit left of* WILL, *he imitates* RICE'S *manner*]. Now you must speak, young man—how can I sublimate your subconscious troubles, if you won't speak? Are you unhappy about Paula, my lad? [*No answer.*] Tell me what's happened between you—relieve your soul, and, as a reward, I may make you co-editor of our magazine. [*No response. He rises and walks to opposite side of table.*] No? Assistant editor you remain. I may even fire you. Yes, I think I will fire you. [*Crossing in front of* WILL *to fireplace.*] Dexter—you're through. Go upstairs and get your check. [*Rubs his hands together in glee.*] God, it gives me a sense of power to fire a man—especially an old friend!

[PAULA *and* KENNETH *come in door right from the garden.*]

PAULA [*amazed to see them*]. Will! But how—! Dennis!

WILL [*rather coolly*]. Hello, Paula.

DENNIS. We came to surprise you. Now that we have surprised you, we can go home.

WILL. Leonie asked me to come.

PAULA. Oh. Well, it's very nice to see you.

WILL. Thanks.

PAULA. When I wired you to come a few weeks ago, you were too busy. It takes Leonie, doesn't it?

DENNIS. You should have tried me, Paula. Hello, Dr. Rice. How's business? Any suppressions today?

KENNETH [*significantly*]. Apparently not.

DENNIS. Well, come on up to my room, Doctor, and we'll play Twenty Questions. [*He goes out.*]

WILL. Hello, Dr. Rice.

KENNETH. How are you?

PAULA. Will—I'm awfully glad to see you. I was just going to write you to thank you for the sweet letter you sent me after Granny died.

KENNETH. I'm afraid it's my fault, Dexter. I do my best

to keep Paula so busy that she finds no time to write letters.

WILL. I was sure I could count on you, Doctor. [WILL *goes out.*]

PAULA. You enjoy hurting Will, don't you?

KENNETH. When there is an obstacle in my path, I do my best to remove it.

PAULA. What makes you think it is only Will that stands between us— That if left to myself I—

KENNETH. Because it is true. Were it not for the squids of idealistic drivel spouted around you by Will and his friends, there would be no issue at all between us. I resent even an imputed rivalry with someone I despise.

PAULA. Rivalry?

KENNETH. Paula— There's no reason any longer why I shouldn't tell you the truth.

PAULA. What is it, Kenneth?

KENNETH [*after a moment—slowly*]. Do you know what I feel like? I feel like a man on a great height, irresistibly tempted to jump over. Do you want the truth really? [*She says nothing. Somehow his words, his voice, his attitude make her feel that really now he may reveal something which before he wouldn't have revealed. He is in a trance-like state almost; she feels it; she is rather horribly fascinated—somehow, though she distrusts him utterly, some instinct tells her that at this moment actually he is tempted by a force, disruptive to himself, to tell her the truth.*] Don't you know it? Don't you feel it? [*Pause.*] Haven't you known it? Haven't you felt it? [*A moment's pause.*] I love you.

PAULA. What?

KENNETH. I love you.

[*A pause. She is too stupefied to speak. She too is under a spell. She is fascinated by him—by the enor-*

mity of this. She rises, walks away from him to stand by sofa.]

PAULA. I suppose I should be afraid of you. I am not afraid of you.

KENNETH. I am afraid of you. You tempt me to venture the impossible. That is impractical. And I have always been eminently practical.

PAULA. I'm sure you have. [*She feels herself talking automatically, as if out of a hypnotic state—at the same time some vanity and shrewdness keeps pounding inside her: "See how far he will go—see how far he will go!"*]

KENNETH. I have lived by a plan. The plan has matured. But I have yearned for a face that would give me joy, for the voice that would soothe me. It is your face. It is your voice.

[PAULA *is fighting not to scream; at the same time she is caught in a nightmarish fascination.*]

PAULA [*very faintly*]. Don't you love Mother?

KENNETH. No. [*A moment's pause.*] You are the youth I have never had, the security I have never had—you are the home I have hungered for. [*Moves toward her—stands over her and a little back.*] That I am standing near you now, that I have achieved a share in your life, that you are listening to me, that you are thinking of me and of what I am, to the exclusion of everything else in the whirling universe—this is a miracle so devastating, that it makes any future possible—Paula—

PAULA. What?

KENNETH. Paula?

PAULA. What *is* it?

KENNETH [*bending over her*]. Paula . . . [*It is as if he got a sexual joy from saying her name.*] I love your name. I love to say your name.

PAULA. I *am* afraid of you. I'm sorry for you.

KENNETH. Do you think me insane?

PAULA. Yes.

KENNETH. Because I am ambitious, because I am forthright, because I deal scientifically with the human stuff around me—you think me insane. Because I am ruthless and romantic, you think me insane. This boy you think you love—who spends his time sniveling about a system he is not strong enough to dominate—is he sane?

PAULA. I don't expect you to—

KENNETH. When I hear the chatter of your friends, it makes me sick. While they and their kind prate of co-operative commonwealths, the strong man takes power, and rides over their backs—which is all their backs are fit for. Never has the opportunity for the individual career been so exalted, so infinite in its scope, so horizontal. House-painters and minor journalists become dictators of great nations. [*With puckish humor—leaning on arm of her chair.*] Imagine what a really clever man could do? See what he has done! [*He smiles, makes a gesture of modest self-assertion, indicating the room as part of his conquest. She laughs, rather choked and embarrassed. He goes on.*] And this I have done alone. From an impossible distance—I have come to you, so that when I speak, you can hear. What might we not do together, Paula—you and I—

[*To her surprise,* PAULA *finds herself arguing an inconceivable point. She loathes the strange fascination she feels in this man, and yet is aware that it might turn to her advantage.*]

PAULA. We don't want the same things.

KENNETH. You want what everyone wants who has vitality and imagination—new forms of power—new domains of knowledge—the ultimate sensations.

PAULA. You *are* romantic, aren't you?

KENNETH. Endlessly. And endlessly—realistic. [*Staring at her.*] What are you thinking?

PAULA [*shrewd against him—against herself*]. I keep thinking—what you want now—what you're after now?

KENNETH [*moving toward her*]. You don't believe then —that I love you?

PAULA [*leaning back in chair—not looking at him*]. You are a very strange man.

KENNETH. I am simple really. I want everything. That's all!

PAULA. And you don't care how you get it.

KENNETH. Don't be moralistic, Paula—I beg you. I am directly in the tradition of your own marauding ancestors. They pass now for pioneers—actually they fell on the true pioneers, and wrested what they had found away from them, by sheer brutal strength. I am doing the same thing—but more adroitly.

PAULA. Why are you so honest with me?

KENNETH [*with his most charming smile*]. Perhaps because I feel that, in your heart, you too are an adventurer.

[*A pause. During these half-spellbound instants a thought has been forming slowly in* PAULA's *mind that crystallizes now. This man is the enemy. This man is infinitely cunning, infinitely resourceful. Perhaps—just the possibility—he really feels this passion for her. If so, why not use this weakness in an antagonist so ruthless? She will try.*]

PAULA. I shouldn't listen to you—

[*A moment. He senses her cunning. He looks at her.*]

KENNETH. You don't trust me?

PAULA. Have I reason to trust you?

KENNETH. What reason would you like? What proof would you like?

PAULA. Aren't you going to marry Mother?

KENNETH. Only as an alternative.

PAULA. Will you—tell her so? Will you give up the alternative?

KENNETH. And if I do?

PAULA. What shall I promise you?

KENNETH. Yourself.

PAULA [*looks at him—speaks*]. And if I do?

KENNETH. Then . . .

PAULA [*taking fire*]. You say you love me! If you feel it —really feel it— You haven't been very adventurous for all your talk! Taking in Mother and Sam! Give up those conquests. Tell her! Tell Mother! Then perhaps I will believe you.

KENNETH. And then?

PAULA. Take your chances!

KENNETH [*quietly*]. Very well.

PAULA. You will?

KENNETH. I will.

PAULA. You'll tell Mother—you love me?

KENNETH. Yes.

PAULA [*going to the foot of the stairs, calls*]. Mother! Mother!

LEONIE [*offstage*]. Yes, Paula. I'm coming right down! I've the most marvelous surprise for you! Wait and see!

[PAULA *walks to end of sofa—looking at* KENNETH. LEONIE *comes in. She is wearing an exquisite old-fashioned silk wedding-dress which billows around her in an immense shimmering circle. She is a vision of enchantment.*]

LEONIE [*in a great flurry of excitement*]. Children, look what I found! It's Mother's. It's the dress she was married in. I was poking around in Granny's room while Sam was talking to me about bonds, and I came upon it. Do you like it, Kenneth? Isn't it adorable? Have you ever . . . What's the matter? Don't you like it?

PAULA. It's very pretty.

LEONIE [*overwhelmed by the inadequacy of this word*]. Pretty! Pretty! [*She hopes for more from* KENNETH.] Kenneth . . . ?

KENNETH. It's exquisite.

LEONIE. Isn't it? [*She whirls around in the dress.*] Isn't it? Yes. Exquisite. Can you imagine the scene? Can you imagine Granny walking down the aisle—and all the august spectators in mutton-chop whiskers and Prince Alberts? We've lost something these days —a good deal—oh, I don't miss the mutton-chops— but in ceremony, I mean—in punctilio and grace. . . .

PAULA [*cutting ruthlessly through the nostalgia*]. Mother!

LEONIE. What is it, Paula?

PAULA. Kenneth has something to tell you.

LEONIE. Kenneth?

PAULA. Yes. He has something to tell you.

LEONIE. Have you, Kenneth?

KENNETH. Yes.

LEONIE. What is it?

KENNETH [*quietly*]. I love Paula. I want to marry Paula.

[*A pause. Granny's wedding dress droops.*]

LEONIE. Do you mean that, Kenneth?

KENNETH. Yes.

LEONIE [*piteously*]. This isn't very nice of you, Paula.

PAULA. I had nothing to do with it. I loathe Kenneth. But I wanted you to know him. Now you see him, Mother, your precious Lothario—there he is! Look at him!

LEONIE. These clothes are picturesque, but I think our modern ones are more comfortable. I think—I feel quite faint—isn't it ridiculous? [*She sways.*]

PAULA. I'm sorry, Mother. I had to. But I love you. I really do.

LEONIE [*very faint*]. Thank you, Paula.

PAULA. You'd better go up and lie down. I'll come to you in a moment.

LEONIE. Yes. I think I'd better. Yes. [*She begins to sob; she goes out, hiding her face in the lace folds of her dress.* PAULA, *having gone with her to the door, rings bell for* ROBERT, *turns to* KENNETH.]

PAULA. I suppose you're going to tell me this isn't cricket. Well, don't, because it will only make me laugh. To live up to a code with people like you is only to be weak and absurd.

KENNETH [*his voice is low and even but tense with hate*]. You, Miss Frothingham, are my *last* miscalculation. I might even say my first. Fortunately, not irreparable!

[ROBERT *enters*.]

PAULA. Robert.

ROBERT. Yes, Miss Frothingham.

PAULA [*still staring fixedly at* KENNETH]. Dr. Rice is leaving. Will you see that his bags are packed, please?

ROBERT. Yes, Miss. [*He goes out*.]

KENNETH. Forgive me—for having overestimated you. [*He goes out door right*.]

[PAULA *comes slowly down and sits on sofa. She gets a reaction herself now from all she has been through; this game hasn't been natural to her; she is trembling physically; she is on the verge of tears.* WILL *comes in*.]

PAULA. Will—Will darling— [*She clings to* WILL.]

WILL [*worried*]. Paula!

PAULA. Put your arms around me, Will—hold me close—

[WILL *obeys.*]

WILL. What's happened?

PAULA. I've tricked him. I made him say in front of Mother that he loved me, that he wanted to marry me. Poor Leonie! But it had to be done! And do you know, Will—at the end I felt—gosh, one has so many selves, Will. I must tell you—for the—well, for the completeness of the record—

WILL [*curious*]. What?

PAULA. At the end I felt I had to do it—not only to save Leonie—but to save myself. Can you understand that? I felt horribly drawn to him, and by the sordid thing I was doing— But it's over. Thank God it's over. Will, darling, these six weeks have been hell without you. When I got your letter about Granny, I sat down and cried. I wanted to go right to New York to be with you. And yet I couldn't. How could I? But now, Will—I don't want to wait for you any longer. I've done what I can. It's cost me almost— Will—I need you terribly—

WILL. And I you, Paula. But listen, darling—I've decided during the weeks I've been away from you— I can't marry you now— I can't face what I'd become—

PAULA. But, Will, I— [*Springing up.*] But, Will, I'll give up the money. I'll live with you anywhere.

WILL. I know that, Paula. But I mustn't. You mustn't let me. I've thought it all out. You say you'd live with me anywhere. But what would happen? Supposing I didn't get a job? Would we starve? We'd take fifty dollars a week from your grandmother's estate. It would be foolish not to. Taking fifty, why not seventy-five? Why not two hundred? I can't let myself in for it, Paula. [*A long pause.*] Paula, darling—do you hate me?

PAULA. No.

WILL. Supposing you weren't rich? Is it a world in which, but for this, I'd have to sink? If it is, I'm going to damn well do what I can to change it. I don't have to scrabble for the inheritance of dead men. That's for Kenneth—one robber baron—after the lapse of several generations—succeeding another. I don't want this damn fortune to give me an unfair advantage over people as good as I am who haven't got it. [*Torn with pity for her.*] Paula—my dearest—what can I do?

PAULA. I see that you can't do anything. I quite see. Still—

WILL. I love you, Paula, and I'll be longing for you terribly, but I can't marry you—not till there's somebody for you to marry. When I've struck my stride, I won't care about Sam, or the money, or anything, because I'll be on my own. If you feel the way I do, you'll wait.

PAULA [*very still voice*]. Of course, Will. I'll wait.

WILL [*overcome with gratitude and emotion—seizes her in his arms passionately*]. Darling—darling—

[LEONIE *comes in.* WILL, *overcome with emotion, goes out.*]

LEONIE. It's easy to say "lie down." But what happens then? Thoughts assail you. Thoughts . . .

PAULA. Mother . . .

LEONIE. Kenneth's going. He's leaving. I suppose you're happy. It's the end—the end of summer.

PAULA [*herself shaken with emotion*]. Mother— [*She wants to talk to* LEONIE, *to tell her what has happened, but* LEONIE *is lost in her own maze.*]

LEONIE. It's cold here. I hate this place. I'm going to sell it. [*She sits, in chair, right of fireplace.*] I've always wanted things around me to be gay and warm and happy. I've done my best. I must be wrong. Why do I find myself this way? With nothing. With nothing.

PAULA [*running to her mother and throwing herself on her knees beside her*]. Mother—Mother darling—

LEONIE [*not responding, reflectively*]. I suppose the thing about me that is wrong is that love is really all I care about. [*A moment's pause.*] I suppose I should have been interested in other things. Good works. Do they sustain you? But I couldn't somehow. I think when you're not in love—you're dead. Yes, that must be why I'm . . . [*Her voice trails off rather.* PAULA *drops her head in her mother's lap and begins to cry.*]

LEONIE [*surprised*]. Paula—what is it? What's the matter? Are you sorry? It's all right, child.

PAULA [*through her tears*]. It's Will—

LEONIE. Will?

PAULA. He's going away.

LEONIE. Why don't you go with him?

PAULA. He doesn't want me.

LEONIE. That's not true. It must be something else.

PAULA. The money.

LEONIE. Oh, the money. Yes, the money. The money won't do anything for you. It'll work against you. It's worked against me. It gives you the illusion of escape—but always you have to come back to yourself. At the end of every journey—you find yourself.

PAULA. What shall I do, Mother?

LEONIE. You and Will want the same things. In the end you will find them. But don't let him find them with someone else. Follow him. Be near him. When he is depressed and discouraged, let it be your hand that he touches, your face that he sees.

PAULA [*breathless*]. Mother—you're right—he told me

last summer—"you must have a shoulder to lean
on"—

LEONIE. Let it be your shoulder, Paula; follow him. Be
near him.

PAULA. Thank you, Mother.

LEONIE [*ruefully*]. I am telling you what *I* should do. It
must be bad advice.

PAULA [*gratefully*]. Darling!

[DENNIS *and* WILL *come in.*]

DENNIS. Here you are! We're off to the boat! Thirty
minutes! Why don't you and Paula come too? What
do you say, Leonie?

LEONIE. You know, all these years I've been coming
up here, and I've never been on the Bar Harbor
boat.

DENNIS. It may be said, Mrs. Frothingham, if you have
never been on the Bar Harbor boat, that you have
not lived!

LEONIE. Really! I'd always heard it was poky.

DENNIS. Poky! The *Normandie* of the Kennebec poky!
Mrs. Frothingham!

LEONIE. It's fun, is it? But doesn't it get into New York
at some impossible hour?

DENNIS. At seven a.m.

LEONIE. Seven! [*She shudders.*]

DENNIS [*the brisk executive*]. Seven! Yes, sir! At my
desk at nine! All refreshed and co-ordinated and
ready to attack my South American correspondence.

LEONIE. I must learn not to believe him, mustn't I?

DENNIS. I am my own master, Leonie. All day for nine
mortal hours I grind out escape fiction for the pulp
magazines. But one day I shall become famous and
emerge into the slicks and then I doubt very much
whether I shall come here.

LEONIE. I shall miss you.

DENNIS. Then I'll come.

LEONIE. I hate to have you go, Dennis. You cheer me up. Why don't you stay?

DENNIS. Impossible, Leonie. I must go to New York to launch the magazine. But for the moment, good-bye, Leonie. As a reward for your hospitality I shall send you the original copy of one of my stories. Would you like to escape from something?

LEONIE [*smiling wanly*]. I would indeed!

DENNIS. Think no more about it. You're as good as free. The story is yours, typed personally on my Underwood. Those misplaced keys—those inaccuracies—how they will bemuse posterity! [*He goes out.*]

WILL [*awkwardly*]. Good-bye, Leonie.

LEONIE. Good-bye, Will. [*He goes out without looking at* PAULA. *In pantomime,* LEONIE *urges* PAULA *to go after him.* PAULA *kisses her quickly and runs after* WILL. *Left alone,* LEONIE *walks to the chair in which her mother sat so often—she looks through the glowing autumn at the darkening sea.* KENNETH *comes in. There is a pause.*]

KENNETH. Leonie—

LEONIE. Yes, Kenneth.

KENNETH. I don't expect you to understand this. I shall not try to make you understand it.

LEONIE. Perhaps I'd better not.

KENNETH. Really I am amused at myself—highly entertained. That I should have almost had to practice on myself what hitherto I have reserved for my patients—that I who have made such a fetish of discipline and restraint so nearly succumbed to an inconsistency. I must revise my notion of myself.

LEONIE. And I too.

KENNETH. Why? Why you?

LEONIE. I seem to be a survival—Paula's directness—and your calculations—they are beyond me.

KENNETH. Nevertheless, it's curious how you and Paula

are alike—no wonder that, for a moment at least, you seemed to me—interchangeable.

LEONIE. Did you know it from the beginning—that it was Paula?

KENNETH. I was attracted by her resemblance to you—for exercising this attraction I hated her. She felt it too—from the beginning and she must have hated me from the beginning. Between us there grew up this strange, unnatural antagonism—

LEONIE. What?

KENNETH. This fused emotion of love and hate. It had to be brought out into the open. It's a familiar psychosis—the unconscious desire of the daughter to triumph over the mother.

LEONIE. But I don't understand—

KENNETH. There is so much in these intricate relationships that the layman can't understand—

LEONIE. You mean that you—felt nothing for Paula?

KENNETH. No, I don't mean that at all. But I saw that what I felt for her was some twisted reflection of what I felt for you. And I saw there was only one way out of it—to let her triumph over you. I told her that I loved her. But this was not enough. I must repeat it in front of you. You must witness her triumph. I made it possible. I gave her her great moment. Well, you see what it's done. It freed her so beautifully that she was able to go to Will. They've gone away together. Perfect cure for her as well as for myself. [*A moment's pause.*]

LEONIE. It all sounds almost too perfect, Kenneth.

KENNETH. I said I didn't expect you to understand it— you have lived always on your emotions. You have never bothered to delve beneath them. You are afraid to, aren't you?

LEONIE. I know this, Kenneth. I heard you say that you loved Paula. I heard your voice. No, I can't accept this, Kenneth! It's not good enough. I've never done that before. I only think now that everything you did, everything you said, was to cover what you felt. And I'd end by telling myself that I believed you. I'd end by taking second best from you. No, I must guard myself from that. I felt this a month ago—that's why I sent for Will.

KENNETH. Some day, Leonie, you will learn that feeling is not enough.

LEONIE. But I trust my instinct, Kenneth.

KENNETH. That, Leonie, is your most adorable trait—

LEONIE. What?

KENNETH. That trust—that innocence. If it weren't for that, you wouldn't be you—and everyone wouldn't love you—

LEONIE. Oh, no, Kenneth—

[DENNIS *comes in.*]

DENNIS. Oh, excuse me. But I left my brief-case. Oh, here it is. [*He picks it up.*] Without my brief-case I am a man without a Destiny. With it I am—

KENNETH. A man with a brief-case.

LEONIE [*crossing rather desperately to* DENNIS—*this straw in the current*]. What's in it—your stories?

DENNIS. Stories—no, that wouldn't matter. I am fertile; I can spawn stories. But the plans for the magazine are in here—the future of Young America is here—

LEONIE. Will you stay and have a whiskey and soda?

DENNIS. Thanks, but if I do, I shall miss the boat.

LEONIE. Suppose you do?

KENNETH. Leonie—that would delay the millenium one day.

DENNIS. The doctor's right. That would be selfish.

LEONIE. Be selfish. Please stay.

DENNIS. No. Once you are enlisted in a cause, you can't live a personal life. It is a dedication.

LEONIE. Kenneth is leaving. I shall be lonely, Dennis. I can't bear to be alone.

KENNETH. Your need for people is poignant, isn't it, Leonie?

LEONIE. Stay for dinner. After dinner we can talk about your magazine.

DENNIS. Oh, well—that makes it possible for me to stay. Thank you, Kenneth. [*He goes to sofa, sits, busying himself with brief-case.*]

[*She goes to console to make highball.*]

KENNETH. Send me your magazine, Dennis. I shall be honored to be the first subscriber.

DENNIS. I'll be glad to. Your patients can read it in the waiting-room instead of the *National Geographic*.

KENNETH. Your first subscriber—and very possibly your last. [*He crosses to door and turns back.*] Good-bye, Leonie. Good luck, Dennis. We who are about to retire—salute you. [*She does not look at him. He bows formally to* DENNIS'S *back, makes a gesture of "good luck" and exits.*]

DENNIS. Trouble with that fellow is—he lives for himself. No larger interest. That's what dignifies human beings, Leonie—a dedication to something greater than themselves.

LEONIE [*coming down to hand him his highball*]. Yes? Here's your whiskey and soda. I envy you, Dennis. I wish I could dedicate myself to something—something outside myself.

DENNIS [*rising to sit beside her*]. Well, here's your opportunity, Leonie—it's providential. You couldn't do better than this magazine. It would give you a new interest—impersonal. It would emancipate you, Leonie. It would be a perpetual dedication to Youth—to the hope of the world. The world is middle-aged and tired. But we—

LEONIE [*wistfully*]. Can you refresh us, Dennis?

DENNIS. Refresh you? Leonie, we can rejuvenate you!

LEONIE [*grateful there is someone there—another human being she can laugh with*]. That's an awfully amusing idea. You make me laugh.

DENNIS [*eagerly selling the idea*]. In the youth of any country, there is an immense potentiality—

LEONIE. You're awfully serious about it, aren't you, Dennis?

DENNIS. Where the magazine is concerned, Leonie, I am a fanatic.

LEONIE. I suppose if it's really successful—it'll result in my losing everything I have—

DENNIS. It'll be taken from you anyway. You'll only be anticipating the inevitable.

LEONIE. Why—how clever of me!

DENNIS. Not only clever but grateful.

LEONIE. Will you leave me just a little to live on—?

DENNIS. Don't worry about that—come the Revolution —you'll have a friend in high office.

[LEONIE *accepts gratefully this earnest of security. They touch glasses in a toast as the curtain falls.*]

IDIOT'S DELIGHT

by Robert E. Sherwood

This play is lovingly dedicated to
Lynn Fontanne and Alfred Lunt

First production, March 9th, 1936,
at the National Theatre, Washington, D.C.,
with the following cast:

DUMPTSY, *George Meader*
ORCHESTRA LEADER, *Stephen Sandes*
DONALD NAVADEL, *Barry Thompson*
PITTALUGA, *S. Thomas Gomez*
AUGUSTE, *Edgar Barrier*
CAPTAIN LOCICERO, *Edward Raquello*
DR. WALDERSEE, *Sydney Greenstreet*
MR. CHERRY, *Bretaigne Windust*
MRS. CHERRY, *Jean Macintyre*
HARRY VAN, *Alfred Lunt*
SHIRLEY, *Jacqueline Paige*
BEULAH, *Connie Crowell*
BEBE, *Ruth Timmons*
FRANCINE, *Etna Ross*
ELAINE, *Marjorie Baglin*
EDNA, *Frances Foley*
MAJOR, *George Greenberg*
FIRST OFFICER, *Alan Hewitt*
SECOND OFFICER, *Winston Ross*
THIRD OFFICER, *Gilmore Bush*
FOURTH OFFICER, *Tomasso Tittoni*
QUILLERY, *Richard Whorf*
SIGNOR ROSSI, *Le Roi Operti*
SIGNORA ROSSI, *Ernestine de Becker*
MAID, *Una Val*
ACHILLE WEBER, *Francis Compton*
IRENE, *Lynn Fontanne*

The scene of the play is the cocktail lounge
of the Hotel Monte Gabriele, in the Italian Alps,
near the frontiers of Switzerland and Austria.

Act I
Afternoon of a winter day in any imminent year.
Act II
Scene 1. *Eight o'clock that evening.*
Scene 2. *Eleven o'clock that evening.*
Scene 3. *After midnight.*
Act III
The following afternoon.

Act one

The cocktail lounge of the Hotel Monte Gabriele.

The hotel is a small one, which would like to consider itself a first-class resort. It was originally an Austrian sanatorium. Its Italian management has refurnished it and added this cocktail lounge and a few modern bedrooms with baths, in the hope that some day Monte Gabriele may become a rival for St. Moritz. So far, this is still a hope. Although the weather is fine, the supply of winter sports enthusiasts at Monte Gabriele is negligible, and the hotel is relying for its trade upon those itinerants who, because of the current political situation, are desirous of leaving Italy.

Near at hand are a railway line into Switzerland, highways into Switzerland and Austria, and an Italian army airport.

At the left, up-stage, is a large doorway, leading to the lobby, in which we can just see the Reception Desk.

At the upper right is a staircase. A few steps up is a landing, above which is a high window with a fine view of the Alpine scenery to the North and West. The panes are fringed with frost. From the landing, the stairs continue up to a gallery which leads to bedrooms off to the upper left.

Downstairs left is a swinging door marked with the word "BAR."

Over this bar entrance are crossed skis and the head of a mountain goat. On the wall at the right is a Fascist emblem with crossed Italian flags. About the Reception Desk, off to the left, are signs assuring the guest that this hotel has been approved by all the automobile associations of Europe and that Travelers' Cheques may be cashed here. Somewhere on the walls are pictures of the Coliseum and the S.S. "Conte de Savoia."

There are small tables and chairs about, with perhaps a couch or two. At the left is a piano, and when the first curtain rises a dismal little four-piece orchestra is playing "June in January."

Note a line in the dialogue along toward the end of Act One: there is something about this place that suggests "a vague kind of horror." This is nothing definite, or identifiable, or even, immediately, apparent. Just an intimation.

Behind the Reception Desk, PITTALUGA *is occasionally visible. He is the proprietor of the hotel—a fussy, worried little Italian in the conventional morning coat and striped pants.*

On the landing at the upper right, looking dolefully out the window, is DONALD NAVADEL, *a rather precious, youngish American, suitably costumed for winter sports by Saks Fifth Avenue. Experienced in the resort business, he was imported this year to organize sporting and social life at Monte Gabriele with a view to making it a Mecca for American tourists. He is not pleased with the way things have turned out.*

DUMPTSY *comes in from the left. He is an humble, gentle little bell-boy, aged about forty, born in this district when it was part of Austria, but now a subject of the Fascist Empire. He has come in to clean the ashtrays. He listens to the music.*

DUMPTSY. Come si chiama questa musica che suonate?

ORCHESTRA LEADER. Il pezzo si chiama: "Giugno in Gennaio."

DUMPTSY. Oh, com'e bello! Mi piace! [*To* DON.] It's good.

DON. Will you please for God's sake stop playing that same damned tiresome thing?

DUMPTSY. You don't like it, Mr. Navadel?

DON. I'm so sick of it, I could scream!

DUMPTSY. I like it. To me, it's good.

DON. Go on, and clean the ash-trays.

DUMPTSY. But they're not dirty, sir. Because there's nobody using them.

DON. There's no need to remind me of *that!* Do as you're told!

DUMPTSY. If you please, sir. [*He whistles the tune and goes out.*]

DON [*to the* LEADER]. You've played enough. Get out!

LEADER. But it is not yet three o'clock.

DON. Never mind what time it is. There's nobody here to listen to you, is there? You can just save the wear and tear on your harpsichord and go grab yourselves a smoke.

LEADER. Very good, Mr. Navadel. [*To the other* MUSICIANS.] E inutile continuare a suonare. La gente non ascolta più. Si potrà invece far quattro chiachiere e fumare una sigaretta.

[*They put away instruments and music and start to go out, as* PITTALUGA *appears bristling.*]

PITTALUGA [*to* LEADER]. Eh, professori? Perchè avete cessato di suonare? Non sono ancora le tre.

LEADER. Il Signor Navadel ci ha detto di andare a fumare egli ne ha avuto abbastanza della nostra musica.

[*The* MUSICIANS *have gone.*]

PITTALUGA [*going to* DON]. You told my orchestra it would stop?

DON [*untroubled*]. I did.

PITTALUGA. My orders to them are they play in here until three o'clock. Why do you take it to yourself to countermand my orders?

DON. Because their performance was just a little too macabre to be bearable.

PITTALUGA. So! You have made yourself the manager of this hotel, have you? You give orders to the musicians. Next you will be giving orders to me—and to the guests themselves, I have no doubt. . . .

DON. The guests! [*He laughs drily.*] That's really very funny. Consult your room chart, my dear Signor Pittaluga, and let me know how many guests there are that I can give orders to. The number when last I counted . . .

PITTALUGA. And you stop being insolent, you—animale fetente. I pay you my money, when I am plunging myself into bankruptcy. . . .

DON. Yes, yes, Signor—we know all about that. You pay me your money. And you have a right to know that I'm fed to the teeth with this little pension that you euphemistically call a high-grade resort hotel. Indeed, I'm fed to the teeth with you personally.

PITTALUGA [*in a much friendlier tone*]. Ah! So you wish to leave us! I'm very sorry, my dear Donald. We shall miss you.

DON. My contract expires on March the first. I shall bear it until then.

PITTALUGA. You insult me by saying you are fed with me, but you go on taking my money?

DON. Yes!

PITTALUGA. Pezzo mascalzone farabutto prepotente canaglia . . .

DON. And it will do you no good to call me names in

your native tongue. I've had a conspicuously successful career in this business, all the way from Santa Barbara to St. Moritz. And you lured me away from a superb job . . .

PITTALUGA [*as* DON *continues*]. Lazzaroné, briccone, bestione. Perdio.

DON. . . . with your glowing descriptions of this handsome place, and the crowds of sportlovers, gay, mad, desperately chic, who were flocking here from London, Paris, New York. . . .

PITTALUGA. Did *I* know what was going to happen? Am *I* the king of Europe?

DON. You are the proprietor of this obscure tavern. You're presumably responsible for the fact that it's a deadly, boring dump!

PITTALUGA. Yes! And I engaged you because I thought you had friends—rich friends—and they would come here after you instead of St. Moritz, and Muerren, and Chamonix. And where are your friends? What am I paying for you? To countermand my orders and tell me you are fed . . . [*Wails from warning sirens are heard from off-stage right.* PITTALUGA *stops short. Both listen.*] Che cosa succede?

DON. That's from down on the flying field.

PITTALUGA. It is the warning for the air raids!

[AUGUSTE, *the barman, is heard in bar off-stage, left.*]

AUGUSTE'S VOICE. Che cosa?

[PITTALUGA *and* DON *rush to the window.*]

PITTALUGA. Segnali d'incursione. La guerra e incominiciata e il nemico viene.

[*Airplane motors are heard off right.*]

DON [*looking through window*]. Look! The planes are taking off. They're the little ones—the combat planes.

[CAPTAIN LOCICERO *enters from the lobby. He is the officer in charge of the frontier station. He is tired,*

quiet, nice. AUGUSTE *enters from the bar.* DUMPTSY
follows the CAPTAIN.]

AUGUSTE. Signor Capitano!

CAPTAIN. Buona sera!

[AUGUSTE *helps him take off his coat.*]

DUMPTSY. Che cosa succede, Signor Capitano? È la
guerra?

CAPTAIN. No—no—datemi cognac.

[DUMPTSY *puts coat on chair right of table and goes up
and exits through arch center.* CAPTAIN *sits chair
left of table.*]

AUGUSTE [*as he goes out*]. Si, Signor Capitano.

[*The* CAPTAIN *sits down at a table.* PITTALUGA *and* DON
cross to him. DUMPTSY *goes.*]

PITTALUGA. Che cosa significano quei terribili segnali?
È, forse, il nemico che arriva?

DON. What's happened, Captain? Is there an air raid?
Has the war started?

CAPTAIN [*smiling*]. Who knows? But there is no raid.
[*The porter's hand-bell in the lobby is heard.*]
They're only testing the sirens, to see how fast the
combat planes can go into action. You understand—
it's like lifeboat drill on a ship.

[DUMPTSY *enters.*]

DUMPTSY. Scusi, padrone. Due Inglesi arrivati. [*He hurries out.*]

PITTALUGA. Scusi. Vengo subito. Presto, presto! [*He
goes.*]

CAPTAIN. Have a drink, Mr. Navadel?

DON. Thank you very much—but some guests are actually arriving. I must go and be very affable. [*He
goes.*]

[DR. WALDERSEE *appears on the gallery above and
comes down the stairs as* AUGUSTE *enters from the
bar and serves the* CAPTAIN *with brandy and soda.*

The DOCTOR *is an elderly, stout, crotchety, sad German.*]

CAPTAIN. Good afternoon, Doctor. Have a drink?

DOCTOR. Thank you very much—no. What is all that aeroplanes?

[AUGUSTE *goes.*]

CAPTAIN. This is a crucial spot, Dr. Waldersee. We must be prepared for visits from the enemy.

DOCTOR. Enemy, eh? And who is that?

CAPTAIN. I don't quite know, yet. The map of Europe supplies us with a wide choice of opponents. I suppose, in due time, our government will announce its selection—and we shall know just whom we are to shoot at.

DOCTOR. Nonsense! Obscene nonsense!

CAPTAIN. Yes—yes. But the taste for obscenity is incurable, isn't it?

DOCTOR. When will you let me go into Switzerland?

CAPTAIN. Again I am powerless to answer you. My orders are that no one for the time being shall cross the frontiers, either into Switzerland or Austria.

DOCTOR. And when will this "time being" end?

CAPTAIN. When Rome makes its decision between friend and foe.

DOCTOR. I am a German subject. I am not your foe.

CAPTAIN. I am sure of that, Dr. Waldersee. The two great Fascist states stand together, against the world.

DOCTOR [*passionately*]. Fascism has nothing to do with it! I am a scientist. I am a servant of the whole damn stupid human race. [*He crosses toward the* CAPTAIN.] If you delay me any longer here, my experiments will be ruined. Can't you appreciate that? I must get my rats at once to the laboratory in Zurich, or all my months and years of research will have gone for nothing.

[DON *enters, followed by* MR. *and* MRS. CHERRY—*a pleas-*

ant young English couple in the first flush of their honeymoon.]

DON. This is our cocktail lounge. There is the American bar. We have a *thé dansant* here every afternoon at 4:30—supper dancing in the evening.

CHERRY. Charming.

DON. All this part of the hotel is new. Your rooms are up there. [*He crosses to the window.*] I think you'll concede that the view from here is unparalleled. We can look into four countries. [*The* CHERRYS *follow him to the window.*] Here in the foreground, of course, is Italy. This was formerly Austrian territory, transferred by the treaty of Versailles. It's called Monte Gabriele in honor of D'Annunzio, Italian poet and patriot. Off there is Switzerland and there is Austria. And far off, you can just see the tip of a mountain peak that is in the Bavarian Tyrol. Rather gorgeous, isn't it?

CHERRY. Yes.

MRS. CHERRY. Darling—*look* at that sky!

CHERRY. I say, it *is* rather good.

DON. Do you go in for winter sports, Mrs. Cherry?

MRS. CHERRY. Oh, yes—I—we're very keen on them.

DON. Splendid! We have everything here.

CHERRY. I've usually gone to Kitzbuhel.

[PITTALUGA *and* DUMPTSY *appear up-stage and speak in Italian through the dialogue.*]

PITTALUGA. Dumptsy, il bagaglio è stato portato su?

DUMPTSY. Si, signore, è già sopra.

PITTALUGA. Sta bene, vattene.

DON. It's lovely there, too.

CHERRY. But I hear it has become much too crowded there now. I—my wife and I hoped it would be quieter here.

DON. Well—at the moment—it is rather quiet here.

PITTALUGA [*coming down*]. Your luggage has been sent

up, Signor. Would you care to see your room now?

CHERRY. Yes. Thank you.

PITTALUGA. If you will have the goodness to step this way. [*He goes up the stairs.*] 'Scuse me.

CHERRY [*pauses at the window on the way up*]. What's that big bare patch down there?

DON [*casually*]. Oh, that's the airport. [PITTALUGA *coughs discreetly.*] We have a great deal of flying here.

PITTALUGA. Right this way, please.

CHERRY. Oh—I see.

[*They continue on up, preceded by* PITTALUGA.]

DON. And do come down for *thé dansant.*

MRS. CHERRY. We should love to.

PITTALUGA. Right straight ahead, please. [*They exit through gallery.*]

DON [*standing on first step*]. Honeymooners.

CAPTAIN. Yes—poor creatures.

DON. They wanted quiet.

DOCTOR [*rises*]. Ach Gott! When will you know when I can cross into Switzerland?

CAPTAIN. The instant that word comes through from Rome. [*The hand-bell is heard.*] You understand that I am only an obscure frontier official. And here in Italy, as in your own Germany, authority is centralized.

DOCTOR. But you can send a telegram to Rome, explaining the urgency of my position.

[DUMPTSY *appears, greatly excited.*]

DUMPTSY. More guests from the bus, Mr. Navadel. Seven of them! [*He goes.*]

DON. *Good God!* [*He goes out.*]

DOCTOR. Ach, es gibt kein Ruhe hier.

CAPTAIN. I assure you, Dr. Waldersee, I shall do all in my power.

DOCTOR. They must be made to understand that time is of vital importance.

CAPTAIN. Yes, I know.

DOCTOR. I have no equipment here to examine them properly—no assistant for the constant observation that is essential if my experiments are to succeed . . .

CAPTAIN [*a trifle wearily*]. I'm so sorry . . .

DOCTOR. Yes! You say you are so sorry. But what do you *do*? You have no comprehension of what is at stake. You are a soldier and indifferent to death. You say you are sorry, but it is nothing to you that hundreds of thousands, *millions*, are dying from a disease that it is within my power to cure!

CAPTAIN. Again, I assure you, Dr. Waldersee, that I . . .

DON'S VOICE. Our Mr. Pittaluga will be down in a moment. In the meantime, perhaps you and the—the others . . . [*He comes in, followed by* HARRY VAN, *a wan, thoughtful, lonely American vaudevillian promoter, press agent, book-agent, crooner, hoofer, barker or shill, who has undertaken all sorts of jobs in his time, all of them capitalizing his powers of salesmanship, and none of them entirely honest. He wears a snappy, belted, polo coat and a brown felt hat with brim turned down on all sides*] . . . would care to sit here in the cocktail lounge. We have a *thé dansant* here at 4:30 . . . supper dancing in the evening. . . .

HARRY. Do you run this hotel?

DON. I'm the Social Manager.

HARRY. What?

DON. The Social Manager.

HARRY. Oh! American, aren't you?

DON. I am. Santa Barbara's my home, and Donald Navadel is my name.

HARRY. Happy to know you. My name's Harry Van [*They shake hands.*]

DON. Glad to have you here, Mr. Van. Are you—staying with us long?

DOCTOR [*rising*]. I shall myself send a telegram to Rome, to the German Embassy.

CAPTAIN. They might well be able to expedite matters. [*The* DOCTOR *goes.*]

HARRY. I've got to get over that border. When I came in on the train from Fiume, they told me the border is closed, and the train is stuck here for tonight and maybe longer. I asked them why, but they either didn't know or they refused to divulge their secrets to me. What seems to be the trouble?

DON. Perhaps Captain Locicero can help you. He's the commander of Italian Headquarters here. This is Mr. Van, Captain.

CAPTAIN [*rising*]. Mr. Van, my compliments.

HARRY. And mine to you, Captain. We're trying to get to Geneva.

CAPTAIN. You have an American passport?

HARRY. I have. Several of them. [*He reaches in his pocket and takes out seven passports, bound together with elastic. He fans them like a deck of cards and hands them to the* CAPTAIN.]

CAPTAIN. You have your family with you?

HARRY. Well—it isn't exactly a family. [*He goes to the right.*] Come in here, girls!

SHIRLEY [*from off-stage*]. Come on in, kids. Harry wants us.

[*Six blonde chorus girls come in. They are named:* SHIRLEY, BEULAH, BEBE, FRANCINE, EDNA *and* ELAINE. *Of these,* SHIRLEY *is the principal, a frank, knowing fan dancer.* BEULAH *is a bubble dancer, and therefore ethereal.* BEBE *is a hard, harsh little number who shimmies.* DON *doesn't know quite how to take this surprising troupe, but the* CAPTAIN *is impressed, favorably.*]

HARRY. Allow me to introduce the girls, Captain. We call them "Les Blondes." We've been playing the Balkan circuit—Budapest, Bucharest, Sofia, Belgrade, and Zagreb. [*He turns to* DON.] Back home, that would be the equivalent of "Pan Time." [*He laughs nervously, to indicate that the foregoing was a gag.*]

CAPTAIN [*bowing*]. How do you do?

HARRY. The Captain is head man, girls.

GIRLS. How do you do? . . . Pleased to meet you. . . . Etc.

HARRY. The situation in brief is this, Captain. We've got very attractive bookings at a night spot in Geneva. Undoubtedly they feel that the League of Nations needs us. [*Another laugh.*] It's important that we get there at once. So, Captain, I'll be grateful for prompt action.

CAPTAIN [*looking at the first passport*]. Miss Shirley Laughlin.

HARRY. Laughlin. This is Shirley. Step up, honey. [*Shirley steps forward.*]

CAPTAIN [*pleased with* SHIRLEY]. How do you do?

SHIRLEY. Pleased to meet you.

CAPTAIN. This photograph hardly does you justice.

SHIRLEY. I know. It's terrible, isn't it!

HARRY [*interrupting*]. Who's next, Captain?

CAPTAIN. Miss Beulah Tremoyne.

HARRY. Come on, Beulah. [*She comes forward in a wide sweep, as* SHIRLEY *goes up and joins the group.*] Beulah is our bubble dancer, a product of the aesthetic school, and therefore more of a dreamer.

CAPTAIN. Exquisite!

BEULAH. Thank you *ever* so much. [*She starts to sit down by the* CAPTAIN. *She is turning it on.*]

HARRY. That'll be all, Beulah.

CAPTAIN. Miss Elaine Messiger—

HARRY. Come on, babe.

CAPTAIN. Miss Francine Merle—

HARRY. No tricks, Francine. This is just identification.

CAPTAIN. Miss Edna Creesh—

HARRY. Turn it off, honey.

CAPTAIN. And Miss Bebe Gould.

HARRY. You'll find Bebe a very, very lovely girl.

BEBE [*remonstrating*]. Harry!

HARRY. A shimmy artiste, and incorrigibly unsophisticated.

CAPTAIN [*summing up*]. Very beautiful. Very, very beautiful. Mr. Van, I congratulate you.

HARRY. That's nice of you, Captain. Now, can we . . .

CAPTAIN. And I wish I, too, were going to Geneva. [*He hands back the passports to* HARRY.]

HARRY. Then it's O.K. for us to pass?

CAPTAIN. But won't you young ladies sit down?

SHIRLEY. Thanks, Captain.

BEULAH. We'd love to.

FRANCINE. He's cute.

EDNA. I'll say. [*They all sit.*]

HARRY. I don't want to seem oblivious of your courtesy, Captain, but the fact is we can't afford to hang around here any longer. That train may pull out and leave us.

CAPTAIN. I give you my word, that train will not move tonight, and maybe not tomorrow night, and maybe never. [*He bows deeply.*] It is a matter of the deepest personal regret to me, Mr. Van, but—

HARRY. Listen, pal. Could you stop being polite for just a moment, and tell us how do we get to Geneva?

CAPTAIN. That is not for me to say. I am as powerless as you are, Mr. Van. I, too, am a pawn. [*He picks up his coat and hat.*] But, speaking for myself, I shall not be sorry if you and your beautiful companions are forced to remain here indefinitely. [*He salutes the girls, smiles and goes out.*]

HARRY. Did you hear that? He says he's a pawn.

BEBE. He's a Wop.

BEULAH. But he's cute!

SHIRLEY. Personally, I'd just as soon stay here. I'm sick of the slats on those stinking day coaches.

HARRY. After the way we've been betrayed in the Balkans, we can't afford to stay any.place. [*He turns to* DON.] What's the matter, anyway? Why can't decent respectable people be allowed to go about their legitimate business?

DON. Evidently you're not fully aware of the international situation.

HARRY. I'm fully aware that the international situation is always regrettable. But what's wrong now?

DON. Haven't you been reading the papers?

HARRY. In Bulgaria and Jugo-Slavia? [*He looks around at the girls, who laugh.*] No.

DON. It may be difficult for you to understand, Mr. Van, but we happen to be on the brink of a frightful calamity.

HARRY. What?

DON. We're on the verge of war.

SHIRLEY. War?

BEBE. What about?

HARRY. You mean—that business in Africa?

DON. Far more serious than that! *World* war! All of them!

HARRY. No lie! You mean—it'll be started by people like that? [*Points after the* CAPTAIN.] Italians?

DON. Yes. They've reached the breaking point.

HARRY. I don't believe it. I don't believe that people like that would take on the job of licking the world. They're too romantic. [PITTALUGA *steps forward.*]

PITTALUGA. You wish rooms, Signor?

HARRY. What have you got?

PITTALUGA. We can give you grande luxe accommo-
dations, rooms with baths. . . .

HARRY. What's your scale of prices?

PITTALUGA. From fifty lira up.

DON. That's about five dollars a day.

HARRY [*wincing*]. What?

DON. Meals included.

HARRY. I take it there's the usual professional discount.

PITTALUGA [*to* DON]. Che cosa significa?

DON. Mr. Van and the young ladies are artists.

PITTALUGA. Ebbene?

DON [*scornfully*]. In America we give special rates to
artists.

PITTALUGA [*grimly*]. Non posso, non posso.

[*The* CHERRYS *appear on the balcony above.*]

DON. I'm sure Mr. Pittaluga will take care of you
nicely, Mr. Van. He will show you attractive rooms
on the *other* side of the hotel. They're delightful.

HARRY. No doubt. But I want to see the accommoda-
tions.

PITTALUGA. Step this way, please.

HARRY. Come on, girls. Now—I want two girls to a
room, and a single room for me adjoining. I promised their mothers I'd always be within earshot. Put
on your shoes, Beulah. [*He goes out right, followed
by the* GIRLS *and* DON.]

BEULAH [*as they go*]. Why's he kicking? I think this
place is *attractive!*

SHIRLEY. Oh—you know Harry. He's always got to have
something to worry about. [*They have gone.*]

MRS. CHERRY [*coming down*]. What an extraordinary
gathering!

CHERRY. There's something I've never been able to understand—the tendency of Americans to travel en

masse. [*They pause to admire the view and each other. He takes her in his arms and kisses her.*] Darling!

MRS. CHERRY. What?

CHERRY. Nothing. I just said, "Darling"! [*He kisses her again.*] My sweet. I love you.

MRS. CHERRY. That's right. [*She kisses him.*]

CHERRY. I think we're going to like it here, aren't we, darling?

MRS. CHERRY. Yes. You'll find a lot to paint.

CHERRY. No doubt. But I'm not going to waste any time painting.

MRS. CHERRY. Why not, Jimmy? You've got to work and—

CHERRY. Don't ask "why not" in that laboriously girlish tone! You know damned well why not!

MRS. CHERRY [*laughing*]. Now really darling. We don't have to be maudlin. We're old enough to be sensible about it, aren't we!

CHERRY. God forbid that we should spoil everything by being sensible! This is an occasion for pure and beautiful foolishness. So don't irritate me by any further mention of work.

MRS. CHERRY. Very well, darling. If you're going to be stinking about it . . . [*He kisses her again.*]

[*The* DOCTOR *comes in from the right and regards their love-making with scant enthusiasm. They look up and see him. They aren't embarrassed.*]

CHERRY. How do you do?

DOCTOR. Don't let me interrupt you. [*He rings a bell and sits down.*]

CHERRY. It's quite all right. We were just starting out for a walk.

MRS. CHERRY. The air is so marvelous up here, isn't it?

DOCTOR [*doubtfully*]. Yes.

[DUMPTSY *comes in from the right.*]

CHERRY. Yes—we think so. Come on, darling. [*They go out at the back.*]

DOCTOR. Mineral water.

DUMPTSY. Yes, sir.

[QUILLERY *comes in and sits at the left. He is small, dark, brooding and French—an extreme-radical-socialist, but still, French.*]

DOCTOR. Not iced—warm.

DUMPTSY. If you please, sir. [*He goes out, left.*]

[*A group of five Italian flying corps officers come in, talking gaily in Italian. They cross to the bar entrance and go out.*]

FIRST OFFICER. Sono Americane.

SECOND OFFICER. Sono belle, proprio da far strabiliare.

THIRD OFFICER. Forse sarranno stelle cinematografiche di Hollyvood.

SECOND OFFICER. E forse ora non ci rincrescerà che abbiano cancellato la nostra licenza. [*They go into the bar.*]

HARRY [*coming in*]. Good afternoon.

DOCTOR. Good afternoon.

HARRY. Have a drink?

DOCTOR. I am about to have one.

HARRY. Mind if I join you? [*He sits down near the* DOCTOR.]

DOCTOR. This is a public room.

HARRY [*whistles a snatch of a tune*]. It's a funny kind of situation, isn't it?

DOCTOR. To what situation do you refer?

HARRY. All this stopping of trains . . . [DUMPTSY *enters from the bar and serves the* DOCTOR *with a glass of mineral water.*] and orders from Rome and we are on the threshold of calamity.

DOCTOR. To me it is not funny. [*He rises with his mineral water.*]

HARRY. Get me a Scotch.

DUMPTSY. With soda, sir?

HARRY. Yes.

DUMPTSY. If you please, sir.

QUILLERY. I will have a beer.

DUMPTSY. We have native or imported, sir.

QUILLERY. Native will do.

DUMPTSY. If you please, sir. [*He goes out.*]

DOCTOR. I repeat—to me it is *not* funny! [*He bows.*] You will excuse me.

HARRY. Certainly. . . . See you later, pal. [*The* DOCTOR *goes.* HARRY *turns to* QUILLERY.] Friendly old bastard!

QUILLERY. Quite! But you were right. The situation *is* funny. There is always something essentially laughable in the thought of a lunatic asylum. Although, it may perhaps seem less funny when you are inside.

HARRY. I guess so. I guess it isn't easy for Germans to see the comical side of things these days. Do you mind if I join you? [*He rises and crosses to the left.*]

QUILLERY. I beg of you to do so, my comrade.

HARRY. I don't like to thrust myself forward—[*He sits down.*]—but, you see, I travel with a group of blondes, and it's always a relief to find somebody to talk to. Have you seen the girls?

QUILLERY. Oh, yes.

HARRY. Alluring, aren't they?

QUILLERY. Very alluring.

[DUMPTSY *comes in with the drinks and goes.* HARRY *takes out his chewing gum, wraps it in paper, places it in a silver snuff box, which he shows to* QUILLERY.]

HARRY. That's a genuine antique snuff box of the period of Louis Quinze.

QUILLERY. Very interesting.

HARRY. It's a museum piece. [*Puts the box in his pocket.*] You've got to hoard your gum here in Europe.

QUILLERY. You've traveled far?

HARRY. Yeah—I've been a long way with that gorgeous array of beautiful girls. I took 'em from New York to Monte Carlo. To say we were a sensation in Monte Carlo would be to state a simple incontrovertible fact. But then I made the mistake of accepting an offer from the manager of the Club Arizona in Budapest. I found that conditions in the South-East are not so good.

QUILLERY. I traveled on the train with you from Zagreb.

HARRY. Zagreb! A plague spot! What were you doing there?

QUILLERY. I was attending the Labor Congress.

HARRY. Yeah—I heard about that. The night club people thought that the congress would bring in a lot of business. They were wrong. But—excuse me— [*Rises.*] My name is Harry Van.

QUILLERY [*rises*]. Quillery is my name.

HARRY. Glad to know you, Mr.—?

QUILLERY. Quillery.

HARRY. Quillery. [*Sits.*] I'm an American. What's your nationality?

QUILLERY. I have no nationality. [*Sits.*] I drink to your good health.

HARRY. And to your lack of nationality, of which I approve. [*They drink.*]

[SIGNOR *and* SIGNORA ROSSI *come in and cross to the bar.* ROSSI *is a consumptive.*]

ROSSI. Abbiamo trascorso una bella giornata, Nina. Beviamo un po'?

SIGNORA ROSSI. Dopo tutto quell' esercizio ti farebbe male. Meglio che tu ti riposi per un'oretta.

ROSSI. Ma, no, mi sento proprio bene. Andiamo. Mi riposerò più tardi. [*They go into the bar.*]

HARRY. I get an awful kick hearing Italian. It's beautiful. Do you speak it?

QUILLERY. Only a little. I was born in France. And I love my home. Perhaps if I had raised pigs—like my father, and all his fathers, back to the time when Caesar's Roman legions came—perhaps, if I had done that, I should have been a Frenchman, as they were. But I went to work in a factory—and machinery is international.

HARRY. And I suppose pigs are exclusively French?

QUILLERY. My father's pigs are! [HARRY *laughs*.] The factory where I have worked made artificial limbs— an industry that has been prosperous the last twenty years. But sometimes—in the evening—after my work —I would go out into the fields and help my father. And then, for a little while, I would become again a Frenchman.

HARRY [*takes out his cigarette case*]. That's a nice thought, pal. [*Offers* QUILLERY *a cigarette*.] Have a smoke?

QUILLERY. No, thank you.

HARRY. I don't blame you. These Jugo-Slav cigarettes are not made of the same high-grade quality of manure to which I grew accustomed in Bulgaria.

QUILLERY. You know, my comrade—you seem to have a long view of things.

HARRY. So long that it gets very tiresome.

QUILLERY. The long view is not easy to sustain in this short-sighted world.

HARRY. You're right about that, pal.

QUILLERY. Let me give you an instance: There we were—gathered in Zagreb, representatives of the workers of all Europe. All brothers, collaborating harmoniously for the United Front! And now—we are rushing to our homes to prevent our people from plunging into mass murder—mass suicide!

HARRY. You're going to try to stop the war?

QUILLERY. Yes.

HARRY. Do you think you'll succeed?

QUILLERY. Unquestionably! This is not 1914, remember! Since then, some new voices have been heard in this world—loud voices. I need mention only one of them—Lenin—Nikolai Lenin!

[*A ferocious looking* MAJOR *of the Italian flying corps comes in and goes quickly to the bar. As he opens the door, he calls "Attention!" He goes into the bar, the door swinging to behind him.*]

HARRY. Yes—but what are you going to do about people like *that?*

QUILLERY. Expose them! That's all we have to do. Expose them—for what they are—atavistic children! Occupying their undeveloped minds playing with outmoded toys.

HARRY. Have you *seen* any of those toys?

QUILLERY. Yes! France is full of them. But there is a force more potent than all the bombing planes and submarines and tanks. And that is the mature intelligence of the workers of the world! There is one antidote for war—Revolution! And the cause of Revolution gains steadily in strength. Even here in Italy, despite all the repressive power of Fascism, sanity has survived, and it becomes more and more articulate. . . .

HARRY. Well, pal—you've got a fine point there. And I hope you stick to it.

QUILLERY. I'm afraid you think it is all futile idealism!

HARRY. No—I don't. And what if I did? I am an idealist myself.

QUILLERY. You too believe in the revolution?

HARRY. Not necessarily in *the* revolution. I'm just in favor of any revolution. Anything that will make people wake up, and get themselves some convictions. Have you ever taken cocaine?

QUILLERY. Why—I imagine that I have—at the dentist's.

HARRY. No—I mean, for pleasure. You know—a vice.

QUILLERY. No! I've never indulged in that folly.

HARRY. I have—during a stage of my career when luck was bad and confusion prevailed.

QUILLERY. Ah, yes. You needed delusions of grandeur.

HARRY. That's just what they were.

QUILLERY. It must have been an interesting experience.

HARRY. It was illuminating. It taught me what is the precise trouble with the world today. We have become a race of drug addicts—hopped up with false beliefs—false fears—false enthusiasms. . . .

[*The four* OFFICERS *emerge from the bar, talking excitedly.*]

SECOND OFFICER. Ma, è state fatta la dichiarazone di guerra attuale?

FIRST OFFICER. Caricheremo delle bombe esplosive?

THIRD OFFICER. Se la guerra è in cominciata, allora vuol dire che noi. . . .

FOURTH OFFICER. La guerra è in cominciata.

MAJOR. Silenzio! Solo il vostro commandante conosce gli ordini. Andiamo! [*All five go out hurriedly.*]

QUILLERY [*jumps up*]. Mother of God! Did you hear what they were saying?

HARRY [*rises*]. I heard, but I couldn't understand.

QUILLERY. It was about war. I know only a little Italian—but I thought they were saying that war has already been declared. [*He grabs his hat.*] I *must* go and demand that they let me cross the border! At once! [*He starts to go.*]

HARRY. That's right, pal. There's no time to lose.

QUILLERY. Wait— I haven't paid. . . . [*He is fumbling for money.*]

HARRY. No, no. This was my drink. You've got to hurry!

QUILLERY. Thank you, my comrade. [*He goes out quickly.*]

[*Airplane motors are heard, off at the right.* HARRY *crosses to the window.* DUMPTSY *comes in to remove the empty glasses.*]

DUMPTSY. Fine view, isn't it, sir?

HARRY. I've seen worse.

DUMPTSY. Nothing quite like it, sir. From here, we look into four nations. Where you see that little village, at the far end of the valley—that is Austria. Isn't that beautiful over there?

HARRY. Are you Italian?

DUMPTSY. Well, yes, sir. That is to say, I didn't used to be.

HARRY. What did you used to be?

DUMPTSY. Austrian. All this part was Austria, until after the big war, when they decided these mountains must go to Italy, and I went with them. In one day, I became a foreigner. So now, my children learn only Italian in school, and when I and my wife talk our own language they can't understand us. [*He gets* HARRY's *drink and brings it over to him.*] They changed the name of this mountain. Monte Gabriele—that's what it is now. They named it after an Italian who dropped poems on Vienna. Even my old father—he's dead—but all the writing on the gravestones was in German, so they rubbed it out and translated it. So now he's Italian, too. But they didn't get my sister. She married a Swiss. She lives over there, in Schleins.

HARRY. She's lucky.

DUMPTSY. Yes—those Swiss are smart.

HARRY. Yeah, they had sense enough to get over there in the first place.

DUMPTSY [*laughs*]. But it doesn't make much difference who your masters are. When you get used to them, they're all the same.

[*The porter's bell rings.* PITTALUGA *appears.*]

PITTALUGA. Dumptsy! Dumptsy! Una gentildonna arriva. Prendi i suoi bagagli. Affretati!

DUMPTSY. Si, Signore. Vengo subito. [*He goes.*]

PITTALUGA [*claps his hands*]. Sciocco! Anna, Per Dio! Dove sei stata, va sopra a preparare la stanza. [ANNA, *the maid, enters with towels.*] Presto, presto!

[ANNA *runs up the steps, exits.* PITTALUGA *goes back into the lobby.*]

IRENE'S VOICE. Vieni, Achille.

DON [*coming in*]. This is our cocktail lounge, madame.

[IRENE *enters. She is somewhere between thirty and forty, beautiful, heavily and smartly furred in the Russian manner. Her hair is blonde and quite straight. She is a model of worldly wisdom, chic, and carefully applied graciousness. Her name is pronounced* "EAR-RAY-NA." . . . *She surveys the room with polite appreciation, glancing briefly at* HARRY.]

DON. Your suite is up there, madame. All this part of the hotel is quite new.

IRENE. How very nice!

DON. We have our best view from this side of the hotel. [*He goes to the window.* IRENE *follows slowly.*] You can see four countries—Italy, Switzerland, Austria and Bavaria.

IRENE. Magnificent!

DON. Yes—we're very proud of it.

IRENE. All those countries. And they all look so very much alike, don't they!

DON. Yes—they do really—from this distance.

IRENE. All covered with the beautiful snow. I think the whole world should be always covered with snow. It would be so much more clean, wouldn't it?

DON. By all means!

IRENE. Like in my Russia. White Russia. [*Sighs, and goes up to the next landing.*] Oh, and—how exciting! A flying field. Look! They're bringing out the big bombers.

DON. Madame is interested in aviation?

IRENE. No, no. Just ordinary flying bores me. But there is no experience in life quite so thrilling as a parachute jump, is there!

DON. I've never had that thrill, I'm ashamed to say.

IRENE. Once I had to jump when I was flying over the jungle in Indo-China. It was indescribable. Drifting down, sinking into that great green sea of enchantment and hidden danger.

[DUMPTSY *comes in.*]

DON. And you weren't afraid?

IRENE. No—no—I was not afraid. In moments like that, one is given the sense of eternity.

HARRY [*viciously*]. Dumptsy! Get me another Scotch.

DUMPTSY. Yes, sir.

HARRY. And put ice in it, this time. If you haven't got any ice, go out and scoop up some snow.

DUMPTSY. If you please, sir. [*He goes into the bar.*]

IRENE [*her gaze wandering about the room*]. But your place is really charming.

DON. You're very kind.

IRENE. I must tell everyone in Paris about it. There's something about this design—it suggests a—an amusing kind of horror.

DON [*not knowing quite how to interpret that*]. Madame is a student of decoration?

IRENE. No, no. Only an amateur, my friend. An amateur, I'm afraid, in everything.

[*The siren sounds from off at the right.* IRENE, *near the top of the staircase, stops to listen.*]

IRENE. What is that?

DON. Oh—it's merely some kind of warning. They've been testing it.

IRENE. Warning? Warning against what?

DON. I believe it's for use in case of war.

IRENE. War? But there will be no war.

[PITTALUGA *enters from the lobby, escorting* ACHILLE WEBER—*which is pronounced* "VAY-BAIR." *He is a thin, keen executive, wearing a neat little mustache and excellent clothes. In his lapel is the rosette of the Legion of Honor. He carries a brief case.*]

PITTALUGA [*as they come in*]. Par ici, Monsieur Weber. Vous trouverez Madame ici . . .

IRENE [*leaning over the railing*]. Achille!

WEBER [*pausing and looking up*]. Yes, my dear?

IRENE. Achille—there will be no war, will there?

WEBER [*amused*]. No, no—Irene. There will be no war. They're all much too well prepared for it. [*He turns to* PITTALUGA.] Where are our rooms?

PITTALUGA. Votre suite est par ici, Monsieur. La plus belle de la maison! La vue est superbe!

IRENE [*to* DON]. There, you see! They will not fight. They are all much too much afraid of each other.

[WEBER *is going up the staircase, ignoring the view.* PITTALUGA *is following.*]

IRENE [*to* WEBER]. Achille—I am mad about this place! Je rafolle de cette place!

WEBER [*calmly*]. Yes, my dear.

IRENE. We must be sure to tell the Maharajah of Rajpipla, Achille. Can't you imagine how dear little "Pip" would love this? [*They go out on the landing above.*]

HARRY. Who was that?

DON [*impressed*]. That was Achille Weber. One of the biggest men in France. I used to see him a lot at St. Moritz.

[*There is a sound of airplane motors off at the right.*]

HARRY. And the dame? Do you assume that is his wife?

DON [*curtly*]. Are you implying that she's not?

HARRY. No, no—I'm not implying a thing. [*He wanders to the piano.*] I'm just kind of—kind of baffled.

DON. Evidently. [*He goes out.*]

[HARRY *at the piano strikes a chord of the Russian song, "Kak Stranna."* DUMPTSY *enters from the bar and serves* HARRY *with Scotch. The off-stage noise increases as more planes take the air.*]

DUMPTSY [*at the window*]. Do you see them—those aeroplanes—flying up from the field down there?

HARRY [*glances toward window, without interest*]. Yes —I see them.

DUMPTSY. Those are the big ones. They're full of bombs, to drop on people. Look! They're going north. Maybe Berlin. Maybe Paris.

[*Harry strikes a few chords.*]

HARRY. Did you ever jump with a parachute?

DUMPTSY. Why, no—sir. [*He looks questioningly at* HARRY.]

HARRY. Well, I have—a couple of times. And it's nothing. But—I didn't land in any jungle. I landed where I was supposed to—in the Fair Grounds.

DUMPTSY [*seriously*]. That's interesting, sir.

[*The* ROSSIS *enter from the bar. He is holding a handkerchief to his mouth. She is supporting him as they cross.*]

SIGNORA ROSSI. Non t'ho detto che dovevi fare attenzione? Te l'ho detto, te l'ho detto che sarebbe accaduto ciò. Vedi, ora ti piglia un accesso di tosse.

ROSSI. 'Scusatemi, Mina. [*Another coughing fit.*]

SIGNORA ROSSI. Va a sdraiarti. Dovresti riposarti a lungo. E adopera il termometro. Scommetto che t'è aumentata la temperatura. [*They go out.*]

DUMPTSY. That Signor Rossi—he has tuberculosis.

HARRY. Is he getting cured up here?

[*The* DOCTOR *appears on the landing above.*]

DUMPTSY. Ja. This used to be a sanatorium, in the old days. But the Fascisti—they don't like to admit that anyone can be sick! [*He starts to go.*]

DOCTOR. Dumptsy!

DUMPTSY. Herr Doctor.

DOCTOR [*coming down*]. Mineral water.

DUMPTSY. Ja wohl, Herr Doctor. [DUMPTSY *goes out, left.*]

[*The* DOCTOR *sits down.* HARRY *takes one more look toward the gallery, where* IRENE *had been. He then looks at the* DOCTOR, *and decides not to suggest joining him. He starts to play "Kak Stranna." The* DOCTOR *turns and looks at him, with some surprise. The uproar of planes is now terrific, but it starts to dwindle as the planes depart.*]

DOCTOR. What is that you are playing?

HARRY. A Russian song, entitled "Kak Stranna," meaning "how strange!" One of those morose ballads about how once we met, for one immortal moment, like ships that pass in the night. Or maybe like a couple of trucks, side-swiping each other. And now we meet again! How strange!

DOCTOR. You are a musician?

HARRY. Certainly. I used to play the piano in picture theatres—when that was the only kind of sound they had—except the peanuts.

[DUMPTSY *brings the mineral water and stops to listen, admiringly.*]

DOCTOR. Do you know Bach?

HARRY. With pleasure. [*He shifts into something or other by Bach.*]

DOCTOR [*after a moment*]. You have good appreciation, but not much skill.

HARRY. What do you mean, not much skill? Listen to

this. [*He goes into a trick arrangement of* "The Waters of the Minnetonka."] "The Waters of the Minnetonka"—Cadman. [*He goes on playing.*] Suitable for Scenics—Niagara Falls by moonlight. Or—if you play it this way—it goes fine with the scene where the young Indian chief turns out to be a Yale man, so it's O.K. for him to marry Lillian "Dimples" Walker. [*Starts playing* "Boola Boola."]

DOCTOR. Will you have a drink?

HARRY. Oh! So you want me to stop playing?

DOCTOR. No, no! I like your music very much.

HARRY. Then, in that case, I'd be delighted to drink with you. Another Scotch, Dumptsy.

DUMPTSY. If you please, sir. [*He goes out.*]

DOCTOR. I'm afraid I was rude to you.

HARRY. That's all right, pal. I've been rude to lots of people, and never regretted it. [*He plays on, shifting back into* "Kak Stranna."]

DOCTOR. The fact is, I am a man who is very gravely distressed.

HARRY. I can see that, Doctor. And I sympathize with you.

DOCTOR [*fiercely*]. You cannot sympathize with me, because you do not know!

HARRY. No—I guess I don't know—except in a general way.

DOCTOR. You are familiar with the writings of Thomas Mann. [*It is a challenge, rather than a question.*]

HARRY. I'm afraid not, pal.

[*The* DOCTOR *opens* "The Magic Mountain," *which he has been reading.*]

DOCTOR. "Backsliding"—he said—"spiritual backsliding to that dark and tortured age—that, believe me, is disease! A degradation of mankind—a degradation painful and offensive to conceive." True words, eh?

HARRY. Absolutely!

[DUMPTSY *comes in with the Scotch.* HARRY *gets up from the piano and crosses.* DUMPTSY *goes.* HARRY *sits down with the* DOCTOR.]

DOCTOR. Have you had any experience with cancer?

HARRY. Certainly. I once sold a remedy for it.

DOCTOR [*exploding*]. There *is* no remedy for it, so far!

HARRY. Well—this was kind of a remedy for everything.

DOCTOR. I am within *that* of finding the cure for cancer! You probably have not heard of Fibiger, I suppose?

HARRY. I may have. I'm not sure.

DOCTOR. He was a Dane—experimented with rats. He did good work, but he died before it could be completed. I carry it on. I have been working with Oriental rats, in Bologna. But because of this war scare, I must go to neutral territory. You see, nothing must be allowed to interfere with my experiments. Nothing!

HARRY. No. They're important.

DOCTOR. The laboratory of the University of Zurich has been placed at my disposal—and in Switzerland, I can work, undisturbed. I have twenty-eight rats with me, all in various carefully tabulated stages of the disease. It is the disease of civilization—and I can cure it. And now they say I must not cross the border.

HARRY. You know, Doctor, it *is* funny.

DOCTOR. What's funny? To you, everything is funny!

HARRY. No—it's just that you and I are in the same fix. Both trying to get across that line. You with rats—me with girls. Of course—I appreciate the fact that civilization at large won't suffer much if *we* get stuck in the war zone. Whereas with you, there's a lot at stake. . . .

DOCTOR. It is for me to win one of the greatest victories of all time. And the victory belongs to Germany.

HARRY. Sure it does!

DOCTOR. Unfortunately, just now the situation in Germany is not good for research. They are infected with the same virus as here. Chauvinistic nationalism! They expect all bacteriologists to work on germs to put in bombs to drop from airplanes. To fill people with death! When we've given our lives to *save* people. Oh—God in heaven—why don't they let me do what is good? Good for the whole world? Forgive me. I become excited.

HARRY. I know just how you feel, Doctor. Back in 1918, I was a shill with a carnival show, and I was doing fine. The boss thought very highly of me. He offered to give me a piece of the show, and I had a chance to get somewhere. And then what do you think happened? Along comes the United States Government and they drafted me! You're in the army now! They slapped me into a uniform and for three whole months before the Armistice, I was parading up and down guarding the Ashokan Reservoir. They were afraid your people might poison it. I've always figured that that little interruption ruined my career. But I've remained an optimist, Doctor.

DOCTOR. *You* can afford to.

HARRY. I've remained an optimist because I'm essentially a student of human nature. You dissect corpses and rats and similar unpleasant things. Well—it has been my job to dissect suckers! I've probed into the souls of some of the God-damnedest specimens. And what have I found? Now, don't sneer at me, Doctor—but above everything else I've found faith. Faith in peace on earth and good will to men—and faith that "Muma," "Muma" the three-legged girl, really has got three legs. All my life, Doctor, I've been selling phony goods to people of meager intelligence and great faith. You'd think that would make me contemptuous of the human race, wouldn't you? But—on the contrary—it has given *me* faith. It has made me sure that no matter how much the meek may be bulldozed or gypped they *will* eventually inherit the earth.

[SHIRLEY *and* BEBE *come in from the lobby.*]

SHIRLEY. Harry!

HARRY. What is it, honey?

[SHIRLEY *goes to* HARRY *and hands him a printed notice.*]

SHIRLEY [*excited*]. Did you see this?

HARRY. Doctor—let me introduce, Miss Shirley Laughlin and Miss Bebe Gould.

SHIRLEY. How do you do?

DOCTOR [*grunts*]. How do you do.

BEBE. Pleased to know you, Doctor.

[HARRY *looks at the notice.*]

SHIRLEY. They got one of those put up in every one of our rooms.

HARRY [*showing it to the* DOCTOR]. Look— "What to do in case of air raids"—in all languages.

DOCTOR. Ja—I saw that.

SHIRLEY. Give it back to me, Harry. I'm going to send it to Mama.

HARRY [*handing it to her*]. Souvenir of Europe.

SHIRLEY. It'll scare the hell out of her.

BEBE. What's the matter with these people over here? Are they all screwy?

HARRY. Bebe—you hit it right on the nose! [*Turns to the* DOCTOR.] I tell you, Doctor—these are very wonderful, profound girls. The mothers of tomorrow! [*He beams on them.* BEULAH *comes in.*]

SHIRLEY. Oh—shut up!

BEULAH. Say—Harry . . .

HARRY. What is it, honey?

BEULAH. Is it all right if I go out with Mr. Navadel and try to learn how to do this ski-ing?

[WEBER *comes out on the gallery and starts down.*]

HARRY. What? And risk those pretty legs? Emphatically—no!

BEULAH. But it's healthy.

HARRY. Not for me, dear. Those gams of yours are my bread and butter. [WEBER *crosses. They look at him. He glances briefly at them.*] Sit down, girls, and amuse yourselves with your own thoughts.

[*The* GIRLS *sit.* WEBER, *at the left, lights his cigar. The* CAPTAIN *comes in, quickly, obviously worried.*]

CAPTAIN. I have been trying to get through to headquarters, Monsieur Weber.

WEBER. And when can we leave?

CAPTAIN. Not before tomorrow, I regret to say.

[IRENE *appears on the gallery.*]

WEBER. Signor Lanza in Venice assured me there would be no delay.

CAPTAIN. There would be none, if only I could get into communication with the proper authorities. But—the wires are crowded. The whole nation is in a state of uproar.

WEBER. It's absurd lack of organization.

[*The* PIANIST *and* DRUMMER *come in from the lobby. The* VIOLINIST *and* SAXOPHONIST *follow.*]

CAPTAIN [*with tense solemnity*]. There is good excuse for the excitement now, Monsieur Weber. The report has just come to us that a state of war exists between Italy and France.

HARRY. What?

CAPTAIN. There is a rumor of war between Italy and France!

HARRY. Rumors—rumors—everything's rumors! When are we going to *know?*

CAPTAIN. Soon enough, my friend.

DOCTOR. And what of Germany?

CAPTAIN. Germany has mobilized. [IRENE *pauses to listen.*] But I don't know if any decision has been reached. Nor do I know anything of the situation anywhere else. But—God help us—it will be serious enough for everyone on this earth.

[IRENE *joins* WEBER, *who has sat down at the left.*]

IRENE [*to* WEBER, *and straight at him*]. But I thought they were all too well prepared, Achille. Has there been some mistake somewhere?

WEBER [*confidentially*]. We can only attribute it to spontaneous combustion of the dictatorial ego.

IRENE [*grimly*]. I can imagine how thrilling it must be in Paris at this moment. Just like 1914. All the lovely soldiers—singing—marching! We must go at once to Paris, Achille.

HARRY [*rises*]. What's the matter with the music, professor? Us young folks want to dance.

[ELAINE *and* FRANCINE *come in.*]

ELAINE. Can we have a drink now, Harry?

HARRY. Sure. Sit down.

[DON *enters, exuding gratification at the sight of this gay, chic throng. The* ORCHESTRA *starts to play "Valencia."*]

WEBER. Will you have a drink, Irene?

IRENE. No, thank you.

WEBER. Will you, Captain Locicero?

CAPTAIN. Thank you. Brandy and soda, Dumptsy.

DUMPTSY. Si, Signor.

BEBE [*yells*]. Edna! We're going to have a drink!

[EDNA *comes in.*]

WEBER. For me, Cinzano.

DUMPTSY. Oui, Monsieur. [*He goes into the bar.*]

DOCTOR. It is all incredible.

HARRY. Nevertheless, Doctor, I remain an optimist. [*He looks at* IRENE.] Let doubt prevail throughout this night—with dawn will come again the light of truth! [*He turns to* SHIRLEY.] Come on, honey—let's dance. [*They dance.*]

[DON *dances with* BEULAH. *The* ORCHESTRA *continues with its spirited but frail performance of* "Valencia." *There are probably* "border incidents" *in Lorraine, the Riviera, Poland, Czecho-Slovakia and Mongolia.*]

CURTAIN

Act two

SCENE I

It is about 7:30 in the evening of the same day.

The CHERRYS *are seated, both of them dressed for dinner.* AUGUSTE *is serving them cocktails.*

CHERRY. Thank you.

AUGUSTE. Thank you, Signor.

CHERRY. Has any more news come through?

AUGUSTE. No, Signor. They permit the wireless to say nothing.

CHERRY. I suppose nothing really will happen.

AUGUSTE. Let us pray that is so, Signor. [AUGUSTE *goes into the bar.* CHERRY *leans over and kisses his wife.*]

CHERRY. My sweet . . . you're really very lovely.

MRS. CHERRY. Yes. [*He kisses her again, then lifts his glass.*]

CHERRY. Here's to us, darling.

MRS. CHERRY. And to hell with all the rest.

CHERRY. And to hell with all the rest. [*They drink, solemnly.*]

MRS. CHERRY. Jimmy—

CHERRY. What is it, darling?

MRS. CHERRY. Were you just saying that—or do you believe it?

CHERRY. That you're lovely? I can give you the most solemn assurance. . . .

MRS. CHERRY. No—that nothing is going to happen.

CHERRY. Oh.

MRS. CHERRY. Do you believe that?

CHERRY. I know this much: they can't start any real war without England. And no matter how stupid and blundering our government may be, our people simply won't stand for it.

MRS. CHERRY. But people can be such complete fools.

CHERRY. I know it, darling. Why can't they all be like us?

MRS. CHERRY. You mean—nice.

CHERRY. Yes—nice—and intelligent—and happy.

MRS. CHERRY. We're very conceited, aren't we?

CHERRY. Of course. And for good and sufficient reason.

MRS. CHERRY. I'm glad we're so superior, darling. It's comforting.

[HARRY *comes in from bar.*]

CHERRY. Oh—good evening, Mr. Van.

HARRY. Good evening. Pardon me— [*He starts to go.*]

CHERRY. Oh—don't run away, Mr. Van. Let's have some music.

MRS. CHERRY. Won't you have a drink with us?

HARRY. No, thanks, Mrs. Cherry—if you don't mind. [*Sits down at the piano.*] I'm afraid I put down too many Scotches this afternoon. As a result of which, I've just had to treat myself to a bicarbonate of soda. [*Starts playing* "Some of These Days."]

MRS. CHERRY. I love that.

HARRY. Thanks, pal—always grateful for applause from the discriminating. [*Finishes the chorus and stops.*]

CHERRY. Do play some more.

HARRY. No. The mood isn't right.

MRS. CHERRY. I can't tell you what a relief it is to have you here in this hotel.

HARRY. It's kind of you to say that, Mrs. Cherry. But I don't deserve your handsome tribute. Frequently, I can be an asset to any gathering—contributing humorous anecdotes and bits of homely philosophy. But here and now, I'm far from my best.

CHERRY. You're the only one here who seems to have retained any degree of sanity.

MRS. CHERRY. You and your young ladies.

HARRY. The girls are lucky. They don't know anything. And the trouble with me is that I just don't give a damn.

MRS. CHERRY. We've been trying hard not to know anything—or not to give a damn. But it isn't easy.

HARRY. You haven't been married very long, have you? I hope you don't mind my asking. . . .

CHERRY. We were married the day before yesterday.

HARRY. Let me offer my congratulations.

CHERRY. Thank you very much.

HARRY. It's my purely intuitive hunch that you two ought to get along fine.

CHERRY. That's our intention, Mr. Van.

MRS. CHERRY. And we'll do it, what's more. You see— we have one supreme thing in common:

HARRY. Yeah?

MRS. CHERRY. We're both independent.

CHERRY. We're like you Americans, in that respect.

HARRY. You flatter us.

MRS. CHERRY. Jimmy's a painter.

HARRY. You don't say!

MRS. CHERRY. He's been out in Australia, doing colossal murals for some government building. He won't show me the photographs of them, but I'm sure they're simply awful. [*She laughs fondly.*]

CHERRY. They're allegorical. [*He laughs, too.*]

HARRY. I'll bet they're good, at that. What do you do, Mrs. Cherry?

MRS. CHERRY. Oh, I work in the gift department at Fortnum's—

HARRY. Behind a counter, eh!

MRS. CHERRY. Yes—wearing a smock, and disgracing my family.

HARRY. Well, what d'ye know!

MRS. CHERRY. Both our families hoped we'd be married in some nice little church, and settle down in a nice little cottage, in a nice little state of decay. But when I heard Jimmy was on the way home I just dropped everything and rushed down here to meet him—and we were married, in Florence.

CHERRY. We hadn't seen each other for nearly a year —so, you can imagine, it was all rather exciting.

HARRY. I can imagine.

MRS. CHERRY. Florence is the most perfect place in the world to be married in.

HARRY. I guess that's true of any place.

CHERRY. We both happen to love Italy. And—I suppose—we're both rather on the romantic side.

HARRY. You stay on that side, no matter what happens.

MRS. CHERRY [*quickly*]. What do you think is going to happen?

HARRY. Me? I haven't the slightest idea.

CHERRY. We've looked forward so much to being here with no one bothering us, and plenty of winter sports. We're both keen on ski-ing. And now—we may have to go dashing back to England at any moment.

MRS. CHERRY. It's rotten luck, isn't it?

HARRY. Yes, Mrs. Cherry. That's what it is—it's rotten. [QUILLERY *enters from the bar, reading a newspaper.*] So they wouldn't let you cross?

QUILLERY. No!

HARRY. Is there any news?

QUILLERY [*glaring*]. News! Not in this patriotic journal. "Unconfirmed rumors"—from Vienna, London, Berlin, Moscow, Tokyo. And a lot of confirmed lies from Fascist headquarters in Rome. [*He slaps the paper down and sits.*] If you want to know what is really happening, ask *him*—up there! [*Indicates the rooms above.*]

CHERRY. Who?

QUILLERY. Weber! The great Monsieur Achille Weber, of the Comité des Forges! He can give you all the war news. Because he *made* it. You don't know who he is, eh? Or what he has been doing here in Italy? I'll tell you. [*He rises and comes close to them.*] He has been organizing the arms industry. Munitions. To kill French babies. And English babies. France and Italy are at war. England joins France. Germany joins Italy. And that will drag in the Soviet Union and the Japanese Empire and the United States. In every part of the world, the good desire of men for peace and decency is undermined by the dynamite of jingoism. And it needs only one spark, set off anywhere by one egomaniac, to send it all up in one final, fatal explosion. Then love becomes hatred, courage becomes terror, hope becomes despair. [*The DOCTOR appears on the gallery above.*] But—it will all be very nice for Achille Weber. Because he is a master of the one *real* League of Nations— [*The DOCTOR slowly comes down steps.*] The League of Schneider-Creusot, and Krupp, and Skoda, and Vickers and Dupont. The League of Death! And the workers of the world are expected to pay him for it, with their sweat, and their life's blood.

DOCTOR. Marxian nonsense!

QUILLERY. Ah! Who speaks?

DOCTOR. *I* speak.

QUILLERY. Yes! The eminent Dr. Hugo Waldersee. A wearer of the sacred swastika. Down with the Communists! Off with their heads! So that the world may be safe for the Nazi murderers.

DOCTOR. So that Germany may be safe from its oppressors! It is the same with all of you—Englishmen, Frenchmen, Marxists—you manage to forget that Germany, too, has a right to live! [*Rings handbell on the table.*]

QUILLERY. If you love Germany so much, why aren't you there, now—with your rats?

DOCTOR [*sitting*]. I am not concerned with politics. [AUGUSTE *enters from the bar.*] I am a scientist. [*To* AUGUSTE.] Mineral water!

[AUGUSTE *bows and exits into the bar.*]

QUILLERY. That's it, Herr Doctor! A scientist—a servant of humanity! And you know that if you were in your dear Fatherland, the Nazis would make you abandon your cure of cancer. It might benefit too many people outside of Germany—even maybe some Jews. They would force you to devote yourself to breeding malignant bacteria—millions of little germs, each one trained to give the Nazi salute and then go out and poison the enemy. You—a fighter against disease and death—you would become a Judas goat in a slaughter house.

[DON *has appeared during this.*]

CHERRY. I say, Quillery, old chap—do we have to have so much blood and sweat just before dinner?

QUILLERY [*turning on him*]. Just before dinner! And now we hear the voice of England! The great, well-fed, pious hypocrite! The grabber—the exploiter— the immaculate butcher! It was *you* forced this war, because miserable little Italy dared to drag its black shirt across your trail of Europe. What do *you* care if civilization goes to pieces—as long as you have your dinner—and your dinner jacket!

CHERRY [*rising*]. I'm sorry, Quillery—but I think we'd better conclude this discussion out on the terrace.

MRS. CHERRY. Don't be a damned fool, Jimmy. You'll prove nothing by thrashing him.

QUILLERY. It's the Anglo-Saxon method of proving everything! Very well—I am at your disposal.

DON. No! I beg of you, Mr. Cherry. We mustn't have any of that sort of thing. [*He turns to* QUILLERY.] I must ask you to leave. If you're unable to conduct yourself as a gentleman, then . . .

QUILLERY. Don't say any more. Evidently I cannot con- duct myself properly! I offer my apologies, Mr. Cherry.

CHERRY. That's quite all right, old man. Have a drink. [*He extends his hand. They shake.*]

QUILLERY. No, thank you. And my apologies to you, Herr Doctor.

DOCTOR. There is no need for apologizing. I am ac- customed to all that.

QUILLERY. If I let my speech run away with me, it is because I have hatred for certain things. And you should hate them, too. They are the things that make us blind—and ignorant—and—and dirty. [*He turns and goes out quickly.* DON *goes with him.*]

MRS. CHERRY. He's so right about everything.

CHERRY. I know, poor chap. Will you have another cocktail, darling?

MRS. CHERRY. I don't think so. Will you, Doctor? [*He shakes his head, indicates the mineral water. She rises.*] Let's dine.

CHERRY. It will be a bit difficult to summon up much relish. [*They go out, hand in hand.*]

HARRY. I find them very appealing, don't you, Doctor? [*The* DOCTOR *doesn't announce his findings.*] Did you know they were married only the day before yesterday? Yeah—they got themselves sealed in Florence—because they love Italy. And they came here hoping to spend their honeymoon on skis. . . . Kind of pathetic, isn't it?

DOCTOR. What did you say?

HARRY. Nothing, pal. [DON *comes in.*] Only making conversation.

DOCTOR [*rising*]. That Communist! Making me a criminal because I am a German!

DON. I'm dreadfully sorry, Dr. Waldersee. We never should have allowed the ill-bred little cad to come in here.

DOCTOR. Oh— It's no matter. I have heard too many hymns of hate before this. To be a German is to be used to insults, and injuries. [*He goes out.* DON *starts to go out left.*]

HARRY. Just a minute, Don.

DON. Well?

HARRY. Have you found out yet who that dame is?

DON. What "dame"?

HARRY. That Russian number with Weber.

DON. I have not inquired as to her identity.

HARRY. But did he register her as his wife?

DON. They registered separately! And if it's not too much to ask, might I suggest that you mind your own damned business?

HARRY. You might suggest just that. And I should still be troubled by one of the most tantalizing of questions—namely, "Where have I seen that face before?" Generally, it turns out to be someone who was in the second row one night, yawning.

DON. I'm sure that such is the case now. [*He starts again to go.*]

HARRY. One moment, Don. There's something else.

DON [*impatiently*]. What is it?

HARRY. I take it that your job here is something like that of a professional greeter.

DON. You're at liberty to call it that, if you choose.

HARRY. You're a sort of Y.M.C.A. secretary—who sees to it that all the guests get together and have a good time.

DON. Well?

HARRY. Well—do you think you're doing a very good job of it right now?

DON [*simply furious*]. Have you any suggestions for improving the performance of my duties?

HARRY. Yes, Don—I have.

DON. And I'd very much like to know just exactly who the hell do you think you are to be offering criticism of my work?

HARRY. Please, please! You needn't scream at me. I'm merely trying to be helpful. I'm making you an offer.

DON. What is it?

HARRY [*looking around*]. I see you've got a color wheel here. [*Referring to the light.*]

DON. We use it during the supper dance. But—if you don't mind, I—

HARRY. I see—well—how would it be if I and the girls put on part of our act here, tonight? For purposes of wholesome merriment and relieving the general tension?

DON. What kind of an act is it?

HARRY. And don't say, "What kind of an act," in that tone of voice. It's good enough for this place. Those girls have played before the King of Rumania. And if some of my suspicions are correct—but I won't pursue that subject. All that need concern you is that we can adjust ourselves to our audience, and tonight we'll omit the bubble dance and the number in which little Bebe does a shimmy in a costume composed of detachable gardenias, unless there's a special request for it.

DON. Do you expect to be paid for this?

HARRY. Certainly not. I'm making this offer out of the goodness of my heart. Of course, if you want to make any appropriate adjustment on our hotel bill . . .

DON. And you'll give me your guarantee that there'll be no vulgarity?

[IRENE *appears on the gallery and starts to come down. She is wearing a dinner dress.*]

HARRY. Now be careful, Don. One more word like that and the offer is withdrawn . . .

[DON *cautions him to silence.*]

DON. It's a splendid idea, Mr. Van. We'll all greatly appreciate your little entertainment, I'm sure. [*To* IRENE]. Good evening, madame.

IRENE [*with the utmost graciousness*]. Good evening, Mr. Navadel. [*She pauses at the window.*] It *is* a lovely view. It's like a landscape on the moon.

DON. Yes—yes. That's exactly what it's like.

[*She comes down.*]

HARRY. You understand, we'll have to rehearse with the orchestra.

DON. Oh, yes—Mr. Van. Our staff will be glad to co-operate in every way. . . . Do sit down, madame.

IRENE [*sitting*]. What became of those planes that flew off this afternoon? I haven't heard them come back. [*Takes out a cigarette.*]

DON. I imagine they were moving to some base farther from the frontier. I hope so. They always made the most appalling racket. [*Lights her cigarette for her.*]

HARRY. About eleven o'clock?

[WEBER *appears on the gallery.*]

DON. Yes, Mr. Van. Eleven will do nicely. You'll have a cocktail, madame?

[HARRY *goes into the lobby.*]

IRENE. No, no. Vodka, if you please.

DON. I shall have it sent right in. [*He goes off at the left into bar.*]

[IRENE *looks slowly off, after* HARRY. *She smiles slightly.* WEBER *comes down the stairs quickly. He is not in evening dress. He too pauses at the window.*]

WEBER. A perfectly cloudless night! They're very lucky. [*He comes on down.*]

IRENE. Did you get your call?

WEBER. Yes. I talked to Lanza.

IRENE. I gather the news is, as usual, good.

WEBER. It is extremely serious! You saw those bombers that left here this afternoon?

IRENE. Yes.

WEBER. They were headed for Paris. Italy is evidently in a great hurry to deliver the first blow.

IRENE. How soon may we leave here?

WEBER. None too soon, I can assure you. The French high command will know that the bombers come from this field. There will be reprisals—probably within the next twenty-four hours.

IRENE. That will be exciting to see.

WEBER. An air raid?

IRENE. Yes—with bombs bursting in the snow. Sending up great geysers of diamonds.

WEBER. Or perhaps great geysers of us.

IRENE [*after a moment*]. I suppose many people in Paris are being killed now.

WEBER. I'm afraid so. Unless the Italians bungle it.

IRENE. Perhaps your sister—Madame d'Hilaire—perhaps she and her darling little children are now dying.

WEBER [*sharply*]. My sister and her family are in Montbeliard.

IRENE. But you said the Italians might bungle it. They might drop their bombs on the wrong place.

WEBER. I appreciate your solicitude, my dear. But you can save your condolences until they are needed. [DUMPTSY *comes in from the bar and serves the vodka.* WEBER *rises.*] I must telegraph to Joseph to have the house ready. It will be rather cold in Biarritz now—but far healthier than Paris. You are going in to dinner now?

IRENE. Yes.

WEBER. I shall join you later. [*He goes out.*]

[DUMPTSY *picks up the* CHERRYS' *glasses.*]

DUMPTSY. We will have a great treat tonight, madame.

IRENE. Really?

DUMPTSY. That American impresario, that Mr. Harry Van—he will give us an entertainment with his dancing girls.

IRENE. Is he employed here regularly?

DUMPTSY. Oh, no, madame. He is just passing, like you. This is a special treat. It will be very fine.

IRENE. Let us hope so. [*She downs the vodka.*]

DUMPTSY. Madame is Russian, if I may say so.

IRENE [*pleased*]. How did you know that I am Russian? Just because I am having vodka?

DUMPTSY. No, madame. Many people try to drink vodka. But only true Russians can do it gracefully. You see—I was a prisoner with your people in the war. I liked them.

IRENE. You're very charming. What is your name?

DUMPTSY. I am called Dumptsy, madame.

IRENE. Are you going again to the war, Dumptsy?

DUMPTSY. If they tell me to, madame.

IRENE. You will enjoy being a soldier?

DUMPTSY. Yes—if I'm taken prisoner soon enough.

IRENE. And who do you think will win?

DUMPTSY. I can't think, madame. It is all very doubtful. But one thing I can tell you: whoever wins, it will be the same as last time—Austria will lose.

IRENE. They will all lose, Dumptsy. [*The* CHERRYS *come in. She greets them pleasantly.*] Good evening.

CHERRY. Good evening, madame. [*The* CHERRYS *start to sit, across from* IRENE.]

IRENE. Bring some more vodka, Dumptsy. Perhaps Mr. and Mrs. Cherry will have some, too.

CHERRY. Why, thank you—we . . .

MRS. CHERRY. I'd love to. I've never tasted vodka.

IRENE. Ah—then it's high time. Bring in the bottle, Dumptsy.

DUMPTSY. Yes, madame. [*He goes in to the bar.*]

IRENE. Come, sit down here. [*The* CHERRYS *sit by her.*] You will find vodka a perfect stimulant to the appetite. So much better than that hybrid atrocity, the American cocktail!

CHERRY. To tell you the truth, madame—we've already dined.

IRENE. It is no matter. It is just as good as a liqueur.

MRS. CHERRY. We didn't really dine at all. We merely looked at the minestrone and the Parmesan cheese—and we felt too depressed to eat anything.

IRENE. It's the altitude. After the first exhilaration there comes a depressive reaction, especially for you, who are accustomed to the heavy, Pigwiggian atmosphere of England.

CHERRY. Pigwiggian?

IRENE. Yes, Pigwig—Oliver Twist—you know, your Dickens?

[DUMPTSY *enters from bar with a bottle of vodka and*

two more glasses, which he places on the table. He returns to the bar.]

CHERRY. You know England, madame?

IRENE [*fondly*]. Of course I know England! My governess was a sweet old ogre from your north country—and when I was a little girl I used to visit often at Sandringham.

CHERRY [*impressed*]. Sandringham?

MRS. CHERRY. The palace?

IRENE. Yes. That was before your time. It was in the reign of dear, gay King Edward, and the beautiful Alexandra. [*She sighs a little for those days.*] I used to have such fun playing with my cousin David. He used to try to teach me to play cricket, and when I couldn't swing the bat properly, he said, "Oh, you Russians will never be civilized!" [*Laughs.*] When I went home to Petersburg I told my uncle, the Tsar, what David had said, and he was so amused! But now—you must drink your vodka. [*They rise, and lift their glasses.*] A toast! To his most gracious Majesty the King. [*They clink glasses.*] God bless him.

CHERRY. Thank you, madame. [*All three drink and MRS. CHERRY coughs violently.*]

IRENE [*to MRS. CHERRY*]. No—no! Drink it right down. Like this. [*She swallows it in a gulp.*] So! [*Refills the glasses from the bottle.*] The second glass will go more easily. [*They sit.*] I used to laugh so at your funny British Tommies in Archangel. They all hated vodka until one of them thought of mixing it with beer.

MRS. CHERRY. How loathsome!

IRENE. It was! But I shall be forever grateful to them— those Tommies. They saved my life when I escaped from the Soviets. For days and nights—I don't know how many—I was driving through the snow—snow—

snow—snow—in a little sleigh, with the body of my father beside me, and the wolves running along like an escort of dragoons. You know—you always think of wolves as howling constantly, don't you?

CHERRY. Why, yes—I suppose one does.

IRENE. Well, they don't. No, these wolves didn't howl! They were horribly, confidently silent. I think silence is much more terrifying, don't you?

CHERRY. You must have been dreadfully afraid.

IRENE. No, I was not afraid for myself. It was the thought of my father. . . .

MRS. CHERRY. Please! I know you don't want to talk about it any more.

IRENE. Oh, no—it is so far away now. I shall never forget the moment when I came through the haze of delirium, and saw the faces of those Tommies. Those simple, friendly faces. And the snow—and the wolves—and the terrible cold—they were all gone— and I was looking at Kew Gardens on a Sunday afternoon, and the sea of golden daffodils—"fluttering and dancing in the breezes."

[WEBER *has come in with the daffodils.*]

WEBER. Shall we go in to dinner now, Irene?

IRENE. Yes, yes, Achille. In a minute. I am coming. [WEBER *goes.* IRENE *rises.*] Now—we must finish our vodka. [CHERRY *rises.*] And you must make another try to eat something.

CHERRY. Thank you so much, madame. [*They drink.*]

IRENE. And later on, we must all be here for Mr. Van's entertainment—and we must all applaud vigorously.

MRS. CHERRY. We shall, madame.

CHERRY. He's such a nice chap, isn't he?

IRENE [*going*]. Yes—and a real artist, too.

CHERRY. Oh—you've seen him?

IRENE. Why—yes—I've seen him, in some *café chantant,* somewhere. I forget just where it was.

[*The three of them have gone out together. The light is dimmed to extinction. The curtain falls.*]

SCENE II

About two hours later.
WEBER *is drinking brandy. The* CAPTAIN *is standing.*

CAPTAIN. I have been listening to the radio. Utter bedlam! Of course, every government has imposed the strictest censorship—but it is very frightening—like one of those films where ghostly hands suddenly reach in and switch off all the lights.

WEBER. Any suggestions of air raids?

CAPTAIN. None. But there is ominous quiet from Paris. Think of it—Paris—utterly silent! Only one station there is sending messages, and they are in code.

WEBER. Probably instructions to the frontier.

CAPTAIN. I heard a man in Prague saying something that sounded interesting, but him I could not understand. Then I turned to London, hopefully, and listened to a gentleman describing the disastrous effects of ivy upon that traditional institution, the oak.

WEBER. Well—we shall soon know. . . . There'll be no trouble about crossing the frontier tomorrow?

CAPTAIN. Oh, no. Except that I am still a little worried about madame's passport.

WEBER. We'll arrange about that. Have a cigar, Captain?

CAPTAIN. Thank you.

[*Irene comes in as the* CAPTAIN *starts to light the cigar.*]

IRENE. Do you hear the sound of airplanes?

[*All stop to listen, intently. The sound becomes audi-*

ble. *The* CAPTAIN *shakes out the match, throws the unlit cigar on the table, and dashes to the window and looks upward.*]

CAPTAIN. It is our bombers. One—two—three. Seven of them. Seven out of eighteen. You will excuse me? [*He salutes and dashes out.*]

WEBER. Seven out of eighteen! Not bad, for Italians.

[IRENE *has gone to the window to look out.*]

IRENE. I'm so happy for you, Achille.

WEBER. What was that, my dear?

IRENE. I said—I'm so happy for you.

WEBER. But—just why am I an object of congratulation?

IRENE. All this great, wonderful death and destruction, everywhere. And you promoted it!

WEBER. Don't give me too much credit, Irene.

IRENE. But I *know* what you've done.

WEBER. Yes, my dear. You know a great deal. But don't forget to do honor to Him—up there—who put fear into man. I am but the humble instrument of His divine will.

IRENE [*looking upward, sympathetically*]. Yes—that's quite true. We don't do half enough justice to Him. Poor, lonely old soul. Sitting up in heaven, with nothing to do, but play solitaire. Poor, dear God. Playing Idiot's Delight. The game that never means anything, and never ends.

WEBER. You have an engaging fancy, my dear.

IRENE. Yes.

WEBER. It's the quality in you that fascinates me most. Limitless imagination! It is what has made you such an admirable, brilliant liar. And so very helpful to me! Am I right?

IRENE. Of course you are right, Achille. Had I been bound by any stuffy respect for the truth, I should never have escaped from the Soviets.

WEBER. I'm sure of it.

IRENE. Did I ever tell you of my escape from the Soviets?

WEBER. You have told me about it at least eleven times. And each time it was different.

IRENE. Well, I made several escapes. I am always making escapes, Achille. When I am worrying about you, and your career, I have to run away from the terror of my own thoughts. So I amuse myself by studying the faces of the people I see. Just ordinary, casual, dull people. [*She is speaking in a tone that is sweetly sadistic.*] That young English couple, for instance. I was watching them during dinner, sitting there, close together, holding hands, and rubbing their knees together under the table. And I saw him in his nice, smart, British uniform, shooting a little pistol at a huge tank. And the tank rolls over him. And his fine strong body, that was so full of the capacity for ecstasy, is a mass of mashed flesh and bones—a smear of purple blood—like a stepped-on snail. But before the moment of death, he consoles himself by thinking, "Thank God *she* is safe! She is bearing the child I gave her, and he will live to see a better world." [*She walks behind* WEBER *and leans over his shoulder.*] But I know where she is. She is lying in a cellar that has been wrecked by an air raid, and her firm young breasts are all mixed up with the bowels of a dismembered policeman, and the embryo from her womb is splattered against the face of a dead bishop. That is the kind of thought with which I amuse myself, Achille. And it makes me so proud to think that I am so close to you—who make all this possible.

[WEBER *rises and walks about the room. At length he turns to her.*]

WEBER. Do you talk in this whimsical vein to many people?

IRENE. No. I betray my thoughts to no one but you. You know that I am shut off from the world. I am a contented prisoner in your ivory tower.

WEBER. I'm beginning to wonder about that.

IRENE. What? You think I could interest myself in someone else—?

WEBER. No—no, my dear. I am merely wondering whether the time has come for you to turn commonplace, like all the others?

IRENE. The others?

WEBER. All those who have shared my life. My former wife, for instance. She now boasts that she abandoned me because part of my income is derived from the sale of poison gas. Revolvers and rifles and bullets she didn't mind—because they are also used by sportsmen. Battleships too are permissible; they look so splendid in the news films. But she couldn't stomach poison gas. So now she is married to an anemic duke, and the large fortune that she obtained from me enables the duke to indulge his principal passion, which is the slaughtering of wild animals, like rabbits, and pigeons and rather small deer. My wife is presumably happy with him. I have always been glad you are not a fool as she was, Irene.

IRENE. No. I don't care even for battleships. And I shall not marry an anemic duke.

WEBER. But—there was something unpleasantly reminiscent in that gaudy picture you painted. I gather that this silly young couple has touched a tender spot, eh?

IRENE. Perhaps, Achille. Perhaps I am softening.

WEBER. Then apply your intelligence, my dear. Ask yourself: why shouldn't they die? And who are the greater criminals—those who sell the instruments of death, or those who buy them, and use them? You know there is no logical reply to that. But all these little people—like your new friends—all of them consider me an arch-villain because I furnish them with what they want, which is the illusion of power. That is what they vote for in their frightened governments—what they cheer for on their national holidays—what they glorify in their anthems, and their monuments, and their waving flags! Yes—they shout bravely about something they call "national honor." And what does it amount to? Mistrust of the motives of everyone else! Dog in the manger defense of what they've got, and greed for the other fellow's possessions! Honor among thieves! I assure you, Irene—for such little people the deadliest weapons are the most merciful.

[*The* CHERRYS *enter. He is whistling* "Minnie the Moocher."]

IRENE. Ah! Mr. and Mrs. Cherry!

CHERRY. Hello there. [*They come down.*]

IRENE. You have dined well!

MRS. CHERRY. Superbly!

CHERRY. We ate everything—up to and including the zabaglione.

IRENE. You can thank the vodka for that. Vodka never fails in an emergency.

CHERRY. And we can thank you, madame, and do so.

IRENE. But—permit me to introduce Monsieur Weber. [WEBER *rises.*] Mrs. Cherry—Mr. Cherry. [*They are exchanging greetings as* DON *comes in.*]

DON. We're going to have a little cabaret show for you now, madame.

WEBER. I don't think I shall wait for it, my dear.

IRENE. But you must—

WEBER. I really should look over Lanza's estimates—

IRENE. Please, Achille—Mr. Van is an artist. You will be so amused.

WEBER [*resuming seat*]. Very well, Irene.

DON [*his tone blandly confidential*]. Between ourselves, I don't vouch for the quality of it. But it may be unintentionally amusing.

IRENE. I shall love it.

CHERRY. This is the most marvelous idea, Mr. Navadel.

DON. Oh, thank you. We try to contrive some novelty each evening. If you'll be good enough to sit here— [DON *goes up to usher in the* ROSSIS *and direct them to their seats.*]

[*The* MUSICIANS *come in and take their places. The* DOCTOR *comes in.* DUMPTSY *is busily moving chairs about, clearing a space for the act.* IRENE *and the* CHERRYS *chat pleasantly.* ANNA, *the maid, appears on the gallery above to watch the entertainment.* HARRY *comes in. He is wearing a tight-fitting dinner jacket, and carries a cane and a straw hat.*]

HARRY. All set, Don?

DON. Quite ready, whenever you are.

HARRY. Okey-doke. Give us a fanfare, professor. [*He goes out. The* BAND *obliges with a fanfare.* HARRY *returns, all smiles.*] Before we start, folks, I just want to explain that we haven't had much chance to rehearse with my good friend, Signor Palota, and his talented little team here. [*He indicates the* ORCHESTRA *with a handsome gesture.*] So we must crave your indulgence and beg you to give us a break if the rhythm isn't all kosher. [*He waits for his laugh.*] All we ask of you, kind friends, is "The Christian pearl of charity," to quote our great American poet, John Greenleaf Whittier. We thank you. Take it away! [*He bows. All applaud. He then sings a song— The* GIRLS *come on in costume and dance.*]

[*During the latter part of the act, the* CAPTAIN, *the*

MAJOR, *and four flying corps* OFFICERS *come in. The latter are dirty and in a fever of heroically restrained excitement. They survey the scene with wonderment and then with delight, saying, in Italian, "What's all this?" and "What brought these blonde bambinos to Monte Gabriele?" etc.* HARRY *interrupts the act and orders the orchestra to play the Fascist anthem, "Giovinezza." The officers acknowledge this graceful gesture with the Fascist salute. The* GIRLS *wave back. The* CAPTAIN *gets the* OFFICERS *seated and then goes to order drinks.* HARRY *and the* GIRLS *resume.*]

[*At the end of the act, all applaud and the* OFFICERS *shout "Brava—Bravissima" and stamp their feet with enthusiasm. The* GIRLS *take several bows and go.* HARRY *returns for a solo bow, waving his straw hat. One of the* OFFICERS *shouts, in Italian, "We want the young ladies!"*]

CAPTAIN [*to* HARRY]. My friends wish to know respectfully if the young ladies will care to join them in a little drink?

HARRY. Certainly! Come back in, girls. Get over there and join the army! [*The* GIRLS *do so.*] Now, folks—with your kind permission—I shall give the girls an interlude of rest and refreshment and treat you to a little piano specialty of my own. Your strict attention is not obligatory. [*He starts his specialty, assisted by* SHIRLEY *and* EDNA. *The* OFFICERS *don't pay much attention. Bottles of champagne are brought for them and the* GIRLS.]

[WEBER *goes and speaks to the* CAPTAIN. *He beckons him up to the landing of the stairs where they converse in low tones, the* CAPTAIN *telling him about the air raid.*]

[HARRY'S *act is interrupted by the entrance of* QUILLERY.]

QUILLERY [*to* HARRY]. Do you know what has happened?

DON. I told you we didn't want you here.

PITTALUGA. We're having an entertainment here.

QUILLERY. Yes! An entertainment!

HARRY. If you'll just sit down, pal . . . [*He and the* GIRLS *continue with their singing.*]

QUILLERY. An entertainment—while Paris is in ruins!

CHERRY [*rises*]. What?

DOCTOR. What are you saying?

QUILLERY. They have bombed Paris! The Fascisti have bombed Paris!

DON. What? It can't be possible—

HARRY. Go on, Shirley. Keep on singing.

QUILLERY. I tell you—tonight their planes flew over and—

CHERRY. But how do you know this?

QUILLERY. It is on the wireless—everywhere. And I have just talked to one of their mechanics, who was on the flight, and saw, with his own eyes—

HARRY. Won't you please sit down, pal? We're trying to give you a little entertainment— [*Stops playing.*]

QUILLERY. For the love of God—listen to me! While you sit here eating and drinking, tonight, Italian planes dropped twenty thousand kilos of bombs on Paris. God knows how many they killed. God knows how much of life and beauty is forever destroyed! And you sit here, drinking, laughing, with *them*— the murderers. [*Points to the* FLYERS, *who ask each other, in Italian, what the hell is he talking about.*] They did it! It was their planes, from that field down there. Assassins!

[*The* OFFICERS *make a move toward* QUILLERY—*one of them arming himself with a champagne bottle.*]

HARRY [*comes down from the piano*]. We can't have any skull-cracking in this club. Hey, Captain, speak to your men before anything starts.

[*The* CAPTAIN *comes down to the* OFFICERS *and pacifies them.* CHERRY *comes down to stand by* QUILLERY.]

MRS. CHERRY. Jimmy! . . . You keep out of this!

MAJOR *and* FIRST *and* THIRD OFFICERS [*jump up*]. Assassini!

HARRY. Now listen, pal . . .

SHIRLEY. Harry! Don't get yourself mixed up in this mess!

QUILLERY. You see, we stand together! France—England—America! Allies!

HARRY. Shut up, France! It's O.K., Captain. We can handle this—

QUILLERY. They don't dare fight against the power of England and France! The free democracies against the Fascist tyranny!

HARRY. Now, for God's sake stop fluctuating!

QUILLERY. England and France are fighting for the hopes of mankind!

HARRY. A minute ago, England was a butcher in a dress suit. Now we're Allies!

QUILLERY. We stand together. We stand together forever. [*Turns to* OFFICERS.] I say God damn you. God damn the villains that sent you on this errand of death.

CAPTAIN [*takes a few steps toward* QUILLERY]. If you don't close your mouth, Frenchman, we shall be forced to arrest you.

QUILLERY. Go on, Fascisti! Commit national suicide. That's the last gesture left to you toy soldiers.

HARRY. It's all right, Captain. Mr. Quillery is for peace. He's going back to France to stop the war.

QUILLERY [*turns on* HARRY]. You're not authorized to speak for me. I am competent to say what I feel. And what I say is "Down with Fascism! Abbasso Fascismo!"

[*There is an uproar from the* OFFICERS.]

CAPTAIN [*ordinarily gentle, is now white hot with rage*]. Attenzione!

QUILLERY. Vive la France! Viv—

CAPTAIN. E agli arresti.

QUILLERY. Call out the firing squad! Shoot me dead! But do not think you can silence the truth that's in me.

CAPTAIN [*grabs* QUILLERY *from the left and calls the* FIRST OFFICER]. Molinari! [FIRST OFFICER *grabs* QUILLERY *from the right. They start to take him out.*]

QUILLERY [*as he is being led out*]. The Empire of the Fascisti will join the Empire of the Caesars in smoking ruins. Vive la France! Vive la France!

[WEBER *goes upstairs and exits. They have gone.*]

CHERRY [*to* HARRY]. You'd better carry on with your turn, old boy.

HARRY. No, pal. The act is cold. [*To the* ORCHESTRA LEADER.] Give us some music, Signor. [*The* ORCHESTRA *starts playing.*] Let dancing become general.

CHERRY. Let's dance, my sweet.

MRS. CHERRY. I can't bear to, Jimmy.

CHERRY. I think we should.

MRS. CHERRY. Very well, darling. [*They dance. The* OFFICERS *dance with the* GIRLS.]

HARRY [*goes over to* IRENE]. Would you care to dance?

IRENE. Why—why, thank you. [*She stands up, and they join the slowly moving mob.*]

[SHIRLEY *is singing as loud as she can. The color wheel turns so that the dancers are bathed in blue, then amber, then red.*]

CURTAIN

SCENE III

Later that night.

IRENE and HARRY are alone. She is sitting, telling the story of her life. He is listening with fascination and doubt.

IRENE. My father was old. The hardships of that terrible journey had broken his body. But his spirit was strong—the spirit that is Russia. He lay there, in that little boat, and he looked up at me. Never can I forget his face, so thin, so white, so beautiful, in the starlight. And he said to me, "Irene—little daughter," and then—he died. For four days I was alone, with his body, sailing through the storms of the Black Sea. I had no food—no water—I was in agony from the bayonet wounds of the Bolsheviki. I knew I must die. But then—an American cruiser rescued me. May God bless those good men! [*She sighs.*] I've talked too much about myself. What about you, my friend?

HARRY. Oh—I'm not very interesting. I'm just what I seem to be.

IRENE. C'est impossible!

HARRY. C'est possible! The facts of my case are eloquent. I'm a potential genius—reduced to piloting six blondes through the Balkans.

IRENE. But there is something that you hide from the world—even, I suspect, from yourself. Where did you acquire your superior education?

HARRY. I worked my way through college selling encyclopedias.

IRENE. I knew you had culture! What college was it?

HARRY. Oh—just any college. But my sales talk was so

good that I fell for it myself. I bought the God-
damned encyclopedia. And I read it all, traveling
around, in day coaches, and depot hotels, and Fox-
time dressing rooms. It was worth the money.

IRENE. And how much of all this have you retained?

HARRY [*significantly*]. I? I—never forget anything.

IRENE. How unfortunate for you! Does your encyclopedia help you in your dealings with the girls?

HARRY. Yes, Mrs. Weber. . . . I got considerable benefit
from studying the lives of the great courtesans, and
getting to understand their technique. . . .

IRENE. Forgive me for interrupting you—but that is
not my name.

HARRY. Oh—pardon me, I thought . . .

IRENE. I know what you thought. Monsieur Weber and
I are associated in a sort of business way.

HARRY. I see.

IRENE. He does me the honor to consult me in matters
of policy.

HARRY. That's quite an honor! Business is pretty good,
isn't it!

IRENE. I gather that you are one of those noble souls
who does not entirely approve of the munitions industry?

HARRY. Oh, no—I'm not noble. Your friend is just another salesman. And I make it a point never to criticize anybody else's racket.

IRENE. Monsieur Weber is a very distinguished man.
He has rendered very distinguished services to all
the governments of the world. He is decorated with
the Legion of Honor, the Order of the White Eagle,
the Order of St. James of the Sword, and the Military Order of Christ!

HARRY. The Military Order of Christ. I never heard of
that one.

IRENE. It is from Portugal. He has many orders.

HARRY. Have you ever been in America?

IRENE. Oh, yes—I've seen it all—New York, Washington, Palm Beach . . .

HARRY. I said America. Have you ever been in the West?

IRENE. Certainly I have. I flew across your continent. There are many White Russians in California.

HARRY. Did you ever happen to make any parachute landings in any places like Kansas, or Iowa, or Nebraska?

IRENE [*laughing*]. I have seen enough of your countrymen to know that you are typical.

HARRY. Me? I'm not typical of anything.

IRENE. Oh, yes, you are. You are just like all of them—an ingenuous, sentimental idealist. You believe in the goodness of human nature, don't you?

HARRY. And what if I do? I've known millions of people, intimately—and I never found more than one out of a hundred that I didn't like, once you got to know them.

IRENE. That is very charming—but it *is* naïve.

HARRY. Maybe so. But experience prevents me from working up much enthusiasm over anyone who considers the human race as just so many clay pigeons, even if he does belong to the Military Order of Christ.

IRENE. If you came from an older culture, you would realize that men like Monsieur Weber are necessary to civilization.

HARRY. You don't say.

IRENE. I mean, of course, the sort of civilization that we have got. [*She smiles upon him benevolently. It is as though she were explaining patiently but with secret enjoyment the facts of life to a backward nephew.*] Stupid people consider him an arch-villain because it is his duty to stir up a little trouble

here and there to stimulate the sale of his products.
Do you understand me, my friend?

HARRY. I shouldn't wonder.

IRENE. Monsieur Weber is a true man of the world. He
is above petty nationalism; he can be a Frenchman
in France—a German in Germany—a Greek—a Turk
—whatever the occasion demands.

HARRY. Yes—that little Quillery was an International-
ist, too. He believed in brotherhood, but the moment he got a whiff of gunpowder he began to spout
hate and revenge. And now those nice, polite Wops
will probably have to shut him up with a firing
squad.

IRENE [*takes out a cigarette from her case*]. It is a painful necessity.

HARRY. And it demonstrates the sort of little trouble
that your friend stirs up. [*He takes out his lighter
and lights her cigarette.*]

IRENE. Do you know that you can be extremely rude?

HARRY. I'm sorry if I've hurt your feelings about Mr.
Weber, but he just happens to be a specimen of the
one per cent that I *don't* like.

IRENE. I was not referring to that. Why do you stare at
me so?

HARRY. Have I been staring?

IRENE. Steadily. Ever since we arrived here this afternoon. Why do you do it?

HARRY. I've been thinking I could notice a funny resemblance to someone I used to know.

IRENE. You should know better than to tell any woman
that she resembles somebody else. We none of us
like to think that our appearance is commonplace.

HARRY. The one you look like wasn't commonplace.

IRENE. Oh! She was someone near and dear to you?

HARRY. It was somebody that occupies a unique shrine
in the temple of my memory.

IRENE. That *is* a glowing tribute. The temple of your memory must be so crowded! But I am keeping you from your duties.

HARRY. What duties?

IRENE. Shouldn't you be worrying about your young ladies?

HARRY. They're all right; they've gone to bed.

IRENE. Yes—but there are several Italian officers about. Aren't you supposed to be the chaperon?

HARRY. I leave the girls to their own resources, of which they have plenty. [*He stares hard at her.*] Have you always been a blonde?

IRENE. Yes—as far as I can remember.

HARRY. You don't mind my asking?

IRENE. Not at all. And now, may I ask you something?

HARRY. Please do so.

IRENE. Why do you waste yourself in this degraded work? Touring about with those obvious little harlots?

HARRY. You mean you think I'm fitted for something that requires a little more mentality?

IRENE. Yes.

HARRY. How do you know so much about me? [*It should be remembered that all through this scene* HARRY *is studying her, trying to fit together the pieces of the jigsaw puzzle of his memory.*]

IRENE. For one thing, I saw your performance tonight.

HARRY. You thought it was punk?

IRENE. I thought it was unworthy.

HARRY. It was unfortunately interrupted. You should have seen . . .

IRENE. I saw enough. You are a very bad dancer.

HARRY. The King of Rumania thought I was pretty good.

IRENE. He is entitled to his opinion—and I to mine.

HARRY. I'll admit that I've done better things in my

time. Would it surprise you to know that I was once
with a mind-reading act?

IRENE. Really?

HARRY. Yeah.

IRENE. Now you're staring at me again.

HARRY. Have you ever been in Omaha?

IRENE. Omaha? Where is that? Persia?

HARRY. No. Nebraska. That's one of our states. I
played there once with the greatest act of my career.
I was a stooge for Zuleika, the Mind Reader. At
least she called me her stooge. But I was the one who
had to do all the brain work.

IRENE. And she read people's minds?

HARRY. I did it for her. I passed through the audience
and fed her the cues. We were sensational, playing
the finest picture houses in all the key cities. Zuleika
sat up on the stage, blindfolded—and usually blind
drunk.

IRENE. Oh, dear. And was *she* the one that I resemble?

HARRY. No! There was another act on the same bill. A
troupe of Russians . . .

IRENE. Russians?

HARRY. Singers, mandolin players, and squat dancers.
One of them was a red-headed girl. She was fascinated by our act, and she kept pestering me to teach
her the code. She said she could do it better than
Zuleika.

IRENE. Those poor Russians. There are so many of
them all over the world. And so many of them completely counterfeit!

HARRY. This dame was counterfeit all right. In fact,
she was the God-damnedest liar I ever saw. She lied
just for the sheer artistry of it. She kept after me so
much that I told her finally to come up to my hotel
room one night, and we'd talk it over.

IRENE. I hope you didn't tell her the code.

HARRY. No. After the week in Omaha the bill split. The Russians went to Sioux Falls and we went on the Interstate Time. I played with Zuleika for another year and then the drink got her and she couldn't retain. So the act busted up. I've always hoped I'd catch up with that red-headed Russian again sometime. She might have been good. She had the voice for it, and a kind of overtone of mystery.

IRENE. It's a characteristic Gypsy quality. And you never saw her again?

HARRY. No.

IRENE. Perhaps it is just as well. She couldn't have been so clever—being duped so easily into going to your room.

HARRY. She wasn't being duped! She knew what she was doing. If there was any duping going on, she was the one that did it.

IRENE. She *did* make an impression!

HARRY [*looking straight at her*]. I was crazy about her. She was womanhood at its most desirable—and most unreliable.

IRENE. And you such a connoisseur. But—it's getting late.

HARRY [*rises*]. Do you know any Russian music? [*He crosses to the piano.*]

IRENE [*rises*]. Oh, yes. When I was a little girl my father used to engage Chaliapin to come often to our house. He taught me many songs.

HARRY. Chaliapin, eh? Your father spared no expense. [*He sits at the piano.*]

IRENE. That was in *old* Russia. [*He plays a few bars of* "Kak Stranna."] "Kak Stranna!"

HARRY. Yeah! How strange! [*He starts to play* "Prostchai."] Do you know this one? [IRENE *sings some of it in Russian.*] How do you spell that name—Irene?

IRENE. I-R-E-N-E. [HARRY *pounds the piano and jumps up.*] What's the matter?

HARRY. That's it! Irene! [*He pronounces it* I-REEN.]

IRENE. But what—?

HARRY. I knew it! You're the one!

IRENE. What one?

HARRY. That red-headed liar! Irene! I knew I could never be mistaken. . . .

IRENE. Irene is a very usual name in Russia. [*She laughs heartily.*]

HARRY. I don't care how usual it is. Everything fits together perfectly now. The name—the face—the voice—Chaliapin for a teacher! Certainly it's you! And it's no good shaking your head and looking amazed! No matter how much you may lie, you can't deny the fact that you slept with me in the Governor Bryan Hotel in Omaha in the fall of 1925. [IRENE *laughs heartily again.*] All right—go ahead and laugh. That blonde hair had me fooled for a while—but now I know it's just as phony as the bayonet wounds, and the parachute jumps into the jungle. . . .

IRENE [*still laughing*]. Oh—you amuse me.

HARRY. It's a pleasure to be entertaining. But you can't get away with it.

IRENE. You amuse me very much indeed. Here we are—on a mountain peak in Bedlam. Tonight, the Italians are bombing Paris. At this moment, the French may be bombing Rome, and the English bombing Germany—and the Soviets bombing Tokyo, and all you worry about is whether I am a girl you once met casually in Omaha.

HARRY. Did I say it was casual?

IRENE [*laughing*]. Oh—it *is* amusing!

HARRY [*angrily*]. I know you're amused. I admit it's all

very funny. I've admitted everything. I told you I was crazy about you. Now when are you going to give me a break and tell me—

IRENE. You! You are so troubled—so—so uncertain about everything.

HARRY. I'm not uncertain about it any more, babe. I had you tagged from the start. There was something about you that was indelible . . . something I couldn't forget all these years.

[WEBER *appears on the gallery, wearing his Sulka dressing gown.*]

WEBER. Forgive me for intruding, my dear. But I suggest that it's time for you to go to bed.

IRENE. Yes, Achille. At once. [WEBER *treats* HARRY *to a rather disparaging glance and exits.* IRENE *starts upstairs.*] Poor Achille! He suffers with the most dreadful insomnia—it is something on his mind. [*She goes up a few more steps.*] He is like Macbeth. Good night, my friend—my funny friend.

HARRY. Good night.

IRENE. And thank you for making me laugh so much—tonight.

HARRY. I could still teach you that code.

IRENE. Perhaps—we shall meet again in—what was the name of the hotel?

HARRY. It was the Governor Bryan.

IRENE. Oh, yes! The Governor Bryan! [*Laughing heartily, she exits.*]

[HARRY *goes to the piano, sits down and starts to play* "Kak Stranna." DUMPTSY *enters from the bar.*]

DUMPTSY. That was wonderful—that singing and dancing.

HARRY [*still playing*]. Thanks, pal. Glad you enjoyed it.

DUMPTSY. Oh, yes, Mr. Van—that was good.

HARRY [*bangs a chord*]. Chaliapin—for God's *sake!*

DUMPTSY. I beg your pardon, sir?

HARRY [*rises*]. It's nothing. Good night, Dumptsy. [*He goes out into the lobby.*]

DUMPTSY. Good night, sir. [*He starts for the bar.*]

CURTAIN

Act three

The following afternoon.

HARRY *is at the piano, idly playing the "Caprice Viennoise," or something similar. His thoughts are elsewhere.*

SHIRLEY *is darning some stockings and humming the tune.* BEBE *is plucking her eyebrows.*

BEULAH, ELAINE, FRANCINE *and* EDNA *are seated at a table.* BEULAH *is telling* ELAINE'S *fortune with cards. The others are watching. All are intensely serious, and all chewing gum.*

SHIRLEY. What's that number, Harry?

HARRY. The "Caprice Viennoise"—Kreisler.

SHIRLEY. It's pretty.

HARRY. You think so? [*He shifts to something jazzier.*]

BEULAH. You are going to marry.

ELAINE. Again?

BEULAH. The cards indicate dis*tinctly* two marriages, and maybe a third.

ELAINE [*chewing furiously*]. For *God's* sake!

SHIRLEY [*to* HARRY]. We certainly need some new stockings.

HARRY. We'll renovate the wardrobe in Geneva.

BEULAH. Now—let's see what the fates tell us next.

BEBE. Say, Harry—when do we lam it out of here?

HARRY. Ask Beulah. Maybe she can get it out of the cards.

BEBE. I hate this place. It's spooky.

BEULAH [*to* HARRY]. What'd you say, honey?

ELAINE. Ah—don't pay any attention to him. What else do they say about me?

BEULAH. Well . . . you'll enter upon a period of very poor health.

ELAINE. When?

BEULAH. Along about your thirty-seventh year.

SHIRLEY. That means any day now. [*She winks broadly at* BEBE, *who laughs.*]

HARRY [*vehemently*]. Listen to me, you nymphs! We can't be wasting our time with card tricks. We've got to do a little rehearsing.

SHIRLEY. Why, Harry—what are you mad about now?

HARRY. Who said I was mad about anything?

SHIRLEY. Well—every time you get yourself into a peeve, you take it out on us. You start in hollering, "Listen, girls—we got to rehearse."

HARRY. I am not peeved. Merely a little disgusted. The act needs brushing up.

BEBE. Honestly, Harry—don't you think we know the routine by now?

HARRY. I'm not saying you don't know it. I'm just saying that your performance last night grieved me and shocked me. You had your eyes on those officers and not on your work. That kind of attitude went big in Rumania, but now we're going to a town where artistry counts. Some day, I'll take the whole bunch of you to watch the Russian ballet, just to give you an idea of what dancing is.

[CAPTAIN LOCICERO *comes in.*]

CAPTAIN. Your pardon, Mr. Van.

HARRY. Ah, Captain. Good afternoon. . . . Rest, girls.

CAPTAIN [*to the* GIRLS]. Good afternoon.

GIRLS. Good afternoon, Captain.

HARRY. You bring us news?

CAPTAIN. Good news, I hope. May I have your passports?

HARRY. Certainly. [*He gets them out of his coat and hands them to the* CAPTAIN.]

CAPTAIN. Thank you. I hope to have definite word for you very shortly. [*He salutes and starts to go.*]

HARRY. What about Mr. Quillery, Captain? What's happened to him?

CAPTAIN. Mr. Quillery was very injudicious. Very injudicious. I am glad that you are so much more intelligent. [*He goes out.*]

SHIRLEY. I don't think they could have done anything cruel to him. They're awfully sweet boys, those Wops.

HARRY. So I observed. . . . Now listen to me, girls. Geneva's a key spot, and we've got to be good. Your audiences there won't be a lot of hunkies who don't care what you do as long as you don't wear practically any pants. These people are accustomed to the best. They're mains—big people, like prime ministers, and maharajahs and archbishops. If we click with them, we'll be set for London and Paris. We may even make enough money to get us home!

BEBE. Oh—don't speak of such a thing! Home!

EDNA. To get a real decent henna wash again!

HARRY. The trouble with all of you is, you're thinking too much about your own specialties. You're trying to steal the act, and wreck it. Remember what the late Knute Rockne said: "Somebody else can have the all-star, all-American aggregations. All *I* want is a team!" Now, you—Beulah. You've got plenty of chance to score individually in the bubble number. But when we're doing the chorus routine, you've got to submerge your genius in the mass.

BEULAH. What do I do wrong, honey?

HARRY. Your Maxie Ford is lackluster. Here—I'll show you. . . . [HARRY *gets up to demonstrate the Maxie Ford.*]

SHIRLEY [*laughs*]. If you do it that way, Beulah, you'll go flat on your face. Here—*I'll* show you.

HARRY. Just a minute, Miss Laughlin. Who's the director of this act, you or me?

SHIRLEY [*amiably*]. You are, you old poop. But you just don't know the steps.

ELAINE. Don't let her get fresh, Harry.

BEBE. Slap her down!

SHIRLEY. Give us the music, Harry.

BEULAH. Please, Harry. Shirley just wants to be helpful.

HARRY. I feel I should resent this—but— [*He returns to the piano.*] Go ahead, Miss Laughlin. Carry on. [*He plays.* SHIRLEY *demonstrates.* BEULAH *tries it.*]

BEULAH. Have I got it right?

SHIRLEY. Sure! He's just shooting his face off!

[*During this, the following conversation goes on.*]

ELAINE. You know that Wop that was giving me a play last night?

FRANCINE. You mean the one with the bent nose?

BEBE. I thought he was terrible. But that boy I had is a Count.

ELAINE. Well, look what he gave me.

EDNA. What is it?

BEBE. Let me see it.

ELAINE. I don't know what it is.

BEBE. Looks like money. What kind of money is that, Harry.

HARRY. It's an old Roman coin.

SHIRLEY. How much is it worth?

HARRY. I haven't looked up the latest rate of exchange on dinars. But I think, dear, you've been betrayed. Now, pay attention, girls. . . . As I said, we've got to improve the act, and with that in view, I'm going to retire from all the dance routine.

BEBE. What?

BEULAH. Why, *Harry*—we couldn't. . . .

SHIRLEY. Oh! I hurt you, didn't I! [*She rushes to him, coos over him.*] Yes, I did, you poor baby. I hurt his feelings—and I'm sorry—I'm very, very sorry.

HARRY. All right, Shirley. We can dispense with the regrets. Save your lipstick. [*He thrusts her away.*]

SHIRLEY. But why . . . ?

HARRY. I've decided that I'm a thinker, rather than a performer. From now on, I shall devote myself to the purely creative end of the act, and, of course, the negotiation of contracts.

BEULAH. But when did you make up your mind to this, honey?

HARRY. I've been considering it for a long time.

SHIRLEY. Say! What were you talking about to that Russian dame?

HARRY. We discussed world politics.

FRANCINE. Oh!

SHIRLEY. And how are politics these days?

BEBE. Did you get anywheres near to first base, Harry?

HARRY. I find it impossible to explain certain things to you girls. You're children of nature.

SHIRLEY. We're *what*?

BEULAH. He means we're natural.

HARRY. Never mind, sweetheart. You'll sing the number, Shirley.

SHIRLEY. Me?

BEBE. With that terrible voice?

HARRY. She handled it fine that time I had bronchitis in Belgrade. And with a little rehearsal, you'll have the whole League of Nations rooting for you. Now—let's have it. [*He plays,* SHIRLEY *sings,* BEBE *disapproves.*]

[DON *comes in, dressed for traveling.*]

DON. Captain Locicero has got the orders to let us through and the train is due to leave about four o'clock. What a relief to be out of this foul place!

HARRY. You going too, Don?

DON. Yes. There's nothing for me here. In fact, I'm sick and tired of Europe as a whole. I was in town this morning when they shot Quillery.

BEBE. Who?

SHIRLEY. It was that little guy that bawled out the Wops.

BEULAH. They *shot* him? Why did they have to do that?

DON. Of course, he asked for it. But even so, it's pretty sickening to see one of your fellow human beings crumpled up in horrible, violent death. Well—there'll be plenty more like him, and right here, too. The French know all about this air base, and they'll be over any minute with their bombs. So—it's California here I come!

HARRY. And run right into the Japs? Better stop off at Wichita.

DON. I'll see you all on the train. [*He goes up the stairs.*]

HARRY. You girls go get yourselves ready.

[*The* CHERRYS *appear on the gallery.* DON *speaks to them, then goes out. The* CHERRYS *come down.*]

ELAINE. O.K., Harry.

EDNA [*going*]. I'm surprised at those Wops. They seemed like such sweet boys.

BEBE. Sure—when they talk they sound like opera. But they're awful excitable.

[BEBE, ELAINE, EDNA *and* FRANCINE *have gone out.*]

BEULAH. But I can't understand—why did they have to shoot that poor boy?

HARRY. It's hard to explain, Beulah. But it seems

there's some kind of argument going on over here, and the only way they can settle it is by murdering a lot of people.

BEULAH. You don't need to tell *me* what it's like. I was in the Club Grotto the night the Purple Gang shot it out with the G's. And was that terrible! Blood all over everything!

[SHIRLEY *and* BEULAH *have gone out.*]

HARRY. You heard what they did to Quillery?

CHERRY. Yes. It seems that he died like a true patriot, shouting "Vive La France."

HARRY. Better if he died like a man—sticking to what he knew was right.

CHERRY. He was a nice little chap.

MRS. CHERRY. The Italians are swine!

[DON *reappears on the balcony and comes down.*]

CHERRY. Oh, they had a perfect right to do it.

MRS. CHERRY. But to kill a man for saying what he thinks!

CHERRY. Many people will be killed for less than that.

HARRY. I'll have to be saying good-bye pretty soon. Did you say the train goes at four, Don?

DON. Four o'clock. Correct! [*He goes.*]

HARRY. I hope all this unpleasantness won't spoil your winter sports.

CHERRY. Oh, that's all washed up. We're going, too—if they'll let us cross the border.

HARRY. So the honeymoon has ended already?

MRS. CHERRY. Yes—I suppose so.

CHERRY. England is coming into this business. We have to stand by France, of course. And so there's nothing for it but . . .

MRS. CHERRY. And so Jimmy will have to do his bit, manning the guns, for civilization. Perhaps he'll join in the bombardment of Florence, where we were married.

CHERRY. You know—after the ceremony we went into the Baptistery and prayed to the soul of Leonardo da Vinci that we might never fail in our devotion to that which is beautiful and true. I told you we were a bit on the romantic side. We forgot what Leonardo said about war. Bestial frenzy, he called it. And bestial frenzy it is.

MRS. CHERRY. But we mustn't think about that now. We have to stand by France. We have to make the world a decent place for heroes to live in. Oh, Christ! [*She starts to sob.* CHERRY *rushes to her.*]

CHERRY. Now, now, darling. We've got to make a pretense of being sporting about it. Please, darling. Don't cry.

HARRY. Let her cry, the poor kid. Let her sob her heart out—for all the God-damned good it will do her. You know what I often think? [*He is trying to be tactful.*] I often think we ought to get together and elect somebody else God. Me, for instance. I'll bet I'd do a much better job.

MRS. CHERRY. You'd be fine, Mr. Van.

HARRY. I believe I would. There'd be a lot of people who would object to my methods. That Mr. Weber, for instance. I'd certainly begin my administration by beating the can off him.

CHERRY. Let's start the campaign now! Vote for good old Harry Van, and his Six Angels!

[*The* CAPTAIN *comes in with a brief-case full of papers and passports. He takes these out and puts them on a table.*]

CAPTAIN. Good afternoon, Mrs. Cherry. Gentlemen.

HARRY. Do we get across?

CAPTAIN. Here is your passport, Mr. Van—and the young ladies', with my compliments. They have been duly stamped. [*He hands them over.*]

HARRY. Thanks, Captain. And how about Mr. Weber

and his—friend? Are they going, too?

CAPTAIN. I have their passports here. I advise you to make ready, Mr. Van. The train will leave in about forty-five minutes.

HARRY. O.K., Captain. See you later, Mr. and Mrs. Cherry. [*He goes.*]

CHERRY. O.K., Harry.

MRS. CHERRY. And what about us, Captain?

CAPTAIN. Due to a slight technicality, you will be permitted to cross the frontier. Here are your passports.

CHERRY. I can't tell you how grateful we are.

[WEBER *appears on the gallery.*]

CAPTAIN. You needn't be grateful to me, Mr. Cherry. The fact that you are allowed to pass is due to the superb centralization of authority in my country. The telegram authorizing your release was filed at 11:43 today, just seventeen minutes before a state of war was declared between Great Britain and Italy. I must obey the order of Rome, even though I know it's out of date. Is your luggage ready?

CHERRY. It's all out here in the hall. We're off now, Captain. Well, good-bye and good luck!

CAPTAIN. And good luck to you—both of you.

CHERRY. I need hardly say that I'm sorry about all this. It's really a damned rotten shame.

CAPTAIN. It is. All of that. Good-bye, my friend. [*He extends his hand and Cherry shakes it.*] Madame. . . . [*He extends his hand to* MRS. CHERRY.]

MRS. CHERRY. Don't call *me* your friend, because I say what Quillery said—damn you—damn your whole country of mad dogs for having started this horror.

CAPTAIN [*bows*]. It is not my fault, Mrs. Cherry.

CHERRY. It's utterly unfair to talk that way, darling. The Captain is doing his miserable duty as decently as he possibly can.

CAPTAIN [*tactfully*]. In this unhappy situation, we are

all in danger of losing our heads.

MRS. CHERRY. I know . . . I know. Forgive me for the outburst. [*She extends her hand to the* CAPTAIN *and they shake.*] I should have remembered that it's everybody's fault.

CHERRY. That's right, my sweet. Come along. [*They go out.*]

CAPTAIN [*to* WEBER]. Frankly, my heart bleeds for them.

WEBER. They're young. They'll live through it, and be happy.

CAPTAIN. Will they? I was their age, and in their situation, twenty years ago, when I was sent to the Isonzo front. And people said just that to me: "Never mind, you are young—and youth will survive and come to triumph." And I believed it. That is why I couldn't say such deceiving words to them now.

WEBER. The cultivation of hope never does any immediate harm. Is everything in order?

CAPTAIN [*rises*]. Quite, Monsieur Weber. Here it is. [*He hands over* WEBER'S *passport.*]

WEBER. And Madame's?

[*The* CAPTAIN *picks up a document on foolscap.*]

CAPTAIN. This is an unusual kind of passport. It has given us some worry.

WEBER. The League of Nations issues documents like that to those whose nationality is uncertain.

CAPTAIN. I understand—but the attitude of Italy toward the League of Nations is not at the moment cordial.

WEBER. Then you refuse to honor Madame's passport?

CAPTAIN. My instructions are to accord you every consideration, Monsieur Weber. In view of the fact that Madame is traveling with you, I shall be glad to approve her visa.

WEBER. Madame is not traveling with me. She has her own passport.

CAPTAIN. But it is understood that you vouch for her, and that is enough to satisfy the authorities.

WEBER [*with cold authority*]. Vouch for her? It is not necessary for anyone to vouch for Madame! She is entirely capable of taking care of herself. If her passport is not entirely in order, it is no affair of mine.

CAPTAIN [*genuinely distressed*]. But—I must tell you, Monsieur Weber—this is something I do not like. This places me in a most embarrassing position. I shall be forced to detain her.

WEBER. You are a soldier, my dear Captain, and you should be used to embarrassing positions. Undoubtedly you were embarrassed this morning, when you had to shoot that confused pacifist, Quillery. But this is war, and unpleasant responsibilities descend upon you and on me as well. However . . . [*He sees* HARRY, *who is coming in.*] I shall attend to my luggage. Thank you, Captain. [*He goes out.*]

CAPTAIN. Don't mention it. [*To* HARRY.] The young ladies are ready?

HARRY. Yes—they're ready. And some of your aviators are out there trying to talk them into staying here permanently.

CAPTAIN [*smiling*]. And I add my entreaties to theirs.

HARRY. We won't have any more trouble, will we?

[*The* DOCTOR *appears on the gallery with coat, hat, books done in a bundle, and umbrella. He comes downstairs.*]

CAPTAIN. Oh, no, Mr. Van. Geneva is a lovely spot. All of Switzerland is beautiful, these days. I envy you going there, in such charming company.

HARRY. Hi, Doctor. Have you got the rats all packed?

DOCTOR. Good afternoon. I am privileged to go now? [*He puts down all of his belongings and crosses.*]

CAPTAIN. Yes, Dr. Waldersee. Here is your passport.

DOCTOR. Thank you. [*He examines the passport carefully.*]

HARRY. I can tell you, Doctor—I'm going to be proud to have known you. When I read in the papers that you've wiped out cancer and won the Nobel prize, and you're the greatest hero on earth, I'll be able to say, "He's a personal friend of mine. He once admired my music."

DOCTOR [*solemnly*]. Thank you very much. [*To the* CAPTAIN.] This visa is good for crossing the Austrian border?

CAPTAIN. Certainly. But you are going to Zurich?

DOCTOR [*rises*]. I have changed my plans. I am going back into Germany. Germany is at war. Perhaps I am needed. [*He crosses to pick up his coat.*]

HARRY. Needed for what?

DOCTOR. I shall offer my services for what they are worth.

[HARRY *goes to help him on with his coat.*]

HARRY. But what about the rats?

DOCTOR [*fiercely*]. Why should I save people who don't want to be saved—so that they can go out and exterminate each other? Obscene maniacs! [*Starts to put on his gloves.*] Then I'll be a maniac, too. Only I'll be more dangerous than most of them. For I know all the tricks of death! And—as for my rats, maybe they'll be useful. Britain will put down the blockade again, and we shall be starving—and maybe I'll cut my rats into filets and eat them. [*He laughs, not pleasantly, and picks up his umbrella and books.*]

HARRY. Wait a minute, Doctor. You're doing this without thinking. . . .

DOCTOR. I'm thinking probably that remedy you sold is better than mine. Hasten to apply it. We are all diseased. . . .

HARRY. But you can't change around like this! Have you forgotten all the things you told me? All that about backsliding?

DOCTOR. No, I have not forgotten the degradation of mankind—that is painful and offensive to conceive. [*He is going out.*] I am sorry to disappoint you about the Nobel prize. [*He has gone.*]

HARRY. Good-bye, Doctor. [*He sits down, wearily.*] Why in the name of God can't somebody answer the question that everybody asks? Why? Why? Oh—I know the obvious answers, but they aren't good enough. Weber—and a million like him—they can't take credit for *all* of this! Who is it that did this dirty trick on a lot of decent people? And why do you let them get away with it? That's the thing that I'd like to know!

CAPTAIN. We have avalanches up here, my friend. They are disastrous. They start with a little crack in the ice, so tiny that one cannot see it, until, suddenly, it bursts wide open. And then it is too late.

HARRY. That's very effective, Captain. But it don't satisfy me, because this avalanche isn't made out of ice. It's made out of flesh and blood—and—and *brains.* . . . It's God-damned bad management—that's what it is! [*This last is half to himself.*]

[IRENE *has appeared on the gallery and started to come down.*]

IRENE. Still upset about the situation, Mr. Van? Ah—good afternoon, my dear Captain Locicero.

CAPTAIN. Good afternoon, madame.

IRENE. I have had the most superb rest here. The atmosphere is so calm, and impersonal, and soothing. I can't bear to think that we're going to Biarritz, with the dull, dismal old sea pounding in my ears.

[WEBER *comes in.*]

IRENE. We are leaving now, Achille?

WEBER. I believe that some difficulties have arisen. [*He looks toward the* CAPTAIN.]

IRENE. Difficulties?

CAPTAIN. I regret, madame, that there must be some further delay.

IRENE. Oh! Then the train is not going through, after all?

CAPTAIN. The train is going, madame. But this passport of yours presents problems which, under the circumstances—

IRENE. Monsieur Weber will settle the problems, whatever they are. Won't you, Achille?

WEBER. There is some question about your nationality, Irene.

CAPTAIN [*referring to the passport*]. It states here, madame, that your birthplace is uncertain, but assumed to be Armenia.

IRENE. That is a province of Russia!

CAPTAIN. You subsequently became a resident of England, then of the United States, and then of France.

IRENE [*angrily*]. Yes—it's all there—clearly stated. I have never before had the slightest difficulty about my passport. It was issued by the League of Nations.

WEBER. I'm afraid the standing of the League of Nations is not very high in Italy at this moment.

CAPTAIN. The fact is, madame, the very existence of the League is no longer recognized by our government. For that reason, we can not permit you to cross the frontier at this time. [*She looks at him and then at* WEBER. *The* CAPTAIN *hands her the passport.*] I'm sure you will appreciate the delicacy of my position. Perhaps we shall be able to adjust the matter tomorrow. [*He salutes and goes out, glad to escape.* HARRY *goes with him, asking, "What's the trouble, Captain? Can't something be done about it?"*]

WEBER. I should of course wait over, Irene. But you

know how dangerous it is for me to delay my return to France by so much as one day. I have been in touch with our agents. The premier is demanding that production be doubled—trebled—at once.

IRENE. Of course.

WEBER. Here— [*He takes out an envelope containing money.*] This will cover all possible expenses. [*He gives her the envelope.*] There is a train for Venice this evening. You must go there and see Lanza. I have already sent him full instructions.

IRENE. Yes, Achille. And I thank you for having managed this very, very tactfully.

WEBER [*smiles*]. You are a genuinely superior person, my dear. It is a privilege to have known you.

IRENE. Thank you again, Achille. Good-bye.

WEBER. Good-bye, Irene. [*He kisses her hand.* HARRY *returns.*] Coming, Mr. Van?

HARRY. In a minute. [WEBER *goes.* IRENE *puts the money in her handbag.*] Tough luck, babe.

IRENE. It's no matter.

HARRY. I just talked to the Captain and he isn't going to be as brutal as the Bolsheviks were. I mean, you won't suffer any bayonet wounds. He'll fix it for you to get through tomorrow.

IRENE. You want to be encouraging, my dear friend. But it's no use. The Italian government has too many reasons for wishing to detain me. They'll see to it that I disappear—quietly—and completely.

HARRY. Yes—I know all about that.

IRENE. All about what?

HARRY. You're a person of tremendous significance. You always were.

[SHIRLEY *appears at the left.*]

SHIRLEY. Hey, Harry! It's time for us to go.

HARRY. I'll be right out.

[SHIRLEY *goes.*]

IRENE. Go away—go away with your friends. If I am to die, it is no concern of yours!

HARRY. Listen, babe—I haven't any wish to . . .

IRENE [*flaming*]. And please don't call me *babe!* [*She stands up and walks away from him. He follows her.*]

HARRY. My apologies, madame. I just call everybody "babe."

IRENE. Perhaps that's why I do not like it!

HARRY. Even if I don't believe anything you say, I can see pretty plainly that you're in a tough spot. And considering what we were to each other in the old Governor Bryan Hotel—

IRENE. Must you always be in Omaha?

HARRY. I'd like to help you, Irene. Isn't there something I can do?

IRENE. I thank you, from my heart, I thank you, for that offer. But it's useless. . . .

HARRY. You don't have to thank me. Tell me—what can I do?

IRENE. You're very kind, and very gallant. But, unfortunately, you're no match for Achille Weber. He has decided that I shall remain here and his decision is final!

HARRY. Is he responsible for them stopping you?

IRENE. Of course he is. I knew it the moment I saw that ashamed look on Captain Locicero's face, when he refused to permit me . . .

HARRY. So Weber double-crossed you, did he! What has the son of a bitch got against you?

IRENE. He's afraid of me. I know too much about his methods of promoting his own business.

HARRY. Everybody knows about his methods. Little Quillery was talking about them last night. . . .

IRENE. Yes—and what happened to Quillery? That's what happens to everyone who dares to criticize him. Last night I did the one thing he could never forgive. I told him the truth! At last I told him just what I think. And now—you see how quickly he strikes back!

[SHIRLEY *and* BEBE *appear.*]

SHIRLEY. Harry! The bus is going to leave.

HARRY. All right—all right!

BEBE. But we got to go this *minute!*

HARRY. I'll be with you. Get out!

SHIRLEY [*as they go*]. Can you imagine? He stops everything to make another pass at that Russian. [*They have gone.*]

IRENE. Go ahead—go ahead! You can't help me! No one can! [*He picks up his coat and hat.*] But—if it will make you any happier in your future travels with Les Blondes, I'll tell you, yes—I did know you, slightly, in Omaha!

HARRY [*peering at her*]. Are you lying again?

IRENE. It was room 974. Does that convince you?

HARRY [*ferociously*]. How can I remember what room it was?

IRENE [*smiling*]. Well, then—you'll never be sure, Mr. Van.

BEBE'S VOICE. Harry!

SHIRLEY'S VOICE. For God's sake, Harry!

DON [*appearing*]. We can't wait another instant! [*DON goes.*]

SHIRLEY'S VOICE. Come *on!*

HARRY [*he turns and starts for the door, addressing the* GIRLS *en route*]. All right, God damn it! [*He goes out.*]

[IRENE *takes out her vanity case, and does something to her face. She takes off her hat and cloak.* DUMPTSY *comes in from the back. He is wearing the uniform of a private in the Italian army, with gas mask at the alert, and a full pack on his back.*]

DUMPTSY. Good afternoon, madame.

IRENE [*turning*]. Why, Dumptsy—what is that costume?

DUMPTSY. They called me up. Look! I'm an Italian soldier.

IRENE. You look splendid!

DUMPTSY. If you please, madame. But why didn't you go on that bus?

IRENE. I've decided to stay and enjoy the winter sports.

DUMPTSY. I don't think this is a good place any more, madame. They say the war is very big—bigger than last time.

IRENE. Yes—I hear that on all sides.

DUMPTSY. The French will be here to drop bombs on everybody.

IRENE. It will be thrilling for us if they do. Won't it, Dumptsy?

DUMPTSY. Maybe it will, madame. But—I came to say good-bye to Auguste, the barman, and Anna, the maid. They're both cousins of mine. They'll laugh when they see me in these clothes. [*He goes to the left.*] Can I get you anything, madame?

IRENE. Yes, Dumptsy. I'll have a bottle of champagne. Bring two glasses. We'll have a drink together.

DUMPTSY. If you please, madame. [DUMPTSY *goes into the bar.*]

[IRENE *lights a cigarette and goes up to the window to look out.* PITTALUGA *comes in.*]

PITTALUGA. Your luggage is in the hall, madame. Will you wish it taken to the same suite?

IRENE. No—I didn't really care much for those rooms. Have you anything smaller?

PITTALUGA [*in a less deferential tone*]. We have smaller rooms on the other side of the hotel.

IRENE. I'll have the smallest. It will be cozier.

PITTALUGA. You wish to go to it now?

IRENE. No. You can send up the luggage. I'll look at it later.

[PITTALUGA *bows and goes.* DUMPTSY *returns with the champagne.*]

DUMPTSY. I was right, madame. Auguste laughed very much.

IRENE [*coming down*]. What will happen to your wife and children, Dumptsy?

DUMPTSY. Oh—I suppose the Fascisti will feed them. They promised to feed all the families with a man who is out fighting for their country. [*He has filled her glass. She sits down.*]

IRENE. Go ahead and pour yourself one, Dumptsy.

DUMPTSY. Thank you so much, madame. I wasn't sure I heard correctly.

IRENE. Here's to you, Dumptsy—and to Austria.

DUMPTSY. And to you, madame, if you please.

IRENE. Thank you. [*They drink.*]

DUMPTSY. And may you soon be restored to your home in Petersburg.

IRENE. Petersburg?

DUMPTSY. Yes, madame. Your home.

IRENE [*with a slight smile*]. Ah, yes. My home! [*They drink again.*] And have no fear for the future, Dumptsy. Whatever happens—have no fear!

DUMPTSY. If you please, madame. [*He finishes his drink.*] And now I must go find Anna, if you will excuse me.

IRENE. Here, Dumptsy. [*She hands him a note of money.*] Good-bye, and God bless you.

DUMPTSY. Thank you so much, madame. [DUMPTSY *leans over and kisses her hand.*] Kiss die hand, madame.

[*The* CAPTAIN *and* MAJOR *come in from the lobby.* DUMPTSY *salutes, strenuously, and goes out. The* MAjor *goes across and into the bar. The* captain *is following him.*]

IRENE. Some champagne, Captain?

CAPTAIN. No, thank you very much.

IRENE. You needn't be anxious to avoid me, Captain. I know perfectly well that it wasn't your fault.

CAPTAIN. You are very understanding, madame.

IRENE. Yes—that's true. I am one of the most remarkably understanding people on earth. [*She swallows her drink.*] I understand so damned much that I am here, alone, on this cold mountain, and I have no one to turn to, nowhere to go. . . .

CAPTAIN. If I can be of service to you in any way . . .

IRENE. I know you'll be kind, Captain Locicero. And faultlessly polite.

CAPTAIN [*with genuine sympathy*]. I realize, madame, that politeness means nothing now. But—under these tragic circumstances—what else can I do?

IRENE [*deliberately*]. What else can you do? I'll tell you what else you can do in these tragic circumstances. You can refuse to fight! Have you ever thought of that possibility? You can refuse to use those weapons that they have sold you! But—you were going into the bar. Please don't let me detain you.

CAPTAIN. You will forgive me, madame?

IRENE. Fully, my dear Captain. . . . Fully.

CAPTAIN. Thank you. [*He salutes and goes into the bar.*]

[IRENE *pours herself another drink. Then she picks it up, goes to the piano, and starts to play a sketchy accompaniment for "Kak Stranna." She seems to be pretty close to tears. Perhaps she does cry a little, thoroughly enjoying the emotion.* HARRY *comes in wearing his snappy overcoat and his hat. He pays no attention to her, as he takes off his coat and hat and throws them down somewhere.*]

IRENE. Did you have some trouble?

HARRY. No. Whose is that champagne?

IRENE. Mine. Won't you have some?

HARRY. Thanks.

IRENE. Dumptsy used that glass.

HARRY. That's all right. [*He fills the glass and drinks.*]

IRENE. What happened? Didn't the train go?

HARRY. Yes—the train went. . . . I got the girls on board. Mr. and Mrs. Cherry promised to look out for them. They'll be O.K.

IRENE. And you came back—to me?

HARRY [*curtly*]. It seems fairly obvious that I did come back. [*He refills his glass.*]

IRENE. You meant it when you said that you wanted to help me.

HARRY. You said I'd never be sure. Well—I came back to tell you I *am* sure! I got thinking back, in the bus, and I came to the conclusion that it *was* Room 974 or close to it, anyway. And somehow or other, I couldn't help feeling rather flattered, and touched, to think that with all the sordid hotel rooms you've been in, you should have remembered that one. [*He has some more champagne.*]

IRENE [*after a moment*]. Bayard is not dead!

HARRY. Who?

IRENE. The Chevalier Bayard.

HARRY. Oh?

IRENE. Somewhere in that funny, music-hall soul of yours is the spirit of Leander, and Abelard, and Galahad. You give up everything—risk your life— walk unafraid into the valley of the shadow—to aid and comfort a damsel in distress. Isn't that the truth?

HARRY. Yes—it's the truth—plainly and simply put. [*He pours himself more champagne and drinks it quickly.*] Listen to me, babe—when are you going to break down and tell me who the hell are you?

IRENE. Does it matter so very much who I am?

HARRY. No.

IRENE. Give me some more champagne. [HARRY *goes to her and pours.*] My father was not one of the Romanoffs. But for many years, he was their guest—in Siberia. From him I learned that it is no use telling the truth to people whose whole life is a lie. But you —Harry—you are different. You are an honest man.

HARRY [*after a short pause*]. I am—am I? [*He crosses to the bar.*] Another bottle of champagne. . . . Hi, Captain.

CAPTAIN'S VOICE [*offstage in bar*]. What has happened, Mr. Van? Did you miss the train?

HARRY. No—just a God-damned fool. [*He closes the bar door.* IRENE *is gazing at him. He goes to her and kisses her.*]

IRENE. All these years—you've been surrounded by blondes—and you've loved only me!

HARRY. Now listen—we don't want to have any misunderstanding. If you're hooking up with me, it's only for professional reasons—see?

IRENE. Yes—I see.

HARRY. And what's more, I'm the manager. I'll fix it with the Captain for us to cross the border tomorrow, or the next day, or soon. We'll join up with the girls in Geneva—and that's as good a place as any to rehearse the code.

IRENE. The code! Of *course*—the code! I shall learn it easily.

HARRY. It's a very deep complicated scientific problem.

IRENE. You must tell it to me at once.

HARRY. At once! If you're unusually smart and apply yourself you'll have a fairly good idea of it after six months of study and rehearsal.

IRENE. A mind reader! Yes—you're quite right. I shall be able to do that very well!

[AUGUSTE *enters from the bar with a bottle of champagne. He refills their glasses, then refills* HARRY'S *glass, gives* HARRY *the bottle and goes back in to the bar.*]

HARRY. And, another thing, if you're going to qualify for this act with me, you've got to lay off liquor. I mean, after we finish this. It's a well-known fact that booze and science don't mix. [*He has another drink.* IRENE *is as one in a trance.*]

IRENE. I don't think I shall use my own name. No—Americans would mispronounce it horribly. No, I shall call myself—Namoura . . . Namoura the Great —assisted by Harry Van.

HARRY. You've got nice billing there.

IRENE. I shall wear a black velvet dress—very plain—My skin, ivory white. I must have something to hold. One white flower. No! A little white prayer book. That's it. A little white . . . [*The warning siren is heard.*] What's that?

HARRY. Sounds like a fire. [*The* CAPTAIN *and* MAJOR *burst out of the bar and rush to the big window, talking excitedly in Italian and pointing to the northwestern sky. The siren shrieks continue. The* MAJOR *then rushes out, the* CAPTAIN *about to follow him.*] What's up, Captain?

CAPTAIN. French aeroplanes. It is reprisal for last night. They are coming to destroy our base here.

HARRY. I see.

CAPTAIN. They have no reason to attack this hotel. But —there may easily be accidents. I advise the cellar.

[AUGUSTE *rushes in from the bar,* PITTALUGA *from the lobby. The latter orders* AUGUSTE *to lower the Venetian blinds.*]

IRENE. Oh, no, Captain. We must stay here and watch the spectacle.

CAPTAIN. I entreat you not to be reckless, madame. I have enough on my conscience now, without adding to it your innocent life!

IRENE. Don't worry, Captain. Death and I are old friends.

CAPTAIN. God be with you, madame. [*He goes out.*]

[HARRY *and* IRENE *empty their glasses.* HARRY *refills them. Airplane motors are heard, increasing. Then the sound of machine guns. Bombs are heard bursting at some distance.* AUGUSTE *and* PITTALUGA *go.*]

IRENE. Those are bombs.

HARRY. I guess so.

IRENE. We're in the war, Harry.

HARRY. What do you think we ought to do about it? Go out and say "Boo"?

IRENE. Let them be idiotic if they wish. We are sane. Why don't you try singing something?

HARRY. The voice don't feel appropriate. Too bad we haven't got Chaliapin here. [*She laughs.*] You know, babe—you look better blonde.

IRENE. Thank you.

[PITTALUGA *runs in.*]

PITTALUGA. The French beasts are bombing us! Everyone goes into the cellar.

HARRY. Thanks very much, Signor.

PITTALUGA. You have been warned! [*He rushes out.*]

IRENE. Ridiculous! Here we are, on top of the world—and he asks us to go down into the cellar. . . . Do you want to go into the cellar?

HARRY. Do you?

IRENE. No. If a bomb hits, it will be worse in the cellar. [*He holds her close to him. She kisses him.*] I love you, Harry.

HARRY. You do, eh!

IRENE. Ever since that night—in the Governor Bryan Hotel—I've loved you. Because I knew that you have a heart that I can trust. And that whatever I would say to you, I would never—*never* be misunderstood.

HARRY. That's right, babe. I told you I had you tagged, right from the beginning.

IRENE. And you adore me, don't you, darling?

HARRY. No! Now lay off—

IRENE. No—of course not—you mustn't admit it!

HARRY. Will you please stop pawing me? [*She laughs and lets go of him.*]

[HARRY *pours more champagne, as she crosses to the window, opens the slats of the blinds, and looks out. There is now great noise of planes, machine guns and bombs.*]

IRENE. Oh, you must see this! It's superb! [*He crosses to the window with his glass and looks out. The light on the stage is growing dimmer, but a weird light comes from the window. The scream of many gas bombs is heard.*] It's positively Wagnerian—isn't it?

HARRY. It looks to me exactly like "Hell's Angels." Did you ever see that picture, babe?

IRENE. No. I don't care for films.

HARRY. I *do*. I love 'em—every one of them. [*He is dragging her to the piano—a comparatively safe retreat.*] Did you know I used to play the piano in picture theatres? Oh, sure—I know all the music there is. [*They are now at the piano—*HARRY *sitting,* IRENE *standing close by him. She is looking toward the window. He starts to accompany the air raid with the "Ride of the Valkyries." There is a loud explosion.*]

IRENE. Harry . . .

HARRY. Yes, babe?

IRENE. Harry—do you realize that the whole world has gone to war? The *whole world!*

HARRY. I realize it. But don't ask me why. Because I've stopped trying to figure it out.

IRENE. I know why it is. It's just for the purpose of killing *us* . . . you and me. [*There is another loud explosion.* HARRY *stops playing.*] Because we are the little people—and for us the deadliest weapons are the most merciful. . . .

[*Another loud explosion.* HARRY *drinks.*]

HARRY. They're getting closer.

IRENE. Play some more. [*He resumes the* "Valkyrie."] Harry—do you know any hymns?

HARRY. What?

IRENE. Do you know any hymns?

HARRY. Certainly. [*He starts to play* "Onward, Christian Soldiers" *in furious jazz time, working in strains of* "Dixie." *There is another fearful crash, shattering the pane of the big window. He drags her down beside him at the piano.* HARRY *resumes* "Onward, Christian Soldiers" *in a slow, solemn tempo.*]

HARRY [*sings*]. Onward, Christian Soldiers—

[IRENE *joins the loud singing.*]

BOTH [*singing*].
　　　　　Marching as to war—
　　　　　With the Cross of Jesus
　　　　　Going on before. . . .

[*The din is now terrific. Demolition-bombs, gas-bombs, airplanes, shrapnel, machine guns.*]

CURTAIN

OF MICE AND MEN

by John Steinbeck

Copyright, 1937, by John Steinbeck
Published by The Viking Press, Inc., New York

First production, November 23, 1937,
at the Music Box Theatre, New York,
with the following cast:

GEORGE, *Wallace Ford*
LENNIE, *Broderick Crawford*
CANDY, *John F. Hamilton*
THE BOSS, *Thomas Findlay*
CURLEY, *Sam Byrd*
CURLEY'S WIFE, *Claire Luce*
SLIM, *Will Geer*
CARLSON, *Charles Slattery*
WHIT, *Walter Baldwin*
CROOKS, *Leigh Whipper*

SYNOPSIS OF SCENES

ACT I
Scene 1. *A Sandy bank of the Salinas River.*
Thursday night.
Scene 2. *The interior of a bunkhouse. Late Friday*
morning.
ACT II
Scene 1. *The same as Act I, Scene 2. About seven-thirty*
Friday evening.
Scene 2. *The room of the stable buck, a lean-to.*
Ten o'clock Saturday evening.
ACT III
Scene 1. *One end of a great barn. Mid-afternoon, Sunday.*
Scene 2. *Same as Act I, Scene 1.*

TIME: *The present.*
PLACE: *An agricultural valley in Southern California.*

Act one

Thursday night.

A sandy bank of the Salinas River sheltered with willows—one giant sycamore right, upstage.

The stage is covered with dry leaves. The feeling of the stage is sheltered and quiet.

Stage is lit by a setting sun.

Curtain rises on an empty stage. A sparrow is singing. There is a distant sound of ranch dogs barking aimlessly and one clear quail call. The quail call turns to a warning call and there is a beat of the flock's wings. Two figures are seen entering the stage in single file, with GEORGE, *the short man, coming in ahead of* LENNIE. *Both men are carrying blanket rolls. They approach the water. The small man throws down his blanket roll, the large man follows and then falls down and drinks from the river, snorting as he drinks.*

GEORGE [*irritably*]. Lennie, for God's sake, don't drink so much. [*Leans over and shakes* LENNIE.] Lennie, you hear me! You gonna be sick like you was last night.

LENNIE [*dips his whole head under, hat and all. As he sits upon the bank, his hat drips down the back*]. That's good. You drink some, George. You drink some too.

GEORGE [*kneeling and dipping his finger in the water*]. I ain't sure it's good water. Looks kinda scummy to me.

LENNIE [*imitates, dipping his finger also*]. Look at them wrinkles in the water, George. Look what I done.

GEORGE [*drinking from his cupped palm*]. Tastes all right. Don't seem to be runnin' much, though. Lennie, you oughtn' to drink water when it ain't running. [*Hopelessly.*] You'd drink water out of a gutter if you was thirsty. [*He throws a scoop of water into his face and rubs it around with his hand, pushes himself back and embraces his knees. LENNIE, after watching him, imitates him in every detail.*]

GEORGE [*beginning tiredly and growing angry as he speaks*]. God damn it, we could just as well of rode clear to the ranch. That bus driver didn't know what he was talkin' about. "Just a little stretch down the highway," he says. "Just a little stretch" —damn near four miles. I bet he didn't want to stop at the ranch gate. . . . I bet he's too damn lazy to pull up. Wonder he ain't too lazy to stop at Soledad at all! [*Mumbling.*] Just a little stretch down the road.

LENNIE [*timidly*]. George?

GEORGE. Yeh . . . what you want?

LENNIE. Where we goin', George?

GEORGE [*jerks down his hat furiously*]. So you forgot that already, did you? So I got to tell you again! Jeez, you're a crazy bastard!

LENNIE [*softly*]. I forgot. I tried not to forget, honest to God, I did!

GEORGE. Okay, okay, I'll tell you again. . . . [*With sarcasm.*] I ain't got nothin' to do. Might just as well spen' all my time tellin' you things. You forgit 'em and I tell you again.

LENNIE [*continuing on from his last speech*]. I tried

and, tried, but it didn't do no good. I remember
about the rabbits, George!

GEORGE. The hell with the rabbits! You can't remember nothing but them rabbits. You remember settin' in that gutter on Howard Street and watchin'
that blackboard?

LENNIE [*delightedly*]. Oh, sure! I remember that . . .
but . . . wha'd we do then? I remember some girls
come by, and you says—

GEORGE. The hell with what I says! You remember
about us goin' in Murray and Ready's and they give
us work cards and bus tickets?

LENNIE [*confidently*]. Oh, sure, George . . . I remember
that now. [*Puts his hand into his side coat-pocket;
his confidence vanishes. Very gently.*] . . . George?

GEORGE. Huh?

LENNIE [*staring at the ground in despair*]. I ain't got
mine. I musta lost it.

GEORGE. You never had none. I got both of 'em here.
Think I'd let you carry your own work card?

LENNIE [*with tremendous relief*]. I thought I put it in
my side pocket. [*Puts his hand in his pocket again.*]

GEORGE [*looking sharply at him; and as he looks, LENNIE brings his hand out of his pocket*]. Wha'd you
take out of that pocket?

LENNIE [*cleverly*]. Ain't a thing in my pocket.

GEORGE. I know there ain't. You got it in your hand
now. What you got in your hand?

LENNIE. I ain't got nothing, George! Honest!

GEORGE. Come on, give it here!

LENNIE [*holds his closed hand away from GEORGE*]. It's
on'y a mouse!

GEORGE. A mouse? A live mouse?

LENNIE. No . . . just a dead mouse. [*Worriedly.*] I didn't
kill it. Honest. I found it. I found it dead.

GEORGE. Give it here!

LENNIE. Leave me have it, George.

GEORGE [*sternly*]. Give it here! [LENNIE *reluctantly gives him the mouse.*] What do you want of a dead mouse, anyway?

LENNIE [*in a propositional tone*]. I was petting it with my thumb while we walked along.

GEORGE. Well, you ain't pettin' no mice while you walk with me. Now let's see if you can remember where we're going. [GEORGE *throws it across the water into the brush.*]

LENNIE [*looks startled and then in embarrassment hides his face against his knees*]. I forgot again.

GEORGE. Jesus Christ! [*Resignedly.*] Well, look, we are gonna work on a ranch like the one we come from up north.

LENNIE. Up north?

GEORGE. In Weed!

LENNIE. Oh, sure I remember—in Weed.

GEORGE [*still with exaggerated patience*]. That ranch we're goin' to is right down there about a quarter mile. We're gonna go in and see the boss.

LENNIE [*repeats as a lesson*]. And see the boss!

GEORGE. Now, look! I'll give him the work tickets, but you ain't gonna say a word. You're just gonna stand there and not say nothing.

LENNIE. Not say nothing!

GEORGE. If he finds out what a crazy bastard you are, we won't get no job. But if he sees you work before he hears you talk, we're set. You got that?

LENNIE. Sure, George . . . sure, I got that.

GEORGE. Okay. Now when we go in to see the boss, what you gonna do?

LENNIE [*concentrating*]. I . . . I . . . I ain't gonna say nothing . . . jus' gonna stand there.

GEORGE [*greatly relieved*]. Good boy, that's swell! Now

say that over two or three times so you sure won't forget it.

LENNIE [*drones softly under his breath*]. I ain't gonna say nothing . . . I ain't gonna say nothing. . . . [*Trails off into a whisper.*]

GEORGE. And you ain't gonna do no bad things like you done in Weed neither.

LENNIE [*puzzled*]. Like I done in Weed?

GEORGE. So you forgot that too, did you?

LENNIE [*triumphantly*]. They run us out of Weed!

GEORGE [*disgusted*]. Run us out, hell! We run! They was lookin' for us, but they didn't catch us.

LENNIE [*happily*]. I didn't forget that, you bet.

GEORGE [*lies back on the sand, crosses his hands under his head. And again* LENNIE *imitates him*]. God, you're a lot of trouble! I could get along so easy and nice, if I didn't have you on my tail. I could live so easy!

LENNIE [*hopefully*]. We gonna work on a ranch, George.

GEORGE. All right, you got that. But we're gonna sleep here tonight, because . . . I want to. I want to sleep out.

[*The light is going fast, dropping into evening. A little wind whirls into the clearing and blows leaves. A dog howls in the distance.*]

LENNIE. Why ain't we goin' on to the ranch to get some supper? They got supper at the ranch.

GEORGE. No reason at all. I just like it here. Tomorrow we'll be goin' to work. I seen thrashing machines on the way down; that means we'll be buckin' grain bags. Bustin' a gut liftin' up them bags. Tonight I'm gonna lay right here an' look up! Tonight there ain't a grain bag or a boss in the world.

Tonight, the drinks is on the ... house. Nice house we got here, Lennie.

LENNIE [*gets up on his knees and looks down at* GEORGE, *plaintively*]. Ain't we gonna have no supper?

GEORGE. Sure we are. You gather up some dead willow sticks. I got three cans of beans in my bindle. I'll open 'em up while you get a fire ready. We'll eat 'em cold.

LENNIE [*companionably*]. I like beans with ketchup.

GEORGE. Well, we ain't got no ketchup. You go get the wood, and don't you fool around none. Be dark before long. [LENNIE *lumbers to his feet and disappears into the brush.* GEORGE *gets out the bean cans, opens two of them, suddenly turns his head and listens. A little sound of splashing comes from the direction that* LENNIE *has taken.* GEORGE *looks after him; shakes his head.* LENNIE *comes back carrying a few small willow sticks in his hand.*] All right, give me that mouse.

LENNIE [*with elaborate pantomime of innocence*]. What, George? I ain't got no mouse.

GEORGE [*holding out his hand*]. Come on! Give it to me! You ain't puttin' nothing over. [LENNIE *hesitates, backs away, turns and looks as if he were going to run. Coldly*]. You gonna give me that mouse or do I have to take a sock at you?

LENNIE. Give you what, George?

GEORGE. You know goddamn well, what! I want that mouse!

LENNIE [*almost in tears*]. I don't know why I can't keep it. It ain't nobody's mouse. I didn' steal it! I found it layin' right beside the road. [GEORGE *snaps his fingers sharply, and* LENNIE *lays the mouse in his hand.*] I wasn't doin' nothing bad with it. Just stroking it. That ain't bad.

GEORGE [*stands up and throws the mouse as far as he can into the brush, then he steps to the pool, and washes his hands*]. You crazy fool! Thought you could get away with it, didn't you? Don't you think I could see your feet was wet where you went in the water to get it? [LENNIE *whimpers like a puppy.*] Blubbering like a baby. Jesus Christ, a big guy like you! [LENNIE *tries to control himself, but his lips quiver and his face works with an effort.* GEORGE *puts his hand on* LENNIE's *shoulder for a moment.*] Aw, Lennie, I ain't takin' it away just for meanness. That mouse ain't fresh. Besides, you broke it pettin' it. You get a mouse that's fresh and I'll let you keep it a little while.

LENNIE. I don't know where there is no other mouse. I remember a lady used to give 'em to me. Ever' one she got she used to give it to me, but that lady ain't here no more.

GEORGE. Lady, huh! . . . Give me them sticks there. . . . Don't even remember who that lady was. That was your own Aunt Clara. She stopped givin' 'em to you. You always killed 'em.

LENNIE [*sadly and apologetically*]. They was so little. I'd pet 'em and pretty soon they bit my fingers and then I pinched their head a little bit and then they was dead . . . because they was so little. I wish we'd get the rabbits pretty soon, George. They ain't so little.

GEORGE. The hell with the rabbits! Come on, let's eat. [*The light has continued to go out of the scene so that when* GEORGE *lights the fire, it is the major light on the stage.* GEORGE *hands one of the open cans of beans to* LENNIE.] There's enough beans for four men.

LENNIE [*sitting on the other side of the fire, speaks patiently*]. I like 'em with ketchup.

GEORGE [*explodes*]. Well, we ain't got any. Whatever we ain't got, that's what you want. God Almighty, if I was alone, I could live so easy. I could go get a job of work and no trouble. No mess . . . and when the end of the month come, I could take my fifty bucks and go into town and get whatever I want. Why, I could stay in a cat-house all night. I could eat any place I want. Order any damn thing.

LENNIE [*plaintively, but softly*]. I didn't want no ketchup.

GEORGE [*continuing violently*]. I could do that every damn month. Get a gallon of whiskey or set in a pool room and play cards or shoot pool. [LENNIE *gets up to his knees and looks over the fire, with frightened face.*] And what have I got? [*Disgustedly.*] I got *you.* You can't keep a job and you lose me every job I get!

LENNIE [*in terror*]. I don't mean nothing, George.

GEORGE. Just keep me shovin' all over the country all the time. And that ain't the worst—you get in trouble. You do bad things and I got to get you out. It ain't bad people that raises hell. It's dumb ones. [*He shouts.*] You crazy son-of-a-bitch, you keep me in hot water all the time. [LENNIE *is trying to stop* GEORGE's *flow of words with his hands. Sarcastically.*] You just wanta feel that girl's dress. Just wanta pet it like it was a mouse. Well, how the hell'd she know you just wanta feel her dress? How'd she know you'd just hold onto it like it was a mouse?

LENNIE [*in panic*]. I didn't mean to, George!

GEORGE. Sure you didn't mean to. You didn't mean for her to yell bloody hell, either. You didn't mean for us to hide in the irrigation ditch all day with guys out lookin' for us with guns. Alla time it's something you didn't mean. God damn it, I wish I could put you in a cage with a million mice and let them pet *you*. [GEORGE'S *anger leaves him suddenly. For the first time he seems to see the expression of terror on* LENNIE'S *face. He looks down ashamedly at the fire, and maneuvers some beans onto the blade of his pocket-knife and puts them into his mouth.*]

LENNIE [*after a pause*]. George! [GEORGE *purposely does not answer him.*] George?

GEORGE. What do you want?

LENNIE. I was only foolin', George. I don't want no ketchup. I wouldn't eat no ketchup if it was right here beside me.

GEORGE [*with a sullenness of shame*]. If they was some here you could have it. And if I had a thousand bucks I'd buy ya a bunch of flowers.

LENNIE. I wouldn't eat no ketchup, George. I'd leave it all for you. You could cover your beans so deep with it, and I wouldn't touch none of it.

GEORGE [*refusing to give in from his sullenness, refusing to look at* LENNIE]. When I think of the swell time I could have without you, I go nuts. I never git no peace!

LENNIE. You want I should go away and leave you alone?

GEORGE. Where the hell could you go?

LENNIE. Well, I could . . . I could go off in the hills there. Some place I could find a cave.

GEORGE. Yeah, how'd ya eat? You ain't got sense enough to find nothing to eat.

LENNIE. I'd find things. I don't need no nice food with ketchup. I'd lay out in the sun and nobody would hurt me. And if I found a mouse—why, I could keep it. Wouldn't nobody take it away from me.

GEORGE [*at last he looks up*]. I been mean, ain't I?

LENNIE [*presses his triumph*]. If you don't want me, I can go right in them hills, and find a cave. I can go away any time.

GEORGE. No. Look! I was just foolin' ya. 'Course I want you to stay with me. Trouble with mice is you always kill 'em. [*He pauses.*] Tell you what I'll do, Lennie. First chance I get I'll find you a pup. Maybe you wouldn't kill it. That would be better than mice. You could pet it harder.

LENNIE [*still avoiding being drawn in*]. If you don't want me, you only gotta say so. I'll go right up on them hills and live by myself. And I won't get no mice stole from me.

GEORGE. I want you to stay with me. Jesus Christ, somebody'd shoot you for a coyote if you was by yourself. Stay with me. Your Aunt Clara wouldn't like your runnin' off by yourself, even if she is dead.

LENNIE. George?

GEORGE. Huh?

LENNIE [*craftily*]. Tell me—like you done before.

GEORGE. Tell you what?

LENNIE. About the rabbits.

GEORGE [*near to anger again*]. You ain't gonna put nothing over on me!

LENNIE [*pleading*]. Come on, George . . . tell me! Please! Like you done before.

GEORGE. You get a kick out of that, don't you? All right, I'll tell you. And then we'll lay out our beds and eat our dinner.

LENNIE. Go on, George. [*Unrolls his bed and lies on his side, supporting his head on one hand.* GEORGE *lays out his bed and sits cross-legged on it.* GEORGE *repeats the next speech rhythmically, as though he had said it many times before.*]

GEORGE. Guys like us that work on ranches is the loneliest guys in the world. They ain't got no family. They don't belong no place. They come to a ranch and work up a stake and then they go in to town and blow their stake. And then the first thing you know they're poundin' their tail on some other ranch. They ain't got nothin' to look ahead to.

LENNIE [*delightedly*]. That's it, that's it! Now tell how it is with us.

GEORGE [*still almost chanting*]. With us it ain't like that. We got a future. We got somebody to talk to that gives a damn about us. We don't have to sit in no barroom blowin' in our jack, just because we got no place else to go. If them other guys gets in jail, they can rot for all anybody gives a damn.

LENNIE [*who cannot restrain himself any longer. Bursts into speech.*] But not us! And why? Because . . . because I got you to look after me . . . and you got me to look after you . . . and that's why! [*He laughs.*] Go on, George!

GEORGE. You got it by heart. You can do it yourself.

LENNIE. No, no. I forget some of the stuff. Tell about how it's gonna be.

GEORGE. Some other time.

LENNIE. No, tell how it's gonna be!

GEORGE. Okay. Some day we're gonna get the jack together and we're gonna have a little house, and a couple of acres and a cow and some pigs and . . .

LENNIE [*shouting*]. And live off the fat of the land! And have rabbits. Go on, George! Tell about what we're gonna have in the garden. And about the rabbits in the cages. Tell about the rain in the winter . . . and about the stove and how thick the cream is on the milk, you can hardly cut it. Tell about that, George!

GEORGE. Why don't you do it yourself—you know all of it!

LENNIE. It ain't the same if I tell it. Go on now. How I get to tend the rabbits.

GEORGE [*resignedly*]. Well, we'll have a big vegetable patch and a rabbit hutch and chickens. And when it rains in the winter we'll just say to hell with goin' to work. We'll build up a fire in the stove, and set around it and listen to the rain comin' down on the roof— Nuts! [*Begins to eat with his knife.*] I ain't got time for no more. [*He falls to eating.* LENNIE *imitates him, spilling a few beans from his mouth with every bite.* GEORGE, *gesturing with his knife.*] What you gonna say tomorrow when the boss asks you questions?

LENNIE [*stops chewing in the middle of a bite, swallows painfully. His face contorts with thought*]. I . . . I ain't gonna say a word.

GEORGE. Good boy. That's fine. Say, maybe you're gettin' better. I bet I can let you tend the rabbits . . . specially if you remember as good as that!

LENNIE [*choking with pride*]. I can remember, by God!

GEORGE [*as though remembering something, points his knife at* LENNIE's *chest*]. Lennie, I want you to look around here. Think you can remember this place? The ranch is 'bout a quarter mile up that way. Just follow the river and you can get here.

LENNIE [*looking around carefully*]. Sure, I can remember here. Didn't I remember 'bout not gonna say a word?

GEORGE. 'Course you did. Well, look, Lennie, if you just happen to get in trouble, I want you to come right here and hide in the brush.

LENNIE [*slowly*]. Hide in the brush.

GEORGE. Hide in the brush until I come for you. Think you can remember that?

LENNIE. Sure I can, George. Hide in the brush till you come for me!

GEORGE. But you ain't gonna get in no trouble. Because if you do I won't let you tend the rabbits.

LENNIE. I won't get in no trouble. I ain't gonna say a word.

GEORGE. You got it. Anyways, I hope so. [GEORGE *stretches out on his blankets. The light dies slowly out of the fire until only the faces of the two men can be seen.* GEORGE *is still eating from his can of beans.*] It's gonna be nice sleeping here. Lookin' up . . . and the leaves . . . Don't build no more fire. We'll let her die. Jesus, you feel free when you ain't got a job—if you ain't hungry.

[*They sit silently for a few moments. A night owl is heard far off. From across the river there comes the sound of a coyote howl and on the heels of the howl all the dogs in the country start to bark.*]

LENNIE [*from almost complete darkness*]. George?

GEORGE. What do you want?

LENNIE. Let's have different color rabbits, George.

GEORGE. Sure. Red rabbits and blue rabbits and green rabbits. Millions of 'em!

LENNIE. Furry ones, George. Like I seen at the fair in Sacramento.

GEORGE. Sure. Furry ones.

LENNIE. 'Cause I can jus' as well go away, George, and live in a cave.

GEORGE [*amiably*]. Aw, shut up.

LENNIE [*after a long pause*]. George?

GEORGE. What is it?

LENNIE. I'm shutting up, George.

[*A coyote howls again.*]

CURTAIN

SCENE II

Late Friday morning.
  The interior of a bunkhouse.

Walls, white-washed board and bat. Floors un-painted.

There is a heavy square table with upended boxes around it used for chairs. Over each bunk there is a box nailed to the wall which serves as two shelves on which are the private possessions of the working men.

On top of each bunk there is a large noisy alarm clock ticking madly.

The sun is streaking through the windows. Note: Articles in the boxes on wall are soap, talcum powder, razors, pulp magazines, medicine bottles, combs, and from nails on the sides of the boxes a few neckties.

There is a hanging light from the ceiling over the table, with a round dim reflector on it.

The curtain rises on an empty stage. Only the ticking of the many alarm clocks is heard.

CANDY, GEORGE *and* LENNIE *are first seen passing the open window of the bunkhouse.*

CANDY. This is the bunkhouse here. Door's around this side. [*The latch on the door rises and* CANDY *enters, a stoop-shouldered old man. He is dressed in blue jeans and a denim coat. He carries a big push broom in his left hand. His right hand is gone at the wrist. He grasps things with his right arm between arm and side. He walks into the room followed by* GEORGE *and* LENNIE. *Conversationally.*] The boss was expecting you last night. He was sore as hell when you wasn't here to go out this morning. [*Points with his handless arm.*] You can have them two beds there.

GEORGE. I'll take the top one . . . I don't want you fall-ing down on me. [*Steps over to the bunk and throws his blankets down. He looks into the nearly empty box shelf over it, then picks up a small yellow can.*] Say, what the hell's this?

CANDY. I don't know.

GEORGE. Says "positively kills lice, roaches and other scourges." What the hell kinda beds you givin' us, anyway? We don't want no pants rabbits.

CANDY [*shifts his broom, holding it between his elbow and his side, takes the can in his left hand and studies the label carefully*]. Tell you what . . . last guy that had this bed was a blacksmith. Helluva nice fellow. Clean a guy as you'd want to meet. Used to wash his hands even *after* he et.

GEORGE [*with gathering anger*]. Then how come he got pillow-pigeons?

[LENNIE *puts his blankets on his bunk and sits down, watching* GEORGE *with his mouth slightly open.*]

CANDY. Tell you what. This here blacksmith, name of Whitey, was the kinda guy that would put that stuff around even if there wasn't no bugs. Tell you what he used to do. He'd peel *his* boiled potatoes and take out every little spot before he et it, and if there was a red splotch on an egg, he'd scrape it off. Finally quit about the food. That's the kind of guy Whitey was. Clean. Used to dress up Sundays even when he wasn't goin' no place. Put on a necktie even, and then set in the bunkhouse.

GEORGE [*skeptically*]. I ain't so sure. What da' ya say he quit for?

CANDY [*puts the can in his pocket, rubs his bristly white whiskers with his knuckles*]. Why . . . he just quit the way a guy will. Says it was the food. Didn't give no other reason. Just says "give me my time" one night, the way any guy would.

[GEORGE *lifts his bed tick and looks underneath, leans over and inspects the sacking carefully.* LENNIE *does the same with his bed.*]

GEORGE [*half satisfied*]. Well, if there's any gray-backs in this bed, you're gonna hear from me!

[*He unrolls his blankets and puts his razor and bar of soap and comb and bottle of pills, his liniment and leather wristband in the box.*]

CANDY. I guess the boss'll be out here in a minute to write your name in. He sure was burned when you wasn't here this morning. Come right in when we was eatin' breakfast and says, "Where the hell's them new men?" He give the stable buck hell, too. Stable buck's a nigger.

GEORGE. Nigger, huh!

CANDY. Yeah. [*Continues.*] Nice fellow too. Got a crooked back where a horse kicked him. Boss gives him hell when he's mad. But the stable buck don't give a damn about that.

GEORGE. What kinda guy is the boss?

CANDY. Well, he's a pretty nice fella for a boss. Gets mad sometimes. But he's pretty nice. Tell you what. Know what he done Christmas? Brung a gallon of whiskey right in here and says, "Drink hearty, boys, Christmas comes but once a year!"

GEORGE. The hell he did! A whole gallon?

CANDY. Yes, sir. Jesus, we had fun! They let the nigger come in that night. Well, sir, a little skinner named Smitty took after the nigger. Done pretty good too. The guys wouldn't let him use his feet so the nigger got him. If he could a used his feet Smitty says he would have killed the nigger. The guys says on account the nigger got a crooked back Smitty can't use his feet. [*He smiles in reverie at the memory.*]

GEORGE. Boss the owner?

CANDY. Naw! Superintendent. Big land company. . . . Yes, sir, that night . . . he comes right in here with a whole gallon . . . he set right over there and says, "Drink hearty, boys," . . . he says. . . . [*The door opens. Enter the* BOSS. *He is a stocky man, dressed in blue jean trousers, flannel shirt, a black unbuttoned vest and a black coat. He wears a soiled brown Stetson hat, a pair of high-heeled boots and spurs. Ordinarily he puts his thumbs in his belt.* CANDY, *shuffling towards the door, rubbing his whiskers with his knuckles as he goes.*] Them guys just come. [CANDY *exits and shuts the door behind him.*]

BOSS. I wrote Murray and Ready I wanted two men this morning. You got your work slips?

GEORGE [*digs in his pockets, produces two slips, and hands them to the* BOSS]. Here they are.

BOSS [*reading the slips*]. Well, I see it wasn't Murray and Ready's fault. It says right here on the slip, you was to be here for work this morning.

GEORGE. Bus driver give us a bum steer. We had to walk ten miles. That bus driver says we was here when we wasn't. We couldn't thumb no rides. [GEORGE *scowls meaningly at* LENNIE *and* LENNIE *nods to show that he understands.*]

BOSS. Well, I had to send out the grain teams short two buckers. It won't do any good to go out now until after dinner. You'd get lost. [*Pulls out his time book, opens it to where a pencil is stuck between the leaves. Licks his pencil carefully.*] What's your name?

GEORGE. George Milton.

BOSS. George Milton. [*Writing.*] And what's yours?

GEORGE. His name's Lennie Small.

BOSS. Lennie Small. [*Writing.*] Le's see, this is the twentieth. Noon the twentieth . . . [*Makes positive mark. Closes the book and puts it in his pocket.*] Where you boys been workin'?

GEORGE. Up around Weed.

BOSS [*to* LENNIE]. You too?

GEORGE. Yeah. Him too.

BOSS [*to* LENNIE]. Say, you're a big fellow, ain't you?

GEORGE. Yeah, he can work like hell, too.

BOSS. He ain't much of a talker, though, is he?

GEORGE. No, he ain't. But he's a hell of a good worker. Strong as a bull.

LENNIE [*smiling*]. I'm strong as a bull.

[GEORGE *scowls at him and* LENNIE *drops his head in shame at having forgotten.*]

BOSS [*sharply*]. You are, huh? What can you do?

GEORGE. He can do anything.

BOSS [*addressing* LENNIE]. What can you do?

[LENNIE, *looking at* GEORGE, *gives a high nervous chuckle.*]

GEORGE [*quickly*]. Anything you tell him. He's a good skinner. He can wrestle grain bags, drive a cultivator. He can do anything. Just give him a try.

BOSS [*turning to* GEORGE]. Then why don't you let *him* answer? [LENNIE *laughs.*] What's he laughing about?

GEORGE. He laughs when he gets excited.

BOSS. Yeah?

GEORGE [*loudly*]. But he's a goddamn good worker. I ain't saying he's bright, because he ain't. But he can put up a four hundred pound bale.

BOSS [*hooking his thumbs in his belt*]. Say, what you sellin'?

GEORGE. Huh?

BOSS. I said what stake you got in this guy? You takin' his pay away from him?

GEORGE. No. Of course I ain't!

BOSS. Hell, I never seen one guy take so much trouble for another guy. I just like to know what your percentage is.

GEORGE. He's my . . . cousin. I told his ole lady I'd take care of him. He got kicked in the head by a horse when he was a kid. He's all right. . . . Just ain't bright. But he can do anything you tell him.

BOSS [*turning half away*]. Well, God knows he don't need no brains to buck barley bags. [*He turns back.*]

But don't you try to put nothing over, Milton. I got
my eye on you. Why'd you quit in Weed?

GEORGE [*promptly*]. Job was done.

BOSS. What kind of job?

GEORGE. Why . . . we was diggin' a cesspool.

BOSS [*after a pause*]. All right. But don't try to put
nothing over 'cause you can't get away with nothing.
I seen wise guys before. Go out with the grain teams
after dinner. They're out pickin' up barley with the
thrashin' machines. Go out with Slim's team.

GEORGE. Slim?

BOSS. Yeah. Big, tall skinner. You'll see him at dinner.
[*Up to this time the* BOSS *has been full of business.
He has been calm and suspicious. In the following
lines he relaxes, but gradually, as though he wanted
to talk but felt always the burden of his position.
He turns toward the door, but hesitates and allows
a little warmth into his manner.*] Been on the road
long?

GEORGE [*obviously on guard*]. We was three days in
'Frisco lookin' at the boards.

BOSS [*with heavy jocularity*]. Didn't go to no night
clubs, I 'spose?

GEORGE [*stiffly*]. We was lookin' for a job.

BOSS [*attempting to be friendly*]. That's a great town
if you got a little jack, Frisco.

GEORGE [*refusing to be drawn in*]. We didn't have no
jack for nothing like that.

BOSS [*realizes there is no contact to establish; grows
rigid with his position again*]. Go out with the grain
teams after dinner. When my hands work hard they
get pie and when they loaf they bounce down the
road on their can. You ask anybody about me. [*He
turns and walks out of the bunkhouse.*]

GEORGE [*turns to* LENNIE]. So you wasn't gonna say a
word! You was gonna leave your big flapper shut. I

was gonna do the talkin'. . . . You goddamn near lost us the job!

LENNIE [*stares hopelessly at his hands*]. I forgot.

GEORGE. You forgot. You always forget. Now, he's got his eye on us. Now, we gotta be careful and not make no slips. You keep your big flapper shut after this.

LENNIE. He talked like a kinda nice guy towards the last.

GEORGE [*angrily*]. He's the boss, ain't he? Well, he's the boss first an' a nice guy afterwards. Don't you have nothin' to do with no boss, except do your work and draw your pay. You can't never tell whether you're talkin' to the nice guy or the boss. Just keep your goddamn mouth shut. Then you're all right.

LENNIE. George?

GEORGE. What you want now?

LENNIE. I wasn't kicked in the head with no horse, was I, George?

GEORGE. Be a damn good thing if you was. Save everybody a hell of a lot of trouble!

LENNIE [*flattered*]. You says I was your cousin.

GEORGE. Well, that was a goddamn lie. And I'm glad it was. Why, if I was a relative of yours— [*He stops and listens, then steps to the front door, and looks out.*] Say, what the hell you doin', listenin'?

CANDY [*comes slowly into the room. By a rope, he leads an ancient drag-footed, blind sheep dog. Guides it from running into a table leg, with the rope. Sits down on a box, and presses the hind quarters of the old dog down*]. Naw . . . I wasn't listenin'. . . . I was just standin' in the shade a minute, scratchin' my dog. I jest now finished swamping out the washhouse.

GEORGE. You was pokin' your big nose into our business! I don't like nosey guys.

CANDY [*looks uneasily from* GEORGE *to* LENNIE *and then back*]. I jest come there . . . I didn't hear nothing you guys was sayin'. I ain't interested in nothing you was sayin'. A guy on a ranch don't never listen. Nor he don't ast no questions.

GEORGE [*slightly mollified*]. Damn right he don't! Not if the guy wants to stay workin' long. [*His manner changes.*] That's a helluva ole dog.

CANDY. Yeah. I had him ever since he was a pup. God, he was a good sheep dog, when he was young. [*Rubs his cheek with his knuckles.*] How'd you like the boss?

GEORGE. Pretty good! Seemed all right.

CANDY. He's a nice fella. You got ta take him right, of course. He's runnin' this ranch. He don't take no nonsense.

GEORGE. What time do we eat? Eleven-thirty?

[CURLEY *enters. He is dressed in working clothes. He wears brown high-heeled boots and has a glove on his left hand.*]

CURLEY. Seen my ole man?

CANDY. He was here just a minute ago, Curley. Went over to the cookhouse, I think.

CURLEY. I'll try to catch him. [*Looking over at the new men, measuring them. Unconsciously bends his elbow and closes his hand and goes into a slight crouch. He walks gingerly close to* LENNIE.] You the new guys my ole man was waitin' for?

GEORGE. Yeah. We just come in.

CURLEY. How's it come you wasn't here this morning?

GEORGE. Got off the bus too soon.

CURLEY [*again addressing* LENNIE]. My ole man got to get the grain out. Ever bucked barley?

GEORGE [*quickly*]. Hell, yes. Done a lot of it.

CURLEY. I mean him. [*To* LENNIE.] Ever bucked barley?

GEORGE. Sure he has.

CURLEY [*irritatedly*]. Let the big guy talk!

GEORGE. 'Spose he don't want ta talk?

CURLEY [*pugnaciously*]. By Christ, he's gotta talk when he's spoke to. What the hell you shovin' into this for?

GEORGE [*stands up and speaks coldly*]. Him and me travel together.

CURLEY. Oh, so it's that way?

GEORGE [*tense and motionless*]. What way?

CURLEY [*letting the subject drop*]. And you won't let the big guy talk? Is that it?

GEORGE. He can talk if he wants to tell you anything. [*He nods slightly to* LENNIE.]

LENNIE [*in a frightened voice*]. We just come in.

CURLEY. Well, next time you answer when you're spoke to, then.

GEORGE. He didn't do nothing to you.

CURLEY [*measuring him*]. You drawin' cards this hand?

GEORGE [*quietly*]. I might.

CURLEY [*stares at him for a moment, his threat moving to the future*]. I'll see you get a chance to ante, anyway. [*He walks out of the room.*]

GEORGE [*after he has made his exit*]. Say, what the hell's he got on his shoulder? Lennie didn't say nothing to him.

CANDY [*looks cautiously at the door*]. That's the boss's son. Curley's pretty handy. He done quite a bit in the ring. The guys say he's pretty handy.

GEORGE. Well, let 'im be handy. He don't have to take after Lennie. Lennie didn't do nothing to him.

CANDY [*considering*]. Well . . . tell you what, Curley's like a lot a little guys. He hates big guys. He's alla time pickin' scraps with big guys. Kinda like he's mad at 'em because *he* ain't a big guy. You seen little guys like that, ain't you—always scrappy?

GEORGE. Sure, I seen plenty tough little guys. But this here Curley better not make no mistakes about Lennie. Lennie ain't handy, see, but this Curley punk's gonna get hurt if he messes around with Lennie.

CANDY [*skeptically*]. Well, Curley's pretty handy. You know, it never did seem right to me. 'Spose Curley jumps a big guy and licks him. Everybody says what a game guy Curley is. Well, 'spose he jumps 'im and gits licked, everybody says the big guy oughta pick somebody his own size. Seems like Curley ain't givin' nobody a chance.

GEORGE [*watching the door*]. Well, he better watch out for Lennie. Lennie ain't no fighter. But Lennie's strong and quick and Lennie don't know no rules. [*Walks to the square table, and sits down on one of the boxes. Picks up scattered cards and pulls them together and shuffles them.*]

CANDY. Don't tell Curley I said none of this. He'd slough me! He jus' don't give a damn. Won't ever get canned because his ole man's the boss!

GEORGE [*cuts the cards. Turns over and looks at each one as he throws it down*]. This guy Curley sounds like a son-of-a-bitch to me! I don't like mean little guys!

CANDY. Seems to me like he's worse lately. He got married a couple of weeks ago. Wife lives over in the boss's house. Seems like Curley's worse'n ever since he got married. Like he's settin' on a ant-hill an' a big red ant come up an' nipped 'im on the turnip. Just feels so goddamn miserable he'll strike at anything that moves. I'm kinda sorry for 'im.

GEORGE. Maybe he's showin' off for his wife.

CANDY. You seen that glove on his left hand?

GEORGE. Sure I seen it!

CANDY. Well, that glove's full of vaseline.

GEORGE. Vaseline? What the hell for?

CANDY. Curley says he's keepin' that hand soft for his wife.

GEORGE. That's a dirty kind of a thing to tell around.

CANDY. I ain't quite so sure. I seen such funny things a guy will do to try to be nice. I ain't sure. But you jus' wait till you see Curley's wife!

GEORGE [*begins to lay out a solitaire hand, speaks casually*]. Is she purty?

CANDY. Yeah. Purty, but—

GEORGE [*studying his cards*]. But what?

CANDY. Well, she got the eye.

GEORGE [*still playing at his solitaire hand*]. Yeah? Married two weeks an' got the eye? Maybe that's why Curley's pants is fulla ants.

CANDY. Yes, sir, I seen her give Slim the eye. Slim's a jerkline skinner. Hell of a nice fella. Well, I seen her give Slim the eye. Curley never seen it. And I seen her give a skinner named Carlson the eye.

GEORGE [*pretending a very mild interest*]. Looks like we was gonna have fun!

CANDY [*stands up*]. Know what I think? [*Waits for an answer.* GEORGE *doesn't answer.*] Well, I think Curley's married himself a tart.

GEORGE [*casually*]. He ain't the first. Black queen on a red king. Yes, sir . . . there's plenty done that!

CANDY [*moves towards the door, leading his dog out with him*]. I got to be settin' out the wash basins for the guys. The teams'll be in before long. You guys gonna buck barley?

GEORGE. Yeah.

CANDY. You won't tell Curley nothing I said?

GEORGE. Hell, no!

CANDY [*just before he goes out the door, he turns back*]. Well, you look her over, mister. You see if she ain't a tart! [*He exits.*]

GEORGE [*continuing to play out his solitaire. He turns to* LENNIE]. Look, Lennie, this here ain't no set-up. You gonna have trouble with that Curley guy. I seen that kind before. You know what he's doin'. He's kinda feelin' you out. He figures he's got you scared. And he's gonna take a sock at you, first chance he gets.

LENNIE [*frightened*]. I don't want no trouble. Don't let him sock me, George!

GEORGE. I hate them kind of bastards. I seen plenty of 'em. Like the ole guy says: "Curley don't take no chances. He always figures to win." [*Thinks for a moment.*] If he tangles with you, Lennie, we're goin' get the can. Don't make no mistake about that. He's the boss's kid. Look, you try to keep away from him, will you? Don't never speak to him. If he comes in here you move clear to the other side of the room. Will you remember that, Lennie?

LENNIE [*mourning*]. I don't want no trouble. I never done nothing to him!

GEORGE. Well, that won't do you no good, if Curley wants to set himself up for a fighter. Just don't have nothing to do with him. Will you remember?

LENNIE. Sure, George . . . I ain't gonna say a word. [*Sounds of the teams coming in from the fields, jingling of harness, croak of heavy laden axles, men talking to and cussing the horses. Crack of a whip and from a distance a voice calling.*]

SLIM'S VOICE. Stable buck! Hey! Stable buck!

GEORGE. Here come the guys. Just don't say nothing.

LENNIE [*timidly*]. You ain't mad, George?

GEORGE. I ain't mad at you. I'm mad at this here Curley bastard! I wanted we should get a little stake together. Maybe a hundred dollars. You keep away from Curley.

LENNIE. Sure I will. I won't say a word.

GEORGE [*hesitating*]. Don't let 'im pull you in—but—if the son-of-a-bitch socks you—let him have it!

LENNIE. Let him have what, George?

GEORGE. Never mind. . . . Look, if you get in any kind of trouble, you remember what I told you to do.

LENNIE. If I get in any trouble, you ain't gonna let me tend the rabbits?

GEORGE. That's not what I mean. You remember where we slept last night. Down by the river?

LENNIE. Oh, sure I remember. I go there and hide in the brush until you come for me.

GEORGE. That's it. Hide till I come for you. Don't let nobody see you. Hide in the brush by the river. Now say that over.

LENNIE. Hide in the brush by the river. Down in the brush by the river.

GEORGE. If you get in trouble.

LENNIE. If I get in trouble.

[*A brake screeches outside and a call: "Stable buck, oh, stable buck!" "Where the hell's that goddamn nigger?" Suddenly* CURLEY'S WIFE *is standing in the door. Full, heavily rouged lips. Wide-spaced, made-up eyes, her fingernails are bright red, her hair hangs in little rolled clusters like sausages. She wears a cotton house dress and red mules, on the insteps of which are little bouquets of red ostrich feathers.* GEORGE *and* LENNIE *look up at her.*]

CURLEY'S WIFE. I'm lookin' for Curley!

GEORGE [*looks away from her*]. He was in here a minute ago but he went along.

CURLEY'S WIFE [*puts her hands behind her back and leans against the door frame so that her body is thrown forward*]. You're the new fellas that just come, ain't you?

GEORGE [*sullenly*]. Yeah.

CURLEY'S WIFE [*bridles a little and inspects her finger-nails*]. Sometimes Curley's in here.

GEORGE [*brusquely*]. Well, he ain't now!

CURLEY'S WIFE [*playfully*]. Well, if he ain't, I guess I'd better look some place else.

[LENNIE *watches her, fascinated.*]

GEORGE. If I see Curley I'll pass the word you was lookin' for him.

CURLEY'S WIFE. Nobody can't blame a person for lookin'.

GEORGE. That depends what she's lookin' for.

CURLEY'S WIFE [*a little wearily, dropping her coquetry*]. I'm jus' lookin' for somebody to talk to. Don't you never jus' want to talk to somebody?

SLIM [*offstage*]. Okay! Put that lead pair in the north stalls.

CURLEY'S WIFE [*to* SLIM, *offstage*]. Hi, Slim!

SLIM [*voice offstage*]. Hello.

CURLEY'S WIFE. I—I'm trying to find Curley.

SLIM'S VOICE [*offstage*]. Well, you ain't tryin' very hard. I seen him goin' in your house.

CURLEY'S WIFE. I—I'm tryin' to find Curley. I gotta be goin'! [*She exits hurriedly.*]

GEORGE [*looking around at* LENNIE]. Jesus, what a tramp! So, that's what Curley picks for a wife. God Almighty, did you smell that stink she's got on? I can still smell her. Don't have to see *her* to know she's around.

LENNIE. She's purty!

GEORGE. Yeah. And she's sure hidin' it. Curley's got his work ahead of him.

LENNIE [*still staring at the doorway where she was*]. Gosh, she's purty!

GEORGE [*turning furiously at him*]. Listen to me, you crazy bastard. Don't you even look at that bitch. I don't care what she says or what she does. I seen 'em poison before, but I ain't never seen no piece of jail bait worse than her. Don't you even smell near her!

LENNIE. I never smelled, George!

GEORGE. No, you never. But when she was standin' there showin' her legs, you wasn't lookin' the other way neither!

LENNIE. I never meant no bad things, George. Honest I never.

GEORGE. Well, you keep away from her. You let Curley take the rap. He let himself in for it. [*Disgustedly.*] Glove full of vaseline. I bet he's eatin' raw eggs and writin' to patent-medicine houses.

LENNIE [*cries out*]. I don't like this place. This ain't no good place. I don't like this place!

GEORGE. Listen—I don't like it here no better than you do. But we gotta keep it till we get a stake. We're flat. We gotta get a stake. [*Goes back to the table, thoughtfully.*] If we can get just a few dollars in the poke we'll shove off and go up to the American River and pan gold. Guy can make a couple dollars a day there.

LENNIE [*eagerly*]. Let's go, George. Let's get out of here. It's mean here.

GEORGE [*shortly*]. I tell you we gotta stay a little while. We gotta get a stake. [*The sounds of running water and rattle of basins are heard.*] Shut up now, the guys'll be comin' in! [*Pensively.*] Maybe we ought to wash up. . . . But hell, we ain't done nothin' to get dirty.

SLIM [*enters. He is a tall, dark man in blue jeans and a short denim jacket. He carries a crushed Stetson hat*

*under his arm and combs his long dark damp hair
straight back. He stands and moves with a kind of
majesty. He finishes combing his hair. Smooths out
his crushed hat, creases it in the middle and puts
it on. In a gentle voice*]. It's brighter'n a bitch outside. Can't hardly see nothing in here. You the new
guys?

GEORGE. Just come.

SLIM. Goin' to buck barley?

GEORGE. That's what the boss says.

SLIM. Hope you get on my team.

GEORGE. Boss said we'd go with a jerk-line skinner
named Slim.

SLIM. That's me.

GEORGE. You a jerk-line skinner?

SLIM [*in self-disparagement*]. I can snap 'em around
a little.

GEORGE [*terribly impressed*]. That kinda makes you
Jesus Christ on this ranch, don't it?

SLIM [*obviously pleased*]. Oh, nuts!

GEORGE [*chuckles*]. Like the man says, "The boss tells
you what to do. But if you want to know how to do
it, you got to ask the mule skinner." The man
says any guy that can drive twelve Arizona jack rabbits with a jerk line can fall in a toilet and come
up with a mince pie under each arm.

SLIM [*laughing*]. Well, I hope you get on my team. I
got a pair a punks that don't know a barley bag
from a blue ball. You guys ever bucked any barley?

GEORGE. Hell, yes. I ain't nothin' to scream about, but
that big guy there can put up more grain alone than
most pairs can.

SLIM [*looks approvingly at* GEORGE]. You guys travel
around together?

GEORGE. Sure. We kinda look after each other. [*Points*

at LENNIE *with his thumb*.] He ain't bright. Hell of a good worker, though. Hell of a nice fella too. I've knowed him for a long time.

SLIM. Ain't many guys travel around together. I don't know why. Maybe everybody in the whole damn world is scared of each other.

GEORGE. It's a lot nicer to go 'round with a guy you know. You get used to it an' then it ain't no fun alone any more.

[*Enter* CARLSON. *Big-stomached, powerful man. His head still drips water from scrubbing and dousing*.]

CARLSON. Hello, Slim! [*He looks at* GEORGE *and* LEN-NIE.]

SLIM. These guys just come.

CARLSON. Glad to meet ya! My name's Carlson!

GEORGE. I'm George Milton. This here's Lennie Small.

CARLSON. Glad to meet you. He ain't very small. [*Chuckles at his own joke*.] He ain't small at all. Meant to ask you, Slim, how's your bitch? I seen she wasn't under your wagon this morning.

SLIM. She slang her pups last night. Nine of 'em. I drowned four of 'em right off. She couldn't feed that many.

CARLSON. Got five left, huh?

SLIM. Yeah. Five. I kep' the biggest.

CARLSON. What kinda dogs you think they gonna be?

SLIM. I don't know. Some kind of shepherd, I guess. That's the most kind I seen around here when she's in heat.

CARLSON [*laughs*]. I had an airedale an' a guy down the road got one of them little white floozy dogs, well, she was in heat and the guy locks her up. But my airedale, named Tom he was, he et a woodshed clear down to the roots to get to her. Guy come over one day, he's sore as hell, he says, "I wouldn't mind if my bitch had pups, but Christ Almighty, this morning she slang a litter of Shetland ponies. . . ." [*Takes off his hat and scratches his head.*] Got five pups, huh! Gonna keep all of 'em?

SLIM. I don' know, gotta keep 'em awhile, so they can drink Lulu's milk.

CARLSON [*thoughtfully*]. Well, looka here, Slim, I been thinkin'. That dog of Candy's is so goddamn old he can't hardly walk. Stinks like hell. Every time Candy brings him in the bunkhouse, I can smell him two or three days. Why don't you get Candy to shoot his ol' dog, and give him one of them pups to raise up? I can smell that dog a mile off. Got no teeth. Can't eat. Candy feeds him milk. He can't chew nothing else. And leadin' him around on a string so he don't bump into things . . . [*The triangle outside begins to ring wildly. Continues for a few moments, then stops suddenly.*] There she goes!

[*Outside there is a burst of voices as a group of men go by.*]

SLIM [*to* LENNIE *and* GEORGE]. You guys better come on while they's still somethin' to eat. Won't be nothing left in a couple of minutes. [*Exit* SLIM *and* CARLSON, LENNIE *watches* GEORGE *excitedly.*]

LENNIE. George!

GEORGE [*rumpling his cards into a pile*]. Yeah, I heard 'im, Lennie . . . I'll ask 'im!

LENNIE [*excitedly*]. A brown and white one.

GEORGE. Come on, let's get dinner. I don't know whether he's got a brown and white one.

LENNIE. You ask him, right away, George, so he won't kill no more of 'em!

GEORGE. Sure! Come on now—le's go. [*They start for the door.*]

CURLEY [*bounces in, angrily*]. You seen a girl around here?

GEORGE [*coldly*]. 'Bout half an hour ago, mebbe.

CURLEY. Well, what the hell was she doin'?

GEORGE [*insultingly*]. She *said* she was lookin' for you.

CURLEY [*measures both men with his eyes for a moment*]. Which way did she go?

GEORGE. I don't know. I didn't watch her go. [CURLEY *scowls at him a moment and then turns and hurries out the door.*] You know, Lennie, I'm scared I'm gonna tangle with that bastard myself. I hate his guts! Jesus Christ, come on! They won't be a damn thing left to eat.

LENNIE. Will you ask him about a brown and white one? [*They exeunt.*]

CURTAIN

Act two

SCENE I

About seven-thirty Friday evening.

Same bunkhouse interior as in last scene.

The evening light is seen coming in through the window, but it is quite dark in the interior of the bunkhouse.

From outside comes the sound of a horseshoe game. Thuds on the dirt and occasional clangs as a shoe hits the peg. Now and then voices are raised in approval or derision: "That's a good one." . . . "Goddamn right it's a good one." . . . "Here goes for a ringer. I need a ringer." . . . "Goddamn near got it, too."

SLIM *and* GEORGE *come into the darkening bunkhouse together.* SLIM *reaches up and turns on the tin-*

shaded electric light. Sits down on a box at the table.
GEORGE *takes his place opposite.*

SLIM. It wasn't nothing. I would of had to drown most of them pups anyway. No need to thank me about that.

GEORGE. Wasn't much to you, mebbe, but it was a hell of a lot to him. Jesus Christ, I don't know how we're gonna get him to sleep in here. He'll want to stay right out in the barn. We gonna have trouble keepin' him from gettin' right in the box with them pups.

SLIM. Say, you sure was right about him. Maybe he ain't bright—but I never seen such a worker. He damn near killed his partner buckin' barley. He'd take his end of that sack [*a gesture*], pretty near kill his partner. God Almighty, I never seen such a strong guy.

GEORGE [*proudly*]. You just tell Lennie what to do and he'll do it if it don't take no figuring.

[*Outside the sound of the horseshoe game goes on: "Son of a bitch if I can win a goddamn game." . . . "Me neither. You'd think them shoes was anvils."*]

SLIM. Funny how you and him string along together.

GEORGE. What's so funny about it?

SLIM. Oh, I don't know. Hardly none of the guys ever travels around together. I hardly never seen two guys travel together. You know how the hands are. They come in and get their bunk and work a month and then they quit and go on alone. Never seem to give a damn about nobody. Jest seems kinda funny. A cuckoo like him and a smart guy like you traveling together.

GEORGE. I ain't so bright neither or I wouldn't be buckin' barley for my fifty and found. If I was bright, if I was even a little bit smart, I'd have my own place and I'd be bringin' in my own crops 'stead of doin' all the work and not gettin' what comes up out of the ground. [*He falls silent for a moment.*]

SLIM. A guy'd like to do that. Sometimes I'd like to cuss a string of mules that was my own mules.

GEORGE. It ain't so funny, him and me goin' round together. Him and me was both born in Auburn. I knowed his aunt. She took him when he was a baby and raised him up. When his aunt died Lennie jus' come along with me, out workin'. Got kinda used to each other after a little while.

SLIM. Uh huh.

GEORGE. First I used to have a hell of a lot of fun with him. Used to play jokes on him because he was too dumb to take care of himself. But, hell, he was too dumb even to know when he had a joke played on him. [*Sarcastically.*] Hell, yes, I had fun! Made me seem goddamn smart alongside of him.

SLIM. I seen it that way.

GEORGE. Why, he'd do any damn thing I tole him. If I tole him to walk over a cliff, over he'd go. You know that wasn't so damn much fun after a while. He never got mad about it, neither. I've beat hell out of him and he could bust every bone in my body jest with his hands. But he never lifted a finger against me.

SLIM [*braiding a bull whip*]. Even if you socked him, wouldn't he?

GEORGE. No, by God! I tell you what made me stop playing jokes. One day a bunch of guys was standin' aroun' up on the Sacramento River. I was feelin' pretty smart. I turns to Lennie and I says, "Jump in."

SLIM. What happened?

GEORGE. He jumps. Couldn't swim a stroke. He damn

near drowned. And he was so nice to me for pullin'
him out. Clean forgot I tole him to jump in, Well,
I ain't done nothin' like that no more. Makes me
kinda sick tellin' about it.

SLIM. He's a nice fella. A guy don't need no sense to
be a nice fella. Seems to be sometimes it's jest the
other way round. Take a real smart guy, he ain't
hardly ever a nice fella.

GEORGE [*stacking the scattered cards and getting his
solitaire game ready again*]. I ain't got no people. I
seen guys that go round on the ranches alone. That
ain't no good. They don't have no fun. After a
while they get mean.

SLIM [*quietly*]. Yeah, I seen 'em get mean. I seen 'em
get so they don't want to talk to nobody. Some ways
they got to. You take a bunch of guys all livin' in
one room an' by God they got to mind their own
business. 'Bout the only private thing a guy's got
is where he come from and where he's goin'.

GEORGE. 'Course Lennie's a goddamn nuisance most
of the time. But you get used to goin' round with a
guy and you can't get rid of him. I mean you get
used to him an' you can't get rid of bein' used to
him. I'm sure drippin' at the mouth. I ain't told
nobody all this before.

SLIM. Do you want to get rid of him?

GEORGE. Well, he gets in trouble all the time. Because
he's so goddamn dumb. Like what happened in
Weed. [*He stops, alarmed at what he has said.*] You
wouldn't tell nobody?

SLIM [*calmly*]. What did he do in Weed?

GEORGE. You wouldn't tell?—No, 'course you wouldn't.

SLIM. What did he do?

GEORGE. Well, he seen this girl in a red dress. Dumb
bastard like he is he wants to touch everything he
likes. Jest wants to feel of it. So he reaches out to

feel this red dress. Girl let's out a squawk and that gets Lennie all mixed up. He holds on 'cause that's the only thing he can think to do.

SLIM. The hell!

GEORGE. Well, this girl squawks her head off. I'm right close and I hear all the yellin', so I comes a-running. By that time Lennie's scared to death. You know, I had to sock him over the head with a fence picket to make him let go.

SLIM. So what happens then?

GEORGE [*carefully building his solitaire hand*]. Well, she runs in and tells the law she's been raped. The guys in Weed start out to lynch Lennie. So there we sit in an irrigation ditch, under water all the rest of that day. Got only our heads stickin' out of water, up under the grass that grows out of the side of the ditch. That night we run outa there.

SLIM. Didn't hurt the girl none, huh?

GEORGE. Hell, no, he jes' scared her.

SLIM. He's a funny guy.

GEORGE. Funny! Why, one time, you know what that big baby done! He was walking along a road— [*Enter* LENNIE *through the door. He wears his coat over his shoulder like a cape and walks hunched over.*] Hi, Lennie. How do you like your pup?

LENNIE [*breathlessly*]. He's brown and white jus' like I wanted. [*Goes directly to his bunk and lies down. Face to the wall and knees drawn up.*]

GEORGE [*puts down his cards deliberately*]. Lennie!

LENNIE [*over his shoulder*]. Huh? What you want, George?

GEORGE [*sternly*]. I tole ya, ya couldn't bring that pup in here.

LENNIE. What pup, George? I ain't got no pup.

[GEORGE *goes quickly over to him, grabs him by the shoulder and rolls him over. He picks up a tiny puppie from where* LENNIE *has been concealing it against his stomach.*]

LENNIE [*quickly*]. Give him to me, George.

GEORGE. You get right up and take this pup to the nest. He's got to sleep with his mother. Ya want ta kill him? Jes' born last night and ya take him out of the nest. Ya take him back or I'll tell Slim not to let you have him.

LENNIE [*pleadingly*]. Give him to me, George. I'll take him back. I didn't mean no bad thing, George. Honest I didn't. I jus' want to pet him a little.

GEORGE [*giving the pup to him*]. All right, you get him back there quick. And don't you take him out no more.

[LENNIE *scuttles out of the room.*]

SLIM. Jesus, he's just like a kid, ain't he?

GEORGE. Sure he's like a kid. There ain't no more harm in him than a kid neither, except he's so strong. I bet he won't come in here to sleep tonight. He'll sleep right alongside that box in the barn. Well, let him. He ain't doin' no harm out there.

[*The light has faded out outside and it appears quite dark outside. Enter* CANDY *leading his old dog by a string.*]

CANDY. Hello, Slim. Hello, George. Didn't neither of you play horseshoes?

SLIM. I don't like to play every night.

CANDY [*goes to his bunk and sits down, presses the old blind dog to the floor beside him*]. Either you guys got a slug of whiskey? I got a gut ache.

SLIM. I ain't. I'd drink it myself if I had. And I ain't got no gut ache either.

CANDY. Goddamn cabbage give it to me. I knowed it was goin' to before I ever et it.

[*Enter* CARLSON *and* WHIT.]

CARLSON. Jesus, how that nigger can pitch shoes!

SLIM. He's plenty good.

WHIT. Damn right he is.

CARLSON. Yeah. He don't give nobody else a chance to win. [*Stops and sniffs the air. Looks around until he sees* CANDY's *dog.*] God Almighty, that dog stinks. Get him outa here, Candy. I don't know nothing that stinks as bad as ole dogs. You got to get him outa here.

CANDY [*lying down on his bunk, reaches over and pats the ancient dog, speaks softly*]. I been round him so much I never notice how he stinks.

CARLSON. Well, I can't stand him in here. That stink hangs round even after he's gone. [*Walks over and stands looking down at the dog.*] Got no teeth. All stiff with rheumatism. He ain't no good to you, Candy. Why don't you shoot him?

CANDY [*uncomfortably*]. Well, hell, I had him so long! Had him since he was a pup. I herded sheep with him. [*Proudly.*] You wouldn't think it to look at him now. He was the best damn sheep dog I ever seen.

GEORGE. I knowed a guy in Weed that had an airedale that could herd sheep. Learned it from the other dogs.

CARLSON [*sticking to his point*]. Lookit, Candy. This ole dog jus' suffers itself all the time. If you was to take him out and shoot him—right in the back of the head . . . [*Leans over and points.*] . . . right there, why he never'd know what hit him.

CANDY [*unhappily*]. No, I couldn't do that. I had him too long.

CARLSON [*insisting*]. He don't have no fun no more. He stinks like hell. Tell you what I'll do. I'll shoot him for you. Then it won't be you that done it.

CANDY [*sits up on the bunk, rubbing his whiskers*

nervously, speaks plaintively]. I had him from a pup.

WHIT. Let 'im alone, Carl. It ain't a guy's dog that matters. It's the way the guy feels about the dog. Hell, I had a mutt once I wouldn't a traded for a field trial pointer.

CARLSON [*being persuasive*]. Well, Candy ain't being nice to him, keeping him alive. Lookit, Slim's bitch got a litter right now. I bet you Slim would give ya one of them pups to raise up, wouldn't ya, Slim?

SLIM [*studying the dog*]. Yeah. You can have a pup if you want to.

CANDY [*helplessly*]. Mebbe it would hurt. [*After a moment's pause, positively.*] And I don't mind taking care of him.

CARLSON. Aw, he'd be better off dead. The way I'd shoot him he wouldn't feel nothin'. I'd put the gun right there. [*Points with his toe.*] Right back of the head.

WHIT. Aw, let 'im alone, Carl.

CARLSON. Why, hell, he wouldn't even quiver.

WHIT. Let 'im alone. [*He produces a magazine*]. Say, did you see this? Did you see this in the book here?

CARLSON. See what?

WHIT. Right there. Read that.

CARLSON. I don't want to read nothing. . . . It'd be all over in a minute, Candy. Come on.

WHIT. Did you see it, Slim? Go on, read it. Read it out loud.

SLIM. What is it?

WHIT. Read it.

SLIM [*reads slowly*]. "Dear Editor: I read your mag for six years and I think it is the best on the market. I like stories by Peter Rand. I think he is a whing-ding. Give us more like the Dark Rider. I don't

write many letters. Just thought I would tell you I
think your mag is the best dime's worth I ever
spen'." [*Looks up questioningly.*] What you want
me to read that for?

WHIT. Go on, read the name at the bottom.

SLIM [*reading*]. "Yours for Success, William Tenner."
[*Looks up at* WHIT.] What ya want me to read that
for?

CARLSON. Come on, Candy—what you say?

WHIT [*taking the magazine and closing it impressively.
Talks to cover* CARLSON]. You don't remember Bill
Tenner? Worked here about three months ago?

SLIM [*thinking*]. Little guy? Drove a cultivator?

WHIT. That's him. That's the guy.

CARLSON [*has refused to be drawn into this conversation*]. Look, Candy. If you want me to, I'll put the
old devil outa his misery right now and get it over
with. There ain't nothing left for him. Can't eat,
can't see, can't hardly walk. Tomorrow you can
pick one of Slim's pups.

SLIM. Sure . . . I got a lot of 'em.

CANDY [*hopefully*]. You ain't got no gun.

CARLSON. The hell, I ain't. Got a Luger. It won't hurt
him none at all.

CANDY. Mebbe tomorrow. Let's wait till tomorrow.

CARLSON. I don't see no reason for it. [*Goes to his
bunk, pulls a bag from underneath, takes a Luger
pistol out.*] Let's get it over with. We can't sleep
with him stinking around in here. [*He snaps a
shell into the chamber, sets the safety and puts the
pistol into his hip pocket.*]

SLIM [*as* CANDY *looks toward him for help*]. Better let
him go, Candy.

CANDY [*looks at each person for some hope.* WHIT
makes a gesture of protest and then resigns himself.

The others look away, to avoid responsibility. At last, very softly and hopelessly]. All right. Take him.
[*He doesn't look down at the dog at all. Lies back on his bunk and crosses his arms behind his head and stares at the ceiling.* CARLSON *picks up the string, helps the dog to its feet*].

CARSON. Come, boy. Come on, boy. [*To* CANDY, *apologetically*.] He won't even feel it. [CANDY *does not move nor answer him*.] Come on, boy. That's the stuff. Come on. [*He leads the dog toward the door*.]

SLIM. Carlson?

CARLSON. Yeah.

SLIM [*curtly*]. Take a shovel.

CARLSON. Oh, sure, I get you.

[*Exit* CARLSON *with the dog.* GEORGE *follows to the door, shuts it carefully and sets the latch.* CANDY *lies rigidly on his bunk. The next scene is one of silence and quick staccato speeches.*]

SLIM [*loudly*]. One of my lead mules got a bad hoof. Got to get some tar on it.

[*There is a silence.*]

GEORGE [*loudly*]. Anybody like to play a little euchre?

WHIT. I'll lay out a few with you.

[*They take places opposite each other at the table but* GEORGE *does not shuffle the cards. He ripples the edge of the deck. Everybody looks over at him. He stops. Silence again.*]

SLIM [*compassionately*]. Candy, you can have any of them pups you want.

[*There is no answer from* CANDY. *There is a little gnawing noise on the stage.*]

GEORGE. Sounds like there was a rat under there. We ought to set a trap there.

[*Deep silence again.*]

WHIT [*exasperated*]. What the hell is takin' him so

long? Lay out some cards, why don't you? We ain't gonna get no euchre played this way.

[GEORGE *studies the backs of the cards. And after a long silence there is a shot in the distance. All the men start a bit, look quickly at* CANDY. *For a moment he continues to stare at the ceiling and then rolls slowly over and faces the wall.* GEORGE *shuffles the cards noisily and deals them.*]

GEORGE. Well, let's get to it.

WHIT [*still to cover the moment*]. Yeah . . . I guess you guys really come here to work, huh?

GEORGE. How do you mean?

WHIT [*chuckles*]. Well, you come on a Friday. You got two days to work till Sunday.

GEORGE. I don't see how you figure.

WHIT. You do if you been round these big ranches much. A guy that wants to look over a ranch comes in Saturday afternoon. He gets Saturday night supper, three meals on Sunday and he can quit Monday morning after breakfast without turning a hand. But you come to work on Friday noon. You got ta put in a day and a half no matter how ya figure it.

GEORGE [*quietly*]. We're goin' stick around awhile. Me and Lennie's gonna roll up a stake.

[*Door opens and the Negro* STABLE BUCK *puts in his head. A lean-faced Negro with pained eyes.*]

CROOKS. Mr. Slim.

SLIM [*who has been watching* CANDY *the whole time*]. Huh? Oh, hello, Crooks, what's the matter?

CROOKS. You tole me to warm up tar for that mule's foot. I got it warm now.

SLIM. Oh, sure, Crooks. I'll come right out and put it on.

CROOKS. I can do it for you if you want, Mr. Slim.

SLIM [*standing up*]. Naw, I'll take care of my own team.

CROOKS. Mr. Slim.

SLIM. Yeah.

CROOKS. That big new guy is messing round your pups in the barn.

SLIM. Well, he ain't doin' no harm. I give him one of them pups.

CROOKS. Just thought I'd tell ya. He's takin' 'em out of the nest and handling 'em. That won't do 'em no good.

SLIM. Oh, he won't hurt 'em.

GEORGE [*looks up from his cards*]. If that crazy bastard is foolin' round too much jus' kick him out.

[SLIM *follows the* STABLE BUCK *out.*]

WHIT [*examining his cards*]. Seen the new kid yet?

GEORGE. What kid?

WHIT. Why, Curley's new wife.

GEORGE [*cautiously*]. Yeah, I seen her.

WHIT. Well, ain't she a lulu?

GEORGE. I ain't seen that much of her.

WHIT. Well, you stick around and keep your eyes open. You'll see plenty of her. I never seen nobody like her. She's just workin' on everybody all the time. Seems like she's even workin' on the stable buck. I don't know what the hell she wants.

GEORGE [*casually*]. Been any trouble since she got here?

[*Obviously neither man is interested in the card game.* WHIT *lays down his hand and* GEORGE *gathers the cards in and lays out a solitaire hand.*]

WHIT. I see what you mean. No, they ain't been no trouble yet. She's only been here a couple of weeks. Curley's got yellow jackets in his drawers, but that's all so far. Every time the guys is around she shows up. She's lookin' for Curley. Or she thought she left somethin' layin' around and she's lookin' for that. Seems like she can't keep away from guys. And Curley's runnin' round like a cat lookin' for a dirt road. But they ain't been no trouble.

GEORGE. Ranch with a bunch of guys on it ain't no place for a girl. Specially like her.

WHIT. If she's give you any ideas you ought to come in town with us guys tomorrow night.

GEORGE. Why, what's doin'?

WHIT. Just the usual thing. We go in to old Susy's place. Hell of a nice place. Old Susy is a laugh. Always cracking jokes. Like she says when we come up on the front porch last Saturday night: Susy opens the door and she yells over her shoulder: "Get your coats on, girls, here comes the sheriff." She never talks dirty neither. Got five girls there.

GEORGE. What does it set you back?

WHIT. Two and a half. You can get a shot of whiskey for fifteen cents. Susy got nice chairs to set in too. If a guy don't want to flop, why he can just set in them chairs and have a couple or three shots and just pass the time of day. Susy don't give a damn. She ain't rushin' guys through, or kicking them out if they don't want to flop.

GEORGE. Might go in and look the joint over.

WHIT. Sure. Come along. It's a hell of a lot of fun—her crackin' jokes all the time. Like she says one time, she says: "I've knew people that if they got a rag rug on the floor and a kewpie doll lamp on the phonograph they think they're runnin' a parlor house." That's Gladys's house she's talkin' about. And Susy says: "I know what you boys want," she says: "My girls is clean," she says. "And there ain't no water in my whiskey," she says. "If any you guys want to look at a kewpie doll lamp and take your chance of gettin' burned, why, you know where to go." She says: "They's guys round here walkin' bowlegged because they liked to look at a kewpie doll lamp."

GEORGE. Gladys runs the other house, huh?

WHIT. Yeah.

[*Enter* CARLSON. CANDY *looks at him.*]

CARLSON. God, it's a dark night. [*Goes to his bunk; starts cleaning his pistol.*]

WHIT. We don't never go to Gladys's. Gladys gits three bucks, and two bits a shot and she don't crack no jokes. But Susy's place is clean and she got nice chairs. A guy can set in there like he lived there. Don't let no Manila Goo-Goos in, neither.

GEORGE. Aw, I don't know. Me and Lennie's rollin' up a stake. I might go in and set and have a shot, but I ain't puttin' out no two and a half.

WHIT. Well, a guy got to have some fun sometimes.

[*Enter* LENNIE. LENNIE *creeps to his bunk and sits down.*]

GEORGE. Didn't bring him back in, did you, Lennie?

LENNIE. No, George, honest I didn't. See?

WHIT. Say, how about this euchre game?

GEORGE. Okay. I didn't think you wanted to play.

[*Enter* CURLEY *excitedly.*]

CURLEY. Any you guys seen my wife?

WHIT. She ain't been here.

CURLEY [*looks threateningly about the room.*] Where the hell's Slim?

GEORGE. Went out in the barn. He was goin' put some tar on a split hoof.

CURLEY. How long ago did he go?

GEORGE. Oh, five, ten minutes.

[CURLEY *jumps out the door.*]

WHIT [*standing up*]. I guess maybe I'd like to see this. Curley must be spoilin' or he wouldn't start for Slim. Curley's handy, goddamn handy. But just the same he better leave Slim alone.

GEORGE. Thinks Slim's with his wife, don't he?

WHIT. Looks like it. 'Course Slim ain't. Least I don't

think Slim is. But I like to see the fuss if it comes off. Come on, le's go.

GEORGE. I don't want to git mixed up in nothing. Me and Lennie got to make a stake.

CARLSON [*finishes cleaning gun, puts it in his bag and stands up*]. I'll look her over. Ain't seen a good fight in a hell of a while. [WHIT *and* CARLSON *exeunt.*]

GEORGE. You see Slim out in the barn?

LENNIE. Sure. He tole me I better not pet that pup no more, like I said.

GEORGE. Did you see that girl out there?

LENNIE. You mean Curley's girl?

GEORGE. Yeah. Did she come in the barn?

LENNIE [*cautiously*]. No—anyways I never seen her.

GEORGE. You never seen Slim talkin' to her?

LENNIE. Uh-uh. She ain't been in the barn.

GEORGE. Okay. I guess them guys ain't gonna see no fight. If they's any fightin', Lennie, ya get out of the way and stay out.

LENNIE. I don't want no fight. [GEORGE *lays out his solitaire hand.* LENNIE *picks up a face card and studies it. Turns it over and studies it again.*] Both ends the same. George, why is it both ends the same?

GEORGE. I don't know. That jus' the way they make 'em. What was Slim doin' in the barn when you seen him?

LENNIE. Slim?

GEORGE. Sure, you seen him in the barn. He tole you not to pet the pups so much.

LENNIE. Oh. Yeah. He had a can of tar and a paint brush. I don't know what for.

GEORGE. You sure that girl didn't come in like she come in here today?

LENNIE. No, she never come.

GEORGE [*sighs*]. You give me a good whorehouse every time. A guy can go in and get drunk and get it over all at once and no messes. And he knows how much it's goin' set him back. These tarts is jus' buckshot to a guy. [LENNIE *listens with admiration, moving his lips, and* GEORGE *continues.*] You remember Andy Cushman, Lennie? Went to grammar school same time as us?

LENNIE. The one that his ole lady used to make hot cakes for the kids?

GEORGE. Yeah. That's the one. You can remember if they's somepin to eat in it. [*Scores up some cards in his solitaire playing.*] Well, Andy's in San Quentin right now on account of a tart.

LENNIE. George?

GEORGE. Huh?

LENNIE. How long is it goin' be till we git that little place to live off the fat of the land?

GEORGE. I don't know. We gotta get a big stake together. I know a little place we can get cheap, but they ain't givin' it away.

[CANDY *turns over and watches* GEORGE.]

LENNIE. Tell about that place, George.

GEORGE. I jus' tole you. Jus' last night.

LENNIE. Go on, tell again.

GEORGE. Well, it's ten acres. Got a windmill. Got a little shack on it and a chicken run. Got a kitchen orchard. Cherries, apples, peaches, 'cots and nuts. Got a few berries. There's a place for alfalfa and plenty water to flood it. There's a pig pen. . . .

LENNIE [*breaking in*]. And rabbits, George?

GEORGE. I could easy build a few hutches. And you could feed alfalfa to them rabbits.

LENNIE. Damn right I could. [*Excitedly.*] You goddamn right I could.

GEORGE [*his voice growing warmer*]. And we could have a few pigs. I'd build a smokehouse. And when we kill a pig we could smoke the hams. When the salmon run up the river we can catch a hundred of 'em. Every Sunday we'd kill a chicken or rabbit. Mebbe we'll have a cow or a goat. And the cream is so goddamn thick you got to cut it off the pan with a knife.

LENNIE [*watching him with wide eyes, softly*]. We can live off the fat of the land.

GEORGE. Sure. All kinds of vegetables in the garden and if we want a little whiskey we can sell some eggs or somethin'. And we wouldn't sleep in no bunkhouse. Nobody could can us in the middle of a job.

LENNIE [*begging*]. Tell about the house, George.

GEORGE. Sure. We'd have a little house. And a room to ourselves. And it ain't enough land so we'd have to work too hard. Mebbe six, seven hours a day only. We wouldn't have to buck no barley eleven hours a day. And when we put in a crop, why we'd be there to take that crop up. We'd know what come of our planting.

LENNIE [*eagerly*]. And rabbits. And I'd take care of them. Tell how I'd do that, George.

GEORGE. Sure. You'd go out in the alfalfa patch and you'd have a sack. You'd fill up the sack and bring it in and put it in the rabbit cages.

LENNIE. They'd nibble and they'd nibble, the way they do. I seen 'em.

GEORGE. Every six weeks or so them does would throw a litter. So we'd have plenty rabbits to eat or sell. [*Pauses for inspiration.*] And we'd keep a few pigeons to go flying round and round the windmill, like they done when I was a kid. [*Seems entranced.*] And it'd be our own. And nobody could can us. If we don't like a guy we can say: "Get to hell out," and by God he's got to do it. And if a friend come along, why, we'd have an extra bunk. Know what

we'd say? We'd say, "Why don't you spen' the night?"
And by God he would. We'd have a setter dog and
a couple of striped cats. [*Looks sharply at* LENNIE.]
But you gotta watch out them cats don't get the
little rabbits.

LENNIE [*breathing hard*]. You jus' let 'em try. I'll break
their goddamn necks. I'll smash them cats flat with
a stick. I'd smash 'em flat with a stick. That's what
I'd do. [*They sit silently for a moment.*]

CANDY [*at the sound of his voice, both* LENNIE *and*
GEORGE *jump as though caught in some secret.*] You
know where's a place like that?

GEORGE [*solemnly*]. S'pose I do, what's that to you?

CANDY. You don't need to tell me where it's at. Might
be any place.

GEORGE [*relieved*]. Sure. That's right, you couldn't find
it in a hundred years.

CANDY [*excitedly*]. How much they want for a place
like that?

GEORGE [*grudgingly*]. Well, I could get it for six hundred bucks. The ole people that owns it is flat bust.
And the ole lady needs medicine. Say, what's it to
you? You got nothing to do with us!

CANDY [*softly*]. I ain't much good with only one hand.
I lost my hand right here on the ranch. That's why
they didn't can me. They give me two hundred and
fifty dollars 'cause I lost my hand. An' I got fifty
more saved up right in the bank right now. That's
three hundred. And I got forty more comin' the end
of the month. Tell you what . . . [*He leans forward
eagerly.*] S'pose I went in with you guys? That's three
hundred and forty bucks I'd put in. I ain't much
good, but I could cook and tend the chickens and
hoe the garden some. How'd that be?

GEORGE [*his eyes half closed, uncertainly*]. I got to

think about that. We was always goin' to do it by
ourselves. Me an' Lennie. I never thought of nobody
else.

CANDY. I'd make a will. Leave my share to you guys in
case I kicked off. I ain't got no relations nor nothing. You fellas got any money? Maybe we could go
there right now.

GEORGE [*disgustedly*]. We got ten bucks between us.
[*He thinks.*] Say, look. If me and Lennie work a
month and don't spend nothing at all, we'll have a
hundred bucks. That would be four forty. I bet we
could swing her for that. Then you and Lennie
could go get her started and I'd get a job and make
up the rest. You could sell eggs and stuff like that.
[*They look at each other in amazement. Reverently.*]
Jesus Christ, I bet we could swing her. [*His voice is
full of wonder.*] I bet we could swing 'er.

CANDY [*scratches the stump of his wrist nervously*]. I
got hurt four years ago. They'll can me pretty soon.
Jest as soon as I can't swamp out no bunkhouses
they'll put me on the county. Maybe if I give you
guys my money, you'll let me hoe in the garden,
even when I ain't no good at it. And I'll wash dishes
and little chicken stuff like that. But hell, I'll be on
our own place. I'll be let to work on our own place.
[*Miserably.*] You seen what they done to my dog.
They says he wasn't no good to himself nor nobody
else. But when I'm that way nobody'll shoot me. I
wish somebody would. They won't do nothing like
that. I won't have no place to go and I can't get no
more jobs.

GEORGE [*stands up*]. We'll do 'er! God damn, we'll fix
up that little ole place and we'll go live there. [*Won-
deringly.*] S'pose they was a carnival, or a circus
come to town or a ball game or any damn thing.
[CANDY *nods in appreciation.*] We'd just go to her.

We wouldn't ask nobody if we could. Just say we'll go to her, by God, and we would. Just milk the cow and sling some grain to the chickens and go to her.

LENNIE. And put some grass to the rabbits. I wouldn't forget to feed them. When we gonna to do it, George?

GEORGE [*decisively*]. In one month. Right squack in one month. Know what I'm gonna do? I'm goin' write to them ole people that owns the place that we'll take 'er. And Candy'll send a hundred dollars to bind her.

CANDY [*happily*]. I sure will. They got a good stove there?

GEORGE. Sure, got a nice stove. Burns coal or wood.

LENNIE. I'm gonna take my pup. I bet by Christ he likes it there.

[*The window, center backstage, swings outward.* CUR-LEY'S WIFE *looks in. They do not see her.*]

GEORGE [*quickly*]. Now don't tell nobody about her. Jus' us three and nobody else. They'll liable to can us so we can't make no stake. We'll just go on like we was a bunch of punks. Like we was gonna buck barley the rest of our lives. And then all of a sudden, one day, bang! We get our pay and scram out of here.

CANDY. I can give you three hundred right now.

LENNIE. And not tell nobody. We won't tell nobody, George.

GEORGE. You're goddamn right we won't. [*There is a silence and then* GEORGE *speaks irritably.*] You know, seems to me I can almost smell that carnation stuff that goddamn tart dumps on herself.

CURLEY'S WIFE [*in the first part of the speech by* GEORGE *she starts to step out of sight but at the last words her face darkens with anger. At her first words every-body in the room looks around at her and remains rigid during the tirade*]. Who you callin' a tart! I come from a nice home. I was brung up by nice people. Nobody never got to me before I was married. I was straight. I tell you I was good. [*A little plaintively.*] I was. [*Angrily again.*] You know Curley. You know he wouldn't stay with me if he wasn't sure. I tell you Curley is sure. You got no right to call me a tart.

GEORGE [*sullenly*]. If you ain't a tart, what you always hangin' round guys for? You got a house an' you got a man. We don't want no trouble from you.

CURLEY'S WIFE [*pleadingly*]. Sure I got a man. He ain't never home. I got nobody to talk to. I got nobody to be with. Think I can just sit home and do nothin' but cook for Curley? I want to see somebody. Just see 'em an' talk to 'em. There ain't no women. I can't walk to town. And Curley don't take me to no dances now. I tell you I jus' want to talk to somebody.

GEORGE [*boldly*]. If you're just friendly what you givin' out the eye for an' floppin' your can around?

CURLEY'S WIFE [*sadly*]. I just wanta be nice.

[*The sound of approaching voices: "You don't have to get mad about it, do you?" . . . "I ain't mad, but I just don't want no more questions, that's all. I just don't want no more questions."*]

GEORGE. Get goin'. We don't want no trouble.

[CURLEY'S WIFE *looks from the window and closes it silently and disappears. Enter* SLIM, *followed by* CURLEY, CARLSON *and* WHIT. SLIM'S *hands are black with tar.* CURLEY *hangs close to his elbow.*]

CURLEY [*explaining*]. Well, I didn't mean nothing, Slim. I jus' ast you.

SLIM. Well, you been askin' too often. I'm gettin' goddamn sick of it. If you can't look after your own wife, what you expect me to do about it? You lay off of me.

CURLEY. I'm jus' tryin' to tell you I didn't mean nothing. I just thought you might of saw her.

CARLSON. Why don't you tell her to stay to hell home where she belongs? You let her hang around the bunkhouses and pretty soon you're goin' to have somethin' on your hands.

CURLEY [*whirls on* CARLSON]. You keep out of this 'less you want ta step outside.

CARLSON [*laughing*]. Why, you goddamn punk. You tried to throw a scare into Slim and you couldn't make it stick. Slim throwed a scare into you. You're yellow as a frog's belly. I don't care if you're the best boxer in the country, you come for me and I'll kick your goddamn head off.

WHIT [*joining in the attack*]. Glove full of vaseline!

CURLEY [*glares at him, then suddenly sniffs the air, like a hound*]. By God, she's been in *here*. I can smell— By God, she's been in here. [*To* GEORGE.] You was here. The other guys was outside. Now, God damn you—you talk.

GEORGE [*looks worried. He seems to make up his mind to face an inevitable situation. Slowly takes off his coat, and folds it almost daintily. Speaks in an unemotional monotone*]. Somebody got to beat the hell outa you. I guess I'm elected.

[LENNIE *has been watching, fascinated. He gives his high, nervous chuckle.*]

CURLEY [*whirls on him*]. What the hell you laughin' at?

LENNIE [*blankly*]. Huh?

CURLEY [*exploding with rage*]. Come on, you big bastard. Get up on your feet. No big son-of-a-bitch is gonna laugh at me. I'll show you who's yellow.

[LENNIE *looks helplessly at* GEORGE. *Gets up and tries*

to retreat upstage. CURLEY *follows slashing at him.
The others mass themselves in front of the two con-
testants:* "That ain't no way, Curley—he ain't done
nothing to you." . . . "Lay off him, will you, Curley.
He ain't no fighter." . . . "Sock him back, big guy!
Don't be afraid of him!" . . . "Give him a chance,
Curley. Give him a chance."

LENNIE [*crying with terror*]. George, make him leave
me alone, George.

GEORGE. Get him, Lennie. Get him! [*There is a sharp
cry. The gathering of men opens and* CURLEY *is
flopping about, his hand lost in* LENNIE'S *hand.*] Let
go of him, Lennie. Let go! ["*He's got his hand!*" . . .
"*Look at that, will you?*" . . . "*Jesus, what a guy!*"
LENNIE *watches in terror the flopping man he holds.*
LENNIE'S *face is covered with blood.* GEORGE *slaps*
LENNIE *in the face again and again.* CURLEY *is weak
and shrunken.*] Let go his hand, Lennie. Slim, come
help me, while this guy's got any hand left.

[*Suddenly* LENNIE *lets go. He cowers away from*
GEORGE.]

LENNIE. You told me to, George. I heard you tell me to.

[CURLEY *has dropped to the floor.* SLIM *and* CARLSON
bend over him and look at his hand. SLIM *looks
over at* LENNIE *with horror.*]

SLIM. We got to get him to a doctor. It looks to me
like every bone in his hand is busted.

LENNIE [*crying*]. I didn't wanta. I didn't wanta hurt
'im.

SLIM. Carlson, you get the candy wagon out. He'll have
to go into Soledad and get his hand fixed up. [*Turns
to the whimpering* LENNIE.] It ain't your fault. This
punk had it comin' to him. But Jesus—he ain't
hardly got no hand left.

GEORGE [*moving near*]. Slim, will we git canned now?
Will Curley's ole man can us now?

SLIM. I don't know. [*Kneels down beside* CURLEY.] You got your sense enough to listen? [CURLEY *nods.*] Well, then you listen. I think you got your hand caught in a machine. If you don't tell nobody what happened, we won't. But you jest tell and try to get this guy canned and we'll tell everybody. And then will you get the laugh! [*Helps* CURLEY *to his feet.*] Come on now. Carlson's goin' to take you in to a doctor. [*Starts for the door, turns back to* LENNIE.] Le's see your hands. [LENNIE *sticks out both hands.*] Christ Almighty!

GEORGE. Lennie was just scairt. He didn't know what to do. I tole you nobody ought never to fight him. No, I guess it was Candy I tole.

CANDY [*solemnly*]. That's just what you done. Right this morning when Curley first lit into him. You says he better not fool with Lennie if he knows what's good for him.

[*They all leave the stage except* GEORGE *and* LENNIE *and* CANDY.]

GEORGE [*to* LENNIE, *very gently*]. It ain't your fault. You don't need to be scairt no more. You done jus' what I tole you to. Maybe you better go in the washroom and clean your face. You look like hell.

LENNIE. I didn't want no trouble.

GEORGE. Come on—I'll go with you.

LENNIE. George?

GEORGE. What you want?

LENNIE. Can I still tend the rabbits, George?

[*They exeunt together, side by side, through the door of the bunkhouse.*]

CURTAIN

SCENE II

Ten o'clock Saturday evening.

The room of the stable buck, a lean-to off the barn. There is a plank door upstage center; a small square window center right. On one side of the door a leather working bench with tools racked behind it, and on the other racks with broken and partly mended harnesses, collars, hames, traces, etc. At the left upstage CROOKS' *bunk. Over it two shelves. On one a great number of medicines in cans and bottles. And on the other a number of tattered books and a big alarm clock. In the corner right upstage a single-barreled shotgun and on the floor beside it a pair of rubber boots. A large pair of gold spectacles hang on a nail over* CROOKS' *bunk.*

The entrance leads into the barn proper. From that direction and during the whole scene come the sounds of horses eating, stamping, jingling their halter chains and now and then whinnying.

Two empty nail kegs are in the room to be used as seats. Single unshaded small-candlepower carbon light hanging from its own cord.

As the curtain rises, we see CROOKS *sitting on his bunk rubbing his back with liniment. He reaches up under his shirt to do this. His face is lined with pain. As he rubs he flexes his muscles and shivers a little.*

LENNIE *appears in the open doorway, nearly filling the opening. Then* CROOKS, *sensing his presence, raises his eyes, stiffens and scowls.*

LENNIE *smiles in an attempt to make friends.*

CROOKS [*sharply*]. You got no right to come in my room. This here's my room. Nobody got any right in here but me.

LENNIE [*fawning*]. I ain't doin' nothing. Just come in the barn to look at my pup, and I seen your light.

CROOKS. Well, I got a right to have a light. You go on and get out of my room. I ain't wanted in the bunkhouse and you ain't wanted in my room.

LENNIE [*ingenuously*]. Why ain't you wanted?

CROOKS [*furiously*]. 'Cause I'm black. They play cards in there. But I can't play because I'm black. They say I stink. Well, I tell you all of you stink to me.

LENNIE [*helplessly*]. Everybody went into town. Slim and George and everybody. George says I got to stay here and not get into no trouble. I seen your light.

CROOKS. Well, what do you want?

LENNIE. Nothing . . . I seen your light. I thought I could jus' come in and set.

CROOKS [*stares at* LENNIE *for a moment, takes down his spectacles and adjusts them over his ears; says in a complaining tone*]. I don't know what you're doin' in the barn anyway. You ain't no skinner. There's no call for a bucker to come into the barn at all. You've got nothing to do with the horses and mules.

LENNIE [*patiently*]. The pup. I come to see my pup.

CROOKS. Well, God damn it, go and see your pup then. Don't go no place where you ain't wanted.

LENNIE [*advances a step into the room, remembers and backs to the door again*]. I looked at him a little. Slim says I ain't to pet him very much.

CROOKS [*the anger gradually going out of his voice*]. Well, you been taking him out of the nest all the time. I wonder the ole lady don't move him some place else.

LENNIE [*moving into the room*]. Oh, she don't care. She lets me.

CROOKS [*scowls and then gives up*]. Come on in and set awhile. Long as you won't get out and leave me alone, you might as well set down. [*A little more friendly.*] All the boys gone into town, huh?

LENNIE. All but old Candy. He jus' sets in the bunkhouse sharpening his pencils. And sharpening and figurin'.

CROOKS [*adjusting his glasses*]. Figurin'? What's Candy figurin' about?

LENNIE. 'Bout the land. 'Bout the little place.

CROOKS. You're nuts. You're crazy as a wedge. What land you talkin' about?

LENNIE. The land we're goin' to get. And a little house and pigeons.

CROOKS. Just nuts. I don't blame the guy you're traveling with for keeping you out of sight.

LENNIE [*quietly*]. It ain't no lie. We're gonna do it. Gonna get a little place and live off the fat of the land.

CROOKS [*settling himself comfortably on his bunk*]. Set down on that nail keg.

LENNIE [*hunches over on the little barrel*]. You think it's a lie. But it ain't no lie. Ever' word's the truth. You can ask George.

CROOKS [*puts his dark chin on his palm*]. You travel round with George, don't you?

LENNIE [*proudly*]. Sure, me and him goes ever' place together.

CROOKS [*after a pause, quietly*]. Sometimes he talks and you don't know what the hell he's talkin' about. Ain't that so? [*Leans forward.*] Ain't that so?

LENNIE. Yeah. Sometimes.

CROOKS. Just talks on. And you don't know what the hell it's all about.

LENNIE. How long you think it'll be before them pups will be old enough to pet?

CROOKS [*laughs again*]. A guy can talk to you and be sure you won't go blabbin'. A couple of weeks and them pups will be all right. [*Musing.*] George knows what he's about. Just talks and you don't understand nothing. [*Mood gradually changes to excitement.*] Well, this is just a nigger talkin' and a busted-back nigger. It don't mean nothing, see. You couldn't remember it anyway. I seen it over and over —a guy talking to another guy and it don't make no difference if he don't hear or understand. The thing is they're talkin'. [*He pounds his knee with his hand.*] George can tell you screwy things and it don't matter. It's just the talkin'. It's just bein' with another guy, that's all. [*His voice becomes soft and malicious.*] S'pose George don't come back no more? S'pose he took a powder and just ain't comin' back. What you do then?

LENNIE [*trying to follow* CROOKS]. What? What?

CROOKS. I said s'pose George went into town tonight and you never heard of him no more. [*Presses forward.*] Just s'pose that.

LENNIE [*sharply*]. He won't do it. George wouldn't do nothing like that. I been with George a long time. He'll come back tonight. . . . [*Doubt creeps into his voice.*] Don't you think he will?

CROOKS [*delighted with his torture*]. Nobody can tell what a guy will do. Let's say he wants to come back and can't. S'pose he gets killed or hurt so he can't come back.

LENNIE [*in terrible apprehension*]. I don't know. Say, what you doin' anyway? It ain't true. George ain't got hurt.

CROOKS [*cruelly*]. Want me to tell you what'll happen? They'll take you to the booby hatch. They'll tie you up with a collar like a dog. Then you'll be jus' like me. Livin' in a kennel.

LENNIE [*furious, walks over towards* CROOKS]. Who hurt George?

CROOKS [*recoiling from him with fright*]. I was just supposin'. George ain't hurt. He's all right. He'll be back all right.

LENNIE [*standing over him*]. What you supposin' for? Ain't nobody goin' to s'pose any hurt to George.

CROOKS [*trying to calm him*]. Now set down. George ain't hurt. Go on now, set down.

LENNIE [*growling*]. Ain't nobody gonna talk no hurt to George.

CROOKS [*very gently*]. Maybe you can see now. You got George. You know he's comin' back. S'pose you didn't have nobody. S'pose you couldn't go in the bunkhouse and play rummy, 'cause you was black. How would you like that? S'pose you had to set out here and read books. Sure, you could play horseshoes until it got dark, but then you got to read books. Books ain't no good. A guy needs somebody . . . to be near him. [*His tone whines.*] A guy goes nuts if he ain't got nobody. Don't make no difference who it is as long as he's with you. I tell you a guy gets too lonely, he gets sick.

LENNIE [*reassuring himself*]. George gonna come back. Maybe George come back already. Maybe I better go see.

CROOKS [*more gently*]. I didn't mean to scare you. He'll come back. I was talkin' about myself.

LENNIE [*miserably*]. George won't go away and leave me. I know George won't do that.

CROOKS [*continuing dreamily*]. I remember when I was a little kid on my ole man's chicken ranch. Had two brothers. They was always near me, always there.

Used to sleep right in the same room. Right in the same bed, all three. Had a strawberry patch. Had an alfalfa patch. Used to turn the chickens out in the alfalfa on a sunny morning. Me and my brothers would set on the fence and watch 'em—white chickens they was.

LENNIE [*interested*]. George says we're gonna have alfalfa.

CROOKS. You're nuts.

LENNIE. We are too gonna get it. You ask George.

CROOKS [*scornfully*]. You're nuts. I seen hundreds of men come by on the road and on the ranches, bindles on their back and that same damn thing in their head. Hundreds of 'em. They come and they quit and they go on. And every damn one of 'em is got a little piece of land in his head. And never a goddamn one of 'em gets it. Jus' like heaven. Everybody wants a little piece of land. Nobody never gets to heaven. And nobody gets no land.

LENNIE. We are too.

CROOKS. It's jest in your head. Guys all the time talkin' about it, but it's jest in your head. [*The horses move restlessly. One of them whinnies.*] I guess somebody's out there. Maybe Slim. [*Pulls himself painfully upright and moves toward the door. Calls.*] That you, Slim?

CANDY [*from outside*]. Slim went in town. Say, you seen Lennie?

CROOKS. You mean the big guy?

CANDY. Yes. Seen him around any place?

CROOKS [*goes back to his bunk and sits down, says shortly*]. He's in here.

CANDY [*stands in the doorway, scratching his wrist. Makes no attempt to enter.*] Look, Lennie, I been figuring something out. About the place.

CROOKS [*irritably*]. You can come in if you want.

CANDY [*embarrassed*]. I don't know. 'Course if you want me to.

CROOKS. Oh, come on in. Everybody's comin' in. You might just as well. Gettin' to be a goddamn race track. [*He tries to conceal his pleasure.*]

CANDY [*still embarrassed*]. You've got a nice cozy little place in here. Must be nice to have a room to yourself this way.

CROOKS. Sure. And a manure pile under the window. All to myself. It's swell.

LENNIE [*breaking in*]. You said about the place.

CANDY. You know, I been here a long time. An' Crooks been here a long time. This is the first time I ever been in his room.

CROOKS [*darkly*]. Guys don't come in a colored man's room. Nobody been here but Slim.

LENNIE [*insistently*]. The place. You said about the place.

CANDY. Yeah. I got it all figured out. We can make some real money on them rabbits if we go about it right.

LENNIE. But I get to tend 'em. George says I get to tend 'em. He promised.

CROOKS [*brutally*]. You guys is just kiddin' yourselves. You'll talk about it a hell of a lot, but you won't get no land. You'll be a swamper here until they take you out in a box. Hell, I seen too many guys.

CANDY [*angrily*]. We're gonna do it. George says we are. We got the money right now.

CROOKS. Yeah. And where is George now? In town in a whorehouse. That's where your money's goin'. I tell you I seen it happen too many times.

CANDY. George ain't got the money in town. The money's in the bank. Me and Lennie and George. We gonna have a room to ourselves. We gonna have a dog and chickens. We gonna have green corn and maybe a cow.

CROOKS [*impressed*]. You say you got the money?

CANDY. We got most of it. Just a little bit more to get. Have it all in one month. George's got the land all picked out too.

CROOKS [*exploring his spine with his hands*]. I've never seen a guy really do it. I seen guys nearly crazy with loneliness for land, but every time a whorehouse or a blackjack game took it away from 'em. [*Hesitates and then speaks timidly.*] If you guys would want a hand to work for nothin'—just his keep, why I'd come and lend a hand. I ain't so crippled I can't work like a son-of-a-bitch if I wanted to.

GEORGE [*strolls through the door, hands in pockets, leans against the wall, speaks in a half-satiric, rather gentle voice*]. You couldn't go to bed like I told you, could you, Lennie? Hell, no—you got to get out in society an' flap your mouth. Holdin' a convention out here.

LENNIE [*defending himself*]. You was gone. There wasn't nobody in the bunkhouse. I ain't done no bad things, George.

GEORGE [*still casually*]. Only time I get any peace is when you're asleep. If you ever get walkin' in your sleep I'll chop off your head like a chicken. [*Chops with his hand.*]

CROOKS [*coming to* LENNIE's *defense*]. We was jus' settin' here talkin'. Ain't no harm in that.

GEORGE. Yeah. I heard you. [*A weariness has settled on him.*] Got to be here ever' minute, I guess. Got to watch ya. [*To* CROOKS.] It ain't nothing against you, Crooks. We just wasn't gonna tell nobody.

CANDY [*tries to change subject*]. Didn't you have no fun in town?

GEORGE. Oh! I set in a chair and Susy was crackin' jokes

an' the guys was startin' to raise a little puny hell.
Christ Almighty—I never been this way before. I'm
jus' gonna set out a dime and a nickel for a shot an'
I think what a hell of a lot of bulk carrot seed you
can get for fifteen cents.

CANDY. Not in them damn little envelopes—but bulk
seed—you sure can.

GEORGE. So purty soon I come back. I can't think of
nothing else. Them guys slingin' money around got
me jumpy.

CANDY. Guy got to have *some* fun. I was to a parlor
house in Bakersfield once. God Almighty, what a
place. Went upstairs on a red carpet. They was big
pichers on the wall. We set in big sof' chairs. They
was cigarettes on the table—an' they was *free*. Purty
soon a Jap come in with drinks on a tray an' them
drinks was free. Take all you want. [*In a reverie.*]
Purty soon the girls come in an' they was jus' as
polite an' nice an' quiet an' purty. Didn't seem like
hookers. Made ya kinda scared to ask 'em. . . .
That was a long time ago.

GEORGE. Yeah? An' what'd them sof' chairs set you
back?

CANDY. Fifteen bucks.

GEORGE [*scornfully*]. So ya got a cigarette an' a whiskey
an' a look at a purty dress an' it cost ya twelve and
a half bucks extra. You shot a week's pay to walk on
that red carpet.

CANDY [*still entranced with his memory*]. A week's pay?
Sure. But I worked weeks all my life. I can't remember none of them weeks. But . . . that was nearly
twenty years ago. And I can remember that. Girl I
went with was named Arline. Had on a pink silk
dress.

GEORGE [*turns suddenly and looks out the door into*

the dark· barn, speaks savagely]. I s'pose ya lookin'
for Curley? [CURLEY'S WIFE *appears in the door.*]
Well, Curley ain't here.

CURLEY'S WIFE [*determined now*]. I know Curley ain't
here. I wanted to ast Crooks somepin'. I didn't know
you guys was here.

CANDY. Didn't George tell you before—we don't want
nothing to do with you. You know damn well Curley ain't here.

CURLEY'S WIFE. I know where Curley went. Got his arm
in a sling an' he went anyhow. I tell ya I come out
to ast Crooks somepin'.

CROOKS [*apprehensively*]. Maybe you better go along to
your own house. You hadn't ought to come near a
colored man's room. I don't want no trouble. You
don't want to ask me nothing.

CANDY [*rubbing his wrist stump*]. You got a husband.
You got no call to come foolin' around with other
guys, causin' trouble.

CURLEY'S WIFE [*suddenly angry*]. I try to be nice an'
polite to you lousy bindle bums—but you're too
good. I tell ya I could of went with shows. An'—an'
a guy wanted ·to put me in pichers right in Hollywood. [*Looks about to see how she is impressing
them. Their eyes are hard.*] I come out here to ast
somebody somepin' an'—

CANDY [*stands up suddenly and knocks his nail keg
over backwards, speaks angrily*]. I had enough. You
ain't wanted here. We tole you, you ain't. Callin' us
bindle stiffs. You got floozy idears what us guys
amounts to. You ain't got sense enough to see us
guys ain't bindle stiffs. S'pose you could get us
canned—s'pose you *could*. You think we'd hit the
highway an' look for another two-bit job. You don't
know we got our own ranch to go to an' our own

house an' fruit trees. An' we got friends. That's what we got. Maybe they was a time when we didn't have nothin', but that ain't so no more.

CURLEY'S WIFE. You damn ol' goat. If you had two bits, you'd be in Soledad gettin' a drink an' suckin' the bottom of the glass.

GEORGE. Maybe she could ask Crooks what she come to ask an' then get the hell home. I don't think she come to ask nothing.

CURLEY'S WIFE. What happened to Curley's hand? [CROOKS *laughs.* GEORGE *tries to shut him up.*] So it wasn't no machine. Curley didn't act like he was tellin' the truth. Come on, Crooks—what happened?

CROOKS. I wasn't there. I didn't see it.

CURLEY'S WIFE [*eagerly*]. What happened? I won't let on to Curley. He says he caught his han' in a gear. [CROOKS *is silent.*] Who done it?

GEORGE. Didn't nobody do it.

CURLEY'S WIFE [*turns slowly to* GEORGE]. So *you* done it. Well, he had it comin'.

GEORGE. I didn't have no fuss with Curley.

CURLEY'S WIFE [*steps near him, smiling*]. Maybe now you ain't scared of him no more. Maybe you'll talk to me sometimes now. Ever'body was scared of him.

GEORGE [*speaks rather kindly*]. Look! I didn't sock Curley. If he had trouble, it ain't none of our affair. Ask Curley about it. Now listen. I'm gonna try to tell ya. We tole you to get the hell out and it don't do no good. So I'm gonna tell you another way. Us guys got somepin' we're gonna do. If you stick around you'll gum up the works. It ain't your fault. If a guy steps on a round pebble an' falls an' breaks his neck, it ain't the pebble's fault, but the guy wouldn't of did it if the pebble wasn't there.

CURLEY'S WIFE [*puzzled*]. What you talkin' about pebbles? If you didn't sock Curley, who did? [*She looks*

at the others, then steps quickly over to LENNIE.]
Where'd you get them bruises on your face?

GEORGE. I tell you he got his hand caught in a machine.

LENNIE [*looks anxiously at* GEORGE, *speaks miserably*].
He caught his han' in a machine.

GEORGE. So now get out of here.

CURLEY'S WIFE [*goes close to* LENNIE, *speaks softly and
there is a note of affection in her voice*]. So . . . it was
you. Well . . . maybe you're dumb like they say . . .
an' maybe . . . you're the only guy on the ranch with
guts. [*She puts her hand on* LENNIE'S *shoulder. He
looks up in her face and a smile grows on his face.
She strokes his shoulder.*] You're a nice fella.

GEORGE [*suddenly leaps at her ferociously, grabs her
shoulder and whirls her around*]. Listen . . . you! I
tried to give you a break. Don't you walk into nothing! We ain't gonna let you mess up what we're
gonna do. You let this guy alone an' get the hell out
of here.

CURLEY'S WIFE [*defiant but slightly frightened*]. You
ain't tellin' me what to do. [*The* BOSS *appears in the
door, stands legs spread, thumbs hooked over his
belt.*] I got a right to talk to anybody I want to.

GEORGE. Why, you—

[GEORGE, *furiously, steps close—his hand is raised to
strike her. She cowers a little.* GEORGE *stiffens, seeing*
BOSS, *frozen in position. The others see* BOSS *too.*
GIRL *retreats slowly.* GEORGE'S *hand drops slowly to
his side—he takes two slow backward steps. Hold
the scene for a moment.*]

CURTAIN

Act three

Mid-afternoon Sunday.

One end of a great barn. Backstage the hay slopes up sharply against the wall. High in the upstage wall is a large hay window. On each side are seen the hay racks, behind which are the stalls with the horses in them. Throughout this scene the horses can be heard in their stalls, rattling their halter chains and chewing at the hay.

The entrance is downstage right.

The boards of the barn are not close together. Streaks of afternoon sun come between the boards, made visible by dust in the air. From outside comes the clang of horseshoes on the playing peg, shouts of men encouraging or jeering.

In the barn there is a feeling of quiet and humming and lazy warmth. Curtain rises on LENNIE sitting in the hay, looking down at a little dead puppy in front of him. He puts out his big hand and strokes it clear from one end to the other.

LENNIE [*softly*]. Why do you got to get killed? You ain't so little as mice. I didn' bounce you hard. [*Bends the pup's head up and looks in its face.*] Now maybe George ain't gonna let me tend no rabbits if he finds out you got killed. [*He scoops a little hollow and lays the puppy in it out of sight and covers it over with hay. He stares at the mound he has made.*] This ain't no bad thing like I got to hide in the brush. I'll tell George I found it dead. [*He unburies the pup and inspects it. Twists its ears and works his fingers in its fur. Sorrowfully.*] But he'll know. George always knows. He'll say: "You done it. Don't try to put nothin' over on me." And he'll say: "Now just for that you don't get to tend no—you-know-whats." [*His anger rises. Addresses the pup.*] God damn you. Why do you got to get killed? You ain't so little as mice. [*Picks up the pup and hurls it from him and turns his back on it. He sits bent over his knees moaning to himself.*] Now he won't let me. . . . Now he won't let me. [*Outside there is a clang of horseshoes on the iron stake and a little chorus of cries.* LENNIE *gets up and brings the pup back and lays it in the hay and sits down. He mourns.*] You wasn't big enough. They tole me and tole me you wasn't. I didn't know you'd get killed so easy. Maybe George won't care. This here goddamn little son-of-a-bitch wasn't nothin' to George.

CANDY [*voice from behind the stalls*]. Lennie, where you at? [LENNIE *frantically buries the pup under the hay.* CANDY *enters excitedly.*] Thought I'd find ya here. Say . . . I been talkin' to Slim. It's okay. We ain't gonna get the can. Slim been talkin' to the boss. Slim tol' the boss you guys is good buckers. The boss got to move that grain. 'Member what hell the boss give us las' night? He tol' Slim he got his eye on you an' George. But you ain't gonna get the can. Oh! an' say. The boss give Curley's wife hell, too. Tole her never to go near the men no more. Give her worse hell than you an' George. [*For the first time notices* LENNIE'S *dejection.*] Ain't you glad?

LENNIE. Sure.

CANDY. You ain't sick?

LENNIE. Uh-uh!

CANDY. I got to go tell George. See you later. [*Exits.*]

[LENNIE, *alone, uncovers the pup. Lies down in the hay and sinks deep in it. Puts the pup on his arm and strokes it.* CURLEY'S WIFE *enters secretly. A little mound of hay conceals* LENNIE *from her. In her hand she carries a small suitcase, very cheap. She crosses the barn and buries the case in the hay. Stands up and looks to see whether it can be seen.* LENNIE *watching her quietly tries to cover the pup with hay. She sees the movement.*]

CURLEY'S WIFE. What—what you doin' here?

LENNIE [*sullenly*]. Jus' settin' here.

CURLEY'S WIFE. You seen what I done.

LENNIE. Yeah! you brang a valise.

CURLEY'S WIFE [*comes near to him*]. You won't tell—will you?

LENNIE [*still sullen*]. I ain't gonna have nothing to do with you. George tole me. I ain't to talk to you or nothing. [*Covers the pup a little more.*]

CURLEY'S WIFE. George give you all your orders?

LENNIE. Not talk nor nothing.

CURLEY'S WIFE. You won't tell about that suitcase? I ain't gonna stay here no more. Tonight I'm gonna get out. Come here an' get my stuff an' get out. I ain't gonna be run over no more. I'm gonna go in pichers. [*Sees* LENNIE'S *hand stroking the pup under the hay.*] What you got there?

LENNIE. Nuthing. I ain't gonna talk to you. George says I ain't.

CURLEY'S WIFE. Listen. The guys got a horseshoe tenement out there. It's on'y four o'clock. Them guys ain't gonna leave that tenement. They got money bet. You don't need to be scared to talk to me.

LENNIE [*weakening a little*]. I ain't supposed to.

CURLEY'S WIFE [*watching his buried hand*]. What you got under there?

LENNIE [*his woe comes back to him*]. Jus' my pup. Jus' my little ol' pup. [*Sweeps the hay aside.*]

CURLEY'S WIFE. Why! He's dead.

LENNIE [*explaining sadly*]. He was so little. I was jus' playin' with him—an' he made like he's gonna bite me—an' I made like I'm gonna smack him—an'—I done it. An' then he was dead.

CURLEY'S WIFE [*consoling*]. Don't you worry none. He was just a mutt. The whole country is full of mutts.

LENNIE. It ain't that so much. George gonna be mad. Maybe he won't let me—what he said I could tend.

CURLEY'S WIFE [*sits down in the hay beside him, speaks soothingly*]. Don't you worry. Them guys got money bet on that horseshoe tenement. They ain't gonna leave it. And tomorra I'll be gone. I ain't gonna let them run over me.

[*In the following scene it is apparent that neither is listening to the other and yet as it goes on, as a happy tone increases, it can be seen that they are growing closer together.*]

LENNIE. We gonna have a little place an' raspberry bushes.

CURLEY'S WIFE. I ain't meant to live like this. I come from Salinas. Well, a show come through an' I talked to a guy that was in it. He says I could go with the show. My ol' lady wouldn't let me, 'cause I was on'y fifteen. I wouldn't be no place like this if I had went with that show, you bet.

LENNIE. Gonna take a sack an' fill it up with alfalfa an'—

CURLEY'S WIFE [*hurrying on*]. 'Nother time I met a guy an' he was in pichers. Went out to the Riverside Dance Palace with him. He said he was gonna put me in pichers. Says I was a natural. Soon's he got back to Hollywood he was gonna write me about it.

[*Looks impressively at* LENNIE.] I never got that letter. I think my ol' lady stole it. Well, I wasn't gonna stay no place where they stole your letters. So I married Curley. Met *him* out to the Riverside Dance Palace too.

LENNIE. I hope George ain't gonna be mad about this pup.

CURLEY'S WIFE. I ain't tol' this to nobody before. Maybe I oughtn' to. I don't like Curley. He ain't a nice fella. I might a stayed with him but last night him an' his ol' man both lit into me. I don't have to stay here. [*Moves closer and speaks confidentially.*] Don't tell nobody till I get clear away. I'll go in the night an' thumb a ride to Hollywood.

LENNIE. We gonna get out a here purty soon. This ain't no nice place.

CURLEY'S WIFE [*ecstatically*]. Gonna get in the movies an' have nice clothes—all them nice clothes like they wear. An' I'll set in them big hotels and they'll take pichers of me. When they have them openings I'll go an' talk in the radio . . . an' it won't cost me nothing 'cause I'm in the picher. [*Puts her hand on* LENNIE'S *arm for a moment*.] All them nice clothes like they wear . . . because this guy says I'm a natural.

LENNIE. We gonna go way . . . far away from here.

CURLEY'S WIFE. 'Course, when I run away from Curley, my ol' lady won't never speak to me no more. She'll think I ain't decent. That's what she'll say. [*Defiantly*.] Well, we really ain't decent, no matter how much my ol' lady tries to hide it. My ol' man was a drunk. They put him away. There! Now I told.

LENNIE. George an' me was to the Sacramento Fair. One time I fell in the river an' George pulled me out an' saved me, an' then we went to the Fair. They got all kinds of stuff there. We seen long-hair rabbits.

CURLEY'S WIFE. My ol' man was a sign-painter when he worked. He used to get drunk an' paint crazy pichers an' waste paint. One night when I was a little kid, him an' my ol' lady had an awful fight. They was always fightin'. In the middle of the night he come into my room, and he says, "I can't stand this no more. Let's you an' me go away." I guess he was drunk. [*Her voice takes on a curious wondering tenderness.*] I remember in the night—walkin' down the road, and the trees was black. I was pretty sleepy. He picked me up, an' he carried me on his back. He says, "We gonna live together. We gonna live together because you're my own little girl, an' not no stranger. No arguin' and fightin'," he says, "because you're my little daughter." [*Her voice becomes soft.*] He says, "Why you'll bake little cakes for me, and I'll paint pretty pichers all over the wall." [*Sadly.*] In the morning they caught us . . . an' they put him away. [*Pause.*] I wish we'd a' went.

LENNIE. Maybe if I took this here pup an' throwed him away George wouldn't never know.

CURLEY'S WIFE. They locked him up for a drunk, and in a little while he died.

LENNIE. Then maybe I could tend the rabbits without no trouble.

CURLEY'S WIFE. Don't you think of nothing but rabbits? [*Sound of horseshoe on metal.*] Somebody made a ringer.

LENNIE [*patiently*]. We gonna have a house and a garden, an' a place for alfalfa. And I take a sack and get it all full of alfalfa, and then I take it to the rabbits.

CURLEY'S WIFE. What makes you so nuts about rabbits?

LENNIE [*moves close to her*]. I like to pet nice things. Once at a fair I seen some of them long-hair rabbits. And they was nice, you bet. [*Despairingly.*] I'd even pet mice, but not when I could get nothin' better.

CURLEY'S WIFE [*giggles*]. I think you're nuts.

LENNIE [*earnestly*]. No, I ain't. George says I ain't. I like to pet nice things with my fingers. Soft things.

CURLEY'S WIFE. Well, who don't? Everybody likes that. I like to feel silk and velvet. You like to feel velvet?

LENNIE [*chuckling with pleasure*]. You bet, by God. And I had some too. A lady give me some. And that lady was—my Aunt Clara. She give it right to me. . . . [*Measuring with his hands.*] 'Bout this big a piece. I wish I had that velvet right now. [*He frowns.*] I lost it. I ain't seen it for a long time.

CURLEY'S WIFE [*laughing*]. You're nuts. But you're a kinda nice fella. Jus' like a big baby. A person can see kinda what you mean. When I'm doin' my hair sometimes I jus' set there and stroke it, because it's so soft. [*Runs her fingers over the top of her head.*] Some people got kinda coarse hair. You take Curley, his hair's just like wire. But mine is soft and fine. Here, feel. Right here. [*Takes* LENNIE's *hand and puts it on her head.*] Feel there and see how soft it is. [LENNIE's *fingers fall to stroking her hair.*] Don't you muss it up.

LENNIE. Oh, that's nice. [*Strokes harder.*] Oh, that's nice.

CURLEY'S WIFE. Look out now, you'll muss it. [*Angrily.*] You stop it now, you'll mess it all up. [*She jerks her head sideways and* LENNIE's *fingers close on her hair and hang on. In a panic.*] Let go. [*She screams.*] You let go. [*She screams again. His other hand closes over her mouth and nose.*]

LENNIE [*begging*]. Oh, please don't do that. George'll be mad. [*She struggles violently to be free. A soft screaming comes from under* LENNIE's *hand. Crying with fright.*] Oh, please don't do none of that. George gonna say I done a bad thing. [*He raises his hand from her mouth and a hoarse cry escapes. An-grily.*] Now don't. I don't want you to yell. You gonna get me in trouble just like George says you will. Now don't you do that. [*She struggles more.*] Don't you go yellin'. [*He shakes her violently. Her neck snaps sideways and she lies still. Looks down at her and cautiously removes his hand from over her mouth.*] I don't wanta hurt you. But George will be mad if you yell. [*When she doesn't answer he bends closely over her. He lifts her arm and lets it drop. For a moment he seems bewildered.*] I done a bad thing. I done another bad thing. [*He paws up the hay until it partly covers her. The sound of the horseshoe game comes from the outside. And for the first time* LENNIE *seems conscious of it. He crouches down and listens.*] Oh, I done a real bad thing. I shouldn't a did that. George will be mad. And . . . he said . . . and hide in the brush till he comes. That's what he said. [*He picks up the puppy from beside the girl.*] I'll throw him away. It's bad enough like it is. [*He puts the pup under his coat, creeps to the barn wall and peers out between the cracks and then he creeps around to the end of the manger and disappears.*]

[*The stage is vacant except for* CURLEY'S WIFE. *She lies in the hay half covered up and she looks very young and peaceful. Her rouged cheeks and red lips make her seem alive and sleeping lightly. For a moment the stage is absolutely silent. Then the horses stamp on the other side of the feeding rack. The halter chains clink and from outside men's voices come loud and clear.*]

CANDY [*offstage*]. Lennie! Oh, Lennie, you in there? [*He enters.*] I been figurin' some more, Lennie. Tell you what we can do. [*Sees* CURLEY'S WIFE *and stops. Rubs his white whiskers.*] I didn't know you was here. You was tol' not to be here. [*He steps near her.*] You oughtn't to sleep out here. [*He is right beside her and looks down.*] Oh, Jesus Christ! [*Goes to the door and calls softly.*] George, George! Come here . . . George!

GEORGE [*enters*]. What do you want?

CANDY [*points at* CURLY'S WIFE]. Look.

GEORGE. What's the matter with her? [*Steps up beside her.*] Oh, Jesus Christ! [*Kneels beside her and feels her heart and her wrist. Finally stands up slowly and stiffly. From this time on through the rest of the scene* GEORGE *is wooden.*]

CANDY. What done it?

GEORGE [*coldly*]. Ain't you got any ideas? [CANDY *looks away.*] I should of knew. I guess way back in my head I did.

CANDY. What we gonna do now, George? What we gonna do now?

GEORGE [*answering slowly and dully*]. Guess . . . we gotta . . . tell . . . the guys. Guess we got to catch him and lock him up. We can't let him get away. Why, the poor bastard would starve. [*He tries to reassure himself.*] Maybe they'll lock him up and be nice to him.

CANDY [*excitedly*]. You know better'n that, George. You know Curley's gonna want to get him lynched. You know how Curley is.

GEORGE. Yeah. . . . Yeah . . . that's right. I know Curley. And the other guys too. [*He looks back at* CURLEY'S WIFE.]

CANDY [*pleadingly*]. You and me can get that little place, can't we, George? You and me can go there and live nice, can't we? Can't we? [CANDY *drops his head and looks down at the hay to indicate that he knows.*]

GEORGE [*shakes his head slowly*]. It was somethin' me

and him had. [*Softly.*] I think I knowed it from the very first. I think I knowed we'd never do her. He used to like to hear about it so much. I got fooled to thinkin' maybe we would.

[CANDY *starts to speak but doesn't.*]

GEORGE [*as though repeating a lesson*]. I'll work my month and then I'll take my fifty bucks. I'll stay all night in some lousy cat-house or I'll set in a pool room until everybody goes home. An' then—I'll come back an' work another month. And then I'll have fifty bucks more.

CANDY. He's such a nice fellow. I didn't think he'd a done nothing like this.

GEORGE [*gets a grip on himself and straightens his shoulders*]. Now listen. We gotta tell the guys. I guess they've gotta bring him in. They ain't no way out. Maybe they won't hurt him. I ain't gonna let 'em hurt Lennie. [*Sharply.*] Now you listen. The guys might think I was in on it. I'm gonna go in the bunkhouse. Then in a minute you come out and yell like you just seen her. Will you do that? So the guys won't think I was in on it?

CANDY. Sure, George. Sure, I'll do that.

GEORGE. Okay. Give me a couple of minutes then. And then you yell your head off. I'm goin' now. [GEORGE *exits.*]

CANDY [*watches him go, looks helplessly back at* CUR-LEY'S WIFE; *his next words are in sorrow and in anger*]. You goddamn tramp. You done it, didn't you? Everybody knowed you'd mess things up. You just wasn't no good. [*His voice shakes.*] I could of hoed in the garden and washed dishes for them guys. . . . [*Pauses for a moment and then goes into a sing-song repeating the old words.*] If there was a circus or a baseball game . . . we would o' went to her . . . just said to hell with work and went to her. And they'd been a pig and chickens . . . and in the winter a little fat stove. An' us jus' settin' there . . . settin' there. . . . [*His eyes blind with tears and he goes weakly to the entrance of the barn. Tries for a moment to break a shout out of his throat before he succeeds.*] Hey, you guys! Come here! Come here!

[*Outside the noise of the horseshoe game stops. The sound of discussion and then the voices come closer: "What's the matter?" . . . "Who's that?" . . . "It's Candy." . . . "Something must have happened." Enter* SLIM *and* CARLSON, *young* WHIT *and* CURLEY, CROOKS *in the back, keeping out of attention range. And last of all* GEORGE. GEORGE *has put on his blue denim coat and buttoned it. His black hat is pulled down low over his eyes.* "What's the matter?" . . . "What's happened?"]

[*A gesture from* CANDY. *The men stare at* CURLEY'S WIFE. SLIM *goes over to her, feels her wrist and touches her cheek with his fingers. His hand goes under her slightly twisted neck.* CURLEY *comes near. For a moment he seems shocked. Looks around helplessly and suddenly he comes to life.*]

CURLEY. I know who done it. That big son-of-a-bitch done it. I know he done it. Why, everybody else was out there playing horseshoes. [*Working himself into a fury.*] I'm gonna get him. I'm gonna get my shotgun. Why, I'll kill the big son-of-a-bitch myself. I'll shoot him in the guts. Come on, you guys. [*He runs out of the barn.*]

CARLSON. I'll go get my Luger. [*He runs out too.*]

SLIM [*quietly to* GEORGE]. I guess Lennie done it all right. Her neck's busted. Lennie could o' did that. [GEORGE *nods slowly. Half-questioning.*] Maybe like that time in Weed you was tellin' me about. [GEORGE *nods. Gently.*] Well, I guess we got to get him. Where you think he might o' went?

GEORGE [*struggling to get words out*]. I don't know.

SLIM. I guess we gotta get him.

GEORGE [*stepping close and speaking passionately*].
Couldn't we maybe bring him in and lock him up?
He's nuts, Slim, he never done this to be mean.

SLIM. If we could only keep Curley in. But Curley
wants to shoot him. [*He thinks.*] And s'pose they
lock him up, George, and strap him down and put
him in a cage, that ain't no good.

GEORGE. I know. I know.

SLIM. I think there's only one way to get him out of it.

GEORGE. I know.

CARLSON [*enters running*]. The bastard stole my Luger.
It ain't in my bag.

CURLEY [*enters carrying a shotgun in his good hand.
Officiously*]. All right, you guys. The nigger's got a
shotgun. You take it, Carlson.

WHIT. Only cover around here is down by the river. He
might have went there.

CURLEY. Don't give him no chance. Shoot for his guts,
that'll double him over.

WHIT. I ain't got a gun.

CURLEY. Go in and tell my old man. Get a gun from
him. Let's go now. [*Turns suspiciously on* GEORGE.]
You're comin' with us, fella!

GEORGE. Yeah. I'll come. But listen, Curley, the poor
bastard's nuts. Don't shoot him, he didn't know
what he was doin'.

CURLEY. Don't shoot him! He's got Carlson's Luger,
ain't he?

GEORGE [*weakly*]. Maybe Carlson lost his gun.

CARLSON. I seen it this morning. It's been took.

SLIM [*looking down at* CURLEY'S WIFE]. Curley, maybe
you better stay here with your wife.

[*The light is fading into evening.* CURLEY *hesitates.
Seems almost to weaken, then he hardens again.*]

CURLEY. Naw, I'm gonna shoot the guts out of that big bastard, I'm gonna get him myself. Come on, you guys.

SLIM [*to* CANDY]. You stay here then, Candy. The rest of us better get goin'.

[*They walk out,* SLIM *and* GEORGE *last. Exeunt all but* CANDY. *He squats in the hay, watching the face of* CURLEY'S WIFE.]

CANDY. Poor bastard.

CURTAIN

SCENE II

Evening.

The river bank again.

Light from the setting sun shines on the low brown hills. Among the trees by the river, the shade is deep with evening feeling.

Sounds: distant barking of dogs and the quiet call of quail.

The curtain rises on an empty stage.

There is a sudden whistle of evening wind that stirs the trees and scuds the leaves on the ground.

The stage is still again. LENNIE *enters as silently as a bear. He is bent over and wary. On stage he looks behind him. Then he takes from under his coat the dead pup, lays it on the ground and, going to the river, lies on his stomach and drinks.*

He returns to the dead pup, sits down beside it.

LENNIE. George gonna give me hell . . . I bet. I . . . won't tell him. I'll bury him. [*Begins to scoop a hole in the sand in front of him. Softly.*] But I didn't forget, you bet. I come right here. Hide in the brush an' wait for George. [*Works carefully at his little grave, shaping the hole. At last he picks up the pup and lays it in the hole. Mourning.*] He gonna give me hell. He gonna wish he was alone. [*Adjusts the puppy in the hole, turning it around to make it fit better. Defiantly.*] Well . . . I can go right up in the hills an' find a cave. 'Course I wouldn't never have no ketchup. [*Begins packing sand down carefully about the pup, patting it as he does in beat with his words.*] I'll—go—away—go—away. [*Every word a pat. Fills the grave carefully, smooths the sand over it.*] There now. [*Gathers leaves and scatters them over the place. Gets up on his knees and cocks his head to inspect the job.*] Now. I won't never tell George. [*Sinks back to a sitting position.*] He'll know. He always knows.

[*Far off sound of voices approaching. They come closer during the scene. Suddenly there is the clicking warning of a cock-quail and then the drum of the flock's wings.* GEORGE *enters silently, but hurriedly.*]

GEORGE [*in a hoarse whisper*]. Get in the tules—quick.

LENNIE. I ain't done nothing, George.

[*The voices are very close.*]

GEORGE [*frantically*]. Get in the tules—damn you.

[*Voices are nearly there.* GEORGE *half pushes* LENNIE *down among the tules. The tops rustle showing his crawling progress.*]

WHIT [*offstage*]. There's George. [*Enters.*] Better not get so far ahead. You ain't got a gun.

[*Enter* SLIM, CARLSON, BOSS, CURLEY, *and three other ranch hands. They are armed with shotguns and rifles.*]

CARLSON. He musta come this way. Them prints in the sand was aimed this way.

SLIM [*has been regarding* GEORGE]. Now look. We ain't

gonna find him stickin' in a bunch this way. We got to spread out.

CURLEY. Brush is pretty thick here. He might be lying in the brush. [*Steps toward the tules.* GEORGE *moves quickly after him.*]

SLIM [*seeing the move, speaks quickly*]. Look—[*pointing*]—up there's the county road and open fields an' over there's the highway. Le's spread out an' cover the brush.

BOSS. Slim's right. We got to spread.

SLIM. We better drag up to the roads an' then drag back.

CURLEY. 'Member what I said—shoot for his guts.

SLIM. Okay, move out. Me an' George'll go up to the county road. You guys gets the highway an' drag back.

BOSS. If we get separated, we'll meet here. Remember this place.

CURLEY. All I care is getting the bastard.

[*The men move offstage right, talking.* SLIM *and* GEORGE *move slowly upstage listening to the voïces that grow fainter and fainter.*]

SLIM [*softly to* GEORGE.] Where is he?

[GEORGE *looks him in the eyes for a long moment. Finally trusts him and points with his thumb toward the tules.*]

SLIM. You want—I should—go away?

[GEORGE *nods slowly, looking at the ground.* SLIM *starts away, comes back, tries to say something, instead puts his hand on* GEORGE's *shoulder for a second, and then hurries off upstage.*]

GEORGE [*moves woodenly toward the bank and the tule clump and sits down*]. Lennie!

[*The tules shiver again and* LENNIE *emerges dripping.*]

LENNIE. Where's them guys goin'? [*Long pause.*]

GEORGE. Huntin'.

LENNIE. Whyn't we go with 'em? I like huntin'. [*Waits for an answer.* GEORGE *stares across the river.*] Is it 'cause I done a bad thing?

GEORGE. It don't make no difference.

LENNIE. Is that why we can't go huntin' with them guys?

GEORGE [*woodenly*]. It don't make no difference. . . . Sit down, Lennie. Right there.

[*The light is going now. In the distance there are shouts of men.* GEORGE *turns his head and listens to the shouts.*]

LENNIE. George!

GEORGE. Yeah?

LENNIE. Ain't you gonna give me hell?

GEORGE. Give ya hell?

LENNIE. Sure. . . . Like you always done before. Like— "If I didn't have you I'd take my fifty bucks . . ."

GEORGE [*softly as if in wonder*]. Jesus Christ, Lennie, you can't remember nothing that happens. But you remember every word I say!

LENNIE. Well, ain't you gonna say it?

GEORGE [*reciting*]. "If I was alone I—could live—so easy. [*His voice is monotonous.*] I could get a job and not have no mess. . . ."

LENNIE. Go on, go on! "And when the end of the month come . . ."

GEORGE. "And when the end of the month come, I could take my fifty bucks and go to—a cathouse. . . ."

LENNIE [*eagerly*]. Go on, George, ain't you gonna give me no more hell?

GEORGE. No!

LENNIE. I can go away. I'll go right off in the hills and find a cave if you don't want me.

GEORGE [*speaks as though his lips were stiff*]. No, I want you to stay here with me.

LENNIE [*craftily*]. Then tell me like you done before.

GEORGE. Tell you what?

LENNIE. 'Bout the other guys and about us!

GEORGE [*recites again*]. "Guys like us got no families. They got a little stake and then they blow it in. They ain't got nobody in the world that gives a hoot in hell about 'em!"

LENNIE [*happily*]. "But not *us*." Tell about us now.

GEORGE. "But not us."

LENNIE. "Because . . ."

GEORGE. "Because I got you and . . ."

LENNIE [*triumphantly*]. "And I got you. We got each other," that's what, that gives a hoot in hell about us.

[*A breeze blows up the leaves and then they settle back again. There are the shouts of men again. This time closer.*]

GEORGE [*takes off his hat; shakily*]. Take off your hat, Lennie. The air feels fine!

LENNIE [*removes his hat and lays it on the ground in front of him*]. Tell how it's gonna be.

[*Again the sound of men.* GEORGE *listens to them.*]

GEORGE. Look acrost the river, Lennie, and I'll tell you like you can almost see it. [LENNIE *turns his head and looks across the river.*] "We gonna get a little place . . . [*Reaches in his side pocket and brings out* CARLSON'S *Luger. Hand and gun lie on the ground behind* LENNIE'S *back. He stares at the back of* LENNIE'S *head at the place where spine and skull are joined. Sounds of men's voices talking offstage.*]

LENNIE. Go on! [GEORGE *raises the gun, but his hand shakes and he drops his hand on to the ground.*] Go on! How's it gonna be? "We gonna get a little place. . . ."

GEORGE [*thickly*]. "We'll have a cow. And we'll have

maybe a pig and chickens—and down the flat we'll have a . . . little piece of alfalfa. . . ."

LENNIE [*shouting*]. "For the rabbits!"

GEORGE. "For the rabbits!"

LENNIE. "And I get to tend the rabbits?"

GEORGE. "And you get to tend the rabbits!"

LENNIE [*giggling with happiness*]. "And live off the fat o' the land!"

GEORGE. Yes. [LENNIE *turns his head. Quickly.*] Look over there, Lennie. Like you can really see it.

LENNIE. Where?

GEORGE. Right acrost that river there. Can't you almost see it?

LENNIE [*moving*]. Where, George?

GEORGE. It's over there. You keep lookin', Lennie. Just keep lookin'.

LENNIE. I'm lookin', George. I'm lookin'.

GEORGE. That's right. It's gonna be nice there. Ain't gonna be no trouble, no fights. Nobody ever gonna hurt nobody, or steal from 'em. It's gonna be—nice.

LENNIE. I can see it, George. I can see it! Right over there! I can see it!

[GEORGE *fires.* LENNIE *crumples; falls behind the brush. The voices of the men in the distance.*]

CURTAIN

THE TIME OF
YOUR LIFE

by William Saroyan

To George Jean Nathan

In the time of your life, live—so that in that good time there shall be no ugliness or death for yourself or for any life your life touches. Seek goodness everywhere, and when it is found, bring it out of its hiding-place and let it be free and unashamed. Place in matter and in flesh the least of the values, for these are the things that hold death and must pass away. Discover in all things that which shines and is beyond corruption. Encourage virtue in whatever heart it may have been driven into secrecy and sorrow by the shame and terror of the world. Ignore the obvious, for it is unworthy of the clear eye and the kindly heart. Be the inferior of no man, nor of any man be the superior. Remember that every man is a variation of yourself. No man's guilt is not yours, nor is any man's innocence a thing apart. Despise evil and ungodliness, but not men of ungodliness or evil. These, understand. Have no shame in being kindly and gentle, but if the time comes in the time of your life to kill, kill and have no regret. In the time of your life, live—so that in that wondrous time you shall not add to the misery and sorrow of the world, but shall smile to the infinite delight and mystery of it.

*First production, October 25, 1939,
at the Booth Theatre, New York City,
with the following cast:*

THE NEWSBOY, *Ross Bagdasarian*
THE DRUNKARD, *John Farrell*
WILLIE, *Will Lee*
JOE, *Eddie Dowling*
NICK, *Charles de Sheim*
TOM, *Edward Andrews*
KITTY DUVAL, *Julie Haydon*
DUDLEY, *Curt Conway*
HARRY, *Gene Kelly*
WESLEY, *Reginald Beane*
LORENE, *Nene Vibber*
BLICK, *Grover Burgess*
ARAB, *Houseley Stevens, Sr.*
MARY L., *Celeste Holme*
KRUPP, *William Bendix*
MCCARTHY, *Tom Tully*
KIT CARSON, *Len Doyle*
NICK'S MA, *Michelette Burani*
SAILOR, *Randolph Wade*
ELSIE, *Cathie Bailey*
A KILLER, *Evelyn Geller*
HER SIDE KICK, *Mary Cheffey*
A SOCIETY LADY, *Eva Leonard Boyne*
A SOCIETY GENTLEMAN, *Ainsworth Arnold*
FIRST COP, *Randolph Wade*
SECOND COP, *John Farrell*

THE PLACE: *Nick's Pacific Street Saloon, Restaurant, and
Entertainment Palace at the foot of Embarcadero,
in San Francisco. A suggestion of room 21 at
The New York Hotel, upstairs, around the corner.*

THE TIME: *Afternoon and night of a day in October, 1939.*

Act one

NICK'S *is an American place: a San Francisco water-front honky-tonk.*

At a table, JOE: *always calm, always quiet, always thinking, always eager, always bored, always superior. His expensive clothes are casually and youthfully worn and give him an almost boyish appearance. He is thinking.*

Behind the bar, NICK: *a big red-headed young Italian-American with an enormous naked woman tatooed in red on the inside of his right arm. He is studying "The Racing Form."*

The ARAB, *at his place at the end of the bar. He is a lean old man with a rather ferocious old-country mustache, with the ends twisted up. Between the thumb and forefinger of his left hand is the Mohammedan tattoo indicating that he has been to Mecca. He is sipping a glass of beer.*

It is about eleven-thirty in the morning. SAM *is sweeping out. We see only his back. He disappears into the kitchen. The* SAILOR *at the bar finishes his drink and leaves, moving thoughtfully, as though he were trying very hard to discover how to live.*

The NEWSBOY *comes in.*

NEWSBOY [*cheerfully*]. Good-morning, everybody. [*No answer. To* NICK.] Paper, Mister? [NICK *shakes his head, no. The* NEWSBOY *goes to* JOE.] Paper, Mister? [JOE *shakes his head, no. The* NEWSBOY *walks away, counting papers.*]

JOE [*noticing him*]. How many you got?

NEWSBOY. Five.

[JOE *gives him a quarter, takes all the papers, glances at the headlines with irritation, throws them away. The* NEWSBOY *watches carefully, then goes.*]

ARAB [*picks up paper, looks at headlines, shakes head as if rejecting everything else a man might say about the world*]. No foundation. All the way down the line.

[*The* DRUNK *comes in. Walks to the telephone, looks for a nickel in the chute, sits down at* JOE's *table.* NICK *takes the* DRUNK *out. The* DRUNK *returns.*]

DRUNK [*champion of the Bill of Rights*]. This is a free country, ain't it?

[WILLIE, *the marble-game maniac, explodes through the swinging doors and lifts the forefinger of his right hand comically, indicating one beer. He is a very young man, not more than twenty. He is wearing heavy shoes, a pair of old and dirty corduroys, a light green turtle-neck jersey with a large letter "F" on the chest, an oversize two-button tweed coat, and a green hat, with the brim up.* NICK *sets out a glass of beer for him, he drinks it, straightens up vigorously saying "Aaah," makes a solemn face, gives* NICK *a one-finger salute of adieu, and begins to leave, refreshed and restored in spirit. He walks by the marble game, halts suddenly, turns, studies the contraption, gestures as if to say, Oh, no. Turns to go, stops, returns to the machine, studies it, takes a handful of small coins out of his pants pocket, lifts a nickel, indicates with a gesture, One game, no more. Puts the nickel in the slot, pushes in the slide, making an interesting noise.*]

NICK. You can't beat that machine.

WILLIE. Oh, yeah? [*The marbles fall, roll, and take their place. He pushes down the lever, placing one marble in position. Takes a very deep breath, walks in a small circle, excited at the beginning of great drama. Stands straight and pious before the contest. Himself vs. the machine. Willie vs. Destiny. His skill and daring vs. the cunning and trickery of the novelty industry of America, and the whole challenging world. He is the last of the American pioneers, with nothing more to fight but the machine, with no other reward than lights going on and off, and six nickels for one. Before him is the last champion, the machine. He is the last challenger, the young man with nothing to do in the world.* WILLIE *grips the knob delicately, studies the situation carefully, draws the knob back, holds it a moment, and then releases it. The first marble rolls out among the hazards, and the contest is on.*

[*At the very beginning of the play "The Missouri Waltz" is coming from the phonograph. The music ends here. This is the signal for the beginning of the play.* JOE *suddenly comes out of his reverie. He whistles the way people do who are calling a cab that's about a block away, only he does it quietly.* WILLIE *turns around, but* JOE *gestures for him to return to his work.* NICK *looks up from "The Racing Form."*

JOE [*calling*]. Tom. [*To himself.*] Where the hell is he, every time I need him? [*He looks around calmly: the nickel-in-the-slot phonograph in the corner; the open public telephone; the stage; the marble game; the bar; and so on. He calls again, this time very loud.*] Hey, Tom.

NICK [*with morning irritation*]. What do you want?

JOE [*without thinking*]. I want the boy to get me a

watermelon, that's what *I* want. What do *you* want?
Money, or love, or fame, or what? You won't get
them studying "The Racing Form."

NICK. I like to keep abreast of the times.

[TOM *comes hurrying in. He is a great big man of
about thirty or so who appears to be much younger
because of the childlike expression of his face: handsome, dumb, innocent, troubled, and a little bewildered by everything. He is obviously adult in years,
but it seems as if by all rights he should still be a
boy. He is defensive as clumsy, self-conscious, over-
grown boys are. He is wearing a flashy cheap suit.
JOE leans back and studies him with casual disap-
proval. TOM slackens his pace and becomes clumsy
and embarrassed, waiting for the bawling-out he's
pretty sure he's going to get.*]

JOE [*objectively, severely, but a little amused*]. Who
saved your life?

TOM [*sincerely*]. You did, Joe. Thanks.

JOE [*interested*]. How'd I do it?

TOM [*confused*]. What?

JOE [*even more interested*]. How'd I do it?

TOM. Joe, you know how you did it.

JOE [*softly*]. I want you to answer me. How'd I save
your life? I've forgotten.

TOM [*remembering, with a big sorrowful smile*]. You
made me eat all that chicken soup three years ago
when I was sick and hungry.

JOE [*fascinated*]. *Chicken soup?*

TOM [*eagerly*]. Yeah.

JOE. Three years? Is it that long?

TOM [*delighted to have the information*]. Yeah, sure.
1937. 1938. 1939. This is 1939, Joe.

JOE [*amused*]. Never mind what year it is. Tell me the
whole story.

TOM. You took me to the doctor. You gave me money

for food and clothes, and paid my room rent. Aw, Joe, you know all the different things you did.

[JOE *nods, turning away from* TOM *after each question.*]

JOE. You in good health now?

TOM. Yeah, Joe.

JOE. You got clothes?

TOM. Yeah, Joe.

JOE. You eat three times a day. Sometimes four?

TOM. Yeah, Joe. Sometimes five.

JOE. You got a place to sleep?

TOM. Yeah, Joe.

[JOE *nods. Pauses. Studies* TOM *carefully.*]

JOE. Then, where the hell have you been?

TOM [*humbly*]. Joe, I was out in the street listening to the boys. They're talking about the trouble down here on the waterfront.

JOE [*sharply*]. I want you to be around when I need you.

TOM [*pleased that the bawling-out is over*]. I won't do it again. Joe, one guy out there says there's got to be a revolution before anything will ever be all right.

JOE [*impatiently*]. I know all about it. Now, here. Take this money. Go up to the Emporium. You know where the Emporium is?

TOM. Yeah, sure, Joe.

JOE. All right. Take the elevator and go up to the fourth floor. Walk around to the back, to the toy department. Buy me a couple of dollars' worth of toys and bring them here.

TOM [*amazed*]. Toys? What *kind* of toys, Joe?

JOE. Any kind of toys. Little ones that I can put on this table.

TOM. What do you want toys for, Joe?

JOE [*mildly angry*]. *What?*

TOM. All right, all right. You don't have to get sore

at *everything.* What'll people think, a big guy like me buying toys?

JOE. *What people?*

TOM. Aw, Joe, you're always making me do crazy things for you, and *I'm* the guy that gets embarrassed. You just sit in this place and make me do all the dirty work.

JOE [*looking away*]. Do what I tell you.

TOM. O.K., but I wish I knew why. [*He makes to go.*]

JOE. Wait a minute. Here's a nickel. Put it in the phonograph. Number seven. I want to hear that waltz again.

TOM. Boy, I'm glad *I* don't have to stay and listen to it. Joe, what do you hear in that song anyway? We listen to that song ten times a day. Why can't we hear number six, or two, or nine? There are a lot of other numbers.

JOE [*emphatically*]. Put the nickel in the phonograph. [*Pause.*] Sit down and wait till the music's over. Then go get me some toys.

TOM. O.K. O.K.

JOE [*loudly*]. Never mind being a martyr about it either. The cause isn't worth it.

[*Tom puts the nickel into the machine, with a ritual of impatient and efficient movement which plainly shows his lack of sympathy or enthusiasm. His manner also reveals, however, that his lack of sympathy is spurious and exaggerated. Actually, he is fascinated by the music, but is so confused by it that he pretends he dislikes it. The music begins. It is another variation of "The Missouri Waltz," played dreamily and softly, with perfect orchestral form, and with a theme of weeping in the horns repeated a number of times. At first* TOM *listens with something close to irritation, since he can't understand what is so attractive in the music to* JOE, *and what is so painful and confusing in it to himself. Very soon, however, he is carried away by the melancholy story of grief and nostalgia of the song. He stands, troubled by the poetry and confusion in himself.* JOE, *on the other hand, listens as if he were not listening, indifferent and unmoved. What he's interested in is* TOM. *He turns and glances at* TOM. KITTY DUVAL, *who lives in a room in The New York Hotel, around the corner, comes beyond the swinging doors, quietly, and walks slowly to the bar, her reality and rhythm a perfect accompaniment to the sorrowful American music, which is her music, as it is* TOM'S. *Which the world drove out of her, putting in its place brokenness and all manner of spiritually crippled forms. She seems to understand this, and is angry. Angry with herself, full of hate for the poor world, and full of pity and contempt for its tragic, unbelievable, confounded people. She is a small powerful girl, with that kind of delicate and rugged beauty which no circumstance of evil or ugly reality can destroy. This beauty is that element of the immortal which is in the seed of good and common people, and which is kept alive in some of the female of our kind, no matter how accidentally or pointlessly they may have entered the world.* KITTY DUVAL *is somebody. There is an angry purity, and a fierce pride, in her. In her stance, and way of walking, there is grace and arrogance.* JOE *recognizes her as a great person immediately. She goes to the bar.*]

KITTY. Beer.

[NICK *places a glass of beer before her mechanically. She swallows half the drink, and listens to the music again.* TOM *turns and sees her. He becomes dead to everything in the world but her. He stands like a lump, fascinated and undone by his almost religious adoration for her.* JOE *notices* TOM.

JOE [*gently*]. Tom. [TOM *begins to move toward the bar, where* KITTY *is standing. Loudly.*] Tom. [TOM *halts, then turns, and* JOE *motions to him to come over to the table.* TOM *goes over. Quietly.*] Have you got everything straight?

TOM [*out of the world*]. What?

JOE. What do you mean, what? I just gave you some instructions.

TOM [*pathetically*]. What do you want, Joe?

JOE. I want you to come to your senses. [*He stands up quietly and knocks* TOM's *hat off.* TOM *picks up his hat quickly.*]

TOM. I got it, Joe. I got it. The Emporium. Fourth floor. In the back. The toy department. Two dollars' worth of toys. That you can put on a table.

KITTY [*to herself*]. Who the hell is he to push a big man like that around?

JOE. I'll expect you back in a half hour. Don't get side-tracked anywhere. Just do what I tell you.

TOM [*pleading*]. Joe? Can't I bet four bits on a horse race? There's a long shot—Precious Time—that's going to win by ten lengths. I got to have money.

[JOE *points to the street.* TOM *goes out.* NICK *is combing his hair, looking in the mirror.*]

NICK. I thought you wanted him to get you a watermelon.

JOE. I forgot. [*He watches* KITTY *a moment. To* KITTY, *clearly, slowly, with great compassion.*] What's the dream?

KITTY [*moving to* JOE, *coming to*]. What?

JOE [*holding the dream for her*]. What's the dream, now?

KITTY [*coming still closer*]. What dream?

JOE. What dream! The dream you're dreaming.

NICK. Suppose he did bring you a watermelon? What the hell would you do with it?

JOE [*irritated*]. I'd put it on this table. I'd look at it. Then I'd eat it. What do you *think* I'd do with it, sell it for a profit?

NICK. How should I know what *you'd* do with *any-thing?* What I'd like to know is, where do you get your money from? What work do you do?

JOE [*looking at* KITTY]. Bring us a bottle of champagne.

KITTY. Champagne?

JOE [*simply*]. Would you rather have something else?

KITTY. What's the big idea?

JOE. I thought you might like some champagne. I myself am very fond of it.

KITTY. Yeah, but what's the big idea? You can't push *me* around.

JOE [*gently but severely*]. It's not in my nature to be unkind to another human being. I have only contempt for wit. Otherwise I might say something obvious, therefore cruel, and perhaps untrue.

KITTY. You be careful what you think about me.

JOE [*slowly, not looking at her*]. I have only the noblest thoughts for both your person and your spirit.

NICK [*having listened carefully and not being able to make it out*]. What are you talking about?

KITTY. You shut up. You—

JOE. He owns this place. He's an important man. All kinds of people come to him looking for work. Comedians. Singers. Dancers.

KITTY. I don't care. He can't call me names.

NICK. All right, sister. I know how it is with a two-dollar whore in the morning.

KITTY [*furiously*]. Don't you dare call me names. I used to be in burlesque.

NICK. If you were ever in burlesque, I used to be Charlie Chaplin.

KITTY [*angry and a little pathetic*]. I *was* in burlesque.

I played the burlesque circuit from coast to coast. I've had flowers sent to me by European royalty. I've had dinner with young men of wealth and social position.

NICK. You're dreaming.

KITTY [*to* JOE]. *I was in burlesque.* Kitty Duval. That was my name. Life-size photographs of me in costume in front of burlesque theaters all over the country.

JOE [*gently, coaxingly*]. I believe you. Have some champagne.

NICK [*going to table, with champagne bottle and glasses*]. There he goes again.

JOE. Miss Duval?

KITTY [*sincerely, going over*]. That's not my *real* name. That's my *stage* name.

JOE. I'll call you by your stage name.

NICK [*pouring*]. All right, sister, make up your mind. Are you going to have champagne with him, or not?

JOE. Pour the lady some wine.

NICK. O.K., Professor. Why you come to this joint instead of one of the high-class dumps uptown is more than I can understand. Why don't you have champagne at the St. Francis? Why don't you drink with a lady?

KITTY [*furiously*]. Don't you call me names—you dentist.

JOE. Dentist?

NICK [*amazed, loudly*]. What kind of cussing is that? [*Pause. Looking at* KITTY, *then at* JOE, *bewildered.*] This guy doesn't belong here. The only reason I've got champagne is because *he* keeps ordering it all the time. [*To* KITTY.] Don't think you're the only one he drinks champagne with. He drinks with *all* of them. [*Pause.*] He's crazy. Or something.

JOE [*confidentially*]. Nick, I think you're going to be all right in a couple of centuries.

NICK. I'm sorry, I don't understand your English.

[JOE *lifts his glass.* KITTY *slowly lifts hers, not quite sure of what's going on.*]

JOE [*sincerely*]. To the spirit, Kitty Duval.

KITTY [*beginning to understand, and very grateful, looking at him*]. Thank you.

JOE [*calling*]. Nick.

NICK. Yeah?

JOE. Would you mind putting a nickel in the machine again? Number—

NICK. Seven. I know. I know. I don't mind at all, Your Highness, although, personally, I'm not a lover of music. [*Going to the machine.*] As a matter of fact I think Tchaikowsky was a dope.

JOE. Tchaikowsky? Where'd you ever hear of Tchaikowsky?

NICK. He was a dope.

JOE. Yeah. Why?

NICK. They talked about him on the radio one Sunday morning. He was a sucker. He let a woman drive him crazy.

JOE. I see.

NICK. I stood behind that bar listening to the God-damn stuff and cried like a baby. *None but the lonely heart!* He was a dope.

JOE. What made you cry?

NICK. What?

JOE [*sternly*]. What made you cry, Nick?

NICK [*angry with himself*]. I don't know.

JOE. I've been underestimating you, Nick. Play number seven.

NICK. They get everybody worked up. They give everybody stuff they shouldn't have. [NICK *puts the*

*nickel into the machine and the waltz begins again.
He listens to the music. Then studies "The Racing
Form."*]

KITTY [*to herself, dreaming*]. I like champagne, and
everything that goes with it. Big houses with big
porches, and big rooms with big windows, and big
lawns, and big trees, and flowers growing everywhere, and big shepherd dogs sleeping in the shade.

NICK. I'm going next door to Frankie's to make a bet.
I'll be right back.

JOE. Make one for me.

NICK [*going to* JOE]. Who do you like?

JOE [*giving him money*]. Precious Time.

NICK. Ten dollars? Across the board?

JOE. No. On the nose.

NICK. O.K. [*He goes.*]

[DUDLEY R. BOSTWICK, *as he calls himself, breaks
through the swinging doors, and practically flings
himself upon the open telephone beside the phonograph.* DUDLEY *is a young man of about twenty-four
or twenty-five, ordinary and yet extraordinary. He
is smallish, as the saying is, neatly dressed in bargain clothes, overworked and irritated by the routine and dullness and monotony of his life, apparently nobody and nothing, but in reality a great
personality. The swindled young man. Educated,
but without the least real understanding. A brave,
dumb, salmon-spirit struggling for life in weary,
stupefied flesh, dueling ferociously with a banal
mind which has been only irritated by what it has
been taught. He is a great personality because,
against all these handicaps, what he wants is simple
and basic: a woman. This urgent and violent need,
common yet miraculous enough in itself, considering the unhappy environment of the animal, is the
force which elevates him from nothingness to great-*

ness. *A ridiculous greatness, but in the nature of things beautiful to behold. All that he has been taught, and everything he believes, is phony, and yet he himself is real, almost super-real, because of this indestructible force in himself. His face is ridiculous. His personal rhythm is tense and jittery. His speech is shrill and violent. His gestures are wild. His ego is disjointed and epileptic. And yet deeply he possesses the same wholeness of spirit, and directness of energy, that is in all species of animals. There is little innate or cultivated spirit in him, but there is no absence of innocent animal force. He is a young man who has been taught that he has a chance, as a person, and believes it. As a matter of fact, he hasn't a chance in the world, and should have been told by somebody, or should not have had his natural and valuable ignorance spoiled by education, ruining an otherwise perfectly good and charming member of the human race. At the telephone he immediately begins to dial furiously, hesitates, changes his mind, stops dialing, hangs up furiously, and suddenly begins again. Not more than half a minute after the firecracker arrival of* DUDLEY R. BOSTWICK, *occurs the polka-and-waltz arrival of* HARRY. HARRY *is another story. He comes in timidly, turning about uncertainly, awkward, out of place everywhere, embarrassed and encumbered by the contemporary costume, sick at heart, but determined to fit in somewhere. His arrival constitutes a dance. His clothes don't fit. The pants are a little too large. The coat, which doesn't match, is also a little too large, and loose. He is a dumb young fellow, but he has ideas. A philosophy, in fact. His philosophy is simple and beautiful. The world is sorrowful. The world needs laughter.* HARRY *is funny. The world needs* HARRY. HARRY *will make the world laugh. He has probably had a year or two of high school. He has also listened to the boys at the pool room. He's looking for* NICK. *He goes to the* ARAB *and says, "Are you Nick?" The* ARAB *shakes his head. He stands at the bar, waiting. He waits very busily.*]

HARRY [*as* NICK *returns*]. You Nick?

NICK [*very loudly*]. I am Nick.

HARRY [*acting*]. Can you use a great comedian?

NICK [*behind the bar*]. Who, for instance?

HARRY [*almost angry*]. Me.

NICK. You? What's funny about you?

[DUDLEY *at the telephone, is dialing. Because of some defect in the apparatus the dialing is very loud.*]

DUDLEY. Hello. Sunset 7349? May I speak to Miss Elsie Mandelspiegel? [*Pause.*]

HARRY [*with spirit and noise, dancing*]. I dance and do gags and stuff.

NICK. In costume? Or are you wearing your costume?

DUDLEY. All I need is a cigar.

KITTY [*continuing the dream of grace*]. I'd walk out of the house, and stand on the porch, and look at the trees, and smell the flowers, and run across the lawn, and lie down under a tree, and read a book. [*Pause.*] A book of poems, maybe.

DUDLEY [*very, very clearly*]. Elsie Mandelspiegel. [*Impatiently.*] She has a room on the fourth floor. She's a nurse at the Southern Pacific Hospital. Elsie Mandelspiegel. She works at night. Elsie. Yes. [*He begins waiting again.* WESLEY, *a colored boy, comes to the bar and stands near* HARRY, *waiting.*]

NICK. Beer?

WESLEY. No, sir. I'd like to talk to you.

NICK [*to* HARRY]. All right. Get funny.

HARRY [*getting funny, an altogether different person, an actor with great energy, both in power of voice, and in force and speed of physical gesture*]. Now,

I'm standing on the corner of Third and Market. I'm looking around. I'm figuring it out. There it is. Right in front of me. The whole city. The whole world. People going by. They're going somewhere. I don't know where, but they're going. I ain't going *anywhere*. Where the hell can you go? I'm figuring it out. All right, I'm a citizen. A fat guy bumps his stomach into the face of an old lady. They were in a hurry. Fat and old. *They bumped.* Boom. I don't know. It may mean war. *War.* Germany. England. Russia. I don't know for sure. [*Loudly, dramatically, he salutes, about faces, presents arms, aims, and fires.*] WAAAAAR. [*He blows a call to arms.* NICK *gets sick of this, indicates with a gesture that* HARRY *should hold it, and goes to* WESLEY.]

NICK. What's on your mind?

WESLEY [*confused*]. Well—

NICK. Come on. Speak up. Are you hungry, or what?

WESLEY. Honest to God, I ain't hungry. All I want is a job. I don't want no charity.

NICK. Well, what can you do, and how good are you?

WESLEY. I can run errands, clean up, wash dishes, anything.

DUDLEY [*on the telephone, very eagerly*]. Elsie? Elsie, this is Dudley. Elsie, I'll jump in the bay if you don't marry me. Life isn't worth living without you. I can't sleep. I can't think of anything but you. All the time. Day and night and night and day. Elsie, I love you I love you. What? [*Burning up.*] Is this Sunset 7-3-4-9? [*Pause.*] 7943? [*Calmly, while* WILLIE *begins making a small racket.*] Well, what's your name? *Lorene?* Lorene Smith? I thought you were Elsie Mandelspiegel. What? Dudley. Yeah. Dudley R. Bostwick. Yeah. R. It stands for Raoul, but I never spell it out. I'm pleased to meet *you,* too. What? There's a lot of noise around here. [WILLIE *stops hitting the marble game.*] Where am I? At Nick's, on Pacific Street. I work at the S. P. I told them I was sick and they gave me the afternoon off. Wait a minute. I'll ask them. I'd like to meet *you*, too. Sure. I'll ask them. [*Turns around to* NICK.] What's this address?

NICK. Number 3 Pacific Street, you cad.

DUDLEY. Cad? You don't know how I've been suffering on account of Elsie. I take things too ceremoniously. I've got to be more lackadaisical. [*Into telephone.*] Hello, Elenore? I mean, Lorene. It's number 3 Pacific Street. Yeah. Sure. I'll wait for you. How'll you know me? You'll *know* me. I'll recognize *you*. Good-by, now. [*He hangs up.*]

HARRY [*continuing his monologue, with gestures, movements, and so on*]. I'm standing there. I didn't do anything to anybody. Why should I be a soldier? [*Sincerely, insanely.*] BOOOOOOOOOM. *WAR!* O.K. War. *I* retreat. *I* hate war. I move to Sacramento.

NICK [*shouting*]. All right, comedian. Lay off a minute.

HARRY [*broken-hearted, going to* WILLIE]. Nobody's got a sense of humor any more. The world's dying for comedy like never before, but nobody knows how to *laugh*.

NICK [*to* WESLEY]. Do you belong to the union?

WESLEY. What union?

NICK. For the love of Mike, where've you been? Don't you know you can't come into a place and ask for a job and get one and go to work, just like that. You've got to belong to one of the unions.

WESLEY. I didn't know. I got to have a job. Real soon.

NICK. Well, you've got to belong to a union.

WESLEY. I don't want any favors. All I want is a chance to earn a living.

NICK. Go on into the kitchen and tell Sam to give you some lunch.

WESLEY. Honest, I ain't hungry.

DUDLEY [*shouting*]. What I've gone through for Elsie.

HARRY. I've got all kinds of funny ideas in my head to help make the world happy again.

NICK [*holding* WESLEY]. No, he isn't hungry.

[WESLEY *almost faints from hunger.* NICK *catches him just in time. The* ARAB *and* NICK *go off with* WESLEY *into the kitchen.*]

HARRY [*to* WILLIE]. See if you think this is funny. It's my own idea. I created this dance myself. It comes after the monologue. [HARRY *begins to dance.* WILLIE *watches a moment, and then goes back to the game. It's a goofy dance, which* HARRY *does with great sorrow, but much energy.*]

DUDLEY. Elsie. Aw, gee, Elsie. What the hell do I want to see Lorene Smith for? Some girl I don't know.

[JOE *and* KITTY *have been drinking in silence. There is no sound now except the soft-shoe shuffling of* HARRY, *the Comedian.*]

JOE. What's the dream now, Kitty Duval?

KITTY [*dreaming the words and pictures*]. I dream of home. Christ, I always dream of home. I've no *home.* I've no place. But I always dream of all of us together again. We had a farm in Ohio. There was nothing good about it. It was always sad. There was always trouble. But I always dream about it as if I could go back and Papa would be there and Mamma and Louie and my little brother Stephen and my sister Mary. I'm Polish. Duval! My name isn't Duval, it's Koranovsky. Katerina Koranovsky. We lost everything. The house, the farm, the trees, the horses, the cows, the chickens. Papa died. He was old. He was thirteen years older than Mamma. We moved to Chicago. We tried to work. We tried to stay together. Louie got in trouble. The fellows he was with killed him for something. I don't know what. Stephen ran away from home. Seventeen years old. I don't know where he is. Then Mamma died. [*Pause.*] What's the dream? I dream of home.

[NICK *comes out of the kitchen with* WESLEY.]

NICK. Here. Sit down here and rest. That'll hold you for a *while*. Why didn't you tell me you were hungry? You all right now?

WESLEY [*sitting down in the chair at the piano*]. Yes, I am. Thank you. I didn't know I was *that* hungry.

NICK. Fine. [*To* HARRY *who is dancing.*] Hey. What the hell do you think you're doing?

HARRY [*stopping*]. That's my own idea. I'm a natural-born dancer and comedian.

[WESLEY *begins slowly, one note, one chord at a time, to play the piano.*]

NICK. You're no good. Why don't you try some other kind of work? Why don't you get a job in a store, selling something? What do you want to be a comedian for?

HARRY. I've got something for the world and they haven't got sense enough to let me give it to them. Nobody knows me.

DUDLEY. Elsie. Now I'm waiting for some dame I've never seen before. Lorene Smith. Never saw her in my life. Just happened to get the wrong number. She turns on the personality, and I'm a cooked Indian. Give me a beer, please.

HARRY. Nick, you've got to see my act. It's the greatest thing of its kind in America. All I want is a chance. No salary to begin. Let me try it out tonight. If I don't wow 'em, O.K., I'll go home. If vaudeville wasn't dead, a guy like me would have a chance.

NICK. You're not funny. You're a sad young punk. What the hell do you want to try to be funny for? You'll break everybody's heart. What's there for you to be funny about? You've been poor all your life, haven't you?

HARRY. I've been poor all right, but don't forget that some things count more than some other things.

NICK. What counts more, for instance, than what else, for instance?

HARRY. Talent, for instance, counts more than money, for instance, that's what, and I've got talent. I get new ideas night and day. Everything comes natural to me. I've got style, but it'll take me a little time to round it out. That's all.

[*By now* WESLEY *is playing something of his own which is very good and out of the world. He plays about half a minute, after which* HARRY *begins to dance.*]

NICK [*watching*]. I run the lousiest dive in Frisco, and a guy arrives and makes me stock up with champagne. The whores come in and holler at me that they're ladies. Talent comes in and begs me for a chance to show itself. Even society people come here once in a while. I don't know what for. Maybe it's liquor. Maybe it's the location. Maybe it's my personality. Maybe it's the crazy personality of the joint. The old honky-tonk. [*Pause.*] Maybe they can't feel at home anywhere else.

[*By now* WESLEY *is really playing, and* HARRY *is going through a new routine.* DUDLEY *grows sadder and sadder.*]

KITTY. Please dance with me.

JOE [*loudly*]. I never learned to dance.

KITTY. Anybody can dance. Just hold me in your arms.

JOE. I'm very fond of you. I'm *sorry*. I *can't* dance. I wish to God I could.

KITTY. Oh, please.

JOE. Forgive me. I'd like to very much.

[KITTY *dances alone.* TOM *comes in with a package. He sees* KITTY *and goes ga-ga again. He comes out of the trance and puts the bundle on the table in front of* JOE.]

JOE [*taking the package*]. What'd you get?

TOM. Two dollars' worth of toys. That's what you sent me for. The girl asked me what I wanted with toys. I didn't know what to tell her. [*He stares at* KITTY, *then back at* JOE.] Joe? I've got to have some money. After all you've done for me, I'll do anything in the world for you, but, Joe, you got to give me some money once in a while.

JOE. What do you want it for?

[TOM *turns and stares at* KITTY *dancing*.]

JOE [*noticing*]. Sure. Here. Here's five. [*Shouting.*] Can you dance?

TOM [*proudly*]. I got second prize at the Palomar in Sacramento five years ago.

JOE [*loudly, opening package*]. O.K., dance with her.

TOM. You mean *her*?

JOE [*loudly*]. I mean Kitty Duval, the burlesque queen. I mean the queen of the world burlesque. Dance with her. She wants to dance.

TOM [*worshiping the name Kitty Duval, helplessly*]. Joe, can I tell you something?

JOE [*he brings out a toy and winds it*]. You don't have to. I know. You love her. You *really* love her. I'm not blind. I know. But take care of yourself. Don't get sick that way again.

NICK [*looking at and listening to* WESLEY *with amazement*]. Comes in here and wants to be a dish-washer. Faints from hunger. And then sits down and plays better than Heifetz.

JOE. Heifetz plays the violin.

NICK. All right, don't get careful. He's good, ain't he?

TOM [*to* KITTY]. Kitty.

JOE [*he lets the toy go, loudly*]. Don't talk. Just dance.

[TOM *and* KITTY *dance.* NICK *is at the bar, watching everything.* HARRY *is dancing.* DUDLEY *is grieving into his beer.* LORENE SMITH, *about thirty-seven, very overbearing and funny-looking, comes to the bar.*]

NICK. What'll it be, lady?

LORENE [*looking about and scaring all the young men*]. I'm looking for the young man I talked to on the telephone. Dudley R. Bostwick.

DUDLEY [*jumping, running to her, stopping, shocked*]. Dudley R. [*Slowly.*] Bostwick? Oh, yeah. He left here ten minutes ago. You mean Dudley Bostwick, that poor man on crutches?

LORENE. Crutches?

DUDLEY. Yeah. Dudley Bostwick. That's what he *said* his name was. He said to tell you not to wait.

LORENE. Well. [*She begins to go, turns around.*] Are you sure *you're* not Dudley Bostwick?

DUDLEY. Who—me? [*Grandly.*] My name is Roger Tenefrancia. I'm a French-Canadian. I never saw the poor fellow before.

LORENE. It seems to me your voice is like the voice I heard over the telephone.

DUDLEY. A coincidence. An accident. A quirk of fate. One of those things. Dismiss the thought. That poor cripple hobbled out of here ten minutes ago.

LORENE. He said he was going to commit suicide. I only wanted to be of help. [*She goes.*]

DUDLEY. Be of help? What kind of help could she be of? [DUDLEY *runs to the telephone in the corner.*] Gee whiz, Elsie. Gee whiz. I'll never leave you again. [*He turns the pages of a little address book.*] Why do I always forget the number? I've tried to get her on the phone a hundred times this week and I still forget the number. She won't come to the phone, but I keep trying anyway. She's out. She's not in. She's working. I get the wrong number. Everything goes haywire. I can't sleep. [*Defiantly.*] She'll come to the phone one of these days. If there's anything to true love at all, she'll come to the phone. Sunset 7349. [*He dials the number, as* JOE *goes on studying the toys. They are one big mechanical toy, whistles, and a music box.* JOE *blows into the whistles, quickly, by way of getting casually acquainted with them.* TOM *and* KITTY *stop dancing.* TOM *stares at her.*]

DUDLEY. Hello. Is this Sunset 7349? May I speak to Elsie? Yes. [*Emphatically, and bitterly.*] No, this is *not* Dudley Bostwick. This is Roger Tenefrancia of Montreal, Canada. I'm a childhood friend of Miss Mandelspiegel. We went to kindergarten together. [*Hand over phone.*] God damn it. [*Into phone.*] Yes. I'll wait, thank you.

TOM. I love you.

KITTY. You want to go to my room? [TOM *can't answer.*] Have you got two dollars?

TOM [*shaking his head with confusion*]. I've got *five* dollars, but I *love* you.

KITTY [*looking at him*]. You want to spend all that money?

[TOM *embraces her. They go.* JOE *watches. Goes back to the toy.*]

JOE. Where's that longshoreman, McCarthy?

NICK. He'll be around.

JOE. What do you think he'll have to say today?

NICK. Plenty, as usual. I'm going next door to see who won that third race at Laurel.

JOE. Precious Time won it.

NICK. That's what you think. [*He goes.*]

JOE [*to himself*]. A horse named McCarthy is running in the sixth race today.

DUDLEY [*on the phone*]. Hello. Hello, Elsie? Elsie? [*His voice weakens; also his limbs.*] My God. She's come to the phone. Elsie, I'm at Nick's on Pacific Street. You've got to come here and talk to me. Hello. Hello, Elsie? [*Amazed.*] Did she hang up? Or was I disconnected? [*He hangs up and goes to bar.* WESLEY *is still playing the piano.* HARRY *is still dancing.* JOE *has wound up the big mechanical toy and is watching it work.* NICK *returns.*]

NICK [*watching the toy*]. Say. That's some gadget.

JOE. How much did I win?

NICK. How do you know you *won*?

JOE. Don't be silly. He said Precious Time was going to win by ten lengths, didn't he? He's in love, isn't he?

NICK. O.K. I don't know why, but Precious Time won. You got eighty for ten. How do you do it?

JOE [*roaring*]. Faith. Faith. How'd he win?

NICK. By a nose. Look him up in "The Racing Form." The slowest, the cheapest, the worst horse in the race, and the worst jockey. What's the matter with my luck?

JOE. How much did you lose?

NICK. Fifty cents.

JOE. You should never gamble.

NICK. Why not?

JOE. You always bet fifty cents. You've got no more faith than a flea, that's why.

HARRY [*shouting*]. How do you like this, Nick? [*He is really busy now, all legs and arms.*]

NICK [*turning and watching*]. Not bad. Hang around. You can wait table. [*To* WESLEY]. Hey. Wesley. Can you play that again tonight?

WESLEY [*turning, but still playing the piano*]. I don't

know for sure, Mr. Nick. I can play *something*.

NICK. Good. *You* hang around, too. [*He goes behind the bar.*]

[*The atmosphere is now one of warm, natural, American ease; every man innocent and good; each doing what he believes he should do, or what he must do. There is deep American naïveté and faith in the behavior of each person. No one is competing with anyone else. No one hates anyone else. Every man is living, and letting live. Each man is following his destiny as he feels it should be followed; or is abandoning it as he feels it must, by now, be abandoned; or is forgetting it for the moment as he feels he should forget it. Although everyone is dead serious, there is unmistakable smiling and humor in the scene; a sense of the human body and spirit emerging from the world-imposed state of stress and fretfulness, fear and awkwardness, to the more natural state of casualness and grace. Each person belongs to the environment, in his own person, as himself:* WESLEY *is playing better than ever.* HARRY *is hoofing better than ever.* NICK *is behind the bar shining glasses.* JOE *is smiling at the toy and studying it.* DUDLEY, *although still troubled, is at least calm now and full of melancholy poise.* WILLIE, *at the marble game, is happy. The* ARAB *is deep in his memories, where he wants to be. Into this scene and atmosphere comes* BLICK. BLICK *is the sort of human being you dislike at sight. He is no different from anybody else physically. His face is an ordinary face. There is nothing obviously wrong with him, and yet you know that it is impossible, even by the most generous expansion of understanding, to accept him as a human being. He is the strong man without strength—strong only among the weak—the weak-*

ling who uses force on the weaker. BLICK *enters casually, as if he were a customer, and immediately* HARRY *begins slowing down.*]

BLICK [*oily, and with mock-friendliness*]. Hello, Nick.

NICK [*stopping his work and leaning across the bar*]. What do you want to come here for? You're too big a man for a little honky-tonk.

BLICK [*flattered*]. Now, Nick.

NICK. Important people never come here. *Here*. Have a drink. [*Whiskey bottle.*]

BLICK. Thanks, I don't drink.

NICK [*drinking the drink himself*]. Well, why don't you?

BLICK. I have responsibilities.

NICK. You're head of the lousy Vice Squad. There's no vice here.

BLICK [*sharply*]. Street-walkers are working out of this place.

NICK [*angry*]. What do you want?

BLICK [*loudly*]. I just want you to know that it's got to stop.

[*The music stops. The mechanical toy runs down. There is absolute silence, and a strange fearfulness and disharmony in the atmosphere now.* HARRY *doesn't know what to do with his hands or feet.* WESLEY'S *arms hang at his sides.* JOE *quietly pushes the toy to one side of the table, eager to study what is happening.* WILLIE *stops playing the marble game, turns around and begins to wait.* DUDLEY *straightens up very, very vigorously, as if to say: "Nothing can scare me. I know love is the only thing." The* ARAB *is the same as ever, but watchful.* NICK *is arrogantly aloof. There is a moment of this silence and tension, as though* BLICK *were waiting for everybody to acknowledge his presence. He is obviously flattered by*

the acknowledgment of HARRY, DUDLEY, WESLEY, *and*
WILLIE, *but a little irritated by* NICK's *aloofness and
unfriendliness.*]

NICK. Don't look at me. I can't tell a street-walker from
a lady. You married?

BLICK. You're not asking *me* questions. *I'm* telling *you*.

NICK [*interrupting*]. You're a man of about forty-five
or so. You *ought* to know better.

BLICK [*angry*]. Street-walkers are working out of this
place.

NICK [*beginning to shout*]. Now, don't start any trouble with me. People come here to drink and loaf
around. I don't care who they are.

BLICK. Well, I do.

NICK. The only way to find out if a lady is a streetwalker is to walk the streets with her, go to bed, and
make sure. You wouldn't want to do that. *You'd*
like to, of course.

BLICK. Any more of it, and I'll have your joint closed.

NICK [*very casually, without ill-will*]. Listen. I've got
no use for you, or anybody like you. You're out to
change the world from something bad to something
worse. Something like yourself.

BLICK [*furious pause, and contempt*]. I'll be back tonight. [*He begins to go.*]

NICK [*very angry but very calm*]. Do yourself a big
favor and don't come back tonight. Send somebody
else. I don't like your personality.

BLICK [*casually, but with contempt*]. Don't break any
laws. I don't like yours, either. [*He looks the place
over, and goes.*]

[*There is a moment of silence. Then* WILLIE *turns and
puts a new nickel in the slot and starts a new game.*
WESLEY *turns to the piano and rather falteringly begins to play. His heart really isn't in it.* HARRY *walks
about, unable to dance.* DUDLEY *lapses into his cus-*

tomary melancholy, at a table. NICK *whistles a little: suddenly stops.* JOE *winds the toy.*]

JOE [*comically*]. Nick. You going to kill that man?

NICK. I'm disgusted.

JOE. Yeah? Why?

NICK. Why should I get worked up over a guy like that? Why should I hate *him?* He's nothing. He's nobody. He's a mouse. But every time he comes into this place I get burned up. He doesn't want to drink. He doesn't want to sit down. He doesn't want to take things easy. Tell me one thing?

JOE. Do my best.

NICK. What's a punk like *that* want to go out and try to change the world for?

JOE [*amazed*]. Does *he* want to change the world, too?

NICK [*irritated*]. You know what I mean. What's he want to bother people for? He's *sick.*

JOE [*almost to himself, reflecting on the fact that* BLICK *too wants to change the world*]. I guess he wants to change the world at that.

NICK. So I go to work and hate him.

JOE. It's not him, Nick. It's everything.

NICK. Yeah, *I know*. But I've still got no use for him. He's no good. You know what I mean? He hurts little people. [*Confused.*] One of the girls tried to commit suicide on account of him. [*Furiously.*] I'll break his head if he hurts anybody around here. This is *my* joint. [*Afterthought.*] Or anybody's *feelings,* either.

JOE. He may not be so bad, deep down underneath.

NICK. I know all about him. He's no good.

[*During this talk* WESLEY *has really begun to play the piano, the toy is rattling again, and little by little* HARRY *has begun to dance.* NICK *has come around the bar, and now, very much like a child—forgetting all his anger—is watching the toy work. He begins to smile at everything: turns and listens to* WESLEY: *watches* HARRY: *nods at the* ARAB: *shakes his head at* DUDLEY: *and gestures amiably about* WILLIE. *It's his joint all right. It's a good, low-down, honkytonk American place that lets people alone.*]

NICK. I've got a good joint. There's nothing wrong here. Hey. Comedian. Stick to the dancing tonight. I think you're O.K. Wesley? Do some more of that tonight. That's fine!

HARRY. Thanks, Nick. Gosh, I'm on my way at last. [*On telephone.*] Hello, Ma? Is that you, Ma? Harry. I got the job. [*He hangs up and walks around, smiling.*]

NICK [*watching the toy all this time*]. Say, that really is something. What is that, anyway?

[MARY L. *comes in.*]

JOE [*holding it toward* NICK, *and* MARY L.]. Nick, this is a toy. A contraption devised by the cunning of man to drive boredom, or grief, or anger out of children. A noble gadget. A gadget, I might say, infinitely nobler than any other I can think of at the moment. [*Everybody gathers around* JOE's *table to look at the toy. The toy stops working.* JOE *winds the music box. Lifts a whistle: blows it, making a very strange, funny and sorrowful sound.*] Delightful. Tragic, but delightful.

[WESLEY *plays the music-box theme on the piano.* MARY L. *takes a table.*]

NICK. Joe. That girl, Kitty. What's she mean, calling me a dentist? I wouldn't hurt anybody, let alone a tooth.

[NICK *goes to* MARY L.'s *table.* HARRY *imitates the toy. Dances. The piano music comes up, the light dims slowly, while the piano solo continues.*]

CURTAIN

Act two

An hour later. All the people who were at NICK'S *when the curtain came down are still there.* JOE *at his table, quietly shuffling and turning a deck of cards, and at the same time watching the face of the* WOMAN, *and looking at the initials on her handbag, as though they were the symbols of the lost glory of the world. The* WOMAN, *in turn, very casually regards* JOE *occasionally. Or rather senses him; has sensed him in fact the whole hour. She is mildly tight on beer, and* JOE *himself is tight, but as always completely under control; simply sharper. The others are about, at tables, and so on.*

JOE. Is it Madge—Laubowitz?

MARY. Is what *what*?

JOE. Is the name Mabel Lepescu?

MARY. What name?

JOE. The name the initials M. L. stand for. The initials on your bag.

MARY. No.

JOE [*after a long pause, thinking deeply what the name might be, turning a card, looking into the beautiful face of the woman*]. Margie Longworthy?

MARY [*all this is very natural and sincere, no comedy on the part of the people involved: they are both solemn, being drunk*]. No.

JOE [*his voice higher-pitched, as though he were growing alarmed*]. Midge Laurie? [MARY *shakes her head.*] My initials are J. T.

MARY [*Pause.*] John?

JOE. No. [*Pause.*] Martha Lancaster?

MARY. No. [*Slight pause.*] Joseph?

JOE. Well, not exactly. That's my first name, but everybody calls me Joe. The last name is the tough one. I'll help you a little. I'm Irish. [*Pause.*] Is it just plain Mary?

MARY. Yes, it is. I'm Irish, too. At least on my father's side. English on my mother's side.

JOE. I'm Irish on both sides. Mary's one of my favorite names. I guess that's why I didn't think of it. I met a girl in Mexico City named Mary once. She was an American from Philadelphia. She got married there. In Mexico City, I mean. While I was *there*. We were in love, too. At least *I* was. You never know about anyone else. They were engaged, you see, and her mother was with her, so they went through with it. Must have been six or seven years ago. She's probably got three or four children by this time.

MARY. Are you still in love with her?

JOE. Well—no. To tell you the truth, I'm not sure. I guess I am. I didn't even know she was engaged until a couple of days before they got married. I thought *I* was going to marry her. I kept thinking all the time about the kind of kids we would be likely to have. My favorite was the third one. The first two were fine. Handsome and fine and intelligent, but that third one was different. Dumb and goofy-looking. I liked *him* a lot. When she told me she was going to be married, I didn't feel so bad about the first two, it was that dumb one.

MARY [*after a pause of some few seconds*]. What do you do?

JOE. Do? To tell you the truth, nothing.

MARY. Do you always drink a great deal?

JOE [*scientifically*]. Not *always*. Only when I'm awake. I sleep seven or eight hours every night, you know.

MARY. How nice. I mean to drink when you're awake.

JOE [*thoughtfully*]. It's a privilege.

MARY. Do you really *like* to drink?

JOE [*positively*]. As much as I like to *breathe*.

MARY [*beautifully*]. Why?

JOE [*dramatically*]. Why do I like to drink? [*Pause.*] Because I don't like to be gypped. Because I don't like to be dead most of the time and just a little alive every once in a long while. [*Pause.*] If I don't drink, I become fascinated by unimportant things— like everybody else. I get busy. Do things. All kinds of little stupid things, for all kinds of little stupid reasons. Proud, selfish, *ordinary* things. I've done them. Now I don't do anything. *I live all the time.* Then I go to sleep. [*Pause.*]

MARY. Do you sleep well?

JOE [*taking it for granted*]. Of course.

MARY [*quietly, almost with tenderness*]. What are your plans?

JOE [*loudly, but also tenderly*]. Plans? I haven't *got* any. *I just get up.*

MARY [*beginning to understand everything*]. Oh, yes. Yes, of course.

[DUDLEY *puts a nickel in the phonograph.*]

JOE [*thoughtfully*]. Why do I drink? [*Pause, while he thinks about it. The thinking appears to be profound and complex, and has the effect of giving his face a very comical and naïve expression.*] That question calls for a pretty complicated answer. [*He smiles abstractly.*]

MARY. Oh, I didn't mean—

JOE [*swiftly, gallantly*]. No. No. I *insist*. I *know* why. It's just a matter of finding words. Little ones.

MARY. It really doesn't matter.

JOE [*seriously*]. Oh, yes, it does. [*Clinically.*] Now, why do I drink? [*Scientifically.*] No. Why does *anybody* drink? [*Working it out.*] Every day has twenty-four hours.

MARY [*sadly, but brightly*]. Yes, that's true.

JOE. Twenty-four hours. Out of the twenty-four hours at *least* twenty-three and a half are—my God, I don't know why—dull, dead, boring, empty, and murderous. Minutes on the clock, *not time of living*. It doesn't make any difference who you are or what you do, twenty-three and a half hours of the twenty-four are spent *waiting*.

MARY. Waiting?

JOE [*gesturing, loudly*]. And the more you wait, the less there is to wait *for*.

MARY [*attentively, beautifully his student*]. Oh?

JOE [*continuing*]. That goes on for days and days, and weeks and months and years, and years, and the first thing you know *all* the years are dead. All the minutes are dead. You yourself are dead. There's nothing to wait for any more. Nothing except *minutes* on the *clock*. No time of life. Nothing but minutes, and idiocy. Beautiful, bright, intelligent idiocy. [*Pause.*] Does that answer your question?

MARY [*earnestly*]. I'm afraid it does. Thank you. You shouldn't have gone to all the trouble.

JOE. No trouble at all. [*Pause.*] You have children?

MARY. Yes. Two. A son and a daughter.

JOE [*delighted*]. How swell. Do they look like you?

MARY. Yes.

JOE. Then why are you sad?

MARY. I was always sad. It's just that after I was married I was allowed to drink.

JOE [*eagerly*]. Who are you waiting for?

MARY. No one.

JOE [*smiling*]. I'm not waiting for anybody, either.

MARY. My husband, of course.

JOE. Oh, sure.

MARY. He's a lawyer.

JOE [*standing, leaning on the table*]. He's a great guy. I like him. I'm very fond of him.

MARY [*listening*]. You have responsibilities?

JOE [*loudly*]. *One*, and *thousands*. As a matter of fact, I feel responsible to everybody. At least to everybody I meet. I've been trying for three years to find out if it's possible to live what I think is a civilized life. I mean a life that can't hurt any other life.

MARY. You're famous?

JOE. Very. Utterly unknown, but very famous. Would you like to dance?

MARY. All right.

JOE [*loudly*]. I'm *sorry*. I don't dance. I didn't think you'd like to.

MARY. To tell you the truth, I don't like to dance at all.

JOE [*proudly—commentator*]. I can hardly walk.

MARY. You mean you're tight?

JOE [*smiling*]. No. I mean *all* the time.

MARY [*looking at him closely*]. Were you ever in Paris?

JOE. In 1929, and again in 1934.

MARY. What month of 1934?

JOE. Most of April, all of May, and a little of June.

MARY. I was there in November and December that year.

JOE. We were there almost at the same time. You were married?

MARY. Engaged. [*They are silent a moment, looking at one another. Quietly and with great charm.*] Are you *really* in love with me?

JOE. Yes.

MARY. Is it the champagne?

JOE. Yes. Partly, at least. [*He sits down.*]

MARY. If you don't see me again, will you be very unhappy?

JOE. Very.

MARY [*getting up*]. I'm so pleased. [JOE *is deeply grieved that she is going. In fact, he is almost panic-stricken about it, getting up in a way that is full of furious sorrow and regret.*] I must go now. Please don't get up. [JOE *is up, staring at her with amazement.*] Good-by.

JOE [*simply*]. Good-by.

[*The* WOMAN *stands looking at him a moment, then turns and goes.* JOE *stands staring after her for a long time. Just as he is slowly sitting down again, the* NEWSBOY *enters, and goes to* JOE's *table.*]

NEWSBOY. Paper, Mister?

JOE. How many you got this time?

NEWSBOY. Eleven.

[JOE *buys them all, looks at the lousy headlines, throws them away. The* NEWSBOY *looks at* JOE, *amazed. He walks over to* NICK *at the bar.*]

NEWSBOY [*troubled*]. Hey, Mister, do you own this place?

NICK [*casually but emphatically*]. I own this place.

NEWSBOY. Can you use a great lyric tenor?

NICK [*almost to himself*]. Great lyric tenor? [*Loudly.*] Who?

NEWSBOY [*loud and the least bit angry*]. Me. I'm getting too big to sell papers. I don't want to holler headlines all the time. I want to *sing*. You can use a great lyric tenor, can't you?

NICK. What's lyric about you?

NEWSBOY [*voice high-pitched, confused*]. My voice.

NICK. Oh. [*Slight pause, giving in.*] All right, then—sing!

[*The* NEWSBOY *breaks into swift and beautiful song:*

"When Irish Eyes Are Smiling." NICK *and* JOE *listen carefully:* NICK *with wonder,* JOE *with amazement and delight.*]

NEWSBOY [*singing*].

> When Irish eyes are smiling,
> Sure 'tis like a morn in Spring.
> In the lilt of Irish laughter,
> You can hear the angels sing.
> When Irish hearts are happy,
> All the world seems bright and gay.
> But when Irish eyes are smiling—

NICK [*loudly, swiftly*]. Are you Irish?

NEWSBOY [*speaking swiftly, loudly, a little impatient with the irrelevant question*]. No. I'm Greek. [*He finishes the song, singing louder than ever.*] Sure they steal your heart away. [*He turns to* NICK *dramatically, like a vaudeville singer begging his audience for applause.* NICK *studies the* BOY *eagerly.* JOE *gets to his feet and leans toward the* BOY *and* NICK.]

NICK. Not bad. Let me hear you again about a year from now.

NEWSBOY [*thrilled*]. Honest?

NICK. Yeah. Along about November 7th, 1940.

NEWSBOY [*happier than ever before in his life, running over to* JOE]. Did you hear it too, Mister?

JOE. Yes, and it's great. What part of Greece?

NEWSBOY. Salonica. Gosh, Mister. Thanks.

JOE Don't wait a year. Come back with some papers a little later. You're a great singer.

NEWSBOY [*thrilled and excited*]. Aw, thanks, Mister. So long. [*Running, to* NICK.] Thanks, Mister. [*He runs out.* JOE *and* NICK *look at the swinging doors.* JOE *sits down.* NICK *laughs.*]

NICK. Joe, people are so wonderful. Look at that kid.

JOE. Of course they're wonderful. Every one of them is wonderful.

[MC CARTHY *and* KRUPP *come in, talking.* MC CARTHY *is a big man in work clothes, which make him seem very young. He is wearing black jeans, and a blue workman's shirt. No tie. No hat. He has broad shoulders, a lean intelligent face, thick black hair. In his right back pocket is the longshoreman's hook. His arms are long and hairy. His sleeves are rolled up to just below his elbows. He is a casual man, easy-going in movement, sharp in perception, swift in appreciation of charm or innocence or comedy, and gentle in spirit. His speech is clear and full of warmth. His voice is powerful, but modulated. He enjoys the world, in spite of the mess it is, and he is fond of people, in spite of the mess they are.* KRUPP *is not quite as tall or broad-shouldered as* MC CARTHY. *He is physically encumbered by his uniform, club, pistol, belt, and cap. And he is plainly not at home in the role of policeman. His movement is stiff and unintentionally pompous. He is a naïve man, essentially good. His understanding is less than* MC CARTHY'S, *but he is honest and he doesn't try to bluff.*]

KRUPP. You don't understand what I mean. Hi-ya, Joe.

JOE. Hello, Krupp.

MC CARTHY. Hi-ya, Joe.

JOE. Hello, McCarthy.

KRUPP. Two beers, Nick. [*To* MC CARTHY.] All I do is carry out orders, carry out orders. I don't know what the idea is behind the order. Who it's for, or who it's against, or why. All I do is carry it out.

[NICK *gives them beer.*]

MC CARTHY. You don't read enough.

KRUPP. I do read. I read *The Examiner* every morning. *The Call-Bulletin* every night.

MC CARTHY. And carry out orders. What are the orders now?

KRUPP. To keep the peace down here on the waterfront.

MC CARTHY. Keep it for who? [*To* JOE.] Right?

JOE [*sorrowfully*]. Right.

KRUPP. How do I know for who? The peace. Just keep it.

MC CARTHY. It's got to be kept for somebody. Who would you suspect it's kept for?

KRUPP. For citizens!

MC CARTHY. I'm a citizen!

KRUPP. All right, I'm keeping it for you.

MC CARTHY. By hitting me over the head with a club? [*To* JOE.] Right?

JOE [*melancholy, with remembrance*]. I don't know.

KRUPP. Mac, you know I never hit you over the head with a club.

MC CARTHY. But you will if you're on duty at the time and happen to stand on the opposite side of myself, on duty.

KRUPP. We went to Mission High together. We were always good friends. The only time we ever fought was that time over Alma Haggerty. Did *you* marry Alma Haggerty? [*To* JOE.] Right?

JOE. Everything's right.

MC CARTHY. No. Did you? [*To* JOE.] Joe, are you with me or against me?

JOE. I'm with everybody. One at a time.

KRUPP. No. And that's just what I mean.

MC CARTHY. You mean neither one of us is going to marry the thing we're fighting for?

KRUPP. *I don't even know what it is.*

MC CARTHY. You don't read enough, I tell you.

KRUPP. Mac, you don't know what you're fighting for, either.

MC CARTHY. It's so simple, it's fantastic.

KRUPP. All right, what are you fighting for?

MC CARTHY. For the rights of the inferior. Right?

JOE. Something like that.

KRUPP. The who?

MC CARTHY. The inferior. The world full of Mahoneys who haven't got what it takes to make monkeys out of everybody else, near by. The men who were created equal. Remember?

KRUPP. Mac, you're not inferior.

MC CARTHY. I'm a longshoreman. And an idealist. I'm a man with too much brawn to be an intellectual, exclusively. I married a small, sensitive, cultured woman so that my kids would be sissies instead of suckers. A strong man with any sensibility has no choice in this world but to be a heel, or a *worker*. I haven't the heart to be a heel, so I'm a worker. I've got a son in high school who's already thinking of being a writer.

KRUPP. I wanted to be a writer once.

JOE. Wonderful. [*He puts down the paper, looks at* KRUPP *and* MC CARTHY.]

MC CARTHY. They *all* wanted to be writers. Every maniac in the world that ever brought about the murder of people through war started out in an attic or a basement writing poetry. It stank. So they got even by becoming important heels. And it's still going on.

KRUPP. Is it really, Joe?

JOE. Look at today's paper.

MC CARTHY. Right now on Telegraph Hill is some punk who is trying to be Shakespeare. Ten years from now he'll be a senator. Or a communist.

KRUPP. Somebody ought to do something about it.

MC CARTHY [*mischievously, with laughter in his voice*]. The thing to do is to have more magazines. Hundreds of them. *Thousands.* Print everything they write, so they'll believe they're immortal. That way keep them from going haywire.

KRUPP. Mac, you ought to be a writer yourself.

MC CARTHY. I hate the tribe. They're mischief-makers. Right?

JOE [*swiftly*]. Everything's right. Right and wrong.

KRUPP. Then why do you read?

MC CARTHY [*laughing*]. It's relaxing. It's soothing. [*Pause.*] The lousiest people born into the world are writers. Language is all right. It's the people who use language that are lousy. [*The* ARAB *has moved a little closer, and is listening carefully. To the* ARAB.] What do you think, Brother?

ARAB [*after making many faces, thinking very deeply*]. No foundation. All the way down the line. What. What-not. Nothing. I go walk and look at sky. [*He goes.*]

KRUPP. What? What-not? [*To* JOE.] What's that mean?

JOE [*slowly, thinking, remembering*]. What? What-not? That means this side, that side. Inhale, exhale. What: birth. What-not: death. The inevitable, the astounding, the magnificent seed of growth and decay in all things. Beginning, and end. That man, in his own way, is a prophet. He is one who, with the help of *beer,* is able to reach that state of deep understanding in which what and what-not, the reasonable and the unreasonable, are *one.*

MC CARTHY. Right.

KRUPP. If you can understand that kind of talk, how can you be a longshoreman?

MC CARTHY. I come from a long line of McCarthys who

never married or slept with anything but the most powerful and quarrelsome flesh. [*He drinks beer.*]

KRUPP. I could listen to you two guys for hours, but I'll be damned if I know what the hell you're talking about.

MC CARTHY. The consequence is that all the McCarthys are too great and too strong to be heroes. Only the weak and unsure perform the heroic. They've *got* to. The more heroes you have, the worse the history of the world becomes. Right?

JOE. Go outside and look at it.

KRUPP. You sure can philos—philosoph— Boy, you can talk.

MC CARTHY. I wouldn't talk this way to anyone but a man in uniform, and a man who couldn't understand a word of what I was saying. The party I'm speaking of, my friend, is *YOU*.

[*The phone rings.* HARRY *gets up from his table suddenly and begins a new dance.*]

KRUPP [*noticing him, with great authority*]. Here. Here. What do you think you're doing?

HARRY [*stopping*]. I just got an idea for a new dance. I'm trying it out. Nick. Nick, the phone's ringing.

KRUPP [*to* MC CARTHY]. Has he got a right to do that?

MC CARTHY. The living have danced from the beginning of time. I might even say, the dance and the life have moved along together, until now we have— [*To* HARRY.] Go into your dance, son, and show us what we have.

HARRY. I haven't got it worked out *completely* yet, but it starts out like this. [*He dances.*]

NICK [*on phone*]. Nick's Pacific Street Restaurant, Saloon, and Entertainment Palace. Good afternoon. Nick speaking. [*Listens.*] Who? [*Turns around.*] Is there a Dudley Bostwick in the joint?

[DUDLEY *jumps to his feet and goes to phone.*]

DUDLEY [*on phone*]. Hello. Elsie? [*Listens.*] You're coming down? [*Elated. To the saloon.*] She's coming down. [*Pause.*] No. I won't drink. Aw, gosh, Elsie. [*He hangs up, looks about him strangely, as if he were just born, walks around touching things, putting chairs in place, and so on.*]

MC CARTHY [*to* HARRY]. Splendid. Splendid.

HARRY. Then I go into this little routine. [*He demonstrates.*]

KRUPP. Is that good, Mac?

MC CARTHY. It's awful, but it's honest and ambitious, like everything else in this great country.

HARRY. Then I work along into this. [*He demonstrates.*] And *this* is where I *really* get going. [*He finishes the dance.*]

MC CARTHY. Excellent. A most satisfying demonstration of the present state of the American body and soul. Son, you're a genius.

HARRY [*delighted, shaking hands with* MC CARTHY]. I go on in front of an audience for the first time in my life tonight.

MC CARTHY. They'll be delighted. Where'd you learn to dance?

HARRY. Never took a lesson in my life. I'm a natural-born dancer. And *comedian*, too.

MC CARTHY [*astounded*]. You can make people *laugh*?

HARRY [*dumbly*]. I can be funny, but they won't laugh.

MC CARTHY. That's odd. Why not?

HARRY. I don't know. They just won't laugh.

MC CARTHY. Would you care to be funny now?

HARRY. I'd like to try out a new monologue I've been thinking about.

MC CARTHY. Please do. I promise you if it's funny I shall *roar* with laughter.

HARRY. This is it. [*Goes into the act, with much energy.*] I'm up at Sharkey's on Turk Street. It's a quarter to nine, daylight saving. Wednesday, the eleventh. What I've got is a headache and a 1918 nickel. What I *want* is a cup of coffee. If I buy a cup of coffee with the nickel, I've got to walk home. I've got an eight-ball problem. George the Greek is shooting a game of snooker with Pedro the Filipino. *I'm in rags.* They're wearing thirty-five dollar suits, made to order. I haven't got a cigarette. They're smoking Bobby Burns panatelas. I'm thinking it over, like I always do. George the Greek is in a tough spot. If I buy a cup of coffee, I'll want another cup. What happens? My *ear* aches! My ear. George the Greek takes the cue. Chalks it. Studies the table. Touches the cue-ball delicately. Tick. What happens? He makes the three-ball! What do I do? I get confused. *I go out and buy a morning paper.* What the hell do I want with a morning paper? What I *want* is a cup of coffee, and a good used car. I go out and buy a morning paper. Thursday, the twelfth. Maybe the headline's about *me.* I take a quick look. *No. The headline is not about me.* It's about Hitler. Seven thousand miles away. I'm here. Who the hell is Hitler? Who's behind the eight-ball? I turn around. *Everybody's behind the eight-ball!*

[*Pause.* KRUPP *moves toward* HARRY *as if to make an important arrest.* HARRY *moves to the swinging doors.* MC CARTHY *stops* KRUPP.]

MC CARTHY [*to* HARRY]. It's the funniest thing I've ever heard. Or *seen,* for that matter.

HARRY [*coming back to* MC CARTHY]. Then, why don't you laugh?

MC CARTHY. I don't know, *yet.*

HARRY. I'm always getting funny ideas that nobody will laugh at.

MC CARTHY [*thoughtfully*]. It may be that you've stumbled headlong into a new kind of comedy.

HARRY. Well, what good is it if it doesn't make anybody laugh?

MC CARTHY. There are *kinds* of laughter, son. I must say, in all truth, that I *am* laughing, although not *out loud*.

HARRY. I want to *hear* people laugh. *Out loud*. That's why I keep thinking of funny things to say.

MC CARTHY. Well. They may catch on in time. Let's go, Krupp. So long, Joe. [MC CARTHY *and* KRUPP *go*.]

JOE. So long. [*After a moment's pause*.] Hey, Nick.

NICK. Yeah.

JOE. Bet McCarthy in the last race.

NICK. You're crazy. That horse is a double-crossing, no-good—

JOE. Bet everything you've got on McCarthy.

NICK. I'm not betting a nickel on him. *You* bet everything you've got on McCarthy.

JOE. I don't need money.

NICK. What makes you think McCarthy's going to win?

JOE. McCarthy's name's McCarthy, isn't it?

NICK. Yeah. So what?

JOE. The *horse* named McCarthy is going to win, *that's all*. Today.

NICK. Why?

JOE. You do what I tell you, and everything will be all right.

NICK. McCarthy likes to talk, that's all. [*Pause*.] Where's Tom?

JOE. He'll be around. He'll be miserable, but he'll be around. Five or ten minutes more.

NICK. You don't believe that Kitty, do you? About being in burlesque?

JOE [*very clearly*]. I believe dreams sooner than statistics.

NICK [*remembering*]. She sure is somebody. Called me a dentist.

[TOM, *turning about, confused, troubled, comes in, and hurries to* JOE's *table.*]

JOE. What's the matter?

TOM. Here's your five, Joe. I'm in trouble again.

JOE. If it's not organic, it'll cure itself. If it is organic, science will cure it. What is it, organic or non-organic?

TOM. Joe, I don't know— [*He seems to be completely broken down.*]

JOE. What's eating you? I want you to go on an errand for me.

TOM. It's Kitty.

JOE. What about her?

TOM. She's up in her room, crying.

JOE. Crying?

TOM. Yeah, she's been crying for over an hour. I been talking to her all this time, but she won't stop.

JOE. What's she crying about?

TOM. I don't know. I couldn't understand anything. She kept crying and telling me about a big house and collie dogs all around and flowers and one of her brothers dead and the other one lost somewhere. Joe, I can't stand Kitty crying.

JOE. You want to marry the girl?

TOM [*nodding*]. Yeah.

JOE [*curious and sincere*]. Why?

TOM. I don't know why, exactly, Joe. [*Pause.*] Joe, I don't like to think of Kitty out in the streets. I guess I love her, that's all.

JOE. She's a nice girl.

TOM. She's like an angel. She's not like those other street-walkers.

JOE [*swiftly*]. Here. Take all this money and run next

door to Frankie's and bet it on the nose of Mc-Carthy.

TOM [*swiftly*]. All this money, Joe? McCarthy?

JOE. Yeah. Hurry.

TOM [*going*]. Ah, Joe. If McCarthy wins we'll be rich.

JOE. Get going, will you?

[TOM *runs out and nearly knocks over the* ARAB *coming back in.* NICK *fills him a beer without a word.*]

ARAB. No foundation, anywhere. Whole world. No foundation. All the way down the line.

NICK [*angry*]. McCarthy! Just because you got a little lucky this morning, you have to go to work and throw away eighty bucks.

JOE. He wants to marry her.

NICK. Suppose she doesn't want to marry *him?*

JOE [*amazed*]. Oh, yeah. [*Thinking.*] Now, why wouldn't she want to marry a nice guy like Tom?

NICK. She's been in burlesque. She's had flowers sent to her by European royalty. She's dined with young men of quality and social position. She's above Tom.

[TOM *comes running in.*]

TOM [*disgusted*]. They were running when I got there. Frankie wouldn't take the bet. McCarthy didn't get a call till the stretch. I thought we were going to save all this money. Then McCarthy won by *two* lengths.

JOE. What'd he pay, fifteen to one?

TOM. Better, but Frankie wouldn't take the bet.

NICK [*throwing a dish towel across the room*]. Well, for the love of Mike.

JOE. Give me the money.

TOM [*giving back the money*]. We would have had about a thousand five hundred dollars.

JOE [*bored, casually, inventing*]. Go up to Schwabacher-Frey and get me the biggest Rand-McNally map of the nations of Europe they've got. On your way back stop at one of the pawn shops on Third Street, and buy me a good revolver and some cartridges.

TOM. She's up in her room crying, Joe.

JOE. Go get me those things.

NICK. What are you going to do, study the map, and then go out and shoot somebody?

JOE. I want to read the names of some European towns and rivers and valleys and mountains.

NICK. What do you want with the revolver?

JOE. I want to study it. I'm interested in things. Here's twenty dollars, Tom. Now go get them things.

TOM. A big map of Europe. And a revolver.

JOE. Get a good one. Tell the man you don't know anything about firearms and you're trusting him not to fool you. Don't pay more than ten dollars.

TOM. Joe, you got something on your mind. Don't go fool with a revolver.

JOE. Be sure it's a good one.

TOM. Joe.

JOE [*irritated*]. What, Tom?

TOM. Joe, what do you send me out for crazy things for all the time?

JOE [*angry*]. They're not crazy, Tom. Now, get going.

TOM. What about Kitty, Joe?

JOE. Let her cry. It'll do her good.

TOM. If she comes in here while I'm gone, talk to her, will you, Joe? Tell her about me?

JOE. O. K. Get going. Don't load that gun. Just buy it and bring it here.

TOM [*going*]. You won't catch me loading any gun.

JOE. Wait a minute. Take these toys away.

TOM. Where'll I take them?

JOE. Give them to some kid. [*Pause.*] No. Take them

up to Kitty. Toys stopped me from crying once.
That's the reason I had you buy them. I wanted to
see if I could find out *why* they stopped me from
crying. I remember they seemed awfully stupid at
the time.

TOM. Shall I, Joe? Take them up to Kitty? Do you
think they'd stop *her* from crying?

JOE. They might. You get curious about the way they
work and you forget whatever it is you're remembering that's making you cry. That's what they're for.

TOM. Yeah. Sure. The girl at the store asked me what
I wanted with toys. I'll take them up to Kitty. [*Tragically*.] She's like a little girl. [*He goes*.]

WESLEY. Mr. Nick, can I play the piano again?

NICK. Sure. Practice all you like—until I tell you to
stop.

WESLEY. You going to pay me for playing the piano?

NICK. Sure. I'll give you enough to get by on.

WESLEY [*amazed and delighted*]. Get money for playing
the piano? [*He goes to the piano and begins to play
quietly.* HARRY *goes up on the little stage and listens
to the music. After a while he begins a soft-shoe
dance*.]

NICK. What were you crying about?

JOE. My mother.

NICK. What about her?

JOE. She was dead. I stopped crying when they gave me
the toys.

[NICK'S MOTHER, *a little old woman of sixty or so,
dressed plainly in black, her face shining, comes in
briskly, chattering loudly in Italian, gesturing.* NICK
is delighted to see her.]

NICK'S MOTHER [*in Italian*]. Everything all right,
Nickie?

NICK [*in Italian*]. Sure, Mamma.

[NICK'S MOTHER *leaves as gaily and as noisily as she came, after half a minute of loud Italian family talk.*]

JOE. Who was that?

NICK [*to* JOE, *proudly and a little sadly*]. My mother. [*Still looking at the swinging doors.*]

JOE. What'd she say?

NICK. Nothing. Just wanted to see me. [*Pause.*] What do you want with that gun?

JOE. I study things, Nick.

[*An* OLD MAN *who looks as if he might have been Kit Carson at one time walks in importantly, moves about, and finally stands at* JOE's *table.*]

KIT CARSON. Murphy's the name. Just an old trapper. Mind if I sit down?

JOE. Be delighted. What'll you drink?

KIT CARSON [*sitting down*]. Beer. Same as I've been drinking. And thanks.

JOE [*to* NICK]. Glass of beer, Nick.

[NICK *brings the beer to the table,* KIT CARSON *swallows it in one swig, wipes his big white mustache with the back of his right hand.*]

KIT CARSON [*moving in*]. I don't suppose you ever fell in love with a midget weighing thirty-nine pounds?

JOE [*studying the man*]. Can't say I have, but have another beer.

KIT CARSON [*intimately*]. Thanks, thanks. Down in Gallup, twenty years ago. Fellow by the name of Rufus Jenkins came to town with six white horses and two black ones. Said he wanted a man to break the horses for him because his left leg was wood and he couldn't do it. Had a meeting at Parker's Mercantile Store and finally came to blows, me and Henry Walpal. Bashed his head with a brass cuspidor and ran away to Mexico, but he didn't die. Couldn't speak a word. Took up with a cattle-breeder named Diego, educated in California. Spoke the language better than you and me. Said, Your job, Murph, is to feed them prize bulls. I said, Fine, what'll I feed them? He said, Hay, lettuce, salt, beer, and aspirin. Came to blows two days later over an accordion he claimed I stole. I had *borrowed* it. During the fight I busted it over his head; ruined one of the finest accordions I ever saw. Grabbed a horse and rode back across the border. Texas. Got to talking with a fellow who looked honest. Turned out to be a Ranger who was looking for me.

JOE. Yeah. You were saying, a thirty-nine-pound midget.

KIT CARSON. Will I ever forget that lady? Will I ever get over that amazon of small proportions?

JOE. Will you?

KIT CARSON. If I live to be sixty.

JOE. Sixty? You look more than sixty now.

KIT CARSON. That's trouble showing in my face. Trouble and complications. I was fifty-eight three months ago.

JOE. That accounts for it, then. Go ahead, tell me more.

KIT CARSON. Told the Texas Ranger my name was Rothstein, mining engineer from Pennsylvania, looking for something worth while. Mentioned two places in Houston. Nearly lost an eye early one morning, going down the stairs. Ran into a six-footer with an iron claw where his right hand was supposed to be. Said, You broke up my home. Told him I was a stranger in Houston. The girls gathered at the top of the stairs to see a fight. Seven of them. Six feet and an iron claw. That's bad on the nerves. Kicked him in the mouth when he swung for my head with the claw. Would have lost an eye except for quick thinking. He rolled into the gutter and pulled a gun. Fired seven times. I was back upstairs. Left the place an hour later, dressed in silk and feathers, with a hat swung around over my face. Saw him standing on the corner, waiting. Said, Care for a wiggle? Said he didn't. I went on down the street and left town. I don't suppose you ever had to put a dress on to save your skin, did you?

JOE. No, and I never fell in love with a midget weighing thirty-nine pounds. Have another beer?

KIT CARSON. Thanks. [*Swallows glass of beer.*] Ever try to herd cattle on a bicycle?

JOE. No. I never got around to that.

KIT CARSON. Left Houston with sixty cents in my pocket, gift of a girl named Lucinda. Walked fourteen miles in fourteen hours. Big house with barbwire all around, and big dogs. One thing I never could get around. Walked past the gate, anyway, from hunger and thirst. Dogs jumped up and came for me. Walked right into them, growing older every second. Went up to the door and knocked. Big Negress opened the door, closed it quick. Said, On your way, white trash. Knocked again. Said, On your way. Again. On your way. Again. This time the old man himself opened the door, ninety, if he was a day. Sawed-off shotgun, too. Said, I ain't looking for trouble, Father. I'm hungry and thirsty, name's Cavanaugh. Took me in and made mint juleps for the two of us. Said, Living here alone, Father? Said, Drink and ask no questions. Maybe I am and maybe I ain't. You saw the lady. Draw your own conclusions. I'd heard of that, but didn't wink out of tact. If I told you that old Southern gentleman was my grandfather, you wouldn't believe me, would you?

JOE. I might.

KIT CARSON. Well, it so happens he wasn't. Would have been romantic if he had been, though.

JOE. Where did you herd cattle on a bicycle?

KIT CARSON. Toledo, Ohio, 1918.

JOE. Toledo, Ohio? They don't herd cattle in Toledo.

KIT CARSON. They don't any more. They did in 1918. One fellow did, leastaways. Bookkeeper named Sam Gold. Straight from the East Side, New York. Sombrero, lariats, Bull Durham, two head of cattle and two bicycles. Called his place The Gold Bar Ranch, two acres, just outside the city limits. That was the year of the War, you'll remember.

JOE. Yeah, I remember, but how about herding them two cows on a bicycle? How'd you do it?

KIT CARSON. Easiest thing in the world. Rode no hands. Had to, otherwise couldn't lasso the cows. Worked for Sam Gold till the cows ran away. Bicycles scared them. They went into Toledo. Never saw hide nor hair of them again. Advertised in every paper, but never got them back. Broke his heart. Sold both bikes and returned to New York. Took four aces from a deck of red cards and walked to town. Poker. Fellow in the game named Chuck Collins, liked to gamble. Told him with a smile I didn't suppose he'd care to bet a hundred dollars I wouldn't hold four aces the next hand. Called it. My cards were red on the blank side. The other cards were blue. Plumb forgot all about it. Showed him four aces. Ace of spades, ace of clubs, ace of diamonds, ace of hearts. I'll remember them four cards if I live to be sixty. Would have been killed on the spot except for the hurricane that year.

JOE. Hurricane?

KIT CARSON. You haven't forgotten the Toledo hurricane of 1918, have you?

JOE. No. There was no hurricane in Toledo in 1918, or any other year.

KIT CARSON. For the love of God, then what do you suppose that commotion was? And how come I came to in Chicago, dream-walking down State Street?

JOE. I guess they scared you.

KIT CARSON. No, that wasn't it. You go back to the papers of November 1918, and I think you'll find there was a hurricane in Toledo. I remember sitting on the roof of a two-story house, floating northwest.

JOE [*seriously*]. Northwest?

KIT CARSON. Now, son, don't tell me *you* don't believe me, either?

JOE [*pause. Very seriously, energetically and sharply*]. Of course I believe you. Living is an art. It's not bookkeeping. It takes a lot of rehearsing for a man to get to be himself.

KIT CARSON [*thoughtfully, smiling, and amazed*]. You're the first man I've ever met who believes me.

JOE [*seriously*]. Have another beer.

[TOM *comes in with the Rand-McNally book, the revolver, and the box of cartridges.* KIT *goes to bar.*]

JOE [*to* TOM]. Did you give her the toys?

TOM. Yeah, I gave them to her.

JOE. Did she stop crying?

TOM. No. She started crying harder than ever.

JOE. That's funny. I wonder why.

TOM. Joe, if I was a minute earlier, Frankie would have taken the bet and now we'd have about a thousand five hundred dollars. How much of it would you have given me, Joe?

JOE. If she'd marry you—*all* of it.

TOM. Would you, Joe?

JOE [*opening packages, examining book first, and revolver next*]. Sure. In this realm there's only one subject, and you're it. It's my duty to see that my subject is happy.

TOM. Joe, do you think we'll ever have eighty dollars for a race sometime again when there's a fifteen-to-one shot that we like, weather good, track fast, they get off to a good start, our horse doesn't get a call till the stretch, we think we're going to lose all that money, and then it wins, by a nose?

JOE. I didn't quite get that.

TOM. You know what I mean.

JOE. You mean the impossible. No, Tom, we won't. We were just a little late, that's all.

TOM. We might, Joe.

JOE. It's not likely.

TOM. Then how am I ever going to make enough money to marry her?

JOE. I don't know, Tom. Maybe you aren't.

TOM. Joe, I got to marry Kitty. [*Shaking his head.*] You ought to see the crazy room she lives in.

JOE. What kind of a room is it?

TOM. It's little. It crowds you in. It's bad, Joe. Kitty don't belong in a place like that.

JOE. You want to take her away from there?

TOM. Yeah. I want her to live in a house where there's room enough to live. Kitty ought to have a garden, or something.

JOE. You want to take care of her?

TOM. Yeah, sure, Joe. I ought to take care of somebody good that makes me feel like *I'm* somebody.

JOE. That means you'll have to get a job. What can you do?

TOM. I finished high school, but I don't know what I can do.

JOE. Sometimes when you think about it, what do you think you'd like to do?

TOM. Just sit around like you, Joe, and have somebody run errands for me and drink champagne and take things easy and never be broke and never worry about money.

JOE. That's a noble ambition.

NICK [*to* JOE]. How do you do it?

JOE. I really don't know, but I think you've got to have the full co-operation of the Good Lord.

NICK. I can't understand the way you talk.

TOM. Joe, shall I go back and see if I can get her to stop crying?

JOE. Give me a hand and I'll go with you.

TOM [*amazed*]. What! You're going to get up already?

JOE. She's crying, isn't she?

TOM. She's crying. Worse than ever now.

JOE. I thought the toys would stop her.

TOM. I've seen you sit in one place from four in the morning till two the next morning.

JOE. At my best, Tom, I don't travel by foot. That's all. Come on. Give me a hand. I'll find some way to stop her from crying.

TOM [*helping* JOE]. Joe, I never did tell you. You're a different kind of a guy.

JOE [*swiftly, a little angry*]. Don't be silly. I don't understand things. I'm trying to understand them.

[JOE *is a little drunk. They go out together. The lights go down slowly, while* WESLEY *plays the piano, and come up slowly on.*]

Act three

A cheap bed in NICK'S *to indicate room 21 of The New York Hotel, upstairs, around the corner from* NICK'S. *The bed can be at the center of* NICK'S, *or up on the little stage. Everything in* NICK'S *is the same, except that all the people are silent, immobile and in darkness, except* WESLEY *who is playing the piano softly and sadly.* KITTY DUVAL, *in a dress she has carried*

*around with her from the early days in Ohio, is seated
on the bed, tying a ribbon in her hair. She looks at
herself in a hand mirror. She is deeply grieved at the
change she sees in herself. She takes off the ribbon,
angry and hurt. She lifts a book from the bed and tries
to read. She begins to sob again. She picks up an old
picture of herself and looks at it. Sobs harder than
ever, falling on the bed and burying her face. There
is a knock, as if at the door.*

KITTY [*sobbing*]. Who is it?

TOM'S VOICE. Kitty, it's me. Tom. Me and Joe.

[JOE, *followed by* TOM, *comes to the bed quietly.* JOE
is holding a rather large toy carousel. JOE *studies*
KITTY *a moment. He sets the toy carousel on the
floor, at the foot of* KITTY'S *bed.*]

TOM [*standing over* KITTY *and bending down close to
her*]. Don't cry any more, Kitty.

KITTY [*not looking, sobbing*]. I don't like this life.

[JOE *starts the carousel which makes a strange, sorrowful, tinkling music. The music begins slowly, becomes swift, gradually slows down, and ends.* JOE
*himself is interested in the toy, watches and listens
to it carefully.*]

TOM [*eagerly*]. Kitty. Joe got up from his chair at
Nick's just to get you a toy and come here. This one
makes music. We rode all over town in a cab to get
it. Listen.

[KITTY *sits up slowly, listening, while* TOM *watches her.
Everything happens slowly and somberly.* KITTY *notices the photograph of herself when she was a little
girl. Lifts it, and looks at it again.*]

TOM [*looking*]. Who's that little girl, Kitty?

KITTY. That's me. When I was seven.

TOM [*looking, smiling*]. Gee, you're pretty, Kitty.

[JOE *reaches up for the photograph, which* TOM *hands*

to him. TOM *returns to* KITTY *whom he finds as
pretty now as she was at seven.* JOE *studies the photograph.* KITTY *looks up at* TOM. *There is no doubt
that they really love one another.* JOE *looks up at
them.*]

KITTY. Tom?

TOM [*eagerly*]. Yeah, Kitty.

KITTY. Tom, when you were a little boy what did you
want to be?

TOM [*a little bewildered, but eager to please her*].
What, Kitty?

KITTY. Do you remember when you were a little boy?

TOM [*thoughtfully*]. Yeah, I remember sometimes,
Kitty.

KITTY. What did you want to be?

TOM [*looks at* JOE. JOE *holds* TOM's *eyes a moment.
Then* TOM *is able to speak*]. Sometimes I wanted to
be a locomotive engineer. Sometimes I wanted to be
a policeman.

KITTY. I wanted to be a great actress. [*She looks up
into* TOM's *face.*] Tom, didn't you ever want to be
a doctor?

TOM [*looks at* JOE. JOE *holds* TOM's *eyes again, encouraging* TOM *by his serious expression to go on talking*]. Yeah, now I remember. Sure, Kitty. I wanted
to be a doctor—once.

KITTY [*smiling sadly*]. I'm so glad. Because I wanted to
be an actress and have a young doctor come to the
theater and see me and fall in love with me and send
me flowers.

[JOE *pantomimes to* TOM, *demanding that he go on
talking.*]

TOM. I would do that, Kitty.

KITTY. I wouldn't know who it was, and then one day
I'd see him in the street and fall in love with him. I
wouldn't know *he* was the one who was in love with

me. I'd think about him all the time. I'd dream
about him. I'd dream of being near him the rest of
my life. I'd dream of having children that looked
like him. I wouldn't be an actress all the time. Only
until I found him and fell in love with him. After
that we'd take a train and go to beautiful cities and
see the wonderful people everywhere and give
money to the poor and whenever people were sick
he'd go to them and make them well again.

[TOM *looks at* JOE, *bewildered, confused, and full of
sorrow.* KITTY *is deep in memory, almost in a trance.*]

JOE [*gently*]. Talk to her, Tom. Be the wonderful
young doctor she dreamed about and never found.
Go ahead. Correct the errors of the world.

TOM. Joe. [*Pathetically.*] I don't know what to say.

[*There is rowdy singing in the hall. A loud young*
VOICE *sings:* "Sailing, sailing, over the bounding
main."]

VOICE. Kitty. Oh, Kitty! [KITTY *stirs, shocked, coming
out of the trance.*] Where the hell are you? Oh,
Kitty.

[TOM *jumps up, furiously.*]

WOMAN'S VOICE [*in the hall*]. Who are you looking for,
Sailor Boy?

VOICE. The most beautiful lay in the world.

WOMAN'S VOICE. Don't go any further.

VOICE [*with impersonal contempt*]. You? No. Not you.
Kitty. You stink.

WOMAN'S VOICE [*rasping, angry*]. Don't you dare to talk
to me that way. You pickpocket.

VOICE [*still impersonal, but louder*]. Oh, I see. Want
to get tough, hey? Close the door. Go hide.

WOMAN'S VOICE. You pickpocket. All of you. [*The door
slams.*]

VOICE [*roaring with laughter which is very sad*]. Oh—
Kitty. Room 21. Where the hell is that room?

TOM [*to* JOE]. Joe, I'll kill him.

KITTY [*fully herself again, terribly frightened*]. Who is it?

[*She looks long and steadily at* TOM *and* JOE. TOM *is standing, excited and angry.* JOE *is completely at ease, his expression full of pity.* KITTY *buries her face in the bed.*]

JOE [*gently*]. Tom. Just take him away.

VOICE. Here it is. Number 21. Three naturals. Heaven. My blue heaven. The west, a nest, and you. Just Molly and me. [*Tragically.*] Ah, to hell with everything.

[*A young* SAILOR, *a good-looking boy of no more than twenty or so, who is only drunk and lonely, comes to the bed, singing sadly.*]

SAILOR. Hi-ya, Kitty. [*Pause.*] Oh. Visitors. Sorry. A thousand apologies. [*To* KITTY.] I'll come back later.

TOM [*taking him by the shoulders, furiously*]. If you do, I'll kill you.

[JOE *holds* TOM. TOM *pushes the frightened boy away.*]

JOE [*somberly*]. Tom. You stay here with Kitty. I'm going down to Union Square to hire an automobile. I'll be back in a few minutes. We'll ride out to the ocean and watch the sun go down. Then we'll ride down the Great Highway to Half Moon Bay. We'll have supper down there, and you and Kitty can dance.

TOM [*stupefied, unable to express his amazement and gratitude*]. Joe, you mean, you're going to go on an errand for *me*? You mean you're not going to send me?

JOE. That's right. [*He gestures toward* KITTY, *indicating that* TOM *shall talk to her, protect the innocence in her which is in so much danger when* TOM *isn't near, which* TOM *loves so deeply.* JOE *leaves.* TOM *studies* KITTY, *his face becoming childlike and som-*

ber. He sets the carousel into motion, listens, watching KITTY, *who lifts herself slowly, looking only at* TOM. TOM *lifts the turning carousel and moves it slowly toward* KITTY, *as though the toy were his heart. The piano music comes up loudly and the lights go down, while* HARRY *is heard dancing swiftly.*]

BLACKOUT

Act four

A little later.
> WESLEY, *the colored boy, is at the piano.*
> HARRY *is on the little stage, dancing.*
> NICK *is behind the bar.*
> *The* ARAB *is in his place.*
> KIT CARSON *is asleep on his folded arms.*
> *The* DRUNKARD *comes in. Goes to the telephone for the nickel that might be in the return-chute.* NICK *comes to take him out. He gestures for* NICK *to hold on a minute. Then produces a half dollar.* NICK *goes behind the bar to serve the* DRUNKARD *whiskey.*

THE DRUNKARD, To the old, God bless them. [*Another.*] To the new, God love them. [*Another.*] To—children and small animals, like little dogs that don't bite. [*Another. Loudly.*] To reforestation. [*Searches for money. Finds some.*] To—President Taft. [*He goes out. The telephone rings.*]

KIT CARSON [*jumping up, fighting*]. Come on, *all* of you, if you're looking for trouble. I never asked for quarter and I always gave it.

NICK [*reproachfully*]. Hey, Kit Carson.

DUDLEY [*on the phone*]. Hello. Who? Nick? Yes. He's here. [*To* NICK.] It's for you. I think it's important.

NICK [*going to the phone*]. Important! *What's* important?

DUDLEY. He sounded like a big-shot.

NICK. Big *what?* [*To* WESLEY *and* HARRY.] Hey, you. Quiet. I want to hear this important stuff.

[WESLEY *stops playing the piano.* HARRY *stops dancing.* KIT CARSON *comes close to* NICK.]

KIT CARSON. If there's anything I can do, name it. I'll do it for you. I'm fifty-eight years old; been through three wars; married four times; the father of countless children whose *names* I don't even know. I've got no money. I live from hand to mouth. But if there's anything I can do, name it. I'll do it.

NICK [*patiently*]. Listen, Pop. For a moment, please sit down and go back to sleep—*for me.*

KIT CARSON. I can do that, too. [*He sits down, folds his arms, and puts his head into them. But not for long. As* NICK *begins to talk, he listens carefully, gets to his feet, and then begins to express in pantomime the moods of each of* NICK'S *remarks.*]

NICK [*on phone*]. Yeah? [*Pause.*] Who? Oh, I see. [*Listens.*] Why don't you leave them alone? [*Listens.*] The church-people? Well, to hell with the church-people. I'm a Catholic myself. [*Listens.*] All right. I'll send them away. I'll tell them to lay low for a couple of days. Yeah, I know how it is. [NICK'S *daughter* ANNA *comes in shyly, looking at her father, and stands unnoticed by the piano.*] What? [*Very angry.*] Listen. I don't like that Blick. He was here this morning, and I told him not to come back. I'll keep the girls out of here. You keep Blick out of here. [*Listens.*] I know his brother-in-law is important, but I don't want him to come down here.

He looks for trouble everywhere, and he always finds it. I don't break any laws. I've got a dive in the lousiest part of town. Five years nobody's been robbed, murdered or gypped. I leave people alone. Your swanky joints uptown make trouble for you every night. [NICK *gestures to* WESLEY—*keeps listening on the phone—puts his hand over the mouthpiece. To* WESLEY *and* HARRY.] Start playing again. My ears have got a headache. Go into your dance, son. [WESLEY *begins to play again.* HARRY *begins to dance.* NICK *into mouthpiece.*] Yeah. I'll keep them out. Just see that Blick doesn't come around and start something. [*Pause.*] O.K. [*He hangs up.*]

KIT CARSON. Trouble coming?

NICK. That lousy Vice Squad again. It's that gorilla Blick.

KIT CARSON. Anybody at all. You can count on me. What kind of a gorilla is this gorilla Blick?

NICK. Very dignified. Toenails on his fingers.

ANNA [*to* KIT CARSON, *with great, warm, beautiful pride, pointing at* NICK]. That's my father.

KIT CARSON [*leaping with amazement at the beautiful voice, the wondrous face, the magnificent event*]. Well, bless your heart, child. Bless your lovely heart. I had a little daughter point me out in a crowd once.

NICK [*surprised*]. Anna. What the hell are you doing here? Get back home where you belong and help Grandma cook me some supper. [ANNA *smiles at her father, understanding him, knowing that his words are words of love. She turns and goes, looking at him all the way out, as much as to say that she would cook for him the rest of her life.* NICK *stares at the swinging doors.* KIT CARSON *moves toward them, two or three steps.* ANNA *pushes open one of the doors and peeks in, to look at her father again. She waves to him. Turns and runs.* NICK *is very sad.*

He doesn't know what to do. He gets a glass and a bottle. Pours himself a drink. Swallows some. It isn't enough, so he pours more and swallows the whole drink. To himself.] My beautiful, beautiful baby. Anna, she is you again. [*He brings out a handkerchief, touches his eyes, and blows his nose.* KIT CARSON *moves close to* NICK, *watching* NICK's *face.* NICK *looks at him. Loudly, almost making* KIT *jump.*] You're broke, aren't you?

KIT CARSON. Always. Always.

NICK. All right. Go into the kitchen and give Sam a hand. Eat some food and when you come back you can have a couple of beers.

KIT CARSON [*studying* NICK]. Anything at all. I know a good man when I see one. [*He goes.*]

[ELSIE MANDELSPIEGEL *comes into* NICK's. *She is a beautiful, dark girl, with a sorrowful, wise, dreaming face, almost on the verge of tears, and full of pity. There is an aura of dream about her. She moves softly and gently, as if everything around her were unreal and pathetic.* DUDLEY *doesn't notice her for a moment or two. When he does finally see her, he is so amazed, he can barely move or speak. Her presence has the effect of changing him completely. He gets up from his chair, as if in a trance, and walks toward her, smiling sadly.*]

ELSIE [*looking at him*]. Hello, Dudley.

DUDLEY [*broken-hearted*]. Elsie.

ELSIE. I'm sorry. [*Explaining.*] So many people are sick. Last night a little boy died. I love you, but— [*She gestures, trying to indicate how hopeless love is. They sit down.*]

DUDLEY [*staring at her, stunned and quieted*]. Elsie. You'll never know how glad I am to see you. Just to see you. [*Pathetically.*] I was afraid I'd never see you again. It was driving me crazy. I didn't want to live. Honest. [*He shakes his head mournfully; with dumb and beautiful affection.* TWO STREETWALKERS *come in, and pause near* DUDLEY, *at the bar.*] I know. You told me before, but I can't help it, Elsie, I love you.

ELSIE [*quietly, somberly, gently, with great compassion*]. I know you love me, and I love you, but don't you see love is impossible in this world?

DUDLEY. Maybe it isn't, Elsie.

ELSIE. Love is for birds. They have wings to fly away on when it's time for flying. For tigers in the jungle because they don't know their end. We know *our* end. Every night I watch over poor, dying men. I hear them breathing, crying, talking in their sleep. Crying for air and water and love, for mother and field and sunlight. We can never know love or greatness. We *should* know both.

DUDLEY [*deeply moved by her words*]. Elsie, I love you.

ELSIE. You want to live. *I* want to live, too, but where? Where can we escape our poor world?

DUDLEY. Elsie, we'll find a place.

ELSIE [*smiling at him*]. All right. We'll try again. We'll go together to a room in a cheap hotel, and dream that the world is beautiful, and that living is full of love and greatness. But in the morning, can we forget debts, and duties, and the cost of ridiculous things?

DUDLEY [*with blind faith*]. Sure, we can, Elsie.

ELSIE. All right, Dudley. Of course. Come on. The time for the new pathetic war has come. Let's hurry, before they dress you, stand you in line, hand you a gun, and have you kill and be killed. [ELSIE *looks at him gently, and takes his hand.* DUDLEY *embraces her shyly, as if he might hurt her. They go, as if*

*they were a couple of young animals. There is a
moment of silence. One of the* STREETWALKERS *bursts
out laughing.*]

KILLER. Nick, what the hell kind of a joint are you
running?

NICK. Well, it's not out of the world. It's on a street in
a city, and people come and go. They bring whatever they've got with them and they say what they
must say.

THE OTHER STREETWALKER. It's floozies like her that
raise hell with our racket.

NICK [*remembering*]. Oh, yeah. Finnegan telephoned.

KILLER. That mouse in elephant's body?

THE OTHER STREETWALKER. What the hell does *he* want?

NICK. Spend your time at the movies for the next couple of days.

KILLER. They're all lousy. [*Mocking.*] All about love.

NICK. Lousy or not lousy, for a couple of days the flat-
foots are going to be romancing you, so stay out of
here, and lay low.

KILLER. I always was a pushover for a man in uniform,
with a badge, a club and a gun.

[KRUPP *comes into the place. The girls put down their
drinks.*]

NICK. O.K., get going.

[*The* GIRLS *begin to leave and meet* KRUPP.]

THE OTHER STREETWALKER. We was just going.

KILLER. We was formerly models at Magnin's. [*They
go.*]

KRUPP [*at the bar*]. The strike isn't enough, so they've
got to put us on the tails of the girls, too. I don't
know. I wish to God I was back in the Sunset holding the hands of kids going home from school, where
I belong. I don't like trouble. Give me a beer. [NICK
gives him a beer. He drinks some.] Right now, Mc-
Carthy, my best friend, is with sixty strikers who

want to stop the finks who are going to try to unload the *Mary Luckenbach* tonight. Why the hell McCarthy ever became a longshoreman instead of a professor of some kind is something I'll never know.

NICK. Cowboys and Indians, cops and robbers, longshoremen and finks.

KRUPP. They're all guys who are trying to be happy; trying to make a living; support a family; bring up children; enjoy sleep. Go to a movie; take a drive on Sunday. They're all good guys, so out of nowhere comes trouble. All they want is a chance to get out of debt and relax in front of a radio while Amos and Andy go through their act. What the hell do they always want to make trouble for? I been thinking everything over, Nick, and you know what I think?

NICK. No. What?

KRUPP. I think we're all crazy. It came to me while I was on my way to Pier 27. All of a sudden it hit me like a ton of bricks. A thing like that never happened to me before. Here we are in this wonderful world, full of all the wonderful things—here we are —all of us, and look at us. Just look at us. We're crazy. We're nuts. We've got everything, but we always feel lousy and dissatisfied just the same.

NICK. Of course we're crazy. Even so, we've got to go on living together. [*He waves at the people in his joint.*]

KRUPP. There's no hope. I don't suppose it's right for an officer of the law to feel the way I feel, but, by God, right or not right, that's how I feel. Why are we all so lousy? This is a good world. It's wonderful to get up in the morning and go out for a little walk and smell the trees and see the streets and the kids going to school and the clouds in the sky. It's wonderful just to be able to move around and whistle a

song if you feel like it, or maybe try to sing one.
This is a nice world. So why do they make all the
trouble?

NICK. I don't know. Why?

KRUPP. We're crazy, that's why. We're no good any
more. All the corruption everywhere. The poor kids
selling themselves. A couple of years ago they were
in grammar school. Everybody trying to get a lot of
money in a hurry. Everybody betting the horses. Nobody going quietly for a little walk to the ocean.
Nobody taking things easy and not wanting to make
some kind of a killing. Nick, I'm going to quit being
a cop. Let somebody else keep law and order. The
stuff I hear about at headquarters. I'm thirty-seven
years old, and I still can't get used to it. The only
trouble is, the wife'll raise hell.

NICK. Ah, the wife.

KRUPP. She's a wonderful woman, Nick. We've got two
of the swellest boys in the world. Twelve and seven
years old.

[*The* ARAB *gets up and moves closer to listen.*]

NICK. I didn't know that.

KRUPP. Sure. But what'll I do? I've wanted to quit for
seven years. I wanted to quit the day they began
putting me through the school. I didn't quit.
What'll I do if I quit? Where's money going to be
coming in from?

NICK. That's one of the reasons we're all crazy. We
don't know where it's going to be coming in from,
except from wherever it happens to be coming in
from at the time, which we don't usually like.

KRUPP. Every once in a while I catch myself being
mean, hating people just because they're down and
out, broke and hungry, sick or drunk. And then
when I'm with the stuffed shirts at headquarters, all
of a sudden I'm nice to them, trying to make an im-

pression. On who? People I don't like. And I feel disgusted. [*With finality.*] I'm going to quit. That's all. Quit. Out. I'm going to give them back the uniform and the gadgets that go with it. I don't want any part of it. This is a good world. What do they want to make all the trouble for all the time?

ARAB [*quietly, gently, with great understanding*]. No foundation. All the way down the line.

KRUPP. What?

ARAB. No foundation. No foundation.

KRUPP. I'll say there's no foundation.

ARAB. All the way down the line.

KRUPP [*to* NICK]. Is that all he ever says?

NICK. That's all he's been saying *this* week.

KRUPP. What is he, anyway?

NICK. He's an Arab, or something like that.

KRUPP. No, I mean what's he do for a living?

NICK [*to* ARAB]. What do you do for a living, brother?

ARAB. Work. Work all my life. All my life, work. From small boy to old man, work. In old country, work. In new country, work. In New York. Pittsburgh. Detroit. Chicago. Imperial Valley. San Francisco. Work. No beg. Work. For what? Nothing. Three boys in old country. Twenty years, not see. Lost. Dead. Who knows? What. What-not. No foundation. All the way down the line.

KRUPP. What'd he say last week?

NICK. Didn't say anything. Played the harmonica.

ARAB. Old country song, I play. [*He brings a harmonica from his back pocket.*]

KRUPP. Seems like a nice guy.

NICK. Nicest guy in the world.

KRUPP [*bitterly*]. But crazy. Just like all the rest of us. Stark raving mad.

[WESLEY *and* HARRY *long ago stopped playing and dancing. They sat at a table together and talked for*

*a while; then began playing casino or rummy. When
the* ARAB *begins his solo on the harmonica, they stop
their game to listen.*]

WESLEY. You hear that?

HARRY. That's *something*.

WESLEY. That's crying. That's crying.

HARRY. I want to make people laugh.

WESLEY. That's deep, deep crying. That's crying a long
time ago. That's crying a thousand years ago. Some
place five thousand miles away.

HARRY. Do you think you can play to that?

WESLEY. I want to *sing* to that, but I can't *sing*.

HARRY. You try and play to that. I'll try to dance.

[WESLEY *goes to the piano, and after closer listening,
he begins to accompany the harmonica solo.* HARRY
*goes to the little stage and after a few efforts begins
to dance to the song. This keeps up quietly for some
time.* KRUPP *and* NICK *have been silent, and deeply
moved.*]

KRUPP [*softly*]. Well, anyhow, Nick.

NICK. Hmmmmmmmm?

KRUPP. What I said. Forget it.

NICK. Sure.

KRUPP. It gets me down once in a while.

NICK. No harm in talking.

KRUPP [*the* POLICEMAN *again, loudly*]. Keep the girls
out of here.

NICK [*loud and friendly*]. Take it easy.

[*The music and dancing are now at their height.*]

CURTAIN

Act five

*That evening. Fog-horns are heard throughout the
scene. A* MAN *in evening clothes and a top hat, and his*
WOMAN, *also in evening clothes, are entering.*

WILLIE *is still at the marble game.* NICK *is behind the
bar.* JOE *is at his table, looking at the book of maps of
the countries of Europe. The box containing the revolver and the box containing the cartridges are on
the table, beside his glass. He is at peace, his hat tilted
back on his head, a calm expression on his face.* TOM *is
leaning against the bar, dreaming of love and* KITTY.
The ARAB *is gone.* WESLEY *and* HARRY *are gone.* KIT
CARSON *is watching the* BOY *at the marble game.*

LADY. Oh, come on, please.
[*The* GENTLEMAN *follows miserably. The* SOCIETY MAN
and WIFE *take a table.* NICK *gives them a menu. Outside, in the street, the Salvation Army people are
playing a song. Big drum, tambourines, cornet and
singing. They are singing "The Blood of the Lamb."
The music and words come into the place faintly
and comically. This is followed by an old sinner
testifying. It is the* DRUNKARD. *His words are not in-
telligible, but his message is unmistakable. He is
saved. He wants to sin no more. And so on.*]
DRUNKARD [*testifying, unmistakably drunk*]. Brothers
and sisters. I was a sinner. I chewed tobacco and
chased women. Oh, I sinned, brothers and sisters.
And then I was saved. Saved by the Salvation Army,
God forgive me.
JOE. Let's see now. Here's a city. Pribor. Czechoslo-

vakia. Little, lovely, lonely Czechoslovakia. I wonder what kind of a place Pribor was? [*Calling.*] Pribor! *Pribor!*

[TOM *leaps.*]

LADY. What's the matter with him?

MAN [*crossing his legs, as if he ought to go to the men's room*]. Drunk.

TOM. Who you calling, Joe?

JOE. Pribor.

TOM. Who's Pribor?

JOE. He's a Czech. And a Slav. A Czechoslovakian.

LADY. How interesting.

MAN [*uncrosses legs*]. He's drunk.

JOE. Tom, Pribor's a city in Czechoslovakia.

TOM. Oh. [*Pause.*] You sure were nice to her, Joe.

JOE. Kitty Duval? She's one of the finest people in the world.

TOM. It sure was nice of you to hire an automobile and take us for a drive along the ocean front and down to Half Moon Bay.

JOE. Those three hours were the most delightful, the most somber, and the most beautiful I have ever known.

TOM. Why, Joe?

JOE. Why? I'm a student. [*Lifting his voice.*] Tom. [*Quietly.*] I'm a student. I study all things. All. All. And when my study reveals something of beauty in a place or in a person where by all rights only ugliness or death should be revealed, then I know how full of goodness this life is. And that's a good thing to know. That's a truth I shall always seek to verify.

LADY. Are you *sure* he's drunk?

MAN [*crossing his legs*]. He's either drunk, or just naturally crazy.

TOM. Joe?

JOE. Yeah.

TOM. You won't get sore or anything?

JOE [*impatiently*]. What is it, Tom?

TOM. Joe, where do you get all that money? You paid for the automobile. You paid for supper and the two bottles of champagne at the Half Moon Bay Restaurant. You moved Kitty out of the New York Hotel around the corner to the St. Francis Hotel on Powell Street. I saw you pay her rent. I saw you give her money for new clothes. Where do you get all that money, Joe? Three years now and I've never asked.

JOE [*looking at* TOM *sorrowfully, a little irritated, not so much with* TOM *as with the world and himself, his own superiority. He speaks clearly, slowly and solemnly*]. Now don't be a fool, Tom. Listen carefully. If anybody's got any money—to hoard or to throw away—you can be sure he stole it from other people. Not from rich people who can spare it, but from poor people who can't. From their lives and from their dreams. I'm no exception. I *earned* the money I throw away. I stole it like everybody else does. I hurt people to get it. Loafing around this way, I *still* earn money. The money itself earns *more*. I *still* hurt people. I don't know who they are, or where they are. If I did, I'd feel worse than I do. I've got a Christian conscience in a world that's got no conscience at all. The world's trying to get some sort of a *social* conscience, but it's having a devil of a time trying to do *that*. I've got money. I'll always have money, as long as this world stays the way it is. I don't work. I don't make anything. [*He sips.*] I drink. I worked when I was a kid. I worked *hard*. I mean hard, Tom. People are supposed to enjoy living. I got tired. [*He lifts the gun and looks at it while he talks.*] I decided to get even on the world. Well, you can't enjoy living unless you work. Unless you do something. I don't do anything. I don't *want* to do anything any more. There isn't anything I can do that won't make me feel embarrassed. Because I can't do simple, good things. I haven't the patience. And I'm too smart. Money is the guiltiest thing in the world. It stinks. Now, don't ever bother me about it again.

TOM. I didn't mean to make you feel bad, Joe.

JOE [*slowly*]. Here. Take this gun out in the street and give it to some worthy hold-up man.

LADY. What's he saying?

MAN [*uncrosses legs*]. You wanted to visit a honky-tonk. Well, *this* is a honky-tonk. [*To the world.*] Married twenty-eight years and she's still looking for adventure.

TOM. How should I know who's a hold-up man?

JOE. Take it away. Give it to somebody.

TOM [*bewildered*]. Do I *have* to *give* it to somebody?

JOE. Of course.

TOM. Can't I take it back and get some of our money?

JOE. Don't talk like a business man. Look around and find somebody who appears to be in need of a gun and give it to him. It's a good gun, isn't it?

TOM. The man said it was, but how can I tell who needs a gun?

JOE. Tom, you've seen good people who needed guns, haven't you?

TOM. I don't remember. Joe, I might give it to the wrong kind of guy. He might do something crazy.

JOE. All right. I'll find somebody myself. [TOM *rises.*] Here's some money. Go get me this week's *Life, Liberty, Time,* and six or seven packages of chewing gum.

TOM [*swiftly, in order to remember each item*]. *Life, Liberty, Time* and six or seven packages of chewing gum?

JOE. That's right.

TOM. All that chewing gum? What kind?

JOE. Any kind. Mix 'em up. All kinds.

TOM. Licorice, too?

JOE. Licorice, by all means.

TOM. Juicy Fruit?

JOE. Juicy Fruit.

TOM. Tutti-frutti?

JOE. Is there such a gum?

TOM. I think so.

JOE. All right. Tutti-frutti, too. Get *all* the kinds. Get as many kinds as they're selling.

TOM. *Life, Liberty, Time*, and all the different kinds of gum. [*He begins to go.*]

JOE [*calling after him loudly*]. Get some jelly beans too. All the different colors.

TOM. All right, Joe.

JOE. And the longest panatela cigar you can find. Six of them.

TOM. Panatela. I got it.

JOE. Give a news-kid a dollar.

TOM. O.K., Joe.

JOE. Give some old man a dollar.

TOM. O.K., Joe.

JOE. Give them Salvation Army people in the street a couple of dollars and ask them to sing that song that goes— [*He sings loudly.*]

Let the lower lights be burning, send a gleam across the wave.

TOM [*swiftly*].

Let the lower lights be burning, send a gleam across
the wave.

JOE. That's it. [*He goes on with the song, very loudly
and religiously.*]

Some poor, dying, struggling seaman, you may rescue,
you may save.

[*Halts.*]

TOM. O.K., Joe. I got it. *Life, Liberty, Time,* all the
kinds of gum they're selling, jelly beans, six panatela
cigars, a dollar for a news-kid, a dollar for an old
man, two dollars for the Salvation Army. [*Going.*]

Let the lower lights be burning, send a gleam across
the wave.

JOE. That's it.

LADY. He's absolutely insane.

MAN [*wearily crossing legs*]. You asked me to take you
to a honky-tonk, instead of to the Mark Hopkins.
You're *here* in a honky-tonk. I can't help it if he's
crazy. Do you want to go back to where people
aren't crazy?

LADY. No, not just yet.

MAN. Well, all right then. Don't be telling me every
minute that he's crazy.

LADY. You needn't be huffy about it.

[MAN *refuses to answer, uncrosses legs. When* JOE *began to sing,* KIT CARSON *turned away from the marble game and listened. While the* MAN *and* WOMAN *are arguing he comes over to* JOE's *table.*]

KIT CARSON. Presbyterian?

JOE. I attended a Presbyterian Sunday School.

KIT CARSON. Fond of singing?

JOE. On occasion. Have a drink?

KIT CARSON. Thanks.

JOE. Get a glass and sit down. [KIT CARSON *gets a glass from* NICK, *returns to the table, sits down,* JOE *pours him a drink, they touch glasses just as the Salvation Army people begin to fulfil the request. They sip some champagne, and at the proper moment begin to sing the song together, sipping champagne, raising hell with the tune, swinging it, and so on. The* SOCIETY LADY *joins them, and is stopped by her* HUSBAND.] Always was fond of that song. Used to sing it at the top of my voice. Never saved a seaman in my life.

KIT CARSON [*flirting with the* SOCIETY LADY *who loves it*]. I saved a seaman once. Well, he wasn't exactly a seaman. He was a darky named Wellington. Heavy-set sort of a fellow. Nice personality, but no friends to speak of. Not until I came along, at any rate. In New Orleans. In the summer of the year 1899. No. Ninety-eight. I was a lot younger of course, and had no mustache, but was regarded by many people as a man of means.

JOE. Know anything about guns?

KIT CARSON [*flirting*]. All there is to know. Didn't fight the Ojibways for nothing. Up there in the Lake Takalooca country, in Michigan. [*Remembering.*] Along about in 1881 or two. Fought 'em right up to the shore of the lake. Made 'em swim for Canada. One fellow in particular, an Indian named Harry Daisy.

JOE [*opening the box containing the revolver*]. What sort of a gun would you say this is? Any good?

KIT CARSON [*at sight of gun, leaping*]. Yep. That looks like a pretty nice hunk of shooting iron. That's a six-shooter. Shot a man with a six-shooter once. Got him through the palm of his right hand. Lifted his

arm to wave to a friend. Thought it was a bird.
Fellow named, I believe, Carroway. Larrimore Carroway.

JOE. Know how to work one of these things? [*He offers*
KIT CARSON *the revolver, which is old and enormous.*]

KIT CARSON [*laughing at the absurd question*]. Know
how to work it? Hand me that little gun, son, and
I'll show you all about it. [JOE *hands* KIT *the revolver. Importantly.*] Let's see now. This is probably
a new kind of six-shooter. After my time. Haven't
nicked an Indian in years. I believe this here place
is supposed to move out. [*He fools around and gets
the barrel out for loading.*] That's it. There it is.

JOE. Look all right?

KIT CARSON. It's a good gun. You've got a good gun
there, son. I'll explain it to you. You see these holes?
Well, that's where you put the cartridges.

JOE [*taking some cartridges out of the box*]. Here.
Show me how it's done.

KIT CARSON [*a little impatiently*]. Well, son, you take
'em one by one and put 'em in the holes, like this.
There's one. Two. Three. Four. Five. Six. Then you
get the barrel back in place. Then cock it. Then all
you got to do is aim and fire. [*He points the gun at
the* LADY *and* GENTLEMAN *who scream and stand up,
scaring* KIT CARSON *into paralysis. The gun is loaded,
but uncocked.*]

JOE. It's all set?

KIT CARSON. Ready to kill.

JOE. Let me hold it.

[KIT *hands* JOE *the gun. The* LADY *and* GENTLEMAN
watch, in terror.]

KIT CARSON. Careful, now, son. Don't cock it. Many a
man's lost an eye fooling with a loaded gun. Fellow
I used to know named Danny Donovan lost a nose.

Ruined his whole life. Hold it firm. Squeeze the trigger. Don't snap it. Spoils your aim.

JOE. Thanks. Let's see if I can unload it. [*He begins to unload it.*]

KIT CARSON. Of course you can.

[JOE *unloads the revolver, looks at it very closely, puts the cartridges back into the box.*]

JOE [*looking at gun*]. I'm mighty grateful to you. Always wanted to see one of those things close up. Is it really a good one?

KIT CARSON. It's a beaut, son.

JOE [*aims the empty gun at a bottle on the bar*]. Bang!

WILLIE [*at the marble game, as the machine groans*]. Oh, boy! [*Loudly, triumphantly.*] There you are, Nick. Thought I couldn't do it, hey? *Now,* watch. [*The machine begins to make a special kind of noise. Lights go on and off. Some red, some green. A bell rings loudly six times.*] One. Two. Three. Four. Five. Six. [*An American flag jumps up.* WILLIE *comes to attention. Salutes.*] Oh, boy, what a beautiful country. [*A loud music-box version of the song "America."* JOE, KIT, *and the* LADY *get to their feet. Singing. "My country, 'tis of thee, sweet land of liberty, of thee I sing." Everything quiets down. The flag goes back into the machine.* WILLIE *is thrilled, amazed, delighted.* EVERYBODY *has watched the performance of the defeated machine from wherever he happened to be when the performance began.* WILLIE, *looking around at everybody, as if they had all been on the side of the machine.*] O.K. How's that? I knew I could do it. [*To* NICK.] Six nickels. [NICK *hands him six nickels.* WILLIE *goes over to* JOE *and* KIT.] Took me a little while, but I finally did it. It's scientific, really. With a little skill a man can make a modest living beating the marble games. Not

that that's what I want to do. I just don't like the
idea of anything getting the best of me. A machine
or anything else. Myself, I'm the kind of a guy who
makes up his mind to do something, and then goes
to work and does it. There's no other way a man can
be a success at anything. [*Indicating the letter "F"
on his sweater.*] See that letter? That don't stand for
some little-bitty high school somewhere. That stands
for *me.* Faroughli. Willie Faroughli. I'm an Assyrian. We've got a civilization six or seven centuries
old, I think. Somewhere along in there. Ever hear
of Osman? Harold Osman? He's an Assyrian, too.
He's got an orchestra down in Fresno. [*He goes to
the* LADY *and* GENTLEMAN.] I've never seen you before in my life, but I can tell from the clothes you
wear and the company you keep [*graciously indicating the* LADY] that you're a man who looks every
problem straight in the eye, and then goes to work
and *solves* it. I'm that way myself. Well. [*He smiles
beautifully, takes the* GENTLEMAN'S *hand furiously.*]
It's been wonderful talking to a nicer type of people
for a change. Well. I'll be seeing you. So long. [*He
turns, takes two steps, returns to the table. Very politely and seriously.*] Good-by, lady. You've got a
good man there. Take good care of him. [WILLIE
goes, saluting JOE *and the world.*]

KIT CARSON [*to* JOE]. By God, for a while there I didn't
think that young Assyrian was going to do it. That
fellow's got something.

[TOM *comes back with the magazines and other stuff.*]

JOE. Get it all?

TOM. Yeah. I had a little trouble finding the jelly
beans.

JOE. Let's take a look at them.

TOM. These are the jelly beans.

[JOE *puts his hand into the cellophane bag and takes*

out a handful of the jelly beans, looks at them, smiles, and tosses a couple into his mouth.]

JOE. Same as ever. Have some. [*He offers the bag to* KIT.]

KIT CARSON [*flirting*]. Thanks! I remember the first time I ever ate jelly beans. I was six, or at the most seven. Must have been in [*slowly*] eighteen—seventy-seven. Seven or eight. Baltimore.

JOE. Have some, Tom.

[TOM *takes some.*]

TOM. Thanks, Joe.

JOE. Let's have some of that chewing gum. [*He dumps all the packages of gum out of the bag onto the table.*]

KIT CARSON [*flirting*]. Me and a boy named Clark. Quinton Clark. Became a Senator.

JOE. Yeah. Tutti-frutti, all right. [*He opens a package and folds all five pieces into his mouth.*] Always wanted to see how many I could chew at one time. Tell you what, Tom. I'll bet I can chew more at one time than you can.

TOM [*delighted*]. All right. [*They both begin to fold gum into their mouths.*]

KIT CARSON. I'll referee. Now, one at a time. How many you got?

JOE. Six.

KIT CARSON. All right. Let Tom catch up with you.

JOE [*while* TOM's *catching up*]. Did you give a dollar to a news-kid?

TOM. Yeah, sure.

JOE. What'd he say?

TOM. Thanks.

JOE. What sort of a kid was he?

TOM. Little, dark kid. I guess he's Italian.

JOE. Did he seem pleased?

TOM. Yeah.

JOE. That's good. Did you give a dollar to an old man?

TOM. Yeah.

JOE. Was he pleased?

TOM. Yeah.

JOE. Good. How many you got in your mouth?

TOM. Six.

JOE. All right. I got six, too. [*Folds one more in his mouth.* TOM *folds one too.*]

KIT CARSON. Seven. Seven each. [*They each fold one more into their mouths, very solemnly, chewing them into the main hunk of gum.*] Eight. Nine. Ten.

JOE [*delighted*]. Always wanted to do this. [*He picks up one of the magazines.*] Let's see what's going on in the world. [*He turns the pages and keeps folding gum into his mouth and chewing.*]

KIT CARSON. Eleven. Twelve. [KIT *continues to count while* JOE *and* TOM *continue the contest. In spite of what they are doing, each is very serious.*]

TOM. Joe, what'd you want to move Kitty into the St. Francis Hotel for?

JOE. She's a better woman than any of them tramp society dames that hang around that lobby.

TOM. Yeah, but do you think she'll feel at home up there?

JOE. Maybe not at first, but after a couple of days she'll be all right. A nice big room. A bed for sleeping in. Good clothes. Good food. She'll be all right, Tom.

TOM. I hope so. Don't you think she'll get lonely up there with nobody to talk to?

JOE [*looking at* TOM *sharply, almost with admiration, pleased but severe*]. There's nobody *anywhere* for *her* to talk to—except *you.*

TOM [*amazed and delighted*]. Me, Joe?

JOE [*while* TOM *and* KIT CARSON *listen carefully,* KIT *with great appreciation*]. Yes, you. By the grace of

God, you're the other half of that girl. Not the angry woman that swaggers into this waterfront dive and shouts because the world has kicked her around. *Anybody* can have *her*. You belong to the little kid in Ohio who once dreamed of living. Not with her carcass, for *money*, so she can have food and clothes, and pay rent. With *all* of her. I put her in that hotel, so she can have a chance to gather herself together again. She can't do that in the New York Hotel. You saw what happens there. There's nobody anywhere for her to talk to, except you. They all make her talk like a whore. After a while, she'll *believe* them. Then she won't be able to remember. She'll get lonely. Sure. People can get lonely for *misery*, even. I want her to go on being lonely for *you*, so she can come together again the way she was meant to be from the beginning. Loneliness is good for people. Right now it's the only thing for Kitty. Any more licorice?

TOM [*dazed*]. What? Licorice? [*Looking around busily.*] I guess we've chewed all the licorice in. We still got Clove, Peppermint, Doublemint, Beechnut, Teaberry, and Juicy Fruit.

JOE. Licorice used to be my favorite. Don't worry about her, Tom, she'll be all right. You really want to marry her, don't you?

TOM [*nodding*]. Honest to God, Joe. [*Pathetically.*] Only, I haven't got any money.

JOE. Couldn't you be a prize-fighter or something like that?

TOM. Naaaah. I couldn't hit a man if I wasn't sore at him. He'd have to do something that made me hate him.

JOE. You've got to figure out something to do that you won't mind doing very much.

TOM. I wish I could, Joe.

JOE [*thinking deeply, suddenly*]. Tom, would you be embarrassed driving a truck?

TOM [*hit by a thunderbolt*]. Joe, I never thought of that. I'd like that. Travel. Highways. Little towns. Coffee and hot cakes. Beautiful valleys and mountains and streams and trees and daybreak and sunset.

JOE. There *is* poetry in it, at that.

TOM. Joe, that's just the kind of work I *should* do. Just sit there and travel, and look, and smile, and bust out laughing. Could Kitty go with me, sometimes?

JOE. I don't know. Get me the phone book. Can you drive a truck?

TOM. Joe, you know I can drive a truck, or any kind of thing with a motor and wheels. [TOM *takes* JOE *the phone book.* JOE *turns the pages.*]

JOE [*looking*]. Here! Here it is. Tuxedo 7900. Here's a nickel. Get me that number.

[TOM *goes to telephone, dials the number.*]

TOM. Hello.

JOE. Ask for Mr. Keith.

TOM [*mouth and language full of gum*]. I'd like to talk to Mr. Keith. [*Pause.*] Mr. Keith.

JOE. Take that gum out of your mouth for a minute. [TOM *removes the gum.*]

TOM. Mr. Keith. Yeah. That's right. Hello, Mr. Keith?

JOE. Tell him to hold the line.

TOM. Hold the line, please.

JOE. Give me a hand, Tom. [TOM *helps* JOE *to the telephone. At phone, wad of gum in fingers delicately.*] Keith? Joe. Yeah. Fine. Forget it. [*Pause.*] Have you got a place for a good driver? [*Pause.*] I don't think so. [*To* TOM.] You haven't got a driver's license, have you?

TOM [*worried*]. No. But I can get one, Joe.

JOE [*at phone*]. No, but he can get one easy enough.

To hell with the union. He'll join later. All right, call him a Vice-President and say he drives for relaxation. Sure. What do you mean? Tonight? I don't know why not. San Diego? All right, let him start driving without a license. What the hell's the difference? Yeah. Sure. Look him over. Yeah. I'll send him right over. Right. [*He hangs up.*] Thanks. [*To telephone.*]

TOM. Am I going to get the job?

JOE. He wants to take a look at you.

TOM. Do I look all right, Joe?

JOE [*looking at him carefully*]. Hold up your head. Stick out your chest. How do you feel?

[TOM *does these things.*]

TOM. Fine.

JOE. You *look* fine, too. [JOE *takes his wad of gum out of his mouth and wraps "Liberty" magazine around it.*]

JOE. You win, Tom. Now, look. [*He bites off the tip of a very long panatela cigar, lights it, and hands one to* TOM, *and another to* KIT.] Have yourselves a pleasant smoke. Here. [*He hands two more to* TOM.] Give those slummers one each. [*He indicates the* SOCIETY LADY *and* GENTLEMAN.]

[TOM *goes over and without a word gives a cigar each to the* MAN *and the* LADY. *The* MAN *is offended; he smells and tosses aside his cigar. The* WOMAN *looks at her cigar a moment, then puts the cigar in her mouth.*]

MAN. What do you think you're doing?

LADY. Really, dear. I'd like to.

MAN. Oh, this is too much.

LADY. I'd *really*, really like to, dear. [*She laughs, puts the cigar in her mouth. Turns to* KIT. *He spits out tip. She does the same.*]

MAN [*loudly*]. The mother of five grown men, and she's still looking for *romance*. [*Shouts as* KIT *lights her cigar.*] No. I forbid it.

JOE [*shouting*]. What's the matter with you? Why don't you leave her alone? What are you always pushing your women around for? [*Almost without a pause.*] Now, look, Tom. [*The* LADY *puts the lighted cigar in her mouth, and begins to smoke, feeling wonderful.*] Here's ten bucks.

TOM. Ten bucks?

JOE. He may want you to get into a truck and begin driving to San Diego tonight.

TOM. Joe, I got to tell Kitty.

JOE. I'll tell her.

TOM. Joe, take care of her.

JOE. She'll be all right. Stop worrying about her. She's at the St. Francis Hotel. Now, look. Take a cab to Townsend and Fourth. You'll see the big sign. Keith Motor Transport Company. He'll be waiting for you.

TOM. O.K., Joe. [*Trying hard.*] Thanks, Joe.

JOE. Don't be silly. Get going.

[TOM *goes.* LADY *starts puffing on cigar. As* TOM *goes,* WESLEY *and* HARRY *come in together.*]

NICK. Where the hell have you been? We've got to have some entertainment around here. Can't you see them fine people from uptown? [*He points at the* SOCIETY LADY *and* GENTLEMAN.]

WESLEY. You said to come back at ten for the second show.

NICK. Did I say that?

WESLEY. Yes, sir, Mr. Nick, that's exactly what you said.

HARRY. Was the first show all right?

NICK. That wasn't a show. There was no one here to

see it. How can it be a show when no one sees it? People are afraid to come down to the waterfront.

HARRY. Yeah. We were just down to Pier 27. One of the longshoremen and a cop had a fight and the cop hit him over the head with a blackjack. We saw it happen, didn't we?

WESLEY. Yes, sir, we was standing there looking when it happened.

NICK [*a little worried*]. Anything else happen?

WESLEY. They was all talking.

HARRY. A man in a big car came up and said there was going to be a meeting right away and they hoped to satisfy everybody and stop the strike.

WESLEY. Right away. *Tonight.*

NICK. Well, it's about time. Them poor cops are liable to get nervous and—shoot somebody. [*To* HARRY, *suddenly.*] Come back here. I want you to tend bar for a while. I'm going to take a walk over to the pier.

HARRY. Yes, sir.

NICK [*to the* SOCIETY LADY *and* GENTLEMAN]. You society people made up your minds yet?

LADY. Have you champagne?

NICK [*indicating* JOE]. What do you think he's pouring out of that bottle, water or something?

LADY. Have you a chill bottle?

NICK. I've got a dozen of them chilled. He's been drinking champagne here all day and all night for a month now.

LADY. May we have a bottle?

NICK. It's six dollars.

LADY. I think we can manage.

MAN. I don't know. I *know* I don't know.

[NICK *takes off his coat and helps* HARRY *into it.* HARRY *takes a bottle of champagne and two glasses to the*

LADY *and* GENTLEMAN, *dancing, collects six dollars, and goes back behind the bar, dancing.* NICK *gets his coat and hat.*]

NICK [*to* WESLEY]. Rattle the keys a little, son. Rattle the keys.

WESLEY. Yes, sir, Mr. Nick.

[NICK *is on his way out. The* ARAB *enters.*]

NICK. Hi-ya, *Mahmed.*

ARAB. No foundation.

NICK. All the way down the line. [*He goes.*]

[WESLEY *is at the piano, playing quietly. The* ARAB *swallows a glass of beer, takes out his harmonica, and begins to play.* WESLEY *fits his playing to the Arab's.* KITTY DUVAL, *strangely beautiful, in new clothes, comes in. She walks shyly, as if she were embarrassed by the fine clothes, as if she had no right to wear them. The* LADY *and* GENTLEMAN *are very impressed.* HARRY *looks at her with amazement.* JOE *is reading "Time" magazine.* KITTY *goes to his table.* JOE *looks up from the magazine, without the least amazement.*]

JOE. Hello, Kitty.

KITTY. Hello, Joe.

JOE. It's nice seeing you again.

KITTY. I came in a cab.

JOE. You been crying again? [KITTY *can't answer. To* HARRY.] Bring a glass.

[HARRY *comes over with a glass.* JOE *pours* KITTY *a drink.*]

KITTY. I've got to talk to you.

JOE. Have a drink.

KITTY. I've never been in burlesque. We were just poor.

JOE. Sit down, Kitty.

KITTY [*sits down*]. I tried other things.

JOE. Here's to you, Katerina Koranovsky. Here's to you. And Tom.

KITTY [*sorrowfully*]. Where *is* Tom?

JOE. He's getting a job tonight driving a truck. He'll be back in a couple of days.

KITTY [*sadly*]. I told him I'd marry him.

JOE. He wanted to see you and say good-by.

KITTY. He's too good for me. He's like a little boy. [*Wearily.*] I'm— Too many things have happened to me.

JOE. Kitty Duval, you're one of the few truly innocent people I have ever known. He'll be back in a couple of days. Go back to the hotel and wait for him.

KITTY. That's what I mean. I can't stand being alone. I'm no good. I tried very hard. I don't know what it is. I miss— [*She gestures.*]

JOE [*gently*]. Do you really want to come back here, Kitty?

KITTY. I don't know. I'm not sure. Everything *smells* different. I don't know how to feel, or what to think. [*Gesturing pathetically.*] I know I don't belong there. It's what I've wanted all my life, but it's too *late.* I try to be happy about it, but all I can do is remember everything and cry.

JOE. I don't know what to tell you, Kitty. I didn't mean to hurt you.

KITTY. You haven't hurt me. You're the only person who's ever been good to me. I've never known anybody like you. I'm not sure about love any more, but I know I love you, and I know I love Tom.

JOE. I love you too, Kitty Duval.

KITTY. He'll want babies. I know he will. I know *I* will, too. Of course I will. I can't— [*She shakes her head.*]

JOE. Tom's a baby himself. You'll be very happy together. He wants you to ride with him in the truck. Tom's good for you. You're good for Tom.

KITTY [*like a child*]. Do you want me to go back and wait for him?

JOE. I can't *tell* you what to do. I think it would be a good idea, though.

KITTY. I wish I could tell you how it makes me feel to be alone. It's almost worse.

JOE. It might take a whole week, Kitty. [*He looks at her sharply, at the arrival of an idea.*] Didn't you speak of reading a book? A book of poems?

KITTY. I didn't know what I was saying.

JOE [*trying to get up*]. Of course you knew. I think you'll like poetry. Wait here a minute, Kitty. I'll go see if I can find some books.

KITTY. All right, Joe.

[*He walks out of the place, trying very hard not to wobble. Fog-horn. Music. The* NEWSBOY *comes in. Looks for* JOE. *Is broken-hearted because* JOE *is gone.*]

NEWSBOY [*to* SOCIETY GENTLEMAN]. Paper?

MAN [*angry*]. No.

[*The* NEWSBOY *goes to the* ARAB.]

NEWSBOY. Paper, Mister?

ARAB [*irritated*]. No foundation.

NEWSBOY. What?

ARAB [*very angry*]. No foundation.

[*The* NEWSBOY *starts out, turns, looks at the* ARAB, *shakes head.*]

NEWSBOY. No foundation? How do you figure?

[BLICK *and two cops enter.*]

NEWSBOY [*to* BLICK]. Paper, Mister?

[BLICK *pushes him aside. The* NEWSBOY *goes.*]

BLICK [*walking authoritatively about the place, to* HARRY]. Where's Nick?

HARRY. He went for a walk.

BLICK. Who are you?

HARRY. Harry.

BLICK [*to the* ARAB *and* WESLEY]. Hey, you. Shut up. [*The* ARAB *stops playing the harmonica,* WESLEY *the piano.*]

BLICK [*studies* KITTY]. What's your name, sister?

KITTY [*looking at him*]. Kitty Duval. What's it to you? [KITTY's *voice is now like it was at the beginning of the play: tough, independent, bitter and hard.*]

BLICK [*angry*]. Don't give me any of your gutter lip. Just answer my questions.

KITTY. You go to hell, you.

BLICK [*coming over, enraged*]. Where do you live?

KITTY. The New York Hotel. Room 21.

BLICK. Where do you work?

KITTY. I'm not working just now. I'm looking for work.

BLICK. What kind of work? [KITTY *can't answer.*] What kind of work? [KITTY *can't answer. Furiously.*] *What kind of work?*

[KIT CARSON *comes over.*]

KIT CARSON. You can't talk to a lady that way in *my* presence.

[BLICK *turns and stares at* KIT. *The* COPS *begin to move from the bar.*]

BLICK [*to the* COPS]. It's all right, boys. I'll take care of this. [*To* KIT.] *What'd you say?*

KIT CARSON. You got no right to hurt people. Who are you?

[BLICK, *without a word, takes* KIT *to the street. Sounds of a blow and a groan.* BLICK *returns, breathing hard.*]

BLICK [*to the* COPS]. O.K., boys. You can go now. Take care of him. Put him on his feet and tell him to behave himself from now on. [*To* KITTY *again.*] Now answer my question. What kind of work?

KITTY [*quietly*]. I'm a whore, you son of a bitch. You

know what kind of work I do. And I know what
kind you do.

MAN [*shocked and really hurt*]. Excuse me, officer, but
it seems to me that your attitude—

BLICK. Shut up.

MAN [*quietly*]. —is making the poor child say things
that are not true.

BLICK. Shut up, I said.

LADY. Well. [*To the* MAN.] Are you going to stand for
such insolence?

BLICK [*to* MAN, *who is standing*]. Are you?

MAN [*taking the* WOMAN's *arm*]. I'll get a divorce. I'll
start life all over again. [*Pushing the* WOMAN.] Come
on. Get the hell out of here! [*The* MAN *hurries his*
WOMAN *out of the place,* BLICK *watching them go.*]

BLICK [*to* KITTY]. Now. Let's begin again, and see that
you tell the truth. What's your name?

KITTY. Kitty Duval.

BLICK. Where do you live?

KITTY. Until this evening I lived at the New York
Hotel. Room 21. This evening I moved to the St.
Francis Hotel.

BLICK. Oh. To the St. Francis Hotel. Nice place. Where
do you work?

KITTY. I'm looking for work.

BLICK. What kind of work do you do?

KITTY. I'm an actress.

BLICK. I see. What movies have I seen you in?

KITTY. I've worked in burlesque.

BLICK. You're a liar.

[WESLEY *stands, worried and full of dumb resentment.*]

KITTY [*pathetically, as at the beginning of the play*].
It's the truth.

BLICK. What are you doing here?

KITTY. I came to see if I could get a job here.

BLICK. Doing what?

KITTY. Singing—and—dancing.

BLICK. You can't sing or dance. What are you lying for?

KITTY. I can. I sang and danced in burlesque all over the country.

BLICK. You're a liar.

KITTY. I said lines, too.

BLICK. So you danced in burlesque?

KITTY. Yes.

BLICK. All right. Let's see what you did.

KITTY. I can't. There's no music, and I haven't got the right clothes.

BLICK. There's music. [*To* WESLEY.] Put a nickel in that phonograph. [WESLEY *can't move*.] Come on. Put a nickel in that phonograph. [WESLEY *does so. To* KITTY.] All right. Get up on that stage and do a hot little burlesque number. [KITTY *stands. Walks slowly to the stage, but is unable to move.* JOE *comes in, holding three books*.] Get going, now. Let's see you dance the way you did in burlesque, all over the country.

[KITTY *tries to do a burlesque dance. It is beautiful in a tragic way*.]

BLICK. All right, start taking them off!

[KITTY *removes her hat and starts to remove her jacket.* JOE *moves closer to the stage, amazed*.]

JOE [*hurrying to* KITTY]. Get down from there. [*He takes* KITTY *into his arms. She is crying. To* BLICK.] What the hell do you think you're doing?

WESLEY [*like a little boy, very angry*]. It's that man, Blick. *He* made her take off her clothes. He beat up the old man, too.

[BLICK *pushes* WESLEY *off, as* TOM *enters.* BLICK *begins beating up* WESLEY.]

TOM. What's the matter, Joe? What's happened?

JOE. Is the truck out there?

TOM. Yeah, but what's happened? Kitty's crying again!

JOE. You driving to San Diego?

TOM. Yeah, Joe. But what's he doing to that poor colored boy?

JOE. Get going. Here's some money. Everything's O.K. [*To* KITTY.] Dress in the truck. Take these books.

WESLEY'S VOICE. You can't hurt me. You'll get yours. You wait and see.

TOM. Joe, he's hurting that boy. I'll kill him!

JOE [*pushing* TOM]. Get out of here! Get married in San Diego. I'll see you when you get back. [TOM *and* KITTY *go.* NICK *enters and stands at the lower end of bar.* JOE *takes the revolver out of his pocket. Looks at it.*] I've always wanted to kill somebody, but I never knew who it should be. [*He cocks the revolver, stands real straight, holds it in front of him firmly and walks to the door. He stands a moment watching* BLICK, *aims very carefully, and pulls trigger. There is no shot.* NICK *runs over and grabs the gun, and takes* JOE *aside.*]

NICK. What the hell do you think you're doing?

JOE [*casually, but angry*]. That dumb Tom. Buys a six-shooter that won't even shoot once. [JOE *sits down, dead to the world.* BLICK *comes out, panting for breath.* NICK *looks at him. He speaks slowly.*]

NICK. Blick! I told you to stay out of here! Now get out of here. [*He takes* BLICK *by the collar, tightening his grip as he speaks, and pushing him out.*] If you come back again, I'm going to take you in that room where you've been beating up that colored boy, and I'm going to murder you—slowly—with my hands. Beat it! [*He pushes* BLICK *out. To* HARRY.] Go take care of the colored boy.

[HARRY *runs out.* WILLIE *returns and doesn't sense that anything is changed.* WILLIE *puts another nickel into the machine, but he does so very violently. The consequence of this violence is that the flag comes up again.* WILLIE, *amazed, stands at attention and salutes. The flag goes down. He shakes his head.*]

WILLIE [*thoughtfully*]. As far as I'm concerned, this is the *only* country in the world. If you ask me, nuts to Europe! [*He is about to push the slide in again when the flag comes up again. Furiously, to* NICK, *while he salutes and stands at attention, pleadingly.*] Hey, Nick. This machine is out of order.

NICK [*somberly*]. Give it a whack on the side.

[WILLIE *does so. A hell of a whack. The result is the flag comes up and down, and* WILLIE *keeps saluting.*]

WILLIE [*saluting*]. Hey, Nick. Something's wrong.

[*The machine quiets down abruptly.* WILLIE *very stealthily slides a new nickel in, and starts a new game. From a distance two pistol shots are heard each carefully timed.* NICK *runs out. The* NEWSBOY *enters, crosses to* JOE'S *table, senses something is wrong.*]

NEWSBOY [*softly*]. Paper, Mister?

[JOE *can't hear him. The* NEWSBOY *backs away, studies* JOE, *wishes he could cheer* JOE *up. Notices the phonograph, goes to it, and puts a coin in it, hoping music will make* JOE *happier. The* NEWSBOY *sits down. Watches* JOE. *The music begins. "The Missouri Waltz." The* DRUNKARD *comes in and walks around. Then sits down.* NICK *comes back.*]

NICK [*delighted*]. Joe, Blick's dead! Somebody just shot him, and none of the cops are trying to find out who. [JOE *doesn't hear.* NICK *steps back, studying* JOE. *Shouting.*] Joe.

JOE [*looking up*]. What?

NICK. Blick's dead.

JOE. Blick? Dead? Good! That goddamn gun wouldn't go off. I *told* Tom to get a good one.

NICK [*picking up gun and looking at it*]. Joe, you wanted to kill that guy! [HARRY *returns.* JOE *puts the gun in his coat pocket.*] I'm going to buy you a bottle of champagne. [NICK *goes to bar.*]

[JOE *rises, takes hat from rack, puts coat on. The* NEWSBOY *jumps up, helps* JOE *with coat.*]

NICK. What's the matter, Joe?

JOE. Nothing. Nothing.

NICK. How about the champagne?

JOE. Thanks. [*Going.*]

NICK. It's not eleven yet. Where you going, Joe?

JOE. I don't know. Nowhere.

NICK. Will I see you tomorrow?

JOE. I don't know. I don't think so.

[KIT CARSON *enters, walks to* JOE. JOE *and* KIT *look at one another knowingly.*]

JOE. Somebody just shot a man. How are you feeling?

KIT. Never felt better in my life. [*Loudly, bragging, but somber.*] I shot a man once. In San Francisco. Shot him two times. In 1939, I think it was. In October. Fellow named Blick or Glick or something like that. Couldn't stand the way he talked to ladies. Went up to my room and got my old pearl-handled revolver and waited for him on Pacific Street. Saw him walking, and let him have it, two times. Had to throw the beautiful revolver into the Bay.

[HARRY, NICK, *the* ARAB *and the* DRUNKARD *close in around him.* JOE *searches his pockets, brings out the revolver, puts it in* KIT'S *hand, looks at him with great admiration and affection.* JOE *walks slowly to the stairs leading to the street, turns and waves.* KIT, *and then one by one everybody else, waves, and the marble game goes into its beautiful American routine again: flag, lights, and music. The play ends.*]

CURTAIN